CAMBRIDGE READINGS IN
THE LITERATURE OF MUSIC

General Editors: John Stevens and Peter le Huray

*Music and Aesthetics in the
Eighteenth and Early-Nineteenth Centuries*

CAMBRIDGE READINGS IN
THE LITERATURE OF MUSIC

Cambridge Readings in the Literature of Music is a series of source materials (original documents in English translation) for students of the history of music. Many of the quotations in the volumes will be substantial, and introductory material will place the passages in context. The period covered will be from antiquity to the present day, with particular emphasis on the nineteenth and twentieth centuries. The series is part of *Cambridge Studies in Music*.

Forthcoming volumes include:

Andrew Barker, *Greek Musical Writings*
John Stevens, *The Middle Ages*
Stanley Boorman, *The Renaissance*
Bojan Bujić, *1850–1910*

Music and Aesthetics in the Eighteenth and Early-Nineteenth Centuries

Edited by

Peter le Huray and James Day

Cambridge University Press

Cambridge
London   New York   New Rochelle
Melbourne   Sydney

Published by the Press Syndicate of the University of Cambridge
The Pitt Building, Trumpington Street, Cambridge CB2 1RP
32 East 57th Street, New York, NY 10022, USA
296 Beaconsfield Parade, Middle Park, Melbourne 3206, Australia

First published 1981

Printed in Great Britain at The Pitman Press, Bath

British Library Cataloguing in Publication Data
Music and aesthetics in the eighteenth and early-
nineteenth centuries. – (Cambridge readings in the
literature of music).
1. Music – Philosophy and aesthetics – Addresses,
essays, lectures
I. Le Huray, Peter   II. Day, James
III. Series
780′.1   ML3845   80–49805
ISBN 0 521 23426 3

Contents

Illustrations

Acknowledgements

We wish to thank the following publishers for granting permission to quote from copyright material: H. Berlioz, 'L'imitation en musique', tr. Jacques Barzun, reprinted from *The Pleasures of Music* by permission of the University of Chicago Press and Cassell Ltd.; C. Baudelaire, 'The Thyrsus' tr. Louise Varèse, reprinted from *Paris Spleen*, Copyright 1947, 1955, © 1962, 1970 by New Directions Publishing Corporation, reprinted by permission of New Directions, New York and Peter Owen, London; Soren Kierkegaard, Either/Or, vol. 1, tr. David F. Swenson and Lillian Marvin Swenson with revisions and a foreword by Howard A. Johnson, copyright 1944 © 1959 by Princeton University Press; Princeton paperback 1971, reprinted by permission of Princeton University Press.

Preface

'In music as well as in literature', as Leon Plantinga has observed in his admirable study of *Schumann as Critic*,[1] 'the word "romantic" is too firmly entrenched in our vocabularies to be rooted out; what we ought to do instead is to clarify what we mean by it. Literary historians have made extensive studies showing what the word has meant, and particularly what it has meant to the romantics themselves. Historians of music have not looked into this matter with comparable thoroughness, even though the word was in regular use in a musical context almost as early as it was in literature. Now there is no reason to think that we should accept on faith the romantics' notion of "romantic", once we find out what it is. But their testimony surely ought to be taken into consideration in any attempts we make to clarify our understanding of the word and the artistic phenomena it designates.'

Our purpose is indeed just that: to present a body of 'evidence' that will serve as the basis for an appreciation of early 'romantic' attitudes. This first collection of materials is designed to illustrate some of the main aesthetic issues that were so hotly and continuously debated during the eighteenth and early-nineteenth centuries. The second – which is to follow – will contain as it were the evidence of the ways in which aesthetic attitudes were given practical expression – evidence in many forms, ranging from the musical novella to evaluations of individual composers and analyses of specific compositions.

Although there have been periods of reaction against an accepted tradition, at no time has there been such a thing as total revolution in the arts. Each age has built, consciously or otherwise, upon the achievements of its immediate past, no matter how vigorously it has protested otherwise. In fact, the more familiar we become with the literature that concerns music – the profusion of articles on aesthetics and criticism in the music journals and dailies, the burgeoning repertory of instruction books, the ever more numerous dissertations in which music is allied to philosophical speculation – the less obvious do the distinctions between historical periods become, and the more we are driven backwards to seek the origins of an idea in an earlier age. Thus, while some commentators have seen the romantic age as one in which emphasis was placed on emotional content rather than form, we find that if there was one point on which every eighteenth-century writer was agreed, it was that music was the art that most immediately appealed to the emotions. Music that failed to engage the emotions, they felt, was of

[1] *Yale Studies in the History of Music*, 4 (New Haven and London 1967), p. 102.

little or no consequence. 'Expression', therefore, was the central theme around which the debate revolved, and against it were measured such time-honoured concepts as 'beauty', 'sublimity' and 'unity'.

It has been argued that aesthetics can never be a proper subject of scientific study. This may or may not be true. The fact remains that it was then considered to be real enough: indeed, it is to Baumgarten that we owe the term aesthetics, in its modern usage.[2] During the course of the eighteenth century, books on aesthetics came from the presses in ever increasing numbers, books written not by remote academics but by intellectuals, many of whom, like André, Du Bos, Beattie, Michaelis, Schopenhauer and Twining, had a very practical understanding and love of music. To read them is to draw a little closer to an appreciation of the impact that music had on the informed musical public of the day.

It would be wrong, moreover, to imagine that such matters went unnoticed by the professional musician. A glance for instance at William Crotch's Oxford lectures (see p. 427) will quickly show how widely a first-rate teacher ranged through the arts and how interested he was in aesthetic ideas of a general nature. Thomas Gray may have contemptuously dismissed the average professional instrumentalist as little more than a 'common lackey', but many of the leading musicians of his day were in fact highly literate and informed. And as time went on the musician took an ever-widening interest in the world around him. Beethoven's declared interests in the idea of freedom have been well documented. As the conversation books show, too, he was aware of the work of his great literary contemporaries: Goethe, Schiller, Lessing and even Kant, if only at second-hand.[3] Weber and Mendelssohn were gifted artists. Mendelssohn attended Hegel's lectures in Berlin and was able to discuss these with Goethe when he visited Weimar in 1830. Berlioz was swept off his feet by Shakespeare, Goethe (and Miss Smithson), and was a master of prose. Schumann, one of the founders of the *Neue Zeitschrift für Musik* (Leipzig 1834–), kept a firm editorial grip on the journal for almost ten years; and although he professed a distrust for aesthetic speculation, it was during the term of his editorship that Gelbcke's important article 'Classic and Romantic' was published (see p. 524); his letter, too, to Clara (see p. 490) suggests that he was very much alive to everything that he encountered and highly susceptible to external influences. Liszt allowed his name to be associated with a quite extraordinary quantity of prose, whilst on the first page of the newly founded *Gazette musicale* (Paris 1833) his name is coupled with those of Chopin, the writer Janin and the publisher Schlesinger, the implication being that together they formed some kind of editorial board. There was in

---

[2] A. G. Baumgarten adopted it as the title – *Aesthetica* – of his study, first published at Frankfurt-an-der-Oder, in 1752.

[3] See for instance, Robert L. Jacobs, 'Beethoven and Kant', *Music and Letters*, vol. 42 (1961), p. 242; W. Kirkendale, 'New Roads to Old Ideas in Beethoven's *Missa Solemnis*', in *The Creative World of Beethoven*, ed. P. H. Lang (New York 1971); and Frida Knight, *Beethoven and the Age of Revolution* (London 1973).

fact no lack of opportunity for theory and practice to meet in the world of the arts, and for common beliefs and attitudes to be shared.

In this first part of our 'testimony' we have chosen to arrange the materials in strictly chronological order. Initially we were to assemble them in 'subject' divisions, but this proved to be less than satisfactory, as few of the chosen extracts centre exclusively on one idea: although for example the first twenty-two paragraphs of Kant's *Kritik der Urteilskraft* come under the general heading of 'Analytic of the beautiful', and paragraphs 23 to 54 'Analytic of the sublime' these are best seen for our purpose in juxtaposition and not in divisions devoted separately to 'The beautiful', and 'The sublime'. The detailed subject index will however, we hope, serve to delineate the various strands in the eighteenth- and early-ninteenth-century debate.

The task of translation has not been an easy one, for the weightier speculations (notably those by German authors) do not readily arrange themselves in fluent English prose. As far as possible our aim has been to strike a balance between stylistic fidelity and readability. We hope of course that in no case we have misrepresented an original; we have, however, taken certain liberties with syntactical structure where the sense of the original would otherwise be impaired, e.g. by subdividing extended sentences and by substituting for indeterminate personal and impersonal pronouns the objects or people to which they refer. Where the meaning of the text is ambiguous the original word or phrase in question is given in the printed text, in brackets.

The anthology is designed not only to represent the various arguments that were put forward in the debate on aesthetics and music, but also to convey something of the flavour of that debate and to indicate the manner in which information and polemic were transmitted. Thus we have chosen, for example, to publish much of Fétis's lengthy survey of music and aesthetics which he published in the Paris *Revue musicale* during the 1830s (see pp. 443–51), rather than briefly to summarise the information that it contains. Thus, too, we have included in full the relevant sections of Lichtenthal's bibliographical dictionary, which gives a particularly clear idea of the extraordinarily comprehensive range of source materials that had at that comparatively early stage been assembled. As a general rule we have chosen wherever possible to quote extended extracts and to avoid making cuts within the quotations: in many cases, cuts would certainly have made for easier reading but they would have tended to falsify the originals, giving them a spurious intensity and even logic that they may not in fact possess.

As the protagonists were in the main English, French, German and (to a lesser extent) Italian, we have largely limited our anthology to a survey of books, dictionaries, encyclopedias, periodicals and newspapers in these languages. Most of the important publications on aesthetics in fact reached an international readership; French was of course the language of much of 'civilised' eighteenth-century Europe.

Our thanks are due to the interest of many kind friends and colleagues. We are particularly indebted to Dr Nicholas Boyle, Dr Roger Scruton and Professor John Stevens for their comments on the structure and contents of the anthology, and to Mrs Jennifer Day, Mr James Wright and Dr J. M. Wilkins for their help with the knottier points of translation. Our grateful thanks are due too, to Miss Erika Weiss and Mrs Eileen French for so cheerfully typing and retyping the translations as they gradually took shape. We cannot fail, too, to acknowledge the patience of the Cambridge University Press, and Mrs Rosemary Dooley in particular for all the thought and care that has gone into the production of the book.

PETER LE HURAY   JAMES DAY

St Catharine's College   *Selwyn College*
Cambridge   *Cambridge*

November 1979

Introduction

During the eighteenth century the discipline of aesthetics gradually took shape – that 'philosophy of the fine arts', as Sulzer put it, 'by which the fundamental laws and general theories of the arts are deduced'. Symptomatic of this was the appearance from the late-eighteenth century onwards of dictionary definitions of the term: Sulzer's own (printed in full pp. 121–3) which he published in his *Allgemeine Theorie der schönen Künste*, of 1771, was the first of its kind. Some indication of the extent to which interest in aesthetics increased during the period can be gathered from the tremendous acceleration that then occurred in publishing activity. In England, for instance, aesthetics and music form a significant part of no more than five books published during the first quarter of the eighteenth century. This number more than doubled during the subsequent twenty-five years, rising to thirty between 1750 and 1775, and to more than forty between 1775 and 1800.[1]

Amongst the various matters that were debated, some half a dozen proved to be of very general interest: the nature of aesthetic experience, the factors that determine aesthetic judgement, the qualities that comprise beauty and sublimity, the necessity for both unity and variety within a work of art, the relevance of the principle of the 'imitation of nature' in the creative process, and from about 1800 onwards, the romantic movement.

One of the most important questions to be debated during the early years of the eighteenth century was that of the nature of aesthetic experience. A key concept to emerge was that of 'disinterestedness', in which the aesthetic object has no cause or function other than that of its own existence. The English philosophers, Shaftesbury and Hutcheson, played an important role in the debate, and all their eighteenth-century successors owe at least something to them, in this respect. A specifically musical illustration of the operation of the principle of disinterest is provided by Kant in his *Kritik der Urteilskraft*: background music at a banquet, he argued, might give pleasure but in no sense could it be described as beautiful and thus as the source of aesthetic experience; such music has a function beyond the experience itself, namely to relax the guests, encourage conversation and aid the digestion (see p. 220). The precondition of 'disinterest' likewise excluded other

---

[1] See John W. Draper, 'Poetry and music in eighteenth-century English aesthetics', *Englische Studien*, vol. 67 (1932–3) pp. 70–85; and also his *Eighteenth-Century English Aesthetics: A Bibliography* (Heidelberg 1931), pt. 5. See, too, Jamie Croy Kassler, *The Science of Music in Britain, 1714–1830: a catalogue of writings, lectures and inventions* (New York 1977).

experiences that had tended in earlier systems to be associated with ideas which eighteenth-century writers were to regard as exclusive to aesthetics: namely goodness and truth. The doing of a good deed, for instance, might arouse feelings that are deeply satisfying, and closely analogous to those of a purely aesthetic kind. Since the deed is inevitably directed, however, to an end that lies beyond the immediate experience, the experience cannot be an aesthetic one. So it was that the principle of 'disinterest' came to provide a yardstick whereby moral, intellectual and aesthetic issues could be separated. The emergence of this principle, moreover, reflects a growing interest, not in the object of the aesthetic experience, but in the pure, subjective response to that object.

The aesthetic response is a response to beauty. But in what ways was it possible to define beauty? There were those, like Hutcheson, who argued that beauty was susceptible to analysis and that it could be defined in certain absolute and universal terms. There were others – and increasingly so as the eighteenth century progressed – who maintained like Edmund Burke that beauty could be best determined 'by an examination of the passions in our breasts'.[2] Philosophical mistrust of the feelings is understandable enough, for subjective reactions – reactions that are liable to vary from person to person – are inimical to systems that are built upon aesthetic universals. Yet subjective feelings could hardly be avoided, at least in discussions involving the idea of music, for as everyone agreed, music was the art that spoke most directly to the feelings, to *le sentiment*, to *das Gefühl*. Thus Hutcheson could hardly avoid acknowledging that 'there is another charm in music to various persons . . . which is occasioned by its raising agreeable passions' (see p. 25), even though he devoted much of his discussion of musical beauty to such objective criteria as unity, form and proportion. And although Kant argued that feelings have absolutely nothing to do with the judgement of beauty, he had somewhat uncomfortably to attempt a reconciliation between this proposition and the inescapable fact that music was universally regarded as a language of the 'affections'. Feelings, therefore, could not wholly be avoided even by those who might have preferred to do so; and it was in the field of musical aesthetics that the feelings most obtruded.

Although Hutcheson was by no means the last to search for universal values that would serve to identify beauty, the realisation steadily grew, as the eighteenth century progressed, that no such thing was possible. Hutcheson had himself recognised that in practice judgements of beauty did differ, and to account for this he drew on the theory of 'association' that had earlier been proposed by Locke, which suggested that judgements could be distorted by such extraneous factors as the personality and individual experience of the judge. The theory of association played an important role

---

[2] See Jerome Stolnitz, '"Beauty": some stages in the history of an idea', *Journal of the History of Ideas*, vol. 22 (1961), p. 185; and 'On the Origins of "Aesthetic Disinterestedness" ', *Journal of Aesthetics*, vol. 20 (1961), p. 131.

in aesthetic theory and especially in Archibald Alison's *Essays on the Nature and Principles of Taste* (1790) (see pp. 209–13) where the author is especially concerned to discriminate between the kinds of association that he considers to be a genuine part of aesthetic judgement, and those that are merely incidental to it.

During the early years of the eighteenth century English writers devoted comparatively little space to a principle that was being continuously debated by their French contemporaries: the Aristotelian principle of 'the Imitation of Nature'. In his *Les beaux-arts réduits à un même principe* (1746) the Abbé Charles Batteux made use of the principle, suitably developed, to establish the concept of 'Les beaux-arts' – fine arts, as the term has come to be translated, having no practical value: he proposed as fine arts, sculpture, painting, music and poetry, in contradistinction to such 'useful' arts as cooking, and such 'mixed' arts as architecture and eloquence. Batteux's categorisation of the arts is to all intents and purposes that which is still currently in use today. The highest artistic manifestation of the principle of 'imitation', Aristotle had argued, was tragedy, which imitated 'action and life' through the media of plot, character, language, thought, spectacle and music.[3] Imitation was designed 'to influence the character and the soul'; the process of imitation therefore had to be highly selective. As Addison bluntly put it, 'fine writing consists of sentiments that are natural without being obvious; the pleasantries of a waterman, the observations of a peasant, the ribaldry of a porter or a hackney coachman, all are natural, but disagreeable'. Beauty, in its highest flights, was regarded in effect as the singular revelation of divine truth; in searching for beauty, man was seen reaching upwards to a knowledge of ultimate truth and perfection. This traditional blend of ethics and aesthetics had a considerable vogue, particularly in France during the late-eighteenth and early-nineteenth centuries, and in the work of such an author as Lamennais (see pp. 517–21) it achieved a quality of longing, of *Sehnsucht* that is closely paralleled in the work of the early romantic German poets.

But in what ways could music possibly imitate nature? The answer was that if music could actually imitate – or rather represent – non-musical things, this was not its prime function; its task was rather to imitate the feelings. Thus, in Batteux's system, expression was music's first priority, whereas in Hutcheson's, the feelings are very much subordinated to abstract considerations of proportion and structure. The musical application of Batteux's system had its practical expression in the so-called doctrine of the affections.[4] The strongly moralistic streak, to which reference has already

[3] See *What is Art? Aesthetic Theory from Plato to Tolstoy*, ed. A. Sesonske (London 1965), pp. 54 and 72; also R. G. Collingwood, *The Principles of Art* (London 1937), chs. 3, 6 and 9; and, R. Scruton, 'Absolute music', and 'Programme music', *The New Grove Dictionary of Music and Musicians*, VI (London 1980).

[4] As stated, for instance, in Johann Mattheson's *Das Neu-Eröffnete Orchester* (Hamburg 1713).

been made, that runs through so much French aesthetic theory at the time goes a long way to explain the comparatively low regard in which purely instrumental music was then held. Rousseau states the classic position in his *Encyclopédie* article on the 'Sonata', which he subsequently revised for the *Dictionnaire de musique* (1767). 'Purely as harmony', he wrote, 'music is of little account. If it is to provide constant pleasure and interest it must be raised to the rank of an imitative art. However the subject of the imitation is not always as immediately obvious as it is in painting and poetry. It is by words that music most frequently defines the idea (*image*) that it is depicting, and it is through the touching sounds of the human voice that the idea evokes in the depths of the human heart the feeling (*sentiment*) that it seeks to arouse. Who does not feel, in this respect', Rousseau continues, 'the inadequacy of instrumental music (*symphonie*) in which brilliance alone is the aim? Can all the trivialities of M. Mondonville's violin be as moving as just two notes sung by Mme le Maure? Instruments may enliven the song and enhance its expression but they can never supplant it. To understand what all the din of a sonata is about we would have to do what the incompetent painter did, when he wrote beneath his works, "This is a tree", "This is a man" and "This is a horse". I shall never forget the witty riposte made by the celebrated Fontenelle after he had been bored to death by an endless succession of instrumental pieces: "Sonate, que me veux-tu?" he exclaimed in passionate impatience.' For many critics then, purely instrumental music was insufficiently precise to handle 'moral' concepts, and its status was inevitably seen as inferior to that of its sister arts, poetry and drama. Such, certainly, was the reason behind Kant's estimate of the relative values of the various fine arts, as also behind that of such conservative nineteenth-century philosophers as Victor Cousin.

During the course of the eighteenth century, interest in the dimension of the sublime steadily rose, as interest in the idea of beauty declined. The idea of the sublime extends back, of course, into classical antiquity, and in particular it was the subject of an influential treatise, the *Peri Houpsous*, attributed to Dionysius Longinus.[5] In his treatise, Longinus was wholly concerned with the sublime 'in writing and discourse', for which he postulated two essentials: 'boldness and grandeur of thought', and 'the Pathetic, or power of raising the passions to a violent and even enthusiastic degree'. Although the work was by no means unknown to earlier generations, it was Boileau's translation, the *Traité du sublime ou du merveilleux dans le discours* (Paris 1674) which marks the beginning of a new interest in the idea of the sublime.

---

[5] See *Longinus on the Sublime: the Peri Houpsous in Translations by Nicholas Boileau Despreaux (1674) and William Smith (1739)* (Scholars Facsimiles and Reprints, New York, 1975); also *On the Sublime*, ed. and trans. W. R. Roberts (2nd edn, Cambridge 1907). See too, S. H. Monk, *The Sublime: A Study of Critical Theories in Eighteenth-Century England* (New York 1935; repr. Ann Arbor Paperbacks, Michigan 1960).

Whereas Longinus had ultimately been concerned with the emotive force of the sublime as a moral agent, as a persuasive power to move and to improve the mind, Boileau's successors showed an ever-increasing interest in the sublime simply for its dynamic, overwhelming and even irrational qualities. As far back as 1704 the English critic and poet, John Dennis, had suggested that Longinus's concept of the sublime was 'impregnated with terrible ideas'. By 1756 Burke was arguing that 'the passion caused by the great and sublime in nature, where those causes operate most powerfully, is astonishment; and astonishment is that state of the soul in which all its motions are suspended, with some degree of horror'. Thus, he argued, the sublime and the beautiful 'are of a very different nature, one being founded on pain, the other on pleasure. . . . Sublime objects are vast in their dimensions, beautiful ones are comparatively small: beauty should be smooth and polished, the great, rugged and negligent . . . beauty should not be obscure; the great ought to be dark and gloomy.' There is, in short, a good deal of the wild and unfathomable about Burke's sublime, and it was with these qualities that the sublime came increasingly to be associated.

Although philosophers and critics were unanimous that of all the arts music spoke most directly to the feelings, they were for the most part hesitant to admit and approve the possibility of a sublime musical style – sublime, that is to say, in the late-eighteenth-century sense of the word. Early-eighteenth-century critics had indeed frequently used it as Longinus might have done to convey the idea of music in the grand style, perfectly composed, deeply moving, certainly, but above all, elevating and uplifting in the way that sublime rhetoric and poetry moved and elevated the mind. Sir John Hawkins's comments on Handel are clearly in this vein: 'Till the most eminent of his contemporaries were taught the contrary', he declared, 'none were aware of that dignity and grandeur of sentiment of which music is capable of conveying, or that there is a sublime in music as there is in poetry.' But even Burke avoids applying his definition of the sublime to composed music, restricting his comments to such 'musical effects' as the beating of drums, and the tolling of midnight bells (see p. 74).

Kant, who respected Burke but who was philosophically more attuned to Longinus, also avoided the sublime in music, even though he both accepted that the emotions had a necessary place in sublime experience, and that of the fine arts, music was pre-eminently the art of the emotions. He argued none the less, that music could not of itself be the source of sublime feelings, but only when allied to the greater dramatic and poetic arts. A significant shift of emphasis however is to be seen in the work of his disciple, C. F. Michaelis, towards a musical definition that Burke himself might well have accepted (see pp. 289–90). For having summarised the Kantian position as regards the beautiful and the sublime, Michaelis went on to discuss in great detail the ways in which composed music could generate sublime impressions. These are aroused, he suggested, when the imagination is elevated to the plane of the infinite, the immeasurable and the insuperable. In music there are, he argued, two ways of doing this: either by establishing a 'uniformity which is so great that it excludes variety' – by for instance the constant repetition of a rhythm, note or chord – or by creating such a 'diversity' of ideas that the mind is overwhelmed by 'thundering torrents of sound'. The practical expression of such ideas is to be found in the creative criticism of a number of Michaelis's poetic contemporaries, amongst whom are numbered Jean-Paul Richter, Ludwig Tieck, Wilhelm Wackenroder and above all, perhaps, E. T. A. Hoffmann. Their concern was not so much with the object – the musical composition itself – but with the feelings which that object aroused in the listener. Hoffmann's famous article on Beethoven's instrumental music (see vol. 2) epitomises the new criticism; in listening to Beethoven Hoffmann experienced fear, horror, suffering even, and a longing for the infinite that he felt was 'the essence of romanticism'. The way was now open for the musically inclined to argue music's pre-eminence over all the arts, on the grounds that it was the most emotive and the least specific of them all – instrumental music, that is, unencumbered by the particularity of words.

The aesthetics of romanticism

A glance at almost any modern musical dictionary will show that musical romanticism is generally thought of as a nineteenth-century phenomenon, one that was heralded by Beethoven perhaps, but which in practice extended from Berlioz and Schubert to the first youthful efforts of the members of the second Viennese School. It comes as something of a shock, therefore, to find that a general history of the romantic movement had already been published by 1829 and that there had been other attempts at the subject before it. Although there may be good reasons for the accepted interpretation of musical history in the late-eighteenth and early-nineteenth centuries, it is important to realise that such a historical viewpoint did not begin to crystallise until the 1840s. Some indication of the way in which this happened can be got from a perusal of dictionaries of aesthetics and music dating from the time. Prior to 1800 the word romantic had been used to describe the fantastic and exotic; it was frequently associated with imaginative literature and especially with the novel or *roman*. This is largely what Millin gives in his 1806 *Dictionnaire des beaux-arts* (see p. 294), though Millin was certainly aware too of a new, romantic movement in England and Germany.

By the time that Schilling published his *Universal Lexicon der Tonkunst*, in 1836, a clear distinction was being drawn between the romanticism of the *roman* and a romantic movement in the world of the arts (see pp. 469–72). Schilling owed a considerable debt to German writers of the late-eighteenth century, writers identified by Mme de Staël in her celebrated study of Germany, *De l'Allemagne* (1810) (see pp. 297–311), notably the Schlegel brothers (see pp. 265–70), F. W. J. von Schelling, and even to a degree,

Goethe and Schiller. Schilling argued, as August Schlegel and Chateaubriand had done, that the phenomenon of romanticism was inextricably bound up with Christianity. As he saw things, the materialistic religion of classical antiquity had produced arts that were earthbound, classically poised, and expressive of nothing more that a 'refined and ennobled sensuality'. The Christian faith, on the other hand, aspired to the eternal, seeking to 'transcend the sphere of cognition so that it might experience something higher, more spiritual'. For those critics who were particularly attuned to music it was a short step from here to the idea that instrumental music was the ideally romantic art, for as we have said, it was unencumbered by the particularity of words, or indeed by the particularities of the materials out of which the other arts were constructed. Schopenhauer was the philosopher to argue this position at greatest length, but others, including Schilling himself, used it as the mainspring for their aesthetic systems.

The first moves towards a historical definition of romanticism, in which romanticism was seen as the successor to and even the antithesis of a previous classicism, date from the late 1830s when many perceptive critics were already lamenting the decay of a truly romantic art. Gelbcke's substantial article in Schumann's *Neue Zeitschrift für Musik*, of 1841, marks a significant step towards the modern definition of historical periods of musical classicism and romanticism (see pp. 524–9). The explicit formulation of such periods had to wait, it would seem, until 1848 when Kahlert published a lengthy article on the subject in the Leipzig *Allgemeine musikalische Zeitung* (see pp. 559–65).

Earlier observers had certainly tended to see the romantic movement as something apart from what had gone before. Yet as the editor of the *Globe* put it, in 1824 (see pp. 423–6), the word romanticism may have been on everyone's lips for some fifteen years or more, but there were probably no two people who attached precisely the same meaning to it. 'Under the banner of romanticism, as under the banner of our crusading ancestors, march many nations in phalanxes that represent opposite extremes. What have these warriors in common with each other', he asked, 'what is the Jerusalem that they seek to conquer, and who is the enemy that they are sworn to fight?' Toreinx, the author of a readable and surprisingly perceptive history of romanticism, flippantly observed some five years later that it was Mme de Staël with her powerful imagination, her ardent spirit and her cutting sense of irony, who first adopted the newborn child, romanticism. 'She saw first of all that it had to have a name, for a name is a rallying point. She knew that people are swayed by words, and especially by words that they do not understand. She accordingly made up a word of no precise meaning, which could consequently be applied to everything. And thus the word "romantique" came to enrich the French language.' Had Toreinx really believed this he would hardly have bothered to produce so substantial a book on the subject (see pp. 406–19). His warning, eloquently restated and developed by Jacques Barzun in his *Classic, Romantic and Modern* (Chicago 1975), of the danger of trying to establish a comprehensive definition of romanticism in terms of positive achievement, is a timely one none the less. He did however believe that a quality of romanticism could be separately observed in every field of creative endeavour and that there was a common bond between the various manifestations of romanticism, in that they each sprang from a reaction to the restraints of outworn conventions. As the editor of the *Globe* observed, a whole volume could be devoted to the definitions of romanticism that have been proposed. What then is the common factor that unites them? It is, he suggests, routine; the Jerusalem that is striven for is liberty. Here, as always, the old struggles against the new, faith against the spirit of enquiry. Toreinx took this as a point of departure for his own detailed account of romanticism, and he argued that in poetry, painting, architecture, music, drama, history, medicine, and even politics, a reaction against a dead past resulted in a new awareness of truth, a heightened consciousness, and an enlivened response to all forms of experience: hence, it was essential to dispense with dramatic allegory and the dramatic unities, he argued, and to create drama that, like nature herself, takes on as many diverse forms as she does personalities; hence, in the field of historical studies could be seen a new concern for detailed observation rather than inexact generalisation, a concern that saw history as the closest possible reflection of the past rather than as a didactic, moralistic tool; hence, there was a need in medicine for a new awareness of the danger of leaning too heavily on the lore of past generations, whilst in politics the desire was growing for freedom from unnecessary restraint, a desire that had so far found its most glorious realisation – for Toreinx at least – in the American War of Independence; it was this new interest in freedom, Toreinx believed, that explained why Beethoven, Weber and Rossini were seen to stand head and shoulders above their routine contemporaries (see pp. 406–19).

In arguing that romanticism was the expression in various ways of a dissatisfaction with outworn conventions, however, Toreinx was in no sense preaching a gospel of total revolution. Indeed, he was keenly aware of the value of a living tradition, and never more so than in the field of music. When we come to think of it, he wrote, does not one idea give rise to another in the realms of intellectual endeavour, the latest idea invariably depending upon the one that preceded it? Where, he asked, would Beethoven have been had he not followed Haydn and Mozart?

Many writers, including Toreinx himself, used the term romanticism from time to time as the synonym for all that was new in contemporary thought. In every century, Toreinx observed, in every age, romanticism will change its form and the romantic works of yesterday often turn out to be the classics of tomorrow. 'As far as we are concerned', he wrote, 'Paisiello, Cimarosa and Mozart are classics, though their contemporaries regarded them as romantics.' As Fétis later maintained in an article that he wrote for the *Revue musicale* in the revolutionary year 1830, the natural tendency was for the young to be romantic, the elderly conservative: for most men are so in love with the ideas that they encountered in their youth, that they arrive at an advanced old age still holding to opinions and tastes that they formed when they were young; indeed, it is precisely for this reason that they lament the times that are passed (see pp. 423–6).

During the first three decades of the nineteenth century and beyond, then, the concept of classical and romantic musical styles as fixed and determinable historical styles, simply did not exist. Wagner, very much under the spell of Schopenhauer, found Palestrina's music every bit as romantic within its own terms of reference as the music of Bach. If the term classical was used in a musical context during this period, it was simply to define those works that had stood the test of time, and which were still listened to with enjoyment.

From the 1840s, classicism and romanticism came to be seen more and more as historical events. This way of thinking, which we are heir to, has its obvious convenience, but if it is not treated with the greatest care it may obscure issues that were at the time held to be of central importance in the process of change. We may in other words be encouraged to an over-simple analysis of the relationship between the much debated concepts of musical form and content that underlie current thinking about classicism and romanticism. It may well be that we experience in the music of Haydn and Mozart a perfect balance between form and content. Musicians of Mozart's day would, however, have been surprised to hear contemporary music spoken of in terms such as these. For in effect the forms used by the composers were those which had evolved because they were found to be most suited to the expression of the content of a composer's thought. Enough will have already been seen, for instance, of the history of the idea of the sublime in the late-eighteenth century, to show that the natural tendency of the age (as indeed of any other) was towards ever more direct and intense means of artistic communication. In Hoffmann's imaginative music criticism, the terms romantic and sublime appear, almost synonymously, in a broad context that embraces not only and obviously the music of Beethoven, but also that of his great predecessors Haydn and Mozart. 'Expression' was throughout the eighteenth century and early-nineteenth century the goal to which musical genius aspired. It was as much a vital issue when Batteux published his contribution to the principle of the 'Imitation of Nature', as it was when Schopenhauer hailed music as the most direct manifestation of the world as 'Will'.

The distance separating these two points is immense, but it was covered by a process of continuous development, one that involved an extension of the principle of conflict within a musical composition. There is much truth in Toreinx's observation that during the time of Gluck a composition was normally based upon a single idea; its particular 'affect' being generated by some characteristic idea suitably developed throughout the composition.

There are, of course, many memorable Baroque compositions to which this does not apply: the great G minor Organ Fantasia of Bach, for instance, or any number of movements from Handel's Op. 6 Concerti Grossi. Even here, however, the ideas tend to follow each other in quick succession, rather than to interact, and it was the process of interaction that perceptive critics saw as one of the hallmarks of the new music of the early-nineteenth century. Earlier music, and that even included some of Mozart's greatest operatic works, took on, in the light of the vivid hues and turbulent contrasts exploited by later composers, a sameness, an uneventfulness that, however perfect it might be, failed to hold the attention.

From about 1830 a note of uncertainty and even of disillusion began to temper the self-confident enthusiasm that had been a characteristic up to then of the highest flights of music criticism. The writer Giuseppe Mazzini, who with Lichtenthal was one of the few Italians to make a major contribution to European music criticism during the early years of the nineteenth century, had by 1832 concluded that music was at a standstill, that current modes of musical expression were completely worked out, and that the way forward to heavens yet unexplored could only be assured by the advent of some as yet undiscovered genius. Mazzini considered that romanticism had been a potent force to break down barriers which had been erected by the exponents of 'bastard' Greek and Roman art and that it had served to restore the human ego, but it had none the less been impotent to create anew. Mazzini felt that true 'Byronian' music had been supplanted by music that sought only obvious effects and which lacked coherence, skimming the surface of feeling. In spite of his very different political and musical background, Mazzini was surprisingly at one with Robert Schumann in seeing the years immediately following the death of Beethoven, Weber, and Schubert as devoid of talent, years in which music was increasingly being equated with empty virtuosity, years in which the Byronian heritage of the immediate past was being squandered. Schilling and Gelbcke were much of the same mind. Meyerbeer, Schilling observed, entitled his *Robert le Diable* a 'romantic' opera; it had however everything, he felt, except the romantic spirit. Its outward trappings of romanticism were obvious enough, yet the soul had for the most part vanished (see pp. 471–2). This was a common criticism of the new music of the 1840s, and it was in part at least blamed on the increasing tendency of composers to seek for pictorial effect, rather than for the inner spirit.

In his important article in the *Neue Zeitschrift*, 'Classisch und Romantisch', Gelbcke argued that any music which sought to reveal feelings and emotions was essentially romantic in spirit, regardless of the time or place of its origin. He felt, however, that the more music attempted to express concepts that lay beyond its natural boundaries, the less effective, the less 'romantic', it was. For this reason he was inclined to describe his immediate contemporaries, notably Berlioz and Liszt, as 'neo-Romantics', primarily because these composers were so attracted to the idea of pictorial representation in music, a process that Gelbcke felt had a distinctly unromantic objectivity about it. Kahlert, too, identified the problem in similar terms some eight years later. He described the decline of musical romanticism in terms of a divergence between the musical imagination and the intellect. On the one hand, he argued, this led to the creation of illustrative miniatures, comprising short-winded ideas loosely fashioned into empty phrases. On the other hand it resulted in introverted, formless compositions, the product of attempts to plumb the profoundest depths of the imagination for hidden treasures. Kahlert, in short, like other perceptive critics of his time, felt that he stood at the end of an era. A romantic concept of the world was, he believed, totally at variance with political reality: the time for dreams was past, the need was for law and order. He ended with the hope that the act of composition would again be concerned with music as a living organism; that it would be bound in short by its own natural laws. If Kahlert then was one of the first to postulate a romantic period in musical history he was also one of the first to announce its demise. The general feeling indeed was one of uncertainty, of disillusion tempered with the hope for the beginning of a new era. That musical romanticism could have a further fifty years to go was an idea that certainly would have been inconceivable to the critics of Kahlert's day.

Cognition and the interpretation of sensations

Even today, with all the resources of modern technical science at our disposal, it is still difficult to describe what precisely happens when we listen and react to a piece of music. The concepts of mind, imagination, and emotion are still elusive of definition. This is so much the case that there are theorists who deny their very existence. If such difficulties exist in the late-twentieth century, how much more did they in the eighteenth. For this reason, it is both necessary and interesting to try to examine what thinkers of the period meant when they used such terms as *emotion, spirit, genius, inspiration, imagination* and *heart*.

There are two main streams of thought regarding the world of the senses, one originating with Descartes in France, the other with Locke in England, which greatly affected theories in our period; and lurking in the background in some cases was the ancient doctrine of the four temperaments – not, perhaps, literally believed in, but still not entirely discounted.

Descartes (1596–1650) thought of mind as a substance; and he defined substance as 'a thing which so exists that it needs no other thing in order to exist' (*Principles of Philosophy*, i, 51). That this was true of the mind, he reached by the famous system of Cartesian doubt. If you doubt the existence of everything, at least one thing is indisputable – the very fact that you are doubting. You cannot doubt without being a doubter; and because you doubt, you do not simply accept the impressions that your senses receive of the world around you. So the fact that you doubt must, he argues, imply that you exist even if the external world does not. The famous phrase 'je pense, donc je suis' might, as has often been pointed out, better have been formulated 'je doute, donc je suis'; but the argument is unaffected – the fact that one can doubt implies the existence of the doubter, or at least of his mind that does the doubting. Self-awareness is, Descartes claimed, the property of mind. What senses perceive is the world of matter, whose property is extension in space. Because mind is not perceived by the senses, it is different from matter; and although man consists of mind and body, his mind cannot be *located* in his material body. The mind can reason and produce clear, distinct and trustworthy ideas. But the image of the world as revealed to us by our senses is complex and by no means reliable — did not our senses seem to tell us that the sun revolved round the earth, for example? (Descartes in fact claimed that neither the earth nor the sun moved; the earth existed in a vortex that revolved around the sun, but this, too, was evidence that the senses deceive us.) Thus the faculty of imagination, by which the mind interprets the data of the senses, is suspect; and so are the passions and emotions: 'all those modes of awareness which often arise in us without our soul making them to be what they are'. However vivid or intense the impressions gained through the senses or the emotions, they are not to be trusted. Only the clear distinct ideas conceived in the mind can lead us to an understanding of reality.

The British empiricists, and particularly Locke (1632–1704) and Hume (1711–76), thought otherwise. The idea that the human mind is a kind of blank sheet on which our experience through the senses writes information about the world which our mind then interpets certainly did not originate with Locke. But Locke maintained that *all* the materials of knowledge are derived from experience and that no kind of human knowledge is innate; none is part of the mind from the very outset.

Many thinkers, including Descartes, had argued that some ideas – such as those of God, of infinity, or of perfection – must be innate, because there is no satisfactory empirical way of explaining their origin. These ideas, it was argued, remained dormant in the human mind until some suitable conditions arose for their actualisation in experience. Locke maintained that our ideas derive from two sources: what our senses tell us about the world around us, and our perception of how our internal mind operates. We can, he argued, think only by means of ideas and all our ideas come from experience. As D. J. O'Connor puts it:[6] 'The mind, like any other natural object, is known to us through the ideas we have of its operations; and these operations are the activation of the dispositional properties which Locke calls "powers" or "faculties". Both minds and material things are substances.' Locke made no pretence to any knowledge of physiology and he was extremely careful not to theorise in any detail about how the powers or faculties operated; but he still wrote of our sense organs conveying into the

---

[6] D. J. O'Connor, *John Locke* (Harmondsworth 1952), p. 107.

mind from external objects the causes of our sensation. The mind might analyse, mix, break down, build up, sort and order the materials given in sensation and reflection, *but it could not add any new materials.*[7]

How David Hume developed this viewpoint in *An Enquiry Concerning Human Understanding,*[8] eliminating the Cartesian distinction between the clear, distinct ideas through which the mind reached truth, and the questionable data of the senses interpreted by the imagination, may be seen from the following passage:

> The imagination has the command over all its ideas, and can join and mix and vary them, in all the ways possible. It may conceive fictitious objects with all the circumstances of place and time. It may set them, in a manner, before our eyes, in their true colours, just as they might have existed. But as it is impossible that this faculty of imagination can ever, of itself, reach belief, it is evident that belief consists not in the peculiar nature or order of ideas, but in the *manner* of their conception, and in their *feeling* in the mind. I confess, that it is impossible perfectly to explain this feeling or manner of conception. We may make use of words which express something near it. But its true and proper name, as we have observed before, is *belief*; which is a term that everyone sufficiently understands in common life. And in philosophy, we can go no farther than assert, that *belief* is something felt by the mind, which distinguishes the ideas of the judgment from the fictions of the imagination. It gives them more weight and influence; makes them appear of greater importance; enforces them in the mind; and renders them the governing principle of our actions. I hear at present, for instance, a person's voice, with whom I am acquainted; and the sound comes as from the next room. This impression of my senses immediately conveys my thought to the person, together with all the surrounding objects. I paint them out to myself as existing at present, with the same qualities and relations, of which I formerly knew them possessed. These ideas take faster hold of my mind than ideas of an enchanted castle. They are very different to the feeling, and have a much greater influence of every kind, either to give pleasure or pain, joy or sorrow.
>
> Let us, then, take in the whole compass of this doctrine, and allow, that the sentiment of belief is nothing but a conception more intense and steady than what attends the mere fictions of the imagination, and that this *manner* of conception arises from a customary conjunction of the object with something present to the memory or the senses: I believe that it will not be difficult, upon these suppositions, to find other operations of the mind analogous to it, and to trace up these phenomena to principles still more general.

Belief, then, 'consists not in the peculiar nature or order of ideas, but in the *manner* of their conception, and their *feeling* in the mind'. According to Hume, it is the intensity and steadiness of the ideas conceived that makes them credible, rather than their clarity or distinctiveness.

In an attempt to explain the nature of genius and inspiration several writers developed a line of argument that was not dissimilar to Hume's, even if it was not directly beholden to Hume, namely that a work of genius

[7] ibid., p. 43.
[8] ed. L. A. Selby-Bigge (Oxford 1894), p. 49.

is the product of intense and steady conceptions. Just how the mind might experience such conceptions was a question that was explored by many eighteenth-century writers. The writings of the British empiricists had aroused much interest in France, and they led to developments, notably by Voltaire (1694–1778), Helvétius (1715–71) and Condillac (1715–80), that Locke certainly and Hume possibly would have thought unjustified. In his *Traité des sensations* (1754), Condillac claimed that the mind did not *reflect* on sensations, but merely compared them through memory. Perception being, according to Condillac, the result of habit rather than the immediate evidence of the senses, reflection was the automatic comparison of former perceptions. The mind was no longer a kind of guiding force, charting a course to objective truth by rationally judging and interpreting the evidence of the senses. It was simply a stock of ideas which had themselves originally been sense-impressions, its continuity merely that of the collection of things which it was feeling and the things which its memory recalled. All ideas were therefore relative to the sense-impressions of the thinker; 'good' and 'beautiful' were not absolute terms, but were relative to the character of the man making the judgement and to the way in which he was organised. Comparisons and judgements, according to Condillac, coalesce into habits; they become stored in the mind, so that more and more associations of ideas are possible. If these associations arouse pleasure, they also arouse the desire to experience again what caused the pleasurable sensation in the first place; and it is thus *desire* that stimulates the memory, determines the operation of our faculties and gives rise to our passions and affections. Reality was thus for Condillac almost a question not so much of *cogito ergo sum*, as the Latin version ran of Descartes's famous phrase, but of *sentio ergo sum*, or even *desidero ergo sum*.

Such relativity of judgement and hence of values was taken a stage further by Helvétius, and similar ideas to his were at one time held by Sulzer (see p. 127), at any rate as far as the man of genius was concerned. In *De l'esprit* (1758) Helvétius argued that the man of genius, the highest type of man, was not the man whose intellect outranked that of his fellows, but the man distinguished by the intensity of his passions, which he then translated into works of art. The passion that drove a genius might equally drive him to splendid virtue or to hideous crime. The advantage held by the man of genius was his habit of concentration and his method of study. These made him more perceptive than and hence superior to ordinary men; and, Helvétius claimed, exempt from the rules that governed ordinary men's conduct. Aspects of these ideas are found in the writings of some German thinkers. In *Die Entwickelung des Begriffs vom Genie* (1762, translated from a French original published five years earlier), Sulzer expresses ideas on genius not far from those of Helvétius, though it will be seen from pp. 127–30 that he had modified his view by the time the *Allgemeine Theorie* was published. K. P. Moritz, too (see p. 185), argued that genius was a capacity to feel with an intensity so great that a desire was aroused to imitate the object stimulating the desire.[9] Moreover the creation of beauty was the highest form of human activity, just as love was the highest form of emotion.[10]

Leibniz (1646–1716) picked up the other end of the stick. In a famous passage he argues that 'even the pleasures of sense are really intellectual pleasures confusedly known' – and it is clear that he invests the term 'mind' with a continuity and a sense of balance and harmony markedly differing from Condillac's definition of the term:

> it is easy to love God as we ought, if we know Him as I have just said [i.e. disinterestedly]. For although God cannot be perceived by our external senses, He is none the less very lovable and He gives very great pleasure. We see how much pleasure honours give to men, although they do not consist in anything that appeals to the external senses. Martyrs and fanatics (though the emotion of the latter is ill-governed) show how much influence mental pleasure (*le plaisir de l'esprit*) can have: and, what is more, even the pleasures of sense are really intellectual pleasures confusedly known. Music charms us, although its beauty consists only in the harmonies (*convenances*) of numbers and in the counting (of which we are unconscious but which nevertheless the soul does make) of the beats or vibrations of sounding bodies, which beats or vibrations come together at definite intervals. The pleasure which sight finds in good proportions is of the same nature; and the pleasure caused by the other senses will be found to amount to much the same thing, although we may not be able to explain it so distinctly.[11]

Pleasure, it seems, may be experienced *through* the senses; but it is experienced *in* the mind. Moreover, there are certain pleasures above and beyond those of the senses.

If Hume, and particularly Condillac, argued that mind was just an aspect of sensation and judgement a matter of association, or even habit, Leibniz is here claiming that emotion, or at any rate pleasure, is an aspect of mind. The ramifications of these ideas, or of aspects of them, can be traced in the following pages.

The term *imagination* has been quoted a number of times in this section as meaning the commonplace imagination that associates ideas and images with one another, sometimes in a way that was at the time unique. With Rousseau (see p. 109), the term takes on a wider meaning. Imagination as he understands the term is not just a matter of having novel powers of association whereby old ideas are associated with other old ideas in a new way. For him, imagination involves the capacity actually to produce novelty; and genius is nothing without this power of *invention*. Imaginative genius creates new ideas *ex nihilo*, as it were, rather than by developing novel combinations of previous ideas. The *Encyclopédie* (see p. 64) also emphasises the part that imagination must play in the work of genius, but it

---

[9] *Ueber die bildende Nachahmung des Schönen* (Brunswick 1788), p. 24.

[10] ibid., p. 42.

[11] *The Monadology and Other Writings*, translated by R. Latta (London 1898; 7th reprint 1971, p. 422).

is clear from the context that this is the older, associative type of imagination that is envisaged. This imagination intensifies the memory of those experiences that first fired it and then relates them to a thousand others that intensify the feelings aroused still further. Kant's section on genius (see p. 227) shows a shift in direction towards the conception of imagination held by Rousseau; and like Helvétius and like the author of the article in the *Encyclopédie*, Kant held that genius had the right not to be bound by rules. He defines genius as 'the aptitude to produce something for which no definite rule can be postulated'; it is, he claims, not explicable in conscious terms, yet its products are such that they may serve as models to others. Not bound by rules itself, it provides models, in fact, from which, in art at any rate, rules may be induced.

Building on the basis established by his study of Kant, Schiller (see pp. 235–6) argued the importance of aesthetic education in human life, not just as a source of pleasure nor for the man of genius alone, but as a training for the emotional and imaginative side of mankind in general so as to make a decisive contribution to a well-balanced society. This training, disciplining the emotions not so much by subjecting them to rigorous intellectual control but by allowing them development and nourishment according to the principles of sound aesthetic judgement, was regarded by Schiller and by later writers such as Herbart (see pp. 452–5) as vital to human education. In Herbart's case, it was for the benefit of the individual human being; with Schiller, it was so that the individual could contribute in harmony and freedom as a balanced and discriminating individual to the good of a just and free social order.

Aesthetic training for the benefit of society and the individuals comprising it became a central feature of romantic speculation. For them, the inventive imagination had a fascination and a significance that was held at times to border on the religious. Certainly in many cases, this particular kind of imagination played a considerable role in the make up of the romantic artist. Forces that were not merely acknowledged to be mysterious and inexplicable, but welcomed because they were so, were felt to be at work in the human soul. By the early years of the nineteenth century, reason had not only been reinterpreted in the light of empiricism, it had been dethroned in favour of the creative imagination stimulated by the emotions. Yet the excerpts quoted in the pages that follow show that this was no sudden violent reaction, but a process of gradual erosion, a process so relentless that by 1819 Arthur Schopenhauer could actually claim that one art – music – was in a strange sense more 'real' than the phenomenal world itself.

See also Bibliography under: Lessem

Jean-Baptiste Du Bos

(b. Beauvais, 21 Dec. 1670; d. Paris, 23 March 1742)

From: *Réflexions critiques sur la poësie et sur la peinture* (Paris 1719), section 45

Having first thought of making a career in the church, Du Bos entered public service in 1695 in the department of affaires étrangères. From 1699 to 1702 he spent much time in Italy, and immediately afterwards he went to England as *chargé d'affaires*, where he made contact with John Locke and many other leading English writers and philosophers. In 1720 he was elected a member of the Académie française, and in 1723 he became its secretary. He published much on political topics, but was most widely known for his *Réflexions critiques*. This went through nine French editions between 1719 and 1770 (the date of the last one), and translations were published in Amsterdam, Leipzig, Berlin, Copenhagen, Breslau and London. The translator of the English version was Thomas Nugent, a close acquaintance of Edmund Burke. After 1770 the book was largely forgotten, partly perhaps because its style was outdated, but also perhaps because the best ideas in it were by then common property;[1] as Chateaubriand was later to remark, 'On vole l'abbé Du Bos sans avouer le larcin.'

Du Bos has been seen as the father of modern aesthetics[2] because he made 'sentiment' – feeling – the *raison d'être* of art; as he put it, 'The most foolish thing that a painter or poet could possibly do would be to select as the principal subject of the imitation, something that is generally looked upon in nature with indifference.'[3]

The 'Author's Advertisement' (as translated by Nugent) may serve to give the outline of the argument.

In the first part of this work I endeavour to explain what the beauty of a picture or poem chiefly consists in, what merit both may draw from conforming to rules, and what assistance their productions may borrow of the other arts in order to shine forth with greater lustre.

In the second part I treat of the qualifications, whether natural or acquired, necessary to form great painters or poets. I inquire here likewise into the reasons of some ages being so fertile and others so barren of celebrated artists. I examine afterwards into the means whereby the reputations of illustrious artists have been raised, by what marks one can foretell whether the fame they have acquired in their days be transient or durable, and finally what these presages are which empower us to predict that the fame of a painter or poet, cried up by his contemporaries, will continue to increase, so as to arrive at a much higher degree of veneration in future ages than at the time he lived.

The third part of this work is laid out entirely in explaining some discoveries which methinks I have made in relation to the theatrical entertainments of the ancients.

[1] See A. Lombard, *L'Abbé Du Bos: Un initiateur de la pensée moderne* (Paris 1913), p. 344.

[2] Lombard, *L'Abbé*, p. 324.

[3] *Réflexions critiques*, ch. 6, p. 52.

Throughout his life Du Bos was an avid opera goer, and he believed that the cultivation of opera in Paris towards the end of the seventeenth century had resulted in a tremendous awakening of interest in music. Although it is the classical principle of 'Ut pictura poesis' that he is debating in the *Réflexions critiques*, it is hardly surprising that he has interesting things to say about music (indeed, Nugent found so many references to music in the book that he gave the work the English title of *Critical Reflections on Poetry, Painting and Music*, London 1746; enlarged edition 1748). Of all the arts, Du Bos found, music was the one that spoke most directly to the feelings. The author was typical of his time in giving pride of place to vocal music, instrumental music lacking the verbal precision exactly to determine the emotion being expressed (a hundred years later the young Berlioz was of a very similar opinion before Habeneck had introduced him to Beethoven's orchestral music). Yet he had a lively appreciation of the power of instrumental music within the operatic context:

> The symphonies of our operas, and especially those of Lully, the greatest musical poet among those whose works are extant, give a probability to the most surprising effects of the music of the ancients. Perhaps the military clangour of Theseus, the soft sounds of Armidas, and several other symphonies of the same author, would have produced such effects as seem fabulous in the accounts given by ancient authors, were they to be heard by people of as great a vivacity of temper as the Athenians, and in entertainments where they had been previously moved by the action of a tragedy. Do not we ourselves feel that these airs make such impressions on us as the musician desires? Do we not perceive that these symphonies enflame us, calm us, soften us, and in short, operate upon us, as effectually almost as Corneille's or Racine's verses?[4]

The particular interest that Du Bos had in 'sentiment' suggests the influence of Locke. He in turn greatly influenced Batteux and the *Encyclopédists*: every artist, Voltaire suggested, could profitably read his work, which was certainly the most useful of its kind ever to have been published. He was also highly regarded in Germany, many of his ideas being taken up in the works of J. U. Koenig, J. J. Bodmer, J. J. Breitinger and particularly Lessing. Frederick the Great is known to have read the *Réflexions critiques* in 1738 and to have much admired it.

Concerning music, as it is properly called

It remains for us to speak of music. This is the third means that man has invented to give a new force to poetry, whereby it is able to make a great impression on us. Just as the painter imitates the forms and colours of nature so the musician imitates the tones of the voice – its accents, sighs and inflections. He imitates in short all the sounds that nature herself uses to express the feelings and passions. All these sounds, as we have already shown, have a wonderful power to move us because they are the signs of the passions that are the work of nature herself, from whence they have derived their energy. Spoken words, on the other hand are only arbitrary symbols of the passions. The spoken word only derives its meaning and value from man-made conventions and it has only limited geographical currency.

---

[4] *Critical Reflections*, p. 66.

In order that the imitation of natural sounds shall be more pleasing and more moving, imitation has centred upon the continuous melody – commonly termed the subject. Two things have nevertheless been found to make melody more pleasing and more moving: the one is harmony, the other is rhythm.

The ear is greatly charmed by the chords that comprise harmony, and the interplay of the different voices of a musical composition (from which the chords are made up) further adds to the expressive power of the sound. The basso-continuo and the other added parts enable the melodic line to express the subject of the imitation much more perfectly.

When the Ancients spoke of rhythm in music they meant what we refer to as metre (*mesure*) and movement (*mouvement*). Now metre and movement as it were give soul to a musical composition. The science of rhythm shows how variety may be given to metre, thus avoiding an otherwise tedious uniformity in the flow (*cadence*) of the music. Rhythm can moreover give added reality to the imitation which is the subject of the composition, since it can imitate the sequence and movement of those noises and natural sounds that music has already imitated in melody and harmony. Rhythm thus adds a further dimension of reality to the imitation.

Music then effects its imitations by means of melody, harmony and rhythm. 'In cantu tria praecipue notanda sunt, harmonia, sermo et rithmus. Harmonia versatur circa sonum: Sermo circa intellectum verborum et enuntiationem distinctam: Rithmus circa concinnum cantici motum'.[5]

The natural signs of the passions that music evokes and which it artfully uses to increase the impact of the words to which it is set, must then make these words more able to touch us, for these natural signs have a marvellous power to move us. They draw their power from nature herself. 'Nihil est enim tam cognatum mentibus nostris, quam numeri atque voces, quibus et excitamur, et incendimur, et lenimur, et languescimus',[6] as one of the most perceptive observers of human affections has said. Thus, the pleasure of the ear becomes the pleasure of the heart. This is the origin of our songs (*chansons*). The words of these things have quite another energy when they are sung, rather than declaimed. This fact has already been observed, and it has led in the theatre to the development of recitative, and ultimately to the singing of a dramatic work from beginning to end. Hence, the opera.

There is thus a truth in operatic recitative, a truth which lies in the imitation of tones, accents, sighs and sounds that naturally relate to the sentiment contained in the words. The selfsame truth is to be found in harmony and in the rhythm of the entire musical composition.

Music has not simply been content to imitate in melody man's inarticulate

[5] In song, three things are particularly to be noted: harmony, words and rhythm. Harmony is a matter of sound; words involve clear enunciation and comprehension of what is being sung; and rhythm, the regular movement of the music.

[6] Nothing is so native to our hearts as words and metre. They arouse us; set us on fire, soothe and pacify us (Cicero, *De oratore*, bk 3).

language, and those natural sounds that he instinctively uses. It has even sought to imitate the many sounds that make a particular impression on him when he hears them in nature. Music uses only instruments to imitate such sounds in which speech has no part. Such imitations are commonly called symphonies. They even now have many different functions in our operas, and they are extremely effective.

In the first place, although this music is purely instrumental, it consistently achieves a truthful imitation of nature. In the second place there are many natural sounds that can be most impressive when heard as part of a dramatic piece.

The imitative truth of a symphony lies in its resemblance to the sound that it seeks to imitate. A symphony that is composed in imitation of a tempest has a truthfulness about it when its melodies, harmonies and rhythms conjure up sounds that are reminiscent of roaring winds and the thunder of waves dashing against each other or breaking against the rocks. The tempest symphony of M. Marais's *Alcione* is just such a work.

Although such symphonies lack articulated sounds, then, they continue to have a role in opera because they serve to further the action, evoking impressions that are analogous to those that are created by the very sounds that are being imitated. For example, the librettist may have inspired us with a lively interest in someone who is about to be engulfed in a raging tempest: the imitation of its sound will affect us in much the way that the sound of a tempest would do if someone for whom we had a warm regard were actually there. We hardly need to be reminded that such a symphony could never make quite the powerful impression upon us that a tempest could, for as I have reiterated above, an imitation can never be as effective as the thing itself. 'Sine dubio in omni re vincit imitationem veritas.'[7]

It is not surprising then that symphonies touch us deeply, although as Longinus has said, they can only be simple imitations of inarticulate sounds, their sounds only having, so to speak, a half life and partial existence.[8]

This is why inarticulate instrumental music has been used everywhere throughout the ages to move men's hearts and to awaken in them certain feelings, notably on those occasions when no way is known of inspiring them with words. Civilised peoples have always made use of instrumental music in their religious rites. Every nation has developed instruments that are suited to war, using them not only to convey the orders of the commanders to the rank and file but also to raise the courage of the combatants, and even on occasion to damp that courage down. Such instruments are played in a manner that conforms to the effect that is being sought, and attempts are made to match sounds to the specific event.

Perhaps we would have studied the art of playing military instruments with the care that the Ancients did, were it not for the fact that the din of

---

[7] In all cases reality undoubtedly surpasses imitation (Cicero, *De oratore*, bk 3).
[8] *Traité du sublime*, ch. 23.

firearms prevents the instruments from being clearly heard. Although we have given little thought to the perfection of military instruments, although we have seriously neglected the art of playing them – one that was so highly valued by the Ancients – and although we now regard the people who play such instruments as of the lowest rank, the basic principles of the art are still alive in our camps. Our trumpeters do not sound the advance in the same manner as the retreat. Our drummers do not beat the parley (*chamade*) at the same speed as the charge.

[p. 433, para. 1 to p. 440, last para. omitted]

The basic principles that govern music are thus similar to those that govern poetry and painting. Like poetry and painting, music is an imitation. Music cannot be good unless it conforms to the general rules that apply to the other arts on such matters as choice of subject and exactness of representation. As Cicero has observed, 'Omnes Artes quae ad humanitatem pertinent, habent quoddam commune vinculum et quasi cognatione quadam inter se continuantur'.[9]

Just as some people are more attracted to the colour of pictures than to the expression of passions, so others are only sensible to the pleasures of melody or even to the richness of harmony, and pay not the slightest attention to whether the melody is an effective imitation, or care whether it is consonant with the words to which it is set. Such people do not require the composer to match his melodic lines to the feelings that the words suggest, but are content that his melodies should be pleasing, and even singular. As far as they are concerned it is enough that the occasional word in a recitative shall be treated expressively. There are far too many musicians who are of this mind, and who act as though music were incapable of anything more. In setting the opening words, 'De torrente in via bibet', from the psalm 'Dixit dominus', they will concentrate wholly upon the idea of the rushing torrent, instead of the sense of the verse as a whole, in which is contained a prophecy of the passion of Jesus Christ. For the expression of a single word can never be as effective as the expression of a feeling unless, that is, the word encapsulates that feeling. If the musician gives expression to a particular word that only forms part of a phrase, he must take care not to lose sight of the meaning of the phrase as a whole.

Musical compositions that fail to move us can unequivocally be equated with pictures that have no merit other than their colouring, or with poems that are no more than well-constructed verses. In poetry and painting, technical excellence must serve to express the insights of genius, and to reveal those imaginative beauties that constitute the imitation of nature. In the same way, harmonic richness and variety, ornamentation and melodic originality must be used solely to create and embellish the musical imitation

---

[9] All the arts relating to man have a common bond and are mutually interconnected by a kind of family relationship.

of the language of nature and the passions. The science of composition is, so to speak, the servant which the genius of the musician must keep under his thumb, just as the poet of genius must control his talent for writing verse. In other words, everything is lost if the slave makes himself the master of the house and if he is allowed to order everything to suit himself, as if the place were built only for him. I believe that all poets and musicians would agree with this were it not easier to produce correct rhymes and to sustain a poetic style, and were it not easier to disregard the truth and to create melodies that are at once smooth and graceful. Genius is essential to expression, whereas even without genius, it is still possible to compose scholarly music and to produce excellent rhymes.

Francis Hutcheson

(b. Drumalig (?) 8 Aug. 1694; d. Glasgow, 1 Nov. 1746)

From: *An Inquiry into the Original of our Ideas of Beauty and Virtue; In Two Treatises. In which the Principles of the late Earl of Shaftesbury are explain'd and defended* (London 1725); text from the 4th edn, 1738, Treatise I, sections 1, 2, 6

Hutcheson studied classics, philosophy, theology and literature at Glasgow, and in 1729 accepted the chair of moral philosophy there, which he held for the rest of his life. He was a self-styled disciple of Shaftesbury, and an important influence on Hume. During the author's lifetime the work ran to four editions, all of which Hutcheson supervised.

Extract (a) illustrates Hutcheson's concern to establish general criteria by which the quality of beauty may be judged: the two central ideas concern aesthetic disinterestedness (i.e. that the experience of beauty is in no way connected with a purpose other than itself) and the principle of unity in variety. Extract (b) illustrates the application of the principle of unity to musical harmony. In (c) Hutcheson discusses music as expression; he recognises the uncomfortable fact that opinions differ considerably on the question of musical beauty, and he suggests that 'persons' tempers and past circumstances' may well affect their judgement. The final extract puts forward the idea that an 'internal sense' apprehends beauty, and that this is something separate from the physical ability to receive sense impressions.

For further reading:
Francis Hutcheson: An Inquiry Concerning Beauty, Order, Harmony, Design, edited with an introduction by Peter Kivy (The Hague 1973).

(a) Treatise I, section 1

XIII. And farther, the ideas of beauty and harmony, like other sensible ideas, are necessarily pleasant to us, as well as immediately so. Neither can any resolution of our own, nor any prospect of advantage or disadvantage, vary the beauty or deformity of an object. For as in the external sensations, no view of interest will make an object grateful, nor view of detriment distinct from the immediate pain in the perception make it disagreeable to the sense. So propose the whole world as a reward, or threaten the greatest evil, to make us approve a deformed object, or disapprove a beautiful one: dissimulation may be procured by rewards or threatenings, or we may in external conduct abstain from any pursuit of the beautiful, and pursue the deformed, but our sentiments of the forms, and our perceptions, would continue invariably the same.

23

This sense antecedent to, and distinct from prospects of interest
XIV. Hence it plainly appears that some objects are immediately the occasions of this pleasure of beauty, and that we have senses fitted for perceiving it, and that it is distinct from that joy which arises upon prospect of advantage. Nay, do not we often see convenience and use neglected to obtain beauty, without any other prospect of advantage in the beautiful form than the suggesting the pleasant ideas of beauty?

Treatise I, section 2

II. That we may more distinctly discover the general foundation or occasion of the ideas of beauty among men, it will be necessary to consider it first in its simpler kinds, such as occurs to us in regular figures; and we may perhaps find that the same foundation extends to all the more complex species of it.

Uniformity with variety
III. The figures which excite in us the ideas of beauty seem to be those in which there is uniformity amidst variety.

(b) Treatise I, section 2

Harmony
XIII. Under original beauty we may include harmony, or beauty of sound, if that expression can be allowed, because harmony is not usually conceived as an imitation of anything else. Harmony often raises pleasure in those who know not what is the occasion of it; and yet the foundation of this pleasure is known to be a sort of uniformity. When the several vibrations of one note regularly coincide with the vibrations of another they make an agreeable composition; and such notes are called concords. Thus the vibrations of any one note coincide in time with two vibrations of its octave; and two vibrations of any note coincide with three of its fifth, and so on in the rest of the concords.

Now no composition can be harmonious in which the notes are not, for the most part, disposed according to these natural proportions. Besides which, a due regard must be had to the key, which governs the whole, and to the time and humour in which the composition is begun, a frequent and inartificial change of any of which will produce the greatest and most unnatural discord. This will appear by observing the dissonance which would arise from tacking parts of different tunes together as one, although both were separately agreeable. A like uniformity is also observable among the basses, tenors, trebles of the same tune.

There is indeed observable, in the best compositions, a mysterious effect of discords: they often give as great a pleasure as continued harmony, whether by refreshing the ear with variety, or by awakening the attention, and enlivening the relish for the succeeding harmony of concords, as shades enliven and beautify pictures, or by some other means not yet known. Certain it is, however, that they have their place, and some good effect in our best compositions. Some other powers of music may be considered hereafter.

(c) Treatise I, section 6

Music, how it pleases differently

XII. There is also another charm in music to various persons, which is distinct from harmony and is occasioned by its raising agreeable passions. The human voice is obviously varied by all the stronger passions: now when our ear discerns any resemblance between the air of a tune, whether sung or played upon an instrument, either in its time, or modulation or any other circumstance, to the sound of the human voice in any passion, we shall be touched by it in a very sensible manner, and have melancholy, joy, gravity, thoughtfulness excited in us by a sort of sympathy or contagion. The same connection is observable between the very air of a tune and the words expressing any passion which we have heard it fitted to, so that they shall both recur to us together, though but one of them affects our senses.

Now in such a diversity of pleasing or displeasing ideas which may be joined with forms of bodies, or tunes, when men are of such different dispositions, and prone to such a variety of passions, it is no wonder that they should often disagree in their fancies of objects, even although their sense of beauty and harmony were perfectly uniform; because many other ideas may either please or displease, according to persons' tempers and past circumstances. We know how agreeable a very wild country may be to any person who has spent the cheerful days of his youth in it, and how disagreeable very beautiful places may be if they were the scenes of his misery. And this may help us in many cases to account for the diversities of fancy, without denying the uniformity of our internal sense of beauty.

[from IX.] The sense of harmony has got its name, viz. a good ear; and we are generally brought to acknowledge this natural power of perception, or a sense some way distinct from hearing. Now it is certain that there is as necessary a perception of beauty upon the presence of regular objects, as of harmony upon hearing certain sounds.

(d) Treatise I, section 1

Beauty and harmony

IX. Let it be observed that in the following papers the word beauty is taken for the idea raised in us, and a sense of beauty for our power of receiving this idea. Harmony also denotes our pleasant ideas arising from composition of sounds, and a good ear (as it is generally taken) a power of perceiving this pleasure. In the following sections, an attempt is made to discover what is the immediate occasion of these pleasant ideas, or what real quality in the objects ordinarily excites them.

Internal sense

x. It is of no consequence whether we call these ideas of beauty and harmony perceptions of the external senses of seeing and hearing, or not. I should rather choose to call our power of perceiving these ideas an internal sense, were it only for the convenience of distinguishing them from other sensations of seeing and hearing which men may have without perception of beauty and harmony. It is plain from experience that many men have in the common meaning the senses of seeing and hearing perfect enough. They perceive all the simple ideas separately, and have their pleasures; they distinguish them from each other, such as one colour from another, either quite different, or the stronger or fainter of the same colour, when they are placed beside each other, although they may often confound their names when they occur apart from each other, as some do the names of green and blue. They can tell in separate notes, the higher, lower, sharper or flatter, when separately sounded; in figures they discern the length, breadth, wideness of each line, surface, angle; and may be as capable of hearing and seeing at great distances as any men whatsoever. And yet perhaps they shall find no pleasure in musical compositions, in painting, architecture, natural landscape, or but a very weak one in comparison of what others enjoy from the same objects. This greater capacity of receiving such pleasant ideas we commonly call a fine genius or taste. In music we seem universally to acknowledge something like a distinct sense from the external one of hearing, and call it a good ear; and the like distinction we should probably acknowledge in other objects, had we also got distinct names to denote these powers of perception by.

Yves Marie André

(b. Chateaulin, 22 May 1675; d. Caen, 26 Feb. 1764)

From: *L'Essai sur le beau* (1741); text from *Oeuvres philosophiques du Père André*, ed. Victor Cousin (Paris 1843), pt 2, pp. 77–96

André studied theology at the college of Clermont and by 1707 was a member of the Jesuit community of La Flèche, Paris. His friendship with the Cartesian scholar Malebranche brought him into conflict with members of his community; he none the less remained a Jesuit and from 1726 until the Order was dissolved in 1762 he lived at Caen, as professeur royale de mathematiques. The *Essai* was reprinted as a new and enlarged edition in 1763, and though by no means as widely read as Du Bos or Batteux it was an influential work.[1] The immediate forerunner of Batteux's *Les beaux-arts* (see p. 40), it foreshadowed Batteux's system of the arts.

The *Essai* is in the form of eight lectures; the first three discuss concepts of artistic and moral beauty; the fourth is wholly devoted to music; the next three analyse the factors that together contribute to the presentation of beauty in its most perfect forms, under the headings of 'modus', 'decorum' and 'grace'; and the series culminates in the ethical question – what power has the love of beauty on the human heart?

The essential points that emerge from the *Essai* are that music is considered to be above all an expressive art, and that its power over the emotions must be harnessed to the common good. As the *Essai* was originally a series of lectures, it is more than usually expansive, even by the accepted standards of the day; and here and there its logic is not impregnable. Even so, it is well worth savouring at length in order to appreciate André's very real enthusiasm for music, to see what it was that fascinated him at a concert, and to understand how he applied the principle of unity both to the natural materials of music (pitch, rhythm and so on), but also to the relationship between music and words. For he believed that music's ethical power could only fully be harnessed with the aid of words, as only words can precisely determine what it is that music expresses.

Gentlemen,

An ancient writer on music whose treatise is one of a group dealing with Greek music, tackles his theme with laudable enthusiasm:

'Flee this place, profane peoples and hasten here, you who admire ethereal beauties. The language of the Gods must only speak to those whose souls are purified' (see his *Gaudent*, ed. Meibom).[2]

This view of music was held by all the ancient philosophers, and notably

---

[1] See P. O. Kristeller, 'The modern system of the arts', pt 2, *Journal of the History of Ideas*, vol. 13 (1952) p. 20.

[2] Marcus Meibomius, *Scriptores Graeci Musicae, Antiqui Musicae Auctores Septem* (Amsterdam 1652) – eds.

by Plato. They placed music above simple speech, and even above poetry. This was on account of the sublimity of the subjects with which it originally dealt: the praises of the Gods, and the praises of famous men whose virtues were sufficiently distinguished to be worthy of remembrance. Music was highly regarded, above all, on account of its harmonic numbers, which – if I may put it this way – shape musical composition, and on account too of the remarkable ecstasies that music inspires in the hearts of those who know how to listen to her. Since the ancient masters saw music in this light it is understandable that they only wished to address this divine language to divine souls, to those that were raised either by genius or taste above the level of common feelings, to those that were more sensible of harmonic consonance than sweetness of sound, and who acquired both theoretical and practical knowledge, the better to understand music's subtleties.

I am aware that some philosophers do not have such an exalted respect for music. Some even hold opinions that are quite to the contrary, claiming that feeling is the sole judge of harmony and that the pleasure of the ear is the only beauty that music affords. They argue moreover, that this pleasure is far too dependent on opinion, prejudice, convention and acquired habit to be the object of firm rules. And, they ask, is not the proof of this obvious enough? Are there two nations whose musical tastes are the same? Europeans and Orientals, French, Italians, Germans, Spaniards and Englishmen, Turks and Tartars even, has not each race its own particular music which it unquestioningly values above all others? Since each nation is evidently charmed and satisfied by its own music, what more is to be said? Nothing indeed, so far as those peoples are concerned who only conduct their lives and their thoughts in a haphazard way. But for thinking people – for men – something more is needed, namely that in all pleasures reason must at least be on an equal footing with the senses. No matter who may deny it – some upstart Midas, for instance, who only brings his ears with him – reason at least will not gainsay it. Let us follow the argument to its logical conclusion, taking as our model the celebrated Pythagoras. Let us strive to banish chance from the world – if not from human affairs then at least from the arts and sciences. This is the plan that I propose to adopt in the following discussion on music: for the sake of orderliness, I shall consider beauty under three headings; in this way the rightness of the argument will become apparent as we go on.

I would propose then: (i) that there is an essential musical beauty that is absolute, wholly independent of human institutions and even divine; (ii) that there is a natural musical beauty that is dependent on the Creator but which is in no way connected with opinion or taste; (iii) that there is an artificial musical beauty that is to some degree arbitrary but which none the less is dependent on the eternal laws of harmony.

Now, what is the precise nature of musical beauty? This is the last question that we shall attempt to resolve. Let us get to grips with it.

A quintessential musical beauty, absolute and in no way related to human institution – divine even! What a paradox this is for so many of us here today! Nothing is however more certain, gentlemen, nothing could be more widely acknowledged in so enlightened a city as yours! To convince any reasonable person of this I would only have to buttonhole him at the end of a concert while the sound of music was still in his ears and in his heart. Sir, I would say, you have just heard some fine music; would you care to tell me in what ways you have found it beautiful? Everything [he would reply]; the vocal melodies and the instrumental symphonies seemed to vie with each other for the honour of pleasing the listener. But in what ways were you pleased? The weight of so many different voices, mixed together, the numerous instruments and contrasting sounds, these surely deaden the ear rather than entertain it? . . . You hardly do justice to our performers. In no way does size lead to confusion. We have all heard how they start together at the initial signal, each distinct, yet blended together. We have heard them rising and falling in time with each other, swelling, sustaining, and each imparting to the other its charms. Above all, we have admired the splendid way in which the consecutive sounds are ordered, the propriety of the progressions, the regularity of the metrical flow, the intervallic proportions, the correctness of the tempi and the perfect balance of the ensemble. . . . Good enough! Order, regularity, proportion, precision, propriety, unity – I begin to comprehend the idea of musical beauty. But such beauty is neither the sound that reached your ear, nor the pleasant sensation that it aroused in your soul, nor the satisfaction that you experienced in your heart upon reflection. What conclusion does this lead you to? . . . It must be that in the concert there is a purer pleasure than the sweetness of the actual sounds, and a beauty that does not have its roots in the senses, a particular beauty that charms the mind and which the mind alone perceives and judges. . . . Do you doubt this? . . . No; but I would like to know by what rule one judges. By what rule have you yourself judged in order to give me so excellent an account of the concert? By what rule? I have done nothing more than pay careful attention to everything. I followed every progression of sound, both simultaneous and successive. I compared them with each other. I noted all the cadences. I was sensible of the music's rise and fall, of its flowing and harmonious style, of its moments of urgency and tranquillity, its recapitulations and restatements, its flights, its returns. In other words, sir, during the time that this large ensemble of sonorous instruments was impressing your ear with pleasurable sounds, you experienced deep down within you a master of music who beat time, if I may put it thus, to show how right the music was, and who revealed its principles by means of a light that was superior to that of the senses. These principles are grounded in order, in the structural beauty of the piece, in harmonic numbers, in the rule of proportion and harmonious progression, and in the idea of propriety, a sacred law that allots each part its position, its conclusion and the right path by which to reach its end. Thus while all those who took part in the concert were reading their individual parts, you were also reading yours, written in eternal and ineffaceable notes from the great book of reason which is open to all receptive minds. In brief, we must either deny music the name of harmony (one that it has undisputedly assumed since the day that the very first concert was given) or we must acknowledge that there is a fundamental and absolute musical beauty which provides music's sacred law, a basic truth that we must establish at the outset for the honour of so fine an art.

I said, secondly, that there is a natural musical beauty that depends on the Creator but which is independent of our opinions and tastes. This can hardly be denied, however little we may know of the structure of sonorous bodies, the sensitivity of the ear, the altogether harmonious make-up of the human body, or above all the sympathy that exists between certain musical sounds and human emotions. Here are four obvious proofs that music is not a purely human institution, to be changed, added to and reduced at will. Let us proceed on the strength of only the most incontestable experiences.

To begin with, what do these tell us about the nature of sonorous bodies? The celebrated Descartes discovered at the beginning of the last century that the sound of a string is never heard on its own but is always accompanied by its upper octave. His friend, the scholarly P. Mersenne, confirmed this observation in several experiments. Afterwards, M. Sauveur, the famous academician, discovered in a single musical sound – that of a harpsichord, for instance – two other highly agreeable consonances: the fifth and the major third. These three can be so clearly distinguished by a trained ear that M. Rameau has made this the basic principle of his new musical system. It is just the same with the voice: there seems to be one sound and yet it is threefold in nature, for in addition to the principal sound, which is the deepest and the strongest, there are also the fifth, major third and octave.

What must the sensitivity be of the organ that distinguishes these sounds so precisely? It is so sensitive, in fact, that if two unison strings were mistuned by no more than one 2,000th part of their length a keen ear would be aware of the dissonance: M. Sauveur has calculated that the difference is no more than 196th part of a tone. M. Dodard, another distinguished academician, cites these figures and confirms them in his excellent memoir on the structure of the voice, published in the Proceedings of 1700. Since then, M. Sauveur has conducted several other experiments on the same subject, and he has given us a second result in which he infers that the sensitivity of the ear to sound is 10,000 times greater than is that of the eye to colour. Can we wonder, then, that music has consistently produced such prodigious results?

Such results will seem less surprising still if it is borne in mind that the entire structure of the human body is harmonic. This is not to suggest that the nerves are stretched over bones as are strings over the soundboards of a musical instrument, nor that the arteries beat time by regulated pulses, nor even that the heart marks out metre and cadence in its precise and reciprocal movements. Such ideas, which may be reasonable enough, even though they are of ancient origin, might seem to be no more than frivolous fancies. I shall keep within the bounds, then, of the obvious.

The science of anatomy reveals that the nerves which form the base of the ear and which are associated with the faculty of hearing, comprise an infinity of delicate fibres. These fibres, which emanate from the eardrum and the labyrinth, run in all directions, some to the brain – the seat of the mind and the imagination – some to the lower part of the mouth where the vocal organs are situated, others to the heart which is the seat of the affections and feelings, and others even to the lower viscera. All these fibres are highly mobile, prompt in response, and under tension, so that they can be disturbed by the slightest movement of the acoustic membrane, rather like strings in a harpsichord that immediately respond to the movement of the keys. Add to this aural nervous system which communicates to all the main parts of the body, those many organs that together form the voice: the hollows of the chest that contain the necessary air; the wind-pipe that serves as a duct; the glottis which produces the voice by means of sonorous vibrations; the buccal cavity and the roof of the mouth which amplify the vibrations by means of resonance; the tongue, the teeth and the lips to modify the voice in every way that art can devise. Now, in all these works of the Creator, in all these organs that are so well adapted to their function (some to create sounds, others to receive them), how many are the obvious signs of a harmonious design, and of a touching and deeply moving harmony!

I mention the question of pathos in harmony, for the good reason that there is a natural sympathy between certain sounds and the emotions of the soul. There is no question here of explaining how this comes about; all that we need to know is this indubitable fact. There are sounds which have a secret understanding with the heart, and this we cannot deny. Lively sounds inspire courage, languishing sounds appease, laughing sounds cheer, mournful sounds sadden, majestic sounds uplift the soul, harsh sounds irritate, gentle sounds soften. There are as many sounds in nature as there are passions to express: love and hate, desire and fear, anger and pity, hope and despair, admiration, terror, boldness.

[p. 83, para. 1 to p. 85, last para. omitted]

In addition to the two kinds of beauty that – as we have just proved – exist independently of the will of man is a third that in some measure depends on him, both in respect of its development and application. I refer to that artificial kind of musical beauty which, having rendered to the eternal law of harmony everything that the voice of nature absolutely requires, unties as it were the hand of genius, concedes much to taste and even a little to the whim of the composer. Is this enough to satisfy our good friends the musicians? We agree with them that there is in music a sort of beauty that belongs to convention and to art: beauty of inspiration, beauty of taste, and under particular circumstances a certain beauty that springs from wit and humour. There is here a huge field in which the musician is free to move. In order, however, to prevent misuse, which could well degenerate into licence, some further explanation is necessary. At this point we must remind ourselves of the basic principles that we established in our opening discussion.

Consonance, which has been our principal concern, must play an essential role in a musical composition. Because there are so few consonances, however, the fear is that they will in the end become distasteful through over-frequent repetition, notwithstanding their sweetness. Either then new consonances must be found from time to time, or the taste for established consonance must be stimulated by some kind of seasoning. As nature has prescribed how many consonances there shall be there can be no question of adding to them. It remains then to season the sweetness with some kind of harmonic spice. In what form (especially in important works) is this harmonic spice to be found, a spice that will provide cohesion, which will bind chords together and enhance the expression by means of piquant modulations? Can you guess? Music has stolen this spice from the very heart of its most bitter enemy. It has sought out individual features to which it can be reconciled. It has developed the art, that is to say, of smoothing roughness and of giving roughness a share in the pleasure of consonance, thereby ensuring that the harmony is not upset. It has learned how to use dissonance, as shadows are used in painting, or as connecting passages are used in a speech to join one point with another. It has found out the art of preparing for suspensions before they are taken, preceding them by sweet and lively sounds that choke the unpleasantness at birth. And when such preparations are either too difficult or altogether impossible it adroitly saves the day with brilliant chords that follow the blemish immediately and cover it up. In a word, the art of handling dissonance in a composition has been developed to such a degree that although the dissonances may hurt the ear a little, they only hurt to please the more. This is the paradox: and here is the explanation.

[p. 86, para. 1 omitted]

There is a still more profound reason for the use of dissonance in music. It has been recognised throughout the ages that if dissonance offends the ear somewhat by its harshness, it is all the more appropriate for certain kinds of expression: violent transports of love, wild anger, troublous dissension, the horrors of battle, tempestuous storms. Now, keeping the discussion on the subject of the human voice, we all know that when the soul is gripped by certain emotions the voice instinctively becomes shrill, it suddenly loses its pleasant tone and gets higher or lower, not gradually but by leaps and bounds. It is in such circumstances as these that dissonance has its place. There are even circumstances in which dissonance is essential, and then – so the most knowledgeable musicians tell us – although it may displease the ear by its harshness, it will please the mind and the heart on account of its expressive power. This is generally acknowledged to be so. The gifted composer will always bear in mind that reason shall be satisfied, and that this is of prime importance to the soul.

[p. 87, last para. omitted]

Thus music becomes a kind of sonorous rhetoric which has its grand gestures to inspire the soul, as words do, its charms to move it, and its playfulnesses, its jokes and its games to divert it. The question is when to make use of these different styles. In the hands of a talented artistic person we can see the three kinds of artificial musical beauty taking shape in response to the matter that is to be expressed: the beauty of genius, the beauty of taste or – if you will pardon the expression – the beauty of caprice.

The beauty of genius concerns noble subjects; in these the music may loftily unfold its grand designs, its images, movements, suspensions and diversions, its fugues and counter fugues, its transitions from key to key that amaze the ear by their very variety. There may be sudden and refreshing silences, unexpected and surprising returns, long, sustained notes that hold the attention, and moments of delightful rapture. Here we have musical eloquence that is, in a word, sublime.

Beauty of taste concerns fine and subtle matters; the musician will then impart an affecting quality to the sounds, quickening them, tempering them, preparing the ear for them, making the ear long for certain consonances the more to increase its enjoyment, giving it a foretaste of others so that it may be granted even more pleasurable ones, leading it astray even, now and again, in order to set it once more on its original path, thereby adding to its enjoyment; the musician may infer, promise or understate in order that the ear may have the gratification of supplying that which is missing or which is only half heard.

Now, if I may be allowed to defer to the musician, the beauty of caprice stems from jocular subjects that involve wit: when for instance some bizarre fancy, some comic action or burlesque passion is to be expressed. His colleague the poet is permitted an element of fantasy in the telling of his adventures; and every day the most serious minds take pleasure in poetic fantasies. Why should not a similar privilege be accorded to musical caprice, in similar circumstances? Why should it not enjoy the same fate as Freni's new opera which has entertained the entire French nation? We should even find musical caprice interesting on occasion, and perhaps justifiably so, if it provided no other satisfaction than that of painting an original with which it was preoccupied.

[p. 89, para. 1 omitted]

Having proved by various arguments the first three propositions concerning musical beauty there remains a final question, namely the precise form that musical beauty takes. Those of you who have done me the honour of attending my first three lectures on beauty will already know my answer to this. Throughout the discussion my principles have remained the same; my conclusions must likewise do so.

I repeat then, with St Augustine, 'Omnis porro pulchritudinis forma unitas est' (moreover, every form of beauty is a unity) (*Epistolae*, 18). In everything that is made, whether by nature or art, the form of true beauty always lies in unity. And as far as music is concerned I have no hesitation in saying that this great principle is more certain than in any other form.

Indeed, gentlemen, let us use our common sense, let us use our ears. What do we automatically look for in a composition? Consonance, ensemble, a general harmony – in other words, total unity. And on the contrary, what gives us such pain during the course of a concert? An out-of-tune voice, a mistuned string, what is called poor intonation, a lack of ensemble: in other words, a breakdown of musical unity. And here is something that is particularly apposite. What do we ask of the musician when he sets words to music? That he should take care to enter into the spirit of the piece; that he should fully appreciate its character, its genre and its mood; that he should express, not only the words but also their meaning, and not only the meaning of each word but the meaning of the entire work.

[p. 90, last five lines to p. 91, last para. omitted]

Finally, to adduce the last piece of evidence in support of our principle, what is it that we admire (at times, almost ecstatically) about those concerts in which so many different voices and instruments perform together, and which might at first sight seem to be so mutually discordant? Is it not the skill with which unity is imposed on so prodigious an array of different sounds? It is said that this large-scale music making originated in the inventive climate of the previous century. But the learned and ingenious Seneca has left us a description which clearly proves, if I am not mistaken, that large ensembles were then no new thing. (Seneca, *Ad Lucillium epistolarum*, No. 84). Certainly, the principle of unity that we have been discussing was fully established in his day.

[p. 92, para. 2 omitted]

In view of the many arguments based on common sense and on the experience of the greatest masters, there can be no doubt that musical beauty exists independently of our opinions and tastes. Nor, I would suggest, can there be the slightest doubt that nature has given musical beauty pride of place over all other forms of sensible beauty. Let us as we finish set music side by side with painting. What a contrast we shall find! Everyone knows that imitation forms the basis of these two kinds of beauty, or – if you prefer – expression. This is the point on which music and painting unite in a common object. What a difference there is however in the way that they achieve it!

What do we see in the finest painting? Solely the surface of a body: a face, eyes, fixed and inanimate colours and a few other features that seem to want to speak. Music lays the soul bare to its very depths – its excitements (expressed in rapid sounds), its struggles (in which sounds conflict) and its repose (sounds that are tranquil and of little variety). Painting only offers to the eyes static objects, objects that are at their best poised for movement: that is the only life that a picture can have. Music depicts movement and even the process of slowing down and speeding up, as the subject or the composer demands. A painting depicts only a split-second action, which is often no more than a small part of the occasion that the painter wishes us to recall. One simple air will recall the whole occasion: its beginning, its continuation and its end. Twenty pictures would be needed to bring together the things that the slightest cantata or sonata would contain. Take for instance a battle scene. The greatest praise that you can bestow on it is to say that you feel you are looking at the original. If a vocal or an instrumental concert attempted the same thing you could imagine that you were right in the midst of the action: you would hear the two armies marching, the call to advance, the clash of arms, the resounding blows as the soldiers strike each other, the triumphant shouts of the conquerors and the plaintive cries of the defeated. It is as if our hearts were there at the scene of the actual battle. There is no more admirable thing in painting than perspective which on a flat surface reveals to us hollow depressions and distant scenes that seem to extend way out of sight. But in truth the imagination must supply a good deal if we are to believe in the distances, despite the evidence of our eyes. Music has its distances, and these are more real. After a unison *coup d'archet* of twenty-four performers, music can make us hear an echo as from a distance, which will completely deceive the ear. A blind man would swear that he heard two ensembles, one of which replied to the other from a long way away.

The painting should not however mourn its defeat. I do not wish to imply that painting fails to achieve a high standard. Indeed, it may well be in a higher state of perfection than music. I only wish to say that it has been less well endowed by nature and that it has had the benefit of less help and fewer lessons than its rival. I do maintain for example that colours are less expressive than sounds; that the hand which guides the brush is less flexible than the glottis which forms the voice; that the eye which guides the painter is less subtle than the ear which guides the musician; that the canvas which carries the colours is less receptive than the air which carries the sounds; that the rays of light which reveal to our eyes the beauties of nature are not so keen or sensitive as the aerial vibrations which bring to us the charms of a concert; nor indeed are the gradations of colour that delineate the characters within the overall design of a picture so easy to measure or calculate as are the pitches that are assigned to voices and instruments within a musical ensemble. Is it surprising then, in the light of such advantages, that musical beauty should have qualities that are more sublime, more delicate, stronger and more refined than the beauties of all the other arts?

[p. 95, last para., to the end of the fourth lecture – p. 96, para. 1 omitted]

James Harris

(b. Salisbury, 20 July 1709; d. Salisbury, 22 Dec. 1780)

From: *Three Treatises. The First Concerning Art, the Second Concerning Music, Painting and Poetry, the Third Concerning Happiness* (London 1744), Ch. 6, sections i–iv

Harris became a gentleman-commoner of Wadham, Oxford in 1726 and later read law at Lincoln's Inn, without, however, any intention to adopt it as a career. Having independent means he subsequently set up house in the cathedral close at Salisbury where he pursued his classical interests, and was both patron and organiser of the annual Salisbury music festival. In 1761 he entered parliament as a representative for Christchurch, and later held minor office in government.

The *Three Treatises* was his most widely read work; by 1794 it had reached its fifth edition and was known on the continent.[1] Like Batteux Harris believed that the generally accepted term, 'the arts' must mean that each of the arts had something in common with the others. He did not adopt, however, the simple Aristotelian idea of the 'imitation of nature' as the solution to the problem, but by a process of dialogue he arrived at the following proposal: that art 'is an habitual power in man, of becoming the cause of some effect, according to a system of various and well-approved precepts. If it is asked us, on what subject art operates? We can answer, on a contingent which is within the reach of the human powers to influence. If it be asked us, for what reason, for the sake of what, art operates? We may reply, for the sake of some absent good, relative to human life, and attainable by man, but superior to his natural and uninstructed faculties.'

The second dissertation treats 'of music, painting and poetry, to consider in what they *agree*, and in what they *differ*, and which upon the whole is more excellent than the other two'. The basic criterion here is 'imitation' and the three arts are exhaustively compared to determine the ways in which they imitate. In the final chapter – given here in full – Harris argues that music is not properly an art of imitation but of expression,[2] that it is an art of motion like poetry, that is inferior to poetry on account of its vagueness, but that it can add a useful dimension to poetry as an art of emotion. In this, Harris was very much at one with Du Bos. Unlike Hutcheson (p. 24), Harris had no interest in abstract definitions of the quality of beauty; he accepted that the impact of a work of art was bound to vary according to the state of mind of the recipient.

Chapter 6

On music considered not as an *imitation*, but as deriving its efficacy from another source. On its joint operation, by this means, with poetry. An objection to music

[1] See Kristeller, 'The modern system of the arts', p. 29; see also the Lichtenthal bibliography, pp. 376–94.

[2] As Twining later pointed out, however, this was in no way contrary to the Aristotelian position; see pp. 197–208.

solved. The advantage arising to it, as well as to poetry, from their being united. Conclusion.

Section i

In the above discourse, music has been mentioned as an ally to poetry.[3] It has also been said to derive its efficacy from another source than imitation.[4] It remains therefore that these things be explained.

Now, in order to do this, it is first to be observed that there are various affections which may be raised by the power of music. There are sounds to make us cheerful, or sad; martial or tender; and so of almost every other affection which we feel.

It is also further observable that there is a reciprocal operation between our affections and our ideas, so that by a sort of natural sympathy certain ideas necessarily tend to raise in us certain affections, and those affections, by a sort of counter operation, to raise the same ideas. Thus ideas derived from funerals, tortures, murders and the like, naturally generate the affection of melancholy. And when by any physical causes that affection happens to prevail, it as naturally generates the same doleful ideas.

And hence it is that ideas derived from external causes have, at different times, upon the same person so different an effect. If they happen to suit the affections which prevail within, then is their impression most sensible and their effect most lasting. If the contrary be true, then is the effect contrary. Thus for instance, a funeral will much more affect the same man if he sees it when melancholy than if he sees it when cheerful.

Now this being premised, it will follow that whatever happens to be the affection or disposition of mind which ought naturally to result from the genius of any poem, the same probably it will be in the power of some species of music to excite. But whenever the proper affection prevails, it has been allowed that then all kindred ideas, derived from external causes, make the most sensible impression. The ideas therefore of poetry must needs make the most sensible impression when the affections peculiar to them are already excited by the music.[5] For here a double force is made cooperate to one end. A poet, thus assisted, finds not an audience in a temper, averse to the genius of his poem, or perhaps at best under a cool indifference, but by the preludes, the symphonies and concurrent operation of the music in all its parts, roused into those very affections which he would most desire.

An audience, so disposed, not only embrace with pleasure the ideas of the poet, when exhibited, but in a manner even anticipate them in their several

---

[3] Harris, *Three Treatises*, p. 93 (eds.)

[4] Harris, p. 69 (eds.)

[5] Quintilian elegantly, and exactly apposite to this reasoning, says of music, 'Namque et voce et modulatione grandia elate, jucunda dulciter, moderate lenitur canit, totaque arte consentit cum eorum, quae dicuntur, affectibus.' (For music sings, through voice and modulation, grand themes loftily, happy themes sweetly, humbler themes gently, and all that her art commands is at one in feeling with the sentiments of those themes) Quintilian, *Institutionum oratoriarum*, I, 10, 24.

imaginations. The superstitious have not a more previous tendency to be frightened at the sight of spectres, or a lover to fall into raptures at the sight of his mistress, than a mind, thus tempered by the power of music, to enjoy all ideas which are suitable to that temper.

And hence the genuine charm of music, and the wonders which it works, through its great professors:[6] a power which consists not in imitations and the raising [of] ideas, but in the raising [of] affections to which ideas may correspond. There are few to be found so insensible, I may even say so inhumane, as when good poetry is justly set to music, not in some degree to feel the force of so amiable a union. But to the muses' friends it is a force irresistible, and penetrates into the deepest recesses of the soul. 'Pectus inaniter angit, irritat, mulcet, falsis terroribus implet.'[7]

Section ii

Now this is that source from whence music was said formerly to derive its greatest efficacy.[8] And here indeed, not in imitation[9] ought it to be chiefly cultivated. On this account also it has been called a powerful ally to poetry.[10] And further, 'tis by the help of this reasoning that the objection is solved which is raised against the singing of poetry (as in operas, oratorios, etc.) from the want of probability and resemblance to nature. To one indeed who has no musical ear this objection may have weight. It may even perplex a lover of music if it happen to surprise him in his hours of indifference. But when he is feeling the charm of poetry so accompanied, let him be angry (if he can) with that which serves only to interest him more feelingly in the subject and support him in a stronger and more earnest attention, which enforces by its aid the several ideas of the poem and gives them to his imagination with unusual strength and grandeur. He cannot surely but confess that he is a gainer in the exchange, when he barters the want of a single probability, that of pronunciation (a thing merely arbitrary and everywhere different), for a noble heightening of the affections which are suitable to the occasion and enable him to enter into the subject with double energy and enjoyment.

---

[6] Such above all is George Frederick Handel, whose genius, having been cultivated by continuous exercise, and being itself far the sublimest and most universal now known, has justly placed him without an equal or a second. This transient testimony could not be denied so excellent an artist, from whom this treatise has borrowed such eminent examples to justify its assertions in what it has offered concerning music.

[7] He tortures his breast over nothing; he rouses it, soothes it, he fills it with imagined terrors. Horace, *Epistolae*, 21, 211.

[8] Harris, p. 69 (eds.)

[9] For the narrow extent and little efficacy of music considered as a mimetic or imitative art, see ch. 2, section iii: viz. 'as to musical imitation in general, it must be confessed that it can from its genius imitate only sounds and motions ... further [that] music does but imperfectly imitate even these . . .; musical imitation is greatly below that of painting, and ... at best it is an imperfect thing'.

[10] Harris, p. 93 (eds.)

Section iii

From what has been said, it is evident that these two arts can never be so powerful singly as when they are properly united. For poetry, when alone, must be necessarily forced to waste many of its richest ideas in the mere raising of affections, when to have been properly relished, it should have found those affections in their highest energy. And music, when alone, can only raise affections, which soon languish and decay if not maintained and fed by the nutritive images of poetry. Yet must it be remembered in this union, that poetry ever have the precedence, its utility as well as dignity being by far the more considerable.

Section iv

And thus much for the present as to music, painting and poetry, the circumstances in which they agree and in which they differ, and the preference due to one of them above the other two.

Charles Batteux

(b. Allend'huy, nr. Rheims, 7 May 1713; d. Paris, 14 July 1780)

From: *Les beaux-arts réduits à un même principe* (Paris 1746), Preface; Table of Contents; pts i, ii and iii

In 1730 Batteux settled in Paris and later was appointed professor of Greek and Latin philosophy at the Collège royale. In 1754 he became a member of the Académie des inscriptions et belles lettres, and in 1761 of the Académie française. *Les beaux-arts*, which has been described as 'the decisive step to the modern system of the fine arts',[1] was widely read and very influential. J. A. Schlegel published a translation of it (Leipzig 1752), and revised German editions appeared in 1759 and 1770; Overbeck, Caspar Ruetz and C. W. Ramler all published commentaries that included discussion of Batteux's ideas on music. In England, an anonymous author plagiarised Batteux as early as 1749, without acknowledgement, in a work entitled *The Polite Arts*. *Les beaux-arts* was still being reissued in France, as late as 1780, though by that time its value was being questioned.[2]

The work is important in that it established categories of arts that are still today accepted: fine arts that are an end in themselves, useful arts that are functional, and mixed arts, incorporating elements from both groups. It is also important, in that it lays unusual emphasis on the idea that the 'imitation' of nature involves a process of selection, that imitation is in fact 'idealisation'.[3] In the search for the ideal, the arts thus acquire an ethical function. This idea had of course been widely debated during the early part of the century, but Batteux undoubtedly did much to pave the way for that efflorescence of neo-classical idealism[4] that preceded the Revolution, in which music's power was to be harnessed, in true Greek fashion, to the needs of the state[5] (see Barthélemy, p. 166; and Leclerc, p. 240).

In applying the principle of the 'imitation of nature' to all the fine arts Batteux failed to make a clear distinction between imitation as representation and imitation as expression.[6] In his discussion of music, for instance, he vacillates between the idea of music as a mimetic art and music as abstract expression. At one point he draws parallels between the various arts and the natural 'objects' that they represent. Words, he argues, are the same both in conversation and poetry; shapes and colours are the same both in natural objects and pictures; just as musical tones are the same, whether the passions be real or simulated. Elsewhere however he comes close

---

[1] See Kristeller, 'The modern system of the arts', p. 20; see also Lichtenthal's bibliography (p. 376).

[2] See the review in the *Correspondance littéraire*, Sept. 1780, p. 483.

[3] *Les beaux-arts*, ch. 3, p. 24.

[4] But see B. H. Bronson, 'When was Neoclassicism?', *Studies in Criticism and Aesthetics (1660–1800)*, ed. Howard Anderson and John S. Shea (Minneapolis 1967) p. 13ff., for a timely warning on the dangers of using this term.

[5] For the repertory of state music, and commentary, see Constant Pierre (ed.), *Musique des fêtes et cérémonies de la révolution française* (Paris 1899).

[6] For a discussion of the distinction between the two, see Scruton, *Grove* vi.

to admitting that musical expression has little or nothing to do with imitation: 'it is true', he remarks, 'that a melodic line can express certain passions ... but for every passion that can be identified there are a thousand others that cannot be verbalised. Such musical expressions are by no means valueless (he continued); it is enough that they are felt. They do not have to be named. The heart has its own understanding that is independent of words. When it is touched, it has understood everything.' Batteux's failure to distinguish clearly between representation and expression, even though the seeds of the distinction are implicit in sections of his book, was readily seized upon by later critics, notably Diderot; and his mimetic theory of musical imitation, in particular, became an Aunt Sally for everyone to shoot at. In effect, however, Batteux was rather subtler than most later commentators would allow.

Preface (Avant-propos)

After so much fruitless research, yet not daring to tackle on my own a problem that seemed on close examination to be so obscure, I decided to have a look at Aristotle's *Poetics*, about which I had heard excellent things. I assumed that the work must have been consulted and copied by every master of the art, but it transpired that many of them had not even read it, and almost no one had drawn upon the ideas that it contained, save for a handful of scholars. From them I took no more than a few embryonic ideas, since they had only referred in their books to such matters as were relevant to the elucidation of specifically textual matters. They expressed themselves, moreover, in such dull, tortuous and obscure language that I all but despaired of finding anywhere a precise answer to the question that I was seeking to resolve, one that in the first instance had seemed so simple.

I was greatly struck, however, by the principle of imitation that Aristotle advanced in connection with the fine arts. I sensed its relevance for painting, which is silent poetry. I compared what Horace, Boileau, and several major authorities had to say on the subject. I took some ideas from other authors; my researches vindicated Horace's proposition: 'Ut pictura poesis'. It seemed that poetry was a complete imitation, as was painting. I went further than this; I applied the same principle to music and to mime, and I was astonished to find how apposite it was. The discovery led to this little book in which poetry occupies the foremost place. It does so because it has been the mainspring for this study, and equally because it merits first place in its own right.

I have divided the book into three sections. The first deals with the nature of the various arts, with their common characteristics and their differences. That the imitation of nature must be their common aim is demonstrated by the quality of the human spirit itself, the arts only differing from each other in the means that they use to achieve their objective. The materials of painting, music and dance are colours, sounds and gestures; the materials of poetry are words. Thus may be seen on the one hand the common bond and intimate relationship in which all the arts are united, all being the children of nature, dedicated to the same ends and governed by the same principles; on the other hand, may be seen their specific differences, ones that separate and distinguish them from each other.

Having determined the character of the arts through the genius of man who has created them, it was natural to seek what evidence could be found to establish the nature of feeling (*sentiment*), all the more because taste (*goût*) is the ultimate arbiter of the fine arts, reason herself only establishing her rules in conjunction with taste and in order to satisfy it. If then taste can be shown to be in agreement with genius (*génie*), prescribing the same rules for all the arts in general and for each in particular, fresh evidence and certainty would be added to the former truth. It is this that provides the substance of the second part of my book. In it is demonstrated that good taste (*bon goût*) in the arts is wholly consonant with ideas that have been established in the first part of the book, and that the rules of taste derive solely from the principle of imitation. For it follows that if the arts imitate beautiful nature (*belle nature*), a taste for beautiful nature must essentially be good taste in the arts. This idea is developed in the course of several chapters, in which attempts are made to define taste, to determine the foundations upon which taste is based, to understand how it is impaired, and so on. All these matters turn upon the general principle of the imitation of nature, which embraces everything. These two parts in the book contain the rational proofs.

To these is added a third part which relates to the conduct and practice of the artists themselves; in this part, theory is verified by practice. General principles are applied to specific things, and most of the accepted rules are related to imitation, forming a kind of chain by which the mind grasps at once the principle and its consequences in a perfectly united whole, the elements of which are mutually supporting.

Thus attempts to define the nature of poetry have led almost accidentally to the present work, by means of a sequence of ideas, the first of which proved to be the seed of all the others.

Table of Contents

Chapter 6: The ways in which eloquence and architecture differ from the other arts

Part 2: In which nature and the rules of taste are used to define the principle of imitation.

Chapter 1: A definition of taste

Chapter 2: That the object of taste is nothing other than nature: logical proofs

Chapter 3: Proofs taken from the history of taste itself

Chapter 4: The laws of taste have nothing but the imitation of beautiful nature as their object
(i) General law of taste: that the arts should imitate nature

Chapter 5: (ii) General law of taste: that the arts should imitate nature well

Chapter 6: That there are rules which are particular to each work, and that taste will only discover these in nature

Chapter 7: (i) Consequence: that although in general terms there is only one kind of good taste, there may be several kinds of good taste in particular

Chapter 8: (ii) Consequence: since the arts imitate nature it is by a process of comparison with her that they must be judged: two methods of comparison

Chapter 9: (iii) Consequence: that as the taste for nature is the same as that for the arts, there is only one taste, embracing everything including even morals

Chapter 10: (iv) Fourth and last consequence: the importance of forming taste early on in life, and the manner in which this may be done

Part 3: In which the principle of imitation is verified by means of its application to the various arts.

Section 1: That the art of poetry lies in the imitation of beautiful nature

Chapter 1: In which objections to the principle of imitation are refuted

Chapter 2: The categories of poetry are determined by imitation

Chapter 3: (i) That the general rules of descriptive poetry derive from imitation; (ii) The rules of high poetic derive from imitation

Chapter 4: The rules of epic poetry are based on imitation

Chapter 5: Concerning tragedy

Chapter 6: Concerning comedy

Chapter 7: Concerning the pastoral

Chapter 8: Concerning the 'Apologue'

Chapter 9: Concerning lyric poetry

Part 1

Chapter 1: The various arts and their origins
[Ch. 1, p. 5 omitted]

The arts may be divided into three categories relating to the objectives that they serve.

Some are designed to fulfil the needs of man, whom nature seems to abandon at the moment of birth; she has willed that man, exposed to cold, hunger and a thousand ills, shall, as a reward for his own industry and labour, secure the remedies and sustenance that he needs. From this have sprung the mechanical arts.

Other arts have as their objective, pleasure. These are the fruits of joy, feelings that spring from plenty and peace. They are *par excellence* the fine arts. They include the arts of music, poetry, painting, sculpture and the art of gesture or dance.

The third category embraces those arts that have as their objective both pleasure and utility, such as eloquence and architecture. They have been born of necessity and perfected by taste. They form a sort of mean between the other two categories, being both functional and pleasurable.

Arts of the first kind make use of nature as she is, and their ends are solely practical. Arts of the third kind use nature in a refined form for practical and pleasurable ends. The fine arts do not use nature but only imitate her, each in its own manner; this is a matter that needs elucidation and one which will be dealt with in the next chapter. Nature is thus the sole object of all the arts. The mechanical and liberal arts have no function other than to serve our needs and pleasures.

We shall only deal here with the fine arts, with those, that is, whose prime object is pleasure. In order to familiarise ourselves with them, let us examine the roots from which they spring.

It is man who has created the arts; he has done so to satisfy his own needs. Finding the pleasures of simple nature too monotonous, and finding himself moreover in a situation in which he could enhance his pleasure, he created out of his own native genius a new order of ideas and feelings, one that would revive his spirits and enliven his taste. For what could the man of genius do? He was on the one hand limited in inventiveness by nature herself, and on the other hand by the people for whom he worked, people whose faculties were similarly limited. He had necessarily to direct his entire effort to a selection from nature of her finest elements, in order to make from them an exquisite, yet entirely natural whole, one that would be more perfect than nature herself. Here is the fundamental principle on which the arts must be based, one that the greatest artists have respected throughout the centuries.

From this I conclude, first, that genius – the father of the arts – must imitate nature. Secondly, that genius may not imitate nature just as she is. Thirdly, that taste, for which the arts are made and by which they are judged, finds satisfaction when the artistic choice and imitation of nature has been well managed. Thus all our arguments must be directed to confirm the principle of the imitation of beautiful nature. This must be done by defining the characteristics of genius and by determining the way in which it operates; and by defining taste, which judges the arts. That is the substance of the first two sections of this book. In the third section general principles will be applied to the various arts: to poetry, painting, music and dance.

Chapter 2: Genius is only able to create art by means of imitation: a definition of imitation

The human mind can only create in a very imperfect manner: all its productions bear the stamp of a model. Even the monsters dreamed up by a disordered imagination are composed of shapes drawn from nature herself. And if genius capriciously gives birth to something that runs counter to natural law, thus degrading nature, it degrades itself and transforms itself into a kind of madness. There are clearly defined limits, beyond which one is lost. If these are exceeded chaos, not order, ensues, and horror rather than pleasure.

Genius then that seeks to please must not and cannot exceed the bounds of nature herself. Its function consists, not in imagining the impossible, but in seeking out what exists. Artistic invention is not a matter of giving substantive form to an object, but in identifying an object and seeing it for what it is. The men of genius who explore the most only uncover that which already existed. They are only creative because they have observed; and conversely, they only observe in order to be in a position to create. They are attracted and wholly absorbed by the very smallest objects, drawing from them new knowledge to widen their mental horizons, and to stimulate their creative powers. Genius is like the earth that brings forth nothing that has not been sown there. . . . The concern of the fine arts is not truth (*vrai*) but that which takes on the appearance of truth (*vraisemblable*). This conclusion is important enough to merit immediate discussion and proof, through concrete example.

What is painting? An imitation of visible objects. It has nothing to do with reality or truth. It is an illusion and its perfection lies only in its resemblance to reality.

Music and dance can well shape the accents and gestures of the orator on his rostrum and the way in which the common man recounts a story in the course of conversation. But it is not for this reason that music and dance are spoken of as fine arts. Both can be misused; sounds can clash together without rhyme or reason to shock, whilst in the dance fantastic jerks and leaps can be used with similar effect.

[p. 11, last three lines to p. 14, line 7 omitted]

In such cases neither art is working within its legitimate boundaries. If they are to fulfil their proper role then, they must get back to imitation, and they should be the artificial portrait of the human passions (*le portrait artificiel des passions humaines*). It is thus that they afford pleasure and express feelings in a manner and to a degree that will be found satisfactory.

[p. 15, para. 2 to p. 29 incl. omitted]

Chapter 4: The state in which genius must be in order to imitate nature
Even the most active genius is not uninterruptedly in the presence of the Muses but goes through arid and sterile periods. The inspired Ronsard, who was a born poet, was silent for months at a time. Milton's muse had its off days, as his works clearly show. And even the great Homer nods in the midst of his heroes and gods, not to mention Stabius, Claudian and countless others. Genius then has its happy moments when the mind, inspired as it were by a divine flame, expresses the whole of nature, imbuing everything with a life that animates them, and lends them those touching qualities that delight and ravish us.

This state of the soul is termed enthusiasm, one that is well enough understood, even if it cannot precisely be defined. The ideas that most authors have developed seem rather to have sprung from an imagination excited and gripped by enthusiasm rather than from a mind that was thoughtful or reflective.

[p. 31, last 11 lines to ch. 6 incl. omitted]

Part 2

Chapter 7: (i) Consequence: that although in general terms there is only one kind of good taste, there may be several kinds of good taste in particular
The first part of this proposition is proved by all that has preceded it. Nature is the sole object of taste; there can then be only one good taste, which is that of nature. The arts themselves can only be perfect when they represent nature; taste, then, which operates in these same arts must be that of nature. Thus, in the broadest sense there can be only one good taste, that

which approves of beautiful nature. Those who do not accept this must necessarily have bad taste.

Nevertheless, men and nations of reputed enlightenment and urbanity do differ in their tastes. Can we be bold enough to condemn the tastes of other people and to prefer our own? That would be a rash and even an unjust thing to do, because individual tastes can differ, and even be in conflict with each other, while yet remaining good in themselves. This can be explained on the one hand by the richness of nature herself; and on the other hand by the limitations of the human heart and mind.

The riches of nature are manifold, and each may be considered from an infinite number of viewpoints. Imagine for instance a model in an artist's studio. The artist may copy it from as many different angles as there are points from which to view it. Change the attitude and the position of the model and a whole new range of features and combinations is revealed to the artist as he draws. And just as the position of the model may be infinitely varied, and just as the variations may be multiplied by an infinite number of viewpoints, so it follows that a single object can be represented in an infinite number of ways, all however entirely regular and wholly conformable to nature and good taste.

Cicero has dealt with the subject of Catiline the conspirator as orator, and as orator-consul, with all the majesty and force that eloquence and authority can muster. He proves; he paints; he exaggerates; his words are arrows of fire. Sallust views the matter from a different angle. He is the historian who dispassionately examines the event; his narrative is a straightforward exposition, the interest of which lies only in its factual content.

French and Italian music each have their own characteristics. It is not that one is good music, the other bad. They are two sisters, or rather two faces of the same object.

[p. 105, para. 1 to the end of ch. 10 omitted]

Part 3, Section 3

Chapter 1: That the character of music and dance are to be defined by means of sound and gesture
[beginning para. 1, p. 258]

From which I conclude, first, that the prime function of music and dance must be the imitation of the feelings or passions (*passions*) whilst poetry on the other hand involves the imitation of action. However, as passions and actions are almost invariably united in nature, and as they must therefore be linked together in the arts, there will be this difference, that in poetry the passions will be used as the motivation for action whilst in music and the dance, action can only be a kind of canvas the purpose of which is to carry, sustain, guide and bind together the different passions that the artist seeks to express.

I conclude, secondly, if vocal inflexion and gesture have a meaning before they are set to metre, they must conserve that meaning in music and dance, just as words preserve their meaning in poetry. All music and dance must in consequence have a meaning.

I conclude, thirdly, that everything which art adds to gesture and vocal inflexion must serve to increase the impact and force of the expression. The first conclusion needs no proof. We shall develop the other two in the following chapters.

Chapter 2: All music and dance must have a meaning and a sense
There is no need to repeat here that melodic lines and dance movements are only imitations, artificial structures of tones and poetic gestures that are merely realistic. The passions are here as imaginary as are actions in poetry. They are equally and wholly the creation of genius and taste: nothing about them is true, everything is artificial. And if it sometimes happens that the musician or dancer is involved in the actual passion that he is expressing this is entirely accidental and it has nothing to do with the purpose of the art; it is like a painting which ought to be on canvas, but which is found to be on a living skin. Art is only created to deceive, a point that has perhaps been sufficiently underlined. We shall only speak here of expressions.

Generally speaking, expressions are in themselves neither natural nor artificial; they are merely signs. No matter whether they are used by art or nature, whether they relate to fiction, truth or untruth, they may change their quality but not their nature or state. Words are the same both in conversation and poetry; shapes and colours are the same in both natural objects and pictures; it follows then that tones and gestures must be identical, be the passions real or simulated. Art neither creates nor destroys expressions, it simply regulates, enhances and refines them. And just as nature may not be exceeded in the creation of objects, nor may she be exceeded in the expression of things: this is axiomatic.

If I were to say that I could derive no pleasure from a lecture that I did not understand, my confession would in no way seem strange. But if I ventured to say the same of a piece of music, people would ask whether I considered myself enough of a connoisseur to appreciate the merits of so carefully constructed and fine a composition. I would dare to reply yes, for it is a matter of feeling. I do not pretend in any way to calculate the sounds, their interrelationships or their connection with the ear. I am speaking here neither of oscillations, string vibrations, nor mathematical proportions. I leave such speculations to learned theorists; these are akin to the grammar and dialectic of a lecture which I can appreciate without going into such details. Music speaks to me in tones: this language is natural to me. If I do not understand it, art has corrupted nature rather than perfected her. A musical composition must be judged in the same way as a picture. In the picture I find shapes and colours that I can comprehend; it charms and touches me. What would we think of a painter who was content to throw on the canvas bold shapes and masses of the liveliest colour without reference to any known object? The same argument can be applied to music. There is no disparity here, and if there were it would strengthen my argument. The ear is said to be much finer than the eye. I am therefore much more capable of judging a musical composition than a painting.

I appeal to the composer himself. What are the musical moments that he most prefers and to which he constantly returns with a kind of secret satisfaction? Are they not those, as it were, in which his music speaks precisely, clearly and unequivocally? Why are certain particular objects and passions preferred to others? It is because these are the easiest to express, and they are the ones which the audience will grasp most readily.

Thus, although the learned musician may congratulate himself if he so wishes on having reconciled, by means of mathematics, sounds that seemed to be irreconcilable, unless those sounds mean something they may be compared to the gestures of an orator which do no more than show that the speaker is alive; they may similarly be compared to verses that are nothing but measured sounds, or to the mannerisms of a writer that are nothing but frivolous ornament. The worst kind of music is that which has no character. There is not a musical sound that does not have its model in nature, and which may not at least be the beginnings of expression, just as is a letter or syllable in speech.[7]

There are two kinds of music. The one merely imitates unimpassioned sounds and noises and is equivalent to landscape painting. The other expresses animated sounds and relates to the feelings. This corresponds to portrait painting.

The musician is no freer than the painter: he is continuously subject in every way to comparison with nature. In depicting a storm or little stream or a gentle breeze, the sounds come from nature, and from nature alone must he take them. If he paints some ideal object, one that has never really existed, such as the groanings of the earth or the shuddering of a ghost as it rises from its tomb, he must do as the poet does: 'Aut famam sequere, aut sibi convenientia finge' [either give some report of it, or make some appropriate representation of it]. Nature can provide him with sounds that correspond to his idea, if it is a musical one. When the composer comes across them he will instantly recognise them for what they are, even though he has not encountered them before: this is a fact. Rich as nature may be for

---

[7] This is equally true of a simple song and a harmonised song: both must have a sense, a meaning. The difference is merely this, that a simple song is like a speech that is addressed to the common man, the understanding of which calls for no special learning, whereas harmonised song calls for some kind of musical erudition and for ears that are trained and exercised. It is like a lecture addressed to a knowledgeable audience that assumes a certain acquired learning without which the merits of the lecture could not be judged. It is a moot point whether a lecture that is addressed solely to the learned can ever be truly eloquent.

the musician, if we are unable to grasp the import of what she can express her riches will mean nothing to us. The idiom will be foreign to us, and hence worthless.

Although music has only a half life, only a part of its being in the symphony, it none the less has meaning. How much more then can it accomplish in song, where it becomes a picture of the human heart. As Cicero observed, every feeling has its sound, its unique sign that reveals it just as every idea has its word: 'Omnis motus animi suum quemdam a natura habet vultum et sonum et gestum'. Thus, sounds in continuity will form a kind of discourse. And if there are expressions that puzzle me because they are inadequately prepared or explained within their particular contexts, if there are distractions, or contradictions, then I certainly will not be satisfied.

It is true, you may say, that a melodic line can express certain passions: love, for instance, or joy, or sadness. But for every passion that can be identified there are a thousand others that cannot be put into words.

That is indeed so, but does it follow that these are pointless? It is enough that they are felt; they do not have to be named. The heart has its own understanding that is independent of words. When it is touched it has understood everything. Moreover, just as there are great things that words cannot reach, so there are subtle things that words cannot capture, above all things that concern the feelings.

We may conclude then that although music may be the most exactly calculated art in respect of its tones, and the most geometrically structured in respect of its consonances, even with these qualities it may well have no significance whatever. The analogy might be with a prism, which produces the finest colours but no picture, or with a colour keyboard the colours and colour-sequences of which might amuse the eye, but which would certainly weary the mind.

Chapter 3: Concerning the expressive qualities that music and dance must have

Sounds and gestures, taken simply as expression, have certain natural qualities in common; art can furnish additional qualities that will make the expression all the more telling and beautiful. Aspects of these natural and artistic qualities will be discussed here.

Musical sounds and dance steps have meaning, just as words have meaning in poetry; expression in music and the dance then must have natural qualities similar to those of eloquence in speech. Everything that will be said here therefore will apply equally to music, dance and eloquence.

Every expression must conform to the thing that it expresses, being the dress tailored for the body. As both unity and variety are essential to poetic or fictitious subjects, the expression must above all have unity and variety.

The fundamental character of the subject will determine the expression, and whether it is to be grandiose or simple, gentle or strong. If joy is the theme every musical turn of phrase, every dance step must take on a smiling colour; and although the songs and airs may vary as they follow and take over from each other, the underlying idea that is common to them all will in no way be altered. Herein lies the unity of the work.[8] A passion never occurs in isolation, however. When one is predominant, the others are so to speak at its command, their function being to introduce and to filter out things that will intensify it, or weaken it. The composer discovers in the very unity of his subject the means to achieve variety. He can call upon love, hate, fear, sadness and hope, each in turn. He imitates the orator who uses every figure of speech, every variation of his art without in any way modifying the underlying tone of his style. In one case all will be dignified, because serious questions are being discussed to do with morals, politics or the law. In another, everything is wholly charming, because the creator is at work on a landscape painting and not a heroic picture. Just imagine what would be said if the first part of a speech were to sound fine from the lips of a magistrate and the conclusion from those of a stage comedian.

Apart from the general tenor of the expression (the style of the music or the dance, as it may be called) there are other qualities that relate to each individual mode of expression.

1. Clarity is of prime importance: 'Prima virtus perspicuitas'. Though there may be a beautiful building in the valley it will mean nothing to me if it lies hidden in the darkness. We do not expect a meaning from each and every detail but we do expect that each ought to contribute to the total sense, be it a phrase, a word or a syllable. Every tone, every modulation and every repetition ought to lead to a feeling or to give expression to one.

2. Each mood must be exactly right. It is the same with feelings as with colours; mezzotints spoil the original colours, changing their character or making them ambiguous.

3. The expression must be lively, and frequently fine and delicate. Everyone is to some extent familiar with the passions. If we only paint the passions half-heartedly, we are no better than the historian or the person who slavishly imitates. We have to search more deeply if we are to discover beautiful nature. In music, dance and even painting there are beauties that artists describe as fleeting and transitory – fine touches that stem from the ecstasy of passion: sighs, emphases, movements of the head. It is these that awaken, enliven and excite the mind.

4. The expression must be straightforward and simple; everything that smacks of effort is painful and tiring. The spectator is at one with the person who speaks or acts; he is not unmoved by the pain and trouble that he witnesses.

[8] Our musicians frequently sacrifice the broad, general mood – that expression of the soul which must inform the entire movement – to a subsidiary idea that is all too often irrelevant to the principal subject. They stop to paint a stream, a zephyr or some other thing that can be pictured in music. Such detail must be subsumed in the subject. If it is to retain its particular identity it must, as it were, blend with the general mood that is being expressed.

5. In conclusion, the expression must be fresh, especially in music. There is no art in which taste is more avid or contemptuous. 'Judicium aurium superbissimum' [the judgement of the ear is proud and disdainful]. The reason for this doubtless lies in the ease with which we take in melody: 'Natura ad numeros ducimur' [we are led to melody by natural instinct]. As the ear conveys the whole force of the feeling to the heart, a second hearing would leave the soul unmoved and indifferent. From this arises the need constantly to vary the modes, the movement and the passions. Happily, these all support each other. As they all have a common cause, one and the same passion takes on all kinds of forms: a roaring lion, gently flowing waters, a blazing fire, jealousy, fury, despair. Vocal sounds and gestures, like words in prose have these natural qualities. Let us now see what art can specifically add to music and dance.

Sounds and gestures are not as free in the arts as they are in nature where there are no rules other than a kind of instinct that easily yields its authority. This instinct governs them, varies them, strengthens and weakens them at will. In the arts there are stringent rules, clear boundaries that may not be transgressed. Everything is calculated (i) by measure, which controls the duration of each sound and gesture; (ii) by movement, which speeds up or slows down this same measure whilst in no way altering the number of sounds or gestures, or changing their quality; (iii) by melody, which unites these sounds or gestures into a successive whole; (iv) and finally by harmony which controls consonance when several lines combine into one. Such rules in no way alter or destroy the natural meaning of sounds and gestures, it should be stressed. They only serve to strengthen that meaning, adding lustre to it and giving it greater energy and charm. 'Cur ergo vires ipsa specie solvi putent, quando res nec ulla sine arte satis valeat' [why then do they believe that vigour can be subdued by beauty alone when nothing can ever have any power without art?] Quintilian, *Institutionum oratoriarum*, 9, 4, 7.

Measure, movement, melody and harmony can equally well govern words, sounds and gestures. They are in other words equally apt for poetry, music and dance. Their relevance to poetry has already been demonstrated.[9] They have a function in dance. Be there one dancer or many, measure controls each step, movement the speed, melody the progression or sequence of steps, and harmony, the concurrence of all these things with the accompanying instrument, and above all the synchronisation of the dancers themselves. For in dance there are solos, duos, choruses, repeats, conjunctions and recapitulations that are subject to the same rules as a concerted musical composition.

Measure and movement give life as it were to a musical composition. The composer manipulates them to imitate the progression and movement of natural sounds, giving to each tone the duration that will fit it for inclusion

---

[9] See the second part of ch. 3.

in the regular structure of musical song, just as words are prepared and measured for their setting in verse. Next, melody places each sound in an appropriate context; it unites, separates or reconciles them in accordance with the nature of the object that the musician is imitating. The stream murmurs, the thunder rolls, the butterfly flutters. There are passions that sigh, some that explode, and others that shudder. Melody accordingly adjusts the notes, intervals and modulations in order to take on the character of these various passions, and it even makes skilful use of dissonance. For as dissonance is to be found in nature side by side with other sounds, it has an equal right to a place in music. Not only does dissonance add salt and seasoning, but it serves in a particular way to characterise the musical expression. Nothing is so irregular as the course of the passions of love, anger and discord. The voice becomes shrill and then suddenly it takes on an explosive quality, in order to express them. Should art not soften such natural asperities, the truthfulness of the expression will compensate for its roughness. It is the composer's task to use dissonance with care, restraint and intelligence.

Finally, harmony contributes to musical expression. All harmonious sound is of its nature threefold, carrying with it the major third and the fifth. On this, Descartes, Father Mersenne, M Sauveur and M Rameau are all agreed, Rameau having adopted it as the basis of his new musical system. It follows from this that even in nature a simple cry of joy has its own harmony and consonance. It is the ray of light which, with the help of a prism, will provide any colour that could go to make the most richly coloured picture. Break up any sound into its constituent parts and the various elements of consonance will be discovered. Do this to the successive notes of an apparently simple song and that song will in some way be multiplied and varied by itself; there will be upper and lower parts that are nothing more than fundamentals of the song itself developed and strengthened into separate parts in order to amplify that basic expression. The several parts that go with the actual song are equivalent to gestures, vocal inflections and words in declamation.

Chapter 4: On the union of the fine arts
Poetry, music and dance are sometimes separated to satisfy the tastes and desires of men. However, as nature has created principles that will lead to unity and the attainment of a common goal – namely the communication of ideas and feelings to the hearts and minds of those whom we seek to reach – these three arts are never more powerful than when they are united. 'Cum valeant multum verba per se, et vox proprium vim adjiciat rebus, et gestus motusque significet aliquid profecto perfectum quiddam, cum omnia coierint fieri necesse est' [if the words have a great power in their own right, if the voice adds appropriate force to the ideas, and if gestures and movement give a certain significance, then naturally something close to

perfection must be created when all these come together] Quintilian, *Institutionum oratoriarum*. 1, 10, 24.

Thus, when artists separated the three arts in order to cultivate and refine them with more care, they should never have lost sight of nature's foremost requirement, nor have imagined that the arts could never completely do without each other. They must be united. Nature demands it: taste requires it. But how, and in what ways? We have here the subject and main headings for a treatise.

When the different arts unite to treat a common theme the situation is parallel to that in which the separate strands of a subject are treated by a single art. The most disparate elements must have a common focus, a point of reference. When painters and poets tell a story, they create a principal character whom they describe as the hero. The hero is presented in the best light and he is the mainspring of everything that goes on around him.

How many warriors there are in the Iliad! What a diversity of roles there are: Diomedes, Ulysses, Ajax, Hector, etc., and yet there is not one that does not have some connection with Achilles. These roles are the steps that the poet has prepared in order to lead up to the sublime bravery of the principal hero. The passing of time would have been less evident if it had not been marked out by such a hierarchy of heroes and Achilles would have seemed a much less imposing and perfect figure without the comparison.

The united arts must be as those heroes. One alone must excel, the others taking a subsidiary place. If poetry takes the form of a play, music and dance[10] may appear in conjunction with it, but only to make it more telling to enhance it and to emphasise the ideas and feelings contained in the verse. There will be no magnificently contrived music nor measured and cadenced gestures to cloud the poetry and distract the attention of the audience. Vocal inflexions will be unfailingly simple, being governed solely by the demands of the words. Bodily movements will be wholly natural seemingly having nothing to do with art.

If the music is to be pre-eminent, it alone has the right to display all its wares. The stage is hers to command. Poetry and dance take the second and third places. There will be no pompous and magnificent verse, no striking narrative or dazzling imagery. The poetry will be simple and straight-forward; it will flow onwards in a gentle and unassuming manner, the wording being almost casual. This is because the verse must follow the song and not the other way about. Although the words are written down before the music is composed, the words in this case are no more than accentual stresses that add clarity and intelligibility to the music: Quinault's poetry must be judged in this light, and if it is condemned as weak, it is up to Lully to redeem it. It is not the finest but the most touching verse that provides the best vehicle for music. As a composer which of the following two pieces by Racine would be the easiest to set to music:

---

[10] By dance we mean here the art of mime, taking the term in its widest sense.

Quel carnage de toutes parts!
On égorge à la fois les enfans, les vieillards,
Et la fille & mère, & la soeur & le frère,
    Le fils dans les bras de son père:
Que de corps entassés! que de membres épars
    Privés de sépulture!

The other follows directly afterwards in the same scene:

Hélas! si jeune encore,
Par quel crime ai-je put mériter mon malheur?
Ma vie à peine a commencé d'éclore,
    Je tomberai comme une fleur
        Qui n'a vu qu'une Aurore.[11]

Need one be a composer to feel the difference?

Dance has an even more modest role in music than poetry. It is at least measured, but gesture rarely contributes as much to music as it does to drama. If on occasion it makes a particular impact this is because the music is more passionate than the poetry. There is consequently more material for it to work on since, as we have said, gesture and vocal inflection relate in a very particular way to the feelings.

Finally, if the dance is to be pre-eminent the music must not be distractingly brilliant. It should merely hold out a helping hand in order to measure with greater precision the character and movement of the dance. The violinist and the dancer must work in concert, and although the violin may lead, it must only act as an accompaniment. The theme belongs by right to the dancer. Whether he leads or follows, nothing must obscure the fact that he is of the foremost importance. The ear must not be engaged more than is absolutely necessary, in order that the eye may not be distracted.

Speech and dance are not commonly linked together but that does not prove that they may not be joined. It is common knowledge that they were joined together in former days: then men danced to the accompaniment of a singer, as today to the accompaniment of instruments, the words having the same rhythm as the dance steps.

It is poetry, music and dance that present to us the image of actions and human passions. But it is architecture, painting and sculpture that set the scene for the drama. They should do so in a way that matches the dignity of the actors and the quality of the subject that is being developed. The gods dwell in Olympus, kings in palaces, simple citizens in their houses, and shepherds in the shady woods. It is the role of architecture to create such scenes and to embellish them with the help of painting and sculpture. The

---

[11] What carnage everywhere! Old men and children are slaughtered, mother and daughter, sister and brother, the son in his father's arms. How many corpses there are, piled up on each other, how many scattered limbs, deprived of burial!
  Alas! Still so young. What is the crime that I have committed that merits this misfortune? My life is hardly begun, and I fall like a flower that has only seen a single dawn!—eds.

entire universe is the province of the fine arts. They can dispense the riches of nature, but they may only do so according to the laws of propriety. Each dwelling must reflect the character, rank, fortune and taste of the person who lives there. This is the rule that must govern the arts in the construction and embellishment of such places. Ovid could not make the Palace of the Sun too brilliant, nor Milton the garden of Eden too delightful; but even as far as a king is concerned such magnificence would be open to criticism as being greatly above his station. 'Singula quaeque locum teneant fortia decentur.'

Jean le Rond d'Alembert

(b. Paris Nov. 1717; d. Paris 29 Oct. 1783)

From: *Encyclopédie, ou dictionnaire raisonné des sciences, des arts et des métiers*, vol. 1 (Paris 1751), pp. xi–xii

The *Encyclopédie*, one of the great cultural, social and scientific achievements of the eighteenth century, originated in a commission from a Paris bookseller, whereby the young man of letters, Denis Diderot, was to translate the *Cyclopedia* (London 1728) of Ephraim Chambers (see p. 354), with such modifications and additions as might be necessary. Diderot enlisted the distinguished scientist and writer, Jean le Rond d'Alembert, as his co-editor. The first volume of what proved to be a wholly new work, was published in 1751. The project involved some 72,000 articles and twenty-eight volumes (seventeen of text and eleven of plates) and was not finished until 1772. During the years 1776–7 five supplementary volumes were published under different editorship.

That so much space was given over to music in the *Encyclopédie* was due doubtless to the interest that both editors had in the subject. Diderot, whom Voltaire described as a 'pantophile', devoted three of the five essays in his early *Mémoires sur différents sujets mathématiques* (The Hague 1748) to music and acoustics. Many of the *Encyclopédie* articles on instruments are his. He took an active part in the Guerre des Bouffons, and later edited, with an informative and amusing commentary, Bemetzreider's *Leçons de clavecin et principes d'harmonie*, which achieved considerable popularity and was reprinted many times, in French and in translation. One of his most important literary achievements was the 'satyr', *Le neveu de Rameau*, in which many technical matters of musical interest are discussed.

D'Alembert became a member of the Paris Académie des sciences in 1741; he was elected to the Académie française in 1754 and in 1772 he became its secretary. The nineteenth-century physicist, Helmholtz, considered that Rameau, and his disciple d'Alembert, together shifted the theory of consonance from metaphysical to physical ground, their work being of the greatest historical importance. In 1747 d'Alembert published his early observations on the vibrations of strings, and it was he who successfully formulated and solved the basic equation of the vibrating string. In 1752 he published a popular exposition of Rameau's harmonic principles under the title *Élémens de musique théorique et pratique, suivant les principes de M Rameau*,[1] which by 1779 had run into five French editions and a number of translations, including one dated 1757 by Marpurg. His *Traité sur la liberté de la musique* came out as part of the *Mélanges de littérature* (Amsterdam 1767–73). D'Alembert contributed some 1,500 articles to the *Encyclopédie* (Rousseau over 800 on music, Diderot some 5,000 and de Jaucourt no less than 17,000): his music articles indicate the breadth of his interests and knowledge, ranging from cacophony to *chaconne*, from cadence to *gigue*. Something of his general attitude to music and its

---

[1] See Jean Philippe Rameau, *Complete Theoretical Writings*, ed. Erwin R. Jacobi (American Institute of Musicology, Rome, 1967–72); vol. 6, pp. 228f and 459f.

relationship to the other arts can be savoured in the Discours préliminaire to the first volume, of which he was the author. Here is to be found Batteux's system of the arts (see p. 41), his unifying principle of the imitation of nature, and the idea of music as the art of the emotions. See also articles from the Encyclopédie on aesthetics (Sulzer p. 121–3), taste (Voltaire p. 66), genius and sensibility (de Jaucourt p. 64).

The Encyclopédie came out in no fewer than nine separate French editions between 1751 and 1782, being published in Paris, Geneva, Lucca, Livorno (it was placed on the Index for its anti-catholic views), Lausanne and Berne. Its contents were copied, plagiarised and adapted in practically every late-eighteenth-century work of reference, and by many distinguished writers including Sulzer (see p. 121) who in turn contributed articles to the later volumes, J. P. Kirnberger, Marpurg, Forkel, J. A. Eberhard, Avison, Burney, Castil-Blaze and Fétis. Rameau refused the invitation of the editors to take charge of the entries on music; Rousseau, who accepted, was persuaded to complete his task before the printing of the first volume had begun: he wrote some 400 articles in the space of a few months, and later had occasion to regret the haste that led to so many inaccuracies and which gave Rameau such just cause for complaint.[2] None the less many of the articles in his later Dictionnaire are taken from the Encyclopédie, and 400 which he wrote specially for the dictionary found their way into the later volumes of the Encyclopédie under the supervision of Frédéric de Castillon.[3]

Discours préliminaire

Of the pursuits that take the form of imitation, painting and sculpture must be regarded as pre-eminent because they most nearly resemble the objects which they portray, and because they communicate most directly to the senses. To these may be added architecture, born of necessity and perfected by luxury. It has been promoted stage by stage from the thatched cottage to the palace, and is, to the philosopher, merely the decorated mask of one of our most essential needs. The imitation of nature is here less obvious and more restricted than it is in the other two arts that have just been mentioned. These openly and fully express every aspect of beautiful nature and they depict her just as she is in her uniformity and variety. Imitation in architecture, on the other hand, is limited to the assembly and union of differing shapes in symmetrical patterns similar to those that nature variously and individually achieves and which contrast so well with the variety that is evident in the whole ensemble.

Poetry, which is only second to painting and sculpture, appeals more to the imagination than to the senses for it imitates solely by the use of words which are arranged in a manner that is pleasing to the ear. It represents the objective phenomena of the universe to the imagination in a vital and touching way, seeming rather to create than to paint, giving them warmth,

---

[2] Jean Phillipe Rameau, Erreurs sur la musique dans l'encyclopédie (Paris 1755).
[3] See A. R. Oliver, The Encyclopedists as Critics of Music (New York 1947); John Lough, The Contributors to the Encyclopédie (London 1973); Essays on the Encyclopédie (London 1968); and The Encyclopédie in Eighteenth-Century England (London 1970).

movement and life. And then music, which takes third place in the order of imitation, appeals both to the imagination and to the senses. This is not because it imitates those objects that it seeks to depict less perfectly but because the opportunities for imitation are apparently so limited. This seems to be due less to music's inherent nature than to a lack of inventiveness and imagination on the part of music's practitioners. One or two observations may not be out of place here. When music began, its function was perhaps merely to represent noise. With the passing of time it became a kind of speech – even a language – by means of which the different feelings, or rather the different passions of the soul are expressed. Why however should this expression be limited to the passions alone and not extended (as far as possible) to the senses? Although the impressions that reach us through our various senses differ quite as much as do the objects that cause them, they could nevertheless be evaluated from the standpoint of the pleasure or pain that they cause, a standpoint that is common to them all. A terrifying object or a frightening sound awakens in each one of us an emotion that enables us to some extent to relate the one to the other; we frequently describe them in similar terms or by means of synonyms. I do not see therefore why a musician who seeks to portray a terrifying object should not find in nature the kind of sound that will arouse emotions similar to those that would be excited by the object itself. The same, I would argue, is true of pleasurable feelings. To argue otherwise would be to seek to place limitations on the art of music and on the pleasure that we find in it. I admit that the kind of portrayal I have in mind would necessitate a detailed and profound study of the nuances that distinguish one feeling from another. Let us hope that such an appraisal will not be undertaken by men of limited talents. Nuances which are seized upon by the man of genius, experienced by the man of taste and comprehended by the man of intellect mean nothing to the multitude. Music that portrays nothing is merely noise, and it would be scarcely more pleasurable than a succession of sonorous words lacking proper order and interconnection.

See also Bibliography under: Weber

Charles Avison

(b. Newcastle upon Tyne, Feb.(?) 1709; d. Newcastle upon Tyne, 10 May 1770)

From: *An Essay on Musical Expression* (London 1753); text from the 3rd edn, 1775, pt I, section 2

Avison became organist of the principal church of St Nicholas, Newcastle upon Tyne in 1736 (see John Brown, p. 82), having spent most of his early years in the city. From then until he died he was responsible for an unusually ambitious series of concerts there. He was an active composer with some fifty concerti grossi to his credit; he is best known perhaps for his *Essay* and for the reaction that it provoked: an anonymous answer from the Oxford professor of music, William Hayes, a 'Reply' from Avison himself, and a 'Letter' in support of Avison from Dr Jortin, all of which were jointly published in the third, 1775 edition of the *Essay*. The *Essay* divides into three parts, the first covering the general question of music's 'force and effects' and suggesting some analogies between music and painting, the second discussing techniques of composition and the need to balance the elements of melody and harmony, the third (and in many ways the most illuminating section of the work) examining questions of performance.

Avison believed above all that music is an expressive art. He observed that melody and harmony of themselves make an impression on the listener. 'Yet when to these is added the force of *musical expression*, the effect is greatly increased; for then they assume the power of exciting all the most agreeable passions of the soul. The force of sound in alarming the passions is prodigious, (pt I, section 1, p. 3).

While Avison has little to say on the theory of the imitation of nature, he was well aware of the work of his French contemporaries; he quotes from Montesquieu, Rameau and (remarkably) from the *Mémoires de littérature, tirez des registres de l'académie royale des inscriptions et belles lettres*, vol. 7, the paper given by M. Burette – 'Dissertation où l'on fait voir que les merveilleux effets, attribuez à la musique des Anciens, ne prouvent point qu'elle fut aussi parfaite que la nôtre', in which he cites the famous passage by Polybius on the music of the Arcadians and the Cynaetheans.[1] A similar breadth of reading is evident in the work of Avison's correspondents: Jortin, for instance, draws upon Voltaire and Du Bos.

The second section of part I (quoted here in full) is Avison's attempt to put into terms that an uninformed reader would be able to understand his views on the nature and purpose of music. Later writers were to see more effective analogies between music and poetry.

---

[1] The passage was quoted by practically every author who subsequently touched upon the subject of ancient Greek music: for the passage in full see below, Henry Home, Lord Kames, p. 77.

On the analogies between music and painting

From this short theory we should now proceed to offer a few observations relating to composition.

But as musical composition is known to very few besides the professors and composers of music themselves, and as there are several resemblances or analogies between this art and that of painting which is an art much more obvious in its principles and therefore more generally known, it may not be amiss to draw out some of the most striking of these analogies, and by this means, in some degree at least, give the common reader an idea of musical composition.

The chief analogies or resemblances that I have observed between these two noble arts are as follows:

First, they are both founded in geometry, and have proportion for their subject. And though the undulations of air which are the immediate cause of sound be of so subtle a nature as to escape our examination, yet the vibrations of musical strings or chords, from whence these undulations proceed, are as capable of mensuration as any of those visible objects about which painting is conversant.

Secondly, as the excellence of a picture depends on three circumstances, design, colouring and expression, so in music, the perfection of composition arises from melody, harmony and expression. Melody of air, is the work of invention, and therefore the foundation of the other two, and directly analogous to design in painting. Harmony gives beauty and strength to the established melodies in the same manner as colouring adds life to a just design. And in both cases the expression arises from a combination of the other two and is no more than a strong and proper application of them to the intended subject.

Thirdly, as the proper mixture of light and shade (called by the Italians, chiaroscuro) has a noble effect in painting, and is indeed essential to the composition of a good picture; so the judicious mixture of concords and discords is equally essential to a musical composition: as shades are necessary to relieve the eye, which is soon tired and disgusted with a level glare of light, so discords are necessary to relieve the ear, which is otherwise immediately satiated with a continued and unvaried strain of harmony. We may add (for the sake of those who are in any degree acquainted with the theory of music) that the preparations and resolutions of discords resemble the soft gradations from light to shade, or from shade to light in painting.

Fourthly, as in painting there are three various degress of distances established, viz. the foreground, the intermediate part and the off-skip; so in music there are three different parts strictly similar to these, viz. the bass (or foreground), the tenor (or intermediate) and the treble (or off-skip). In consequence of this, a musical composition without its bass is like a landscape without its foreground; without its tenor it resembles a landscape deprived of its intermediate part; without its treble it is analogous to a landscape deprived of its distance or off-skip. We know how imperfect a picture is when deprived of any of these parts; and hence we may form a judgement of those who determine on the excellence of any musical composition without seeing or hearing it in all its parts, and understanding their relation to each other.

Fifthly, as in painting, especially in the nobler branches of it and particularly in history painting, there is a principal figure which is most remarkable and conspicuous and to which all the other figures are referred and subordinate, so in the greater kinds of musical composition there is a principal or leading subject or succession of notes which ought to prevail and be heard through the whole composition, and to which both the air and harmony of the other parts ought to be in like manner referred and subordinate.

Sixthly, so again, as in painting a group of figures, care is to be had, that there be no deficiency in it but that a certain fullness or roundness be preserved, such as Titian beautifully compared to a bunch of grapes, so in the nobler kinds of musical composition there are several inferior subjects which depend on the principal: and here the several subjects (as in painting the figures do) are as it were to sustain and support each other: and it is certain that if any one of these be taken away from a skilful composition, there will be found a deficiency highly disagreeable to an experienced ear. Yet this does not hinder but there may be perfect composition in two, three, four or more parts, in the same manner as a group may be perfect though consisting of a smaller or greater number of figures. In both cases the painter or musician varies his disposition according to the number of parts or figures which he includes in his plan.

Seventhly, as in viewing a picture you ought to be removed to a certain distance, called the point of sight, at which all its parts are seen in their just proportions, so in a concert there is a certain distance at which the sounds are melted into each other and the various parts strike the ear in their proper strength and symmetry. To stand close by a bassoon or double-bass when you hear a concert, is just as if you should plant your eye close to the foreground when you view a picture, or, as if in surveying a spacious edifice, you should place yourself at the foot of a pillar that supports it.

Lastly, the various styles in painting – the grand – the terrible – the graceful – the tender – the passionate – the joyous – have all their respective analogies in music. And we may add in consequence of this, that as the manner of handling differs in painting, according as the subject varies, so in music there are various instruments suited to the different kinds of muscial compositions and particularly adapted to and expressive of its several varieties. Thus, as the rough handling is proper for battles, sieges, and whatever is great or terrible, and on the contrary the softer handling and more finished touches, are expressive of love, tenderness, or beauty: so in music, the trumpet, horn or kettle-drum are most properly employed on the first of these subjects, the lute or harp on the last. There is a short story in the *Tatler*[2] which illustrates this analogy very prettily. Several eminent painters are there represented in picture as musicians with those instruments in their hands which most aptly represent their respective manner in painting.

See also Bibliography under: Bardez

Chevalier de Jaucourt

From: *Encyclopédie, ou dictionnaire raisonné des sciences, des arts et des métiers*, vol. 7 (Paris 1757), pp. 582–3

This article includes sections on military genius, genius in architecture and painting, and the quality of national genius, but contains no specific reference to music, though Rousseau included a high-flown article on musical genius in his *Dictionnaire* (see below, p. 108). Both de Jaucourt and Rousseau believed that genius must of its nature break with rules and conventions: both place great weight on *sensibilité* as a central attribute of genius.

For further discussion of the *Encyclopédie* see p. 57 above – the editorial introduction to the Discours préliminaire.

After studies in Geneva, the Chevalier de Jaucourt spent some time at Cambridge and at Leyden, where he graduated as an M.D. in 1730. He settled in Paris, and became the most prolific of the *Encyclopédie* contributors, with some 17,000 articles to his name. He was subsequently elected an honorary member of academies at Bordeaux, Stockholm and Berlin, and of the Royal Society in London.

For further reading: Lough, *Encyclopédie in England*, ch. 2.

Genius (Génie)

Intellectual breadth, imaginative power and an active soul, these are the qualities of genius. The manner in which ideas are recalled depends upon the way that they are assimilated. Thrown headlong into the universe man takes in ideas that are the common property of all people, together with sensations of varying intensity. Most men only experience strong feelings when the cause of these has a direct connection with their particular needs and tastes. Things that are unrelated to their desires and which have no analogy with their way of life are either unperceived or are briefly noted without in any way being felt, and are then forgotten.

Genius is particularly responsive to all creatures; having an interest in everything natural, it never entertains an idea without experiencing some related feeling. Everything excites it and makes a lasting impression on it.

When the soul has been touched by a particular thing it is also touched by the remembrance of it. As far as the man of genius is concerned, however, the imagination goes much further than this. He recollects things with much livelier feelings than he did at the time, because he relates these things to a thousand others that arouse the feelings even more effectively.

The things that surround and engross him are not just memories; he actually sees them, indeed, he is moved by them. In the gloomy silence of his study he delights in the joyful and fruitful countryside; he is frozen by the whistling winds; he is scorched by the sun; he is terrified by the storms.

[p. 582, col. 1, para. 8 to p. 582, col. 2, para. 5 omitted]

The man of genius is cramped by rules and laws of taste. He breaks them so that he can fly upwards to the sublime – to things that are great and intensely moving. As far as he is concerned, taste is a love of the eternal beauty that characterises nature; it is his passion to ensure that the pictures he creates conform to a model that he has set up, upon which he builds his ideas and feeling for beauty. He is constantly thwarted in his desire to express the passions that excite him, by grammar and convention. Often the idiom in which he is writing cannot express an image that would in another form be sublime. Homer could not find in just one dialect the expressions that his genius demanded. Milton continually violated the rules of language and sought energetic expression in three or four different idioms. In short, energy, abundance, all kinds of harshness, irregularity, pathos and sublimity, all these characterise artisitic genius. It is never weak; it never pleases without astonishing. It even amazes by its very defects.

[p. 583, col. 1, para. 1 to p. 583, col. 2, para. 4 omitted]

One quality that is particularly essential to those who govern is a cool head. Without it, means will often be ineptly applied to circumstances, inconsistencies will arise and there will be no effective thought. A cool head subordinates the movements of the soul to reason, in every eventuality. It frees a man from fear, from ecstasy and from untoward haste. Only those who have mastery of the imagination have the power to do this. Is not such a quality totally at odds with genius? The fount of genius is extreme sensibility. This enables it to assimilate a host of new impressions that may well serve to deflect it from its initial objective, that may well result in broken trust, that may drive it beyond the bounds of reason, and that may well – on account of its very unpredictability – rob it of the natural advantage that it would otherwise have enjoyed on account of its superior insight. Men of genius seem to me to be better suited to overthrow and establish governments than to sustain them, to re-establish order rather than to conform to it, since they make decisions on the strength of feelings, tastes, likes and dislikes, since they are distracted by a thousand things, since they rely too much on guesswork and too little on foresight, and since they carry to extremes their desires and hopes.

[p. 583, col. 2, last para. to the end omitted]

Voltaire

(b. Paris 21 Nov. 1694; d. Paris 30 May 1778)

From: *Encyclopédie, ou dictionnaire raisonné des sciences, des arts et des métiers*, vol. 7 (Paris 1757), p. 761

Voltaire contributed no more than forty articles to the *Encyclopédie*, all in vols. 5–8. His discussion is a classic statement of the issues involved: the man of taste has great discrimination born of innate sensibility, acquired knowledge and a mature national culture. Voltaire addresses himself equally to Batteux's fine arts of poetry, painting, music and drama, though paying little attention to the principle of imitation.

For further information on the *Encyclopédie* see the Discours préliminaire, on p. 57.

Taste (Goût)

In the previous article we examined the phenomenon of physical taste. This sense, this ability to discriminate where food is concerned has given rise in every known language to a metaphor which expresses by the use of the word taste a feeling for the beauties and defects of the arts. This taste is as immediate in its action as that of the tongue and palate, and it too precedes reflection. It enjoys and is sensible to good things moreover, and it, too, indignantly rejects the bad. It is often uncertain and misguided, also, not knowing even whether it ought to be pleased with what is offered, for there is a need to get accustomed to some things if taste is to be acquired.

It is not enough to see and become familiar with the beauty of a work, as far as taste is concerned. We must feel it and be touched by it. Nor will it suffice to feel and be touched in some undefined and general way. The various nuances must precisely be distinguished. Nothing must escape immediate notice. The parallel between intellectual, artistic and sensual tastes can be pushed still further, for just as the gourmet instantly senses and recognises a blend of two liqueurs, so will the connoisseur instantly spot a mixture of two differing styles. He at once takes note of defects and charms. This verse, for instance, by Horace will immediately fire his enthusiasm: 'Que vouliez vous qu'il fit contre trois? qu'il mourût'. On the other hand he will experience an involuntary aversion for the following verse: 'Ou qu'un beau déséspoir alors le secourût'.[1]

---

[1] This comes from Corneille's *Horace*, Act III, Sc. vi; the point here is that the first sentence – a beautifully measured Alexandrine ending with a terse response of dreadful finality – is immediately followed by a cumbersome line of obscure meaning–eds.

66

A poor taste for good is only stimulated by excessively piquant and recherché seasonings; similarly, a poor taste in the arts only finds pleasure in studied embellishment, and it has no feeling for the beauty of nature.

A depraved taste for food demands things that would disgust others: it is a kind of illness. A depraved artistic taste takes pleasure in subjects that revolt well-formed minds. It prefers the burlesque to the noble, the precious and affected to the simple and natural. It is an illness of the mind. Artistic taste is much more consciously formed than is sensual taste, for although we may eventually develop a liking for things that originally were distasteful to us, nature has decreed that in general men should only like those things for which they have a need. The formation of an intellectual taste, by comparison, takes a much longer time. A sensitive but uneducated young man will not at first be able to distinguish the various parts of a grand chorus; his eyes will at first see none of the subtleties of a picture: its colour, perspective, its light and shade, the correctness of its composition. Gradually however his ears will learn to listen, and his eyes to see. He will be moved when he watches his first great tragedy, but he will know nothing about the merits of the unities; the absence of pointless entrances and exits will escape him, as also will the still greater art which focuses the various interests on a central one. Nor indeed will he be aware of the innumerable difficulties that have been surmounted. Only after much experience and reflection will he succeed in feeling with sudden pleasure all the things that formerly he was unable to unravel. Taste imperceptibly establishes itself on a national level, through the influence of good minds and good artists. We become accustomed to looking at pictures with the eyes of a Lebrun, a Poussin or a Lesueur, to listening with Lully's ears to declamatory settings of scenes by Quinault, and with Rameau's ears to airs and symphonies. We read books with the same attitude of mind as good authors have.

If in the early stages of its cultural development a nation is united in its respect for authors whose work is full of faults and which is later held in contempt, it is because their work had natural beauties that were generally recognised and which it was beyond the public to disentangle from the attendant imperfections. So it was that Lucilius was cherished by the Romans before Horace superseded him. Régnier was enjoyed by the French until Boileau appeared. And if ancient authors who stumbled through each page are still highly reputed, it is because no pure and polished writer has come to the fore to open the eyes of his countrymen, as Horace did in Rome and Boileau in France.

It is said that there is no point in arguing about taste. This is so when the question is merely one of sensual taste: the dislike of a certain food, that is, or the preference for another. There can be no argument, because there is no defect of the senses to correct. It is not so in the arts, where real beauties can be discerned by good taste and overlooked by bad taste. It is often possible to correct the defect of mind that leads to ill-formed taste. But there are frigid souls, false spirits that can neither be corrected nor excited. It is pointless to argue matters of taste with them, as they have none.

In many matters taste is purely arbitrary: in dress, ornament and things that are not ranked as fine arts. In such cases fancy rather than taste is the source of new fashions.

The taste of a nation can be impaired. This misfortune commonly happens after centuries of perfection. Artists develop a dread of imitation and they seek out untrodden paths. They lose touch with those natural beauties that their predecessors seized upon. Their efforts are not without merit, and the defects remain hidden. Enamoured with novelty the public runs after them but soon wearies of them. Other artists appear and in a new effort to please depart still further from nature. Taste is engulfed in a rapid succession of novelties and is ruined. The public no longer knows where it is and vainly laments that past age of good taste which can never return. A few good minds, who keep themselves apart from the crowd, keep it in trust.

There are vast countries in which taste has not yet been formed. They are countries in which society has not yet been perfected, in which men and women do not gather together and in which certain arts – such as sculpture and the painting of living things – are proscribed by religion. When society is yet young the mind is cramped, its edge blunted, there being nothing on which to form taste. When several fine arts are lacking the others rarely have much sustenance, because the arts go hand in hand, each supporting the other. That is why the peoples of Asia have lacked well-made works of practically every kind, and why taste has remained the property of certain European peoples.

Edmund Burke

(b. Dublin, 12 Jan. 1729; d. Beaconsfield, 9 July 1797)

From: *A Philosophical Enquiry into the Origin of our Ideas of the Sublime and the Beautiful* (London 1757), pts 2–4

Fig. 1. *The Indian Widow* (Wright of Derby, 1734–97). An example of the pathetic sublime: the Indian warrior's widow, set in a formidable hostile landscape, alone and in stoic calm while the storm rages round her. Rousseau's noble savage, the noble simplicity and silent grandeur that Winckelmann found in classical art and Burke's 'sublime' all in the one composition. (Derby Art Gallery)

Burke began the *Philosophical Enquiry* whilst a student at Trinity College, Dublin (1743–8). It was his first major published work and it proved to be immensely influential. Some fourteen separate English printings have been identified dating from Burke's lifetime, together with French (Paris 1765) and German (Riga and Leipzig 1773) translations.[1]

---

[1] See *Edmund Burke. A Philosophical Enquiry*, ed. J. T. Boulton (London 1958), the editor's introduction, and the appendix of published editions, p. 179.

69

The work divides into four parts. The first identifies the various passions and suggests how it is that passions which are aroused by the sublime can none the less be a source of delight. The second treats of the various manifestations of the sublime, and the third, of beauty. The fourth examines the ways in which the sublime and the beautiful make an impact on the emotions, whilst the fifth and final section centres on the verbal arts.

Kant, who devoted much attention to the concepts of beauty and sublimity, thought sufficiently highly of Burke's study to single it out for special comment in his *Kritik der Urteilskraft* (see p. 214). Whereas Burke was principally concerned with the psychology of aesthetic perception, Kant sought to determine standards whereby beauty and sublimity could be judged, and from there he went on to explore the relationship between the moral life and aesthetic sensibility. In this respect Kant was critical of Burke: 'Empirical investigation [he wrote] can only show us how we judge; it cannot tell us how we ought to judge', for 'if the pleasure in some object is utterly and completely invested in the attraction it has or the emotional effect it arouses, then no one may commit anyone else to his own aesthetic judgements, for each person would merely depend on the evidence of his own sense organs'.[2] Schlegel was also critical, arguing the empirical judgements – if they were to have any authority – would require the weight of majority opinion the determination of which would be an impossible task.

Burke differs markedly from Longinus in his concept of the sublime (see p. 71, the editorial introduction). Both agreed that the emotional impact of the sublime was intense – even violent. Longinus's sublimity was man-made and morally uplifting. Burke's however was overwhelming, terrifying, painful; it could be man-made but was as likely to stem from the action of purely sensible phenomena on the imagination, phenomena drawn from nature, not as she ought to be, but as she is.

During the second half of the century, artists, writers (even musicians) were opening up new avenues of aesthetic experience in which Burke's sublimity is in some form or other present, whether in Anton Koch's mountainscapes, Friedrich's romantic nature scenes, Goya's visionary grotesques, Piranesi's prison studies, Goethe's novels (and above all his *Faust*), Weber's operas or Beethoven's symphonies.

As far as the ear is concerned, Burke seems to reserve the category of the sublime for sounds, rather than for composed music, but in fact he sets out an effective system that could be applied directly to composition (see, for example, Michaelis, pp. 289–90).

Part 3

Section xxvii: The sublime and beautiful compared

On closing this general view of beauty, it naturally occurs that we should compare it with the sublime, and in this comparison there appears a remarkable contrast. For sublime objects are vast in their dimensions, beautiful ones comparatively small: beauty should be smooth and polished; the great, rugged and negligent; beauty should shun the right line yet deviate from it insensibly; the great in many cases loves the right line; and when it deviates, it often makes a strong deviation: beauty should not be obscure; the great ought to be dark and gloomy: beauty should be light and delicate;

[2] *Kritik der Urteilskraft*, ed. G. Lehmann (Stuttgart 1966).

the great ought to be solid and even massive. They are indeed ideas of a very different nature, one being founded on pain, the other on pleasure; and however they may vary afterwards from the direct nature of their causes yet these causes keep up an eternal distinction between them, a distinction never to be forgotten by any whose business it is to affect the passions. In the infinite variety of natural combinations we must expect to find the qualities of things the most remote imaginable from each other united in the same object. We must expect also to find combinations of the same kind in the works of art. But when we consider the power of an object upon our passions, we must know that when anything is intended to affect the mind by the force of some predominant property, the affection produced is like to be the more uniform and perfect if all the other properties or qualities of the object be of the same nature and tending to the same design as the principal.

> If black and white blend, soften, and unite,
> A thousand ways, are there no black and white?

If the qualities of the sublime and beautiful are sometimes found united, does this prove that they are the same; does it prove that they are any way allied; does it prove even that they are not opposite and contradictory? Black and white may soften, may blend; but they are not therefore the same. Nor, when they are so softened and blended with each other, or with different colours, is the power of black as black, or of white as white, so strong as when each stands uniform and distinguished.

Part 2

Section i: Of the passion caused by the sublime

The passion caused by the great and sublime in nature, when those causes operate most powerfully, is astonishment; and astonishment is that state of the soul in which all its motions are suspended with some degree of horror.[3] In this case the mind is so entirely filled with its object that it cannot entertain any other, nor by consequence reason on that object which employs it. Hence arises the great power of the sublime, that far from being produced by them, it anticipates our reasonings and hurries us on by an irresistible force. Astonishment, as I have said, is the effect of the sublime in its highest degree; the inferior effects are admiration, reverence and respect.

Part 3

Section xxv: The beautiful in sounds

In this sense we find an equal aptitude to be affected in a soft and delicate

---

[3] Burke, pt 1, sections iii, iv and vii–eds.

manner; and how far sweet or beautiful sounds agree with our descriptions of beauty in other senses, the experience of everyone must decide. Milton has described this species of music in one of his juvenile poems.[4] I need not say that Milton was perfectly well versed in that art, and that no man had a finer ear, with a happier manner of expressing the affections of one sense by metaphors taken from another. The description is as follows:

> And ever against eating cares,
> Lap me in soft Lydian airs;
> In notes with many a winding bout
> Of linked sweetness long drawn out;
> With wanton heed, and giddy cunning,
> The melting voice through mazes running;
> Untwisting all the chains that tie
> The hidden soul of harmony.

Let us parallel this with the softness, the winding surface, the unbroken continuance, the easy gradation of the beautiful in other things; and all the diversities of the several senses, with all their several affections, will rather help to throw lights from one another to finish one clear, consistent idea of the whole, than to obscure it by their intricacy and variety.

To the above-mentioned description I shall add one or two remarks. The first is, that the beautiful in music will not bear that loudness and strength of sounds which may be used to raise other passions, nor notes which are shrill or harsh or deep; it agrees best with such as are clear, even, smooth and weak. The second is that great variety and quick transitions from one measure or tone to another are contrary to the genius of the beautiful in music. Such transitions often excite mirth or other sudden and tumultuous passions but not that sinking, that melting, that languor which is the characteristical effect of the beautiful as it regards every sense. The passion excited by beauty is in fact nearer to a species of melancholy than to jollity and mirth.[5] I do not here mean to confine music to any one species of notes or tones, neither is it an art in which I can say I have any great skill. My sole design in this remark is to settle a consistent idea of beauty. The infinite variety of the affections of the soul will suggest to a good head and skilful ear a variety of such sounds as are fitted to raise them. It can be no prejudice to this, to clear and distinguish some few particulars that belong to the same class and are consistent with each other, from the immense crowd of different and sometimes contradictory ideas that rank vulgarly under the standard of beauty. And of these it is my intention to mark such only of the leading points as show the conformity of the sense of hearing, with all the other senses in the article of their pleasures.

[4] *L'Allegro*, line 135.
[5] I ne'er am merry, when I hear sweet musick. Shakespeare.

Part 4

Section xi: The artificial infinite
We have observed that a species of greatness arises from the artificial infinite, and that this infinite consists in an uniform succession of great parts: we observed too that the same uniform succession had a like power in sounds. But because the effects of many things are clearer in one of the senses than in another, and that all the senses bear analogy to and illustrate one another, I shall begin with this power in sounds as the cause of the sublimity from succession is rather more obvious in the sense of hearing. And I shall here once for all observe that an investigation of the natural and mechanical causes of our passions, besides the curiosity of the subject, gives, if they are discovered, a double strength and lustre to any rules we deliver on such matters. When the ear receives any simple sound, it is struck by a single pulse of the air which makes the ear-drum and the other membranous parts vibrate according to the nature and species of the stroke. If the stroke be strong, the organ of hearing suffers a considerable degree of tension. If the stroke be repeated pretty soon after, the repetition causes an expectation of another stroke. And it must be observed that expectation itself causes a tension. This is apparent in many animals who, when they prepare for hearing any sound, rouse themselves and prick up their ears: so that here the effect of the sounds is considerably augmented by a new auxiliary, the expectation. But though after a number of strokes we expect still more, not being able to ascertain the exact time of their arrival, when they arrive they produce a sort of surprise which increases this tension yet further. For I have observed that when at any time I have waited very earnestly for some sound that returned at intervals (as the successive firing of cannon), though I fully expected the return of the sound, when it came it always made me start a little; the ear-drum suffered a convulsion and the whole body consented with it. The tension of the part thus increasing at every blow by the united forces of the stroke itself, the expectation and the surprise [are] worked up to such a pitch as to be capable of the sublime; it is brought just to the verge of pain. Even when the cause has ceased, the organs of hearing being often successively struck in a similar manner, continue to vibrate in that manner for sometime longer; this is an additional help to the greatness of the effect.

Part 2

Section xvii: Sound and loudness
The eye is not the only organ of sensation by which a sublime passion may be produced. Sounds have a great power in these as in most other passions. I do not mean words, because words do not affect simply by their sounds but by means altogether different. Excessive loudness alone is sufficient to overpower the soul, to suspend its action and to fill it with terror. The noise of vast cataracts, raging storms, thunder or artillery awakes a great and

awful sensation in the mind, though we can observe no nicety or artifice in those sorts of music. The shouting of multitudes has a similar effect; and, by the sole strength of the sound, so amazes and confounds the imagination that, in this staggering and hurry of the mind, the best established tempers can scarcely forbear being borne down and joining in the common cry and common resolution of the crowd.

Section xviii: Suddenness
A sudden beginning or sudden cessation of sound of any considerable force has the same power. The attention is roused by this and the faculties driven forward as it were, on their guard. Whatever either insights or sounds makes the transition from one extreme to the other easy, causes no terror, and consequently can be no cause of greatness. In everything sudden and unexpected, we are apt to start; that is, we have a perception of danger, and our nature rouses us to guard against it. It may be observed that a single sound of some strength, though but of short duration, if repeated after intervals, has a grand effect. Few things are more awful than the striking of a great clock when the silence of the night prevents the attention from being too much dissipated. The same may be said of a single stroke on a drum repeated with pauses; and of the successive firing of cannon at a distance. All the effects mentioned in this section have causes very nearly alike.

Jean Philippe Rameau

(b. Dijon, Sept. 1683; d. Paris, 12 Sept. 1764)

From: 'Nouvelles réflexions sur le principe sonore', in *Code de musique pratique* (Paris 1760), Introduction, p. 189

It may seem odd that the greatest composer of the day, and a theorist of considerable importance, should be represented here by no more than a brief paragraph from his last published treatise. Throughout his life Rameau steadily extended a principle that he had proposed in his earliest theoretical work – the *Traité de l'harmonie réduite à ses principes naturels* – namely that the unity of harmony and melody stem from the harmonic constituents of a single note. The natural principles were first extended to account for the existence of major and minor modes; and then in the *Démonstration du principe de l'harmonie* (1750) to explain the acoustic structure of musical instruments and the human voice. Four years later, Rameau suggested that the principle applied to all the arts of taste which have the senses for judge and proportion for rule. Finally in 1760 Rameau came to see the principle as the foundation of all proportion. It was the later extensions of the early 'principes naturels' that were hotly disputed.

For further reading:
Cuthbert Girdlestone, *Jean Philippe Rameau. His Life and Work* (London 1957), ch. 14.

One principle governs everything. Any thinking person will have sensed the truth of this, though no one has yet explained it. In the conviction that there must be a universal principle, the earliest philosophers turned to music in their search for it. Pythagoras followed the Egyptians in applying the laws of harmony to the motions of the planets. Plato believed that the disposition of the soul was governed by these laws. Aristotle, his disciple, described music as a divine and heavenly thing, and added that it provided the explanation of the system on which the world was built. So impressed were these philosophers by the marvellous way in which the constituent parts of the universe harmonise, that they continued to look for the explanation in music, as the one thing in which proportion dwelt. For those objects that are perceived by the other senses are only the image of proportion, properly speaking. Movement, action, temporal relationships, and analogies, these can only be expressed in acoustic symbols. Unfortunately the system that these great men adopted – far from bringing them nearer to the desired goal – only served to distance them further from it. There can be absolutely no doubt that they were unaware of the phenomenon of the resonant body (*corps sonore*).

75

Henry Home, Lord Kames

(b. Berwickshire 1696; d. Kincardine, Perthshire, 27 Dec. 1782)

From: *Elements of Criticism* (Edinburgh 1761); text from the 6th edn, Edinburgh 1785, vol. 1, ch. 2, pts 1 and 4; vol. 2, ch. 23

Henry Home was called to the Scottish bar in 1724, and after an active legal career took a seat on the Scottish Bench, holding this from 1752 until his death. He was a prolific writer on legal topics. Perhaps his most widely read book was the *Elements of Criticism*, which by 1807 had reached its eighth English edition and had been translated into German (Leipzig 1763–6 and 1772). Abridged editions were still available well into the nineteenth century. Johnson was of the opinion that it was a 'pretty essay', though most of it 'chimerical'. As Home observed in his dedication to George III, the book 'treats of the Fine Arts, and attempts to form a standard of Taste, by unfolding those principles that ought to govern the taste of every individual'. Home is to be associated with the many late-eighteenth-century writers who linked aesthetics to ethics.

   The work divides into two volumes. The first examines as it were the psychology of aesthetic perception, and contains definitions of such key concepts as idea, emotion, passion, beauty, grandeur, sublimity, motion, force, novelty, humour, uniformity, variety and sentiment. The second volume is primarily devoted to the verbal arts, though gardening and architecture are assigned a separate chapter. Home became aware after the third edition had been published that music deserved more attention than he had given it, and in an attempt to remedy the deficiency he inserted an additional section in vol. 1, ch. 2, pt 1, section ii of which p. 52 to p. 55, line 14 are quoted below (a). This supplements such musical comment as is to be found elsewhere, notably in vol. 1, ch. 2, pt 4 (see (b) below) – the section entitled 'Coexistent emotions and passions' – and vol. 2, ch. 23, pp. 420–2 (see (c) below) the chapter on 'The Three Unities'. Home would seem to have been greatly influenced by Avison and Harris, and he is of importance more on account of the extent to which his *Elements* was read, than for any original views that it might contain.

(a) Power of sounds to raise emotions and passions

Upon a review, I find the foregoing section almost wholly employed upon emotions and passions raised by objects of sight, though they are also raised by objects of hearing. As this happened without intention, merely because such objects are familiar above others, I find it proper to add a short section upon the power of sounds to raise emotions and passions.

   I begin with comparing sounds and visible objects with respect to their influence upon the mind. It has already been observed, that of all external objects, rational beings, especially of our own species, have the most powerful influence in raising emotions and passions; and, as speech is the most powerful of all the means by which one human being can display itself to another, the objects of the eye must so far yield preference to those of the ear. With respect to inanimate objects of sight, sounds may be so contrived as to raise both terror and mirth beyond what can be done by any such object. Music has a commanding influence over the mind, especially in conjunction with words. Objects of sight may indeed contribute to the same end but more faintly; as where a love poem is rehearsed in a shady grove or on the bank of a purling stream. But sounds, which are vastly more ductile and various, readily accompany all the social affections expressed in a poem, especially emotions of love and pity.

Music having at command a great variety of emotions, may like many objects of sight, be made to promote luxury and effeminacy, of which we have instances without number, especially in vocal music. But with respect to its pure and refined pleasures, music goes hand in hand with gardening and architecture, her sister arts, in humanising and polishing the mind, of which none can doubt who have felt the charms of music. But if authority be required, the following passage from a grave historian, eminent for solidity of judgement, must have the greatest weight. Polybius, speaking of the people of Cynaetha, an Arcadian tribe, has the following train of reflections.

'As the Arcadians have always been celebrated for their piety, humanity, and hospitality, we are naturally led to inquire, how it has happened that the Cynaetheans are distinguished from the other Arcadians, by savage manners, wickedness and cruelty. I can attribute this difference to no other cause, but a total neglect among the people of Cynaetha, of an institution established among the ancient Arcadians with a nice regard to their manners and their climate: I mean the discipline and exercise of that genuine and perfect music which is useful in every state but necessary to the Arcadians, whose manners originally rigid and austere, made it of the greatest importance to incorporate this art into the very essence of their government. All men know that in Arcadia, the children are early taught to perform hymns and songs composed in honour of their gods and heroes; and that when they have learned the music of Timotheus and Philoxenus, they assemble yearly in the public theatres, dancing with emulation to the sound of flutes, and acting in games adapted to their tender years. The Arcadians, even in their private feasts, never employ hirelings, but each man sings in his turn. They are also taught all the military steps and motions to the sound of instruments, which they perform yearly in the theatres, at the public charge. To me it is evident that these solemnities were introduced, not for idle pleasure, but to soften the rough and stubborn temper of the Arcadians occasioned by the coldness of a high country. But the Cynaetheans, neglecting these arts, have become so fierce and savage that there is not another city in Greece so remarkable for frequent and great enormities. This consideration ought to engage the Arcadians never to relax in any degree their musical discipline; and it ought to open the eyes of the Cynaetheans and make them sensible of what importance it would be to restore music to their city, and every discipline that may soften their manners; for otherwise they can never hope to subdue their brutal ferocity.'

(b) Concerning the emotions that are proper to music

It must be premised that no disagreeable combination of sounds is entitled to the name of music: for all music is resolvable into melody and harmony which imply agreeableness in their very conception.[1] Secondly, the agreeableness of vocal music differs from that of instrumental: the former, being intended to accompany words, ought to be expressive of the sentiment that they convey; but the latter, having no connection with words, may be agreeable without relation to any sentiment; harmony, properly so called, though delightful when in perfection, hath no relation to sentiment; and we often find melody without the least tincture of it.[2] Thirdly, in vocal music, the intimate connection of sense and sound rejects dissimilar emotions, those especially that are opposite. Similar emotions produced by the sense and the sound, go naturally into union; and at the same time are concordant or harmonious: but dissimilar emotions, forced into union by these causes intimately connected, obscure each other, and are also unpleasant by discordance.

These premises make it easy to determine what sort of poetical compositions are fitted for music. In general, as music in all its various tones ought to be agreeable, it never can be concordant with any composition in language expressing a disagreeable passion or describing a disagreeable object: for here the emotions raised by the sense and by the sound, are not only dissimilar but opposite; and such emotions forced into union produce always an unpleasant mixture. Music accordingly is a very improper companion for sentiments of malice, cruelty, envy, peevishness or of any other dissocial passion; witness among a thousand King John's speech in Shakespeare, soliciting Hubert to murder Prince Arthur, which even in the most cursory view will appear incompatible with any sort of music. Music is a companion no less improper for the description of any disagreeable object, such as that of Polyphemus in the third book of the Æneid, or that of Sin in the second book of *Paradise Lost*: the horror of the object described, and the pleasure of the music, would be highly discordant.

With regard to vocal music, there is an additional reason against associating it with disagreeable passions. The external signs of such passions are painful; the looks and gestures to the eye, and the tone of pronunciation to the ear; such tones therefore can never be expressed musically, for music must be pleasant, or it is not music.

On the other hand, music associates finely with poems that tend to inspire

---

[1] Sounds may be so contrived as to produce horror, and several other painful feelings, which in a tragedy, or in an opera, may be introduced with advantage to accompany the representation of a dissocial or disagreeable passion. But such sounds must in themselves be disagreeable; and upon that account cannot be dignified with the name of music.

[2] It is beyond the power of music to raise a passion or a sentiment: but it is in the power of music to raise emotions similar to what are raised by sentiments expressed in words pronounced with propriety and grace; and such music may justly be termed sentimental.

pleasant emotions: music for example in a cheerful tone is perfectly concordant with every emotion in the same tone; and hence our taste for airs expressive of mirth and jollity. Sympathetic joy associates finely with cheerful music, and sympathetic pain no less finely with music that is tender and melancholy. All the different emotions of love, namely, tenderness, concern, anxiety, pain of absence, hope, fear, accord delightfully with music: and accordingly, a person in love, even when unkindly treated, is soothed by music; for the tenderness of love still prevailing, accords with a melancholy strain. This is finely exemplified by Shakespeare in the fourth act of Othello, where Desdemona calls for a song expressive of her distress. Wonderful is the delicacy of that writer's taste, which fails him not even in the most refined emotions of human nature. Melancholy music is suited to slight grief, which requires or admits consolation: but deep grief, which refuses all consolation, rejects for that reason even melancholy music.

Where the same person is both the actor and the singer, as in an opera, there is a separate reason why music should not be associated with the sentiments of any disagreeable passion, nor the description of any disagreeable object; which is, that such association is altogether unnatural: the pain, for example, that a man feels who is agitated with malice or unjust revenge, disqualifies him for relishing music or any thing that is pleasing; and therefore to represent such a man, contrary to nature, expressing his sentiments in a song, cannot be agreeable to any audience of taste.

For a different reason, music is improper for accompanying pleasant emotions of the more important kind, because these totally engross the mind and leave no place for music nor for any sort of amusement: in a perilous enterprise to dethrone a tyrant, music would be impertinent, even where hope prevails and the prospect of success is great: Alexander attacking the Indian town and mounting the wall, had certainly no impulse to exert his prowess in a song.

It is true that not the least regard is paid to these rules either in the French or Italian opera; and the attachment we have to operas may at first be considered as an argument against the foregoing doctrine. But the general taste for operas is no argument: in these compositions the passions are so imperfectly expressed as to leave the mind free for relishing music of any sort indifferently; and it cannot be disguised that the pleasure of an opera is derived chiefly from the music, and scarce at all from the sentiments: a happy concordance of the emotions raised by the song and by the music is extremely rare; and I venture to affirm that there is no example of it, unless where the emotion raised by the former is agreeable as well as that raised by the latter.

(c) A proposal for the heightening of dramatic tension in opera by the use of interval music

But to open a larger view, I am ready to show, that a representation with proper pauses is better qualified for making a deep impression, than a continued representation without a pause. This will be evident from the following considerations: representation cannot very long support an impression of reality, for when the spirits are exhausted by close attention and by the agitation of passion, an uneasiness ensues which never fails to banish the waking dream. Now supposing the time that a man can employ with strict attention without wandering to be no greater than is requisite for a single act, a supposition that cannot be far from truth, it follows that a continued representation of longer endurance than an act, instead of giving scope to fluctuation and swelling of passion, would overstrain the attention and produce a total absence of mind. In that respect the four pauses have a fine effect, for by affording to the audience a seasonable respite when the impression of reality is gone, and while nothing material is in agitation, they relieve the mind from its fatigue, and consequently prevent a wandering of thought at the very time possibly of the most interesting scenes.

In one article, indeed, the Grecian model has greatly the advantage: its chorus during an interval not only preserves alive the impressions made upon the audience, but also prepares their hearts finely for new impressions. In our theatres, on the contrary, the audience, at the end of every act, being left to trifle time away, lose every warm impression, and they begin the next act cool and unconcerned, as at the commencement of the representation. This is a gross malady in our theatrical representations, but a malady that luckily is not incurable. To revive the Grecian chorus would be to revive the Grecian slavery of place and time; but I can figure a detached chorus coinciding with a pause in the representation, as the ancient chorus did with a pause in the principal action. What objection, for example, can there lie against music between the acts, vocal and instrumental, adapted to the subject? Such detached chorus, without putting us under limitation of time or place, would recruit the spirits, and would preserve entire the tone, if not the tide of passion: the music, after an act, should commence in the tone of the preceding passion and be gradually varied till it accord with the tone of the passion that is to succeed in the next act. The music and the representation would both of them be gainers by their conjunction, which will thus appear. Music that accords with the present tone of mind, is on that account doubly agreeable; and accordingly, though music singly hath not power to raise a passion, it tends greatly to support a passion already raised. Further, music prepares us for the passion that follows, by making cheerful, tender, melancholy or animated impressions, as the subject requires. Take for an example the first scene of the *Mourning Bride*, where soft music, in a melancholy strain, prepares us for Almeria's deep distress. In this manner, music and representation support each other delightfully: the impression made upon the audience by the representation is a fine preparation for the music that succeeds, and the impression made by the music is a fine preparation for the representation that succeeds. It appears to me evident that by some such contrivance, the modern drama may be improved so as to enjoy the advantage of the ancient chorus without its slavish limitation of place and time. And as to music in particular, I cannot figure any means that would tend more to its improvement: composers, those for the stage at least, would be reduced to the happy necessity of studying and imitating nature; instead of deviating, according to the present mode, into wild, fantastic and unnatural conceits.

John Brown

(b. Rothbury, Northumberland, 5 Nov. 1715; d. Newcastle upon Tyne, 23 Sept. 1766)

From: *A Dissertation on the Rise, Union and Power . . . of Poetry and Music* (Dublin 1763), section iv

After graduating from St John's College, Cambridge, in 1735, Brown became a minor canon and lecturer of Carlisle Cathedral and later, Chaplain to the Bishop. He subsequently held a small living in the Colchester area, before moving to St Nicholas' Church, Newcastle upon Tyne, where Avison was organist (see p. 60). Avison is said to have consulted Brown when at work on his *Essay on Musical Expression*. Brown was sufficiently known in his day to receive an invitation from the Empress of Russia to act as an adviser on general education; ill health however prevented him from taking up the task, and in a subsequent fit of depression he committed suicide.

Two editions of the *Dissertation* were published during Brown's lifetime, the second (1764) shorn of its musical section (quoted here). Brown's interpretation of music history is one of the earliest of a family of late-eighteenth-century studies, of which Rousseau's *Essai sur l'origine des langues* (p. 89) and Barthélemy's *Voyages* (p. 166) were the most influential. Brown works on the premise that music and poetry were separated in Roman times and that a reunion of the two is vital if the two arts are to regain their former power. Whilst it is easy to smile at this kind of speculative writing, its practical effect on later educational theory should not be underestimated; Pestalozzi was to use music as a basic tool of moral education; others – notably Mainzer – were to promote the cause of music among the working classes.[1] And whilst 'classical' arguments of this kind tended to result in the denigration of contemporary music (see Toreinx, p. 416), in combating the idea of music as merely pleasurable amusement they indirectly served to enhance the status of the art.

The titles of the principal sections are as follows: Of Music, Dance, and Poem in the Savage State; Of the Natural Consequences of a Supposed Civilisation; Music and Poetry in Ancient Greece; Of the Natural Union and Progression of Music and Poetry in other European Countries; in China, Peru and India; The Music of the Ancient Hebrews; Of the State and Separation of Music and Poetry in Ancient Rome; Of the State and Separation of Music and Poetry Among the Polished Nations of Europe through the Succeeding Ages; Of the Possible Re-Union of Poetry and Music.

Of the natural consequences of a supposed civilisation

While these free and warlike savages continue in their present unlettered state of ignorance and simplicity, no material improvements in their

[1] See B. Rainbow, *The Land without Music* (London 1967).

song-feasts can arise. But let us suppose that the use of letters should come among them, and as a cause or consequence of civilisation be cultivated with that spirit which is natural to a free and active people; and many notable consequences would appear. Let us consider the most probable and striking among these natural effects.

1. Their ideas of music, in its most enlarged sense, would comprehend the three circumstances of melody, dance and song. For these three, as we have seen, being naturally conjoined, because naturally producing each other, would not separately command the attention of such a people at their public festivals. Therefore, instrumental melody without song would be little attended to and of low esteem, because it would want all those attractions which must arise from the correspondent dance and song.

2. In the early periods of such a commonwealth, the chiefs or legislators would often be the principal musicians. The two characters would commonly coalesce, for we find that among the savage tribes, the chiefs are they who most signalise themselves by dance and song, and that their songs dwell principally on the great actions and events which concern their own nation.

3. Hence their most ancient Gods would naturally be styled singers and dancers. For the most ancient Gods of civilised pagan countries are generally their legislators who taught their people the first arts of life. These deceased legislators, therefore, when advanced to the rank of Gods, would naturally be delivered down to posterity with the same attributes and qualities by which they had distinguished themselves in life; and it appears from the last article that these qualities would naturally be those of dance and song.

4. Measured periods, or in other words, rhythm, numbers and verse, would naturally arise. For measured cadence, or time, is an essential part of melody, into which the human ear naturally falls. And as the same force of ear would lead the action or dance to correspond with the melody, so the words or song must, on a like principle, keep pace with both. Among the savage Americans we see the first rudiments of poetic numbers emerging from this source. For 'as the means of adjusting the words to the air or melody, they sometimes strike off syllables from their words'. And such is the natural generation of rhythm and verse.

5. Their earliest histories would be written in verse. For we see that among the savage tribes, the action of their heroes and Gods and the great events of their nation, make a principal part of their songs. Whenever therefore the use of letters should come among such a people, these ancient songs would naturally be first recorded, for the information and use of future times.

6. Their most ancient maxims, exhortations, proverbs or laws, would probably be written in verse. For these would naturally make a part of their songs of celebration, and would by degrees be selected from thence, would in time become the standard of right and wrong, and as such be treasured up and appealed to by the improving tribe.

7. Their religious rites would naturally be performed or accompanied by dance and song. For it appears from fact that the great actions of their Gods and heroes are the most general subject of the savage dance and song, and the common end of pagan rites hath ever been to praise the Gods of the country, and by these means (as well as by sacrifice) to appease their wrath or secure their favour.

8. Their earliest oracles would probably be delivered in verse and sung by the priest or priestess of the supposed God. For these oracles being supposed to be inspired by a deceased chief (now a deity) who had himself delivered his exhortations in this enthusiastic manner, and being addressed to a tribe, among whom this mode of instruction universally prevailed, no other vehicle but that of verse and song could at first gain these oracles either credit or reception.

9. Their melody would be simple and derive a considerable part of its power from its rhythm or measure, without any mixture of artifical composition. First, because this kind would be most suited to the powers of the barbarous legislators or bards, at once composers and performers, among whom nothing artificial or refined could as yet take place. Secondly, because this simplicity of manner would be best adapted to the capacity of the surrounding people, incapable in this early period to be attracted or moved by anything but what nature dictates.

10. The force of this simple melody would be much increased by the power of early association and continued habit. For this, by appropriating certain sounds to certain subjects, would raise their melody into a kind of natural and expressive language of the passions.

11. Their songs would be of a legislative cast, and being drawn chiefly from the fables or history of their own country, would contain the essential parts of their religious, moral and political systems. For we have seen above that the celebration of their deceased heroes would of course grow into a religious act: that the exhortations and maxims intermixed with these celebrations and founded on the example of their hero Gods would naturally become the standard of right and wrong: that is, the foundation of private morals and public law. And thus the whole fabric of their religion, morals and polity would naturally arise from and be included in their songs, during their progress from savage to civilised life.

12. Music, in the extended sense of the word (that is including melody, dance and song) would make an essential and principal part in the education of their children. For the important principles of their religion, morals and polity being delivered and inculcated in their songs, no other method could be devised which would so strongly impress the youthful mind with the approved principles of life and action.

13. Music therefore (in this extended sense) must gain a great and universal power over the minds and actions of such a people. For through the force of early and continued habit, together with the irresistible contagion of general example, while everything pleasing, great and impor-

tant was conveyed through this medium and through this only, such strong impressions would strike themselves into the growing mind as would give it its ruling colour through life, and such as no future incidents could easily weaken or efface.

14. In the course of time and the progress of polity and arts, a separation of the several parts or branches of music (in its extended sense) would naturally arise. Till a certain period of civilisation, letters and art, the several kinds would of course lie confused, in a sort of undistinguished mass, and be mingled in the same composition, as inclination, enthusiasm, or other incidents might impel. But repeated trial and experiment would naturally produce a more artificial manner, and thus by degrees the several kinds of poem would assume their legitimate forms.

15. If their warlike character continued, the dance would naturally separate from the song, and would in itself become a distinct exercise or art, for the sake of increasing their strength and ability of body as the means of rendering them invincible in war. For the dance, or action, of their song-feasts, being only secondary and merely an appendage to the song would not be of a character sufficiently severe for the fierce and stubborn contention of those who were destined to the immediate toils of warlike service.

16. After a certain period of civilisation, the complex character of legislator and bard would separate or be seldom united. For as the society grew more populous, and the increasing arts of life increased the labours and cares of government, the musical art (in its extended sense) would of course be delegated by the civil magistrate to such men of genius and worth as might apply it to its proper ends, the instruction and welfare of mankind.

17. Hymns or odes would be composed and sung by their composers at their festal solemnities. For these in their simple state are but a kind of rapturous exclamation of joy, grief, triumph or exaltation, in consequence of some great or disastrous action known, alluded to or expressed: a species of composition which naturally ariseth from the song-feast.

18. The epic poem would naturally arise and be sung by its composers at their public solemnities. For it appears above that their earliest histories would be written in verse and make a part of their public song-feasts. Now the epic poem is but a kind of fabulous history, dwelling chiefly on the great actions of ancient Gods and heroes and artificially composed under certain limitations with respect to its manner, for the ends of pleasure, admiration and instruction.

19. From the union of these two a certain rude outline of tragedy would naturally arise. We may see the first seeds or principles of this poem in the conduct of the savage song-feast. A chief sings some great action of a God or hero: the surrounding choir answer him at intervals by shouts of sympathy or concurrent approbation.

20. In process of time this barbarous scene would improve into a more perfect form. Instead of relating, they would probably represent by action

and song united those great or terrible achievements which their heroes had performed. For of this too we find the seeds or principles in the savage state. 'After a chief of war hath recounted the battles he had fought, they who are present will often rise up to dance, and represent those actions with great vivacity.' If to this we add the usual exclamations of the surrounding choir, we here behold the first rude form of savage tragedy.

21. If the choir should be established by general use, and should animate the solemnity by dance as well as song, the melody, dance and song would of course regulate each other, and the ode or song would fall into stanzas of some particular kind. This appears from the third article.

22. Another consequence of an established choir would be an unvaried adherence to the unities of place and time. For a numerous choir, maintaining their station through the whole performance, must give so forcible a conviction to the senses, of the sameness of place and shortness of time, that any deviation from this apparent unity must shock the imagination with an improbability too gross to be endured.

23. Not only the part of the tragic choir, but the episode or interlocutory part would also be sung. For as the ode and epic would be sung from the earliest periods, so when they became united, and by that union formed the tragic species, they of course maintained the same appendage of melody which nature and custom had already given them.

24. While the nation held its fierce and warlike character, the tragic representations would chiefly turn on subjects distressful or terrible. For thus they would animate each other to victory and revenge by a representation of what their friends had done and suffered. These subjects would likewise be accommodated to the natural taste of the poetic chiefs of such a people whose achievements must produce and abound with events of distress and terror. They also would be best suited to the genius and ends of their state and polity: for as the leading view of such a fierce and warlike people must be to destroy pity and fear so this would effectually be done by making themselves familiar with distressful and terrible representations. The gentle passions and less affecting actions which might fill the spectacles of a mild and peaceful nation, would be insipid to the taste and incompatible with the character of such a warlike people.

24. As their tragedy would be intended as a visible representation of their ancient Gods and heroes, so it would be natural for them to invent some means of strengthening the voice and aggrandising the visage and person, as the means of completing the resemblance. For in all savage countries the tallest and strongest men are generally selected as their chiefs.

26. As their tragic poets would be singers, so they would be actors, and perform some capital part in their own pieces for the stage. For we see these different characters are naturally united in the savage state. Therefore, till some extraordinary change in manners and principles should ensue, this union would of course continue.

27. Musical contests would be admitted as public exercises in such a

state. For we have seen that the important articles of religion, morals and polity would naturally make a part of their public songs: therefore public contests of this kind would be regarded as the best and surest means of raising an emulation of a most universal nature, and of strengthening the state by enforcing all the fundamental principles of society in the most striking and effectual manner.

28. The profession of bard or musician would be held as very honourable and of high esteem. For he would be vested with a kind of public character, and if not an original legislator, yet still would be regarded as a subordinate and useful servant of the state.

29. Odes or hymns would naturally make a part of their domestic entertainments, and the chiefs would be proud to signalise themselves by their skill in melody and song. For their songs being enriched with all the great and important subjects relative to the public state, nothing could be more suitable to a high station in the commonwealth than a proficiency in this sublime and legislative art.

30. When music had attained to this state of relative perfection it would be regarded as a necessary accomplishment. And if any man or society of men were unacquainted with the practice and power of music, their ignorance of this art would be regarded as a capital defect, for it would imply a deficiency in the three great leading articles of education: religion, morals and polity.

31. The genius of their music would vary along with their manner. For manners being the leading and most essential quality of man all his other tastes and acquirements naturally correspond with these, and accommodate themselves to his manners, as to their chief and original cause.

32. As a change of manners must influence their music, so by a reciprocal action a change in their music must influence manners. For we have seen that music was the established vehicle of all the great principles of education. Therefore a change in music must tend to bring on a change in these.

33. A provident community of principles, uncommonly severe, would probably fix both the subjects and movements of song and dance by law. This would arise from their knowledge of the mutual influence of manners and music on each other.

34. In a society of more libertine and relaxed principles, the corruption of music would naturally arise, along with the corruption of manners, for the reasons now assigned, and the musicians, bards or poets would be the immediate instruments of this corruption. For being educated in a corrupt state, they would be apt to debase their art to vile and immoral purposes, as the means of gaining that applause which would be the natural object of their ambition.

35. In consequence of this corruption a gradual and total separation of the bard's or musician's complex character would ensue. For the chief would now no longer pride himself on the character of poet or performer,

nor the man of genius and worth descend to the profession of lyrist, singer or actor, because these professions, which had formerly been the means of inculcating everything laudable and great, would now (when perverted to the contrary purposes) be disdained by the wise and virtuous.

36. Hence the power, the utility and dignity of music would sink into a general corruption and contempt. This consequence is so plain as to need no illustration.

Jean-Jacques Rousseau

(b. Geneva, 28 June 1712; d. Ermenonville, Paris, 2 July 1778)

From: *Essai sur l'origine des langues,* in *Oeuvres complètes*, vol. 12, ed. P. R. Auguis (Paris 1825), chs. 12–15, 19

He has only felt during the course of his life, and in this respect his sensibility rises to a pitch beyond what I have seen any example of; but it still gives him a more acute feeling of pain than pleasure.   David Hume.

After a turbulent childhood, and an uncompleted apprenticeship as an engraver, Rousseau dreamed of being a professional musician. He had the temerity to set up as a music teacher in Lausanne after a brief and not altogether satisfactory period of study with the organist of Annecy Cathedral, and he even allowed himself to be persuaded to compose some pieces for a local group of amateurs in Lausanne, the result being a totally illiterate concoction that proved to be altogether unperformable, to his intense chagrin and embarrassment.[1] Music none the less went on to play an important role in his life. His earliest earnings came from music copying, and his first published work – *Dissertation sur la musique moderne* (Paris 1743) – was the substance of a paper that he had delivered the previous year to the Académie des sciences on the need for a reform of musical notation; the subject was one that remained dear to his heart, his concern being that music should reach as wide a public as possible (a very real line of descent can in fact be traced from Rousseau to Curwen, and to present day tonic sol fa notations). In 1748 he was commissioned to provide the articles on music for the great *Encyclopédie* – Rameau having declined the invitation – and these he dispatched in the space of a few months; he later regretted that he had not insisted, as other contributors had done, that he be allowed to space out his contributions over the ten years that it took to complete publication of the *Encyclopédie*. In 1767 he published a musical dictionary that included material, suitably revised, from the *Encyclopédie*.

His prize essay for l'Académie de Dijon on the theme, 'Has progress in the arts and sciences contributed to an improvement of morals?' (1750) was his first work to attract widespread attention, and it marked the beginning of a major series of moral, philosophical and political writings.

His influence in many different spheres was enormous. His *Contrat social* (Amsterdam 1762) was of immense importance in the pre-history of the French Revolution. His romantic novel *Julie ou la nouvelle Héloïse* went through more than seventy editions between 1761 and 1800 (the averagely successful novel would have been reprinted three or four times). His little piece for the Opéra, *Le Devin du village* (1752) – a practical demonstration of the singability of the French language – was still being performed half a century later, and when it was finally pensioned off in 1829 (Berlioz reports how a large *perruque* was thrown on to the stage at the last

---

[1] The whole acutely uncomfortable episode is vividly recounted in the autobiography: see *The Confessions of Jean-Jacques Rousseau*, tr. J. M. Cohen (Harmondsworth 1953).

performance) it had been given more than 400 times. Even his writings on music continued to be widely read and quoted well into the nineteenth century. Within two years of its appearance, his dictionary had been published in Dutch and English versions – Fétis suggested that the absence of a German edition was due to the fact that French was so widely spoken in Germany at the time. Its contents were pillaged by later French and English scholars, including Framery, Burney (for Rees's *Cyclopedia*, 1801) and Castil-Blaze, who lifted and adapted no fewer than 340 articles from it for his *Dictionnaire de musique* (1821). That the elder Fétis could still praise it in his *Biographie universelle* (1862) is remarkable proof of its continuing usefulness.

Charles Burney had a particularly high regard for Rousseau, remarking that if in other respects he was eccentric, 'his taste and views, particularly in dramatic music are admirable and supported with more wit, reason and refinement than by any other writer on the subject that I am able to read'. Garrick produced Burney's *The Cunning Man* – his translation of *Le Devin du village* – at Drury Lane in 1766, and a number of times after that, with great success. *Le Devin du village* was even the subject of praise by Gluck, who in a letter to the Paris *Mercure* of February 1773 (see p. 149), had this to say: 'The language of nature is a universal language. M Rousseau has used it with the greatest success in a simple piece, *Le Devin du village*. It is a model that no author has yet imitated.' Mme de Staël, who was a particularly influential figure in the early romantic movement in France, was a later admirer of his, publishing as her first work, *Lettres sur J. J. Rousseau* (1788) (see p. 297).

Rousseau is particularly known to musicians for his aggressive denunciation of French music in the *Lettre sur la musique française* (1753).[2] The principles that led him to make this denunciation are substantially revealed in the *Essai sur l'origine des langues* (pub. 1764). The first sounds that primitive man used, he suggested, had the purpose of communicating feelings, and it was from these sounds that music sprang. In the earliest times, speech was music, and the two long continued a close association. The legendary power of music in ancient Greece was to be explained by its union with words, and its use was strictly controlled to ensure the maximum good to society. As Rousseau himself remarked elsewhere, 'C'est la raison qui fait l'homme, c'est le sentiment qui le conduit' (It is reason that makes man, and feelings that guide him); words spoke to reason, and music to the feelings.

Rousseau was an impulsive writer, all too prone to short-sightedness when in hot pursuit of some favoured theme. In the *Essai*, Rousseau was less concerned with musical practicalities than with theories of social behaviour. If the music of ancient Greece was purely melodic, as all the evidence suggested, and if the power of Greek music was as great as ancient writers asserted, then logically, for the purposes of the *Essai* any non-melodic musical elements – harmony, counterpoint, instrumentation, and even instrumental music – could only distract the attention from expressive melody. Rousseau was unconcerned with appearances of self-consistency – having composed the highly successful *Le Devin du village*, for instance, he was not afraid to decry the French language as unsingable, one year later. As far as his attitude to harmony was concerned, this was coloured by his dislike for the high priest of harmony, Rameau, who had openly disparaged his *Muses galantes* before the influential *La Pouplinière* in 1747. In fact, Rousseau was by no means as blind to the value of both harmony and instrumental music as he is often made out to be: this is evident enough from his later admiration for Gluck; less well known perhaps is the following passage from a letter which he wrote to d'Alembert in 1754, just one year

[2] *Source Readings in the History of Music*, selected by Oliver Strunk (New York 1950), p. 636.

after the *Lettre sur la musique française*: 'The symphony itself has learned to speak without the help of words, and often the feelings that come from the orchestra are no less lively than those that come from the mouths of the actors.'

In the *Essai* Rousseau is ultimately concerned with moral issues, and like Barthélemy (see pp. 166–75) he examines the question of music's function as a moral agent. If, he argues, music is merely a sensual, pleasurable art, how is it that a savage could be totally unmoved by a piece of music that a Frenchman might find deeply affecting? Clearly, our reaction to music is not purely a matter of physical response. So it was that after arguing that passions, not needs, generated the first articulated sounds, and that these sounds were both words and music, having outlined the way in which he believed the southern and northern languages had taken shape, and having discussed the relationship of music to words (see below, chs. 12–19) Rousseau took as the title of his final and culminating chapter, 'The relationship of language to government'.

Rousseau's opinions on music were later to be subject to much hostile comment (much of it, indeed, wilfully misguided). No critic was more outspoken than G. A. Villoteau, whose extensive *Recherches sur l'analogie de la musique avec les arts qui ont pour objet l'imitation du langage* (Paris 1807) contains a detailed commentary on chapters 13–14 of the *Essai*. Villoteau published Rousseau's original text, adding extensive footnotes to it, and italicising the particular passages to which he took exception; these two chapters are given here with Villoteau's annotation.

Guillaume André Villoteau (1759–1839) sang in the choir at Notre-Dame while a student at the Sorbonne. In 1792 he joined the chorus at the Opéra. He is principally remembered for his work as a member of the Institut de l'Egypte which between 1809 and 1826 published twenty folio volumes on every aspect of Egyptian civilisation; the sections on ancient and modern Egyptian music in these volumes are by him. The first of his two books on musical aesthetics was the result of a paper which he read to the Société libre des sciences et des arts entitled, *Mémoire sur la possibilité et l'utilité d'une théorie exacte des principes naturels de la musique* (Paris 1807). The second, the *Recherches*, was a mammoth, two-volume work which was greatly decried by Fétis. It is a prolix and wayward work, but of interest in reflecting the way in which eighteenth-century doctrines involving the principle of the imitation of nature were then being challenged.

For further reading:

A translation of Rousseau's *Essai* in its entirety, coupled to Johann Gottfried Herder's essay on the same topic are in *On the Origin of Language*, tr. John H. Moran and Alexander Gode (New York 1966). Rousseau's relationship to Rameau is discussed in Eve Kisch, 'Rameau and Rousseau', *Music and Letters*, vol. 22 (1947), p. 97. A useful survey is provided by H. V. F. Somerset, 'Rousseau as a Musician' *Music and Letters*, vol. 17 (1936), p. 37.

See also articles on Rousseau in *The New Grove Dictionary of Music and Musicians*, VI, and *Musik in Geschichte und Gegenwart*; and Lionel Gossman, 'Time and History in Rousseau', *Studies on Voltaire and the Eighteenth Century*, vol. 30 (1964), p. 311, and especially pp. 319–33 for a fascinating comparison of Rousseau and Rameau as representative of 'two completely different ways of understanding the world'.

Chapter 12   The common origins of poetry, song and speech

As the voice developed, the differing passions generated the first articulations or sounds. Anger gives rise to threatening cries which are articulated by the tongue and the palate; tenderness is expressed in softer tones which are modified by the glottis. The sounds become utterances and are formed by accents and inflections of varying frequency, emphasis and pitch, according to the feelings that are to be conveyed. In this way sounds, inflections and syllables are formed. Feelings make the organs of speech spring to life, imparting to the voice all their vibrancy. Thus poetry, song and speech have a common origin. Those first exchanges I spoke of were the first song. Poetry, music and language sprang alike from the regular and periodic nature of rhythm, and from the melodious rise and fall that goes with accentuation: or rather, all this was language in those happy climes and times when spontaneous desire was the only motivation for seeking the cooperation of others.

The first stories, the first speeches, the first laws were in verse. Poetry preceded prose. That had to be, since the passions were in evidence before reason was. As far as music was concerned, it was necessarily the same. There was at first no other music than melody nor other melody than the varied sounds of speech; accents combined to form the tune, quantities formed its rhythms, and people spoke as much by means of natural sounds and rhythms as by articulations and words. According to Strabo, singing and speaking were one and the same thing in earlier times, and he argues from this that poetry is the source of eloquence. He ought to have said that poetry and eloquence sprang from the same source, and at first were one and the same thing. In view of the way in which primitive societies were bound together it is hardly surprising that the first stories were told in verse and that the first laws were sung. It is no wonder that the first grammarians subordinated their art to music and were teachers of both.

A language which has only articulations and vocalisations has only half of its potential richness. It conveys ideas, certainly, but to express feelings and impressions (*images*) it needs rhythm and sound (*sons*), that is to say, melody, something that the Greek language had and which ours lacks.

We are constantly astonished by the prodigious effects that eloquence, poetry and music had on the Greeks. We can never envisage them because we have never experienced such things. The best that we can do, seeing that these effects have been so well authenticated, is to pretend a belief in them, out of deference to our scholars. When Burette had to the best of his ability transcribed certain bits of Greek music, he rather naively had them performed at the Académie des belles-lettres, and the academicians had the patience to listen to them. I admire such enterprise in a country whose native music is unintelligible abroad. Ask any foreign musicians you may choose to perform a monologue from a French opera, and I defy you to recognise any of it. And these are the selfsame Frenchmen who presume to judge the melody of an ode of Pindar set to music 2,000 years ago!

[the final para. of ch. 12 omitted]

Chapter 13   Concerning melody

Nobody denies that man is swayed by his senses, but we confuse the causes for want of distinguishing the effects. We place far too little weight on the function of the senses; we do not see that they affect us, not only as sensations but as signs or images, and that they have moral effects that spring from moral causes. Just as the feelings that painting excites in us do not come from colour, no more does music's power over us simply derive from sounds.[3] Beautiful and well-graded colours please the sight, but the pleasure is purely one of sensation. It is the drawing, the representation that gives life and soul to these colours. We are moved and affected by the feelings that are expressed, and the objects that are represented. Interest and feeling do not depend on colour. The features of a striking picture would still touch us if the work were a print: take away these features from the picture, and the colours have no value.

Melody is the musical equivalent of design in painting; it is melody that delineates the features and forms, harmonies and timbres being only the colours. But, you may say, melody is only a succession of sounds. No doubt. And similarly, design is only an arrangement of colours. Merely because a speaker uses ink, though, to write out his speech, can the ink be said to be a very eloquent liquid?[4]

Let us imagine a country where the idea of drawing was unknown, and where many men spent their lives combining, mixing and blending colours, believing themselves to excel in painting. These people would argue about our painting just as we do about Greek music. When they were told about the emotions that we experience from a fine picture, and about the delight that we take in a pathetic subject, their scholars would launch into a

---

[3] This comparison straightway annuls Jean-Jacques's definition of music, for if music's power over us does not derive from sounds, it is pointless to combine them in order to make them pleasing. But there is no parallel between sounds and colours in this comparison, and the conclusion that Rousseau draws can only be true in a relative and particular sense. It is false when applied in a general and absolute sense, for there are sounds that are in themselves disagreeable, and others that make a pleasing impression on the senses. No one has such a poor ear that he cannot distinguish between the two. On the other hand it is a very different matter with colours, which in themselves are not found to be relatively more or less pleasing than others.

[4] Jean-Jacques well knows how to turn an argument round when he senses a fault in the principle that he has proposed! He is very careful to avoid the same mode of comparison that he used earlier on, for it would have brought him up with a jerk. Had he said that 'an orator makes persuasive use of a range of vocal timbres during the course of his speech', is that not to say that the sounds of his voice 'are most eloquent'? The logical outcome would then have been quite different.

ponderous investigation; they would compare their colours to ours,[5] asking whether our green was more tender, or our red more exciting. They would strive to discover what combination of colours could bring tears to the eyes and which others could give rise to anger.[6] The Burettes of that country would gather together a few mutilated fragments of our pictures and they would ask, with some surprise, what was so marvellous about the colours.

And if a neighbouring country began to develop a kind of sketchy drawing, or rough outline, this would be taken for mere scribbling – capricious and baroque. In order to preserve taste, people would adhere to the simple style that indeed expresses nothing,[7] but which comprises a glowing array of colours, huge slabs of colour, and extended sequences of carefully graded but totally featureless colours.

Finally perhaps, in the course of progress, they would discover the prism, and straightway some celebrated artist would found some beautiful system upon it. Gentlemen, he would say, in order to be truly philosophical we must embark upon a study of physics. Here you see the light broken down into its constituent parts. Here are the primary colours; this is how they relate to each other; these are their proportions. Here are the true principles that underlie the pleasure which painting gives you.[8] All those mysterious words about design, representation and figure are the delusions of French painters who seek to arouse I know not what movements of the soul by their imitations, though as we know, only sensation is involved. They talk to you about the marvels of their pictures, but look at my range of colours.

French painters, he would continue, have possibly noticed the rainbow, and they may perhaps have been able to get some feeling for colour and some sensitivity to shading, from nature. But I have shown you the great and true principles of art, of all the arts, gentlemen, and of all the sciences. An analysis of colour and a calculation of prismatic refractions will give you the

---

[5] Had their scholars gone into the matter more deeply they would have found out; but if they had done as Jean-Jacques suggested they would merely have skimmed the surface of the subject.

[6] As yet this has not been done with music; if it had, the art would have been fully mastered. Experience shows that sounds are sad, touching, violent and so on; this alone negates what Jean-Jacques has said.

[7] Was it necessary for Jean-Jacques to equate simple beauty with total and grievous poverty, in this context?

[8] Jean-Jacques is obviously referring to Rameau's system of harmony, but he consistently mishandles comparisons. The argument here is totally false when it is applied to music. It is true that musical expression depends on the choice and ordering of sounds just as expression in painting depends on the selection and arrangement of colours. But in painting the truth of expression does not wholly depend on this, in the way that music depends on sounds. For whatever colours the painter may use for the forms that he seeks to represent, the resemblance will still be easily recognisable if he has correctly captured the outlines and contours, and the effects of lighting. It is not so, however, with musical sounds. Their individual qualities and interrelationships are so irrevocably determined by nature that the slightest misjudgement of dynamics, or the smallest miscalculation of range will be enough to transform the expression. When a song is sung in a different, though analogous key, it will always sound quite different.

only exact relationships that are to be found in nature; these give you the rules that govern all relationships.[9] The universe is nothing but such interrelationships. One therefore knows everything when one knows how to paint. One knows everything when one knows how to arrange colours.

What would we say of the painter who had so little feeling and taste that he could reason in such an absurd manner, limiting our pleasure in painting to matters of physics?[10] What would we say of the musician who, full of prejudice, thought he saw in harmony alone the source of music's power? We would send the first fellow off to paint a bit of wood, and the other should be sentenced to composing French operas.[11]

Since, then, painting is not the art of combining colours in an agreeable manner, neither is music the art of combining sounds in an agreeable manner.[12] If there were nothing more to it than this, both would belong to the natural sciences,[13] rather than to the fine arts. Imitation alone raises them to this plane. Now in what way is painting also an art of imitation? It is through design. And in what way is music also an art of imitation? It is through melody.[14]

Chapter 14   Concerning harmony

The beauty of sound is natural and the effect purely physical. It derives from the diverse particles of air that are set in motion by the sonorous body and its aliquots – possibly to infinity. The total effect is pleasing. Everyone takes pleasure in listening to beautiful sounds, but if the experience is not animated by melodious and familiar inflections it will in no way be delightful or sensually pleasing.[15] The most beautiful songs will only make a

[9] If there do exist such fundamental and precisely determined natural relationships between colours, these have so far escaped notice and investigation, and will doubtless continue to do so. For whether we study the flowers, the plumage of birds or any other coloured object we can distinguish no such fixed and invariable order that can be related to all material objects. It is not so with sounds. These have a constant and invariable relationship to the size of the body, the rapidity of its movement, and the density of the air that carries the sounds. Vocal sounds similarly have a constant relationship to the feelings and passions that they express.

[10] Jean-Jacques here pronounces sentence upon himself in associating the musician with all the absurdities that he has condemned in the painter.

[11] In this connection, Jean-Jacques has had more success than he can have expected, from his *Le Devin du village*.

[12] I came to this conclusion before discovering that Jean-Jacques had beaten me to it. I am delighted to find myself in agreement with him on this point.

[13] In effect the Ancients accorded music this status, although they numbered it among the fine arts, together with philosophy, and so on.

[14] This argument ceases to be valid when applied in a specific and absolute manner: it is too general to be applied to melody and too restricted to be applied to music.

[15] This is true. I became convinced of this when I was in Egypt. This does not in any way disprove, however, the expressive and imitative principles of melody; for as long as the melody remains simple and as long as its naturally expressive accents are recognisable, its inflections will be familiar to all peoples.

slight impression on an ear that is not accustomed to them. A dictionary is needed to comprehend the language.[16]

Harmony in its strictest sense is even less favourably placed. Since its beauties derive only from convention, it gives no pleasure to the ear that is unaccustomed to it. Considerable experience is needed if a taste and feeling for it are to be developed. Our consonances are but noise to the uncultured ear. When natural proportions are impaired it is hardly surprising that natural pleasures can no longer be derived from them.[17]

One note carries with it all its associated harmonics, which together in their relative strengths and pitches give the note the most perfectly harmonious sound. Add to that the third, the fifth or some other consonance, and you are not adding but merely doubling. You are leaving the intervals unchanged but simply altering the strengths relative to one another. In reinforcing one consonance and not the others you are destroying the proportions of the sound. In seeking to improve nature you are spoiling her. Your ear and your taste are impaired by an art that

[16] A veritable dictionary of music's language would be required to list the musical equivalents of all the natural accents of expression. These accents were known to the Greeks and Romans but they were not written down, as the musical notation that they used was inadequate. It was the 'Phonasques' or 'Masters of Song and Declamation' who taught by practical example how to link together the musical words that make up the natural accents of expression. Such knowledge could only be the fruit of long study, enquiry and experience of natural and imitative expression. The contemporary musician who has familiarised himself with the words of the language of music, and who knows how to make proper use of them will have reached his goal, namely that perfection which once again is allied to nature, though in a way which is the precise opposite of that which pertained in its first infancy. Without this knowledge musical expression will never recover its truly original and emotive character. Otherwise it will be coloured, not only by the peculiar customs, tastes and habits of each people, but it will also be affected by all those incidental factors that are born of caprice, fashion and bad taste. It is these that make expression unrecognisable, so that those who are not familiar with it cannot savour it.

Most indigenous music today is far removed from nature; it is imbued with an arbitrary mode of expression that completely distorts any natural qualities that may be left, excepting only those songs that are not intended for dancing, by the Barbras people, mountain dwellers of the Nubia, who live above the first waterfalls on the river Nile. These melodies represent music in its first infancy; they are of the sweetest and most melancholy kind, and in a way are simply long, modulated sighs, during which the voice gently ascends and then slowly descends again by imperceptible steps of no precise pitch, only to begin again as many times as there are couplets to be sung. To form an idea of the quality of this music we have only to recall the sounds that children make before they have learned to speak, when in a sort of ecstasy of happiness they softly rock their voices. The only difference is that the Barbras people use the full compass of the voice, whereas children span no more than three or four notes.

[17] This is indeed a fact that we have proved in Egypt. However, there is no denying that when with practice the effects of various chords have been determined, felt and appreciated, our harmony definitely adds a new power and interest to melodic expression; this is so because it can imitate and enhance the most obscure as well as the most obvious movements, the most secret as well as the most evident actions that concern each animate and inanimate thing that is on the stage, where the action referred to in the music takes place.

is misunderstood. In nature there is no other harmony than the unison.[18]

M Rameau believes that a simple treble line will naturally suggest its own bass, and that an untrained person with a good ear will instinctively sing that bass. This is a musician's assumption that is altogether contradicted by experience. The person who has never heard a bass or a harmony will find neither, unaided, and if he were made to listen to them, he would find them displeasing and would prefer the simple unison. Though one were to calculate for a thousand years the relationship between sounds and the laws of harmony, how could that possibly result in the conclusion that music is an art of imitation?[19] Upon what principle is this supposed imitation based? What does harmony signify? And can chords have anything in common with our emotions?

If similar questions are asked in respect of melody the answers are self-evident; they are already present in the mind of the reader. By imitating the inflections of the voice, melody can express cries of grief, complaints, threats and groans. It is concerned with all the vocal expressions of passion.[20] It imitates the accents of language and the turns of phrase that reflect every movement of the soul. Not only does it imitate but it speaks, and its language, though inarticulate, is lively, ardent and passionate, and it

---

[18] I am not at all of Rousseau's opinion on this matter. On the contrary I believe that the unison is more a part of art than nature, in which everything is harmoniously varied. Is there not a natural harmony when the day star sinks towards the horizon and soft breezes begin to waken nature, gently stirring first grass, plants and shrubs, then trees and at length the very forests; or when birds, after hopping from branch to branch for a while and calling to one another, suddenly take flight, making the heavens ring with their thousand different songs; or when the doors of the stable and the sheepfold are opened, and the sheep jostle their way out, bleating and leaping round the shepherd who is leading them; or when oxen, herded along by the labourers, bellow to each other in long, drawn-out tones. And are all these sounds, these bird songs, these cries, in unison? The error lies, as in so many other cases, in the fact that Rousseau has confused the basic principles of harmony with the basic principles that relate to the use of that harmony; he has assumed in other words that both are derived from the resonance of sonorous bodies. As I have observed in the preceding footnote, musical harmony is essentially the imitation of natural and concurrent sounds such as those that I have just described. To avoid confusion, simultaneously sounding notes are drawn from a common generating tone, and these form harmonies. The diversity of sounds that go to make up harmony is thus in conformity with natural harmony, just as the sounds in a chord relate to each other and are prescribed by laws affecting the resonance of sonorous bodies. The harmonics that sound together with the principal generating tone are thus only the means and not the end of musical harmony. Musical harmony, like other kinds of harmony, is to do with variety and not with uniformity. The unison cannot therefore give rise to harmony.

[19] This is the inevitable consequence of the erroneous principle that has been established concerning the purpose of harmony. I have in the previous note demonstrated its falsity. If, as I maintain, its consequences have been logically deduced, there is no need to demonstrate the error of this statement.

[20] Musical expression does not, then, derive wholly from melodic design but also from the imitation of those sounds and vocal inflections that are appropriate to the feelings and passions. The function of music is thus by no means limited to 'the pleasurable satisfaction of the ear'.

has a hundred times more energy than the word itself. This is the source of the power of musical imitation; this is the mainspring of the power that song has over sensitive hearts.[21]

In certain systems harmony can be an integrating force, binding together successions of sounds by certain laws of modulation. It can improve intonation, it can provide the ear with definite evidence of that exactness; in the case of suspensions and consonant intervals it can bring together and determine the subtlest of inflections. But in fettering melody, harmony saps it of its energy and expression. It substitutes for the passionate accent the harmonic interval; it binds within two scale-formations melodies that should have as many notes as there are intonations in speech. It eliminates and destroys a multitude of sounds and intervals that lie outside its system. In a word, it so separates song from speech that the two languages conflict, and take from each other their essential truth, it being impossible to conjoin them in the expression of a pathetic subject without a feeling of absurdity. That is why people always find the expression of deep and sincere passions in song so ridiculous, for they know that there are no musical inflections for these passions in our language, and that the inhabitants of the northern climes do not die singing, any more than do swans.[22]

Harmony is certainly inadequate of itself to express the many things that seem wholly to depend on it. Thunder, the murmur of running waters, winds, storms, all these are badly portrayed by simple harmonies. Whatever is done, the noise alone will say nothing to the mind.[23] Objects must speak if

[21] In truth, Jean-Jacques is no less adroit at changing his opinion from moment to moment than was Proteus in changing his form. Only a moment ago the philosopher was telling us that the most beautiful songs would make little impression on an ear that was unfamiliar with them if they were composed of inflections that were foreign to it, that music was a language for which a dictionary was essential, and that an imitative art could never be based on harmony. But then, he argued, melody imitates all the inflections of the voice that express the different feelings and passions; that it does not merely imitate but that it speaks; that its inarticulate language, lively, ardent and passionate has, none the less, a hundred times more energy than language itself. And now, he says, this is the source from which song derives its power over sensitive hearts. Where, then, do Jean-Jacques's feelings come from, after all that?

[22] Oh! Why then do people not find music out of place in sad and serious situations, above all at the time of death, when scholars claim and artists prove that music is purely and solely the art of 'pleasing the ear'? It seems to me that ordinary people are much nearer the truth than are the philosophers and learned musicians, who set out to reconcile expressions of the bitterest grief with an art that they believe to have been created, or that they themselves create, 'to give pleasure to the ear'.

I have already proved in many ways that music is nothing but the art of imitating natural expression, and that it must be aided in every way that can add to its vitality and interest. I have also proved – and the passage that I quoted from Plutarch, vol. 13, p. 70, supports my point – that music is best suited to the expression of intense passions, especially sorrowful ones, and that it is far less apt at expressing affections of a moderate kind. Many authorities have convincingly shown that song was once nothing more than artistic expression, and that it could never have been otherwise. There is thus no point in discussing here J. J. Rousseau's erroneous statement.

[23] This is one of the main objections that certain people have against music. To them the mind is all important even in the matter of the emotions they experience. Thus,

they are to be heard; imitation always calls for a kind of discourse that supplies what is lacking in the voice of nature. The musician who seeks to portray noise by noise deceives himself. He knows neither the strengths nor weaknesses of his art. He judges without taste or understanding.

Tell him that he must portray noise by song: that if he wishes to portray the croaking of frogs he must make them sing. For it is not enough that he should imitate: he must touch and please. Otherwise his dull imitation is worthless, and since it will interest no one it will make no impression.

Chapter 15   That our keenest sensations are often activated by moral impressions

As long as sounds are only considered as having effect on the nerves, the true principles of music will be no more understood than the power that music has over our hearts. The sounds of a melody do not only act on us as sounds but as signs of our affections and feelings. Thus do sounds excite in us the emotions that they express and which we recognise. Something of the moral effect of sounds is even discernible in animal behaviour. A dog barks, and in doing so attracts another. If I imitate the miaowing of my cat the animal straightway is alert, anxious and agitated. Having discovered that I am imitating one of its fellow creatures it sits down again and relaxes. How can this be accounted for? There was no difference in the way that the nerves were excited since the cat was at first deceived.

If it is correct that our sensations have nothing to do with moral causes why is it that we are so sensitive to impressions that mean nothing to a barbarian? Why is it that a West Indian finds our most moving music nothing but meaningless sound? Are his nerves of a different make-up to ours? Why are they not excited as our are? Why do the same vibrations affect one person so much and another so little?

[paras. 3 and 4 omitted]

I know of only one sense that remains unaffected by moral considerations: taste. Gluttony is the vice of men who are totally insensitive.

Anyone, then, who wishes to play the philosopher and to examine the power of our sensations, must begin by distinguishing purely sensual impressions from those intellectual and moral impressions that we receive through the senses, but which are but rarely caused by them. Let him then avoid the trap of attributing to objective phenomena powers that they do not possess, or which they only derive from the affections of the soul that they symbolise. Colours and sounds can be very effective as signs and

music will strive in vain to move them, to make them shed sweet tears or to excite passions of the most violent and impetuous kind. But, these gentlemen will say, music in no sense speaks to the mind, and so it cannot paint, it cannot imitate, and it is therefore a conventional and frivolous art. Who knows indeed where they may lead us with their absurd conclusions!

symbols, but they can do little simply as objects of the senses. I may be amused for a while by particular successions of notes or chords, but something more is needed than sounds and chords if I am to be moved and charmed, something that will effectively move me, in spite of myself. Even songs will lose their interest if they merely give pleasure and say nothing, for it is not so much that the ear gives pleasure to the heart, but rather the reverse. In developing these ideas we have spared ourselves those absurd arguments that involve ancient music. This is an age that seeks to prove that the workings of the soul spring from material causes, and that there is no morality in human feelings: if I am not very much mistaken, the new philosophy will prove as disastrous for good taste as it will for virtue.

Chapter 16   A false analogy between colour and sound

There is no sort of absurdity that has not been put forward during discussions about the physical causes which relate to the Fine Arts. Parallels have been found between sound and light, and these have instantly been seized upon, without reference to experience or reason. The search for a system has bedevilled everything. When we are unable to paint with the ears we decide to sing with the eyes. I have seen that famous keyboard on which they claim to make music with colours. Failure to recognise that colours owe their effect to permanence and sounds to successiveness shows a total misunderstanding of the workings of nature.

The whole richness of colour is spread before us at a single moment. Everything can be seen at a first glance. But the more we look, the more we are delighted; all that we have to do is endlessly to admire and to contemplate.

It is not so with sound. Nature does not analyse harmonies, and in no way does she separate them out. On the contrary, she hides them under cover of the unison. Now if at times she does separate them, as in human song and the warblings of certain birds, she does so successively, one sound after another. She inspires songs, not chords; she dictates melodies, not harmonies. Colours adorn inanimate things; all matter is coloured. Sounds, however, imply movement; the voice announces the presence of a living being, and only animate bodies sing. The flute is not played by an automaton but by the mechanic [i.e. God] who tempered the winds and gave movement to the fingers.

Thus, each sense occupies its own particular field. Music moves in time, whilst painting occupies space. To build up simultaneous sounds or to develop colours, one after the other is to change their disposition. It is to put the eye in place of the ear and the ear in place of the eye.

But, you may say, just as each colour is determined by the refractive angle of light, so each sound is determined by the frequency with which the sonorous body vibrates. Now there is an evident analogy here, as the relationships between the angles and numbers is similar. This is indeed so, but the analogy is made on rational rather than empirical grounds; and reason has no place here. To begin with, the angle of refraction can be experienced and is measurable, whilst the frequency of the vibrations can not. Sonorous bodies are subject to the action of the air, and continuously change their dimensions and pitch. Colours are durable, sounds are evanescent, and there can never be any certainty that the next sound will be the same as that which preceded it. Each colour, moreover, is absolute and independent. Each sound, on the other hand, is related to others, and can only be identified by a process of comparison. In itself no sound has an absolute character of its own; it is low or high, soft or loud in relation to others. Of itself it has no such properties. In a harmonic system a single sound is nothing either, naturally; it is neither tonic, nor dominant, harmonic nor fundamental, because all these qualities are nothing but relationships. Because the whole system can vary widely in pitch each sound will change its order and place according to how the system itself changes. The properties of colours, on the other hand, in no way depend on such relationships. Yellow is yellow, without reference to red or blue. It is everywhere identifiable as such, and once its angle of refraction has been determined, that particular yellow can be produced at will.

Colour derives, not from the coloured object, but from the light, for if the object is to be visible it must be well lit. Sounds, though, have need of movement, and in order that they may exist, sonorous bodies must be set in motion. Sight thus has this further advantage that the stars furnish it with a perpetual source of stimulation, whereas unaided nature gives rise to few sounds. Indeed, if we discount the theory of the harmony of the spheres, sound can only come from living beings.

It thus follows that painting is closer to nature, and that music is a more human art. The one is felt to be of more interest than the other because it brings men more closely together, and affords them endless insights into their fellow beings. Painting is often dead and inanimate. It can transport the viewer to the midst of a desert, but the existence of a fellow human being is instantly recognised when a voice is heard. The voice is, so to speak, the organ of the soul, and if voices were to portray solitude they would none the less say that we were not alone. The birds chirrup but man alone sings. We can hear neither song nor symphony without being immediately aware of the existence of another intelligent being.

It is one of the musician's particular advantages that he can represent things that could never be understood, whilst the painter can never depict things that cannot be seen. The most staggering thing about an art that only acts through movement is that it can even manage to portray repose. Sleep, nocturnal peace, solitude, silence itself, all these can be illustrated in music. Certainly, noise can convey the effect of silence, and silence the effect of noise; if one falls asleep, for instance, during the course of a monotonously delivered lecture, one awakes immediately it is over. Music tends to act inwardly upon us, awakening through one sense feelings that are similar to those which can be awakened by another. Painting cannot imitate music in the way that music can imitate painting; only when the impression that results from such imitation is a strong one can the relationship be felt, and painting lacks this power. Were the whole of nature to sleep, the man who contemplated her would yet be awake. The musician's art consists in substituting for the lifeless image of an object such impressions as the object excites in the heart of the beholder. It will whip up the sea, fan the inferno, make the rivulets flow, rains fall, and floods swell; it will moreover paint the horrors of a frightening desert, darken the walls of a subterranean prison, subdue the tempest, bring tranquillity and serenity, and impart from the orchestra new fragrance to the groves. The art of music does not directly represent such things but it excites in the soul feelings such as those one experiences on seeing them.

Chapter 17   An error which musicians make that is harmful to the art of music

You see that we return, time and again, to the moral effects of which I have spoken. How far removed those musicians are from a true understanding of the power of their art who think of music merely as movements of the air and excitements of the nerves! The more interested they become in purely physical causes the further removed they are from its origins and the more they deprive it of its basic energy. As music becomes increasingly concerned with harmony at the expense of vocal inflection it is rougher on the ear, and less pleasing to the heart. Already it has ceased speaking; soon it will cease to sing, and then, for all its consonance and all its harmony, it will make absolutely no impression on us.

Chapter 18   To show that the musical system of the Greeks has no parallel with our own

How is it that this has come about? By a natural change in the quality of language. Our harmony is a Gothic invention. Those who claim that our system is based on that of the Greeks are making fun of us. The Greek system had absolutely no harmonic quality about it, in our sense of the word, other than that which was needed to tune instruments to perfect consonances. Those peoples who play stringed instruments are obliged to tune them by consonances. Those who do not have such instruments make use of melodic inflections that seem false to us because they do not lie within our own system, and because therefore we are unable to note them down. The songs of the American natives are a case in point. Many Greek intervals must similarly have been foreign to our system, a fact that might emerge if only this music could be studied with less bias towards our own.

The Greeks divided their system into tetrachords as we divide our keyboard into octaves, and they repeated these divisions exactly as we do our octave. Such an extension would not have been possible, nor could it even have been envisaged within the unit of the harmonic mode. As the voice makes use of smaller pitch intervals when speaking than when singing the Greeks naturally repeated tetrachords in their sung speech (*mélodie orale*) as we repeat octaves in our harmonic melody (*mélodie harmonique*).

They only recognised those consonances that we call 'perfect', rejecting thirds and sixths. Why so? It was because the interval of the minor tone [semitone] was unknown to them or at least forbidden in practice. Since their consonances were not tempered, all the major thirds would have been sharp by the span of a comma, and their minor thirds flat. Their major and minor sixths would also have been too wide or too narrow as a result of this. We may imagine then what concepts they could have of harmony, and what harmonic modes they could establish, discounting as they did the consonances of the third and sixth. As for those consonances that they did recognise, had they thought of them in terms of harmony they would at least have made implicit use of them beneath their melodies, and the term consonance would have been applied to the diatonic steps of the fundamental progressions.[24] Far from having fewer consonances than us they would have had more, so that, for instance, stemming from their interest in the interval of the fifth it would follow that the interval of the second would have been described as a consonance.

But, you may say, why did they have diatonic steps? The spoken language being so well inflected and tuneful, they made an instinctive choice of the most convenient intervals. For the voice finds a middle course between the over-large movements that the glottis has to make to span the wider consonances, and the smallest intervals, the intonation of which is difficult to regulate. It therefore adopts intervals that are smaller than those of the consonances, but simpler than those of the comma, whilst at the same time not ruling out the use of the smaller intervals in the more pathetic genres.

Chapter 19   How music has degenerated

As language perfected itself, melody weighed itself down with new rules and imperceptibly lost its ancient power, finesse of inflection being sacrificed to the calculation of intervals. Thus, for instance, the enharmonic genre gradually fell into disuse. When the theatres had taken on a regular form, only certain prescribed modes were used, and the more the rules of imitation multiplied, the less effective was the imitative language.

In perfecting grammar, the study of philosophy and logic took away from language that lively and passionate accent that had at first made it so songlike. From the time of Menalippides and Philoxenus, the musicians who had formerly been in the service of the poets and who were so to speak under their direction, became independent of them. This is the license of

---

[24] Rousseau is referring here to the *marches fondamentales*, a term that Rameau used to describe his theory of the basic harmonic structure of chord progressions (eds.)

which Music complained so bitterly in a comedy of Pherecrates, a passage from which has been preserved for us by Plutarch. Thus, whilst melody had begun by being closely modelled on speech, it gradually took on a separate existence, and music became increasingly independent of words. So it was that those marvels gradually disappeared that music had achieved when it had been no more than the accent and harmony of poetry. No longer did it give poetry power over the passions, and words only had an effect on reason. Thus, although Greece was full of sophists and philosophers, there were no longer poets or famous musicians. In cultivating the art of persuasion, men lost the art of arousing the emotions. Plato himself, jealous of Homer and Euripides, decried the one and was unable to imitate the other.

Servitude soon came to influence philosophy. The Greek people, now in chains, no longer possessed the fire that only warms free spirits, and they could not find the voice to praise their tyrants that they had used to sing their heroes. Roman influence still further weakened what remained of the language of harmony and accent. Latin, being a heavier and less musical language, did violence to music in adopting it. The melodies that were used in the capital gradually modified those that were sung in the provinces. The Roman theatres harmed those of Athens. When Nero carried off the prize, the Greeks were no longer worthy of it, and the same melody, shared between two languages, suited neither.

Finally came that catastrophe which disrupted the progress of the human spirit without removing those defects which were the product of progress. Europe, invaded by the barbarians and enslaved by ignorant peoples, lost at the same time its sciences, its arts, and that universal instrument of both, namely perfected, harmonious language. Those coarse men from the north gradually accustomed everyone to the roughness of their speech; their hard and expressionless voices sounded rough, and lacked sonority. The Emperor Julian compared Gallic speech to the croaking of frogs. Since their articulation was as harsh as their voices, being nasal and heavy, they were only able to give one sort of character to their song, accenting the vowels in order to cover the roughness of the innumerable consonants.

This harsh song, along with the vocal monotony, obliged these newly arrived peoples and their subjects, who imitated them, to slow down their speech in order to make themselves intelligible. Laboured articulation and heavy accentuation combined to drive all feeling for rhythm and phrasing from melody. As the transition from one sound to another was always the hardest thing to pronounce they had no alternative but to stop on each sound as much as possible, to expand on it and to make it as distinct as they could. Song soon came to be nothing more than a slow and tedious succession of forced and drawn-out sounds, lacking sweetness, shape and grace. And although some scholars said that 'longs' and 'breves' in Latin chant should be respected, people certainly sang verse as if it had no poetic feet, poetic rhythm or any kind of measure.

Thus deprived of melody, song consisted solely of volume and duration of sound, and as such it must at last have suggested ways, with the help of consonance, in which more sonority could be achieved. Groups of voices at the unison, dragging out sounds of endless duration, found by accident concords which seemed to them to be agreeable, since they added to the total sound. Thus began the practice of descant and counterpoint.

I cannot say how many centuries passed during which they worried over fruitless questions bearing upon the known effect of a principle that they had forgotten. The most indefatigable reader would not stand the verbiage that Jean de Muris put into eight or ten chapters over the question of whether the fourth or the fifth should be the lower of two intervals within the octave. Four hundred years later we find Bontempi enumerating – no less tediously – all the basses that can carry the sixth above them instead of the fifth. However, harmony insensibly took the path that analysis had prescribed for it, until finally the invention of the minor scale and dissonance, introduced an arbitrariness of which it is full, and which prejudice alone prevents us from admitting.

Melody being forgotten, all attention being directed at harmony, everything gradually centred on this novelty. The genres, the scales, the modes were all given a new look. Part writing was controlled by harmonic progression. This development having usurped the name of melody, it was in fact impossible to recognise in the new melody, the features of its mother. Our musical system has thus by steps become purely harmonic. It is hardly surprising then that it has lost its verbal accentuation and almost all its energy.

This is how song has by degrees become wholly separated from words, its source of origin. This is how the harmonics of sound have led us to forget vocal inflection and how, finally, its effect being limited to the purely physical concurrence of vibrations, music has found itself shorn of those moral effects that it had produced when it was in two senses the voice of nature.

See also Bibliography under: Babbitt

Chevalier de Jaucourt

From: *Encyclopédie, ou dictionnaire raisonné des sciences, des arts et des métiers*, vol. 15 (Paris 1765), pp. 52, 566–7

In the official *Dictionnaire de l'académie française* (Paris 1694), the sublime was defined as follows: 'Exalted, lofty. The term is only used in connection with spiritual matters that concern the intellect: thus, a man of sublime virtue, a sublime genius, a sublime spirit, a sublime thought, a sublime style, the sublime sciences, the most sublime understanding.' The word is also used substantively: thus, a sublime style, sublime thoughts. Longinus has written a dissertation on the sublime, parts of which are sublime. The *Encyclopédie* definition follows this, rather than the interpretation proposed by Burke (see pp. 69–73).

For information on the *Encyclopédie* see the editorial preface to d'Alembert's *Discours préliminaire* (pp. 57–9), and that prefacing the *Encyclopédie* article on genius (pp. 64–5) for a note on the author, the Chevalier de Jaucourt.

Sensibility (Sensibilité)

A tender and delicate inclination of the soul which disposes it to be moved and touched readily.

As the author of *Des Moeurs* has rightly said, sensibility of the soul leads to a kind of wisdom in honourable matters that goes much deeper than purely intellectual comprehension. Sensible souls may fall into errors that calculating men would never commit, simply because they are so responsive. However, they do infinitely more good. They are more fully alive than others, and in their hands both good and evil can thrive. Contemplation can make a man upright, but sensibility makes him virtuous. Sensibility is the mother of humanity and generosity. It adds to excellence, it sustains the mind; finally it convinces.

The sublime (Sublime)

What, asks La Bruyère, is the sublime? Has it been defined? Despréaux [Boileau] has at least described it.

He believes that the sublime is a certain power of speech that elevates and enraptures the soul and which is the product either of great thoughts and noble feelings, imposing words, or vital, animated and mellifluous expression. It derives from any one of these things, in other words, or from a combination of them all in sublime perfection.

In his treatise on the subject, M. Sylvain argues that the sublime takes the form of an extraordinary, lively and spirited oration which lifts up the soul,

106

enraptures it, and gives it a most exalted concept of itself by means of noble thoughts and lofty sentiments.

In brief, the sublime can broadly be said to be that which lifts us above ourselves and which at the same time makes us aware of our exalted state.

The sublime depicts the truth as it is embodied in a noble subject. It fully reveals the cause and effect of truth and it is the worthiest expression or image of that truth. It is an altogether extraordinary and marvellous quality of speech that transfixes, ravishes and transports the soul, giving it the profoundest self-knowledge. Two dimensions of the sublime will be discussed here: sublimity of phenomena (*images*) and sublimity of feelings. This is not to say that the two are mutually exclusive; both, after all, are sublime for the very reason that they lay open to view the soul and the heart. It is none the less necessary to distinguish which quality of the sublime is pre-eminent, for the phenomenal sublime only concerns static objects, whilst the other involves a movement of the heart.

[p. 566, col. 1, para. 7 to p. 567, col. 1, para. 1 omitted]

Feelings are sublime when they are based on true virtue, when they appear to be almost superhuman and when, as Seneca said, they reveal the constancy of God through the frailty of human nature. The righteous man is at peace, even when the very heavens are falling in upon him. Such tranquillity, when set against the surrounding chaos, gives rise to a sublime picture, whereas the sublimity of the righteous person is the source of sublime feelings.

Jean-Jacques Rousseau

From: *Dictionnaire de musique* (Geneva 1767, Paris 1768)

During the latter part of the eighteenth century this was probably the most widely known work of its kind. Castil-Blaze used its contents as the basis of his own 1821 dictionary, particularly the articles dealing with aesthetic matters. Rousseau had himself borrowed heavily from his earlier work in the *Encyclopédie*. His *Dictionnaire* was translated into several languages, the English version by William Waring dating from 1770.[1] (i) Genius: this is one of Rousseau's most passionate effusions; it more than compensates for the lack of specific reference to musical genius in the *Encyclopédie* (see pp. 64–5). (ii) Imitation: Rousseau touched upon this central concept in practically all his articles of an aesthetic nature. This particular article was reprinted verbatim (as were many others in the dictionary) in the *Encyclopédie méthodique* (Paris 1791, 1818), together with appended comments by one or more of the editors: Framery, Ginguené and Marmontel: as Fétis pointed out (see p. 000) good as the idea may have been in theory, it proved in practice to be thoroughly confusing, particularly as the quality of much of the comment was low. Framery's addendum to Rousseau's article on imitation is given here, as an example of the *Encyclopédie méthodique* at its best. (iii) Natural: Rousseau expanded the article from one in the *Encyclopédie* that was under the general editorship of de Jaucourt, amplifying somewhat the discussion of key signatures, and adding a final paragraph on Italian recitative. It was subsequently reprinted in this form in the *Encyclopédie* supplement. Millin took the original *Encyclopédie* article as it stood (see pp. 293–6) Castil-Blaze reprinted Rousseau's revision, however. (iv) Taste: the translation is essentially that of William Waring (the 1779 edition): Castil-Blaze printed the article in his 1821 dictionary together with brief comments of his own to the effect that Taste was then very much an upper-class attribute! (v) Unity of melody: Rousseau's naive condemnation of harmony and counterpoint may blind us to the main premise of the article, namely that if a composition is to be coherent, it must have a unity. The topic was frequently aired at the time, and it was demonstrated practically in the art of keyboard improvisation. Numerous books on the subject were published, notably Czerny's *L'Art d'improviser* (Paris 1829); amongst the criteria that were proposed, that of unity in variety was perhaps foremost: it is not perhaps altogether misguided to see the technique of thematic transformation (as developed notably by Liszt and Wagner) as originating here.

See also Rousseau's *Essai sur l'origine des langues* (1764), and the editorial introduction to it (pp. 89–105).

Genius (Génie)

Seek not, young artist, the meaning of *genius*. If you possess it you will sense

[1] See facsimile reprint by the American Musicological Society Press (New York 1975).

it within you. If not, you will never know it. The musician of genius encompasses the entire universe within his art. He paints his pictures in sound; he makes the very silence speak; he expresses ideas by feelings and feelings by accents, and the passions that he voices move us to the very depths of our hearts. With his help, pleasure affords fresh delights; his expressions of grief draw from us cries of sympathy. He continuously burns and yet is never consumed. He expresses with fire the hoar-frost and the ice. Even when he paints the horrors of death he experiences in his heart a feeling for life that never leaves him and which he communicates to those who possess responsive hearts. But, alas, he knows of nothing to say to those in whom his seed is not planted, and his prodigies are hardly comprehensible to those who cannot imitate him. Would you like to know then whether any spark of this devouring flame inspires you? Run, fly to Naples! Listen to the masterpieces of Leo, Durante, Jomelli and Pergolesi. If your eyes brim with tears, if your heart pounds, if you are seized with trembling, if in the middle of your rapture oppressive feelings weigh you down, then take Metastasio and set to work. His genius will warm yours. You will build upon the model that he has given you. This is what genius knows; and soon, other eyes will repay you those tears which the great masters have drawn from you. But if the charms of this great art leave you unmoved, if you are neither delighted nor ravished, if that which carries you away seems to you to be merely beautiful, dare you ask what *genius* is? Vulgar mortal! Do not profane that sublime word! What point would there be in you knowing it, you would never feel it!

[Castil-Blaze prefaced Rousseau's article with the following paragraph by Voltaire:]

It seems that the term *genius* ought not to be applied in a very general way to all highly talented people, but only to those who are gifted with invention. In ancient times invention was particularly regarded as a gift of the Gods, a sort of divine inspiration or 'ingenium qua si ingenitum'. However perfect an artist may be, he will never be thought a *genius* if he lacks originality, if he is wanting in invention. He will only be looked upon as a man who has been inspired by his artistic predecessors, even though he may surpass them.

Imitation (Imitation)

Dramatic or theatre music is as much a matter of imitation as are poetry and painting. As M Batteux has shown, all the fine arts have the principle of imitation in common, though the imitation is not of the same kind in each case. The domain of poetry extends over everything that the imagination can envisage. Painting, which does not address the imagination but the senses – and one sense alone – only depicts visible objects. Music would seem to be similarly limited in respect to the ear, and yet it portrays everything, even those objects that are purely visible. By means of almost inconceivable powers it seems to give the ear eyes. The most marvellous thing of all is that though music is in essence movement, it can even conjure up an atmosphere of repose. Night, sleep, solitude and silence are numbered amongst music's greatest pictures. It is well known that noise can create an impression of silence and silence an impression of noise; we slumber for instance during the course of a reading that is delivered in an unvaried and monotonous voice, only to waken the instant it ceases.

Music however makes a more subjective impression on us, awakening through the medium of one of the senses responses similar to those that may be aroused by another. Such parallels are only possible when the impressions are strong, and since painting lacks this strength, it cannot give back to music those imitations that it draws from her. Were the whole realm of nature asleep, the person who contemplated it would be awake. The musician's art is to substitute for the insensate image of the object the movements that the object excites in the heart of the beholder.

Not only will the musician stir up the sea, fan the blaze, make rivulets flow, rains fall and torrents rage, but he will paint the horrors of a fearful desert, he will darken the walls of a subterranean prison, calm the tempest, make the air tranquil and serene, and he will make the orchestra spread abroad a new and pleasing fragrance. He will not literally imitate things, but he will excite in the soul feelings similar to those that it experiences when it sees them.

In the article on harmony I have observed that harmony itself does not have anything to do with musical imitation, since there can be no connection between chords and the objects that are to be depicted or the passions that are to be expressed. I shall demonstrate, in the article on melody, what natural elements are used in music to depict objects and passions, and what is the principle of imitation that harmony lacks.

Framery's commentary on Rousseau's article on imitation
One of Rousseau's presumptions is that melody alone is imitative, and harmony in no way so. There is an implied contradiction here for what is harmony if not a combination of several separate melodies? What is melody then? None other than the foremost of the melodies that together form the harmony. It is consequently absurd to attempt to argue that the principal line of a texture imitates objects in some way or other, and that the whole texture which contains this part and all the others can neither paint nor imitate.

It is obvious that Rousseau has reduced the idea of harmony here to nothing more than a succession of wholly undistinguished chords, altogether devoid of melodic interest and expression. But this is not what is understood, nor what ought to be understood by the term 'harmony', for harmony is none other than the totality of the parts which whilst assuming a distinct and recognisable character of their own in no way fail to make up a genuine ensemble.

A very monotonous melody might well be the principal part of a harmony that was equally devoid of expression; with a more effective choice of chords and individual lines it might none the less form part of an interesting ensemble. How then can the philosopher Rousseau, a man of feeling, a musician and a sublime writer, maintain that there is no connection between chords and the objects that are to be depicted or the passions that are to be expressed? Do not the sounds of chords and melodies both come from the same scale?

Rousseau unveils his secret in the article on melody. It is there that he backs up the paradox in which melody is favoured at the expense of harmony. He does this with all the burning fire of his eloquence, but not with the whole weight of his intellect, for to do so would be against his nature. It is the inflection of speech, he claims, that imbues melody with the magic charm that makes it a vehicle for the imitation of the feelings and passions. From this it follows that there is no melody other than that for the voice. If a melody when set to words expresses something when sung by a voice but nothing when played by an instrument, then the musical expression ought not to be attributed to the melody but to the words and their inflections. When voice, words and inflections have no unity, then no expression can be attributed to those successions of sounds that comprise the melody. If on the other hand the melody has a truly moving and expressive quality as the result of a felicitous combination of notes, even when played on various instruments, the expression may be attributed to the notes of the scale and not to the inflections of speech.

Inasmuch as a beautiful voice may be suitably united to fine words, the expressive powers of voice and words will be enhanced (or at least each will retain its power) when so united. It is essential however to avoid confusing the qualities of the one with the other; one might otherwise declaim a reasoned argument in impassioned tones, thereby proving nothing even though one might succeed by such fallacious means in deceiving those who were not sufficiently on their guard against the power of words and of specious reasoning.

Was it not the philosopher of Geneva who declared in print that painting does not address the imagination but only the senses – and one sense alone which concerns only visible objects? There would be no need to refute so ill-grounded an opinion were it not that even the most profound thinkers can sometimes be absent-minded enough to speak as if they were wholly unthinking people. It is through the eyes that painting speaks to the soul, the heart and the imagination; painting does not aim merely to speak to the eyes, any more than music is solely intended for the ear. Suppose the ear were deaf to nature, would it offer nothing to the mind?

Can it be that on their own, visual images have nothing to say to the imagination? Is that not to suggest that for the greatest of all painters, painting is dumb?

Do we not hear the thunder of the waves as we look at this picture? Do we not see in those static forms that represent the crew of the sinking ship, a turmoil of activity?

What! And do all those shapes that pursue me in my dreams go no further than the retina of my eye? Do they not go down to the depths of my soul? Is it not quite overwhelmed?

What! And that madonna which inspires such a pure and sweet devotion in the young maid kneeling before her, and whose pretty face awakens such ardent desires in this lover of painting and beauty who gazes so intently at her – are these things expressed merely from the eyes of one person to those of another?

The convention of language has undoubtedly a great advantage over the natural languages of music and painting, when it is not confined to the description of objects, to the portrayal of their movements or to such similar matters. Language can express everything through a medium that is wholly one of convention. Language's advantages are none the less outweighed in certain circumstances by an actual portrait of something in sound or colour. On occasion, the feeblest picture can say more than the most brilliant description.

Natural (Naturel)

In music this word has several meanings: (i) natural music is vocal music, whilst artificial music is performed on instruments; (ii) a song is said to be natural when it is effortless, sweet, graceful, and uncomplicated; a harmony is natural when it contains few inversions and few dissonances, and when it is the product of the essential and natural chords of the mode; (iii) all melodies that are neither contrived nor baroque are said to be natural, too – melodies that go neither too high nor too low, too slow or too fast; (iv) finally the word is most commonly used (and this is the only definition the Abbé Brossard did not discuss) to indicate those tones or modes that are built upon the ordinary scale without any alteration – those that is to say that make use neither of flats or sharps. In a particular sense there is only one natural mode, the one that is built upon Ut or C with the major third; the term natural however is applied to all those modes in which the essential chords carry neither flats nor sharps, provided that the key signature is open – these comprise the major modes of G and F and the minor modes of A and D.

The Italians always notate their recitative in the open key. The key changes are so frequent and the modulations so abrupt that whatever key signature was supplied, sharps and flats could not be avoided; considerable confusion would then ensue during the course of a modulation from a conflict between the key signature and the added accidentals.

Taste (Goût)

Of all natural gifts, taste is that which is most felt and least explained. It would not be what it is if it could be defined; for it judges of objects in which the judgement is not concerned, and serves as it were as spectacles to reason.

There are in melody some airs more agreeable than others, though equally well modulated. There are, in harmony, things striking, and others not so, all equally regular. There is in the interweaving of pieces, an exquisite art of making the one receive a power from the other, which depends on something more subtle than the law of contrasts. There are, in the execution of the same piece, different methods of rendering it, without ever straying from its character: of these methods the one pleases more than the others, and far from being able to submit them to rules, we cannot even determine them. Reader, give me an explanation of their differences, and I will explain to you what is taste.

Each man has his peculiar taste, by which he gives to things which he calls beautiful and excellent, an order which belongs to himself alone. One is more touched with pathetic pieces; the other prefers a gay air. A sweet and flexible voice will fill its tunes with agreeable ornaments; a sensible and strong voice will animate them with the accents of passion. The one will seek simplicity in melody, the other will value elaborate expression, and each will call that an elegance of taste, which he has preferred.

This diversity comes sometimes from the different dispositions of the organs which taste teaches us to make use of: sometimes from the particular character of each man, which renders him more sensible to one pleasure or failing, than to another; sometimes from the diversity of age or sex, which turns the desires towards different objects. In all these cases, each having only his own taste to oppose to that of another, it is evident, that there is no dispute to be made.

But there is also a general taste, about which all well-ordered people agree, and to this alone can the name of taste absolutely be given. Let a concert be heard by ears that are sufficiently trained, and by men who are reasonably knowledgeable, and the majority will usually agree, in judging the pieces, on their order of merit. Ask each one the reason for his judgement, and there will be points on which they are almost unanimously agreed. These are the matters that are subject to rules, and the artist and connoisseur are commonly agreed on them. But among those things that they agree to be good or bad there are some to which they cannot apply the authority of any sound principles: the final verdict stems from having preferences of taste. It seems to me that these people are not divided in their opinion. They agree on finding a work good or bad, but they cannot find why. When there is not perfect unanimity, this is because not everyone is equally well endowed with sound judgement; not all have equally good taste, because the order of natural beauties is often randomly affected by prejudices that are born of convention and education. Since there is only one true 'taste', this is a proper object for discussion. But I see no means of settling the dispute other than asking for a show of hands when there is disagreement on the taste of nature herself. In regard to this taste, we may dispute on it by another method of determining the variance than that of counting the notes, when we do not even agree to that of nature. Here, then, is what ought to decide, in respect to the preference of French and Italian music.

Genius creates, but taste makes the choice; and a too abundant genius is often in want of a severe censor to prevent it from abusing its riches. We can do great things without taste, but it is that alone which renders them interesting. It is taste that makes the composer catch the ideas of the poet; it is taste which makes the executant catch the ideas of the composer.

It is taste which furnishes to each whatever may adorn and augment their subject; and it is taste which gives the audience the sentiment of their agreements.

Taste however is by no means sensibility. We may have much taste with a frigid soul; and a man transported with things really passionate is little touched with the pleasing. It seems that taste is most readily to be attached to restraint, and sensibility to boldness of expression.

Have the French good musical taste? Yes, as far as the great world of high society is concerned; but, as far as ordinary people are concerned, no, a thousand times, no!

Those who belong to the best society frequent concerts and musical events, and they punctiliously attend the Théâtre Italien in order to hear the sublime compositions of Mozart, Cimarosa and Paer. They enjoy grand opera when there is dancing, they only go to the Feydeau on good days, and they fly from the Vaudeville as they would fly from leprosy and the plague. Men of the world thus familiarise themselves with fine music and good performances, and in the salon they are pleased to search out the melodies that have charmed them in the theatre. They could still further purify their taste, none the less, if they banned those insipid *romances* that dare to display themselves alongside the most elegant compositions, and above all if they asked those people who have rasping Parisian accents, and who imagine that they can sing, to keep silent.

As for most Parisians, they are essentially barbarians. They frequent the places where the miserable refrains of the pleasure gardens and the Pont-Neuf are endlessly repeated. They only praise an opera if it contains songs similar to the ones that they like. The vaudeville does not corrupt common taste; that has already been done. It does however keep it low.

How can one have an ear that is attuned to the Feydeau or the Académie royale, if one has for a long time been accustomed to the fearful cacophony of boulevard bravura? In our lyric theatres one could sing out of tune and unrhythmically, lacking any attack, missing beats, breathing in the middle of long, sustained notes, one could mangle a chorus or a finale, and no one would say anything: everything would be accepted, thanks to the ignorance of the rabble in the pit.

I am well aware that there are connoisseurs in the pit, but they do not whistle; when they can in all conscience do so, they are content to applaud. In resorting to our lyric theatres they well know that they will encounter there a goodly number of honest hacks, truly insignificant little songsters, who make every effort to please and who therefore merit the unlimited indulgence of a man of breeding. In taverns and public places only gothic refrains are to be heard, bawled out in unison and repeated even more discordantly by the barrel organs. As nature has apparently denied the Parisians any musical discrimination, should they, surrounded as they are by perennial cacophony, be the arbiters of French taste? When singers are employed in the theatres in which singing is the principal activity, when music is played there instead of the strings of ditties that make up so many of our operettas (and which in truth are no more than blown-up ballads), then the general musical taste will improve, little by little, as it has already done in respect of poetry and dancing.

Unity of melody (Unité de mélodie)

All the fine arts have a certain unity of purpose, and this is a source of pleasure to the mind. For a divided attention cannot settle anywhere. When two objects claim our attention this is proof that neither satisfies us. In music there is a successive unity that relates to the subject and by means of which all the parts, being well joined together, form a single whole in which both the ensemble and the interrelationship of the various constituents can be seen.

But there is a subtler and more immediate unity of purpose from which springs (without one attending to it) music's energy and expressive power.

On hearing the psalms sung to four-part harmony I am always to begin with overwhelmed and ravished by the full and vigorous harmony. When the opening chords are properly sung I am moved to the extent that I tremble all over. But hardly has the music continued for a minute than my attention begins to wander; little by little my head begins to swim, the noise stuns my brain, and in no time I grow weary of listening merely to chords.

This does not happen when I listen to good modern music though the harmony may be less forceful. I recall that at the opera in Venice, far from being bored with a fine air when it was well performed, I was constantly attentive, no matter what its length, and at the end I was listening with greater pleasure even than at the beginning.

The difference springs from the character of the two kinds of music, one being merely a succession of chords, the other an extended melody. Now the pleasure of harmony is only a pleasure of pure sensation, and the pleasure of the senses lasts for only a short while. Surfeit and boredom soon follow. But the pleasure that springs from melody and song is a pleasure of interest and feeling that speaks to the heart, one that the artist can always sustain and renew by the power of his genius.

If the music then is to sustain the interest and attention, if it is to move and to please, it must sing. But how can music sing, given our system of chords and harmony? If each part has its own melody, they will be mutually destructive, and there will no longer be melody. If all the parts are one and the same melody, there will no longer be harmony, and the concert will be wholly in unison.

It is quite remarkable how musical instinct – an insensible feeling on the part of genius – has got round the difficulty and even used it to advantage, without realising that it exists. The harmony, which ought to choke the melody, gives it life, strengthens it, shapes it. The different parts contribute to the one effect without becoming entangled. Though each line seems to have its own melody, yet when they are put together only one single melody is heard. It is this that I mean by unity of melody.

This is how the harmony contributes to this unity, without compromising it. The modes determine the character of our melodies, and the modes are based on harmony. Every time, then, that the harmony adds to or defines the feeling of the mode and the modulation, it makes the melody more expressive, provided that the melody is not swamped.

As far as unity of melody is concerned, then, the composer's art is: (i) when the mode is not adequately defined by the melody, to define it by the use of harmony; (ii) to choose and manipulate the chords in such a way that the singing part is pre-eminent, its progress being most effectively governed by the bass; (iii) if the expression is harsh, to add to its energy by means of harsh chords, and by sweet chords if the expression is peaceful; (iv) to have respect for the dynamics of the melody in the disposition of the accompaniment; (v) to arrange it that the lines of the other parts, far from getting in the way of the principal melody, sustain it, support it and give to it the liveliest possible accent.

In order to prove that music's energy springs wholly from harmony M Rameau gives an example in which a single interval (which he calls a melody) assumes different characteristics according to the accompaniment that is set to it. M Rameau did not see that he has proved quite the contrary to what he intended, for in all the examples he cites it is the bass line, and that alone, which determines the melodic line. A simple interval is no melody. It only becomes a melody when it is assigned a place within a mode; and it is the bass line that dictates whether the interval is of this or that melodic kind, by determining the mode and the position of that interval within the mode. If the place that the interval occupies in the modulation can be determined by referring to the notes that precede it, then the interval will make its effect without any bass line. The one function of harmony here, then, is to determine that the melody is of such and such kind; only as melody does the interval assume different expressions, according to the place that it occupies in the mode.

Unity of melody demands that two melodies must never be heard simultaneously. This is not to say however that the melody may not pass from one part to another; on the contrary a skilful change is often tasteful and elegant, even from melody to accompaniment, provided that the words are constantly audible. There are even learned and well-contrived harmonies in which the melody is simply the result of the whole texture; the melody in such a case belongs to no single part. This crude example may suffice to illustrate the point.

A treatise would be needed to show the detailed application of the principle to duos, trios, quartets, choruses and symphonies. Men of genius will find out enough about its extent and use, and their works will instruct others. To summarise then, it follows from the principle of unity of melody that all music is tedious which does not sing, no matter what the harmonies may be, and that all music in which several melodic lines may simultaneously be determined is bad, producing the same effect as two or more conversations going on at the same time. This judgement, which admits no exception, tells us what to think of those marvellous compositions in which one melody serves as the accompaniment to another.

It is this principle of melodic unity that the Italians instinctively respected and followed, whereas the French have neither known nor observed it. The essential difference between French and Italian music lies in this great principle; any impartial judge who devoted equal attention to both (assuming this were possible) would I believe admit as much.

See also Bibliography under: Maniates, Mornet

Daniel Webb

(b. Maidstone, co. Limerick, 1719(?); d. Bath, 2 Aug. 1798)

From: *Observations on the Correspondence between Poetry and Music*
(London 1769), pp. 8–12

Webb matriculated from New College, Oxford in 1735, and he subsequently settled in Bath. Prior to the *Observations* he had published *An Inquiry into the Beauties of Painting* (London 1760) and some *Remarks on the Beauties of Poetry* (London 1762). The *Observations* was considered sufficiently important to merit a German translation (Leipzig 1771).

As the titles of these books clearly show, Webb was particularly interested in the ways in which the arts interrelated. As he puts it in his dedicatory Preface, 'The beauty of order in the disposition of visible objects, the powerful effects of arrangement in the succession of our ideas, of measure and proportion in the successions of sounds, are but different modifications of one common principle.' He proposes that the mind, 'under particular affections, excites certain vibrations in the nerves, and impresses certain movements on the animal spirits', and he argues that music 'in its original purity' was particularly used 'as a mode of conveying or enforcing sentiment'.

Webb had catholic musical tastes and was one of the few writers of his day openly to admit that instrumental music could be just as 'delightful', 'exalted' – sublime even – as vocal music. He believed none the less that poetry and music had parted company and that the time was ripe for their reunion (see Brown, pp. 82–8). Unusually, though, he placed the blame for the separation as much on poetry as on music, observing that so much poetry of the time was 'a school for painters, not musicians'.

In my *Remarks on the Beauties of Poetry*, I have observed:

That in music we are transported by sudden transitions, by an impetuous reiteration of impressions.

That we are delighted by a placid succession of lengthened tones, which dwell on the sense, and insinuate themselves into our inmost feelings.

That a growth or climax in sounds exalts and dilates the spirits and is therefore a constant source of the sublime.

If an accent of notes be in accord with the sublime, then their descent must be in unison with those passions which depress the spirits.

All musical impressions which have any correspondence with the passions may, I think, be reduced under one or other of these four classes.

If they agitate the nerves with violence, the spirits are hurried into the movements of anger, courage, indignation and the like.

The more gentle and placid vibrations shall be in unison with love, friendship and benevolence.

118

If the spirits are exalted or dilated, they rise into accord with pride, glory and emulation.

If the nerves are relaxed, the spirits subside into the languid movements of sorrow.

From these observations it is evident that music cannot of itself specify any particular passion, since the movements of every class must be in accord with all the passions of that class: for instance, the tender and melting tones which may be expressive of the passion of love will be equally in unison with the collateral feelings of benevolence, friendship and pity; and so on, through the other classes.

On hearing an overture by Jomelli or a concerto by Geminiani, we are in turn transported, exalted, delighted; the impetuous, the sublime, the tender take possession of the sense at the will of the composer. In these moments, it must be confessed, we have no determinate idea of any agreement or imitation; and the reason of this is, we have no fixed idea of the passion to which this agreement is to be referred. But let eloquence cooperate with music and specify the motive of each particular impression, while we feel an agreement in the sound and motion with the sentiment, song takes possession of the soul, and general impressions become specific indications of the manners and the passions.

Johann Georg Sulzer

(b. Winterthur, 16 Oct. 1720; d. Berlin, 27 Feb. 1779)

From: *Allgemeine Theorie der schönen Künste, in einzelnen, nach alphabetischer Ordnung der Künstwörter aufeinanderfolgenden Artikeln abgehandelt*, 2nd edn, 4 vols., Leipzig, 1792–4, vol. 1, pp. 47–9; 271–4; 349–56; vol. 2, pp. 97–8; vol. 3, pp. 233–4; 363–6; 421–34; 511–14

The first successful attempt to produce a comprehensive guide to the arts in German was the *Allgemeine Theorie der schönen Künste* of 1771. The man responsible for this impressive work was Johann Georg Sulzer; and, like a number of the leading figures in German art and aesthetics in the eighteenth century, Sulzer was Swiss. His father intended him to be a theologian, but before the boy could complete his studies, both his parents died. So at the age of fourteen, he came under the tutelage of Johann Jakob Bodmer, teacher, city councillor at Zurich and one of the leading progressive literary critics of the early Enlightenment in German-speaking countries.

Bodmer and his friend and colleague Johann Jakob Breitinger were well aware of the work of their French contemporaries on aesthetics and ethics, and their views on 'imitation' in the arts coincided in many respects with those of such influential writers as Du Bos and André. None the less they were also among the most influential representatives of a new taste in German literature which reacted strongly against the French-oriented classicism of writers such as J. S. Bach's Leipzig colleague Johann Christoph Gottsched, in favour of models based on contemporary English taste. Bodmer himself translated *Paradise Lost* in 1732, turning his prose version into verse in 1742. His taste in art criticism was influenced both by French and German writers.

Long after Bodmer and Breitinger ceased to be of any significance in German letters, Sulzer remained faithful to the idea that poetry is an imitation of nature and its aim is moral teaching. This viewpoint is integral to the *Allgemeine Theorie*; and when the *Allgemeine Theorie* appeared in 1771, it was strongly criticised (by Goethe among others) for its old-fashioned moralistic outlook.

Sulzer took holy orders in 1741, moved to Magdeburg in 1743 as tutor to the two sons of a rich merchant, and was appointed head of mathematics at the Joachimsthal Gymnasium, Berlin, in 1747, becoming a member of the Prussian Akademie der Wissenschaften. At this time, Prussia was a centre of the second phase of the German Enlightenment, with figures such as Moses Mendelssohn, the composer's grandfather, and Gotthold Ephraim Lessing. Sulzer's concern to relate aesthetics to ethics brought him into controversy with Mendelssohn and Lessing, both of whom thought his moralistic attitude to the purpose of poetry to be outdated.

Sulzer married in 1750; and on the death of his wife in 1761, he returned to Switzerland to begin work on the *Allgemeine Theorie*. He later returned to Berlin, however, and was appointed director of the philosophical section of the Prussian Akademie der Wissenschaften in 1775.

In the Preface to the work, Sulzer states that the two bases of human happiness are the intellect and the moral sense. His interpretation of the idea of the imitation of

120

nature was that the artist had to portray the 'moral intentions that can be discerned in nature' (vol. 3, p. 91). He continues:

> Since the artist is nature's servant, and since his aims are identical to hers, he needs similar means to achieve them. Nature, the first and most perfect of artists, invariably chooses the best way to go about her task; indeed, a better way is impossible to imagine. The artist must therefore model himself on her . . . nature is the true school in which the artist must discover the principles of his art by imitating her universal procedures.

The *Allgemeine Theorie* owed not a little to the French *Encyclopédistes*, just indeed as the supplementary volumes of the *Encyclopédie* owed something to Sulzer. If the *Allgemeine Theorie* was not Sulzer's greatest work, it was certainly his most substantial one. Though he may have been considered old fashioned by his younger contemporaries, his *Allgemeine Theorie* continued to be read for some years after it was published: indeed it was even reprinted in 1792. Its moralistic tone is in line with his other works, notably the *Versuch einiger moralischen Betrachtungen über die Werke der Natur (Essay on some moral observations concerning the Works of Nature)* (Berlin 1780).

The *Allgemeine Theorie* was the first work on aesthetics to give much space to music. Alexander Gottlieb Baumgarten hardly mentioned music at all in his *Aesthetica*. Sulzer's advisers on music were Johann Philipp Kirnberger, Heinrich Christoph Koch and Johann Abraham Schulz.

Sulzer uses a number of terms that require a little elucidation. The word *Gegenstand* seems to be used both in the sense of a material object and of the object that inspires or is portrayed by the artist. The context generally makes clear which of the two meanings is implied. The word *Geist* (spirit) is easy to translate, but it should be remembered that Sulzer and other writers were using it before the days of depth psychology and modern biochemistry, and according to contemporary theories about the nature of the human mind and body. A fuller explanation of these will be found in the General Introduction. Similarly, the word *Gemüt*, roughly equivalent to the English *personality* or *temperament*, really stands for that overall combination of responsive faculties that includes the brain, the nervous system and the mind; what in an early number of the *Allgemeine musikalische Zeitung* (7 July 1802) is defined as 'the inner organisation of our nature which determines whether we feel pleasure or distaste at a sensation'. The word *Vorstellung* we have taken to mean, here as elsewhere, *image* in the sense of an idea projected before the creative or perceptive imagination. We have tended therefore to translate it by the English word *concept*, sometimes preferring the compound *imaginative concept* where the context needs the additional qualification.

Our quotations are from the second (1792) edition of the *Allgemeine Theorie*. Certain passages that contain further examples of a general point that has already been amply illustrated are abbreviated.

Aesthetics (Aesthetik)

This is a new term that has been coined to identify a science that came into being only a few years ago. Aesthetics is the philosophy of the fine arts by which their fundamental laws and general theories are deduced. The word is of Greek origin: the original meaning is feeling (*Gefühl*). Aesthetics is then basically the science of the feelings. The highest goal of the fine arts is to awaken a keen sense of the good and the true. The theory of the fine arts must be founded on the theory of the feelings and upon those concepts that come to us through the medium of our various senses.

Aristotle already realised that artistic practice precedes artistic theory. Indeed it could be argued that specific rules are evolved long before the general principles from which they stem are identified. Many great works of genius have given pleasure long before men have thought to enquire into the sources of their pleasure. Aristotle was one of the first to establish rules based upon a study of specific examples; but neither in the field of poetics nor rhetoric did he establish a complete theory. He was most careful to note in the work of Greek poets and orators – both of his day and of earlier generations – those qualities that had met with general approval; upon these he based his rules. He went no further, however, than the experience of feeling itself; he was not interested in tracing it back to its source, nor did he consider whether poets and orators had in fact fully exploited the resources of their arts.

Subsequent critics followed the path that he had mapped out. They made new observations and added to the established rules, but they discovered no new principles. If I am not mistaken, M. Du Bos was the first of our modern critics to have sufficient initiative to deduce from a general principle the theory of the fine arts and to demonstrate rules from it. In his excellent treatise, the *Réflexions critiques sur la poésie et sur la peinture,* this celebrated author bases his theory on the fact that under certain circumstances men experience the need to occupy their minds and to exercise their feelings. From this general principle he has derived a number of rules; for the rest, however, he has been content to adopt the empirical methods of his predecessors. Even so, his book is full of excellent observations and sensible rules.

A. G. Baumgarten – a professor at the University of Frankfurt-an-der Oder – has been the first to use philosophical methods in an attempt to establish a general science of the fine arts, a science to which he has given the name aesthetics. He takes as the basis of his system Wolff's theory concerning the origin of pleasurable feelings, one that Wolff confuses with the question of perfection. In the theoretical part of his work – the only one that has yet appeared – he handles with great perception the entire theory relating to beauty and the perfection of phenomena. He examines the various aspects of beauty, and at the same time he demonstrates the contrasting qualities of ugliness. It is most unfortunate that he lacks an intimate understanding of the arts, and is thus unable to extend his enquiry beyond the realms of poetry and eloquence.

Aesthetics must be numbered amongst the sciences that are as yet imperfectly developed. It is all the more important, then, that we try here to outline the general plan upon which this new science is constructed, and attempt some observations on its detailed organisation.

The first step is to determine the purpose and nature of the fine arts.

Having proved that the role of the arts is to establish a hold over our hearts through the medium of our feelings of pleasure and displeasure, the next step must be to enquire into the origins of the feelings, either deducing the quality of pleasure from the nature of the soul, or seeing what philosophers have had to say on this matter.

This having been done, the many types of pleasant and unpleasant object would have to be categorised in the minutest detail. If neither theory, nor the careful study of works of taste actually produced solutions to problems, at least in this way the problems could be defined. All this would comprise the theoretical part of the philosophy of the fine arts.

As far as the practical side is concerned, the various limits and qualities of the fine arts would need to be determined: such arts as poetry, eloquence, music and painting. At the same time it would be necessary to define the qualities of genius and the kinds of natural and acquired taste that are appropriate to each kind of artist, determining the ways in which genius, imagination, invention, taste (and so on) contribute to artistic success.

Emotions (Leidenschaften)

Emotions play such a significant role in the fine arts that their place in aesthetic theory merits special and fairly detailed consideration. It is the artist's immediate purpose to excite or to temper emotions; to illustrate their true nature and expression; and to demonstrate their various good and evil effects as vividly as possible. As this article will be somewhat wide-ranging, here for the sake of clarity is a preliminary statement of its main points:

The aim here is to show: (1) how the artist excites and tempers the emotions; (2) the nature of each emotion, its good or evil effect and the ways in which it is to be portrayed. The first of these points is subdivided into two, for two questions relate to it: question one deals with the way that dormant emotion can be aroused in a person, or how emotion once stimulated can be tempered; and question two examines how individual sensitivities are to be sharpened or dulled in order to produce the most intense and beneficial response both to sustained and transient emotional states. If the fine arts, as has always been believed, are truly the means of shaping and even, in special cases, of controlling human character, then the artist must necessarily be in full command of the points that have been discussed already as a means to such an end. Polybius says that music was necessary so as to refine the somewhat crude sensibility of the Arcadians; and everybody knows that this particular art is used in special circumstances to arouse or to modify the emotions. All the fine arts have this end in view and for that reason every good artist must have to be able to control the means to this end.

[p. 223, col. 2, para. 1 to p. 224, col. 1, para. 1 omitted]

Basically, emotions are simply powerful feelings which are accompanied by pleasure or displeasure, thus leading either to desire or revulsion. They invariably spring from sensations or from undefined images of certain things that we consider good or evil. Our feelings are not engaged by images that are wholly clear. Anything that is designed to move the heart and awaken our sensibility must at the same time offer a great deal to the imagination, the object of the emotion must be comprehended as a whole. We must feel that we are reacting both to the good and evil in it; the object must be comprehended as an entity, our attention must not be drawn to the individual details so that these become the object of our contemplation. Anyone who analyses an object, contemplating and consequently examining each of its separate parts to discover how it is constructed, does so completely dispassionately; if we are to feel, our efforts should be directed not towards the contemplation or analysis of the object but towards the effect that it has on us. Objects of emotions resemble the bundle of rods that the Scythian king showed his son: their strength lies in the combination of their several parts; individually they could easily be smashed to pieces.

The imagination, then, must make the greatest contribution to emotion, for when a strong emotion is felt it is the imagination that gives birth to the great mass of simultaneously associated images.

Expression in music (Ausdruck in der Musik)

The principal, if not indeed the sole function of a perfect musical composition is the accurate expression of emotions and passions in all their varying and individual nuances. A composition that merely fills the imagination with a sequence of harmonious sounds, without touching the heart, is like a picture of a beautiful sky in the glow of the setting sun. The attractive kaleidoscope of colours pleases us; but the heart is not involved by the cloudscape. If, on the other hand, we are also aware of a melodic language whose perfectly-shaped and uninterrupted flow of notes reveals the out-pourings of a sensitive heart, our sense of hearing is pleasantly stimulated. Our soul is borne to rest, undisturbed, on a kind of couch of sound, and can abandon itself to every emotion that is aroused in it by the expressive melody. The attention is totally held by the play of harmony, and the ear is induced into a state of complete self-forgetfulness, so that it concentrates only on the refined emotions that take possession of the soul.

Expression is the soul of music; without it, music is just a pleasant toy; with it, music becomes an overwhelmingly powerful language which engulfs the heart. It compels us in turn to tenderness, resolution and courage. It successively arouses our sympathy and our admiration. At times it enhances and exalts the soul; at others, it takes it captive so that it dissolves in languorous emotion. How, though, does the composer acquire this miraculous skill to dominate our hearts so completely? The foundations of his power must have been laid in him by nature herself. His soul must be responsive to every emotion and passion, for he can only effectively express what he himself keenly feels. The extent to which personality affects art is illustrated in the work of two much-admired German composers – Graun and Hasse. Nature endowed Graun with a tender, gentle, complaisant soul; though he may have mastered all the skills of his craft, he was at home only in the gentle, the pleasant and the charming emotions; and more than once he ran into problems when he had to express boldness, pride or resolution. Nature endowed Hasse, on the other hand, with loftier courage, bolder emotions and stronger desires, and he was most at home with the emotions that were consistent with his character rather than with those that were gentle and pleasant.

It is very important for the artist to know himself, and, if the decision lies with him, to undertake nothing that is inconsistent with his personality. Unfortunately, the decision does not always lie with him. The epic poet must be able to capture every emotion, and, indeed, conflicting emotions when he portrays a submissive, a daring, or even a cowardly character. The composer, too, will encounter similar situations, so he must be able to help himself by diligent practice whenever Nature affords him little support.

In such circumstances, the musician must closely study how each passion is expressed. This point has already been dealt with in the article on the problem of expression in the arts in general. He must see people only from this point of view. Each emotion has its special character, its musical formulation (*Gedanke*) and its vocal quality, pitch, relative tempo and rhetorical accentuation. Those who have studied this closely will often be able to grasp the correct sense of a speech even if they do not understand the words. They will know whether the individual sounds express joy or sorrow; they may even, in fact, be able to identify intense and moderate pain, deep-rooted tenderness, overwhelming or restrained joy. The musician must pay the most scrupulous attention to a study of natural expression; speech invariably has something about it that melody can imitate, however much the two may differ. Joy is expressed in sonorous tones, unhurried tempi and in limited gradations of pitch and dynamics. Sadness unburdens itself slowly, from the depths of the heart, and is of sombre hue. Every emotion, then, has its own character, one that the composer must observe and get to know as intimately as he can. Only in this way will he achieve correctness of expression.

Next, he should make every effort to determine how the various emotions affect the personality itself, its sequence of thoughts and emotions. Every emotion involves a sequence of images (*Vorstellungen*) somewhat akin to motion; the very phrase 'motions of the affections' already indicates as much. There are emotions in which the images flow evenly like a gentle stream; there are others in which the sequence of images resembles a raging and turbulent flood, swollen with heavy rain, a flood that sweeps every obstruction before it. At times, the images within us resemble a wild sea that dashes violently against the shore, and then falls back, only to surge forward again with renewed force.

Music is ideally suited to the portrayal of all such movements. If the composer is sufficiently aware of them and if he is skilled enough to follow every movement in melody and harmony, these subjective changes will be aurally perceptible. To this end, he has at his disposal many and varied means – provided he also has the skill. These means are: 1. The actual harmonic progressions, whatever the metre. The harmony must move easily and naturally, without great complexity or ponderous suspensions, if the mood is gentle or pleasant. If the mood is violent or recalcitrant, however, the progressions should move haltingly, and there should be fairly frequent modulations into more remote keys; the progressions should also be more complex, with frequent and unexpected dissonances, and suspensions which are rapidly resolved. 2. The metre, by means of which all kinds of movement may be imitated in general terms. 3. The melody and the rhythm, which are of themselves equally capable of portraying the language of every emotion. 4. Dynamic variations, too, contribute significantly to expression. 5. The choice of accompaniment, with particular regard to the choice of instruments and the way in which they interact, and 6. Modulations into, and extended passages in other keys.

The composer should carefully consider all these elements, judging the effect of each of them with care and precision; in this way, he will be in a position to express every emotion as accurately and as tellingly as possible. Despite the fineness of nuance that differentiates certain emotions, there are many emotions that are not beyond music's power to express. In the aria 'Dalle labbre del mio bene', from the operetta *Europa Galante*, for example, Graun has expressed to perfection that kind of tenderness, combined with complete submission to the master's will, that is so eminently typical of an Ottoman seraglio. Here is triumphant proof that music has the capacity to express the most difficult emotions.

Nonetheless, careful thought and extreme diligence are called for if perfect expression is to be achieved, for this great composer and others of the front rank have frequently lapsed in the matter of correct expression. We would recommend anyone who wishes to achieve this essential artistic goal to take careful note of the foregoing remarks and of what is to follow.

Every piece of music must have a definite character and evoke emotions of a specific kind. This is so both of instrumental and vocal music. Any composer would be misguided if he started work before deciding on the character of his piece. He must know whether the language he is to use is that of a man who is proud or humble, bold or timid, violent or gentle. He must know if the character is a supplicant or one in authority. Even if he comes upon his theme by accident, he should still examine it carefully if he is to sustain its character throughout the piece. Having determined the character of his piece, he must put himself into the emotional state that he wishes others to experience. His best course of action is to imagine some drama, happening or situation that will naturally induce the kind of state that he has in mind; and if his imagination is sufficiently fired by this, he should at once set to work, taking care not to introduce a musical passage (*Periode*) or figure (*Figur*) that is out of character with the piece.

Many composers have been led astray by an over-fondness for certain pleasant-sounding and skilfully-contrived formulae that express particular emotions. It should be borne in mind that such repetitions are often detrimental to expression and are suitable only for certain obsessive emotions and passions. Other emotions, however, involve impressions that are constantly changing, variable and transient. In such cases, frequent reiteration of the same expressive formula is unnatural.

If the composer is to set a given text to music, he should first of all study its true spirit, character and mood. He should give detailed consideration to the circumstances and intentions of the person speaking; and he should determine the overall character of his vocal line. He should choose the most effective key, an appropriate tempo, rhythms that are intrinsic to the emotion, and intervals that are best suited to its ebb and flow. The expressive element characteristic of the piece (*dieses Charakteristische*) must prevail throughout, especially where the text calls for some specific emphasis.

Genius (Genie)

It seems that the people who are generally credited with genius are those who have greater skill and spiritual insight than others in the tasks and occupations for which they are gifted. The man of genius sees more than other people do in those things that interest him, he discovers more easily than they the securest means of achieving his aim; he finds a happy way round all obstacles; he has greater control over the powers of his soul; his cognitive powers are sharper and more sensitive than those of other people; and, what is more, he has a finer control over his imaginative concepts and emotions, whereas men who lack genius are controlled and governed by theirs. Basically, the genius seems to consist of nothing other than generous spiritual endowment; the terms *a great spirit, a great mind*, and *a man of genius*, can therefore be considered as synonymous.

Yet greatness worthy to be called *genius* is not always just a matter of spiritual capacity. There are those extremely rare people in whose souls everything is great. There are others in whose souls only certain particular faculties are highly developed; they are consequently much more efficient at certain things than others. Such people are generally accredited, not with genius as such, but with a special kind of genius for those things in which they are particularly gifted.

In both cases, genius normally implies a particular ability to focus imaginative concepts with sharpness, or, as the case demands, to highlight those of particular importance. The clear full light of day shines in the soul of the man of genius and illuminates every object as a brilliantly lit close-up image, one that can easily be scanned and every detail of which can be made out clearly. As far as a few very fortunate people are concerned, this light illuminates the entire soul. With most, however, the light reaches only a few areas of the soul. In one case, it illuminates the upper realms of the spirit, the seat of concepts that are general and abstract; it may on the other hand shed light over empirical concepts, or perhaps even penetrate the darker regions of the emotions. Wherever the light falls, the powers and main-springs of the soul unite; and inspiring fire burns within the man of genius which effectively arouses all his faculties; he discovers within himself ideas, imaginative images and emotions that inspire awe in others; they are no surprise to him since without a painstaking search he has perceived them in himself rather than invented them.

It is questionable whether philosophy will ever discover the real root causes of genius. Nature seems to lay its foundations first by making the people whom she has endowed with special genius outstandingly sensitive to particular things, so that the appreciation of these things becomes to some extent a need. It is generally agreed that something akin to genius is found even in animals, and a search for evidence of such genius in brute creation is not to be despised. We notice that an animal goes about every activity relevant to its needs with a skill and efficiency suggestive of genius. As far as the animal is concerned, the root cause is an extremely delicate feeling, an exceptional sensitivity. Deprive the dog of his fine sense of smell and you will instantly rob him of his genius. In man, genius seems to require similar support. Imaginative powers, however strong, do not constitute genius; there must also be some stimulus that effectively directs and concentrates the powers of genius. What have been described as imaginative powers are simply and more specifically spiritual aptitudes or potentials which come into play only if some internal or external need arouses and sustains them. The soul of limited sensitivity which cannot be stimulated into activity, one that has no especial needs, is not a genius, no matter how powerful the intellect may be; genius requires great intellect to be consis-tently stimulated by some desire. The various faculties of the soul lie in relaxed inactivity until some emotion stimulates them, after which they are operative as long as this emotion persists. Just as the most cunning and lively animal stretches out in a lethargic stupor once it is replete and satisfied, so all the powers of the spirit sink into drowsy inactivity, whatever their potential, if the sensitive area of the soul is not stimulated to excite them into effective action.

Wherever a certain inner need reinforces and adequately stimulates the imaginative power that is strongest in the soul, genius manifests itself, acquiring its especial disposition from the character of that need. The man of intellect and lively imagination whose principal need is love will either become a gallant or a tender lover according to the intensity of that need, a model and a genius of his kind. Similarly, the man of intellect and lively imagination whose soul takes particular pleasure in the beauty of visible forms will become a great draughtsman and a genius of his kind. Ardent emotions are essential to genius, then if these are wanting the spirit cannot express itself as effectively as it might. Where such emotions manifest themselves only fleetingly in people of outstanding spiritual gifts, genius also manifests itself sporadically; all true genius calls for a sustained level of emotional intensity.

Of course a man of intellect can well engage dispassionately in activities to which genius would feel emotionally committed merely from convention or the desire to imitate, or some other cause than emotion. But intellectual considerations apart, he will fall far short of true genius; contrivance born of cold calculation will certainly be apparent, as well as the somewhat stilted character of the work. He will thus reveal himself as a man of intellect: a thinker, but not a genius. It will be evident that although a work of true genius bears the stamp of nature itself, his own is the product of craftsmanship and imitation. He who plays the lover to some beautiful woman but who has no genuine feeling of love for her will always reveal himself as an actor or a fop. Similarly, he who imitates genius but himself lacks genius will all too soon give himself away.

These observations suggest that outstanding spiritual powers, combined with a special sensitivity to certain kinds of images, are the necessary preconditions of genius. For the sake of brevity, let us confine the application of these general observations to the types of genius that find expression in the fine arts.

Basically, each of the fine arts affects the external senses. If our ear were merely an opening through which dead sound was given access to the soul, if the eye merely an aperture on which light fell, music would be no different from speech and painting identical with writing. Music and painting are fine arts simply because the ear is moved by rhythm and harmony and the eye by the harmony of colours and beauty of form. Music is mere noise to the person whose ear is unaffected by harmony and rhythm. From this can be inferred the basis of the particular genius that is appropriate to each art, one that depends on special sensitivity of the senses and nervous system. A person who is so stimulated by music's power that he cannot forgo its pleasures has the potential of true musical genius. A person who is so intensely moved by the harmony of colours that he too experiences an extreme pleasure in it has the genius of the colourist. He whose emotions are aroused by the passionate and harmonious tones of eloquence is potentially a poetic genius. But these various kinds of excitement relate only to the mechanical aspects of artistic genius, which are still closely akin to the animal instincts. An artist who possesses only this genius is no more than a talented technician. His work consequently lacks the spirit which has a specific effect on those who are themselves not artists. A piece of music may be sound in rhythm and harmony and yet be devoid of expressive power; in the way that a poem with the finest versification may be utterly trivial.

The greatest artist, who seeks a place among those men of genius who shine like stars of the first magnitude in the history of the human spirit, must, like Homer, or Phidias, or Handel, possess not only genius but a great mind. He must be a man who would still have been a genius if in some other field than his chosen art. His great mind provides him with great inspirations, great ideas, and his artistic genius develops these in ways that are artistically appropriate. Thus originate those splendid works of art which are admired not only by the artist, but also by every man of feeling and intellect.

Inspiration (Begeisterung)

All artists of any genius claim that from time to time they experience a state of extraordinary psychic intensity which makes work unusually easy, images arising without great effort and the best ideas flowing in such profusion as if they were the gift of some higher power. This is without doubt what is called inspiration. If an artist experiences this condition, his object appears to him in an unusual light; his genius, as if guided by a divine power, invents without effort, shaping his invention in the most suitable form without strain; the finest ideas and images occur unbidden in floods to the inspired poet; the orator judges with the greatest acumen, feels with the greatest intensity, and the strongest and most vividly expressive words rise to his tongue. The inspired painter finds the picture he has sought painted most vividly in his mind; he needs only to copy it; his very hand seems to be guided by some extraordinary art; and the work acquires a new lease of life with every movement of his hand.

What is to be made of such a strange phenomenon, which is so very important to the philosopher in its origin and to the artist in its effect? Whence comes this extraordinary intensity of the soul and how can it effect such happy results? This enhanced intensity shows itself either in the soul's powers of desire or its powers of imagination, in each case with a special result. In the former case it does so through reverent or political or tender or voluptuous states of enthusiasm; in the latter through the genius's enhanced capacities, through the richness, efficiency, power and brilliance of his images and ideas. Thus inspiration is of two kinds, one affecting principally the emotions, the other the imagination. Both have their origin in the vivid impression made by an object of especial aesthetic power upon the soul. If the object is vague, so that the imagination can develop little in it; if the emotions react with more vigour than cognition does in its judgement of the type of objects of the commonest emotions, then all attention is directed towards the emotion, all the soul's powers are fused into an emotional state of great intensity. If, however, the object that has made this powerful impression manifests itself so brightly that the spirit can apprehend its various parts, the imagination is aroused alongside the emotions and intensely powerfully focused on the object; intellect and emotion strive to comprehend it as an entity with the greatest clarity and vigour. The first case gives rise to emotional enthusiasm; the other to the inspiration of the genius. Both merit somewhat more detailed attention, both to their nature and to their effects.

Emotional enthusiasm, or supercharged intensity of the soul, which expresses itself mainly via the emotions, is aroused by significant objects in which we see nothing clearly, where the imagination finds nothing to do, where our attention is distracted from the object itself and directed towards what the soul feels, towards its own efforts.[1] In doing so, the spirit loses sight of the object, feeling its effect proportionately more intensely. The soul immediately becomes all emotion; it is aware of nothing but itself and everything within itself. All images of things apart from it fall into darkness; it sinks into a dream which in large measure inhibits the effects of the intellect but proportionately increases the vigour of the emotions. In such a state it is capable neither of precise calculation nor of correct judgement, but its inclinations express themselves with greater freedom and vigour and all the springs of its powers of desire are allowed proportionately freer play.

Now since the imagination is no longer capable of differentiating between what is really there and what is merely imaginary, what is merely potential appears as actual; even the impossible becomes possible; the relationship between things is no longer assessed by an act of judgement, but according to emotion; the *absent* becomes actual and the future already becomes present. Anything that once affected the soul in some manner similar to the present emotion the soul now recalls.

In this kind of inspiration, nothing is distinct in the soul save emotion and all its close or remote associations. Thus the uncommon case originates in expressing what lies within the soul, the vigour and power of expression, the sweet eloquence in gentle emotions; the savage, astonishing or deeply moving expression of vehement passions; the great variety of tender or powerful images; the variegated lights and shades of emotion, the odd and dream-like combinations of tone, so precisely suited to each emotion, and everything else that reveals itself in this kind of inspiration.

[p. 351, col. 1, para. 1 to p. 352, col. 1, para. 1 omitted]

The other type of inspiration manifests similar phenomena in the imagination. It is founded in the strong attraction that swiftly attacks this faculty. It may be generated by the size, the richness, or the beauty of the object. If it affects the spirit principally, not just the emotions, it must be capable of lucid development. The imagination must perceive the variety latent within it and be stimulated to visualise everything with the greatest

---

[1] See the article, *Emotions* (pp. 123–4).

But the matter has been more comprehensively dealt with in the proceedings of the Königliche Preussische Akademie der Wissenschaften for the year 1764 under the title: *Observations sur les divers états où l'âme se trouve en exerçant ses facultés primitives, celle d'appercevoir et celle de sentir.*

clarity. This occasions an extraordinary tension of all its forces, and, if we may put it thus, an increased elasticity of the soul, which now aspires to expand enough to comprehend such an object completely. The spirit concentrates all its powers, ignores all other objects and endeavours only to perceive clearly. . . .

Nobody has explored the depths of the human soul sufficiently to explain this fully. Yet the little that observation has revealed about it deserves to be assessed accurately. From the theory of emotions, it can be understood how certain objects arouse a desire, and how our attention, by sustained effort, can be focused on them. It is also known that not only the inner quality of a thing, but also quite random advantages related to it, of which honour and praise are examples, possess great power to rivet the soul's concentration completely to such objects. Now if the spirit has been subject to such a definite impulse, reinforced by concentrated effort, its own efforts gain not only power, but also concentration. The object floats continuously before its perception; all other subjects appear only in relation to it. Just as the miser considering everything that affects his senses is aware of nothing but its money value, and the ambitious man of nothing but what flatters his vanity, so the artist strongly stimulated by an object is aware of nothing in nature except in relation to it; nothing escapes him of what he is required to notice and comprehend in proportion to the capacity of his genius to do so.

Now it is a well-known fact from experience, however difficult it is to explain, that ideas and images arising from sustained contemplation of an object, whether they are obscure or clear, store up in the soul, germinate unobserved like grains of seed in fertile soil, gradually develop and finally emerge into the light as required. We immediately see the object to which they belong, which up till then, like a shapeless phantom, has hovered, dark and confused, in our minds, in a bright and well-shaped form before us. This is the real moment of inspiration.

It is now that the object is perceived in an unusual light; things are seen in it that have never been seen before; what one had so long wished to see now appears without effort; one is inclined to believe that a benevolent being of a higher kind has sharpened our senses or has in some supernatural manner placed the desired object before our imagination. But how does this happy moment come about? How does the artist achieve this assistance from the Muse? . . . In the unceasing concentration of the imaginative powers on one single object, it certainly happens – perhaps often at random, even in dreams – that an unusually vivid idea is generated. The great desire with which one has so long wished to see the object in a clearer light is suddenly most vigorously stimulated; all the nerves are now tensed; attention is withdrawn from all other objects; all images not connected with the one object of interest sink into obscurity. Even the effect of the external senses is so weakened that the spirit need fear no distraction from them. Every concept related to the main object grows brighter and more vigorous; all the collected images now surge up out of obscurity and, as in a dream at night, when all distraction suddenly ceases, the image that we have seen veiled while awake stands before our eyes as clear as the broadest daylight, so, in the sweet dream of inspiration, the artist sees the desired object before his vision, he hears sounds when all is silent, and feels a body which is real only to his imagination.

From this at any rate it can be understood whence the intensified psychic powers in the state of inspiration acquire their strength, and why the latter influences works of taste to such advantage; how it comes about that every individual image becomes unusually vivid; why things not actual as present, past or future seem imminent. If, however, the artist has such vivid and perfect images in his inspiration, it is also easy for him, according to the canons of his art, to express them in words, or through line and colour, or through mere sounds.

Music (Musik)

A proper idea of this charming art must begin with an attempt to trace its origins in nature. Since we can in some degree observe the process of tracing its origins in nature daily, and since we are in the process of discovering how partly civilised people refine the raw material of song through the principles of taste, this task is less difficult than it might be. Nature has established a direct link between the ear and the heart; each emotion is expressed by particular sounds, each of which awakens in the listener's heart the original experience that gave rise to it. A cry of terror terrifies us; joyful sounds awaken happiness. The cruder senses – smell, touch and taste – affect the body, not the soul; they arouse nothing but blind pleasure or displeasure; their energies are absorbed in enjoyment or revulsion. The visual and aural senses, however, affect the spirit and the heart. In these two senses lie the mainsprings of rational and moral behaviour. The aural sense is certainly the more powerful of the two. Dissonance is far more easily perceived than is a clash of colours; the charming chromatic harmony of the rainbow is by no means as moving as a triad, for example. So the sense of hearing is by far the most effective path to the emotions. Who would claim that clashing or unharmonious colours have ever caused pain? But the ear can be so adversely affected by dissonance as almost to bring the listener to despair.

This is doubtless because the material that affects the aural nerves – air – is much coarser and more physical than ethereal light, which affects the eye. The aural nerves consequently transmit to the entire body the impact of the shock they receive. This is not the case with visual effects. Hence it is understandable that the body, and consequently the soul, can be intensely affected by sounds. Little thought or experience is needed to discover the power of sound; the most inobservant of men feel it. A man who is a prey to strong emotions similarly often tries to intensify them with cries of joy, rage, etc. Children and very primitive peoples likewise express themselves spontaneously, inflaming and intensifying not only their own emotions but those of others by means of a whole range of varying sounds. Although a sequence of such cries may not constitute an actual song, it clearly has the makings of song.

The point at issue here is the very close link that subsists between movement, rhythm and sounds. The measured movement of sustained physical effort, which occurs with regular emphasis in a discernible repeated pattern, relieves monotony, assists concentration and serves to enlighten tasks that would otherwise become tedious, such as carrying or dragging a heavy load or, as Ovid observed, rowing a boat. The relief is even greater, however, when the movement is rhythmically accentuated, i.e. when the smaller strokes that constitute each step or beat vary almost imperceptibly in strength and weakness, as is the case in a blacksmith's hammering, or a team threshing. This is how the burden of toil is lightened, as the pleasure derived from unity in variety facilitates the continuation of the task in hand.

Such rhythms and measures may be applied to a sequence of sounds, since they inevitably convey the notion of movement. This is the origin of accompanied song and it is the natural link between song and dance. So it is not at all surprising on reflection that even the most primitive peoples have discovered music and to some extent developed it.

Music is thus deeply rooted in man's nature. As a notated art, it has its own principles which must be observed to ensure the progress of the art and the composition of music of quality. The first thing that we must do, therefore, is dispose of a widespread and common misconception concerning the immutability of musical principles. The Chinese are said to have no taste for European music; Europeans, on the other hand, cannot stand Chinese music. This is said to be because music is not based on universal principles that are rooted in human nature. We shall see.

If music had no aim other than that of arousing fleeting impressions of joy, fear or terror, then a simple spontaneous cry from a large crowd would suffice. The effect of a shout of jubilation or terror from a large crowd is violent, however undisciplined, dissonant, odd or unruly the sound may be. Laws and principles are irrelevant here.

But such noises do not last long; they soon lose their impact and thus our attention. They would do so even if they were prolonged. If sounds are to affect us, they must be subject to metre. This is a common experience of all sensitive peoples, Indians, Iroquois, Siberians and ancient Greeks alike. Metre and rhythm provide order and regular measure, the basic principles of which are respected by all peoples. But as rhythm (*Metrische*) is infinitely variable, each people has its own idea of rhythm, a fact that can be illustrated from the dance melodies of various peoples; but the universal rules of regularity and order are common to all. . . .

As we have seen, music is essentially a sequence of sounds which are excited by passionate emotion and which are capable of arousing, sustaining and illustrating such emotion. Let us now investigate what makes music an art and the purpose that musical works can serve.

Music's aim is to arouse the emotions; this it does by means of sequences of sounds that are appropriate to the natural expression of the emotion; and its application must suitably conform to the intentions of nature in emotional matters. We must examine each of these points in more detail.

There is no doubt about music's purpose, for its first seeds certainly sprang from the pleasure that was experienced in prolonging and intensifying an emotional state. The expression of joy was apparently a first step towards music. The wish to lighten arduous toil was the second; this could be done in one of two ways: either passively, by diverting the attention from the burden to pleasurable things through variety in unity, or actively by exciting actual joy by means of rousing sounds and energetic movement. In the first case, music seeks to captivate or charm the senses; in the second, it seeks to stimulate bodily and spiritual powers. The music of nature (*die bloss natürliche Musik*) hardly ever seems to lead to tenderness, sadness or anger. Once it was found, however, that these emotions could be forcefully portrayed in art and thus aroused, this was done. Moreover, as the moral character of individuals and nations alike can be powerfully affected by the various ways in which people express them, music can be said to contain an ethical element in so far as that element can be emotionally felt and expressed. And, in fact, national songs and their associated dances faithfully reflect the mores of the people who create them.

There is no justification, though, for the idea that music can influence the conceptual imagination (*Vorstellungskraft*) in matters that are altogether unrelated to emotion, or which are related to them only through cognitive reflection. Language was invented to express ideas and concepts; it is language that constructs and projects images in the imagination, not music. The portrayal of such images is altogether foreign to music's aim. It is not rational man, a thinking and imaginative creature, that music influences therefore, but man as a sentient being. However learned, correct or well-wrought, then, a composition may be, it is not a piece of genuine music if it fails to stimulate the emotions. All that the listener needs is a sensitive heart; with this he may judge whether a work is good or bad, even if he lacks all musical knowledge. If music reaches his heart, it has achieved its purpose, and whatever serves to achieve this aim is good. Leave the experts to judge whether the music might have done so more effectively had the composer not weakened or spoilt it through lack of taste or skill. For only such experts know the means to the end and can judge whether good or bad use has been made of them.

Those, then, who have mastered the art as well as those who are connoisseurs may need to be reminded of music's aim, since the former often seek applause by purely technical devices, by leaps, runs and harmonies, which are perhaps difficult to manage but which communicate nothing. At the very most a singer or instrumentalist who has mastered such technical difficulties arouses a reaction in the audience similar to that aroused by a skilful tight-rope dancer or bareback rider in full gallop. How much more natural it is to prefer the song of a real nightingale to an imitation.

Those who doubt the ancient stories of music's marvellous powers are either ignorant of, or insensitive to good music. The emotions are excited, as is well known, by the action of the nerves and by the rapid circulation of the blood. Music unquestionably and genuinely affects both. Since music involves the movement of air and the impact of air on the highly sensitive aural nerves, it affects the body; how, indeed, could it fail to do so, since it can shatter even inorganic matter – not merely fragile windows, but even strong walls? Why doubt, therefore, that it can affect sensitive nerves in a manner unparalleled by any other art, or that through the nerves it can stimulate a feverish, tormented pulsing of the blood; that it can even, as we have read in the transactions of the Paris Académie des Sciences, actually cure a musician of a fever? . . .

It must not be forgotten, however, that although music enjoys this evident advantage over the other arts, its effect is more transient. It is easier to recall things that have been read or heard in speech than it is to recall sound as such. So it is that poetry and painting leave a lasting impression even though the actual works are no longer before us. If a piece of music is to make a lasting impression, it must be frequently repeated. On the other hand, where an immediate but transient impact is desired, music is supremely effective.

It follows, then, that this divine art might be put to effective use in the service of politics. What an incomprehensible waste simply to treat music as a pleasurable pastime for the leisured! Is further proof required that rich as an age may be in scholarship, mechanical ingenuity and intellectual achievement, it can yet be very poor in common sense?

Natural (Natürlich)

This adjective is applied to artistic objects which seem to owe their existence to some stroke of nature, rather than to art. When a painting strikes the eye as lifelike we describe it as natural; we do the same when we observe the dramatic action of a play and forget that we are watching a work of art, or when we read the description of a character which gives us a first-hand impression of his actions, or when we listen to a melodic line, imagining as we do so that we can hear actual cries of anger or tenderness or expressions of true joy or grief – all such things are called natural. The unforced, fluent power of representation is sometimes described as natural, because in fact everything that is the direct product of nature is inherently of this character. An object may be called 'natural', then, if the artist has not taken it from nature but has fashioned it with his poetic imagination, provided that he has learned how to give it the stamp of natural authenticity.

In other fields we describe as natural those things or events that are spontaneous, that are not straitjacketed by deducible rules, but which exist or occur in such a way that they directly and immediately reveal the hand of nature. So a natural man is one whose speech, gestures and movements are governed with perfect sincerity and spontaneity by his emotions, without reference to any acquired system of conduct.

Naturalness is one of the most important prerequisites of a work of art, because in itself it already has power to please and because any work that lacks it is not complete. These two observations call for amplification.

The object of the fine arts is to place interesting material before us, material that will rivet the attention and create an impression that is consonant with the aim in view. Now human beings relate to natural objects in the way that the physique of an animal relates to its environment. Nature has exactly adapted our senses and sensitivities (from which all desires stem), to the objects in the material world that may be of interest to us. We react, then, only to things which have been created for us by nature herself. If, therefore, a person seeks to move us through the medium of the arts he must set before us objects that look natural and have a natural character. The more precisely the artist achieves this, the more he may expect his work to realise his intentions.

It follows, therefore, that he should represent nothing bizarre, fantastic or contrary to nature; it follows, too, that objects copied from nature must be quite natural if they are to have their full effect. They must deceive us into thinking of them as real. A person who hid his face in his hands and pretended to cry might move a child, but an adult would soon notice the deception.

[p. 512, col. 2, line 6 to p. 513, col. 2, para. 1 omitted]

There is something else of importance to mention before concluding. In moral issues, nature can be either cruder, as is the case with relatively primitive peoples whose powers of reasoning are but little; or comparatively refined, according to the length of time over which the arts, sciences, ways of life and customs of a people have been developed. Crude moral nature is stronger: a Huron Indian's emotions are far more violent, his actions bolder, than would be those of a European in similar circumstances. Homer's warriors acted with more vigour and expressed themselves with more vehemence than we do. In recent times some German poets and critics seem to have exalted a preference for this cruder nature into an artistic principle on account of the superior energy of its poetic imagery. Our readers will already have been reminded of this in the article entitled *Emphasis* (*Nachdruck*). We would add here, however, that if the poet is to make an appropriate choice of materials for his work he must give full consideration to the objective that he has in mind. If he sets out merely to provide descriptions which are to move us by the power of the natural emotions, material drawn directly from nature will furnish all that is needed. His descriptions will afford pleasure and they cause us to comment on them much as we are astonished by and driven to comment on the stories that travellers tell of their encounters with savage people and of extraordinary calamities that have befallen them. We shall read such poems as we read the descriptions of a Homer, an Ossian or a Theocritus. But as soon as the poet no longer wishes merely to interest us, but to be useful, he will have to confine himself to nature as she is and as she is seen herself today. There would be little point in producing on a European stage a drama about, say, Caribbeans or Hurons in all their natural forcefulness. Such a work might serve to instruct a philosopher who wished to see man perfectly portrayed in his completely natural state. But this lies far beyond the scope of the fine arts.

Sublime (Erhaben)

In works of taste, apparently, the term sublime is generally applied to whatever in its way is much greater and more powerful than might have been expected; for this reason, the sublime arouses our astonishment and admiration. We enjoy those things which are simply good and beautiful in nature; they are pleasurable or edifying; they create an impression that is tranquil enough for us to enjoy without disturbance. The sublime, however, works on us with hammer-blows; it seizes us and irresistibly overwhelms us. This effect, however, is not confined to the initial impact of surprise; it persists. The longer the close contemplation of the sublime, the more intense its effect. The relationship between a charming landscape and the breathtaking vista of lofty mountains, or between the tender gentleness of a Fidli and the raging passion of a Sappho, is similar to that between the beautiful and the sublime.

The sublime is thus the highest thing that there is in art. It should be resorted to only when the psyche is to be attacked with hammer-blows, when admiration, awe, powerful longing, high courage, or even fear or terror are to be aroused, whenever the aim is to intensify the powers of the soul or violently to curb them. Hence, an important aspect of the theory of the fine arts must be the detailed examination of the categories of the sublime, the sources from which it springs, its treatment and application.

Since the sublime invariably arouses astonishment by its size, but since a sense of size originates only when we realise how big something is, the size of the sublime object should not be totally beyond our conception; for admiration of size arises only from the ability to compare. We are moved as little by the wholly inconceivable as if it had never existed. If we are told that God created the world *ex nihilo*, or that God rules the world by His Will, we experience nothing at all, since this lies totally beyond our comprehension. But when Moses says: 'And God said: Let there be light; and there was light', we are overcome with astonishment because we can at least form some idea of such greatness; we hear to some extent words of command and feel their power; and if we are made to see instead of the mere Divine Will some empirical symbol of it: as in Homer, and, after him, Horace, when they give the image of Jove setting everything in motion with the blink of an eyelid – 'cuncta supercilio moventis' – we are astonished at such power . . . We must have a yardstick by which we seek to measure the extent of the sublime, even if unsuccessfully. Where this yardstick is lacking, its grandeur evaporates or degenerates into mere bombast.

Sir William Jones

(b. Westminster, 28 Sept. 1746; d. Calcutta, 28 April 1794)

From: *Poems, consisting chiefly of translations from the Asiatik Languages, with two Essays on the Poetry of the Eastern Nations and on the Arts called Imitative* (Oxford 1772), Essay II

Sir William, a student of classics and oriental languages, became a Fellow of University College, Oxford in 1776. One of his first publications was a translation, in French, of the life of Nadir Shah from the Persian, the result of a commission from Christian VII of Denmark. In 1772 he became a Fellow of the Royal Society, and a member of the Literary Club, alongside Reynolds, Burke, Johnson, and Hawkins. In 1774 he was called to the bar, and after being knighted in 1783 he settled in India as High Court judge of Calcutta. He had a prodigious knowledge of languages, being said to have mastered thirteen languages 'thoroughly' and twenty-eight 'fairly well'. The second essay is given below in its entirety: not surprisingly it reveals a wide grasp of classical and French literature. Towards the end Sir William is at pains to stress the difference between imitation as pure description, and imitation as the process of awakening affections or sentiments analogous to those which arise in us when we encounter natural objects and events. While supporting the idea put forward by many of his predecessors that 'there is one uniform standard of taste' he acknowledged none the less that the fine arts did arouse a 'great diversity' of responses in people, responses that were conditioned by individual 'inclinations' and interests.

On the arts, commonly called imitative

It is the fate of those maxims which have been thrown out by very eminent writers, to be received implicitly by most of their followers and to be repeated a thousand times for no other reason than because they once dropped from the pen of a superior genius: one of these is the assertion of Aristotle that all poetry consists in imitation, which has been so frequently echoed from author to author, that it would seem a kind of arrogance to controvert it; for almost all the philosophers and critics, who have written upon the subject of poetry, music, and painting, how little soever they may agree in some points, seem of one mind in considering them as arts merely imitative: yet it must be clear to any one, who examines what passes in his own mind, that he is affected by the finest poems, pieces of music and pictures, upon a principle which, whatever it be, is entirely distinct from imitation. M le Batteux has attempted to prove that all the fine arts have a relation to this common principle of imitating: but, whatever be said of painting, it is probable that poetry and music had a nobler origin; and if the

140

first language of man was not both poetical and musical, it is certain, at least, that in countries where no kind of imitation seems to be much admired, there are poets and musicians both by nature and by art: as in some Mahometan nations where sculpture and painting are forbidden by the laws, where dramatic poetry of every sort is wholly unknown, yet where the pleasing arts of expressing the passions in verse and of enforcing that expression by melody, are cultivated to a degree of enthusiasm. It shall be my endeavour in this paper to prove that though poetry and music have certainly a power of imitating the manners of men and several objects in nature, yet that their greatest effect is not produced by imitation but by a very different principle, which must be sought for in the deepest recesses of the human mind.

To state the question properly we must have a clear notion of what we mean by poetry and music; but we cannot give a precise definition of them till we have made a few previous remarks on their origin, their relation to each other, and their difference.

It seems probable then that poetry was originally no more than a strong and animated expression of the human passions, of joy and grief, love and hate, admiration and anger, sometimes pure and unmixed, sometimes variously modified and combined: for if we observe the voice and accents of a person affected by any of the violent passions, we shall perceive something in them very nearly approaching to cadence and measure, which is remarkably the case in the language of a vehement orator, whose talent is chiefly conversant about praise or censure, and we may collect from several passages in Tully, that the fine speakers of old Greece and Rome had a sort of rhythm in their sentences, less regular but not less melodious than that of the poets.

If this idea be just, one would suppose that the most ancient sort of poetry consisted in praising the deity; for if we conceive a being created with all his faculties and senses, endued with speech and reason, to open his eyes in a most delightful plain, to view for the first time the serenity of the sky, the splendour of the sun, the verdure of the fields and woods, the glowing colours of the flowers, we can hardly believe it possible that he should refrain from bursting into an ecstasy of joy and pouring his praises to the creator of those wonders, and the author of his happiness. This kind of poetry is used in all nations but as it is the sublimest of all when it is applied to its true object, so it has been perverted to impious purposes by pagans and idolaters: everyone knows that the dramatic poetry of the Europeans took its rise from the same spring, and was no more at first than a song in praise of Bacchus; so that the only species of poetical composition (if we except the epic), which can in any sense be called imitative, was deduced from a natural emotion of the mind, in which imitation could not be at all concerned.

The next source of poetry was probably love, or the mutual inclination which naturally subsists between the sexes and is founded upon personal beauty: hence arose the most agreeable odes and love-songs, which we admire in the works of the ancient lyric poets, not filled like our sonnets and madrigals, with the insipid babble of darts and Cupids, but simple, tender, natural, and consisting of such unaffected endearments and mild complaints.

> Teneri sdegni, e placide e tranquille
> Repulse, e cari vezzi, e liete paci,[1]

as we may suppose to have passed between the first lovers in a state of innocence, before the refinements of society and the restraints which they introduced had made the passion of love so fierce, and impetuous, as it is said to have been in Dido, and certainly was in Sappho, if we may take her own word for it.[2]

The grief which the first inhabitants of the earth must have felt at the death of their dearest friends and relations gave rise to another species of poetry which originally, perhaps, consisted of short dirges, and was afterwards lengthened into elegies.

As soon as vice began to prevail in the world, it was natural for the wise and virtuous to express their detestation of it in the strongest manner and to show their resentment against the corrupters of mankind: hence moral poetry was derived, which at first, we find, was severe and passionate but was gradually melted down into cool precepts of morality or exhortations to virtue: we may reasonably conjecture that epic poetry had the same origin, and that the examples of heroes and kings were introduced to illustrate some moral truth by showing the loveliness and advantages of virtue or the many misfortunes that flow from vice.

Where there is vice, which is detestable in itself, there must be hate, since the strongest antipathy in nature, as Mr Pope asserted in his writings and proved by his whole life, subsists between the good and the bad: now this passion was the source of that poetry which we call satire, very improperly and corruptly, since the satire of the Romans was no more than a moral piece, which they entitled Satura or Satyra,[3] intimating that the poem, like a dish of fruit and corn offered to Ceres, contained a variety and plenty of fancies and figures; whereas the true invectives of the ancients were called Jambi, of which we have several examples in Catullus and in the Epodes of Horace, who imitated the very measures and manner of Archilochus.

These are the principal sources of poetry, and of music also, as it shall be my endeavour to show: but it is first necessary to say a few words on the

---

[1] Tender disdains, serene and mild denials,
   delightful wiles, surrenders of all bliss
   smiled-at, sweet sounding words and dewey drops
   of tears, and languid kisses, broken sighs,
   these things she took and blended into one;
   [from *Torquato Tasso's Jerusalem delivered*, tr. into verse by Joseph Tusiani, (1970), Canto 16, Stanza 25—ed.]

[2] See the ode on Sappho, quoted by Longinus, and translated by Boileau.

[3] Some Latin words were spelled either with a u or a y, as Sulla or Sylla.

nature of sound, a very copious subject which would require a long dissertation to be accurately discussed. Without entering into a discourse on the vibrations of chords or the undulations of the air, it will be sufficient for our purpose to observe that there is a great difference between a common sound and a musical sound, which consists chiefly in this, that the former is simple and entire in itself like a point, while the latter is always accompanied with other sounds, without ceasing to be one – like a circle, which is an entire figure, though it is generated by a multitude of points flowing at equal distances round a common centre. These accessory sounds which are caused by the aliquots of a sonorous body vibrating at once, are called harmonics, and the whole system of modern harmony depends upon them, though it were easy to prove that the system is unnatural, and only made tolerable to the ear by habit: for whenever we strike the perfect accord on a harpsichord or an organ, the harmonics of the third and fifth have also their own harmonics which are dissonant from the principal note.[4]

Now let us conceive that some vehement passion is expressed in strong words, exactly measured and pronounced in a common voice, in just cadence and with proper accents, such an expression of the passion will be genuine poetry; and the famous ode of Sappho is allowed to be so in the strictest sense: but if the same ode, with all its natural accents, were expressed in a musical voice (that is, in sounds accompanied with their harmonics), if it were sung in due time and measure in a simple and pleasing tune that added force to the words without stifling them, it would then be pure and original music, not merely soothing to the ear but affecting to the heart, not an imitation of nature but the voice of nature herself. But there is another point in which music must resemble poetry, or it will lose a considerable part of its effect: we all must have observed that a speaker, agitated with passion, or an actor who is indeed strictly an imitator, are perpetually changing the tone and pitch of their voice, as the sense of their words varies: it may be worth while to examine how this variation is expressed in music. Everybody knows that the musical scale consists of seven notes, above which we find a succession of similar sounds repeated in the same order, and above that, other successions, as far as they can be continued by the human voice or distinguished by the human ear: now each of these seven sounds has no more meaning when it is heard separately than a single letter of the alphabet would have; and it is only by their succession and their relation to one principal sound, that they take any rank in the scale or differ from each other, except as they are graver, or more acute: but in

---

[4] Suppose C, E and G are struck together: then E gives G♯, B; and G gives B, D: which G♯, B, D are dissonant from C, the first being its superfluous fifth, and the two last its seventh and second. And to complete the harmony, as it is called, G♯ and G♮ are heard together, than which, nothing can be more absurd. These horrid dissonances are indeed almost overpowered by the natural harmonics of the principal chord, but that does not prove them agreeable. Since nature has given us a delightful harmony of her own, why should we destroy it by the additions of art? It is like painting a face naturally beautiful.

the regular scale each interval assumes a proper character, and every note stands related to the first or principal one by various proportions. Now a series of sounds relating to one leading note is called a mode, or a tone, and, as there are twelve semitones in the scale, each of which may be made in its turn the leader of a mode, it follows that there are twelve modes; and each of them has a peculiar character arising from the position of the modal note, and from some minute difference in the ratios, as of 81 to 80, or a comma; for there are some intervals, which cannot easily be rendered on our instruments yet have a surprising effect in modulation or in the transitions from one mode to another.

The modes of the ancients are said to have had a wonderful effect over the mind; and Plato, who permits the Dorian in his imaginary republic on account of its calmness and gravity, excludes the Lydian because of its languid, tender, and effeminate character: not that any series of mere sounds has a power of raising or soothing the passions but each of these modes was appropriated to a particular kind of poetry and a particular instrument; and the chief of them, as the Dorian, Phrygian, Lydian, Ionian, Eolian, Locrian, belonged originally to the nations from which they took their names: thus the Phrygian mode, which was ardent and impetuous, was usually accompanied with trumpets, and the Mixolydian, which, if we believe Aristoxenus, was invented by Sappho, was probably confined to the pathetic and tragic style: that these modes had a relation to poetry as well as to music, appears from a fragment of Lasus, in which he says, 'I sing of Ceres, and her daughter Meliboea, the consort of Pluto, in the Eolian mode, full of gravity'; and Pindar calls one of his Odes an Eolian song. If the Greeks surpassed us in the strength of their modulations, we have an advantage over them in our minor scale, which supplies us with twelve new modes, where the two semitones are removed from their natural position between the third and fourth, the seventh and eighth notes, and placed between the second and third, the fifth and sixth; this change of the semitones, by giving a minor third to the modal note, softens the general expression of the mode and adapts it admirably to subjects of grief and affliction: the minor mode of D is tender, that of C, with three flats, plaintive, and that of F, with four, pathetic and mournful to the highest degree, for which reason it was chosen by the excellent Pergolesi in his 'Stabat Mater'. Now these twenty-four modes, artfully interwoven and changed as often as the sentiment changes, may, it is evident, express all the variations in the voice of a speaker, and give an additional beauty to the accents of a poet. Consistently with the foregoing principles we may define original and native poetry to the language of the violent passions, expressed in exact measure, with strong accents and significant words; and true music to be no more than poetry, delivered in a succession of harmonious sounds so disposed as to please the ear. It is in this view only that we must consider the music of the ancient Greeks, or attempt to account for its amazing effects, which we find related by the gravest historians, and philosophers; it was wholly passionate or descriptive, and so closely united to poetry that it never obstructed but always increased its influence: whereas our boasted harmony with all its fine accords and numerous parts, paints nothing, expresses nothing, says nothing to the heart, and consequently can only give more or less pleasure to one of our senses; and no reasonable man will seriously prefer a transitory pleasure which must soon end in satiety or even in disgust, to a delight of the soul arising from sympathy, and founded on the natural passions, always lively, always interesting, always transporting. The old divisions of music into celestial and earthly, divine and human, active and contemplative, intellective and oratorial, were founded rather upon metaphors and chimerical analogies than upon any real distinctions in nature; but the want of making a distinction between the music of mere sounds and the music of the passions has been the perpetual source of confusion and contradictions both among the ancients and the moderns: nothing can be more opposite in many points than the systems of Rameau and Tartini, one of whom asserts that melody springs from harmony, and the other deduces harmony from melody; and both are in the right, if the first speaks only of that music which took its rise from the multiplicity of sounds heard at once in the sonorous body, and the second, of that which rose from the accents and inflexions of the human voice, animated by the passions: to decide, as Rousseau says, whether of these two schools ought to have the preference, we need only ask a plain question, Was the voice made for the instruments or the instruments for the voice?

What has been said of poetry may with equal force be applied to music, which is poetry dressed to advantage; and even to painting, many sorts of which are poems to the eye, as all poems, merely descriptive, are pictures to the ear: and this way of considering them will set the refinements of modern artists in their true light; for the passions which were given by nature, never spoke in an unnatural form, and no man, truly affected with love or grief, ever expressed the one in an acrostic, or the other in a fugue: these remains, therefore, of the false taste which prevailed in the dark ages, should be banished from this, which is enlightened with a just one.

It is true that some kinds of painting are strictly imitative, as that which is solely intended to represent the human figure and countenance; but it will be found that those pictures have always the greatest effect which represent some passion, as the 'Martyrdom of St Agnes' by Domenichino, and the various representations of the Crucifixion by the finest masters of Italy; and there can be no doubt but that the famous 'Sacrifice of Iphigenia' by Timanthes was affecting to the highest degree; which proves, not that painting cannot be said to imitate, but that its most powerful influence over the mind, arises, like that of the other arts, from sympathy.

It is asserted that descriptive poetry and descriptive music, as they are called, are strict imitations; but, not to insist that mere description is the meanest part of both arts, if indeed it belongs to them at all, it is clear, that words and sounds have no kind of resemblance to visible objects: and what is an imitation but a resemblance of some other thing? Besides, no unprejudiced hearer will say that he finds the smallest traces of imitation in the numerous fugues, counterfugues and divisions which rather disgrace than adorn the modern music: even sounds themselves are imperfectly imitated by harmony, and if we sometimes hear the murmuring of a brook or the chirping of birds in a concert, we are generally apprised beforehand of the passages where we may expect them. Some eminent musicians indeed have been absurd enough to think of imitating laughter and other noises, but if they had succeeded, they could not have made amends for their want of taste in attempting it; for such ridiculous imitations must necessarily destroy the spirit and dignity of the finest poems, which they ought to illustrate by a graceful and natural melody. It seems to me that as those parts of poetry, music and painting which relate to the passions, affect by sympathy, so those which are merely descriptive, act by a kind of substitution, that is, by raising in our minds, affections or sentiments, analogous to those which arise in us when the respective objects in nature are presented to our senses. Let us suppose that a poet, a musician, and a painter are striving to give their friend or patron a pleasure similar to that which he feels at the sight of a beautiful prospect. The first will form an agreeable assemblage of lively images, which he will express in smooth and elegant verses of a sprightly measure; he will describe the most delightful objects, and will add to the graces of his description a certain delicacy of sentiment and a spirit of cheerfulness. The musician who undertakes to set the words of the poet will select some mode which on his violin has the character of mirth and gaiety, as the Eolian, or E flat, which he will change as the sentiment is varied: he will express the words in a simple and agreeable melody which will not disguise but embellish them without aiming at any fugue or figured harmony: he will use the bass to mark the modulation more strongly, especially in the changes, and he will place the tenor generally in union with the bass, to prevent too great a distance between the parts: in the symphony he will above all things avoid a double melody, and will apply his variations only to some accessory ideas which the principal part, that is the voice, could not easily express: he will not make a number of useless repetitions, because the passions only repeat the same expression and dwell upon the same sentiments, while description can only represent a single object by a single sentence. The painter will describe all visible objects more exactly than his rival but he will fall short of the other artists in a very material circumstance, namely that his pencil, which may indeed express a simple passion, cannot paint a thought or draw the shades of sentiment: he will however finish his landscape with grace and elegance; his colours will be rich and glowing, his perspective striking, and his figures will be disposed with an agreeable variety but not with confusion: above all, he will diffuse over his whole piece such a spirit of liveliness and festivity, that the beholder shall be seized with a kind of rapturous delight, and for a moment mistake art for nature.

Thus will each artist gain his end, not by imitating the works of nature but by assuming her power and causing the same effect upon the imagination which her charms produce to the senses: this must be the chief object of a poet, a musician and a painter, who know that great effects are not produced by minute details but by the general spirit of the whole piece, and that a gaudy composition may strike the mind for a short time but that the beauties of simplicity are both more delightful and more permanent.

As the passions are differently modified in different men, and as even the various objects in nature affect our minds in various degrees, it is obvious that there must be a great diversity in the pleasure which we receive from the fine arts, whether that pleasure arises from sympathy or substitution; and that it were a wild notion in artists to think of pleasing every reader, hearer or beholder, since every man has a particular set of objects and a particular inclination which direct him in the choice of his pleasures, and induce him to consider the productions, both of nature and of art as more or less elegant, in proportion as they give him a greater or smaller degree of delight: this does not at all contradict the opinion of many able writers that there is one uniform standard of taste; since the passions and consequently sympathy, are generally the same in all men, till they are weakened by age, infirmity or other causes.

If the arguments used in this essay have any weight, it will appear that the finest parts of poetry, music and painting are expressive of the passions, and operate on our minds by sympathy; that the inferior parts of them are descriptive of natural objects and affect us chiefly by substitution; that the expressions of love, pity, desire and the tender passions, as well as the descriptions of objects that delight the senses, produce in the arts what we call the beautiful; but that hate, anger, fear and the terrible passions, as well as objects which are unpleasing to the senses, are productive of the sublime when they are aptly expressed or described.

These subjects might be pursued to infinity, but if they were amply discussed it would be necessary to write a series of dissertations instead of an essay.

Christoph Willibald [von] Gluck

(b. 2 July 1714; d. 15 Nov. 1787)

From: *Mercure de France*, February 1773, p. 182: Lettre de M le Chevalier Gluck, sur la musique

Gluck's letter preceded the first Paris performance of any of his operas by a year or so. It was obviously designed as publicity for *Iphigénie*, and to whet Parisian appetites for the new style of opera that was enjoying such success in Vienna. Gluck's tribute to Rousseau may have been a diplomatic move: it is none the less remarkable testimony to Rousseau's fame and to the popularity of his ideas on musical expression. See also Gluck's preface to *Alceste*, tr. Strunk, *Source Readings*, p. 673.

Sir, I could be justly reproached, and I would deeply reproach myself, if having read in the *Mercure* of October last the letter addressed to one of the directors of the Académie royale about the opera *Iphigénie*, and having paid my respects to the author of the letter for the praise that he has seen fit to bestow on me, I did not hasten to declare that his friendship towards me and his partiality have carried him away, and that I am far from flattering myself that I merit the eulogies that he has showered upon me. I should reproach myself still more if I allowed the invention of the new genre of Italian opera – the success of which has justified the attempt – to be attributed to me. It is to M Calzabigi that the principal merit belongs. If my music has had some success, I attribute this to him, since he has made it possible for me to develop the resources of my art. This author, of great genius and talent, has followed a path that is little known to the Italians, in the poems that treat of Orpheus, Alceste and Paris. These works are full of happy situations and of terrible and deeply moving features that furnish the composer with the means to express the great passions, and to compose music that is full of energy and pathos. Whatever talent the composer may have, he will only produce mediocre music if the poet does not waken in him that enthusiasm without which all the arts are weak and sickly. The imitation of nature is the acknowledged end to which they must all address themselves. It is this that I strive for; my music is consistently as natural and simple as I can make it; it aims to be as expressive as possible and to underline the poetic declamation. That is why I avoid the trills, passages and cadences that are so beloved of the Italians. Their tongue, which readily lends itself to such things, has in this respect then no advantage, as far as I am concerned. It may well have others, but as I am a German, whatever study I have been able to make of the German and French languages, I do not believe I can recognise those fine

148

nuances that might give the advantage to either one or the other. All foreigners, I believe, must abstain from judging this matter. I do believe that it is possible to say this, however, that I find the most suitable words are those in which the poet has given me the most varied means of expressing the passions. This I believe is the advantage that I have found in the text of *Iphigénie*, the poetry of which has for me all the energy that is necessary to inspire in me good music. Although I have never been in the situation of offering my works to any theatre, I can hardly be displeased with the letter that the author addresses to one of the directors, proposing my *Iphigénie* for your Académie de musique. I confess that I would gladly have it produced in Paris. With the help of the famous M. Rousseau of Geneva, whom I would propose to consult, we would perhaps – in the search for a noble, sensitive and natural melody, and for declamation that exactly matches the prosody of each tongue and the character of each people – be able to determine the way that I have in mind, to produce music that is suited to every nation, thereby dispensing with absurd distinctions of national styles. I have studied the works of this great man on music, amongst which is the letter in which he analyses the monologue in Lully's *Armide*;[1] these have filled me with admiration, and have proved the sublimity of his knowledge and the surety of his taste. I am left with the deep conviction that had he wished to apply himself to the practice of music he would have been able to achieve those prodigious effects that were in ancient times attributed to music. I am delighted to have the opportunity here, to pay public tribute to one who I, believe, so much deserves it.

I beg you, Sir, to have the goodness to include this letter in your forthcoming *Mercure*.

I have the honour to be, etc.,
    Chevalier Gluck.

---

[1] In *Lettre sur la musique française* (1753), *Oeuvres complètes*, ed. P. R. Auguis (Paris 1825); excerpts tr. Strunk, *Source Readings*, p. 636, though not this passage (eds.)

James Beattie

(b. Laurencekirk, Kincardine, 25 Oct. 1735; d. Aberdeen, 18 Aug. 1803)

From: *An Essay on Poetry and Music as they affect the Mind* (Edinburgh 1776) Pt 1, ch. 6, sections i–iii, pp. 122–35; 155–62

In 1760 Beattie took the chair of moral philosophy at Marischal College, Aberdeen, having graduated from Aberdeen seven years previously as a student of classics. He remained there for the rest of his career, and was an active member of the Wise Club which met regularly for the reading of papers on philosophical and scientific matters. His biographers[1] speak of his love for 'romantic' scenery and of the fact that he would pass whole nights out under the stars. He was a keen amateur musician, and on terms of friendship with Burney. In 1770, after several poetic works, Beattie ventured into philosophy, in an aggressively worded attack on Hume – the *Essay on Truth*; this rapidly passed through five editions and was translated into French, German, Dutch and Italian. To the 1776 edition were added three *Essays*, of which the *Essay on Poetry and Music* was the first. It divides into two parts. Chapters 1–5 of part 1 examine the question of poetry and imitation, whilst the sixth, from which the extracts are taken, is in three sections: (i) 'Of Imitation. Is music an imitative art?'; (ii) How are the pleasures we derive from music to be accounted for?'; and (iii) 'Conjectures on some peculiarities of national music'. The first part of the work ends with a final chapter, examining the role of 'sympathy' in aesthetic experience. Part 2 explores every factor that bears upon the quality of poetic language. Beattie attacked the idea that music could in any significant sense be regarded as an imitative art, and he was at one with his contemporaries in arguing that 'the end of all genuine music is to introduce into the human mind certain affections or susceptibilities of affection' (see pp. 151–2). He took the view – one that was very fashionable in French circles – that musical expression should be directed toward the improvement of society. It followed then that purely instrumental music was greatly inferior to vocal music, for while an effective piece of instrumental music will certainly 'incline the heart to sensibility', only poetry or language can 'improve that sensibility into a real emotion by fixing the fancy on some definite and affecting ideas'. Beattie also examines the function of 'association' in aesthetic appreciation (see pp. 154–6) amplifying by specific example Hutcheson's earlier comment (see pp. 23–6). The quality of Beattie's argument is on a much higher plane than that of most of his immediate predecessors, and it reveals a genuine understanding of musical processes, and a familiarity with contemporary music.

The *Essay* was translated into German (Leipzig 1779) and French (Paris 1799): see Lichtenthal's bibliography for further details (p. 391).

---

[1] See A. H. Bullen, *Dictionary of National Biography*, s.v., 'Beattie'.

Remarks on music

Of imitation. Is music an imitative art?
Man, from his birth, is prone to imitation, and takes great pleasure in it. At a time when he is too young to understand or attend to rules, he learns by imitating others, to speak and walk and do many other things equally requisite to life and happiness. Most of the sports of children are imitative, and many of them dramatical. Mimickry occasions laughter; and a just imitation of human life upon the stage is highly delightful to persons of all ranks, conditions and capacities.

[p. 122, para. 2 to p. 127, line 15 omitted]

Since imitation is so plentiful a source of pleasure, we need not wonder that the imitative arts of poetry and painting should have been greatly esteemed in every enlightened age. The imitation itself, which is the work of the artist, is agreeable; the thing imitated, which is nature, is also agreeable; and is not the same thing true of the instrument of imitation? Or does any one doubt, whether harmonious language be pleasing to the ear or certain arrangements of colour beautiful to the eye?

Shall I apply these and the preceding reasonings to the musical art also, which I have elsewhere called and which is generally understood to be imitative? Shall I say that some melodies please, because they imitate nature, and that others which do not imitate nature are therefore unpleasing: that an air expressive of devotion, for example, is agreeable because it presents us with an imitation of those sounds by which devotion does naturally express itself? Such an affirmation would hardly pass upon the reader, notwithstanding the plausibility it might seem to derive from that strict analogy which all the fine arts are supposed to bear to one another. He would ask, What is the natural sound of devotion? Where is it to be heard? When was it heard? What resemblance is there between Handel's 'Te Deum' and the tone of voice natural to a person expressing, by articulate sound, his veneration of the Divine Character and Providence? In fact, I apprehend that critics have erred a little in their determinations upon this subject, from an opinion that music, painting, and poetry are all imitative arts. I hope at least I may say without offence that while this was my opinion, I was always conscious of some unaccountable confusion of thought whenever I attempted to explain it in the way of detail to others.

But while I thus insinuate that music is not an imitative art, I mean no disrespect to Aristotle who seems in the beginning of his *Poetics* to declare the contrary. It is not the whole but the greater part of music which that philosopher calls imitative; and I agree with him so far as to allow this property to some music, though not to all. But he speaks of the ancient music, and I of the modern; and to one who considers how very little we know of the former, it will not appear a contradiction to say that the one might have been imitative though the other is not.

Nor do I mean any disrespect to music when I would strike it off the list of imitative arts. I allow it to be a fine art and to have great influence on the human soul: I grant that by its power of raising a variety of agreeable emotions in the hearer it proves its relation to poetry, and that it never appears to the best advantage but with poetry for its interpreter: and I am satisfied that though musical genius may subsist without poetical taste and poetical genius without musical taste, yet these two talents united might accomplish nobler effects than either could do singly. I acknowledge too, that the principles and essential rules of this art are as really founded in nature, as those of poetry and painting. But when I am asked what part of nature is imitated in any good picture or poem, I find I can give a definite answer: whereas when I am asked what part of nature is imitated in Handel's 'Water-music', for instance, or in Corelli's eighth concerto, or in any particular English song or Scotch tune, I find I can give no definite answer, though no doubt I might say some plausible things, or perhaps after much refinement be able to show that music may by one shift or other be made an imitative art, provided you allow me to give any meaning I please to the word imitative.

Music is imitative when it readily puts one in mind of the thing imitated. If an explication be necessary, and if after all we find it difficult to recognise any exact similitude, I would not call such music an imitation of nature, but consider it as upon a footing in point of likeness with those pictures wherein the action cannot be known but by a label proceeding from the mouth of the agent, nor the species of animal ascertained without a name written under it. But between imitation in music and imitation in painting, there is this one essential difference: a bad picture is always a bad imitation of nature and a good picture is necessarily a good imitation; but music may be exactly imitative and yet intolerably bad; or not at all imitative and yet perfectly good. I have heard that the 'Pastorale' in the eighth of Corelli's concertos (which appears by the inscription to have been composed for the night of the Nativity) was intended for an imitation of the song of angels hovering above the fields of Bethlehem, and gradually soaring up to heaven. The music however is not such as would of itself convey this idea: and even with the help of the commentary it requires a lively fancy to connect the various movements and melodies of the piece with the motions and evolutions of the heavenly host, as sometimes flying off, and sometimes returning, singing sometimes in one quarter of the sky, and sometimes in another, now in one or two parts, and now in full chorus. It is not clear that the author intended any imitation; and whether he did or not, is a matter of no consequence, for the music will continue to please when the tradition is no more remembered. The harmonies of this 'pastorale' are indeed so uncommon and so ravishingly sweet that it is almost impossible not to think of heaven when one hears them. I would not call them imitative, but I believe they are finer than any imitative music in the world.

How are the pleasures we derive from music to be accounted for?
Natural sensibility is not taste, though it be necessary to it. A painter discovers both blemishes and beauties in a picture in which an ordinary eye can perceive neither. In poetical language and in the arrangement and choice of words, there are many niceties whereof they only are conscious who have practised versification, as well as studied the works of poets and the rules of the art. In like manner, harmony must be studied a little in its principles by every person who would acquire a true relish for it; and nothing but practice will ever give that quickness to his ear which is necessary to enable him to enter with adequate satisfaction or rational dislike, into the merits or demerits of a musical performance. When once he can attend to the progress, relations and dependencies of the several parts, and remember the past and anticipate the future at the same time he perceives the present, so as to be sensible of the skill of the composer and dexterity of the performer, a regular concerto, well executed, will yield him high entertainment even though its regularity be its principal recommendation. The pleasure which an untutored hearer derives from it is far inferior: and yet there is something in harmony that pleases, and in dissonance that offends every ear; and were a piece to be played consisting wholly of discords or put together without any regard to rule, I believe no person whatever would listen to it without great disgust.

After what has been briefly said of the agreeable qualities of musical notes, it will not seem strange that a piece either of melody or of harmony, of little or no expression, should when elegantly performed give some delight, not only to adepts, who can trace out the various contrivances of the composer, but even to those who have little or no skill in this art and must therefore look upon the whole piece as nothing more than a combination of pleasing sounds.

Conjectures on some peculiarities of national music
But pathos or expression is the chief excellence of music. Without this, it may amuse the ear, it may give a little exercise to the mind of the hearer, it may for a moment withdraw the attention from the anxieties of life, it may show the performer's dexterity, the skill of the composer, or the merit of the instruments; and in all or any of these ways it may afford a slight pleasure: but without engaging the affections, it can never yield that permanent, useful and heart-felt gratification, which legislators, civil, military and ecclesiastical, have expected from it. Is it absurd to ascribe utility and permanence to the effects produced by this noble art? Let me expatiate a little in its praise. Did not one of the wisest and least voluptuous of all ancient legislators give great encouragement to music?[2]

Does not a most judicious author ascribe the humanity of the Arcadians to the influence of this art, and the barbarity of their neighbours the

[2] Lycurgus, *Lives*; see Plutarch.

Cynethians to their neglect of it?[3] Does not Montesquieu, one of the first names in modern philosophy, prefer it to all other amusements as being that which least corrupts the soul?[4]

Quintilian is very copious in the praise of music, and extols it as an incentive to valour, as an instrument of moral and intellectual discipline, as an auxiliary to science, as an object of attention to the wisest men, and a source of comfort and an assistant in labour, even to the meanest.[5] The heroes of ancient Greece were ambitious to excel in music; and it is recorded of Themistocles, as something extraordinary that he was not. Socrates appears to have had checks of conscience for neglecting to accomplish himself in this art, for he tells Cebes, a little before he swallowed the deadly draught, that he had all his life been haunted with a dream in which one seemed to say to him, 'O Socrates, compose and practise music'; in compliance with which admonition he amused himself while under sentence of death with turning some of Aesop's fables into verse and making a hymn in honour of Apollo – the only sort of harmonious composition that was then in his power.[6] In armies, music has always been cultivated as a source of pleasure, a principle of regular motion and an incentive to valour and enthusiasm. The Son of Sirach declares the ancient poets and musicians to be worthy of honour, and ranks them with the benefactors of mankind.[7] Nay, Jesus Christ and his apostles were pleased to introduce this art into the Christian worship; and the church has in every age followed the example.

Music however would not have recommended itself so effectually to general esteem if it had always been merely instrumental. For if I mistake not, the expression of music without poetry is vague and ambiguous, and hence it is that the same air may sometimes be repeated to every stanza of a long ode or ballad. The change of the poet's ideas, provided the subject continue nearly the same, does not always require a change of the music: and if critics have ever determined otherwise, they were led into the mistake by supposing what every musician knows to be absurd, that in fitting verses to a tune or a tune to verses, it is more necessary that particular words should have particular notes adapted to them than that the general tenor of the music should accord with the general nature of the sentiments.

It is true that to a favourite air, even when unaccompanied with words, we do commonly annex certain ideas which may have come to be related to it in consequence of some accidental associations: and sometimes we imagine a resemblance (which however is merely imaginary) between certain melodies and certain thoughts or objects. Thus a Scotchman may fancy that there is some sort of likeness between that charming air which he calls 'Tweedside' and the scenery of a fine pastoral country: and to the same

---

[3] Polybius, *Historiarum libri quinque*, bk. 4.
[4] *Esprit des lois* (Geneva 1748), bk. 4, ch. 3.
[5] *Institutionis Oratoriae*, bk. 1, ch. 8.
[6] Plato, *The Phaedo*, section iv.
[7] Ecclesiasticus, xliv. 1–8.

air, even when only played on an instrument he may annex the ideas of romantic love and rural tranquillity, because these form the subject of a pretty little ode which he has often heard sung to that air. But all this is the effect of habit. A foreigner who hears that tune for the first time, entertains no such fancy. The utmost we can expect from him is to acknowledge the air to be sweet and simple. He would smile if we were to ask him whether it bears any resemblance to the hills, groves and meadows adjoining to a beautiful river; nor would he perhaps think it more expressive of romantic love than of conjugal, parental or filial affection, tender melancholy, moderate joy, or any other gentle passion. Certain it is that on any one of these topics an ode might be composed which would suit the air most perfectly. So ambiguous is musical expression.

It is likewise true that music merely instrumental does often derive significancy from external circumstances. When an army in battle-array is advancing to meet the enemy, words are not necessary to give meaning to the military music. And a solemn air on the organ, introducing or dividing the church-service, may not only elevate the mind and banish impertinent thoughts but also, deriving energy from the surrounding scene, may promote religious meditation.

Nor can it be denied that instrumental music may both quicken our sensibility and give a direction to it; that is, may both prepare the mind for being affected, and determine it to one set of affections rather than another, to melancholy, for instance, rather than merriment, composure rather than agitation, devotion rather than levity, and contrariwise. Certain tunes too, there are, which having been always connected with certain actions do, merely from the power of habit, dispose men to those actions. Such are the tunes commonly used to regulate the motions of dancing.

Yet it is in general true that poetry is the most immediate and most accurate interpreter of music. Without this auxiliary, a piece of the best music, heard for the first time, might be said to mean something but we should not be able to say what. It might incline the heart to sensibility: but poetry or language would be necessary to improve that sensibility into a real emotion, by fixing the fancy upon some definite and affecting ideas. A fine instrumental symphony well performed is like an oration delivered with propriety but in an unknown tongue; it may affect us a little, but conveys no determinate feeling; we are alarmed perhaps, or melted, or soothed, but very imperfectly because we know not why: the singer, by taking up the same air and applying words to it, immediately translates the oration into our own language; then all uncertainty vanishes, the fancy is filled with determinate ideas, and determinate emotions take possession of the heart.

A great part of our fashionable music seems intended rather to tickle and astonish the hearers than to inspire them with any permanent emotions. And if that be the end of the art, then to be sure, this fashionable music is just what it should be, and the simpler strains of former ages are good for nothing. Nor am I now at leisure to inquire whether it be better for an audience to be thus tickled and astonished than to have their fancy impressed with the beautiful images and their hearts melted with tender passions or elevated with sublime ones. But if you grant me this one point, that music is more or less perfect in proportion as it has more or less power over the heart, it will follow that all music merely instrumental, and which does not derive significancy from any of the associations, habits or outward circumstances above mentioned, is to a certain degree imperfect; and that while the rules hinted at in the following queries are overlooked by composers and performers, vocal music, though it may astonish mankind or afford them a slight gratification, will never be attended with those important effects that we know it produced of old in the days of simplicity and true taste.

Sir John Hawkins

(b. London, 30 Mar. 1719; d. London, 21 May 1789)

From: *A General History of the Science and Practice of Music* (London 1776, 5 vols.), 'Preliminary Discourse'

After studying for a while under the architect, Hopper, Hawkins embarked upon a career as attorney and solicitor in the city of London. He was an enthusiastic amateur musician, involving himself in the activities of the Academy of Ancient Music, the Madrigal Society, and many private musical gatherings, including the one arranged by the celebrated type founder, Caslon. He became a close friend of John Stanley, the blind composer, and a member of Joshua Reynolds' Literary Club to which Samuel Johnson, Edmund Burke and Oliver Goldsmith also belonged. By 1776 he had been knighted, and was chairman of the Middlesex Quarter Sessions. His *History* was the first serious attempt in English at music history (Burney's first volume came out in the same year but was completed only in 1789). Hawkins was by no means as familiar as Burney with the pre-eighteenth-century literature on music, though he was certainly acquainted with the work of many French and German scholars of his day, as well as with the writings of a number of English aestheticians. He offers no profound thoughts on the nature of music. He was obviously conversant with the principle of imitation, though he does no more than examine the question of literal imitation, concluding – as most others did – that painting and poetry are more suited to it than is music. That he chose to preface the entire work with such remarks – slight as they are – is an indication of the general currency that the principle of imitation then had.

Preliminary discourse

The powers of the imagination, with great appearance of reason, are said to hold a middle place between the organs of bodily sense and the faculties of moral perception; the subjects on which they are severally exercised are common to the senses of seeing and hearing, the office of which is simply perception; all pleasure thence arising being referred to the imagination.

The arts which administer to the imaginative faculty the greatest delight are confessedly poetry, painting and music, the two former exhibiting to the mind by their respective media, either natural or artificial,[1] the resemblances of whatever in the works of nature is comprehended under the general division of great, new and beautiful; the latter as operating upon the mind by the power of that harmony which results from the concord of sounds,

[1] The natural media seem to consist only in colour and figure, and refer solely to painting: the artificial are words, which are symbols by compact of ideas, as are also in a limited sense musical sounds, including in the term the accident of time or duration.

157

and exciting in the mind those ideas which correspond with our tenderest and most delightful affections.

These, it must be observed, constitute one source of pleasure; but each of the above arts may in a different degree be said to afford another, namely that which consists in a comparison of the images by them severally and occasionally excited in the mind with their archetypes; thus for instance in poetry, in comparing a description with the thing described; in painting, a landscape and the scene represented by it, or a portrait and its original; and in music, where imitation is intended, as in the songs of birds or in the expression of those various inflexions of the voice which accompany passion or exclamation, weeping, laughing and other of the human affections, the sound and the thing signified.

It is easy to discover that the pleasures above described are of two distinct kinds, the one original and absolute, the other relative; for the one we can give no reason other than the will of God, who in the formation of the universe and the organization of our bodies has established such a relation as is discoverable between man and his works; the other is to be accounted for by that love of truth which is implanted in the human mind.[2] In poetry and painting therefore we speak, and with propriety, of absolute and relative beauty; as also of music merely imitative; for as to harmony, it is evident that the attribute of relation belongs not to it, as will appear by a comparison of each with the others.[3]

---

[2] In this sentiment liberty has been taken to differ from Mr Harris, who with his usual accuracy has analysed this principle of the human mind in the following note on a passage in the second of his three celebrated *Treatises*:

That there is an eminent delight in this very recognition itself, abstract from any thing pleasing in the subject recognised, is evident from hence that in all the mimetic arts, we can be highly charmed with imitations, as whose originals in nature we are shocked and terrified. Such, for instance, as dead bodies, wild beasts and the like.

The cause assigned for this seems to be the following kind: we have a joy, not only in the sanity and perfection, but also in the just and natural energies of our several limbs and faculties. And hence, among others, the joy in reasoning as being the energy of that principal faculty, our intellect or understanding. This joy extends, not only to the wise, but to the multitude. For all men have an aversion to ignorance and error and in some degree, however moderate, are glad to learn and to inform themselves.

Hence therefore the delight arising from these imitations; as we are enabled in each of them to exercise the reasoning faculty; and by comparing the copy with the architype in our minds, to infer that this is such a thing, and that another; a fact remarkable among children, even in their first and earliest days.

[3] Nevertheless there have not been wanting those who, not contemplating the intrinsic excellence of harmony, have resolved the efficacy of music into the power of imitation; and to gratify such, subjects have been introduced into practice that to injudicious ears have afforded no small delight; such, for instance, as the noise of thunder, the roaring of the winds, the shouts and acclamations of multitudes, the wailings of grief and anguish in the human mind; the song of the cuckoo, the hooting of the screech-owl, the cackling of the hen, the notes of singing-birds, not excepting those of the lark and nightingale. Attempts also have been made to imitate motion by musical sounds; and some have undertaken in like manner to relate histories, and

With regard to poetry, it may be said to resemble painting in many respects, as in the description of external objects and the works of nature; and so far it must be considered as an imitative art; but its greatest excellence seems to be its power of exhibiting the internal constitution of man, and of making us acquainted with characters, manners and sentiments, and working upon the passions of terror, pity and various others. Painting is professedly an imitative art; for setting aside the harmony of colouring and the delineation of beautiful forms, the pleasure we receive from it, great as it is, consists in the truth of the representation.

But in music there is little beyond itself to which we need or indeed can refer to heighten its charms. If we investigate the principles of harmony, we learn that they are general and universal; and of harmony itself, that the proportions in which it consists are to be found in those material forms which are beheld with the greatest pleasure, the sphere, the cube and the cone, for instance, and constitute what we call symmetry, beauty and regularity; but the imagination receives no additional delight; our reason is exercised in the operation and that faculty alone is thereby gratified. In short, there are few things in nature which music is capable of imitating, and those are of a kind so uninteresting that we may venture to pronounce that as its principles are founded in geometrical truth and seem to result from some general and universal law of nature, so its excellence is intrinsic, absolute and inherent, and, in short, resolvable only into His will who has ordered all things in number, weight and measure.[4]

Seeing therefore that music has its foundation in nature, and that reason recognises what the sense approves, what wonder is it, that in all ages and even by the least enlightened of mankind, its efficacy should be acknowledged; or that, as well by those who are capable of reason and reflection as those who seek for no other gratifications than what are

> to describe the various seasons of the year. Thus, for example, Froberger, organist to the emperor Ferdinand III is said to have in an allemand represented the passage of Count Thurn over the Rhine, and the danger he and his army were in, by twenty-six cataracts or falls in notes. Kuhnau, another celebrated musician, composed six sonatas, entitled *Biblische Historien*, wherein, as it is said, is a lively representation in musical notes of David manfully combating Goliath. Buxtehude of Lübeck also composed suites of lessons for the harpsichord, representing the nature of the planets. Vivaldi, in two books of concertos has striven to describe the four seasons of the year. Geminiani has translated a whole episode of Tasso's *Jerusalem* into musical notes. And Mr Handel himself, in his *Israel in Egypt*, has undertaken to represent two of the ten plagues of Egypt by notes, intended to imitate the buzzing of flies and the hopping of frogs.
>
> But these powers of imitation, admitting them to exist in all the various instances above enumerated, constitute but a very small part of the excellence of music; wherefore we cannot but applaud that shrewd answer of Agesilaus, king of Sparta, recorded in Plutarch, to one who requested him to hear a man sing that could imitate the nightingale, 'I have heard the nightingale herself.' The truth is, that imitation belongs more properly to the arts of poetry and painting than to music; for which reason Mr Harris has not scrupled to pronounce of musical imitation, that at best it is but an imperfect thing. See his *Discourse on Music, Painting, and Poetry*, p. 69.

[4] Wisdom, xi. 20.

obvious to the senses, it should be considered as a genuine and natural source of delight? The wonder is that less of that curiosity, which leads men to enquire into the history and progress of arts and their gradual advances towards perfection, has been exercised in the instance now before us than in any other of equal importance.

F.D.C.

From: *Supplément à l'encyclopédie*, vol. 2 (Amsterdam 1776), pp. 924–6

Rousseau's article on 'Expression' in the *Supplément* was taken verbatim from his *Dictionnaire* with an addendum by F.D.C. This addendum is concerned to show, by reference to specific technical procedures, the musical processes that govern expression. Many of the points that F.D.C. makes – somewhat naively – have been taken up by later writers, and most recently by Deryck Cooke in his *The Language of Music* (London 1959). F.D.C. may well be Frédéric de Castillon, a Berlin academician to whom the editors of the *Supplément* were indebted for help on the music articles. This contributor's initials, however, were normally given as F.C.

For further discussion of the *Encyclopédie* see the editorial introduction to d'Alembert's Discours préliminaire p. 57.

[Addendum to 'Expression']

Perhaps I may be allowed here to add my views on expression in music. These may be no more than extensions of ideas that have been put forward by M Rousseau, but his ideas do merit further development.

Musical expression derives from three things: melody, harmony, and the style of the accompaniment.

If the expressive potential is fully to be realised, the musician must be a poet, or the poet a musician. A man who was equally talented in both spheres would be adept, not only at drawing a portrait but at capturing the colour, attitude and dress of the original. There are few men today, however, who are equally gifted in music and poetry although the illustrious M Rousseau has shown that such a thing is possible. An air, then, is the work of two masters: the first (the poet) draws the features of the original in exact detail. The second makes the picture more lifelike by capturing the complexion of the sitter, adding further to the illusion by catching him in some characteristic pose. In short, by dressing up his copy as the model he achieves a striking resemblance. This then is the task of the musician, which he accomplishes by means of melody, harmony and accompaniment.

Concerning melodic expression
Melodic expression derives from two sources: (a) imitation of the kind that only properly relates to the sense of hearing; melody can thus only imitate sounds, their durations and interrelationships. If the composer wishes to imitate some noise or other such as that of a storm or a mill, he must study the natural sound and imitate it to the best of his ability. No rules can be given, however, for this kind of imitation.

161

If the composer wishes to imitate the inflexions of the voice – if, that is, he is trying to compose a truly excellent musical declamation – he must himself know how to declaim. It is the good actor then who will furnish him with the rules for this sort of imitation.

(b) analogy, in which melody produces an aural effect that is analogous to one that is produced upon another organ, and by another cause. Analogy may be practical when imitation is impossible.

If someone persists in playing a slowly moving melody, the notes of which are of equal length and similar pitch, he will eventually put the listener to sleep. In such a case the melody could hardly be said to imitate poppy juice or a third-rate book, but its effect on the ear is similar. If, having put you to sleep, the musician changes his tune to one that is lively and varied, the odds are a thousand to one that you will suddenly awaken, just as if someone had grabbed you by the arms and pulled you to your feet. Can it be said that music imitates such actions? Nature herself is the source of musical expression that is based on analogy. We must search out with all our power the ways in which analogy may be used.

Melody either comprises a single note that is repeated many times – in which case it is merely movement, such as that produced by the beating of a drum – or a number of different notes of equal length in succession, or a number of different notes having different rhythms.

A melody that is composed of slow notes, equal in length and of identical pitch is boring and displeasing.

Increase the speed of these notes and the displeasure will lessen; a tranquil feeling may even take its place, one that is therefore pleasurable.

If the speed is further increased the listener will become increasingly agitated, ultimately to the point of violence; the melody will be fatiguing; it will deaden the senses and renew a feeling of displeasure.

Thus, two kinds of displeasure can be produced by means of simple, unvaried movement, the one producing boredom, the other, boredom coupled with fatigue. Such movement can also produce a pleasurable, or at least a restful feeling. It is clear enough that if these various kinds of movement are sustained for any length of time they will cease to have any effect, for the listener will have become familiar with them. The person who lives near a water mill sleeps and goes about his daily business just as if there were no noise at all within earshot.

If paired groups are substituted for notes of equal length, the first of which is dotted and thus three times the length of the second, a different effect results. If the mood is sad, the rhythms produce a sombre effect; if the speed is moderate the effect is rather grand, whereas if it is more lively the effect is more spirited. This kind of rhythm is not effective when it is taken very fast.

I do not proposed to discuss here the grouping of whole and half notes in succession. This rhythm is only found in a particular kind of metre, namely triple metre. I am only discussing metre in general terms.

A sound that begins pianissimo and steadily increases to a fortissimo similarly makes us agitated; the reverse is true of a diminuendo. When a musician mixes up various rhythms and dynamics he is able, not only to amuse and distract us, but also to bore us, to make us good tempered, gay, angry, furious, tired, stupefied and after that to make us bored again, though now the boredom results not solely from a lack of variety as at first, but also from fatigue.

The different marches and airs that a good drummer can perform will serve to illustrate the point. This is further proved by the music of the savages which predominantly involves percussion having but a single note, but which none the less accompanies all the dancing. Perhaps the best way to determine the true principles of analogical expression would be carefully to study the music of the savages. In the process of embellishing nature we have so covered her with ornament that we have almost stifled her. Let us hasten to her rescue, or we shall be left with nothing more than a gorgeously dressed corpse.

If a diatonic succession of ascending notes is placed in the midst of a series of slow and equal ones, sounding at the same pitch, this melodic feature will give rise to less displeasure than one based upon only one note. Depending on the speed at which it is taken this succession of ascending notes will produce an effect of gaiety, anger, or even fury, provided that it is essentially diatonic. Repeat it too often and too quickly and the effect will be unpleasant and shattering. A succession of ascending notes, then, gives rise to effects that are similar to those produced by movement alone. As this succession of notes can only be effective when it is given rhythmic shape, the conclusion must surely be that it enhances the rhythmic impact.

A diatonic succession of descending notes creates a sadder impression than one that ascends. By altering the lengths of these descending notes in various ways you may produce sombre effects, effects of anger and fury. It is a sure thing that ascending and descending notes produce very different effects.

Of all melodies that move by leaps those that span an ascending major triad must be the most pleasurable and the least disturbing, since all the sounds that follow in succession are contained in the first note. A diatonically moving melody is more disturbing. One that moves downwards, triadically, is less natural and is also sadder. If a melody moves by dissonant rather than consonant steps its effect is more striking. In the ascent it expresses astonishment and distraction; in the descent, gravity, sadness or horror. The upward leap of the diminished fifth is sweet and sad; that of the tritone is harsh and it gives rise to astonishment mixed with anger. Small leaps have less impact than large ones. Upward leaps of the minor and major sixth give rise to altogether different effects. Sharpen the fourth of an upward scale to produce a tritone (C, D, E, F♯, A, G, F, for instance) and, provided that the notes move rapidly, you will feel disturbed and angry. Move downwards a fifth, flattening the second note (C, B♭, A,

G, F, for instance), and you will experience feelings of sadness. Move slowly upwards in semitones and a deep sadness comes over you; go downwards at a similar speed and that sadness will reach its ultimate limits. Speed up the two and the first will arouse fury, the second horror.

Let us call a halt at this point to our discussion of movement and shape in simple melody. Enough has been said to show how the two can by analogy add to the expressive qualities of a work. If I were to say more I would run the risk of losing my way.

Metre, too, is one of the principal sources of melodic expression. Very slowly moving quadruple metre is sad; at a slightly faster speed the effect is merely solemn; a little less slowly still and the effect is grand and majestic; taken at an allegro it becomes stately and proud; faster still and it becomes impetuous, uncontrolled and furious. Triple metre never loses a certain quality of sweetness whatever the speed at which it is taken. Slow triple metre expresses an affecting sadness; less slowly, tenderness; a little more quickly, contentment; faster still, gaiety but never anger, provided that the natural sweetness of the metre is not obscured by the melodic line or by its accompaniment.

6/8 metre is both ternary and binary for it comprises two equal beats each of which is divided into three. In moderate tempi this metre is suited to pastoral subjects. At a faster speed it becomes gay; but whatever one does it never becomes as furious as quadruple metre. 6/8 time is very appropriate for the expression of despair, above all for despair mingled with tenderness. It does not work at extremes of speed.

Before going further it must be said that the poet is often at fault in obliging the musician to choose the wrong metre. When the verbal rhythm is ternary and when at the same time the musical expression calls for quadruple metre the composer finds himself in an embarrassing situation. He commonly chooses the metre that conforms to the verbal rhythm, and he is right to do so, for whilst it is possible to get round the misuse of musical metre it is wholly impossible to compensate for errors of verbal stress.

Major keys are suited to gaiety, solemnity, anger, passion and even to sadness, but not for that sweet and touching sadness that is the province of the minor keys.

Minor keys are soft and tender; they have something about them that is deeply moving; they are able to express the painful emotions but never anger or fury.

What however do so many musicians do? They pervert these natural characteristics. They try to express profound sadness in major keys and violent anger in minor ones. But, people often say to me, they succeed. Indeed they do, just as a woman succeeds in becoming a man by donning a man's clothes.

I would go further than this. I would argue that it is these musical *tours de force* that are the ruination of the art. In what ways can the composer counteract the power of the major mode in a sad and moving air? He can be prodigal with minor dissonances; he can interlace his harmony with minor chords and accompany his melody with flutes, horns and muted strings. In doing so he unseasonably accustoms us to the use of all these artistic resources, ones which can produce the most powerful effects when properly managed, within the major mode, and as a substitute for the more correct minor mode.

This is not all. A melody produces differing effects when it is at different pitches. If a melody expresses joy, the lower the pitch the more its effect will be impaired. The effect could indeed be wholly nullified. Beyond this point it could even be ridiculous on account of the conflict between pitch and melodic line, just as the declaration of tender and passionate love sounds absurd from the lips of an old man.

A soft and tender melody will always be especially effective when it is played on the flute or the violin. The violin will take away less of its sweetness than will an oboe, and an oboe, less than a trumpet. As for the *cor de chasse*, it has I believe considerable potential. Few melodies can however be performed on this instrument in their entirety, and for this reason it is of greatest use as an accompanying instrument.

A warlike march is much more effective with trumpets than oboes, with oboes than violins, with violins than flutes.

Jean Jacques Barthélemy

(b. Cassis, 20 June 1716; d. Paris, 25 April 1795)

From *Entretiens sur l'état de la musique grecque au quatrième siècle* (Paris 1777); text taken from the 1788 *Voyages du jeune Anacharsis*, pp. 245–69

Barthélemy settled in Paris, where he held office in the Académie des inscriptions et belles lettres as a numismatist, and where in 1753 he became keeper of the royal collection of medals, in which capacity he made important visits to Herculaneum and Pompeii. In 1758 he entered the service of M. de Stainville, later Duc de Choiseul, French ambassador to Italy, where he spent three years in archaeological research. In 1788 he published his celebrated *Voyages du jeune Anacharsis en Grèce dans le milieu du quatrième siècle*, an imaginative study of every aspect of ancient Greek civilisation, couched in the form of a travelogue in which the hero, a young Scythian – a descendant of the famous philosopher Anacharsis – goes to Greece for his early education, and then to the republics, the colonies and the islands, returning home in old age to write the book. It became an instant best-seller, and by 1893 had reached forty-two French editions and numerous translations and abridgements.

Barthélemy had already published a section of the *Voyages*, in 1777 – the section on music, entitled *Entretiens sur l'état de la musique grecque au quatrième siècle*; this was warmly received by the *Correspondance littéraire* (Nov. 1777, p. 28), and was published in a splendid edition by Diderot. The young Anacharsis is in conversation with Philotime, a pupil of Plato: their conversation is a condemnation, not only of the later forms of ancient Greek music but also, by implication, modern French music. There are two conversations, the first on purely technical matters, the second (quoted here) on music as a moral agent in society. The main argument is that music – an art of powerful emotional appeal – should be in the service of the state. The book is the theoretical forerunner of Leclerc's practical essay on the need for state control of music, the *Essai sur la propagation de la musique en France* (1796) (see pp. 240–5); it did much to pave the way for the idea of a state academy of music – the Conservatoire, which was founded by the Convention nationale, on 3 August 1795. Without it, too, one wonders whether Jacques Louis David, the 'pageant master of the republic', would have made such lavish use of music in the ceremonial of the Republic.

For further reading:

A. L. Ringer, 'J. J. Barthélemy and musical utopia in revolutionary France', *Journal of the History of Ideas*, vol. 22 (1961), pp. 355–68.
David L. Dowd, *Pageant Master of the Republic, Jacques Louis David* (Lincoln 1948).
J. G. Prod'homme, 'Napoleon, music and musicians', *Musical Quarterly*, VII (1921) p. 584.
Pierre (ed.), *Musique*.

As long as music was intended to preserve the soundness of morals, as long as it was closely associated with poetry and, like poetry, was serious and respectable, it could be expected to produce effects of the kind that have just been mentioned. But now that music has made such great progress it has lost the noble privilege of instructing and improving men.

I have heard this complaint more than once, I replied, but it has more often than not been dismissed as a matter of idle fancy. Some people lament the fact that music has been corrupted; others rejoice in its perfection. Ancient music has its admirers, but far more people are on the side of the new music. In earlier times the rulers looked upon music as an essential part of education;[1] most modern philosophers[2] only regard music as an honest amusement. How is it that an art which has so much power over our souls should be less and less useful as it becomes increasingly pleasurable?

You may perhaps understand this [Philotime said] if you compare ancient music with the music that has been composed in more recent times. It was originally simple. Subsequently it became richer and more varied and it successively enlivened the verse of Hesiod, Homer, Archilocus, Terpander, Simonides and Pindar. It was inseparable from poetry. It borrowed its charm from poetry or rather it lent poetry its own charms, for its whole ambition was to adorn its companion.

The full force of an image or feeling could only be expressed in one way. Since this expression alone could make the voice of nature resound in our hearts, the emotions that it excited were all the more vivid. How is it that unhappy people so easily discover the secret of moving us to pity and piercing our souls? It is because their cries, their accents are the very language of grief. The sole means of expression in vocal music is the quality of intonation that is given to each word, to each verse.[3] Now the ancient poets never lost sight of this fact; they were at once musicians, philosophers and rulers. It was their task to create the kind of melody that was appropriate to their verse. One person alone controlled the three powerful agents that music uses in order to imitate:[4] words, melody and rhythm. The result of this was that all three contributed equally to the unity of expression.

At an early stage in music's development the poets were familiar with the diatonic, chromatic and enharmonic genres. After determining their characteristics they assigned to each the sort of poetry that was most suited to it.[5] They made use of our three principal modes, preferring them almost always for the three kinds of subject that they were required to handle. They had to

[1] 'Timaeus Locrus', p. 104a–b.
[2] Aristotle, *Politics*, bk 8. ch. 3, p. 1338a.
[3] Giuseppe Tartini, *Trattato di musica*, p. 141.
[4] Plato, *Republic*, bk 3, p. 398d; Aristotle, *Poetics*, ch. 1, p. 1447a; Aristides Quintilianus, *De musica*, bk 1 (ed. Meibom, Amsterdam 1652, p. 6).
[5] Plutarch, *De musica*, p. 1142d; *Mémoires de l'académie des inscriptions et belles-lettres*, vol. 15, p. 372.

call a warlike nation to arms, or to recount its exploits: for this they found strength and majesty in the Dorian mode.[6] They had to teach the people about adversity, placing before them great examples of misfortune; their elegies and lamentations owed their penetrating and moving sounds to the Lydian mode.[7] They had also to fill the people with gratitude to the Gods and respect for them; they accordingly reserved the Phrygian mode for sacred canticles.[8]

Most of these songs or *nomes* (rules, or models,[9] that is to say) were divided into several parts and they comprised a story. As the character of the particular deity to whom homage was being paid in the canticle was acknowledged to be immutable, the prescribed rules of song were rarely departed from.[10] Song was strictly subject to the word. It was accompanied by the instrument that was best suited to it, playing in unison with the voice.[11] When dance accompanied the song it was a faithful visual representation of the feelings or images that were conveyed to the ear.

The lyre only had a limited range of notes and the song had little variety. The simplicity of the music assured the supremacy of the poetry. Poetry was a great teacher of courage, prudence and honour, for it was more philosophical and instructive than history, selecting as it did finer models[12] and delineating nobler characters.

At this point Philotime broke off to let me hear some bits of this ancient music, and especially the airs of a poet called Olympus who lived about nine centuries ago. They only then used a limited number of strings,[13] Philotime added, and yet they are the despair of our modern composers.

The art of music progressed. It gathered more modes and rhythms. The lyre acquired more strings but for a long time poets rejected such innovations, or otherwise used them with caution. They always stuck to the spirit of the ancient principles, taking particular care not to stray from the propriety and dignity[14] that characterises this music.

When the fine arts are not limited in their effect to merely sensuous pleasure, two qualities are essential to them: firstly, order; and secondly, beauty. Considerations of propriety and suitability establish an acceptable balance between style and subject. They ensure that each object, each idea and each passion has its colour, tone and movement.[15] They consequently rejected as defective such beauties as are out of context, and they never

---

[6] Plato, *Republic*, bk 3, p. 399a; Plutarch, *De musica*, p. 1136d–f.
[7] Plutarch, *De musica*, p. 1136c.
[8] Plato, *Republic*, bk 3, p. 399b.
[9] *Mémoires de l'académie*, vol. 10, p. 218.
[10] Plutarch, *De musica*, p. 1133b–c; Plato, *Laws*, bk 3, p. 700a–b.
[11] Plutarch, *De musica*, p. 1141b.
[12] Aristotle, *Poetics*, ch. 9, p. 1451b.
[13] Plutarch, *De musica*, p. 1137a–b.
[14] Plutarch, *De musica*, p. 1140f; Athenaeus, *Deipnosophistae*, bk 14, p. 631e.
[15] Dionysius of Halicarnassus, *De compositione verborum*, section 20.

allowed the primary objective to be vitiated by random ornamentation. As dignity is related to exalted ideas and feelings, the poet who bears its stamp in his soul will never stoop to servile imitation.[16] The poet's ideas are high and his words are those of a mediator who speaks with the Gods and who instructs mankind.[17]

The first poets of ancient Greece assiduously observed their double role. Their hymns inspired piety, their poems a desire for glory, their elegies resolution in adversity. Precepts and examples were easily planted in the mind by these songs, which were simple, noble and expressive. The young were accustomed to repeating them from their earliest youth, and it was from these that they learned with pleasure of the love of duty, and from which they took their ideas of true beauty.

It seems to me, I then said to Philotime, that so rigorous a music was hardly able to excite the passions.

You think then, he smilingly replied, that the Greeks were not passionate enough? The nation was proud and sensitive. The risk was that vice and virtue might be pushed to extremes. Its lawgivers also had the profound conviction that music should serve to moderate enthusiasm in the midst of pleasure and on the path to victory. Why, ever since the remotest past has it been customary to sing of the Gods and heroes at feasts, if not to circumvent an excess of wine,[18] which could be all the more disastrous the more a person is inclined by nature towards violence. Why did the Lacedemonian generals station a certain number of flautists alongside the soldiers, and why did the soldiers advance on the enemy to the sound of the flute, rather than to the strident trumpet? Was it not to keep in reserve the impetuous courage of the young Spartans and to ensure that they should not break their ranks?[19]

Small wonder then that even before the development of philosophy the best regulated societies watched so carefully over an unchanging and wholesome music,[20] and that since then the wisest men have been convinced that the passions must be kept in check rather than excited, recognising that under the guidance of philosophy music is one of the finest gifts of the Gods and one of the best institutions of mankind.[21]

Music only serves today to give pleasure. You will have guessed that at the end of its reign it was threatened by imminent corruption, having

---

[16] Plato, *Republic*, bk 3, p. 395c.

[17] Plutarch, *De musica*, p. 1140a–b.

[18] Plutarch, *De musica,* p. 1146f; Athenaeus, *Deipnosophistae,* bk 14, p. 627e.

[19] Thucydides, bk 5, ch. 70; Aulus Gellius, *Attic Nights,* bk 1, ch. 11, pp. 1–5; 17–19, quoting Aristotle; Plutarch, *De cohibenda ira,* p. 458e; Polybius, bk 4, ch. 20, p. 6; Athenaeus, *Deipnosophistae,* bk 12, p. 517a; Athenaeus, *Deipnosophistae,* bk 14, p. 627d.

[20] Plutarch, *De musica,* p. 1146b.

[21] 'Timaeus Locrus', 104a–b; Plato, *Republic,* bk 3, p. 411e; Diotogenes the Pythagorean quoted by Stobaeus, *Anthology,* in the section on 'Politics', item 95.

acquired new riches. Polymnestes, tuning the strings of his lyre at will, introduced chords that were unknown before his time.[22] One or two musicians involved themselves in the composition of wordless airs for the flute;[23] soon afterwards, in the Pythean games only the sounds of instruments were heard.[24] Finally, poets tortured language, melody and rhythm in order to screw themselves up to a mad frenzy, and especially the poets who wrote that forceful, turbulent genre known as the dithyramb.[25] The ancient taste still prevailed, however. Pindar, Pratinas, Lamprus and other celebrated lyricists sustained it during the age of decadence.[26] Pindar flourished at the time of Xerxes's expedition about 120 years ago. He lived long enough to witness the revolution that had been prepared for by his innovatory predecessors and fostered by a spirit of independence, inspired by our Persian conquests. The thing that accelerated it most was the sudden and wild passion for instrumental music and the dithyramb. The first taught us to do without words; the second to stifle them with irrelevant ornament.

Music, till then the servant of poetry, shook off its yoke with the audacity of a rebel slave.[27] Musicians began to think of nothing more than attracting attention to themselves by their innovations. The more they complicated the art the further removed it became from nature.[28] They drew a larger number of sounds from the lyre and cithara. They confused the essential qualities of the genres, modes, voices and instruments. The chants that once had been assigned to particular types of poetry were now used indiscriminately.[29] Unknown consonances and unusual modulations were to be found, together with vocal inflexions that often lacked harmony.[30] The fundamental and precious law of rhythm was openly violated, and several sounds were set to one syllable.[31] Extravagances such as these ought to be as objectionable in music as they are in declamation.

As Anaxilas recently said, in one of his comedies, in the face of such rapid change music, like Libya, brought forth each year some new monster.[32]

The principal authors of change lived in the last century, and are still with us.

[p. 255, para. 2 to p. 258 incl. omitted]

In our society workmen and mercenaries decide the fate of music. They

---

[22] Plutarch, De musica, p. 1141b; Mémoires de l'académie, vol. 15, p. 318.
[23] Plutarch, De musica, pp. 1134d; 1141c–d.
[24] Pausanias, bk 10, ch. 7, p. 4; Mémoires de l'académie, vol. 32, p. 444.
[25] Plato, Laws, bk 3, p. 700d; Scholion on Aristophanes, Clouds, 1.333.
[26] Plutarch, De musica, p. 1142b.
[27] Athenaeus, Deipnosophistae, bk 14, p. 617b–c, quoting Pratinas.
[28] Tartini, Trattato, p. 148.
[29] Plato, Laws, bk 3, p. 700d–e.
[30] Plutarch, De musica, 1141e, quoting Pherecrates.
[31] Aristophanes, Frogs, ll. 1314, 1348, and scholion.
[32] Athenaeus, Deipnosophistae, bk 14, p. 623f.

fill the theatres; they attend the musical competitions and they set themselves up as arbiters of taste. As they look for shocks rather than emotions,
the rougher, the wilder, the more highly coloured the music, the more
intense is their rapture.[33] The philosophers were right when they declared
that the adoption of such innovations undermined the foundations of the
state.[34] Dramatists vainly launched a thousand arrows at the innovators[35]
but as no decrees were issued in support of the ancient music, the
blandishments of its enemy finally won the day. The fates of these two were
identical to those of virtue and pleasure when they came into conflict.

But be frank with me, I said to Philotime, have you not occasionally felt
its general seductiveness?

Often, he replied. I accept that modern music is superior to the old in its
richness and attractiveness, but I would claim that it has no moral objective.
As far as the ancients are concerned I esteem the poet who inspires me with
a love of duty; as for the moderns, I admire the composer who gives me
pleasure.

But surely, I replied with some heat, music should be judged by the
pleasure that it gives![36]

Certainly not, he replied, if that pleasure is harmful or if it supplants
others that are less intense but more useful. You are young and you need
emotional experiences that are strong and frequent.[37] However, as you
would blush to abandon yourself to those emotions that do not conform to
order, it is clear that you have to submit your pleasures and pains to the
judgement of your reason before deciding on the way you conduct yourself.

I believe a principle can be established, namely that an object is not
worthy of our assiduous attention unless, above and beyond the immediate
pleasure that it affords, it embraces some inherent goodness and is truly
useful.[38]

[p. 260, line 25 to p. 261, line 17 omitted]

Let us give practical application to this principle. Imitation, which is the
aim of the arts, affects us in different ways. One such way has already been
described. There can also be another of which the spectator and artist are
often unaware. This transforms the soul, imperceptibly moulding it to a way
of life that is either beneficial or harmful to it.[39] If you have never reflected

---

[33] Aristotle, *Politics*, bk 8, ch. 7, p. 1342a.
[34] Plato, *Republic*, bk 4, p. 424b–c.
[35] Aristophanes, *Clouds*, l.971; Aristophanes, *Frogs*, ll.1309ff and scholia; Athenaeus,
Deipnosophistae, bk 14, p. 617b–c, quoting Pratinas; Plutarch, *De musica*,
pp. 1141d–1142a, quoting Pherecrates.
[36] Plato, *Laws*, bk 2, p. 668a–b.
[37] Plato, *Laws*, bk 2, p. 664e.
[38] Plato, *Laws*, bk 2, p. 667b.
[39] Aristotle, *Politics*, bk 8, ch. 5, p. 1340b.

on the immense power of imitation, just think how two of our senses – sight and hearing – transmit to our souls the impressions that they receive. How easily a child copies the conversation and manners of slaves that are close to him; how readily he adopts their disposition and their servility.[40]

Although painting has nowhere like the same impact as reality I am none the less present at the scenes which are depicted. Most spectators are only concerned with the realism of the representation and the pleasure of a passing sensation. Philosophers often see, however, in the fascination that art holds for us, traces of a hidden poison. To listen to them it seems that our virtues are either so pure or so weak that the slightest breath of contagion will wither and destroy them. Whilst therefore young men may be permitted to gaze at leisure on the pictures of Denys and to return, again and again, to those of Polygnotes they will be discouraged from paying any attention to the pictures of Pauson.[41] Denys paints men as we see them: his imitation is realistic, pleasant to look at, and without either danger or value to morals. Pauson, however, degrades man for he gives ignoble features and actions to the characters he depicts. He has painted man smaller than he is. He has robbed heroism of its brilliance, and virtue of its dignity. Polygnotes, by representing man as greater and more virtuous than in real life, uplifts the mind and feelings to sublime models; he firmly implants in the soul the idea of moral beauty and a love of decency and order.

The impression that music makes is more immediate, profound and durable than that of painting.[42] Its imitations, however, are rarely in tune with our true needs, and are thus rarely instructive. Indeed, what lesson can the flute player teach me, as he counterfeits in the theatre the song of the nightingale,[43] or as in the games he imitates the hiss of the serpent?[44] What can I learn from a performance in which my ear is stunned by a multiplicity of sounds that rapidly build up, one upon another?[45] I have seen Plato ask the meaning of such noise. Whilst most of those in the audience have rapturously applauded the musician for his audacity[46] Plato has taxed him for his ignorance and ostentation – for, on the one hand, his lack of any understanding of true beauty, and on the other for the lack of any ambition apart from that of the vain glory of conquering difficulties.

What effect, moreover, can the words have when they are dragged along behind the music, dismembered and their progress interrupted? They can only attract attention as vocal inflexions and ornaments belonging solely to the melodic line. I refer particularly here to the sort of music that can be

---

[40] Plato, *Republic*, bk 3, p. 395c–d.
[41] Aristotle, *Politics*, bk 8, ch. 5, p. 1340a; Aristotle, *Poetics*, ch. 2, p. 1448a.
[42] Aristotle, *Politics*, bk 8, ch. 3, p. 1340a.
[43] Aristophanes, *Birds*, after l.222.
[44] Strabo, *Geography*, bk 9, ch. 3, p. 10.
[45] Plato, *Laws*, bk 2, p. 669d–e.
[46] Aristotle, *Politics*, bk 8, ch. 6, p. 1341a.

heard in the theatre[47] and at the games, for in several of our religious ceremonies music still preserves something of its ancient character.

Just then a melodious song stole upon our ears. That day there was a festival in honour of Theseus,[48] and several choirs, comprising the most brilliant youth of Athens, had gone to the temple of the hero. They were recalling his victory over the Minotaur, his arrival in the town, and the return of the young Athenians whose swords he had broken.

After listening attentively I said to Philotime, I do not know whether I more admire the poetry, the melody, the rhythmic precision, the interest of the subject itself or the ravishing beauty of the voices themselves,[49] but I feel as though this music fills and elevates my soul.

That, replied Philotime ardently, is because it does not just amuse us by exciting our own petty passions but awakens from the very depths of our hearts man's most honourable feelings, those that are of the greatest use to society: courage, gratitude, respect and patriotism. Music takes on a quality of imposing grandeur, because it is felicitously linked to poetry, rhythm and those many other things that you have just mentioned. Such a quality never loses its effect, and because it particularly appeals to those who are receptive to it, it heightens their self-respect. This is the justification for Plato's teaching. He wished that the arts, the games, the theatre and all external things should furnish us with pictures that would unceasingly fix our gaze on true beauty. The habitual contemplation of beauty would for us become a sort of instinct, and the soul would be constrained to direct its efforts according to the order and harmony which shine in the divine model.[50]

Ah! How far our artists are from achieving this high ideal! Not satisfied with destroying the properties of the various kinds of music, they even violate the most common rules of decorum. The dance, which is already subject to their caprice, has become riotous and impetuous when it ought to be grave and decorous. Into the entr'actes of our tragedies they now insert fragments of poetry and music that have nothing to do with the piece, whilst the choruses have no connection with the action.[51]

I am not arguing that such disorders as these are the result of our depravity. They do none the less sustain and fortify it. Those who watch all this unconcernedly, fail to recognise that the rules are upheld as much by ritual and behaviour as by principle. Customs have their forms as do laws, and a contempt for form gradually destroys the bonds that unite men.

Modern music must none the less be criticised for its sweet indolence and enticing sonority, which enrapture the multitude, and for its expression, which, lacking a determined object, is always interpreted in terms of the

---

[47] Plutarch, *De musica*, p. 1136b.
[48] Plutarch, *Life of Theseus*, ch. 36, pp. 2–3.
[49] Xenophon, *Memorabilia*, bk 3, ch. 3, p. 13.
[50] Plato, *Republic*, bk 3, p. 401d.
[51] Aristotle, *Poetics*, ch. 18, p. 1456a.

dominant passion. Music's effect is more and more to sap the vitality of a nation, whose listless spirits lack character and can only be distinguished, one from another, by their differing degrees of ineffectualness.

Well then, I said to Philotime, since ancient music has such overwhelming advantages, and since modern music has so much charm, why have not the two been combined?

I know a musician named Telesias, he replied, who set out to do this several years ago.[52] In his youth he was brought up on the austere beauties of Pindar and certain other lyric poets. Later he was caught up with the works of Philoxenus, Timotheus and the other modern poets, and he wished to reconcile these different styles. In spite of his efforts he has always fallen back on the older masters, and he has gathered no other fruit from his vigils than the displeasure of both ancients and moderns.

No, music will never rise again after its fall. We would have to change our ideas and regain our virtues. Now it is much more difficult to reform a nation than to police it. We no longer have morals, he added, so we will have pleasures. Ancient music suited the Athenians who were conquerors of Marathon; the new befits the Athenians who have been vanquished at the river Aegos.[53]

I have only one more question to put to you, I said: why do you teach your pupils such a baleful art? What is the good of doing so?

What is the good? he exclaimed, laughing. It is a toy for children of all ages, to stop them breaking up the furniture.[54] It occupies the minds of those whose idleness would be fearful in such a society as ours. It amuses those who are dangerous, if only on account of the boredom that they carry around with them and because they do not know what to do with their lives.

Being destined to occupy high office in the Republic Lysis learns music because he has to ensure that he will be able to give advice on the pieces that are to be publicly performed, both in the theatre and at the musical competitions. He will familiarise himself with all kinds of harmony and he will only give his approval to those that may influence morals.[55] For decadent as it is, music can still teach us useful lessons.[56] I shall never weary my pupils with those painful procedures, those difficult melodies that we were once happy to admire in the theatre and which today are so laboriously taught to the children.[57] I will allow him the use of musical instruments on condition that he never becomes as skilled in them as a professional. It is my wish that a specially chosen music should agreeably occupy such leisure as he has, that music should refresh him after work,

---

[52] Plutarch, *De musica*, p. 1142b.
[53] The Thracian river near which Lysander destroyed the Athenian fleet at the end of the Peloponnesian war, 405 B.C. (eds.)
[54] Aristotle, *Politics*, bk 8, ch. 6, p. 1340b.
[55] Aristotle, *Politics*, bk 8, ch. 7, p. 1342a.
[56] Aristotle, *Politics*, bk 8, ch. 6, p. 1340b.
[57] Aristotle, *Politics*, bk 8, ch. 6, p. 1341a.

rather than give him additional labour, and that it should calm him down if he is too emotional.[58] I wish, in short, that he would constantly have this maxim in mind: that music calls him to pleasure and philosophy to virtue, and that it is by means of pleasure and virtue that nature calls us to happiness.[59]

[58] Aristotle, *Politics*, bk 8, ch. 7, pp. 1341b–1342a.
[59] Aristotle, *Politics*, bk 8, ch. 5, p. 1339b.

Johann Nicolaus Forkel

(b. Meeder, Saxe-Coburg, 22 Feb. 1749, d. Göttingen, 20 Mar. 1818)

From: *Ueber die Theorie der Musik, insofern sie Liebhabern und Kennern der Kunst notwendig und nützlich ist* (Göttingen 1777), pp. 4–7

Forkel is probably best known as the first biographer of Johann Sebastian Bach. Self-taught as a musician, he read law at Göttingen, but while he was an undergraduate, he became organist at the university church and in 1778 Director of Music to the University. He took a doctorate in philosophy in 1780 and remained at Göttingen until his death.

Ueber die Theorie der Musik, from which this passage is taken, is the first of Forkel's works on music. It is, in fact, more a prospectus than a theory book, saying what ought to be taught in a series of university lectures on music rather than setting out a corpus of musical theory. A man of wide learning and interests, he was also somewhat of a pessimist regarding the development of music since the death of his idol J. S. Bach. It is clear from the philosophical outlook in *Ueber die Theorie der Musik* that he was a true enlightenment figure, strongly influenced in his ideas by Locke. Forkel has been described, with some justification, as the founder of modern musicology. He was certainly one of the earliest writers to draw the attention of the Germans to the richness of their musical past.

Marcus Manilius, to whom Forkel refers, lived in the first century A.D., and was the author of *De Astronomia*, a poem in five books that deals with the nature and movement of the stars and with the design of the cosmos. Sebastian Cesar de Menezes (d. 1672) was sometime Bishop of Coimbra, Archbishop of Lisbon and Portuguese Inquisitor General.

If music is a language of the passions and emotions, if not a single person's emotions exactly coincide with those of another, would it not then follow that, in default of suitable precepts and rules deduced from nature and from experience, art would have to be left to the caprice and wilfulness of each individual? How conflicting would the demands then be that the artist would have to fulfil! Pope tells us that our intellects and emotions are like our watches; they do not keep exact time with one another, but all differ, though everyone thinks that his own watch keeps the best time: "Tis with our judgements as our watches, none go just alike, yet each believes his own.'[1] The novice bases his needs as much on the extent of his experience as does the expert: he insists that art should accommodate itself to his crude and untested emotions just as does the more refined connoisseur and man of taste and judgement. Which path should the perplexed artist then choose? Where is the artist to find order, truth, exactness, beauty and those many

[1] Pope's *Essay on Criticism* (London 1711).

other potent artistic charms if everyone has an equal right to prescribe in such various and contradictory ways? Dare a critic examine and assess the value of a work of art? Dare he judge it? Will the work not suit someone's taste, however bad it may be?[2] Would this not conclusively prove the assertion of an English writer earlier in the century 'that a composer should fit his Music to the genius of the people, and consider that the delicacy of hearing, and taste of harmony has been formed upon those sounds which every country abounds with: In short, that music is of a relative nature, and what is harmony to one ear, may be dissonance to another'.[3]

Every man is born with the basic capacity to speak, but only a few men are orators. Similarly, almost everybody can sing, without claiming to reach a professional standard. Anyone who gives the matter careful thought will thus realise that the poet's and orator's entire art is based on the restricted range of sounds that a culture produces just as much as is the musician's. Nobody, however, would dream of inferring the basic principles of oratory or poetry from such limited materials. The simplest fundamentals of all the arts and sciences, or at any rate the basic material for them, are to be found there, but if we simply adopted such material as we found it, what would become of art and science? They would resemble the human mind in its childhood state – just as the mind is a blank sheet on which experience imprints concepts and images, so the arts and sciences as nature reveals them to us are no more than raw material that artists must mould to the design they have in mind so as to give it the shape of art. In other words, they must impose order and create beauty: 'Ars a natura materiem, ab arte formam natura mutuatur' (Art derives its material from nature, nature its form from art).[4]

So if these resources with which nature provides us – this raw, untreated material – are to serve our spirit's needs, and provide it with adequate sustenance, they must, like that spirit itself, be shaped to achieve certain ends, and gradually brought to greater beauty and perfection. They must be freed from their imperfect childhood state, first of all in order to develop simple, individual characteristics of beauty and then more varied, complex ones. But what principles should underlie this process? On what basic premises should these principles rest?

The manner in which the human mind acquires sure knowledge in most other arts and sciences may be the surest guide here. Attentive study of the nature of the heart and the sense of beauty, truth and sublimity in art and learning alike leads to the inference of rules and precepts that take us some way on the path to perfection. In music similarly, attention must be given to the nature of the emotions and the feeling for the beautiful. These will

---

[2] '. . . Ainsi qu'en sots Auteurs,
Notre siècle est fertile en sots Admirateurs.' Boileau, *l'Art poetiqué* (Paris 1674) I, 225–6.

[3] Spectator, no. 29, p. 113.

[4] Seb. Caesar de Menezes.

gradually provide a yardstick by which we may infer and establish from repeated experience the precepts and principles that apply to it: 'Per varios usus artem experientia fecit, Exemplo monstrare viam' (Through various practical applications experience created art, obviously to point out a way).[5] Constant study of an object reveals more than any number of superficial observations: The face of nature may be read; but it is less obvious than it is claimed to be by those say who claim that they can read it. We must proceed with caution – I had almost said with timidity.[6] Such constant attention to an object, then, such unceasing investigation and observation, develops mastery. The master spirit achieves maturity by dint of industry and unremitting study of nature's secrets, then leaves as his legacy the means by which he reached his goal and provides laws that show the way which others may follow. In this way, they are enabled in like manner to search out nature's hidden depth for the magic beauties of art. Genius does not invent these laws; it merely discovers them. The man of genius does not distance himself from nature; what he does is penetrate more deeply into her mysteries, enticing her more recondite secrets from her and revealing them to others. In short, he adapts and orders the gifts that nature has so prodigally dispensed; he teaches the human spirit to use this prodigality of material more efficiently and to apply it to specific aims.

---

[5] Manilius, *De Astronomia*, bk. 1.
[6] Burke, *Essay on the Sublime*, Preface.

Bernard Germain Étienne de la Ville sur Illon, Comte de la Cépède

(b. Agen, 26 Dec. 1756; d. Epinay, 6 Oct. 1825)

From: *La poétique de la musique*, 2 vols. (Paris 1785) pp. 71–190.

La Cépède developed an early interest in music and natural sciences under the tutelage of the Bishop of Agen. When at work on his first opera he wrote to Gluck for advice, and later, in 1776, he was the composer's guest at a performance of *Alceste*, at the Paris Opéra. He subsequently studied with Gossec. It is clear that *La poétique* greatly influenced Berlioz's teacher, Le Sueur.[1] It was enthusiastically though not uncritically reviewed in the *Correspondance littéraire* (May 1785, p. 140):

> the two volumes aim to demonstrate – with great spirit and in great detail, in places with a profusion of metaphor and imagery and over-emphasis – that the principles that guide poetic genius are the same as those that guide musical genius. The idea is without doubt as true as it is new and useful. The author has extensively developed it in the three main areas of theatrical music, church music and concert music. When however the author comes to discuss the particular ways in which music may produce those effects that by rights the poet may expect of the composer, he is too vague and general. The clearest part of the work deals with the way in which Gluck himself approaches the task of composing an opera . . . possibly this is the most original part of the work, too.

The two volumes divide into four 'books'; the first (from which the following extract comes) treats of music's origins and effects, and the relationship between nature and music; the second deals with theatre music (some 580 pages); the third with church music (sixteen pages); and the fourth with all forms of concert music, both vocal and instrumental (vocal music, seven pages; symphonies and concertos, twelve; instrumental chamber music, ten).

The work is important, not only for its influence on Le Sueur and Berlioz, but because it is one of the earlier attempts to relate aesthetic theory to practical composition: the theory of symmetry, discussed here, relates to earlier discussion of unity, and the handling of symmetry and asymmetry to 'nature', to the beautiful and to the sublime. La Cépède's interest in the dramatic function of the orchestra doubtless reflects the influence of Gluck.[2] Amongst those who commended *La poétique* were Sacchini and Frederick the Great.

---

[1] Ora F. Saloman, 'La Cépède's La poétique de la musique and Le Sueur', *Acta Musicologica*, vol. 47 (1975), pp. 144ff.

[2] It will be evident, however, from a study of Du Bos, pp. 17–22, and Rousseau, pp. 89–105, above, that Saloman, 'La Cépède's La poétique', overstates the case in arguing that the writings of La Cépède and Le Sueur represent 'an entirely different . . . response to the challenge posed by the customary defence of *le chant*'.

179

A phrase in the art with which we are dealing is the smallest section of a song or a piece of music that is self-sufficient – one that cannot be subdivided or heard in part without leaving something to be desired. It makes sense, of itself, and it ends with a perfect consonance in its home key. A piece of music – no matter what it is – must contain phrases. To put this rather better, whatever the manner in which the music is composed, it has to be built up out of a succession of phrases, following one after the other. Such music can only properly be described as phrased (*phrasé*) however when the constituent phrases assume a specific form: when they observe a determined order, when they have a certain regularity and proportion and when they are linked together according to rule.

A melodic harmonic fragment can be very beautiful without being phrased, as will subsequently be shown. A piece that is designed to touch and please will only produce all the effects of which it is capable when it has the merit of being phrased, as well as the other merits that are appropriate to it. Such a piece is termed an 'air'. This is the word for a composition of outstanding excellence. This is why an air for one or more voices always follows after a series of monologues and scenes of increasingly violent passion, when that passion has managed to raise itself imperceptibly above those other passions that disturbed and fought against it so that finally it gains sole command, and fearlessly exercises its formidable power.

But what are those rules that relate to the proportion of phrases, rules that the musician must observe? This is a subject on which there is less information than there ought to be. Let us draw our rules from the two sources of these same proportions.

The proportion of a phrase is none other than its relative grandeur or extensiveness, *vis-à-vis* other phrases. The extent of a phrase can only be gauged by the number of beats that it contains: by its duration, that is to say, in performance. The number of notes that a phrase contains, and their quality and pitch appertain to quite different matters.

There are two reasons for seeking a precise relationship between the lengths of musical phrases. The first is the desire to combine the charms of song (*chanson*) with the power of serious music, the second a wish to obey the law of symmetry which is the sovereign ruler of taste. The law of symmetry holds greater sway in all the arts than has generally been recognised; it governs almost every aspect of beauty and is the source of great charm. The power of symmetry is all the greater because she is the cherished daughter of nature; symmetry adorns practically all her productions.

As song only came into being as the partner of dance and its accompaniment, it follows that the relationship between the phrases of a musical composition is regulated by dance and by symmetry. Every piece of music that is intended to accompany the dance must be divided into small and equal divisions. Following from this, though every piece of music may not have been constructed of very short phrases of equal length, at least the phrases must have been composed in such a way that the ear can easily divide them up, whether by taking the phrases separately, or by thinking of them as linked.

Symmetry, in turn, requires that the corresponding sections of a composition shall have the same structure and the same number of components; it is essential at least that the music is composed in such a way that the ear can easily connect and divide phrases and thus discover parallel arrangements and groupings of sections. These goals have only been attained – as those who have given thought to the matter will clearly see – when the length of phrase has been based on the number two and its multiples. It is agreed therefore that all phrases must be constructed of two, four, eight or sixteen measures, and so on. The ear is easily able then to divide the pieces into equal phrases of four or two measures, or to build four bar phrases from successions of two, on the assumption that the ear wishes to be guided by the laws of song or of symmetry.

This is the rule that the greatest masters everywhere have observed. Only in special circumstances (about which more will shortly be said) have they disregarded it in short sections of their works. The simplicity or grandeur of the subject and the size of the building in which the music is to be performed will determine a preference for phrases of sixteen, eight or two bars – and so on. Pleasant, small-scale subjects that are to be studied closely require detailed work and delicate brush strokes, whilst large canvases that are to be viewed from a distance call for bold brush strokes and grand gestures. Similarly, musical compositions that are only to be performed in small rooms, compositions that are miniature paintings and which are only intended to charm the ears of those who perform them, such pieces call for short phrases – those, that is, of two and eight measures. Longer, though not colossal phrases will be used in such large-scale works as are designed to display the charms of melody and harmony in vast theatres, or to voice the praises of the Eternal One beneath the lofty vaults of immense temples.

Despite everything that has been said, musicians who wish to introduce greater variety into their compositions may scatter phrases here and there that are built on other models than those that have already been discussed: phrases of five, seven, and nine measures, for instance. These should only be used sparingly however, and this kind of freedom is only permissible when the new phrases display the finest harmony and the most pleasing or touching melody. The precaution should be taken moreover of placing two or four of these irregular phrases in succession. In hearing two or four five-bar phrases in succession, then, a listener could deceive himself into hearing five of two, or four.

It is essential to note that these rules of proportion may easily be dispensed with if they would cause the music to flag, or if the music is required to be no more than a shadowy background or a perfunctory transition to which, consequently, hardly any attention is paid. The composer will be exempt from these rules, too, when he is carried away by the intermittent and volatile passions that he is striving to paint. Under such circumstances, will not perfection merely result in frigidity?

It is not the intention here to trace the path that leads to genius. It is a difficult one to follow, and nature alone must be the guide. The path is interrupted by so many precipitous gaps that can only be crossed on the wings of feeling, and there are so many false turnings, that only a happy instinct can determine the correct way. We can only attempt then to remove some of the obstacles that might hinder genius and feeling.

Let us first simply consider the passions in general terms before we discuss how to depict them. They are the affections that take the soul out of its natural state, those feelings that move it, gladden or sadden it, inflame it, and so on. Each of these is a feeling. When a feeling lasts for a certain length of time, or rather when several feelings succeed each other practically without interruption, a passion is kindled. How is it represented? Just as one of those feelings would be depicted, of which it is composed.

But how to depict a feeling? Let us first remind ourselves of what has been said about music's effects, for some preliminary ideas have already been proposed as to how the feelings may be expressed. Let us turn first of all to melody (*le chant*). In nature, is not a particular cry or sound the expression of a feeling? This cry or sound will be employed then in the melody; or rather, the melody will be formed out of phrases that most closely and continuously reflect the sound.

If a melody is composed in this way it is bound to express the feeling that is sought; it will awaken the idea of the feeling and even stir up its fires within the listener's soul. It will move the listener in just the way that he would be affected and torn apart by the cries and sobs of someone who wept bitterly.

But the musician is not properly fulfilling his role if he is simply content to paint in his melody the feeling that he strives to express. For the melody must always please the soul, and never shock. The musician must be skilled enough to capture all the signs of the feeling, all the accents that are part of the affection, all the phrases that encompass the accents and which bear a resemblance to them. Yet when these passions are too powerful or too heated, when they can only be expressed by frenetic shrieks, these cries must surely be concealed in some way beneath a veil of pleasing melody, melody that is sufficiently regular in its construction, which embraces intervals that are easy enough to grasp, and which has all the qualities that are needed to please. This veil must none the less be transparent enough to reveal that expression, the colours of which must be softened but never obliterated.

In order to paint the feelings the musician will also make use of accompaniments against which to set his melodies. As these accompaniments will always form a kind of melody, may they not reproduce cries and sounds that are proper to the feeling, may they not contain phrases that represent these cries and sounds? The extent to which phrases and sounds, both in the melody and its accompaniment, are disguised by pleasing qualities will depend on the extent to which a literal and faithful portrayal of feeling would be distasteful, marring the pleasure that ought to be got from every theatrical representation.

The musician will also use the accompaniments to paint those details that are incidental to the feeling: violent gestures, tears, sobs, palpitations of the heart, abrupt movements. The rate at which the music moves will also have a bearing on the fidelity of the expression, since it parallels to a greater or lesser degree the movement of the passions within us.

The mode that the musician selects, too, will surely contribute to the fidelity of the picture. We have already discovered what a musical mode is, and we have seen that the differences between modes depend on the pitch at which the mode occurs. The modes vary in another way, however, and this we must examine now.

Not only may the fundamental note of the scale be placed now higher, now lower, but the note may stand at the head either of a major or a minor scale. Let us see what distinguishes them.

The scale that we have adopted is constructed of notes that spring from the natural resonance of sounding bodies. The scale is designed to make use of and to present the notes as follows: in its fundamental form its first two intervals are a major third and a minor third. For the sake of musical variety and in order to tap new sources of musical expression the order of the thirds was reversed, the minor third coming first in the scale. To do this the second [*sic*] note of this fundamental scale was lowered by a semitone. There resulted from this a new scale, the remaining intervals of which were virtually identical to those of the natural scale. It was called the minor scale. Like the major scale, it was played at various pitches, and like the major scale it owed its existence to the fundamental natural scale.

When the musician seeks to portray a feeling in which there is a trace of sadness he will do well, if everything else is equal, to give preference to the minor mode. He will certainly be well advised never, or hardly ever, to use it for feelings of gaiety or any affection that has no element of sadness in it.

On its own, the minor mode very faithfully portrays sadness and for this reason it easily evokes feelings of sadness. Here is the reason why this is so. When the soul listens to the minor mode it is never satisfied, nor can it ever be. It is always wishing for something, and even the most final ending of a piece always leaves something to be desired. Every musician will have observed this fact. Let us try to understand why this is so.

The ear is only fully satisfied when it is presented with a piece of music that is constructed of perfect consonances similar to those that nature herself produces. All other consonances are only conceived and used to throw into relief the natural and fundamental consonances. The soul is unsettled at the sound of these others, or if at times it does take great pleasure in contrived consonances, this is only because it feels it will soon get back to pure, perfect and natural consonances, that the cause of its anxiety will soon be removed, that it has only been deprived of the things it loves in order to lay hold of them soon again, that in doing so it will find them more beautiful and touching still, and that only for a few moments was it being led astray, from surprise to surprise. Without being assured of a return to natural consonance the soul will never cease to torment itself. It will find no pleasure other than that which is afforded by a trace of pain; it is the pleasure of one who suffers a gentle melancholy. Now the major mode is the only one in which perfect, natural consonance is to be heard. The most that the minor mode can offer is a somewhat impaired consonance, because of the nature of its scale. In the minor mode melody and harmony can only be a source of inner pain. The ear will never find true and perfect repose. The soul cannot but be somewhat unsettled as it listens. It must always long for something; it can never enjoy pure pleasure and must continuously give itself up to melancholy. The minor mode must always inspire and paint sadness then; it must always throw a kind of mourning veil over the object that it portrays.

Karl Philipp Moritz

(b. Hamelin, 15 Sept. 1757; d. Berlin, 26 June 1793)

From: 'Versuch einer Vereinigung aller schönen Künste und Wissenschaften unter dem Begriff des in sich selbst Vollendeten', from the *Berlinische Monatsschrift*, vol. 5 (Berlin 1785), pp. 225–30

Moritz was a man of wide experience. He was apprenticed to a hatmaker, afterwards becoming first an actor and then a schoolmaster under the educational reformer Basedow. He was promoted to the post of assistant headmaster of the Greyfriars Gymnasium in Berlin and then to a professorship at the Köllnisches Gymnasium there. Active as a journalist and writer, he produced novels and plays. In 1786, he gave up his teaching post to visit Italy, where he met Goethe, who later invited him to Weimar. From 1789 till his death, Moritz was a professor at the Akademie der Künste in Berlin.

His most important theoretical writing is probably *Ueber die bildende Nachahmung des Schönen* (Brunswick 1788), in which he claims that true imitation in art is neither a copy nor a parody, but a penetration to the essence of the object imitated, a penetration which the artist achieves by a process of empathy. In imitating an object, the artist 'seeks to compete with it. Its image simply raises one's sights above oneself.' Imitation, he contends, acquires its value when the imitation is of noble moral qualities rather than surface features. All beauty, however, is a microcosmic reflection of nature's macrocosmic beauty; the contemplation of beauty stimulates the imitation of nature:

> the man who is filled with the sense of nature's creative power, and who is aware of the *extent* of the beautiful, is not content merely to contemplate her; he must imitate her, he must strive to follow her, to observe her in her secret workshop and with heart aflame, to shape and create, like her (p. 49).

True appreciation of beauty then, leads to action, to an attempt to discern the inner relationship between the 'parts' of the model, and to make them visible or audible. To appreciate beauty, in nature as in art, creative imagination (*Bildungskraft*) and sensitivity (*Empfindungsfähigkeit*) are needed. The appreciation of beauty is an activity that transcends the intellect because it includes not only the capacity to think but also to feel and to give shape to things. But, wherever possible, the creative genius must 'himself comprehend all the latent proportions of that grand harmony which so transcends in scale his own individuality' (p. 37). This theme, in which the individual is subsumed in the whole, runs strongly throughout the essay. Moritz had however defended what he understood by the principle of imitation in art, some three years before this essay was published, in a letter addressed publicly to Felix Mendelssohn-Bartholdy's grandfather (see p. 187); it is from this letter that our quotation is taken.

Mendelssohn himself was a significant thinker in the tradition of Leibniz. The kind of opinion against which Moritz was reacting may perhaps best be demonstrated by the following quotation from Mendelssohn's essay *On Emotions*, which appears in part 1 of his *Philosophical Writings* (1771; reprinted in his *Werke*, Stuttgart 1971, vol. 1, p. 246):

> My motto is, *select, experience, reflect* and *enjoy*: from the objects that surround you choose those that contribute to your welfare. *Experience* them; become familiar with cognitive concepts and judgements of their nature. Reflect on them. Form a clear idea of their constituent parts and measure their relationships to each other and to the whole. And then, *enjoy*; direct your attention to the object itself. Avoid considering the nature of individual parts at this juncture. Allow your soul's faculties free rein. By considering the whole the parts will lose their bright hues, but they will leave behind traces that illuminate the concept of the whole, thereby providing greater intensity to the pleasure derived from it.

What Mendelssohn thought of music can be inferred from another passage in the same essay (p. 280) in which he refers to music as 'divine', combining 'all kinds of satisfaction . . . a sweet amalgam of perfection, sensuous pleasure and beauty.'

To Moses Mendelssohn, Esq.

The principle of the imitation of nature has been rejected as the basic objective of the fine arts and sciences, and subordinated to that of pleasure, which has replaced it as the primary, basic law of the fine arts. The sole aim of the fine arts, it is claimed, is really the provision of pleasure, just as that of the mechanical arts is solely utility. But if we derive pleasure from what is beautiful as well as from what is useful, how do we differentiate between them?

In the case of useful objects, my pleasure stems far more from the idea of the comfort or convenience that they afford than from the objects themselves. I turn myself, as it were, into the focal point to which all parts of the object relate. That is to say, I regard the object simply as a means and myself as its end, in so far as the object contributes to my own fulfilment. So a merely useful object is not complete or perfect in itself; it only becomes so if it achieves the end I have for it or it contributes to my fulfilment.

When, however, I contemplate a beautiful object, I deflect the aim from myself back on to the object itself. I consider it as something that fulfils not me, but *itself*. It thus constitutes an entity in itself, affording me pleasure *on its own account*. I consider, not the beautiful object in relation to me, but rather myself in relation to the beautiful object. Now since I enjoy a beautiful object more on its own account and a useful one only on my account, the beautiful affords me a higher and less self-centred pleasure than the merely useful. Pleasure taken in what is useful is coarser and lower; that taken in what is beautiful is finer and rarer. The former we enjoy to some degree as animals do; the latter raises us above them.

Since a useful object is not so much an end in itself but the means to an end extrinsic to itself, the fulfilment of which is enhanced by the object, then anyone who wishes to create something useful must have an extrinsic aim constantly before him. And as long as the work achieves its extrinsic aim, it may take any conceivable shape: its shape does not matter as long as it is a useful object. If a watch tells the time accurately, or a knife cuts keenly, I have no interest in whether the watch case or knife handle are exquisitely made, nor whether the knife blade or the watch mechanism are beautiful. The purpose of the watch or the knife is an extrinisic one, centred on the person whose convenience the object serves. Watch and knife are not complete in themselves; they have no real value other than that which arises from their actual or potential extrinsic function. Only when considered in conjunction with their function and as an entity that includes that function do they afford pleasure; divorced from that function, they are a matter of total indifference. I contemplate the watch and the knife with pleasure only in so far as I can use them and I do not need them just for purposes of contemplation.

The opposite is the case with the beautiful. This has no extrinsic purpose. It is not there to fulfil anything else, but it exists on account of its own perfection. We do not contemplate it to discover what use we may make of it; we use it only to the extent that we can contemplate it. It is not so much we who need a beautiful object for the pleasure that we derive from it as the beautiful object that needs us, so that it may be appreciated. We can perfectly well exist without contemplating works of fine art, but the latter can hardly exist independently of our contemplation. So the more we do without them, the more, as it were, we consider them for their own sake, in order to provide them for the first time with a real rounded existence of their own when we contemplate them. For our increasing recognition of the beauty of a work of fine art increases its actual beauty, as it were, investing it with greater and greater value. Hence the impatience with which we desire a beautiful thing once we have recognised that it is so; the more universally its beauty is recognised and admired, the more value it acquires in our eyes. Hence our displeasure when a theatre auditorium is empty, however good the performance. If we took pleasure in the beautiful on our own account rather than for the sake of the beautiful object, what would it matter if its beauty were acknowledged by nobody apart from ourselves? We make use of and enthuse over something beautiful so as to win over admirers for it whenever we encounter it – indeed, we feel a kind of pity when contemplating a work of art that has been ground into the dust and regarded with indifference by passers-by. Even that sweet astonishment, that *pleasurable self-oblivion* that we feel when contemplating a work of art is an indication that our pleasure is something that absorbs us completely. While a beautiful object attracts our complete attention, it draws us for a time out of ourselves, so that we lose ourselves in it. It is precisely this self-forgetting which constitutes that supreme degree of disinterested pleasure which beauty affords us. At such a moment we sacrifice our circumscribed individual existence for a kind of higher existence. Pleasure in the beautiful must thus more and more resemble unselfish *love* if it is to be genuine.

Sir Joshua Reynolds

(b. Plympton-Earl's, Devon, 16 July 1723; d. London, 23 Feb. 1792)

From: *Discourse* XIII; delivered to the students of the Royal Academy, on the distribution of prizes, 11 Dec. 1786, in *The Literary Works of Sir Joshua Reynolds* (London 1835), vol. 2, pp. 65–8

Reynolds, the first president of the Royal Academy, had occasion to give fifteen such discourses during his term as president. They had a wide circulation and were constantly reprinted. William Crotch referred to them a number of times during his Oxford and London lectures (see p. 427). The subjects that Reynolds treated, whilst centering on painting, ranged widely over general questions of aesthetics and the arts. We may be sure that they were the fruit of much preliminary discussion between the distinguished members of his Literary Club (a club which he founded in 1764, as he remarked, to give Dr Johnson unlimited opportunities for talking). On this particular occasion Sir Joshua enlarged upon the idea that art is 'not merely imitation, but under the direction of the imagination', and that in many ways it 'departs from nature'.

It is the lowest style only of arts, whether of painting, poetry or music, that may be said in the vulgar sense to be naturally pleasing. The higher efforts of those arts, we know by experience do not affect minds wholly uncultivated. This refined taste is the consequence of education and habit; we are born only with a capacity of entertaining this refinement, as we are born with a disposition to receive and obey all the rules and regulations of society; and so far it may be said to be natural to us, and no further.

What has been said, may show the artist how necessary it is when he looks about him for the advice and criticism of his friends, to make some distinction of the character, taste, experience and observation in this art, of those from whom it is received. An ignorant uneducated man may, like Apelles's critic, be a competent judge of the truth of the representation of a sandal; or to go somewhat higher, like Molière's old woman, may decide upon what is nature, in regard to comic humour; but a critic in the higher style of art ought to possess the same refined taste which directed the artist in his work.

To illustrate this principle by a comparison with other arts, I shall now produce some instances to show that they, as well as our own art, renounce the narrow idea of nature and the narrow theories derived from that mistaken principle, and apply to that reason only which informs us not what imitation is, a natural representation of a given object, but what is natural for the imagination to be delighted with. And perhaps there is no better way of acquiring this knowledge than by this kind of analogy: each art will corroborate and mutually reflect the truth on the other. Such a kind of juxtaposition may likewise have this use, that whilst the artist is amusing himself in the contemplation of other arts, he may habitually transfer the principles of those arts to that which he professes; which ought to be always present to his mind, and to which every thing is to be referred.

So far is art from being derived from or having any immediate intercourse with particular nature as its model, that there are many arts that set out with a professed deviation from it.

This is certainly not so exactly true in regard to painting and sculpture. Our elements are laid in gross common nature, an exact imitation of what is before us: but when we advance to the higher state, we consider this power of imitation, though first in the order of acquisition, as by no means the highest in the scale of perfection.

Poetry addresses itself to the same faculties and the same dispositions as painting, though by different means. The object of both is to accommodate itself to all the natural propensities and inclinations of the mind. The very existence of poetry depends on the licence it assumes of deviating from actual nature in order to gratify natural propensities by other means which are found by experience full as capable of affording such gratification. It sets out with a language in the highest degree artificial, a construction of measured words, such as never is, nor ever was, used by man. Let this measure be what it may, whether hexameter or any other metre used in Latin or Greek – or rhyme, or blank verse varied with pauses and accents, in modern languages – they are all equally removed from nature, and equally a violation of common speech. When this artificial mode has been established as the vehicle of sentiment, there is another principle in the human mind, to which the work must be referred, which still renders it more artificial, carries it still further from common nature, and deviates only to render it more perfect. That principle is the sense of congruity, coherence, and consistency, which is a real existing principle in man; and it must be gratified. Therefore, having once adopted a style and a measure not found in common discourse, it is required that the sentiments also should be in the same proportion elevated above common nature, from the necessity of there being an agreement of the parts among themselves, that one uniform whole may be produced.

To correspond, therefore, with this general system of deviation from nature, the manner in which poetry is offered to the ear, the tone in which it is recited, should be as far removed from the tone of conversation, as the words of which that poetry is composed. This naturally suggests the idea of modulating the voice by art, which I suppose may be considered as accomplished to the highest degree of excellence in the recitative of the Italian opera; as we may conjecture it was in the chorus that attended the ancient drama. And though the most violent passions, the highest distress, even death itself, are expressed in singing or recitative, I would not admit as sound criticism the condemnation of such exhibitions on account of their being unnatural.

If it is natural for our senses and our imaginations to be delighted with singing, with instrumental music, with poetry and with graceful action, taken separately (none of them being in the vulgar sense natural, even in that separate state); it is conformable to experience, and therefore agreeable to reason as connected and referred to experience, that we should also be delighted with this union of music, poetry and graceful action, joined to every circumstance of pomp and magnificence calculated to strike the senses of the spectator. Shall reason stand in the way and tell us that we ought not to like what we know we do like, and prevent us from feeling the full effect of this complicated exertion of art? This is what I would understand by poets and painters being allowed to dare everything; for what can be more daring than accomplishing the purpose and end of art by a complication of means, none of which have their archetypes in actual nature?

So far, therefore, is servile imitation from being necessary, that whatever is familiar, or in any way reminds us of what we see and hear every day, perhaps does not belong to the higher provinces of art, either in poetry or painting.

Charles Burney

(b. Shrewsbury, 7 Apr. 1726; d. Chelsea, London, 12 Apr. 1814)

From: *A General History of Music*, vol. 3 (London 1789); the prefatory 'Essay on Musical Criticism'

Burney showed considerable musical talent at an early age. He was articled at the age of eighteen to Thomas Arne in London, where he gained much professional experience in the London theatres and orchestras. Ill health forced him in 1751 to retire to King's Lynn where he remained for some nine years as organist. Back in London he rapidly established a position as a fashionable teacher. His admiration for French culture led him to send his daughters to Paris in 1764 to finish their education. Throughout his life he retained a great respect for Rousseau; in 1766 he prepared an English version of *Le Devin du village* for performance at Drury Lane under Garrick; later he used Rousseau's dictionary as the basis for much of his work for Rees's *Cyclopedia* (1800–5). Amongst his friends were Burke, Beattie, Johnson, Garrick, Reynolds, Rousseau and Diderot; amongst the honours he collected were a Fellowship of the Royal Society of Arts, the position of musician in ordinary to George III (with whom he was on good terms), and a foreign membership of the Institut de France (1810).

As music may be defined the art of pleasing by the succession and combination of agreeable sounds, every hearer has a right to give way to his feelings and be pleased or dissatisfied without knowledge, experience or the fiat of critics; but then he has certainly no right to insist on others being pleased or dissatisfied in the same degree. I can very readily forgive the man who admires a different music from that which pleases me, provided he does not extend his hatred or contempt of my favourite music to myself, and imagine that on the exclusive admiration of any one style of music and a close adherence to it, all wisdom, taste and virtue depend.

Criticism in this art would be better taught by specimens of good composition and performance than by reasoning and speculation. But there is a certain portion of enthusiasm connected with a love of the fine arts which bids defiance to every curb of criticism; and the poetry, painting or music that leaves us on the ground and does not transport us into the regions of imagination beyond the reach of cold criticism, may be correct but is devoid of genius and passion. There is however a tranquil pleasure, short of rapture, to be acquired from music, in which intellect and sensation are equally concerned; the analysis of this pleasure is therefore the subject of the present short essay, which it is hoped will explain and apologise for the critical remarks which have been made in the course of this history, on the

191

works of great masters, and prevent their being construed into pedantry and arrogance.

Indeed, musical criticism has been so little cultivated in our country that its first elements are hardly known. In justice to the late Mr Avison, it must be owned that he was the first and almost the only writer who attempted it. But his judgement was warped by many prejudices. He exalted Rameau and Geminiani at the expense of Handel, and was a declared foe to modern German symphonies. There have been many treatises published on the art of musical composition and performance but none to instruct ignorant lovers of music how to listen or to judge for themselves. So various are musical styles that it requires not only extensive knowledge and long experience but a liberal, enlarged, and candid mind to discriminate and allow to each its due praise:

> Nullius addictus jurare in verba magistri. (A man given to making up his own mind, heedless of the words of any instructor.)

A critic should have none of the contractions and narrow partialities of such as can see but a small angle of the art; of whom there are some so bewildered in fugues and complicated contrivances that they can receive pleasure from nothing but canonical answers, imitations, inversions and counter-subjects, while others are equally partial to light, simple, frivolous melody, regarding every species of artificial composition as mere pedantry and jargon. A chorus of Handel and a graceful opera song should not preclude each other: each has its peculiar merit, and no one musical production can comprise the beauties of every species of composition. It is not unusual for disputants in all the arts to reason without principles; but this I believe happens more frequently in musical debates than any other. By principles, I mean the having a clear and precise idea of the constituent parts of a good composition and of the principal excellencies of perfect execution. And it seems as if the merit of musical productions, both as to composition and performance, might be estimated according to De Piles' steel-yard, or test of merit among painters. If a complete musical composition of different movements were analysed, it would perhaps be found to consist of some of the following ingredients: melody, harmony, modulation, invention, grandeur, fire, pathos, taste, grace and expression; while the executive part would require neatness, accent, energy, spirit and feeling; and in a vocal performer, or instrumental where the tone depends on the player, power, clearness, sweetness, brilliancy of execution in quick movements and touching expression in slow.

But as all these qualities are seldom united in one composer or player, the piece or performer that comprises the greatest number of these excellences and in the most perfect degree, is entitled to pre-eminence: though the production or performer that can boast of any of these constituent qualities cannot be pronounced totally devoid of merit. In this manner, a composition, by a kind of chemical process, may be decompounded as well as any other production of art or nature.

Prudent critics without science seldom venture to pronounce their opinion of a composition decisively till they have heard the name of the master or discovered the sentiments of a professor; but here the poor author is often at the mercy of prejudice or envy. Yet the opinion of professors of the greatest integrity is not equally infallible concerning every species of musical merit. To judge minutely of singing, for instance, requires study and experience in that particular art. Indeed, I have long suspected some very great instrumental performers of not sufficiently feeling or respecting real good singing. Rapid passages neatly executed seem to please them infinitely more than the finest *messa di voce* or tender expression of slow notes, which the sweetest voice, the greatest art and most exquisite sensibility can produce. They frequently refer all excellence so much to their own performance and perfections, that the adventitious qualities of singers who imitate a hautbois, a flute, or violin, are rated higher than the colour and refinements that are peculiar to vocal expression; which instrumental performers ought to feel, respect and try to imitate, however impossible it may be to equal them: approximation would be something when more cannot be obtained. Of composition and the genius of particular instruments, whose opinion but that of composers and performers, who are likewise possessed of probity and candour, can be trusted? There are alas but too many professors who approve of nothing which they themselves have not produced or performed. Old musicians complain of the extravagance of the young; and these again of the dryness and inelegance of the old.

And yet among the various styles of composition and performance, the partial and capricious tastes of lovers of music and the different sects into which they are divided, it seems as if the following criteria would admit of little dispute.

In church music, whether jubilation, humility, sorrow or contrition are to be expressed, the words will enable the critic to judge; but of the degree of dignity, gravity, force and originality of the composition, few but professors can judge in detail though all of the general effect.

In hearing dramatic music little attention is pointed by the audience to anything but the airs and powers of the principal singers; and yet if the character, passion and importance of each personage in the piece is not distinctly marked and supported, if the airs are not contrasted with each other and the part of every singer in the same scene specifically different in measure, compass, time and style, the composer is not a complete master of his profession.

Good singing requires a clear, sweet, even and flexible voice, equally free from nasal and guttural defects. It is but by the tone of voice and articulation of words that a vocal performer is superior to an instrumental. If in swelling a note the voice trembles or varies its pitch, or the intonations are false, ignorance and science are equally offended; and if a perfect shake, good taste in embellishment and a touching expression be wanting, the singer's reputation will make no great progress among true judges. If in rapid divisions the passages are not executed with neatness and articulation; or in *adagios*, if light and shade, pathos and variety of colouring and expression are wanting, the singer may have merit of certain kinds, but is still distant from perfection.

Of perfect performance on an instrument, who can judge accurately but those who know its genius and powers, defects and difficulties? What is natural and easy on one instrument is often not only difficult but impracticable on an other. *Arpeggios*, for instance, which are so easy on the violin and harpsichord, are almost impossible on the hautbois and flute. And the rapid iteration of notes which give the violin player such little trouble are impracticable on the harpsichord with the same finger. Those instruments of which the tone and intonation depend on the player, as the violin, flute, hautbois, etc., are more difficult than harps and keyed-instruments where the player is neither answerable for the goodness of the tone nor truth of intonation. However, there are difficulties on the harpsichord of another kind, to balance the account, such as the two hands playing two different parts in dissimilar motion at once, and often three or four parts with each hand. Of a good shake, a sweet tone and neat execution, almost every hearer can judge; but whether the music is good or bad, the passages hard or easy, too much or too little embellished by the player, science and experience can only determine.

In chamber music, such as cantatas, single songs, solos, trios, quartets, concertos and symphonies of few parts, the composer has less exercise for reflection and intellect, and the power of pleasing in detached pieces by melody, harmony, natural modulation, and ingenuity of contrivance, fewer restraints and fewer occasions for grand and striking effects and expression of the passions, than in a connected composition for the church or the stage. Many an agreeable lesson, solo, sonata and concerto, has been produced by musicians who would be unable to compose a 'Te Deum' for voices and instruments or to interest and satisfy an audience during a single act of an opera. We never have heard of Corelli, Geminiani, or Tartini attempting vocal melody, and the music merely instrumental of the greatest vocal composers is often meagre, common and insipid. There are limits set to the powers of every artist, and however universal his genius, life is too short for universal application.

It was formerly more easy to compose than play an *adagio*, which generally consisted of a few notes that were left to the taste and abilities of the performer; but as the composer seldom found his ideas fulfilled by the player, *adagios* are now made more *chantant* and interesting in themselves, and the performer is less put to the torture for embellishments.

In 1752, Quantz classed *quartettos* at the head of instrumental music, calling them the touch-stone of an able composer; adding, that they had not yet been much in fashion. The divine Haydn however has since that time removed all kinds of complaint on that account, having produced such quartets for number and excellence as have never been equalled in any species of composition at any other period of time.

In composing and playing a solo, the least complicated of all music in parts, much knowledge, selection, invention and refinement are necessary. Besides consulting the genius of the instrument and power of the performer, new, interesting and shining passages must be invented, which will at once please and surprise the hearer and do honour to the composer and performer. And who can judge of the originality of the composition, its fitness for the instrument or degree of praise due to the performer, but those who have either studied composition, practised the same instrument or heard an infinite variety of music and great performers of the same kind?

The famous question therefore of Fontenelle: 'Sonate, que [me] veux-tu?' to which all such recur as have not ears capable of vibrating to the sweetness of well-modulated sounds, would never have been asked by a real lover or judge of music. But men of wit of all countries being accustomed to admiration and reverence in speaking upon subjects within their competence, forget, or hope the world forgets, that a good poet, painter, physician or philosopher is no more likely to be a good musician without study, practice and good ears than another man. But if a lover and judge of music had asked the same question as Fontenelle, the sonata should answer: 'I would have you listen with attention and delight to the ingenuity of the composition, the neatness of the execution, sweetness of the melody and the richness of the harmony, as well as the charms of refined tones, lengthened and polished into passion.'

There is a degree of refinement, delicacy and invention which lovers of simple and common music can no more comprehend than the Asiatic's harmony.[1] It is only understood and felt by such as can quit the plains of simplicity, penetrate the mazes of art and contrivance, climb mountains, dive into dells or cross the seas in search of extraneous and exotic beauties with which the monotonous melody of popular music has not yet been embellished. What judgement and good taste admire at first hearing, makes no impression on the public in general but by dint of repetition and habitude. A syllogism that is very plain to a logician, is incomprehensible to a mind unexercised in associating and combining abstract ideas. The extraneous and seemingly forced and affected modulation of the German composers of the present age is only too much for us because we have heard too little. Novelty has been acquired and attention excited, more by learned modulation in Germany than by new and difficult melody in Italy. We dislike both perhaps only because we are not gradually arrived at them; and difficult and easy, new and old, depend on the reading, hearing and

---

[1] The Chinese, allowed to be the most ancient and longest civilised people existing, after repeated trials, are displeased with harmony, or music in parts; it is too confused and complicated for ears accustomed to simplicity.

knowledge of the critic. The most easy, simple and natural is new to youth and inexperience, and we grow nice and fastidious by frequently hearing compositions of the first class, exquisitely performed.

Thomas Twining

(b. London, 8 Jan. 1735; d. Colchester, 6 Aug. 1804)

From: *Aristotle's Treatise on Poetry Translated: with Notes on the Translation, and on the Original; and two Dissertations, on Poetical and Musical, Imitation* (London 1789), Dissertation II

Twining graduated from Sidney Sussex College, Cambridge, in 1760 and shortly afterwards became a Fellow of the college. In 1764 he accepted the living of Fordham, near Colchester, where he remained until 1790 when he moved to the rectory at Colchester. His two interests were classics and music; he played violin, organ, harpsichord and the new pianoforte, and he corresponded with Burney, making the results of his researches available for the *History*. Apart from three sermons, the *Treatise* is Twining's only publication. It is easily the most informed and balanced account in English of the principle of imitation, making, as it does, the essential distinction between representation and expression. Since the time of Batteux indeed most scholars had defined 'imitation' far too narrowly. Twining pointed out, as Batteux had done, that Aristotle considered musical imitation to be the imitation of human affections or passions. Twining had not only a thorough grasp of classical Greek theory, but also a wide knowledge of eighteenth-century discussions of musical imitation, including d'Alembert's interesting essay on musical freedom,[1] his Discours préliminaire from the *Encyclopédie* (see pp. 57–9), articles from Rousseau's *Dictionnaire*, the same author's *Lettre sur la musique française* (see Strunk, *Source Readings*, p. 636), all in the original language, and most of the English literature, including Hutcheson's *Inquiry* (see pp. 23–6).

Although Twining was prepared to accept that the fine arts were united in the common principle of imitation, interpreting the word in its fullest sense, he felt the principle had produced more misunderstanding than illumination and that the time was ripe for its demise. From this time onwards the idea of music as an expressive art was to be stated in other ways, as part of the growing debate on romanticism.

Dissertation II

On the different senses of the word imitative, as applied to music by the ancients and by the moderns.

The whole power of music may be reduced I think to three distinct effects – upon the ear, the passions and the imagination: in other words it may be considered as simply delighting the sense, as raising emotions, or as raising ideas. The two last of these effects constitute the whole of what is called the

[1] Published in d'Alembert, *Mélanges de littérature*, vol. 5; a contribution to the French–Italian controversy.

moral[2] or expressive power of music; and in these only we are to look for anything that can be called imitation. Music can be said to imitate no further than as it expresses something. As far as its effect is merely physical and confined to the ear, it gives a simple, original pleasure; it expresses nothing, it refers to nothing; it is no more imitative than the smell of a rose or the flavour of a pineapple.

Music can raise ideas immediately[3] only by the actual resemblance of its sounds and motions to the sounds and motions of the thing suggested.[4] Such music we call imitative in the same sense in which we apply the word to a similar resemblance of sound and motion in poetry.[5] In both cases the resemblance, though immediate, is so imperfect that it cannot be seen till it is in some sort pointed out; and even when it is so, is not always very evident. Poetry, indeed, has here a great advantage; it carries with it of necessity its own explanation: for the same word that imitates by its sound, points out or hints at least, the imitation by its meaning. With music it is not so. It must call in the assistance of language or something equivalent to language for its interpreter.[6]

Of all the powers of music, this of raising ideas by direct resemblance is confessed to be the weakest and the least important. It is indeed so far from being essential to the pleasure of the art that unless used with great caution, judgement, and delicacy, it will destroy that pleasure by becoming, to every competent judge, offensive or ridiculous. It is, however, to music of this kind only that Mr Harris and most other modern writers allow the word imitative to be applied.[7] The highest power of music and that from which 'it

---

[2] Moral, merely as opposed to physical: as affecting the mind, not as ethic, or influencing the manners.

[3] Music may raise ideas immediately by mere association; but I pass over the effect of this principle, important and powerful as it is in music as in everything else, as having nothing to do with imitation. If to raise an idea of any object by casual association be to imitate, any one thing may imitate any other. I inserted the word, immediately, because music has also a power of raising ideas to a certain degree through the medium of emotions which naturally suggest correspondent ideas – that is, such ideas as usually raise such emotions; see James Harris, *Three Treatises*, ch. 6.

[4] Harris, *Three Treatises*, ch. 2, where this subject is treated with the author's usual accuracy and clearness.

[5] See *Dissertation* I.

[6] When the idea to be raised is that of a visible object, the imitation of that object by painting, machinery or other visible representation may answer the same end. A visible object, strongly characterised by motion may be suggested by such musical motion as is analogous to it. Thus a rapid elevation of sounds bears, or is at least conceived to bear some analogy to the motion of flame; but this analogy must be pointed out. 'The listener must be advised, either verbally, visually or by some other means that he must substitute the idea of flame for that of sound.' See M d'Alembert's *Mélanges de littérature*, vol. 5, p. 158, where the philosophical reader will perhaps be pleased with some very ingenious and uncommon observations on the manner in which the imitative expression even of music without words may be influenced by the phraseology of the language in which the hearer thinks.

[7] Dr Beattie, *An Essay on Poetry and Music*, p. 138, *et passim* (see pp. 150–6); Lord Kames, *Elements of Criticism*, vol. 2, p. 1 (see pp. 76–8); Avison, *An Essay on*

derives its greatest efficacy', is undoubtedly its power of raising emotions. But this is so far from being regarded by them as imitation that it is expressly opposed to it.[8]

The ideas and the language of the ancients on this subject were different. When they speak of music as imitation, they appear to have solely or chiefly in view, its power over the affections. By imitation they mean, in short, what we commonly distinguish from imitation and oppose to it, under the general term of expression.[9] With respect to Aristotle in particular this will clearly appear from a few passages which I shall produce from another of his writings; and at the same time, the expressions made use of in these passages will help us to account for a mode of speaking so different from that of modern writers on the subject.

What Aristotle, in the beginning of his *Treatise on Poetry*[10] calls 'mimésis' – imitation – he elsewhere in the same application of it to music, calls 'homiōma', resemblance. And he also clears up his meaning further, by adding the thing resembled or imitated[11] – 'homoiōma tois ēthesi – homoiōmata tōn ēthōn'[12] (representation of human character – representations of human character) i.e. dispositions or tempers; for what he means by these 'ēthē' (dispositions) he has likewise clearly explained by these expressions, 'homoiōmata orgēs kai praotētos; eti d'andrias kai sōphrosunēs' (resemblances of the irascible and the gentle disposition, of fortitude and temperance, etc.[13] This resemblance, he expressly tells us, is 'in the rhythm and the melody' – 'homoiōmata' – 'en tois ruthmois kai tois melesin, orgēs kai praotētos' (resemblances in the rhythm and melody of anger and gentleness).[14] In these passages Aristotle differs only in the mode of expression from Mr Harris when he affirms that there are sounds to make us cheerful or sad, martial or tender, etc.[15] – from Dr Beattie when he says,

---

Musical Expression (see pp. 60–3). There is but one branch of this imitation of sound by sound that is really important, and that has been generally overlooked. I mean the imitation of the tones of speech. Of this presently.

[8] Harris, *Three Treatises*, pp. 69, 99, 100.

[9] 'If we compare imitation with expression the superiority of the latter will be evident', Beattie, *Essay*, pp. 139ff.; Avison, *Essay*, pt II, section 3.

[10] 'kai tēs aulētikēs hē pleistē kai kitharistikēs-mimēseis' (and most flute-playing and harp-playing . . . may be said to be . . . artistic representation).

[11] In the same passage he uses the word mimēsis as synonymous with homoiōma.

[12] Aristotle, *De republica*, bk. 8, ch. 5, p. 455, ed. Duval. Plato uses 'mimēmata tropōn' (artistic representations of behaviour) in the same sense – *De legibus*, bk 2, p. 655.

[13] The word 'ēthē', taken in its utmost extent, includes everything that is habitual and characteristic, but it is often used in a limited sense for the habitual temper or disposition. That it is here used in that sense appears from Aristotle's own explanation. I therefore thought it necessary to fix the sense of the word manners, which has the same generality as 'ēthē' and is its usual translation, by adding the words 'dispositions or tempers'.

[14] The same expressions occur in the *Problems*, sections 19, 27 and 29.

[15] Ch. 6.

'Music may inspire devotion, fortitude, compassion – may infuse a sorrow', etc.[16]

It appears then in the first place that music, considered as affecting or raising emotions, was called imitation by the ancients because they perceived in it that which is essential to all imitation, and is indeed often spoken of as the same thing – resemblance.[17] This resemblance, however, as here stated by Aristotle, cannot be immediate;[18] for between sounds themselves and mental affections there can be no resemblance. The resemblance can only be a resemblance of effects: the general emotions, tempers, or feelings produced in us by certain sounds are like those that accompany actual grief, joy, anger, etc. And this, as far at least as can be collected from the passage in question, appears to be all that Aristotle meant.

But secondly, the expressions of music considered in itself, and without words, are within certain limits vague, general and equivocal. What is usually called its power over the passions is in fact no more than a power of raising a general emotion, temper, or disposition, common to several different though related passions, as pity, love, anger, courage etc.[19] The effect of words is to strengthen the expression of music by confining it – by giving it a precise direction, supplying it with ideas, circumstances, and an object, and by this means raising it from a calm and general disposition or emotion into something approaching at least to the stronger feeling of a particular and determinate passion. Now among the ancients music, it is well known, was scarce ever heard without this assistance. Poetry and music were then far from having reached that state of mutual independence and separate improvement in which they have now been long established. When an ancient writer speaks of music he is almost always to be understood to mean vocal music – music and poetry united. This helps greatly to account for the application of the term imitative by Aristotle, Plato and other Greek writers to musical expression, which modern writers oppose to musical imitation. That emotions are raised by music, independently of words, is certain,[20] and it is as certain that these emotions resemble those of actual

---

[16] *Essay.* In another place Dr Beattie approaches very near indeed to the language of Aristotle; he says, 'After all, it must be acknowledged that there is some relation at least, or analogy, if not similitude between certain musical sounds and mental affections', p. 143.

[17] 'Imitations or resemblances of something else', Francis Hutcheson, *An Inquiry into the Original of our Ideas of Beauty and Virtue*, p. 15. 'Taking imitation in its proper sense as importing a resemblance between two objects', Kames, *Elements* ch. 18, section 3. Imitation indeed necessarily implies resemblance; but the converse is not true.

[18] See *Dissertation* I, the first pages.

[19] The expression of Aristotle seems therefore accurate and philosophical. It is everywhere 'homoiōma ēthōn', not 'pathōn' (a resemblance 'to manners or tempers', not 'to passions').

[20] This is expressly allowed by Aristotle in the problem which will presently be produced, 'kai gar ean ē aneu logou melos, homōs echei ēthos' (for if the melody is without words, yet still has some sort of human character).

passion, temper, etc. But in the vague and indeterminate assimilations of music purely instrumental, though the effect is felt and the emotion raised, the idea of resemblance is far from being necessarily suggested; much less is it likely that such resemblance if it did occur, having no precise direction, should be considered as imitation.[21] Add words to this music and the case will be very different. There is now a precise object of comparison presented to the mind; the resemblance is pointed out; the thing imitated is before us. Further, one principal use of music in the time of Aristotle was to accompany dramatic poetry – that poetry which is most peculiarly and strictly imitative,[22] and where manners and passions (ēthē kai pathē) are peculiarly the objects of imitation.

It is then no wonder that the ancients, accustomed to hear the expressions of music thus constantly specified, determined, and referred to a precise object by the ideas of poetry, should view them in the light of imitations; and that even in speaking of music properly so called, as Aristotle does, they should be led by this association to speak of it in the same terms and to attribute to it powers which, in its separate state do not in strictness belong to it. With respect, however, even to the instrumental music of those times,

[21] I observed (p. 49) that music is capable of raising ideas to a certain degree, through the medium of those emotions which it raises immediately. But this is an effect so delicate and uncertain – so dependent on the fancy, the sensibility, the musical experience, and even the temporary disposition of the hearer, that to call it imitation is surely going beyond the bounds of all reasonable analogy. Music here is not imitative, but, if I may hazard the expression, merely suggestive. But whatever we may call it, this I will venture to say – that in the best instrumental music, expressively performed, the very indecision itself of the expression, leaving the hearer to the free operation of his emotion upon his fancy, and as it were to the free choice of such ideas as are to him most adapted to react upon and heighten the emotion which occasioned them, produces a pleasure which nobody, I believe, who is able to feel it will deny to be one of the most delicious that music is capable of affording. But far the greater part even of those who have an ear for music, have only an ear; and to them this pleasure is unknown. The complaint so common, of the separation of poetry and music, and of the total want of meaning and expression in instrumental music was never, I believe, the complaint of a man of true musical feeling: and it might perhaps be not unfairly concluded that Aristotle, who expressly allows that 'music, even without words, has expression' (see the problem below), was more of a musician than his master Plato, who is fond of railing at instrumental music, and asks with Fontenelle – 'Sonate, que me veux-tu.' – 'pangchalepon aneu logou gignomenon ruthmon te kai harmonian gignōskein ho ti bouletai' (it is extremely difficult without words to make out what the rhythm and harmony is . . . I mean, what they are trying to show), *De legibus*, bk 2, p. 669. The story of Fontenelle is well known: 'I shall never forget', says Rousseau, 'the witticism of the celebrated Fontenelle, who having been wearied by an unending series of in-strumental pieces, cried out impatiently, 'Sonata, what do you want with me?', *Dictionnaire de musique*, 'Sonate'. I would by no mean be understood to deny that there is now and has been at all times much unmeaning trash composed for instruments that would provoke such a question. I mean only to say what has been said for me by a superior judge and master of the art: 'There is some kind, even of instrumental music, so divinely composed and so expressively performed, that it wants no words to explain its meaning.' Charles Burney, *History of Music*, vol. 1, p. 85.

[22] *Dissertation* I.

it should be remembered that we cannot properly judge of it by our own nor suppose it to have been in that simple state of the art what is now in its state of separate improvement and refinement. It seems highly probable that the music of the ancients, even in performances merely instrumental, retained much of its vocal style and character and would therefore appear more imitative than our instrumental music: and perhaps, after all, a Greek solo on the flute or the cithara was not much more than a song without the words, embellished here and there with a little embroidery or a few sprinklings of simple *arpeggio*, such as the fancy and the fingers of the player could supply.

But there is another circumstance that deserves to be considered. Dramatic music is often strictly imitative. It imitates not only the effect of the words by exciting correspondent emotions but also the words themselves immediately, by tones, accents, inflexions, intervals and rhythmical movements, similar to those of speech. That this was peculiarly the character of the dramatic music of the ancients seems highly probable, not only from what is said of it by ancient authors but from what we know of their music in general; of their scales, their genera, their fondness for chromatic and enharmonic intervals, which approach so nearly to those sliding and unassignable inflections (if I may so speak) that characterize the melody of speech.

I am indeed persuaded, that the analogy between the melody and rhythm of music and the melody and rhythm of speech,[23] is a principle of greater extent and importance than is commonly imagined. Some writers have extended it so far as to resolve into it the whole power of music over the affections. Such appears to have been the idea of Rousseau. He divides all music into natural and imitative; including under the latter denomination all music that goes beyond the mere pleasure of the sense and raises any kind or degree of emotion an effect which he conceives to be wholly owing to an imitation more or less perceptible, of the accents and inflexions of the voice in animated or passionate speech.[24] Professor Hutcheson was of the same opinion. In his *Inquiry* [section 6, p. 83], he says:

There is also another charm in music to various persons, which is distinct from the harmony, and is occasioned by its raising agreeable passions. The human voice is obviously varied by all the stronger passions;[25] now when our ear discerns any

[23] legetai gar dē kai logōdes ti melos, to sungkeimenon ek tōn prosōdiōn tōn en tois onomasi (People also speak of a melody based on speech, a melody that rests on the modulations of the voice in spoken phrases), Aristoxenus, *Harmonia*, bk 1, p. 18, ed. Meibomii. To this he opposes 'mousikon melos' (musical melody).

[24] Rousseau, *Dictionnaire*, 'Musique', 'Melodie', etc.

[25] Thus Theophrastus, in a curious passage cited by Plutarch in his *Symposiacs*, p. 623, 'mousikes archas treis einai, lupen, hedonen, enthusiasmon: hos hekastou touton paratrepontos ek tou sunethous kai engklinontos ten phonen' (There are three principles of music, grief, love and enthusiasm; for each of these passions turns the voice from its usual course and gives it inflexions different from those of ordinary speech). 'Only the passions sing' says Rousseau, 'Understanding only speaks'. This passage of Theophrastus is introduced to resolve the question, in what sense love is

resemblance between the air of a tune whether sung or played upon an instrument, either in its time or modulation or any other circumstance, to the sound of the human voice in any passion, we shall be touched by it in a very sensible manner and have melancholy, joy, gravity, thoughtfulness, excited in us by a sort of sympathy or contagion.

This ingenious and amiable writer seems to have adopted this opinion from Plato, to whom indeed in a similar passage in his *System of Moral Philosophy*[26] he refers, and who in the third book of his *Republic* speaks of a warlike melody, inspiring courage, as 'imitating the sounds and accents of the courageous man'; and of a calm and sedate melody, as imitating the sounds of a man of such a character.[27]

With respect to Aristotle – whether this was his opinion or not cannot, I think be determined from any thing he has expressly said upon the subject. In the passage above produced,[28] where so much is said of the resemblance of melody and rhythm to manners or tempers, not a word is said from which it can be inferred that he meant a resemblance to the tones and accents by which those manners are expressed in speech. On the contrary, the expressions there made use of are such as lead us naturally to conclude that he meant no more than I have above supposed him to mean; i.e. that the music produces in us, immediately, feelings resembling those of real passion, etc. For after having asserted that there is a 'resemblance in rhythms and melodies to the irascible and the gentle disposition', he adds – 'This is evident from the manner in which we find ourselves affected by the performance of such music; for we perceive a change produced in the soul while we listen to it.'[29] And again – 'In melody itself there are imitations of human manners: this is manifest from the melodies or modes which have evidently their distinct nature and character; so that when we hear them, we feel ourselves affected by each of them in a different manner, etc.'[30] But the

said to teach music? 'No wonder' says the resolver, 'if love, having in itself all these three principles of music – grief, pleasure and enthusiasm – should be more prone to vent itself in music than any other passion.' Aristoxenus, describing the difference between the two motions of the voice in speaking and singing – the motion by slides and that by intervals – says, 'dioper, en to dialegesthai pheugomen to histanai ten phonen, an me dia pathos pote eis toiaiten kinesin anangkasthomen elthein' (because in speech we avoid raising the voice unless through an emotional shock we are forced to such a change), p. 9, ed. Meibomii.

[26] Vol. 1, p. 16.

[27] *De republica*, bk 3, p. 399. The expressions are – 'hē (harmonia) en tē polemikē praxei ontos andreiou-prepontōs an mimēsaito phthoggous te kai prosōdias' (which mode would suitably imitate the sounds and accents of the courageous man). And again – 'sōphronōn, andreiōn, phthoggous mimēsontai' (they will imitate the utterances of the self-controlled and the brave).

[28] p. 51.

[29] 'Dēlon de ek tōn ergōn: metaballomen gar tēn psuchēn akroōmenoi toutōn' (this is clear from practice. For we perceive a change produced in the soul while we listen to it).

[30] 'En de tois melesin autois esti mimēmata tōn ēthōn; kai tout' esti phaneron: euthus gar hē tōn harmoniōn diestēke phusis: hōste akouontas allōs diatithesthai kai mē ton auton tropon echein pros hekastēn autōn'. The 'harmoniai', i.e. melodies, – or more

passage furnishes, I think, a more decisive proof that the resemblance here meant was not a resemblance to speech. Aristotle asserts here, as in the problem of which I shall presently speak, that of all that affects the senses, music alone possesses this property of resemblance to human manners. In comparing it with painting he observes that this art can imitate, immediately, only figures and colours; which are not resemblances (omoiomata) of manners and passions but only signs and indications of them (semeia) in the human body: whereas in music, the resemblance to manners 'is in the melody itself'.[31] Now whatever may be the meaning of this last assertion – for it seems not quite philosophical to talk of such a resemblance as being in the sounds themselves – whatever may be its meaning, it cannot well be that the melody resembles manners as expressed by speech; because this would destroy the distinction between music and painting: for words are exactly in the same case with colours and figures; they are not resemblances of manners or passions but indications only. We must then, I fear, be contented to take what Aristotle says as a popular and unphilosophical way of expressing a mere resemblance of effect.

In one of his musical problems, indeed, he advances a step further and inquires into the cause of this effect of music upon the mind. The text of these problems is, in general, very incorrect and often absolutely unintelligible; this problem however, seems not beyond the reach of secure emendation, though it may possibly be beyond that of secure explanation. As it has not that I know of been noticed by any writer on the subject, and may be regarded at least as a curiosity not uninteresting to the musical and philosophical reader, I shall venture to give the entire problem as I think it should be read, and to subjoin a translation.[32]

properly perhaps, enharmonic melodies – here spoken of must not be confounded with what are usually called the modes, and described by the writers on ancient music under the denomination of 'tonoi', i.e. pitches or keys: these were mere transpositions of the same scale or system; the 'harmoniai' appear to have been, as the name implies, different melodies – scales, in which the arrangement of intervals and the divisions of the tetrachord (or genera) were different. Aristides Quintilianus is the only Greek writer who has given any account of these 'harmoniai' (p. 21, ed. Meibomii). He asserts that it is of these, not of the 'tonoi' that Plato speaks in the famous passage of his Republic, bk 3, where he rejects some of them and retains others. This at least is clear, that whatever the harmoniai of Plato were, Aristotle here speaks of the same; see his Republic, bk 8, p. 459. Their distinctive names, Lydian, Dorian, etc. were the same with those of the 'tonoi', that of Syntono-Lydian excepted, which I think is peculiar to the 'harmoniai'. This coincidence of names seems to have been the chief cause of the confusion we find in the modern writers on this subject. The distinction has been pointed out in Dr Burney's History of Music, vol. 1, p. 32. See also Rousseau's dictionary articles, 'Syntono-Lydien' and 'Genre'.

[31] 'ouk esti tauta homoiōmata tōn ēthōn alla sēmeia mallon, ta ginomena schēmata kai chrōmata, tōn ēthōn; kai tauta estin epi tou sōmatos en tois pathesin, en de tois melesin autois esti mimēmata tōn ēthōn' (these are not likenesses of moral character, these are physical shapes and colours of moral characters. And in the body, these lie in the passions. But in the melodies themselves there are representations of moral qualities), p. 455, ed. Duval.

[32] This passage is remarkable. It is exactly the language of Rousseau: 'there is no

Dai ti to akouston monon ēthos echei tōn aisthētōn (kai gar ean e aneu logou melos, omiōs echei ēthos), all' ou to chrōma, oude e osme oude o chumos, echei? ē oti kinēsin echei monon? ouch hēn ho psophos hēmas kinei. toiautē men gar tois allois huparchei; kinei gar to chrōma tēn opsin. alla tēs hepomenēs tōi toioutōi psophōi aisthanometha kinēseōs. autē de echei homoiotēta (tois ēthesin) en te tois ruthmois kai en tēi ton phthongōn taxei tōn oxeōn kai bareōn (ouk en tei mixei, alla hē sumphonia ouk echei ēthos). en de tois allois aisthētois touto ouk estin. hai de kinēseis autai praktikai eisin: hai de praxeis ēthous semasia esti (Problem 27 of section 19).

Why, of all that affects the senses, the audible only has any expression of the manners; (for melody, even without words, has this effect) – but colours, smells, and tastes, have no such property? – Is it because the audible alone affects us by motion? – I do not mean that motion by which as mere sound it acts upon the ear; for such motion belongs equally to the objects of our other senses; – thus, colour

connection between sounds and the objects that are to be painted or the passions that are to be expressed', *Dictionnaire de musique*, 'Imitation'; see also the last paragraph of the article, 'Harmonie'. Thus, too, Lord Kames: 'Harmony properly so called, though delightful when in perfection, hath no relation to sentiment', *Elements of Criticism*, vol. 1, p. 128. But how is this? The same intervals are the material both of melody and harmony. These intervals have each of them their peculiar effect and character, and it is by the proper choice of them in succession, and by that only, that melody considered abstractly from rhythm or measure, becomes expressive, or has any 'relation to sentiment'. Do these intervals then lose at once as by magic all their variety and striking difference of character as soon as they are heard in the simultaneous combinations of harmony? If this be the case, the vocal composer is at once relieved from all care of adapting the harmonies of his accompaniment to the expression of the sentiment conveyed in the words, and it must be a matter of perfect indifference whether for example he uses the major or the minor third, the perfect or the false fifth, the common chord or the chord of the diminished seventh, etc. With respect to Rousseau it is not easy to see how this assertion of his can be reconciled with what he has said elsewhere. In his letter *Sur la musique française*, he expressly allows that every interval, consonant or dissonant, 'has its peculiar character, that is to say, a manner of affecting the soul that is peculiar to it'. And upon this depends entirely all the admirable observations he has there made concerning the ill effects which a crowded harmony and an 'excess' of chords have upon musical expression. In another article of his dictionary this inconsistence is still more striking. One would not think it possible for the same writer who in one place talks of intervals 'suitable, through their harshness to express rage, anger and the painful passions', and of 'a plaintive harmony to soften the heart', and in another part of the same work that 'there is no connection between harmonies and the passions that are to be expressed'.

Had these writers contented themselves with saying that harmony has much less relation to sentiment than melody, they would not have gone beyond the truth. And the reason for this difference in the effect of the same intervals, in melody and in harmony, seems plainly this, that in melody, these intervals being formed by successive sounds, have of course a much closer and more obvious relation to the tones and inflections by which sentiments are expressed in speech than they can have in harmony where they are formed by sounds heard together.

As to the assertion of Aristotle, it seems only to furnish additional proof that the ancients did not practice anything like our counterpoint or continued harmony in different parts. Where the utmost use of harmony seems to have been confined to unisons, octaves, fourths and fifths, where at least no discords – the most expressive materials of modern harmony – were allowed, we cannot wonder that the 'mixture' of sounds in consonance should be thought to have no relation to sentiment, and that all the power of music over the passions should be confined to melodious and rhythmical succession.

acts by motion upon the organs of sight, &c. But I mean another motion which we perceive subsequent to that; and this motion bears a resemblance to human manners, both in the rhythm, and in the arrangement of sounds acute and grave: – not in their mixture; for harmony has no expression. With the objects of our other senses this is not the case. Now these motions are analogous to the motion of human actions; and those actions are the index of the manners.

In this problem, the philosopher plainly attributes the expressive power of musical sounds to their succession – to their motion in measured melody. He also distinguishes the rhythmical from the melodious succession; for he says expressly, that this motion is 'both in the rhythm (or measure) and in the order or arrangement of sounds acute and grave'. But whence the effect of these motions? He answers, from their analogy to the motions of human actions[33] by which the manners and tempers of men are expressed in common life. With respect to the analogy of rhythmic movement to the various motions of men in action this indeed is sufficiently obvious. But Aristotle goes further and supposes that there is also such analogy in the motion of melody considered merely as a succession of different tones, without any regard to time: en te tōn phthongōn taxei, tōn oxeōn kai bareōn. He plainly asserts that this succession of tones also is analogous to the motion of human actions. Now it seems impossible to assign any human action to which a succession of sounds and intervals, merely as such, has or can have any relation or similitude, except the action (if the expression is allowable) of speaking, which is such a succession. If this be Aristotle's meaning – and I confess myself unable to discover any other – I do not see how we can avoid concluding that he agreed so far with Plato as to attribute part at least of the effect of music upon the affections to the analogy between melody and speech.

This analogy is indeed a curious subject, and deserves perhaps a more thorough examination and development than it has yet received.[34] But I shall not trust myself further with a speculation so likely to draw me wide from the proper business of this dissertation, than just to observe that the writers above mentioned who resolve all the pathetic expression of music

---

[33] The original is short and rather obscure. It says, literally, 'these motions are practical motions' – 'praktikai eisin'. But that I have given Aristotle's true meaning in my translation is evident from a clearer expression in problem 19, which is a shorter solution of the same question. His expression there is, 'kinēseis eisin (sc. hoi ruthmoi kai ta mele) hōsper kai hai praxeis' (rhythm and melody are motions, as actions also are).

[34] Much light has been thrown upon this subject as far as relates to speech by Mr [Joshua] Steele in his curious and ingenious *Essay on the Melody and Measure of Speech* [London 1775]. But the object of his enquiry was speech, not music. His purpose in tracing the resemblance between them was only to show that speech is capable of notation, not to examine how far the effect of music on the passions depends on that resemblance. His notation is extremely ingenious; but with respect to his project of accompanying the declamation of tragedy by a drone bass, I must confess that for my own part I cannot reflect without some comfort upon the improbability that it will ever be attempted.

into this principle, though they assert more than it seems possible to prove, are yet much nearer to the truth than those who altogether overlook or reject that principle;[35] a principle of which instances so frequent and so palpable are to be traced in the works of the best masters of vocal composition – in those of Purcell, for example, of Handel and above all of Pergolesi – that I have often wondered it should have been neglected by so exact a writer as Mr Harris, though it lay directly in his way, and in one place he actually touched it as he passed.[36] He seems here to have deserted those ancients whom in general he most delighted to follow.

But to return to Aristotle and his treatise on poetry: the reader will observe that he does not there assert in general terms that 'music is an imitative art', but only that the music 'of the flute and the lyre' is imitative, and even that not always but 'for the most part'.[37] I just mention this because I have observed in many of the commentators as well as in other writers, a disposition to extend and generalise his assertions by which they

[35] After allowing that 'different passions and sentiments do indeed give different tones and accents to the human voice,' Dr Beattie asks, 'but can the tones of the most pathetic melody be said to bear a resemblance to the voice of a man or woman speaking from the impulse of passion?' I can only answer, that to my ear such a resemblance, in the 'most pathetic melody,' is often even striking: and I have no doubt that in many passages we are affected from a more delicate and latent degree of that resemblance, sufficient to be felt in its effect though not to be perceived. Dr Beattie also asks, 'if there are not melancholy airs in the sharp key, and cheerful ones in the flat?' Undoubtedly the peculiar and opposite characters of these keys may be variously modified and tempered by the movement, the accent, and the manner of performance, in general: but they can never be destroyed; much less can they be changed, as Dr Beattie supposes, to their very opposites. A cheerful air in a flat key, I confess, I never heard. If Dr Beattie thinks the jig in the fifth solo of Corelli cheerful, because the movement is allegro, I would beg of him to try an experiment: let him only play the first bar of that jig (with the bass) upon a harpsichord, etc. in G major: and when he has attended to the effect of that, let him return to the minor key, and hear the difference. As to 'melancholy airs in a sharp key,' the word melancholy is I think used with considerable latitude, and comprehends different shades. In the lightest of these shades it may perhaps be applied to some airs in a major key; that key may by slowness of movement, softness and smoothness of tone, etc. become solemn, tender, touching, but I cannot say I recollect any air in that key which makes an impression that can properly be called melancholy. But we must be careful in this matter to allow for the magic of association, which no one better understands or has described with more feeling and fancy than Dr Beattie himself. See *Essay*, p. 173, etc. With respect to 'a transition from the one key to the other' [from major to minor, etc.] 'in the same air, without any sensible change in the expression,' I must also confess that it is to me totally unknown. One word more: Dr Beattie is 'at a loss to conceive how it should happen that a musician, overwhelmed with sorrow, for example, should put together a series of notes, whose expression is contrary to that of another series which he had put together when elevated with joy,' p. 180. But is not Dr Beattie equally at a loss to conceive how it should happen that any man overwhelmed with sorrow should put together, in speaking (as he certainly does), a series of tones whose expression is contrary to that of another series which he had put together when elevated with joy? The two facts are equally certain, and even at the first view so nearly allied, that whoever can account for the one need not, I am persuaded, be at the trouble of trying to account separately for the other.

[36] Ch. 2, section 1; particularly note 1.

[37] tēs aulētikēs hē pleistē kai kitharistikēs' (and in most flute-playing and harp-playing).

have sometimes involved the subject and themselves in unnecessary difficulties.

With respect to modern writers at least, there seems to be a manifest impropriety in denominating music an imitative art while they confine the application of the term imitative to what they confess to be the slightest and least important of all its powers. In this view, consistence and propriety are certainly on the side of Dr Beattie when he would 'strike music off the list of imitative arts'.[38] But perhaps even a further reform may justly be considered as wanting in our language upon this subject. With whatever propriety, and however naturally and obviously the arts both of music and of poetry may be separately and occasionally regarded and spoken of as imitative, yet when we arrange and class the arts, it seems desirable that a clearer language were adopted. The notion that painting, poetry, and music,[39] are all arts of imitation, certainly tends to produce, and has produced, much confusion. That they all in some sense of the word or other imitate, cannot be denied; but the senses of the word when applied to poetry or music are so different both from each other and from that in which it is applied to painting, sculpture and the arts of design in general – the only arts that are obviously and essentially imitative – that when we include them all without distinction under the same general denomination of imitative arts, we seem to defeat the only useful purpose of all classing and arrangement; and instead of producing order and method in our ideas, produce only embarrassment and confusion.[40]

---

[38] Beattie, *Essay*, p. 129.

[39] What shall we say to those who add architecture to the list of imitative arts? One would not expect to find so absurd a notion adopted by so clear and philosophical a writer as M. d'Alembert. Yet in his Discours préliminaire of the *Encyclopédie* he not only makes architecture an imitative art, but even classes it with painting and sculpture. He allows indeed that the imitation of 'beautiful nature is less obvious and more limited than in the other arts'; but how is it any imitation at all? Only because it imitates 'by the assembly and union of the different bodies that it uses'. What? – 'the symmetrical order that is naturally found, to a greater or lesser degree, in each thing', *Mélanges de littérature*, bk 1, p. 63. I can only say that upon this principle the joiner, the smith, the mechanic of almost every kind, have a fair claim to be elevated to the rank of imitative artists: for if a regular building be an imitation of 'beautiful nature', so is a chair, a table or a pair of fire-tongs.

[40] See *Dissertation* I, pp. 19–20.

Archibald Alison

(b. Edinburgh, 1757; d. Edinburgh, 17 May, 1839)

From: *Essays on the Nature and Principles of Taste* (Dublin 1790), Essay I,
pp. 3–4; Essay II, ch. 2, pp. 265–75.

Alison graduated from Balliol, Oxford, taking his LL.B in 1784. He spent much of
his life as a country parson in the counties of Durham, Northamptonshire and
Shropshire, finally settling in Edinburgh as minister of the episcopal chapel,
Cowgate. By 1825 his *Essays* had reached a sixth edition. The book has the form
of two essays, the first of which defines the emotions of sublimity and beauty, the
second treating of the sublimity and beauty of the material world. Chapter 2 of this
second part is devoted to sound and music.

One of Alison's main arguments is that beauty is not a quality of things that exists
independently of the observer. Alison therefore rejected the idea that beauty could be
defined by 'any single principle'; he made 'association' the uniquely crucial element
in aesthetic experience, even when it concerned purely 'private affections or
remembrances'.[1] He accepted that music can express not only beauty but sublimity
(pp. 250–1); he drew some interesting analogies between eloquence and music that
were parallel to those that Momigny worked out in his fascinating analysis of the
first movement of Mozart's D minor quartet, K. 421:[2] he suggested too that music
could heighten verbal expression through modulation, intermediate key changes
creating tensions that could only be released by a final return to the tonic. Alison
implied moreover that instrumental music could mean even more to the educated
listener than vocal music, since 'words lead us always to think of the sentiment, and
rarely of anything else'.

Although he wrote 'with the greatest diffidence' about an art on which he had no
theoretical knowledge, his comments prove him to have been a sensitive and
intelligent listener, fully aware of the ways in which pitch, rhythm, metre, harmony,
timbre and dynamics can determine the musical 'affection'.

Essay I

The effect of the different arts of taste is similar. The landscapes of Claude
Lorraine, the music of Handel, the poetry of Milton, excite feeble emotions
in our minds when our attention is confined to the qualities they present to
our senses, or when it is to such qualities of their composition that we turn
our regard. It is then, only, we feel the sublimity or beauty of their
productions when our imaginations are kindled by their power, when we
lose ourselves amid the number of images that pass before our minds, and

---

[1] Quoted by Jerome Stolnitz, in his valuable study, 'Beauty', p. 200ff.

[2] See Jérôme Joseph de Momigny, *Cours complet d'harmonie et de composition* (Paris
1806), vol. 3, p. 109ff.

when we waken at last from this play of fancy, as from the charm of a romantic dream. The beautiful apostrophe of the Abbé de Lille upon the subject of gardening,

> N'avez-vous pas souvent, aux lieux infrequentés,
> Rencontré tout-à-coup, ces aspects enchantés,
> Qui suspendent vos pas, dont l'image chérie
> Vous jette en une douce et longue rêverie?

> [Have you not often in unfrequented places suddenly come across enchanting views that halt you in your tracks, the treasured sight of which transport you into a sweet and protracted dream?]

Essay II

Although its real power consists in its imitation of those signs of emotion or passion which take place in the human voice, yet from its nature it possesses advantages which these signs have not, and which render it within these limits one of the most powerful means which can be made use of in exciting emotion. As far as I am able to judge, these advantages principally consist in the two following circumstances.

1. In that variety of sounds which it admits of, in conformity to the key or fundamental tone. In the real expression of passion in the human voice, the sound is nearly uniform or at least admits of very small variation. In so far therefore as mere sound is concerned, the tone of any passion would in a short time become unpleasing from its uniformity; and if this effect were not forgot in our attention to the language and sentiments of the person who addresses us, would be perceived by every ear. In music, on the contrary, the variety of related sounds which may be introduced, not only prevents this unpleasing effect of uniformity, and preserves the emotion which the prevailing tone is of itself able to excite, but by varying the expression of it, keeps both our attention and our imagination continually awake. The one resembles what we should feel from the passion of any person who uniformly made use of the same words to express to us what he felt. The other, what we feel from that eloquence of passion, where new images are continually presenting themselves to the mind of the speaker, and a new source of delight is afforded to our imagination in the perception of the agreement of those images with the emotions from which they arise. The effect of musical composition, in this light, resembles in some measure the progress of an oration, in which our interest is continually kept alive: and if it were possible for us, for a moment, to forget that the performer is only repeating a lesson, were it possible for us to imagine that the sounds we hear were the immediate expressions of his own emotion, the effect of music might be conceived in some measure to approach to the effect of eloquence. To those who have felt this influence, in the degree in which, in some seasons of sensibility, it may be felt, there is no improbability in the accounts of the effects of music in early times when the professions of poetry

and music were not separated; when the Bard, under the influence of some strong and present impression, accommodated his melody to the language of his own passion, and when the hearers, under the influence of the same impression, were prepared to go along with him in every variety of that emotion which he felt and expressed himself.

2. But besides this, there is another circumstance in which the expression of music differs materially from the expression of natural signs, and which serves to add considerably to the strength of its effect. Such natural sounds express to us immediately, if they express at all, the emotion of the person from whom they proceed, and therefore immediately excite our own emotion. As these sounds however have little or no variety, and excite immediately their correspondent emotion, it necessarily happens that they become weaker as they proceed until at last they become positively disagreeable. In musical composition, on the contrary, as such sounds constitute a whole, and have all a relation to the key, or fundamental note in which they close, they not only afford us a satisfaction as parts of a regular whole, but what is of much more consequence, they keep our attention continually awake and our expectation excited until we arrive at that fundamental tone which is both the close of the composition and the end of our expectation. Instead therefore (as in the former case) of our emotion becoming more languid as the sounds proceed, it becomes in the case of musical composition on the contrary more strong. The peculiar affection we feel is kept continually increasing by means of the expectation which is excited for the perfection of this whole, and the one and the other are only gratified when we arrive at this desired and expected end.

In this respect indeed musical expression is in itself superior even to the expression of language, and were the passions or affections which it can express as definite or particular as those which can be communicated by words, it may well be doubted whether there is any composition of words which could so powerfully affect us as such a composition of sounds. In language, every person under the influence of passion or emotion naturally begins with expressing the cause of his emotion, an observation which every one must have made in real life, and which might easily be confirmed by instances from dramatic poetry. In this case, our emotion is immediately at its height, and as it has no longer any assistance from curiosity, naturally cools as the speaker goes on. In music, on the contrary, the manner of this communication resembles the artful but interesting conduct of the epic or dramatic poem where we find ourselves at once involved in the progress of some great interest, where our curiosity is wound up to its utmost to discover the event, and where at every step, this interest increases, from bringing us nearer to the expected end. That the effect of musical composition is similar, that while it excites emotion from the nature of the sounds it excites also an increasing expectation and interest from the conduct of these sounds, and from their continued dependence upon the close, has I am persuaded been felt in the strongest manner by every person of common sensibility, and indeed is in itself extremely obvious, from the effect which is universally produced by any pathetic composition upon the audience. The increasing silence, the impatience of interruption, which are so evident as the composition goes on, the arts by which the performer is almost instinctively led to enhance the merit of the close, by seeming to depart from it, the suppression of every sign of emotion till the whole is completed, and the violence either of sensibility or applause, that are immediately displayed whenever a full and harmonious close is produced, all testify in the strongest manner the increasing nature of the emotion and the singular advantage which music thus possesses in keeping the attention and the sensibility so powerfully awake.

Such seems to me the natural effect of music on the human mind in expressing to us those affections or emotions which are signified by the tones of the voice and the progress of articulate sounds; limited indeed in the reach of its imitation or expression and far inferior to language, in being confined to the expression only of general emotions; but powerful within those limits beyond any other means we know, both by the variety which it can afford, and the continued and increasing interest which it can raise.

It is obvious that the observations which I have now offered relate principally to vocal music, and to that simple species of composition which is commonly called song or air. I believe it will be found that this is in reality not only the most expressive species of composition but the only one which affects the minds of uninstructed men. It is the only music of early ages, the only music of the common people, the only music which pleases us in infancy and early youth. It is a considerable time before we discern the beauties of more artificial composition, or indeed before we understand it. In such kinds of composition a young person, whatever may be his natural taste, seldom discovers any continued relation. He is disposed to divide it in his own mind into different parts, to consider it as a collection of distinct airs, and he is apt to judge of it, not as a whole but as the separate parts of it are expressive to him or not. There is nothing, accordingly, more common than to find young people expressing their admiration of a particular strain or division of the composition, and such strains are always the most simple, and those which approach most to the nature of airs: but it is seldom, I believe, that they are able to follow the whole of a concerto, or that they are found to express their admiration of it as a whole.

With such a species of composition however, they who are instructed in music have many and very interesting associations. A song or an air leads us always to think of the sentiment, and seldom disposes us to think of any thing else. An overture or a concerto disposes us to think of the composers. It is a work in which much invention, much judgement and much taste may be displayed; and it may have therefore, to those who are capable of judging of it, all that pleasing effect upon the mind which the composition of an excellent poem or oration has upon the minds of those who are judges of such works. The qualities of skill, of novelty, of learning, of invention, of taste, may in this manner be expressed by such compositions, qualities, it is obvious, which are the foundation both of sublimity and beauty in other cases, and which may undoubtedly be the foundation of such characters in musical composition even although it should have no other or more affecting expression to recommend it. Nor is this all: such compositions are not read in private but are publicly recited. There is therefore the additional circumstance of the performance to be attended to, a circumstance of no mean consequence and of which every man will acknowledge the importance who recollects the different effects the same composition has produced on him when performed by different people. There is therefore the judgement, the taste, the expression of the performer, in addition to all those different qualities of excellence which may distinguish the composition; and the whole effect is similar to that which every one has felt from any celebrated piece of poetry when recited by an able and harmonious declaimer. Even to the very worst music, this gives an effect, and the effect may easily be conceived when the music also is good.

Immanuel Kant

(b. Königsberg, 22 Apr. 1724; d. Königsberg, 12 Feb. 1804)

From: *Kritik der Urteilskraft* (Berlin/Libau 1790), ed. Gerhard Lehmann
(Stuttgart, 1966), pt 1, bks 1 and 2

Although Leibniz had touched on what might be described as aesthetic issues, and
Moses Mendelssohn, grandfather of the composer Felix, had speculated on aesthetic
matters, Kant was the first German thinker of world significance to devote a
considerable part of his philosophical system to the theme of aesthetics. The term
aesthetics itself is generally attributed to A. G. Baumgarten. His *Meditationes
philosophicae de nonnullis ad poema pertinentibus* (1735) contains the following
passage:

115. Philosophical poetics is the branch of learning that sets standards for sensate
discourse; and since in speaking we communicate through images, philosophical
poetics must also imply some lower cognitive faculty possessed by the poet. The
task of logic, taking the term in the broader sense, must, in consequence, be the
establishment of standards to assist this faculty in the cognition of things through
the senses. Anyone with any knowledge of modern logic, however, will realise
how little this field has been cultivated. What is to be done? If logic be defined as
strictly as present-day usage requires, it must surely be considered only as the
science of knowing things philosophically; in other words, as that branch of
knowledge that directs the higher cognitive faculty towards the apprehension of
truth. Nevertheless, philosophers might well find it amply rewarding to investigate
criteria for the development and sharpening of the lower cognitive faculty, so that
it may then be more generally exploited for the benefit of all. A science must surely
exist to set standards for this lower cognitive faculty, based on the reliable
principles provided by psychology, for the assessment of things experienced
through the senses.

116. We are now almost in a position to define and devise a name for this branch
of knowledge. The Greeks and the Church Fathers carefully distinguished between
things perceived (aistheta) and *things known (noeta)*. Clearly, they did not equate
things known with things perceived through the senses, for they applied the term
to things removed from sense-perception (i.e. images) as well. *Things known*,
then, are those known by the superior faculty; they come within the ambit of
logic. *Things perceived* come within the ambit of the science of perception and are
the object of the lower faculty. These may be termed *aesthetic*.

It was only later, in his *Aesthetica* of 1758, that Baumgarten applied this word
that he had invented to a whole body of theory and knowledge in the sense in which
we understand it today; and the field that he opened up was to be greatly expanded
in the century after he invented the term. Kant's contribution was to be significant;
but he was building on foundations laid by others of far less significance in the world
of learning than himself.

Kant was educated at Königsberg; first at the Collegium Fredericanum and then at the university. The Collegium was strongly influenced by the doctrines of pietism, and the university by Leibnizian rationalism. He began his university studies in 1740, taught privately for a number of years and became a Privatdozent, a licensed, unsalaried lecturer, in 1755. In 1770, he became professor of logic and philosophy. He never travelled more than a dozen or so miles from his native city throughout his life.

He was a man of wide interests. In addition to his passion for rational and moral philosophy, he had an interest in the physical sciences and was greatly attracted to, though critical of, both the English empiricists, notably Locke and Hume, and Rousseau. His other interests included international politics – particularly the establishment of a world citizenship – religion and morality; the three great critiques, however, remain his greatest and most influential works.

The *Kritik der reinen Vernunft* (1781) is an investigation into the sources of human knowledge. In it, Kant sets out to prove that our experience of the world through our senses presupposes certain *a priori* principles which, taken together, constitute an interpretation of nature as a mechanistic system. The natural world, then, can be known through the senses, and it is self-consistent. But knowledge through the senses is knowledge of *appearances* (phenomena), not of reality. If there is (and Kant thinks it is obvious that there is) a source of all phenomena beyond any consciousness we have of individual things, bounded by the world of space, time and movement, that source cannot be known by us. We can know things only as they appear to us, not as they are *in themselves*; we cannot *know* the *Ding an sich*. Although this conception of the *Ding an sich* is largely negative, therefore, Kant was generally understood by his contemporaries and successors to be referring by it not to the limitations on our knowledge, but to the existence of a transcendent, unknowable Something. However, it has to be admitted that Kant's formulations are far from clear; and some of them lend credence to this misunderstanding, which was espoused in particular by Schopenhauer.

The *Kritik der praktischen Vernunft* (1786) sets out to examine the sources of morality. If the view of the universe as a mechanistic system is a view justified by the necessary principles of our thought, how can we be sure that such a thing as moral freedom exists, and that we are not merely the creatures of some deterministic process? Kant's answer to this is that we cannot be 'sure' of our moral freedom in the same way that we can be 'sure' of a fact of natural science. Moral freedom, however, is something that we have to postulate if we are to believe in the possibility of moral judgement and moral action at all; and philosophy can at least show that moral freedom is not incompatible with natural determinism. If we believe in the possibility of moral action, then – Kant says – we must believe in the absolute bindingness of the moral law, independently of any considerations of 'natural' factors. This is why he calls the 'imperative' which enjoins moral action a 'categorical' imperative, the basis of which is that all moral actions should be such that any of them could be set up as a universal moral precept. (When we come to consider his definition of genius, we shall see that he follows very similar lines about the principles through which genius operates.) Moral actions may well be pleasurable – as a side-effect – but pleasure and well-being are not the aim of morality. The whole basis of morality, and hence of freedom, as Kant saw it, was not self-realisation, but *duty*.

In the second *Kritik*, then, Kant maintained that freedom was the principle of obedience to rational laws which were at the same time self imposed. These laws were binding on any rational agent, whatever his desires. The third *Kritik*, the *Kritik der Urteilskraft*, sets out to establish the relationship between nature and freedom, based, not just on evidence or argument, but on *a priori* principles. Kant, like many of his predecessors, saw beauty as a symbol of moral virtue, and hence for him, aesthetics was an aspect of, or at any rate an adjunct to, ethics. In the first part of the *Kritik der Urteilskraft*, his concern is to establish absolute principles regulating beauty and its appreciation. The third *Kritik*, then, is no mere appendage to the other two; it is in a sense the culmination of them.

Kant's style is complex, but the complexity is due to the density of his thought rather than any prolixity on his part. Certain terms may need a short explanation.

Throughout the *Kritik der Urteilskraft* Kant uses the word *Gemüt* (usually translated *temperament* or *personality*) in contexts where he is clearly thinking of the body-mind-soul complex that constitutes a whole human being and his reactions to the phenomenal world. We have tended either to omit the term altogether where this could be done without damaging the sense of the original, or to translate it according to that aspect of the concept that was uppermost in his mind in a particular context. He also uses the word *Verstand* (intellect) and *Vernunft* (reason) in contrast to one another. The word *angenehm*, a key concept in the *Kritik* which he uses to categorise a particular kind of art, is usually translated *pleasant*. We have preferred the word *pleasurable*, for it is clear that Kant's use of the word *angenehm* implies 'pleasure-providing' rather than just 'agreeable' or 'inoffensive'.

Another important term that needs some explanation to the modern reader is the German word *Spiel*. It is usually translated 'play'. It has nothing of the modern idea of sport, but really stands for the spontaneous interaction of dynamic forces without any ulterior purpose. We have therefore preferred the English term *interplay*.

Part 1, Book 1: Analytic of the beautiful

Section 5: The three different types of pleasure

What is pleasurable to a person is that which satisfies some *need*; what is beautiful, simply what *pleases*; what is good is what he *esteems* (*geschätzt*), i.e. that on which he places some objective value. Even animals experience pleasure, though they possess no reason; beauty can be experienced only by mankind, i.e. by beings that are animal and yet rational. Goodness, however, is essentially a matter for rational beings.

Section 2: Any judgement of taste must be devoid of interest

Interest is that pleasure which we associate with a representation of the existence of some object.

Quite obviously everyone must admit that any judgement on beauty remotely tinged with interest is very partisan and no genuine judgement of taste. One should not be in the slightest degree involved in the object's existence, but quite impartial in this respect if one is to act as a judge in matters of taste.

This proposition is of paramount importance; and we can explain it in no better way than by contrasting the pure disinterested pleasure enjoyed in a judgement of taste with one involving interest, particularly if we know at the same time that the categories of interest are limited to those mentioned below.

Section 3: Pleasurable reactions are not disinterested

The pleasurable is whatever gratifies the senses when they react to it. This provides an immediate opportunity to draw attention to and condemn a prevalent confusion arising from the use of the word 'sensation' with two different meanings. People say or think that all pleasure is a sensation (of some pleasure or other). Everything therefore that pleases is pleasurable simply because it pleases; it is charming, attractive, delightful, gratifying and so on, according to the degree [of pleasure] that it affords, or according perhaps to the association that it has with other pleasurable sensations. But if this is accepted, then it does not matter at all whether as far as the feeling of enjoyment is concerned, the effect arises from sense-impressions conditioning inclination, from rational principles affecting the will, or merely from reflective forms of perception affecting the faculty of judgement. For the resultant pleasure would be that engendered by a particular state; and since in the last resort all processes in our faculties must have a practical starting point and combine to achieve a practical goal, the only standard by which something could be assessed or valued would be the pleasure that it promises. How this pleasure is secured is in the long run immaterial since the only thing that can make any difference is the choice of means; men could certainly condemn each other for stupidity and lack of judgement, but never for evil intent or wickedness, for, after all, whatever way they look at it they are all pursuing the same goal, namely pleasure.

The term sensation is applied to the conditioning of some feeling of pleasure or displeasure. It means something quite different, however, when I call a sensation the representation of a thing by the senses, in their role as the receptive faculty in the cognitive process. For in this latter case, the representation relates to the object, whereas in the former, it relates solely to the subject, and it does not contribute in any way to the process of cognition, not even in the sense of the subject *being aware* of itself.

But in the above explanation, we understand the term sensation to mean an objective representation by the senses. In order, therefore, to avoid any risk of misunderstanding, the generally accepted term 'emotion' will be used to describe anything that can never be other than purely subjective, and which can therefore quite simply never constitute a representation of an object. The green colour of meadows is a matter of *objective* sensation, being empirical perception of an object; the pleasure that the meadows afford, however, since no object is represented, is *subjective*, i.e. a matter of the emotion with which the object is contemplated (and this pleasure is not cognitive).

So when I judge an object as pleasurable, my judgement expresses interest; this is obvious from the fact that through sensation it arouses desire for similar objects; thus the pleasure is not simply an assessment of the object but a matter of relating its existence to my condition insofar as this is affected by the object. Hence the pleasurable is not said merely to *please*, but to *satisfy a need*. I am not merely demonstrating approval of it; it is arousing a disposition in me towards it. Pleasure that is intensely felt, then, has nothing to do with the character of the object. So anyone who has enjoyment as his sole aim (for that is what the word means that describes the inner core of satisfaction) will happily evade judging it in any respect.

Section 4: Delight in the good is connected with interest

A thing is *good* if it pleases purely as a rational concept (*vermittelst der Vernunft*). Those things are called *good for something* (useful) that please only as a means; others, however, are called *good in themselves*, that please on their own account. In either case there is the concept of some end, or at any rate (potential) desire: a connection, that is, between reason and some pleasure taken in the *existence* of an object or process, i.e. an interest of some kind.

To discover the good in something, I must always know what sort of thing the object is supposed to be, i.e. I must have some concept of it. This is not necessary if I wish to discover its beauty. Floral designs (*Blumen*), random arabesques, technically called leafwork (*Laubwerk*), mean nothing, do not depend on any definite concept, and yet they provide pleasure. Delight in the beautiful must derive from consideration of an object before any rational concept (as yet undefined) is reached; and it differs in this even from what is pleasant, which depends entirely on sensation.

Section 7: Comparison of the beautiful with the pleasurable and the good

With regard to what is *pleasurable*, everyone has his own standard, admitting when he says that an object pleases him that his judgement is based on personal emotion. If he were to say that canary wine is pleasurable, he would not object if someone corrected him, by reminding him that he ought to say: the wine is pleasurable *to him*. This is so not only in judgements of the tongue and the palate but also in cases of what is pleasurable to the ear and the eye. One person may feel that purple is soft and attractive; another may consider it lifeless and faded. One may like the sound of wind instruments; another may prefer strings. To argue over such matters, and to condemn someone else's judgement as mistaken on logical grounds if it differed from ours would be stupid; so as far as the pleasurable is concerned, therefore, the principle holds good: *to each his own taste* (based on sense).

As far as beauty is concerned, matters are quite different. It would (matters being completely different) be quite absurd if someone who prided himself on his taste sought to justify himself by saying: 'This object (the building we are looking at, the garment someone is wearing, the concert we are listening to, the poem submitted to our judgement) is *beautiful to me*.' For he should not call it *beautiful* if it pleases only him. It does not matter that many things may attract and charm him; but if he states that something is beautiful, he is implying that others will find the same pleasure in it; he is making not merely a personal and independent assessment, but one that is binding on everyone else. The moment he does this he is speaking of beauty as if it were a quality of things. Hence he says the *thing* is beautiful, not counting on the agreement of others with this judgement of pleasure simply because he has found them in agreement with him on a number of occasions, but demanding that they should agree with him. He censures them if they judge differently; he denies them taste, although he still expects it of them.

To this extent, then, it cannot be said: 'each has his own taste'. This would be tantamount to claiming that taste does not exist at all, i.e. no aesthetic judgement could be made that called on everyone to accept it.

Section 13: A pure judgement of taste is independent of charm or emotion

Interest of any kind spoils the judgement of taste, robbing it of its impartiality, especially when that interest is based on preferring what affords immediate pleasure, not, as reason does, preferring what suits the situation. This often happens in aesthetic judgements on things. Judgements that are thus swayed by emotion may make no claim whatever to universal validity, or at any rate they will stand in inverse proportion to the influence that the emotions exert over them. Standards of taste are still barbaric if they require an admixture of, let alone a total dependence on, *physical attraction (charm) and emotional appeal*. Not only is charm often considered to be a component of beauty contributing to universal aesthetic pleasure (and beauty should surely be a question only of form), but that attraction is actually considered as beautiful in itself, hence as form rather than matter. This is a misconception which, like so many others, yet possesses an element of truth in it; it is one which may be eliminated by careful definition of these concepts.

Any judgement of taste which is uninfluenced by (charm) and emotion (whether or not it is connected with pleasure taken in the beautiful), and which, therefore, is based purely on suitability of form, is a *pure judgement of taste.*

Section 14: Examples [of components in aesthetic judgements: what beauty is and what it is not]

Any form of an empirically perceived object (whether external or internal) is either a *pattern* or an *interplay*. In the latter case the interplay is either of shapes (in space: mime and dance) or simply of emotions (in time). The *charm of* colours or the pleasurable sounds of instruments may also be involved; but in the first case the *design* constitutes the actual object of any pure judgement of taste and in the second, the composition. Beauty may seem to be enhanced by the purity, variety or contrast of colours and sounds. Colours and sounds do more indeed than just add something extra to the pleasure taken in the form. They attract our attention to the object and keep it there, by giving greater precision and clarity to the form and by adding at the same time life to the representation.

That which is only incidental to and not an inner component of the complete representation, is called a *decoration* (*parerga*). It increases the pleasure of taste, though only by its form; such are picture-frames, draperies for statues, or colonnades round palaces. If however the decoration is not integral to the beautiful form itself, if as with the golden frame it is there as an attraction simply to arouse admiration for the painting, it is then termed an *embellishment* (*Schmuck*) and it has nothing to do with beauty.

Beauty has nothing to do with *being moved*, a sensation, that is, in which pleasure is aroused only by a momentary damming of vital force followed by a more powerful surge. But the judgement of sublimity (with which the sense of being moved is connected) requires a different yardstick from that required by the judgement of taste. A pure judgement of taste is thus conditioned neither by charm nor emotion. No sensation is, in short, the substance of aesthetic judgement.

Part 1, Book 2: Analytic of the sublime

Section 44: The fine arts. The pleasurable and fine arts compared
Pleasurable arts are those intended merely for enjoyment. (Among pleasures of this kind may be included those associated with entertaining at table, and with banquet *Tafelmusik*, an odd convention which is supposed to entertain by providing a pleasant accompaniment to put the guests in a cheerful mood, encouraging relaxed conversation between neighbours at table without requiring them to devote any attention to the music itself.) Fine art, on the other hand, is a manner of representation that is an end in itself. It is one that promotes the development of the personality and its capacity for social communication, regardless of ulterior motive.

The very idea that pleasure is universally communicable already implies that such pleasure does not depend on the enjoyment of mere emotion, but that it must involve reflection; hence because aesthetic art is fine art, it takes its standards not from the emotions of the senses, but from the reflective power of judgement.

Section 51: The divisions of the fine arts [Whether painting and music are fine arts]
If the art of the *beautiful interplay of the emotions* (generated by external stimuli) is to be universally communicable, it can only be concerned with the various degrees of mood (tension) in the particular physical sense through which we experience the emotion; thus broadly defined, the term may be sub-divided into a skilfully designed interplay of the emotions of hearing and of sight, i.e. into *music* and the *art of colour*. It is remarkable that these two senses, sight and hearing, are not only sensitive to impressions (and are thereby able to conceptualise external objects) but they are capable of responding to another special sensation. Whether this sensation is based on perception or on reflexion is uncertain. Moreover, this capacity to respond

may well be lacking even though the sense may otherwise be perfectly efficient or even outstandingly perceptive as far as the cognition of objects is concerned. This means that it cannot be stated with certainty whether a note (sound) or colour arouses merely pleasurable emotions or whether in itself it is already a beautiful interplay of emotions, involving pleasure in the form when it is judged aesthetically. Taking into account the speed of the vibrations of light (or, in the second instance, those of sound), which are probably far too rapid for us to form any direct estimate of the time each occupies, one might believe that it was only the *effect* of these vibrations on the elastic parts of our body that was perceived by the senses, the time interval between them being neither observed nor submitted to a process of judgement by those organs, and that everything connected with the pleasantness of sounds and colours relates to pleasure rather than to beauty of composition. However, consider *first of all* the mathematical relationship of these vibrations in music and the way they are judged and, by analogy, the judgement of colour gradations. Consider secondly those men, rare though they be, who possess the sharpest sight and yet cannot differentiate colours, and those who have the keenest hearing yet cannot differentiate sounds. Evidently those who can differentiate the various intensities on the scale of colour or pitch perceive a definite change in quality (and not merely a change in the degree of emotion). Indeed, only a limited number of such qualities can be *comprehensibly* differentiated. So both kinds of sensation might have to be regarded not merely as empirical impressions, but as the effect of a judgement of form arising from the interplay of a number of sensations. Whichever opinion one holds as to the basis of music the definition would only be modified to the extent that it could either, as we have said, be a *beautiful* interplay of emotions (via the sense of hearing) or a beautiful interplay of *pleasurable* emotions. Only in the first respect can music be fully defined as a *fine* art; in the second, it is none the less in part, at any rate, a *pleasurable* one.

Section 53: A comparison of the relative aesthetic value of the fine arts
As far as charm and stimulation go, I should place after poetry that art which comes closer to it than any of the other arts of eloquence and which can thus very naturally be combined with it: *music.* For although it communicates by means of mere sensations without concepts, and therefore does not, like poetry, leave anything to reflect on, it nevertheless moves us in more ways and with greater intensity than poetry does, even if its effect is more transient. Admittedly, it is enjoyable rather than civilising (the incidental play of thought it arouses being merely the effect of what might be termed mechanical associations); in rational terms, then, music is of less value than any other of the fine arts. Thus, like any pleasure, it requires fairly constant change; nor does it bear frequent repetition without surfeiting the appetite. Its charm, which can so universally be communicated, appears to come about in the following way: every verbal expression has a

note or timbre that is appropriate to it; a particular sound or note symbolises more or less an emotional reaction in the speaker, which in turn is induced in the listener. The idea expressed in language by the sound or note is then evoked by a reverse process in the listener's mind; hence, just as melody is a universally comprehensible language of the emotions, so music by itself communicates this language of the affections (*Affekten*) in its most intensive form; thus, by association, it universally communicates the aesthetic ideas that are naturally connected with those affections. Since aesthetic ideas are not concepts or definite ideas, however, the form (harmony and melody) in which the emotions are arranged serves not so much as the framework of a language, but as the means by which an aesthetic idea may coherently be shaped in all its inexpressible fullness, in conformity with a specific theme constituting the dominant emotional mood of the piece. It does this by means of a balanced mood-combination of these emotions (a combination that can be mathematically subjected to certain rules, since it is based on the numerical relationship of simultaneously- or successively-sounding notes, and thus on the numerical relationship between the vibrations of the air at a given instant). It is on these mathematical relationships alone, even though they are not expressed by means of precise concepts, that the satisfaction depends which is caused by the mere contemplation of the interplay of so many simultaneous or successive emotions and which constitute a universal criterion of beauty; and it is in this form alone that taste can lay claim to the right to judge on behalf of all men.

Yet mathematics has nothing at all to do with the way that music charms and stimulates us; it is only the indispensable condition (*conditio sine qua non*) whereby impressions, both simultaneous and successive may be balanced so that they may be grasped as a whole. This prevents them from cancelling each other out so that they refresh us in uninterrupted harmonious combination by means of consonant emotional reactions (*Affekten*). In this way, they produce a sense of inner enjoyment and well-being.

If, on the other hand, we judge the value of the fine arts by the culture they provide, by which is meant the development of those faculties that must combine in the act of cognition when judgement is being exercised, then music is least amongst the fine arts, because it plays merely with emotions (just perhaps as it is greatest among those arts prized for the pleasure they afford). Hence in this respect the representational arts greatly excel it, for they freely stimulate the play of the imagination in a way that is suited to the intellect. They thus fulfil a function by creating at the same time a product which is permanent, an autonomous vehicle for intellectual concepts, and one, at the same time, that has both imaginative and sensuous appeal. Thus they promote, as it were, the 'good breeding' (*Urbanität*) of the superior cognitive faculties. The two kinds of art take quite different paths. Music moves from emotions to indefinite ideas; the formative arts move from definite ideas to emotions. The formative arts create lasting impressions, music creates only transient ones. The impressions of the former can be recalled and enjoyed by the imagination; the impressions of the latter vanish altogether, or, if they are involuntarily recalled by the imagination, are more tiresome than pleasurable. Besides which, music to some extent lacks good breeding in that it obtrudes unnecessarily [on those in the neighbourhood], forcing itself on them, as it were, and thus restricting the freedom of those who are not a party to the music-making. This is something that the visual arts do not, for it is only necessary to avert the eye if one wishes not to become involved.

Section 23: [The sublime: a comparison with the beautiful]
The beautiful and the sublime have this in common that they both please in themselves. Moreover, they also have this in common, that they both presuppose a judgement based not on empirical or logical standards, but on those of reflexion. Consequently, pleasure in the sublime does not depend on a sensation, whereas the pleasant does, nor on a precise concept, as does pleasure in the good. Concepts are none the less involved, even though they are imprecise. Hence the pleasure is solely linked with the faculty of perception, or the faculty of the imagination, so that the capacity to create images – the imagination – is thought to harmonise with the *cognitive capacity* of the intellect or of reason, the cognitive capacity assisting the imagination. Hence the judgements of both intellect and imagination are *individual*, yet they can be considered as universally applicable to every subject, even though they apply only to pleasurable emotions rather than to any cognition of the object.

Yet there are also notable and striking differences between the two. Beauty in nature concerns the form of the object; and this consists in limitation. The sublime, on the other hand, may be discerned even in a formless object in so far as it has or evokes the idea of limitlessness even though the object's totality may be adduced as well. It appears, therefore, that the term beautiful is used to represent an indeterminate intellectual concept, whereas the term sublime represents a rational concept that is imprecise. Hence pleasure in the beautiful is a matter of quality, and pleasure in the sublime a matter of quantity. Similarly, the kind of pleasure deriving from the experience of beauty differs greatly from pleasure in the sublime, the former (the beautiful) directly involving a sense of enhanced vitality. It is thus something that may be experienced in combination with charm and the play of the imagination. As far as the sublime is concerned, however, feelings of pleasure are only generated indirectly and come from a momentary damming of the vital forces, immediately followed by a proportionately stronger outpouring of them. Hence, the emotional reaction is apparently an activity of the imagination more serious than mere play. It is incompatible with charm; and because the object is not necessarily attractive, but can even be repulsive, pleasure in the sublime involves not so much positive desire but rather admiration or respect, i.e. it deserves to be termed negative pleasure.

But the most significant and fundamental difference between the sublime and the beautiful is probably this: if, as is reasonable, we confine consideration of the sublime to natural objects (the sublime in art being of course restricted to situations that are consonant with nature), natural beauty (on its own account) seems to have a finality in its form that as it were preconditions our powers of judgement, and which thus constitutes in itself an object of pleasure. On the other hand whatever arouses a sense of the sublime in us merely as we apprehend it, without rationalisation (*ohne zu vernünfteln*), will be considered sublime to the extent that it resists judgement, is incompatible with the interpretative faculties and does violence, as it were, to the imagination.

Section 24: Concerning sublime feelings

. . . the analysis of the sublime calls for a subdivision that is unnecessary for the beautiful, namely the *mathematically* and the *dynamically* sublime.

For the emotion engendered by the sublime involves a *change* in the temperament associated with the judgement of the object, whereas taste in respect of the beautiful presupposes and sustains a mood of *calm* contemplation; this change should however be judged as subjectively appropriate (because the sublime pleases); hence it is related by the imagination either to the *faculty of cognition* or the *capacity for desire*. But in both of these cases the appropriateness of the given representation is judged only in respect of the *faculty or capacity* (without ulterior motive or interest); since then the faculty of cognition presents the object to the imagination as a *mathematical* condition, and the capacity for desire as a *dynamic* condition, the object may be considered sublime in either of these two senses.

Part 1, Book 2, A: The mathematical sublime

Section 25: A definition of the term sublime

The sublime is that which makes everything else seem small in comparison with it. So it is obvious that nothing can exist in nature, however large, that might not be infinitesimally small by some other standard; and, conversely, nothing so small that, by some still smaller standard, might not be magnified in our imagination to the size of the world itself. Telescopes have provided us with ample evidence of the first, microscopes with evidence of the second kind of observation. Nothing, then, can by this criterion be called sublime that can be perceived empirically. Yet there is in our imagination a latent urge to reach out towards the infinite and in our reason a call for some concept of absolute phenomenal totality. The very fact, then, that our capacity to evaluate the size of things cannot match the concept itself is the first awakening in us of a feeling of some supra-sensible faculty.

Judgement naturally makes use of certain objects to enhance this faculty; and it does so by using scale, large in the absolute sense, not just by the standard of the object itself, whereas as far as everything else is concerned it uses a comparatively small scale. So what should be called sublime is the state of being that is generated by a particular image rather than the object itself. We may thus add to the foregoing definitions of the sublime the following: *The sublime is that which indicates some capacity to transcend all empirical standards merely by thinking of it.*

Section 26: The estimate of the magnitude of natural things that is consonant with the idea of the sublime

The infinite is not merely comparatively great, but absolutely so. Compared with it, anything else (of the same kind of magnitude) is small. But the most significant point is that the capacity even to think of the infinite *as a totality* represents a capacity transcending any empirical scale. For to do so would require a capacity to comprehend that was based on a unity that bore a precise numerical relationship to infinity, which is impossible. None the less, the capacity *even to think of infinity* without inconsistency requires a faculty in the human temperament that in itself transcends the empirical . . .

Nature, therefore, is sublime when she conveys to us the idea of infinity as we contemplate her. This can only happen when the very mightiest effort of our imagination is inadequate to estimate an object's size. But our imagination is competent to measure the mathematical size of any object because the mind is able through progressive upgrading of the unit of measurement to adapt itself to any suitable numerical scale. Whenever an attempt is made to comprehend an object, using a valid basic scale of measurement – one that can be applied with the minimum of intellectual effort – and when that attempt produces an increasing awareness of our inability to comprehend its infinite scale, then this attempt transcends the imaginative powers and the assessment must therefore be an *aesthetic* one. But since this basic scale is a self-contradictory concept (because an unlimited progression towards absolute totality is impossible), then the size of any natural object on which our comprehension and the entire resources of our imagination are vainly focused must raise our idea of nature to a plane transcends the empirical. This plane which underlies both nature and our capacity to think, is so gigantic that it transcends the capacity of our senses to grasp it. Hence it is not so much the object that must be considered *sublime* as our mood when we apprehend it. . . .

It is obvious from this that true sublimity should be sought only in the character of the person making the judgement, not in the natural object arousing the sense of the sublime. Anyway, who could possibly describe a dark, tempestuous ocean as sublime, or formless mountain ranges, towering over one another in wild disorder, and capped with icy peaks? Yet in judging such things man experiences a sense of exaltation, regardless of their form, when he abandons himself to his imagination and reason and still cannot match them, although his reason is not following any clear course but merely enlarging the horizons.

Every case in which our imagination is presented with a larger unit of measurement rather than a numerical concept that is comparatively greater (to simplify the mathematical series) provides an example of the mathematically sublime. A tree measured by the height of a man provides at any rate a scale for a mountain; and if the latter were about a mile high, it could be used as a scale on which to measure the earth's diameter so as to make that comprehensible; the earth's diameter could be used as a scale for the planetary system known to us; the planetary system for the Milky Way; and the immeasurable host of such galactic systems, or nebulae, as they are called, which probably constitute yet another system in themselves, permit us to conceive of no limits. Now in the aesthetic judgement of such an immeasurable whole, the sublime lies not so much in the number as in the fact that we are judging on a progressively larger scale. When reason creates ideas on an appropriate scale, nature herself dwindles into insignificance in our imagination. The systematic structure of the cosmos contributes to this, by representing everything great in nature as small, or rather, small in comparison with the limitless imagination – the ideas reason creates to establish a scale adequate to their representation.

Part 1, Book 2, B: The dynamically sublime in nature

Section 28: Nature as power

In judging nature as dynamically sublime, we must imagine her as arousing fear (though the converse is not true; not every object arousing fear is considered aesthetically sublime). For when we judge a thing aesthetically (no concept being involved) our victory over the forces in our way can be judged only in proportion to the size of the resistance we meet with. But what we endeavour to resist is a threat; and if we discover our capacity to resist is inadequate, it is an object of fear. So our faculty of aesthetic judgement can consider nature as a force, and hence as dynamically sublime, only to the extent that she is an object of fear.

But an object may be considered *terrifying* without *causing* fear in us if we judge it simply by *supposing* some situation in which we should wish to resist it and then finding that such resistance was totally futile. So a virtuous man fears God without being afraid of Him, because he cannot think of a situation in which he would wish to defy God and His commandments. But in every case that he thinks of as not in itself impossible, he recognises Him as an object of fear.

The sublime can no more be judged by someone who is afraid than can the beautiful by someone who is absorbed by his appetite and his desires. The former person will flee from the sight of an object that arouses his fear; and it is impossible to take pleasure in actual terror. Hence the pleasure when some unease is relieved is *gladness*. But this becomes gladness at the sense of being liberated from some danger, accompanied by a resolve never again to be exposed to it; in fact we do not even enjoy the memory of such a sensation, let alone the prospect of encountering it again.

Prominent, overhanging, menacing cliffs, towering stormclouds from which come lightning flashes and thunderclaps as they roll by, volcanoes in all their destructive violence, hurricanes leaving devastation in their trail, the boundless, raging ocean, a lofty waterfall on some mighty river, all render our capacity to resist insignificantly small in comparison to their power. But their aspect becomes ever more attractive the safer we feel ourselves to be; and we are happy to call such objects sublime because they elevate the powers of our soul above their normal state, causing us to discover within ourselves a capacity to resist, of quite another order, giving us courage to measure ourselves against the apparent omnipotence of nature. . . .

So sublimity is contained, not in any natural object, but in ourselves in so far as we become aware of nature and thus of our superiority over nature (to the extent that she influences us).

General observation on the exposition of aesthetic reflective judgements
The moral law which so powerfully preconditions every important characteristic in us is the object of pure and unqualified intellectual pleasure; and since this power really makes its presence felt aesthetically only through sacrifice . . . any aesthetic pleasure deriving from it is negative, i.e. against the interest of the senses; yet from the intellectual standpoint, however, it is positive and involves an interest of some kind. It follows from these aesthetic considerations that something both morally good and self-consistent is to be thought of not so much as beautiful than as sublime. It arouses respect (which despises charm) rather than love or affection. The reason for this is the mighty power that the mind exercises over sensual desire, for human nature of itself does not incline to such goodness. Conversely, what we call sublime in external nature, or even in ourselves (e.g. certain emotional states (*Affekten*)) takes form only as a power in our character capable of overcoming *certain* obstacles of sense attraction by moral principles, thereby becoming as objects of interest.

Section 46: Fine art is the art of genius
Genius is the aptitude (natural gift) that gives the arts their rules. Since this aptitude, the artist's inborn creative (*produktiv*) capacity, is itself part of nature, it might well be defined thus: *Genius* is the inborn human aptitude (ingenium) *through which* nature provides art with rules.

Whether this definition is appropriate or not, whether it is merely arbitrary, or whether it is in keeping with the usual interpretation of the term genius or not . . . at any rate it can be shown from the start that the fine arts must necessarily be regarded as arts of *genius*, as we have defined the term.

For each and every art presupposes rules on which a product must be based if it is in any way to be called artistic. But the beauty of a work of fine art may not be judged on the basis of a concept derived from some rule or other, nor can any concept be formed of how it is created. Thus the fine art itself cannot devise the rules governing the creation of its product. But equally, no product can ever be termed art unless some rule pre-exists it, since nature must supply the individual, and through him art, with rules (by virtue of the sensitivity of his faculties), i.e. fine art is only possible as the product of some genius.

From this it is evident that genius (1) is an *aptitude* to produce something for which no definite rule can be postulated; it is not a capacity or skill for something that can be learnt from some rule or other. Its prime quality, then, must be *originality*. (2) Since there is such a thing as original nonsense, the products of genius must at the same time be models, i.e. they should be *exemplary*; and therefore, while not being products of imitation themselves, they should serve as models for others, i.e. they should provide a standard or rule of assessment. (3) The aptitude cannot of itself describe how it creates its products, or demonstrate the process theoretically, though it provides the rules by itself being a part of *nature*. Thus the progenitor of a work of art is indebted to his own genius and he does not himself know how the ideas for it came to him, nor does it lie within his power to calculate them methodically or, should he so wish, to communicate them to others by means of principles that would enable others to create works of equal quality. . . . (4) It is through genius that nature prescribes the rules of art though not of scholarship or science, and only here in so far as the art is a fine art.

Section 52: On the combination of fine arts in one and the same product
Rhetoric may be combined with a pictorial representation of people and things alike, in a *play*; poetry may be combined with music in *song*; both may be combined with a pictorial (theatrical) representation in an *opera* as may the interplay of emotions in a piece of music with dance steps, and so on. The representation of the sublime, too, in so far as it is part of fine art, can be combined with beauty in an *edifying poem*, in a *verse tragedy* or an *oratorio*; and when so linked, the fine arts become even more artistic. Whether, however, they gain in beauty (as so many and varied kinds of pleasure interact with one another) is in some cases debatable. Yet in all fine arts, the essential thing is the form, which is the starting point for observation and judgement where pleasure is at the same time culture, attuning the spirit to ideas, and so making it receptive to more such pleasure and entertainment. The physical experience is not the issue (that is to say what charms or moves us). Where the aim is merely enjoyment, no ideas are left behind, the spirit is blunted, the object gradually becomes tedious and one becomes dissatisfied and ill-tempered with oneself, being conscious of one's resistance to the exercise of the rational powers of judgement.

If the fine arts are not associated with moral ideas, either closely or distantly, ideas which alone imply some independent pleasure, this is bound to happen. In such cases they serve only as amusements, and one comes increasingly to depend on them the more one exploits them to banish dissatisfaction; in so doing one becomes increasingly dissatisfied with oneself and ever more ineffectual. Natural beauties in particular are most conducive to moral improvement (*der ersteren Absicht*) if one becomes accustomed to observing, judging and admiring them from an early stage.

See also Bibliography under: Dahlhaus, Knox, Koerner

Karl Heinrich Heydenreich

(b. Stolpen, 19 Feb. 1764; d. Leipzig, 26 Apr. 1801)

From: *System der Aesthetik* (Leipzig 1790), pp. 150; 154–7; 160–6

Heydenreich, rather than Sulzer, seems to be mentioned in later articles and publications as the pioneer of musical aesthetics in Germany; both Nauenberg, in Volume 1 of the *Neue Zeitschrift für Musik* (Leipzig 1834) and Schilling pay tribute to him. Educated at St Thomas's School, Leipzig and at Leipzig University, where he read philosophy and philology, he proceeded to his Master's degree in 1785 and succeeded to the chair of philosophy not long afterwards. He held the post until 1798, when he ran into debt, resigned his appointment and degenerated into an alcoholic.

Both as a teacher and as a writer, Heydenreich enjoyed considerable initial success. Soon, however, he was accused of sentimentality in his attempts to reconcile the categories of Kantian philosophy with the claims of the emotions. His writings include, as well as his *System der Aesthetik*, works on moral philosophy and a series of *Briefe über den Atheismus* (Leipzig 1796).

Like Sulzer, Heydenreich was an eclectic; and like other thinkers of his age, he regarded music as the art most suitable to the portrayal of the motions and passions of the soul. He regarded its potential in this respect as great because of its directness in communication without recourse to any image or object, the notes themselves being the symbols that convey the intended emotion. As such, despite the fact that he had no connection whatever with the literary romantics of the late 1790s and the early years of the nineteenth century, he is one of the most important precursors of the romantic movement in music.

See also Lichtenthal, *Bibliography*, p. 378

As a general rule man's aims and needs are twofold: one concerns the body and its maintenance in the healthiest possible state for as long as possible; the other concerns the spirit, its free expression and development and the fulfilment of man's basic spiritual aspirations.

Man's physical needs give rise to the mechanical arts, which satisfy them.

Man's spiritual needs involve his emotions and his cognitive powers. As a cognitive creature man is inescapably driven to discover more about himself, and to instruct his fellow men. As a creature of feeling he is driven to express and to develop his emotions. In the former case, works of learning are the result; in the latter, works of art. Every work of fine art is therefore a representation of a particular state of sensibility. . . .

The representation of a specific state of sensibility can generally be achieved in three ways:

1. I may merely wish to imitate my emotion or passion, its nature, the way it progresses, changes, develops and combines with others, but without any indication or description of the objects that may have aroused them.

2. I may wish merely to depict the object that has affected my sensibility without illustrating the emotion or passion that it aroused.

3. I may wish to combine both aims in one work, and to portray at one and the same time the object and the emotion or passion that it arouses, or each in turn.

In this case, I may aim to give particular emphasis to either (a) the illustration of the object or (b) the description or illustration of the emotion or passion. . . . Such a division can be universally applied to representations of states of sensibility, not only as they have been expressed in works of this kind up to the present, but also as they might conceivably be expressed at any time.

The following requirements are thus essential to any medium (*Zeichen*) capable of illustrating emotion and passion:

1. It must be subject to the constraints of time (*die Form der Zeit*) and observe all its laws and conditions. It must be adaptable and able to mirror whatever rapidly-passing changes we may observe in those emotions and passions of which we are clearly conscious.

2. It must be sensitive to the whole range of emotions and passions, whether weak or strong, coarse or refined, gentle or violent.

3. It must have the same potential constancy and consistency as the natural emotions and passions themselves have.

4. It must none the less be potentially as variable as the passions and emotions themselves without losing the coherence that results from its constancy and consistency.

A medium that satisfies all these demands must necessarily be able to imitate emotions and passions comprehensively and consistently. Its imitations will be unfailingly effective as long as it lasts and as long as the sensibility for which it is intended is capable of reacting to variations in its intensity. These are basic requirements. Unless, however, our spirit is in the first place so disposed that conscious perception of the imitation immediately transports us into a state of emotion or passion identical to that represented by the imitation, our reaction will be merely one of cold admiration at the accuracy of the imitation. Now musical sounds do satisfy all these demands and in the following ways:

1. Notes are necessarily subject to the constraints of time and to all its laws and conditions; successions of notes can move just as quickly or slowly as the emotions and passions of which we are conscious. If therefore melancholy moves with slow, dragging steps, or sublime emotion with solemn measured ones, and emotions of hope or joy light and skipping ones, notes can in this sense perfectly imitate their various states.

2. Sounds can exhibit every shade of strength and feebleness, coarseness and refinement, gentleness and violence that we find in the emotions and passions. If, for example, mood melts into mood, as it were, in feelings of tenderness, sounds can imitate this. If, on the other hand, the soul is tossed savagely by some tempestuous emotions which batter against one another at random, as it were, sounds can equally well imitate such a state. It is not just the melodic contour and its development that effects this, however, but also the harmony. If a predominantly powerful emotion is to be evoked, what can richness and fullness of harmony not achieve? What powers do dissonances (and these may of course be resolved) not have in the expression of a savagely exuberant and volatile passion? Again, what powers do not smooth sequences of consonances have to express gentle, uniform, peacefully flowing emotions?

3. Sounds may have as much continuity as natural emotions and passions by means of:

(a) melodic unity; (b) consistency of the tonality in which a piece is written; (c) unity of rhythm and metre; (d) unity of tempo; and certainly through (e) unity of performing style; they may also have continuity

(a) because of the relationship between the melodic phrases; (b) because of the relationship between the tonalities; (c) because of the continuity of time itself.

4. Sounds may be as varied as emotions and passions themselves without prejudice to the potential unity that may be achieved of which they are capable through persistence and continuity. Variety springs from the constitution of sounds, partly from melodic structure and partly from harmony. In this respect, variety within a composition may be divided into (a) successive variety and (b) simultaneous variety.

Sounds can work only through the sense of hearing. The characteristic nature of hearing really determines the effect that works constituted from sounds will have. The sense of hearing is (a) sufficiently sensitive to respond to simultaneous sequences of sounds (*Tonreihen*); (b) acute and responsive enough to act to the most rapid sequences of sounds. Musical works have an irresistible power to move us. This mainly derives from the close connection that exists between the hearing, the memory and our poetic capacity for feelings and emotions.

1. Sequences of sounds arouse memories of former emotions and passions. After what has been said about the correlation between sounds and emotions and passions, the most commonly accepted laws governing the recall of ideas and emotions must all the more necessarily apply in view of that correlation.

2. Through experience, we possess a poetic capacity for passions and emotions: we can re-create in ourselves, that is, a passionate or emotional state illustrated for us by external symbols. We can do this by concentrating on the recollections of previous states and experiences, and by making

appropriate use of them. We can also do so through the power that we have to induce in ourselves the capacity for new feelings and desires. That this is actually what happens when musical works are played nobody will deny. Sounds are thus symbols that truthfully imitate emotions and passions in a universally comprehensible manner, awakening reactions that the human heart is powerless to resist. No other medium can rival it in this respect; music is thus the only art that can fully imitate emotions, and passions. Who cannot but admire nature's wisdom in creating this medium, one that is so similar to the emotions and passions that any emotion or passion, once aroused, can be translated into sound in the effort to express itself? The intimate connection that exists between the capacity to feel music and the capacity to feel emotion and desire is beyond further explanation. Experience merely teaches us that the connection is really there and that in this respect all men are alike.

Fig. 2. *Schubertiade* (Moritz von Schwind, 1804–71). Schwind was a friend of
Schubert; and this engraving – entitled *Ein Schubertabend bei Ritter von Spaun* – is
an elaboration of an unfinished oil-painting that conveys the atmosphere of a
Schubertiade. The various ways in which the listeners are enraptured by Schubert's
music are very striking. The engraving dates from 1868. (Hochschule der Künste,
Berlin)

Christian Gottfried Körner

(b. Leipzig, 2 July 1756; d. Berlin, 13 May 1831)

From 'Ueber Charakterdarstellung in der Musik', *Die Horen, eine Monatsschrift* (Stuttgart 1795), no. 5, pp. 97 *et seq*, in *Christian Gottfried Körner ein Musikästhetiker der deutschen Klassik*, ed. Wolfgang Seifert (Regensburg 1960), pp. 147–9; 154–8

The Golden Age of German literature was dominated by the work of Johann Christian Friedrich von Schiller (1759–1805) and Johann Wolfgang von Goethe (1749–1832). Schiller is best known to musicians as the author of the ode, *An die Freude* (1785), part of which was set by Beethoven in the finale of the Ninth Symphony, and as the great dramatist, many of whose plays were transformed into operas by such nineteenth-century composers as Donizetti and Verdi. Goethe was unquestionably the greatest of all German lyric poets and a man of extraordinarily wide interests: dramatist, novelist, botanist, aesthetic theorist, efficient civil servant, essayist and epic poet.

During the 1780s and 90s, these two great figures were at the height of their powers; and, as W. H. Bruford explains in his *Culture and Society in Classical Weimar, 1775–1806* (Cambridge 1962), they devoted a good deal of their attention to the place of the arts in the moral and even the political education of man. They were both very receptive to music; and while neither of them left any profoundly original ideas on music in any developed form, a number of passages from their works attest to the kind of music that they appreciated and the effect that it had on them.

Goethe moved to Weimar in 1776; Schiller joined him eleven years later; and the interchange of ideas between the two of them and with Herder, who was court preacher there, was intense. When Schiller died in 1805, Goethe felt the loss severely; yet it is interesting to note that they never used the familiar 'du' form to one another, for all the intimacy of their intellectual contact. Schiller was much influenced by Kant, and among the various works that Kant inspired was an important set of letters, *Über die ästhetische Erziehung des Menschen*, usually referred to as the *Erziehungsbriefe*, of which Bruford gives an excellent account on pp. 270–84 of his study. In the *Erziehungsbriefe*, Schiller

> gets completely away from the 'imitation theory' and helps considerably to clarify the thought of his time about the nature of a work of art. He calls it a 'semblance' (*Schein*), something that interests us above all through its pattern, the relationship between its parts, not through the material of which it is made or the references to real-life experience that it may suggest.[1]

In the twenty-second letter, Schiller writes of music:

> In its highest state of refinement, music must become form and affect us with the calm power of antiquity; representative art must aspire to become music and

[1] Bruford, *Culture and Society*, p. 282.

235

move us by direct sensuous presence; poetry, like music, must seize us powerfully, but also, like representational art, surround us with calm clarity. In a truly beautiful work of art, this must be achieved by form alone, not by content, for form affects *universal*, content only *specific* powers.[2]

Bruford's summary of the argument should be consulted by those who wish to know the details of this important work. Bruford himself wrily admits that 'we cannot follow Schiller into the intricate details of his argument'. Schiller postulates two drives in man: the drive towards *form* and the drive towards *matter*. These may be roughly equated with the mental forming of experience and the desire for experience through the senses. There is, however, another aspect of human character, which Schiller calls the drive towards *play*, which he says can suspend or balance the other two drives. In doing so, it allows men to be truly free, free, as Bruford puts it, 'from the compulsion exercised by natural laws, and equally free from the dictates of reason – in particular . . . Kant's "practical reason" and the "categorical imperative"'. It is this play impulse that lies at the root of artistic creation and enjoyment; and it is 'only when actively or passively engaged in aesthetic activity that man becomes in the fullest sense human – which means . . . made in God's image, and so semi-divine – because he attains here totality'.[3]

Schiller's claims on behalf of the play impulse and of aesthetic activity go much further than this. It is only through such 'play' and the true humanity that results from it that the ordinary sensual man can be granted the rational insight and strength of character that are necessary to a satisfactory political order. This is not to claim that art has a practical political aim; but aesthetic education, Schiller maintains, is an intermediate stage 'having passed through which a man only needs the appropriate occasion for the exercise of these qualities [rational insight and strength of character] and he will find that he possesses them'.[4]

Although susceptible to music, Schiller was suspicious of its strong emotional appeal and deplored what he regarded as current trends in emphasising 'its sensual appeal, pandering to prevalent taste, which seeks only to be pleasantly titillated, rather than gripped, powerfully moved, edified'. (*Ueber das Pathetische* (1793), in *Sämtliche Werke* (Leipzig n.d.), vol. xi, *Kleine Schriften vermischten Inhalts*, p. 230). He had no doubt that music *could* appeal, by virtue of its form, to a higher aesthetic taste, but he did not feel that it was the most significant of the arts in the task of aesthetic education.

It was Christian Gottfried Körner, the acknowledged expert on music in the Weimar circle, who tried to apply Schiller's theories to music. Körner was a close friend of Schiller; he was a successful lawyer and a well-trained musician of near-professional standard when he first met the poet in 1784. He composed three settings of *An die Freude* which was written while Schiller was staying with Körner's family, and the exchange of correspondence between him and Schiller, published in 1847, shows the bond of sympathy that existed between the two men.

We differentiate in what we call the *soul* between the permanent and the transient, between the character and its emotions: character – *ethos* – and emotional states – *pathos*. Is it a matter of indifference which of the two the musician seeks to portray?

The first requirement of a work of art is indisputably that, as a human

---

[2] J. C. F. von Schiller, *Sämtliche Werke* (Leipzig n.d.), vol. 12, pp. 57–8.
[3] Bruford, *Culture and Society*, pp. 279–80.
[4] Ibid.

product, it should be differentiated from the effects of blind chance by evidence that it has been properly constructed. This is the basis of the law of unity. The superior composer tries to give his works this quality, though not always with equal success.

By the nature of things, poets and artists cannot portray a situation except through the medium of the personality. The musician, however, may easily cherish the illusion that emotions can be portrayed in the abstract. It is an easy enough game, admittedly, to dish up a disconnected jumble of emotions by means of a motley collection of sounds, but if the composer is content with this, he cannot claim to be an artist. If, on the other hand, he recognises the need for unity, he will seek it in vain in a series of emotional states: these concern nothing but variety, constant change, growth and decline. If he wishes to capture and to sustain an individual mood, his work will become monotonous, dull and drawn out. If he wishes to portray change, something constant must be implied against which to project change; indeed, the constant element is often there, though the artist himself may not have consciously chosen it. But all too often he sinks to a state of raw nature simply because he neglects to make this choice. He is led astray, he misuses his talents, because the very lowest mode of expression is the one that is most generally understood. He frequently earns the loudest applause when he has sinned most grievously against Art; and this distances him still further from his goal. If the arts are content to copy slavishly the things of the phenomenal world, this is sufficient proof that they are at a very low ebb. Such imitations may be of value in recalling an impression that has previously been experienced, but the value is not an aesthetic one; when we anticipate enjoyment from a work of art, we demand more than this. The artist has to compensate for our want of perception in respect of individual phenomena; he must idealise his subject matter. He must portray the dignity of human nature in the products of his creative imagination. He must raise us to his level from our lowly, circumscribed state of dependence and represent to us the Infinite, an Infinite that can otherwise come to us only by intuition (*Anschauung*).

But an emotional state has limitations by its very nature. All its power is focused, as it were, on the endeavour to achieve a specific goal. In such a case, the imagination cannot enrich the subject matter with new material, but merely strengthens and intensifies the endeavour.

Attempts have often been made to idealise misery, joy, desire and revulsion. But in these attempts, what was, in fact, the element of the ideal? Was it the *emotion* in itself? Or the person through whom we experienced the emotion? If we divest ourselves of any ideas of masculine power or of feminine gentleness, how much of the ideal still remains?

Nothing is infinite in human nature but *freedom*, freedom which operates on a unique scale and with unique power, freedom from the external world and all the tempestuous internal world of emotions, and which is embodied for us in the representation of character.

If it is true that music, of its very nature, forgoes the advantages that the other arts have in the representation of character, the reason for this must lie in the specific qualities of the art. We should examine this more closely.

It has been said that music gives us nothing to think about. If there were any substance in this, music would no more be able than the other arts to portray human character. Indeed, many people still believe this. They still consider that poetry, drama, or dance must necessarily supplement music's imprecision; and the meaning of self-sufficient musical compositions is misconstrued because that meaning cannot be translated into words and concrete forms.

[pp. 150–3 omitted]

The particular way in which the language of gesture gives expression to a specific aim undoubtedly lends the representation a clarity which is lacking in a sequence of notes. Perception of this aim evokes a clear idea of the object of desire: fear, wrath or love. Music, too, has a specific aim – that of regaining the home tonic. The ear's satisfaction increases or diminishes to the extent that the musical progression approaches or moves away from it. This objective towards which music moves does not, however, symbolise anything in the visible world. It symbolises the unknown something which can be imagined as an individual object, as the sum of many objects, or as the external world in its entirety.

Granted, however, that musical representation is in this respect less complete, and that it leaves more to the imagination than the arts of dance and mime do, we have none the less seen that a representation does not have to be comprehensive in order to be precise. Even in the language of gesture, the *kind of movement* indicates enough, though the purpose of the movement is not explicit; and the question arises whether precision of this kind may not be considered analogous to what we discern in the simple outlines of a shape.

In the language of gesture, the airy gait of joy and the heavy tread of grief are universally understood even if in neither case does the gesture provide us with a precise image. The symbols acquire meaning because we have noticed a connection between these differentiated movements and our own differentiated moods; and this connection can be transferred from ourselves to other human beings. In the movements of an alien form we recognise ourselves.

The difference between a shout of jubilation and a forced cry of pain is of a similar nature. Our own experience tells us the emotional state that is being expressed; and a certain sympathy which finds its expression in the language of gesture, however tenuously it does so, reinforces that experience.

If, then, we assume that objective criteria exist by which even the least sensitive and skilful person may differentiate between signals of joy and those of pain, by the same token, specific signals exist that convey infinite nuances of these contrasted emotions. A person of fine and receptive sensibility will compare unfamiliar gestures and sounds with those that are universally understood, and he will discover that they correspond to a greater or lesser extent to the accepted signals of joy and pain. In this way, the language of gesture is enriched, and the language of sounds can also be enriched as long as the opportunity exists to train the sense of hearing as well as that of sight. Though the ear cannot be said to discriminate less subtly than the eye, the individual may well find himself more frequently having to compare images rather than sounds. He will therefore more readily understand dance and drama than he will music. Music, on the other hand, will convey more to someone whose attention is more readily held by sounds than by shapes.

Jean Baptiste Leclerc

(b. Chalonnes, Maine-et-Loire, 1755; d. Chalonnes, Nov. 1826)

From: *Essai sur la propagation de la musique en France, sa conservation, et ses rapports avec le gouvernement* (Paris 1796), pp. 1–33

Leclerc represented Chalonnes in the Convention nationale that was responsible for the execution of Louis XVI in 1792. He was returned by Chalonnes to the Conseil des Cinq-Cents in 1795 and he was for a short while its president. In the same year he was expelled from France as a regicide, but he was eventually permitted to return to Chalonnes. He was something of a poet, a novelist and a religious mystic, a 'théophilanthropique' as he has been described, who believed that the necessary basis of morality was belief in the immortality of the soul, and in a God. His *Essai*, the outcome of a paper that he had prepared for discussion by the central committee for public education (of which he was a member) is the logical successor to Barthélemy's *Entretiens* (see pp. 166–75). It was published only a year after the Convention had accepted the proposal – passionately argued by Sarrette on similar lines – for a national music Conservatoire, to further the well-being of the nation. There is no record to show how Leclerc's fellow committee members reacted to his idealistic and bigoted naivety. Already, however, the State had gone a long way in the direction that Leclerc proposed.

For further reading:
Constant Pierre, *Sarrette et les origines du Conservatoire* (Paris 1895); also his *Musique* and his *Les Hymnes et chansons de la révolution française* (Paris 1904).

The argument

There comes an opportune moment for the establishment of an institution: once this is passed, that institution will prosper only with the greatest difficulty. The time is almost ripe, perhaps, for the establishment of a national music. The government has a duty to seize the opportunity. When our enemies are forced to sue for peace, when at last they let us enjoy the fruits of perseverance and victory, when national enthusiasm is roused again by the glory of the French name and the prospect of better fortune, all hearts will be receptive to similar feelings, and for a moment everyone will be swept up in a common ecstasy. Let a comprehensive plan be prepared, in order that this new access of feeling may profitably be exploited. Let the government consolidate the achievements of this movement, and in some way or other establish moral unity throughout the Republic.

[pp. 4–7, line 5 omitted]

Although the constitutive laws of modern society take no account of

240

music's influence, music is no less powerful than it was in ancient times; we believe that it plays a much greater part in modern politics than is generally supposed.

[p. 7, line 13 to p. 10, line 15 omitted]

Antoinette, a victim of national pride, attracted to France some years ago the celebrated German to whom we are indebted for the creation here of dramatic music. This was an unwise thing to do. It is not too much to say that Gluck's musical revolution must have made the government tremble. His vigorous harmonies stirred the warm hearts of the French, which were moved to lament past errors. There were signs then of a power which was to burst forth, shortly afterwards. The throne was shaken. The friends of liberty in their turn enlisted music's help – music which employed those manly accents that the German composer had taught it. The Champ de Mars[1] was founded upon the sound of the clarinet. The Marseillaise triumphed on France's frontiers; civic songs taught the people that they had a fatherland; men developed a deep love of liberty.

[p. 11, para. 1 to p. 14, para. 2 omitted]

All the national institutions that are concerned with morals must be united in a comprehensive plan and organised in such a way that they have an equal influence on every member of the community.

The problem that must be solved then is this: the restoration of an equilibrium between the townsfolk and the countryfolk, or rather the discovery of a half-way point at which music will serve to restrain the former and advance the latter, a point at which the music will be acceptable to both.

Before proposing a solution to this problem it will be good to ask whether, on the one hand, music is suited to rustic simplicity, rural customs and labours, and whether on the other it may not be destroyed if it is forced to retrace its steps.

In doing so we must look for a moment at the state of contemporary music. In the final analysis we will find that it is of two distinct kinds. One corrupts and is already too decadent to be regenerated. The other is still pure enough to deserve protection. If prudence does not allow us to banish the first, at least there can be no objection to abandoning it, so to speak, to its unhappy fate, whilst the second will be preserved for the welfare of the community.

This will become clearer as we go on. Before doing so it will be appropriate to say something of the French aptitude for music. It is a

---

[1] Sited between the École militaire and the left bank of the Seine; it was the parade ground where troops were reviewed on the anniversary of the storming of the Bastille. It was there that Louis XVI swore, before the *députés* of the 83 *départements*, on 14 July 1790, to uphold the new constitution (eds.)

mistake to believe that nature has denied us gifts that it has apparently showered on other peoples. The philosopher who used to claim that the French language was the enemy of music was discountenanced when the sublime compositions of Gluck were heard. Those of us who are equally mistaken in referring to the so-called grosser faculties of the French peasant, would renounce our opinions, too, if we were to look around carefully at the various regions of the Republic.

Who has not often been charmed during his travels by the songs of the shepherds and the ploughboys? Who is unaware of the sweetness of Provençal folksong? And in the theatre, who has not been thrilled with the songs of the mountainfolk, songs that our modern composers have adapted with scarcely a change? The ease with which these people memorise tunes, many of which are quite difficult, the joyful pleasure that a group of people take in a folksong or a hurdy-gurdy tune, the love that the French have of dancing, are these not proof enough that we have an innate disposition for music? Everything from the galoubet[2] to the musette, from a farandole to a Breton dance, proves that the French only lack instruction to be as successful as other nations in an art whose first master is nature but out of which men have made a science.

[p. 17, para. 1 to p. 19, para. 1 omitted]

Nowhere in the Republic are the French inferior to the Swiss or the Germans in discernment and sensitivity. If these peoples have progressed somewhat further in music it is because they are more musically educated than we are. When we decide to teach our children music at the age that they are taught to read and write, in both our city and our village schools, then within a few years France will leave Switzerland and Germany far behind.

But can this be done without harming the simple manners of our countryfolk?

Ah! We have a very different idea of music than the ancients had if we doubt it for a moment! It is true that we only yet know a defective kind of music; certainly, if I felt that music had nothing to offer but that licentiousness with which it prostitutes itself in the theatre I should think twice before introducing it into the countryside. But I have in mind a young virgin, not a votary of Bacchus.

Would a village be perverted simply because an ensemble comprising ten or twelve military instruments graced its festivals and regulated the marching of its national guard? If each district maintained a group of singers to perform patriotic hymns, and if the greater part of the populace had sufficiently practised ears to join in simple and easy choruses, would there be any impropriety in this? It is surely desirable, moreover, that a young man going about his business, and a young woman in the midst of

[2] A three-holed, Provençal flute (eds.)

her domestic chores, should soothe the pains of their parents by moral, yet graceful songs. It is surely right they should find a useful pastime in this exercise of their nascent sensibilities, or rather, easy and pleasurable instruction whereby their emotions, which are ready to take wing, can be directed toward some happy goal!

[p. 21, line 11 to p. 22, line 7 omitted]

The function of a purer music would be to lead us, by pleasurable means, to the practice of all the private and public virtues. In order that this should never be lost sight of, its limits would be prescribed by law, its development would be governed by rule, and there would be a special magistrate with responsibility for administering the laws and regulations.

We would banish, not only the harmful, but also the trivial and worthless. In order that music shall become – I will not say, more expressive, or more imitative, for music imitates but imperfectly and it expresses only generalities – in order, then, that it should become more positive and inspiring, we would inseparably unite it to poetry, without which it almost invariably lacks any sense of purpose. Following Plato's example we would ban purely instrumental music; we would only allow it to lead the marches of the national guard battalions, and to accompany dancing at public festivals if it had originally been set to words that were of a moral or political flavour.

[p. 23, para. 1 to p. 25, para. 3 omitted]

The variety to be observed in the spirit and behaviour of the French people stems more from the diversity of their laws and customs than from differences of climate and soil. By implanting in all hearts a common aim, a united response, one will unite the passions. It is music's especial task to complete this important work. Let music operate in a similar way throughout the Republic; let it draw to a central point all the diverse interests that must converge there; the excitability of the southerner, the stolidity of the northerner, the stubbornness of the Breton, the volatility of other regional peoples, all the many nuances of temperament will gradually give place to one unified, national character.

To argue that each region should have music and musical instruction appropriate to its particular genius would be to propose the retention of a multiplicity of dialects, and this would to some extent create barriers between the borderlands and the central provinces of the Republic.

[p. 27, paras. 2–3 omitted]

The priests, to whom we refer again in this connection, felt the need for uniformity. With a few exceptions the church tunes were the same everywhere, and the towns and villages were on an equal footing. The southerner and the well-to-do would find in the northern regions and in the hamlets, the same nourishment for their religious fervour as would the northerner and the countryman in the south and in the cities, should they by chance be taken there. This kind of communion would help considerably in untold ways to strengthen the moral links that bound them to their faith, and to extend its domain.

Let us then like the priests have a liturgy that is common to us all.

[p. 28, para. 1 to p. 29, para. 1 omitted]

Before the revolution there were only two kinds of music, properly speaking: all kinds of instrumental music – symphonies, quartets, trios, and keyboard pieces – and dramatic music, which we believed subsumed every kind of vocal music (for the chanson only gained a public hearing after it had been sung on the stage, or else it was so like an operatic aria that it usually provoked an enquiry as to the opera from which it had been taken).

We have already put forward our views on purely instrumental music. Now we are going to be equally frank about purely dramatic music.

It is above all in the theatre that music is daily becoming more and more degenerate as it gets further away from the kind of music that the legislator has a right to demand for the improvement of morals.

Music's purpose must be to re-establish an equilibrium between the passions, moderating those that are harmful when taken to excess, and stimulating those that have a beneficial effect. In the theatre, its function is to express the passions, there being no question of any choice or discernment. Jealousy, hate, vengeance, lust – all these are feelings the portayal of which earns music the loudest applause. Yet she rarely employs the colours that are best suited to her subject. More often than not, she substitutes terror for energy; as the faithful companion of degenerate poetry she shares in her licence, and like her – no longer innocent – she lards herself with ornament and seduces instead of using her natural charms. Philosophers and artists generally are aware of the fact that music can go astray, and it is this that leads them to fear that music is hastening to her downfall. The public's avidity for novelty, and the ease with which composers discover extraordinary devices to astonish it, have resulted in the kind of orchestral licence that often degenerates into mere noise, ruining the ear and causing it to lose its taste for pure harmony. All artistic efforts are bent towards incidental effects; melody is almost despised, and the organ that nature has given us to express the affections is the medium that our modern musicians employ the least often. Composers have so expanded the orchestra, moreover, that not even the smallest comic opera can be put on, except in four or five of the largest cities in the Republic.

[p. 31, Para. 1 to p. 33 line 3 omitted]

The Revolution has seen the birth of a new genre of 'hymn', which enshrines that elevated character that the subject demands. It is the hymn – we suggest – that should be wholly reserved for our national music.

As Plutarch observed, 'Like all whose prime concern is the care of public mores, the Ancients preferred and esteemed above all, a solemn music that was not affected.' We read, in discussions of Greek music, that Olympus, who lived some nine centuries before the celebrated Timotheus, only made use of a very few notes in his sacred songs, which were the despair of the modern poets.[3]

---

[3] Leclerc then quotes extensively from Barthélemy – the passage beginning, 'Just then a melodious song stole upon our ears', down to 'it heightens their self-respect'; see p. 173 above (eds.)

(Karl Wilhelm) Friedrich von Schlegel

(b. Hanover, 10 Mar. 1772, d. Dresden, 11 Jan. 1829)

From: 1. *Kritische Schriften*, ed. Wolfdietrich Rasch (Munich 1956) and
2. *Das Athenäum* (Jena 1798–1800), pp. 302, 320

August Wilhelm von Schlegel's younger brother was apprenticed to a Leipzig banker
before his parents gave him leave to attend university. He read law and classics at
Göttingen and Leipzig and then joined his brother at Jena in 1796. His earliest
critical studies were all on classical themes, but the periodical, *Das Athenäum*, which
he founded with August Wilhelm in 1798, became the organ of early literary
romanticism in Germany.

In 1802, Friedrich moved to Paris for two years, where he worked as a literary
journalist and a lecturer in philosophy as well as studying oriental languages. He
became a Roman Catholic in 1808 and entered the service of the Austrian
government. Much of the rest of his life was spent in diplomatic and administrative
service.

Schlegel's creative works are of little importance, but his critical essays and the
pointed aphorisms which he contributed to *Das Athenäum* show him as an
imaginative and original critic.

For further reading:
Lilian R. Furst, *European Romanticism* (London & New York 1980).

1. [Romantic poetry]

Romantic poetry is a progressive, all-embracing poetry. It is not concerned
merely to reunite the many disparate genres of poetry, and to establish links
with philosophy and rhetoric. It rightly aims in one instance to fuse poetry
with prose, and in another to mix the two together. A similar fusion and
juxtaposition is to be seen in the realms of critical analysis and spontaneous
creativity, and in the poetry of nature and of art. Romantic poetry
is concerned to bring life and social relevance to poetry, to saturate the
forms of art with materials that aptly delineate all kinds of character;
it is concerned to poeticise wit, and to infuse artistic forms with vibrant
humour. . . .

Romantic poetry is related to the other arts in the way that companionship, friendship and love are to life. Other kinds of poetry are
complete and can now be fully and critically analysed. Romantic poetry is
constantly developing. That in fact is its true nature: it can forever only
become, it can never achieve definitive form. No exhaustive theories about
it are possible, and only a critic with oracular powers of analysis would be
entitled to dare a definition of it. It alone is infinite. It alone is free. Its

246

overriding principle is that the poet's fantasy is subject to no agreed principles. Romantic poetry is the only poetry that is more than a poetic genre. It is, so to speak, the very art of poetry itself. Indeed, in a certain sense, all poetry is – or should be – romantic.

2. The philosophical nature of music

All pure music must be philosophical and instrumental.

Many people tend to find it curious and absurd that musicians should talk of the *ideas* in their compositions; and yet it may frequently occur that one is apparently more conscious of their thoughts *in* their music than of their thoughts *about* it. Anyone who is aware of the wonderful ways in which the arts and sciences relate to one another will at any rate mistrust the dull idea that the arts are based on the concept of so-called 'naturalness'. According to this, music is supposed to be merely the language of the emotions. The person who goes more deeply into the question will discern that a certain element of philosophical speculation is not at all foreign to the spirit of pure instrumental music. Must not purely instrumental music create its own text? And is not its theme developed, confirmed, varied and contrasted, just as is the object of a sequence of philosophical speculations?

See also Bibliography under: Piert

Wilhelm Heinrich Wackenroder

(b. Berlin, 13 July 1773; d. Berlin, 13 Feb. 1798)

From: (1) a letter to Ludwig Tieck, 5 May 1792, quoted in *Mit der ganzen Ungeduld des Herzens, Briefe deutscher Klassiker*, ed. Kurt Fassmann (Munich 1969) p. 691; (2) *Phantasien über die Kunst für Freunde der Kunst* (Hamburg 1799) in *Sämtliche Schriften*, ed. Curt Grützmacher and Sybille Claus (Munich 1968), pp. 146–7

The publication of Wackenroder's *Herzensergiessungen eines kunstliebenden Klosterbruders* in 1797 was a landmark in German literature because it announced a quite new type of aesthetic criticism. Romanticism had arrived. The collection of eighteen essays, fourteen by Wackenroder himself, the other four by his friend Ludwig Tieck (1773–1853) deals exclusively with aesthetic issues in painting and music. Its main theme was that art, and especially music, was not just an imitation of nature, but a holy mystery; and this was particularly so of music.

The best known of the essays is probably that entitled 'Das Leben des Tonkünstlers Joseph Berglinger', in which three themes are apparent. The first theme is that art is a luxury whilst the daily routine and work are the true realities. The second is that art is the *only* reality. Berglinger is prone to this attitude when he takes up his post as a Kapellmeister; but he then discovers that art too, in such a context, becomes a drudgery and a routine. The third theme is that the artist must transcend even imagination by the force of his creative power, suffusing his workaday world with that creative power. Berglinger, then dying, achieves this by the composition of a magnificent Requiem Mass. It is strange how the events of Wackenroder's life and even of his death parallel those of this work.

Wackenroder went to school at the Friedrichs-Werder Gymnasium in Berlin where he first met Tieck. His musical gifts were soon recognised, and he was taught by Karl Friedrich Christian Fasch (1763–1800), friend and colleague of C. P. E. Bach (1714–88) and teacher of Karl Friedrich Zelter (1758–1832). Zelter was a friend of Goethe and the teacher of Felix Mendelssohn. Zelter himself wrote of Fasch that he:

> required a work of art to be real work of art – aiming not simply to give pleasure, but to have a discernible value to the expert . . . As an instructor, he was eloquent, precise about detail and dependable, yet in any other respect it was very difficult to obtain any systematic musical credo from him, especially if it ran counter to current tastes. Anything he could not praise with his whole heart, he preferred to pass over in silence, but his praise was precise and carefully thought out.[1]

It is not difficult to imagine what kind of a musician Fasch was, nor where his tastes lay.

Both in music and in his more academic studies, Wackenroder was gifted and industrious. He became interested in Germanic literature and art; and in September 1792, he and Tieck set out on a walking tour, on which they visited a number of art

[1] *Gedenkschrift an Karl Friedrich Christian Fasch* (Berlin 1801).

248

galleries. They then began their university studies at Erlangen. Although Wackenroder kept up his literary, musical and art studies throughout his time at university, writing novels (*Die Unsichtbaren,* 1794; *Der Demokrat,* 1796 and *Das Schloss Montford,* 1796) and composing music, he graduated in law and began legal practice in 1794. However, a visit with Tieck to the Dresden Art Gallery in 1796 resulted in the *Herzensergiessungen,* and he expressed the wish to devote himself to music and the arts. His father, later to become *Geheimrat,* remained adamant that the young man should continue legal practice. In February 1798 Wackenroder died of what was termed a nervous fever. All his other works are substantially devoted to music, including the *Phantasien über die Kunst,* from which the following extract is taken.

Wackenroder regarded art as something ineffable and sacred, and he believed that however logically conceived it might be, it could only properly be appreciated when there was a bond of empathy between creator and recipient, a bond that sprang from an act of imagination. This is very evident in the first extract, which comes from a letter that he wrote to Tieck in Berlin, dated 5 May 1792. It is not a little curious that although Wackenroder wrote much on Raphael, Dürer and Michelangelo, he failed to mention a single composer in his many discussions of music.

[1. A letter to Ludwig Tieck]

Whenever I go to a concert, I find that I always enjoy the music in two ways. Only one of these is the true one. This involves attentively following the progression of sounds, yielding completely to this stream of overwhelming sensations, and banishing and withdrawing from every disturbing thought and every alien sense-impression. A certain effort is involved when one drinks in the sounds so avidly, and it cannot be sustained for any length of time. For this reason, I believe I can confidently claim that an hour's music is all that we can absorb, at the very most. Concerts, operas and operettas, therefore, exceed the bounds of nature.

The other way in which music gives me pleasure comes not from direct enjoyment, not from a passive acceptance of tonal impressions, but from a certain spiritual activity which is generated and sustained by the music. In such cases, I do not feel the prevalent emotion of the piece; my thoughts and fantasies are, so to speak, borne away on the waves of melody, and are lost in some remote hiding-place. The remarkable thing is that when I am in this mood, I am best able to reflect aesthetically [*sic*] on the music as I hear it. It is as if universal ideas are being prised loose from the emotions that are induced by the composition, ideas that are then projected rapidly and clearly before my soul.

[2. Colours]

Sculpture, painting and music are separate arts and each has a validity and a quality of its own. I have always felt, however, that music could lead a separate existence of its own whereas poetry could not. Certainly a musical counterpart can easily be found to every fine painting, the two having but a single soul. Whenever the musical composition is heard the picture takes on a new life. An intenser art speaks to us from the canvas. Sound, light and colour intermingle in ardent union. When this happens we may indeed be face to face with art as the counterpart to nature, nature refined to its highest degree and speaking to our purest and loftiest emotions. This is surely why, from time to time, pictures that in themselves may be quite insignificant make such a remarkable impact. When the deep silence that surrounds the picture is broken by sounds that have an affinity to it, the picture takes on as it were a living soul, and every line and point of colour breaks into tumultuous life. Sculpture seeks only to express forms. It scorns colour and speech. It is too ideal to have any purpose other than its own existence. Music is the breath of the spiritual in its highest form, its finest manifestation, the invisible stream as it were from which the soul draws sustenance for its deepest dreams. Music engulfs the human spirit. It means both everything and nothing. It is a finer and perhaps subtler medium than language. The spirit can no longer use it as a vehicle, as a means to an end, for it is substance itself and this is why it lives and moves in its own enchanted realm. Painting is too simple, and it holds a place virtually on its own between sculpture and music. It sets out as it were to create an illusion through form; it strives to imitate the sounds of the living world; it endeavours to depict life and movement; it is tense, yet it has no strength; it seeks in music a powerful life, movement and strength. It is almost impossible therefore to describe a painting. The words are dead; they explain nothing, even when the painting is before us. A genuinely poetic description, however, evokes a new joy and understanding of the painting, because it arouses a response that is similar to the one that music arouses, the music being replaced here by images, brilliant forms and words.

Johann Gottfried Herder

(b. Mohrungen, 25 August 1744; d. Weimar, 11 December 1803)

From: 1. *Allgemeine musikalische Zeitung*, Leipzig, vol. 15, no. 1, 6 Jan. 1813, p. 1; 2. *Kalligone* in *Sämtliche Werke*, ed. B. Suphan (Berlin 1877–99), vol. 22; text taken from an edition by Heinz Begenau (Weimar 1955) pp. 39–42; 144–54

Herder was one of the most significant influences on German life and letters in the last quarter of the eighteenth century. There is hardly an aspect of German literature that he did not touch upon; to see him simply as an early romantic is greatly to underestimate his vigour and range. He studied philosophy and theology at Königsberg, where he attended Kant's lectures (it was Kant who aroused his interest in anthropology), and critical analysis and investigation. At Königsberg, too, he met Johann Georg Hamann (1730–88), one of the champions of instinct and intuition who thought that poetry was 'the mother-tongue of the human race' and was known to his friends as the Magus of the North. In 1764, Herder entered holy orders and was appointed as a teacher at the cathedral school in Riga where he soon became noted as a fine preacher. He lived and worked in Riga until 1769, publishing in 1767 an essay on recent German literature that was both original and influential. In 1768 he set about systematising his ideas on art and literature in a series of four *Sylvanae* (*Kritische Wälder, oder Betrachtungen, die Wissenschaft und Kunst des Schönen betreffend, nach Massgabe neuerer Schriften*). Only the first three of the *Sylvanae* were published in Herder's lifetime; the fourth, which included his ideas on music, appeared posthumously in 1846.

Herder was already aware of the need for a dynamic and empathetic approach to the appreciation of literature and art, taking account of the emotional and cultural environment against which works were produced; and this attitude was deepened and reinforced by a long sea voyage to France which he now undertook. On the return trip, he was shipwrecked; and the whole experience gave him a first-hand insight into the world of the ancient Nordic sagas. For the rest of his life he pressed the claims of ancient non-classical cultures and folk-art, publishing an extensive corpus of traditional material (*Stimmen der Völker in Liedern*, 1778–9 – the work is always known under this title, though the title itself was first applied only to the second edition of 1807). Herder was certain that the key to the study of humanity lay in the study of art and culture and that the emotional appeal of the great literature of all ages and cultures was one of the foundations of this study.

In 1771, Herder became court preacher at the court of Schaumburg-Lippe in Bückeburg, where J. S. Bach's youngest-but-one son, Johann Christoph Friedrich (1732–95), was Kapellmeister. Intensely responsive to music as he was, Herder collaborated with Bach on a number of works, such as a cantata-oratorio *Die Auferweckung Lazarus*; an opera (now unhappily lost) on the subject of *Brutus*; *Die Kindheit Jesu*; and another oratorio (also unfortunately lost) with the interesting title *Der Fremdling auf Golgotha*.

In 1776, at the invitation of Goethe, whom he had met in Strassburg in 1771,

251

Herder accepted the post of general superintendent and court preacher at Weimar, where he stayed until his death in 1803.

Folk-poetry, gothic architecture, intuition and imagination, Shakespeare – these were four of the territories that Herder's vital and imaginative approach really opened out to German intellectuals of his age. To Herder, emotion (*Gefühl*) was the original state of psychic awareness; hence music was the art that appealed to the innermost part of man. The ideas that he published during his lifetime were set out most comprehensively in his treatise *Kalligone* (Weimar 1800), written as a vehement counter-offensive to Kant's *Kritik der Urteilskraft*. *Gefühl*, Herder argued, was not simply emotional indulgence; it was the inner psychic process of experiencing phenomena, the basis of apprehending not merely sensations but truth, goodness and beauty as well. Aesthetics was thus for Herder the most fruitful of studies, the science not merely of man's body and mind but of his very soul – the unconscious, spontaneous and deepest part of his whole being. Herder sensed the need to challenge the epistemology and thus the shared assumptions of most eighteenth-century thinkers, though he was in fact unable to do this. Herder's rejection of Pythagorean aesthetics – as instanced in his espousal of pure instrumental music – is a radical departure from much pre-romantic musical thought.

For further reading:

R. T. Clark, *Herder's life and Work* (Berkeley and Los Angeles 1955).

[1. Allgemeine musikalische Zeitung]

Whatever form is given permanent physical shape (as in the arts of sculpture and painting), judgement must constantly be sharpened, tested and perfected against that form. But the situation seems to be different with things that are transient – such as music and language. Who can take in at a glance those rolling seas in which each surging wave instantly recedes? Moreover, every nation, every age, every individual judges music and poetry by widely differing criteria. This is why judgements of nations, individuals and eras differ so widely. This may be so; yet the materials of art are none the less inseparably linked by empathy to the person who enjoys them and who experiences *emotion* through them, an emotion that is always purely *human*. Harmonic relationships are the same to all peoples; the susceptibility of our sense-organs can be gradually developed and thus taken into account and compensated for; hence some universal standard, some *empathy* is possible. And even if the masters of the art from various eras and peoples did not wish to deny their individuality, the intellect's musical ear will still correlate them, appreciating each in its individuality and raising it to the sphere of the universal. *Languages* float on a cloud of arbitrary conventions; to the uninitiated their sounds are often actually repellent; but once they are fully understood, the *ear of the soul* is opened up, and transcending all such arbitrary conventions, hears them as the pure music of thoughts and reflections. So we brazenly step in front of a work of art, even of language, forget it for what it is, and in it, with our intellect, appreciate only what is the product of the intellect. Peoples and eras vanish before our eyes. Obviously, the ideal of the beautiful becomes loftier and loftier with each age; like a sun it rises before humanity, shining on all peoples and all ages. The more works of art from different ages and peoples stand before us for comparison, the more clearly we see what each one lacks and what this and that one excel in. Of visible forms, sculpture stands in the forecourt of the great temple, drama and her sisters in the foyer; the spirit of the epic hovers over the entire building and the lyric chorus encloses its two wings. Today, one people and one language will excel in one art; yesterday, another people and another language in another art. Anyone who admires one particular era to the exclusion of all else, who holds its forms to be eternally valid and apt for the times in which he lives, whether these be Greek, or French, anyone who transplants himself from his own living soil into its frail earthen vessels, will remain apart and estranged from that ineffable, living ideal: *the ideal that extends to all peoples and all ages.*

[2. Kalligone]

[p. 154]
The memory of pictures fades and foresakes us; music travels with us as our most intimate companion, enlivening and uplifting our existence from childhood onwards, cheering and comforting us.

[p. 146]
Everything . . . that we hear in nature . . . contains the elements of music, only a hand is needed to draw forth music, an ear to hear it and the capacity to respond to it. No artist has ever invented a sound, nor has he been able to invest one with a power that does not relate to nature or to some musical instrument; what he does is irresistibly to coax it forth by his sweet power. The composer discovers sequences of sounds and subtly but skilfully compels us to respond to them. The musical sensations are not 'evidenced from without', but are within us, inside us. What comes to us from without is merely the sweet sound that moves everything; this sound is generated by harmony and melody, and it awakens harmony and melody in everything that responds to it.

[pp. 39–41]
A. A blow disturbs a body; what message does that body's sound communicate?

B. 'I have been disturbed; my members are consequently vibrating and eventually coming to rest.'

A. Is that what they say to us?

B. Every fibre of our being is capable of responding; our ear, the hearing-chamber of the soul, is extraordinarily sensitive, an echo-chamber of the finest kind.

A. So if single sounds *arouse* us, what do intermittent sounds do?

B. They renew and reinforce the stimulus, like a trumpet; they reawaken.

A. And *long-sustained* sounds?

B. They sustain the emotion by prolonging the stimulus. They create an extraordinarily powerful effect.

A. What about sounds that get louder or softer, faster or slower, sounds that rise or fall, that are increasingly or decreasingly intense, harsh or soft, regular or irregular, sadder or gayer; what about blows, accents, waves, emotion and pleasure – what effect do all these have on us?

B. As every involuntary reaction of our emotions to music proves, these all produce similar responses. The tide of our passions ebbs and flows, it floods, it meanders and trickles. At one moment the passions are intensified, at another they are aroused now gently, now powerfully; at yet another moment they are satisfied; their movement and the way they move varies in response to every melodic nuance, and every forceful accent, let alone every change of key. Music performs on the clavichord within us which is our own inmost being.

A. Might it not be *Castel's* colour-keyboard, or a keyboard of visual shapes that is played within us?

B. Visual shapes indeed! What have these to do with our inner responsiveness to emotional currents, vibrations and passions? You are implying that sounds *illustrate* things.

A. Does every person who is responsive to nature experience a similar reaction to sounds?

B. I should imagine so. A certain kind of music makes everyone sad; another flowing or lilting kind makes everyone cheerful, lively and gay. One person may be more responsive to the former kind of music, another to the latter, according to his mood at the time. A person's response to music that is fast or slow, harsh or gentle, powerful or tender, grave or gay may depend on his physical build or character, but every person is none the less endowed with a basic pattern of varying emotional and tonal responses.

[pp. 149–50]

Word and sound, sound and gesture, are intimately related to each other, and they affect us most powerfully in the three specific spheres of religious awe, love and dynamic power (*wirkende Macht*). Religious awe can involve every shade of feeling, from fainting submission to overwhelming and irresistible strength, from heavy grief to exuberant joy. The simplest word, sound or gesture here achieves the most effective and far-reaching results. Love, too, finds its most intense manifestation in longing and fulfilment, struggle and victory, mourning and joy. Last but not least it is *dynamic power* that transforms nature. It creates and re-creates through courage, through decision and action. The dimensions in which it operates are those of judgement and change. All three spheres of religious awe, love and dynamic power have given us superb masterpieces, and thus to prefer one before the other would be an act of tasteless insensitivity and sinful ingratitude. Let each have its appointed space and time. Given that both time and place are right, even descriptive music, as it is called, is not to be despised if it strengthens our faltering resolve and lends further power to words, like the voice of invisible spirits, by holding back or releasing the energies of nature. Even light music may be of some value, for is not our most sparkling and cheerful plane of existence that of fun and joy?

[pp. 146–7]

Sound, the summoner of the passions, has a power that we all experience; we respond to it both physically and spiritually. It is nature's voice, an inner dynamism that draws forth a response from the entire human race; it is *harmonious movement*.

The dance depends on this; the musical sounds consist of regular vibrations which affect the body to the extent that they reflect, develop or subdue the emotions. Musical rhythm relates to bodily rhythm or emotional expression. Natural man can scarcely avoid associating music with movement when he is deeply moved: his face, his posture, the way he moves his body and beats time with his hands all express what he hears. The dances of primitive peoples and of warm-blooded, vigorous races alike all take the form of mime. This was true even of the Greeks, who spoke of music as the 'leader of the dance', a dance that involved every response of which the soul was capable.

Since nature has bound together *music, dancing* and *movement* so intimately as primeval expressions of communal energy, it was surely inevitable that these should be accompanied by singing and by the primeval voice of one who was deeply moved. We tend to join in when we hear voices singing; the impact of the *chorus,* particularly when it first enters or re-enters after a long rest, is quite beyond words, as is also the magical sound of voices singing in parts. They are one, yet not one. They part company, they pursue each other, harass each other, clash, they conflict, they support and overwhelm each other; they stimulate, they enliven, comfort, flatter and re-embrace each other until they die away in eventual union. Such textures, for two or more voices, tonal contests, both with and without words, are the sweetest images of a sweet and total union, images of seeking and finding, of friendly conflict and reconciliation, of loss and longing, of despair and recognition. Nor in the case of vocal music, do the words just passively interpret the elegant labyrinth of meaning; they contribute equally to the total effect.

[pp. 41–2]

B. Harmony is certainly the basis of music, just as fixed proportions are the basis of architecture; none the less the power and impact of music does not wholly depend on harmony. We must therefore formulate a law that will serve to explain how harmony plays on the emotions by means of its purely musical qualities, its functions, its procedures, fluctuations of power, its ebb and flow, its rise and fall, its strength, its weakness, its vitality, its languor.

A. Might we not be able to discover this law? Might it not be the cycle that binds all sounds and progressions indissolubly together? We hear a multiplicity of sounds in one sound that comprehends not just one melody, but an infinity of potential melodies; we have a scale as firmly and solidly based as a rock. May this be perhaps the law that we sense? In the realm of sound, harmony performs, as it were, the function that the straight line does in relation to other kinds of line, or the square or rectangle in relation to other geometrical figures: it is the foundation of correctness, yet it can generate of itself no form of organic beauty. Harmony, the architecture of music, could never generate a dynamic and stirring melody within the strictly circumscribed pattern of tonal relationships if the emotion itself did not have its own shape, its own focus, its aim and procedures. Melodic progressions are equivalent, in terms of beauty, to lines, which range from the straight to the circle. None can be substituted for any other, but all, are subject to one eternal law: the harmonic series.

[p. 38]

It has been found that harmony is the basis of the structure of physical bodies, the overtones of which sound in every note; this can actually be seen in the vibration of a bowed string and in *Chladni's* experiments on glass plates. The notes take on visual shape and can be identified by their simple relationships and easily understood proportions. I willingly admit that neither *Rameau* nor *Tartini* has quite satisfied me on the question of melody; *Rousseau's* doubts about these two theorists and others seem to me well-founded. If it were true that music is nothing more than a mathematical sleight of hand in which musical pleasure derives from numerical relationships and intervallic calculations – an idea that I find quite meaningless – I should be frightened off it for ever. Whoever counts or calculates when he experiences music's deepest and life-giving joys? Listen to a composer improvising in the fiery intensity of inspiration; watch him composing with genius and passion; he is preoccupied with other matters than counting and calculating. It is scarcely credible that a *Mozart*, a *Gluck*, or a *Haydn*, could calculate thus and at the same time create such magic.

[pp. 150–1]

In the light of what has been said it would be wrong to conclude that word and gesture must always be linked to music and that they are indispensable in every minute detail to the interpretation of its meaning. Were this so they would soon make tedious company. And what would be the purpose of interpreting every note in word and gesture? Speech is for the formulation of *thoughts*; *emotions* it can merely stammer out, expressing them more by what is left unsaid rather than by what is said. Emotion that is expressed by a profusion of words is insupportable, for the words engulf the emotion and in so doing demonstrate its insincerity. Sounds can absorb one another, pursue one another, clash with one another and imitate one another; the quintessence of music is indeed the coming and going of these magic spirits of the air, for music creates its effect through the ebb and flow of the emotions (*Schwingung*). Words are empty and inappropriate, whether in speech or in music, when the emotions press upon each other, especially if they are an attempt by an undemonstrative people at self-expression, and every intake of breath, every bow stroke is laboured at. Music must be free to speak without encumbrance, as is the tongue. Song and speech do not adopt the same means. Music has developed into a self-sufficient art, *sui generis*, dispensing with words. Pan, who summoned Echo on his reed pipe without either words or gestures, was the Pan who called forth and declaimed the music of the universe. When Apollo, with only a single swan as his audience, invented the lyre, he became by virtue of that lyre and his own character the progenitor of all the choruses of the Muses. Orpheus moved Orcus by the eloquence of his lute; the Eumenides would never have responded to a mortal's *words*.

Those of you, then, who despise pure music and cannot respond to wordless music, those of you who find nothing in it, should avoid it. Treat it as a game that is played with or without purpose by living instruments. But musicians should, like Plato, inscribe these words over their studio door: 'Let the inartistic keep their distance!'

The slow progress of music's history amply demonstrates how hard it has been for music to cut herself free from her sisters – mime and the word – and to establish herself as an independent art. One single compelling force was needed to give her independence and to free her from alien help.

In ancient Greece, in fact, music was usually the accompanying hand-maid of poetry; and tended to take the form of recitative. Music gained much by this freedom of declamation, but only in being tied to poetry. In the dance, where she was apparently the dominant partner, she was subservient to the rite, to the grouping, the form and the gestures of the performer. What was it that helped her to rise, to trust in her own power and to take flight with her own wings? What was that something that freed her from all external control, from spectacle, dance, mime, and even from the accompanying voice? It was *religious awe*. Religious awe raises the individual above words and gestures so that nothing remains to express the emotions but – *sounds*.

See also Bibliography under: Begenau, Marks, Wiora

Pierre Simon Ballanche

(b. Lyon, 4 Aug. 1776; d. Paris, 12 June 1847)

From *Du sentiment considéré dans ses rapports avec la littérature et les arts*
(Lyon 1801), pp. 12–33; 46–64

Ballanche was the only son of Hughes Jean Ballanche, an associate of one of the principal printing houses in France's second city, Lyon. He was dogged by ill health in early life and left very much to his own devices. He was an avid reader, developing at an early age an informed interest in ethics and aesthetics, and the writings of such influential figures as Hutcheson, Du Bos, Batteux, Barthélemy, Goethe and Kant (though he admitted to having only a second-hand acquaintance with Kant's work). *Du sentiment* was his first published work, and it was the one that deals most directly with aesthetic problems: later important publications include the *Essai sur les institutions sociales* (1818) and *Palingénésie sociale* (1832).

Much of *Du sentiment* is a restatement of ideas that had already been developed by earlier writers: the imitation of beautiful nature, the relationship between the good and the beautiful, and the purpose of the fine arts. Ballanche chose however to place particular emphasis on the quality of 'sentiment' (though he claimed to have been guided by Kant, in so doing). The idea had already been well explored of course by Du Bos (see pp. 19–20); yet no previous writer had so explicitly praised *le sentiment* at the expense of *la raison* in the context of aesthetics. In *Du sentiment* we find a process of natural growth that links eighteenth- and nineteenth-century concepts of 'feeling', even though Ballanche saw himself as a member of a new romantic movement that had made a radical break with 'classical' expressions of feeling.[1]

Without doubt, Ballanche's distrust of *la raison* was greatly sharpened by the post-revolutionary disillusion that so many idealists were then experiencing, and he is highly critical of 'reason' in those passages that refer directly to political events. 'Sentiment' he argued, was the benificient power that kept watch 'over the mysterious sanctuary of illusion, guarding it against the impious curiosity of lofty reason', and it was 'sentiment' that the revolutionary forces had destroyed. Whilst he offered no original comment on music as 'sentiment' he quoted André at length[2] on the subject.

When it was first published, *Du sentiment* attracted little notice, though there is evidence that it influenced several major figures, including Chateaubriand, whose *Génie du Christianisme* came out a year later, and Charles Nodier, editor of the influential Parisian *Journal des Débats*. From 1817 onwards, however, Ballanche moved in the circle of Mme Recamier, and after the 1830 revolution he achieved a wider recognition. Amongst those who acknowledged his influence were the Polish poet, Mickiewicz (whom Chopin admired), Sainte-Beuve, and George Sand, who

---

[1] See Albert J. George, *Pierre Simon Ballanche, Precursor of Romanticism* (Syracuse 1945), pp. 73ff.
[2] See pp. 27–35.

found, when she came to know Liszt, that Ballanche was one of his favourite authors, his works standing 'unblushingly on the shelves, alongside Montaigne, Voltaire, Lammenais and Lamartine'.[3]

Introduction

[pp. 19–20]
There is a French book on moral feelings (*sentimens moraux*) by an anonymous author. Its plan is a very limited one and its title is inaccurate, for the work only deals with thoughts and maxims as they are expressed in terms of feelings, not moral feelings. Though it is full of excellent things I shall dispense with an analysis because I plan to say more about it in my notes. I shall simply pause over a very astute observation – one that I believe has not been made before – that there are four classes of idea to which the term sentiment (*sentiment*) is applied: sentiment is the synonym of opinion, the expression of a judgement; it stands for feelings of the senses – for sensations; for feelings of passion or pathos; and for moral feelings. In reality, however, these four classes of ideas are not far removed from each other, for they all have a common origin.

[p. 12]
This now is my attempt at a definition of sentiment (*sentiment*): it is the moral power that judges instinctively and without premeditation, and which conforms to the law of our nature, a nature in which there is a threefold relationship between animality (*animalité*), personality (*personnalité*) and spirituality (*spiritualité*). Sentiment never separates the three but apperceives them in a single instant. The first of the three defines the domain of physical sensibility or sensation; the second, that of individuality or consciousness (*conscience*); the third, that of the intellectual faculties or soul. In the first we are in contact with visible nature; in the second we arrive at self-knowledge and become aware of good and bad; in the third we envisage a superior order of things of which our own existence seems to be but a shadow, and it is here that our domain extends outwards into the infinite. Out of these three springs a fourth, our humanity (*notre humanité*), which is no more nor less than a union of the three.

[p. 17]
In comparing the ancients with the moderns I find that the present age has been the first to bring the torch of analysis to sentiment. The ancients did not use the term, nor any other that was analogous to it. This may explain why our ideas on the subject are so unformed. Indeed, when the great masters are silent we can only stammer. Even so, we must rejoice that they were unaware of the subject of this essay; the discovery of this rich vein has

---

[3] George, *Ballanche*, p. 134.

been reserved for us by fate as some small compensation for the vast mine that the ancients opened up for us. Recent progress in metaphysics has undoubtedly led us to the discovery of the faculty of sentiment; there are other causes, too, which we shall have occasion to examine.

[pp. 31–3]

In his *Principes de littérature* Lebatteux has proved that all the arts boil down to one principle: namely the imitation of beautiful nature (*la belle nature*). This is doubtless why the arts borrow their most common terms, as also their most brilliant metaphors, from each other. 'Ut pictura poésis erit', said the poet, who was the richest source of maxims that have since become proverbs in the world of letters, maxims having the greatest intellectual substance and expressed in the original form of 'sentiment'.

Here are some corollaries that immediately spring from this principle.

The imitation of beautiful nature produces what has been called ideal beauty. The faculty that perceives in nature the things that must contribute to the composition of ideal beauty is called *genius* or *talent*. The faculty to discern beauty in nature before imitating it, the faculty that precedes observation, which is the motivating power of genius and which becomes the habit of being moved by beauty is precisely that power of feeling (*cette puissance du sentiment*) which we have defined above. At a certain level of energy or exaltation sentiment becomes enthusiasm.

The fine arts then have created in us a new faculty by which we can assess the extent to which the artist approaches ideal perfection in the imitation of nature. This faculty holds such a sway over our ways of being, feeling and judging that often we are as moved by the imitation of nature as by nature itself, and sometimes even more so. This faculty is a modification of feeling, for the person who admires artistic masterpieces does so because his ready perception demonstrates the truth of the imitation, confirming that what he feels deep inside him is indeed what he has seen in nature. It is this that produces the critic of sentiment.

Prologue

[pp. 46–8]

The greatest benefit that sentiment has afforded us, however, is not the immortal gift of the fine arts; that which undoubtedly merits the greatest recognition is the invaluable way in which it has lodged in our hearts the immutable principles of virtue and morals, by which our happiness is measured.

It is not by reason, of which we are so proud, that we are able to raise ourselves to the sphere of spiritual beings; it is not solely by the power of reason that we flatter ourselves in the discovery of useful truths; reason, that man has so frequently deified simply because he wished to lay exclusive claim to it, is only a vain abstraction unless it is allied to sentiment.

Was it reason that brought men together, that formed the first societies of men, that built the first towns and raised the first temples to the Gods? Is it reason that has revealed to us nature's harmony, and unveiled the hand of God in the marvels of creation? Is it reason that has invented the arts, and most astonishingly, the means whereby we communicate with our fellows? Is it reason that speaks a common language to all men in every age, of which conscience is the immortal interpreter? Is it reason that commands virtue in our hearts and which awakens in the hearts of the guilty, floods of remorse. When impious dogmas shackle whole nations in the yoke of superstition, is it reason that makes man just, despite an unjust God, and which shields innocence and modesty from the voluptuous teachings of Venus and the contagious cult of wordly love?

There is within us a power that is stronger than despotic human law or superstitious and immoral cults. It is a power that still watches over us when the frail bark of reason is tossed about by tempestuous passions. It is the power of sentiment.

The philosophy of reason is vain and subject to great error; its pliability makes it the slave of governments and vulgar opinion. Universal morality stems from sentiment and it is free of governments and opinion. The wisdom of reason is speculative and remote. The wisdom of sentiment is practical and open hearted. It is vain if a man is convinced by reason. Unless he is persuaded by sentiment, a good thought will never become a good deed. Oh! I have discovered within my heart a comforting maxim, one no doubt that is engraved on all hearts, that all truths essential to the happiness of humanity are truths of sentiment. I have also found, deep in my heart, this other truth, that the beautiful and the good are one, and that the man of genius can only win the approval of his contemporaries and the admiration of posterity by using moral principles as the basis of his work. Thus, the laws of taste and morality are but one.

[pp. 55–6]

We have seen that sentiment was of the greatest benefit in lodging within the heart the principles of morality and virtue. Another benefit however has been insufficiently valued, but which none the less is very real, namely that sentiment keeps watch over the mysterious sanctuary of illusion, guarding it against the impious curiosity of lofty reason. Eh! And who is aware that nature has linked our greatest pleasures to some of these precious illusions, in order to keep us within certain bounds? Who knows that impious systematic philosophy, having torn off the salutary bandage of illusion, and taught to dare all, soon carries its audacity to the point of wishing to overthrow with sacrilegious hand the arch of eternal truth? Ignorance and simplicity are the guarantee of happiness in this life and the next. Woe to us who have destroyed all our magic charms and who have plucked from the fateful tree the bitter fruits of science! Cold rationalists, behold your work! You sought mathematical explanations for the origin and truth of your cult, for the springs of your affections and for the state of your being, before and after death. Then the altars lay in ruins, the thrones were overturned in the dust, the most generous passions, the purest affections were only motivated by self-interest. The final misfortune was that when refuge had been sought in the bosom of immortality, only the horror of nothingness was revealed behind the curtain of death.

[pp. 56–8]
I have watched the French Revolution become the fruit of this cruel war waged on all illusion. I have seen philosophers, emboldened by the superiority of their intellect, attempt to determine the bounds of truth and error, saying to the people: This colossus of six thousand years is but a shadow. Ungodly ones! Where are your credentials? Why has truth chosen you to reveal it rather than the millions of other people, who are better than you?

Sentiment, a thousand times more clear sighted than reason, has enlightened that astonishing man who alone has had the gift to found a sect without involving it in the allure of religious innovation. Sentiment, I would argue, has enlightened J. J. Rousseau, the man who spent his entire life laboriously struggling against the chimera of his imagination and the torments of his sensibility, the man who has poured out in his writings the turmoils of every passion and the seeds of every virtue, about whose works (strong with so much sap) can be said this: misfortune to those who have read them without being powerfully moved, for they are dead to all sensibility! Woe, too, to those who have read them with profound emotion, for they have lost innocence of soul and simplicity of heart! And yet, Rousseau used all the force of his genius to fight sentiment. From this springs the unheard-of inconsistency of the misanthropist's deeds and writings. The evidence of sentiment cried out from the depths of his heart, but he was dissatisfied with this great witness and sought the assent of proud reason which rebelled at its own inadequacy and nothingness.

Soon a whole nation became imbued with the principles of the philosopher of Geneva; nourished by the paradoxes of his most fervid disciples, a prey to corruption and lax morals, all too ready therefore to abuse the best things, and avidly taking to itself philosophical doubts and impious precepts, the nation has been punished by the loss of all that it took to be mere illusion, all that it had dared to call vain prejudice. All was taken away – culture, social bonds, everything that was sacred to mankind – because society has made them the object of injudicious mockery and impious sarcasm. Chastised by providence, it has been punished by the realisation of the dreams of those that it had called its wise men. Thus, the politest and most rational people on earth, clothed in luxurious garments and rags of misery, proud of its progress in the arts and sciences, has been seen to exchange its paternal government for anarchy and the religion of its fathers for the prostitution of the most hideous idols. This people has been seen as a loathsome flock led by the vilest rabble, stumbling under the weight of so many scourges, defenceless against persecution, decimated by its hangman, morally dried up, despicably letting itself be dragged to an ignominious death, and at length expiring at the hands of torturing slaves, like the tyrant of Samos. He was proud of such great prosperity, and he still placed his trust in the continuing goodness of fortune at the moment when Nemesis dragged him into the most staggering catastrophe. I carefully avoid colouring in this sketch of the most terrible political phenomenon that has been known in social history.

[pp. 61–4]

At one of those moments when all thought takes on a sentimental hue, when our lives, like a peaceful stream, flow between banks of flowers in the paradise of the imagination, in one of those happy moments that are so familiar to sensitive souls, I thought I beheld a spirit, lovely as a vernal inspiration. It presented me with a book inscribed in ancient characters. It was the sacred book from which Pythagoras had drawn certain of his moral laws. I was enraptured, running through the pages of this immortal book, but on being returned to the world of external sensations I remember no more than these two axioms: 'Everything makes harmony in nature. Everything in nature is open to feelings' (*Tout est sensible dans la nature*).

Pythagoras, the founder of the Italian school, had travelled abroad before giving the laws to Croton. He had gathered together the traditions of all the peoples. He had visited the wise and the simple. He had frequented the temples of the Gods and the hovels of the poor; he had spoken with priests and philosophers; he had collected the traditions of various nations, the allegories of poets and the maxims of the wise. But above all, he had studied nature.

Often the hours sped by, their rapid passage unnoted by the philosopher who was lost in ravishing dreams. He observed the periodic return of the seasons, the unceasing and constant progress of the constellations, and the succession of days and nights. He had a feeling for the harmony of nature.

Sometimes, deep in sweet meditation, he watched the setting day star enveloped in clouds of gold, opal and azure, sinking silently beneath the shadow of the horizon, whilst on earth his ear was caressed by an undefined and steady sound. In the morning he had seen the sun burst forth from the bosom of the horizon like the thoughts of a God; he had seen the shadows flee from the valleys into the depths of the forests; he had heard a thousand winged songsters saluting the dawn, their voices more melodious no doubt than that of Memnon. Often in the long night watches, marvelling at the array of celestial spheres, he had felt how close to the throne of the eternal being this half light, this deep silence, this coolness, this solitude sometimes brought the soul, and how at other times it turned the soul inwards in self-contemplation. How many times had he not compared the calm of his consciousness (*sa conscience*) to the peaceful passage of the moon, hovering silently over the mountain tops, gliding over the surface of the diaphanous clouds, and balancing on the tresses of the trees.

During the storm he watched the clouds, fearfully black, projecting themselves through the sky like aerial islands; he watched the lightning which, swift as thought, travels from one pole to another in an instant of time or darts with a twisting flash through the heavens. He never feared to lose himself in the profound obscurity that threatened all nature; he never feared to hear the raging tempest, its brazen chariot now making the horizon tremble, now wheeling above the imperturbable philosopher as he meditated in the midst of the universal disorder, likening the stormy movements of human passions to the terrible spectacle of the tempest. He had been moved by the imposing voice of the thunder echoing through the air a thousand times and drowning beneath its majestic and sombre harmonies the unleashed winds, the mournful cries of the furious hurricane, and the groans of nature in her agony. It was particularly after these great scenes of terror when the rainbow of reconciliation was visible in the sky and when the earth's inhabitants opened their hearts to hope and joy that he understood this truth: that the whole of nature is in harmony with itself. He understood, too, that man alone has the sentiment for this sublime harmony, from which he believed it possible to conclude that man is the earthly pattern of all harmony and that he unites them all in the unfathomable sanctuary of his intelligence.[4]

This is the basis of the musical system developed in the school at Croton. The most sublime concert is that of the universe itself, and it is only given to wise men and poets to hear its ravishing harmony. Linus, Orpheus, Homer, and Pythagoras – you divine men – your exquisite nature surely made you sensible to the melody of the heavenly bodies as they rolled in concert through the immensities of space. Yet if for humbler mortals this melody has only the charm of magnificent allegory, there yet remains the pleasure of more immediate phenomena in which we can still sense divine harmony.

---

[4] Ballanche quotes extensively in an appendix on p. 255 from André the passage on music translated here on pp. 27–35. He himself has little to say of music, though he was known to have some practical knowledge of the subject (eds.)

August Wilhelm von Schlegel

(b. Hanover, 8 Sept. 1767; d. Bonn, 12 May 1845)

From 1. *Vorlesungen über schöne Literatur und Kunst* (1801), in *Die Kunstlehre*, ed. Edgar Lohner (Stuttgart 1963), pp. 220–1; 2. *Vorlesungen über dramatische Kunst und Literatur* (1808), in *Schriften*, ed. Walther Flemmer (Munich n.d.), pp. 161–3 and 165–7

The two Schlegel brothers came of a family with literary traditions; but their efforts in the cause of romanticism give them a place in German letters far above that of any of their relatives. August Wilhelm, the elder of the two, is assured of a permanent place in the history of Western literature for his part in what remains one of the supreme feats of translation: the version of Shakespeare's plays which he made in collaboration with Ludwig Tieck over the years 1797–1810. August Wilhelm, however, did not restrict his activities to translating Shakespeare. He was also a gifted translator from other languages and the most influential propagandist of German romanticism. It was, in fact, his influence on Madame de Staël, whom he accompanied from 1804 onwards in various journeys across Europe, that indirectly led to the arousal in France of interest in German romantic literature.

August Wilhelm was educated in Hanover and at the University of Göttingen. He was active as a teacher, taking up a post at Jena University in 1796, moving to Berlin in 1801 and to Vienna in 1808. He was ennobled in 1815 and took up the chair of oriental languages in Bonn in 1817. He remained at Bonn, translating and studying oriental texts, till his death.

A man of enormous breadth of interest and fine literary judgement, August Wilhelm was an aesthetic theorist of originality and sensitive insight. The *Vorlesungen über dramatische Kunst und Literatur* were delivered during his stay in Vienna and are generally considered to be his most important work of literary criticism. The *Vorlesungen über schöne Literatur und Kunst* date from his Jena years and constitute one of the first significant coherent critical manifestos of German romanticism.

It is with romanticism that music comes into its own as the *supreme* art; and the 'mystery' of music – particularly its powerful and inexplicable emotional appeal – was one of the reasons for this. Schlegel's division of art history into two contrasting epochs: the ancient or 'classical' and the modern or 'romantic' is part of his belief that the human spirit develops and deepens its experience throughout history. For all its perfection, Schlegel claims, Greek art is inferior to modern, romantic art because it is pre-Christian. The 'noble simplicity and tranquil grandeur' which Winckelmann (1717–68) claimed to be the essential qualities of Greek sculpture, and which Schlegel refers to obliquely in the passage quoted on p. 269, were insufficient. Christianity had added the dimension of eternity to the whole of human life, including art; and the highest type of modern music created an effect which was nothing less than a foreshadowing of the bliss of eternity. No higher claim could be made for any art.

Moreover, the fact that music could only be apprehended as a sequence of sounds in time made it a peculiarly 'romantic' art. August Wilhelm's brother Friedrich (see p. 246) points out that a romantic work is always in a state of *becoming* – which is precisely what a piece of music is while it is being performed. What could be more romantic? Mysterious, evanescent, palpably at its technical zenith in the era in which Schlegel was living (the great age of Viennese 'classicism'), both opening out vistas of eternity and inducing intense introspective and subjective reactions in the listener, music could be shown to be 'romantic', according to Schlegel's conception of the term, in a way that no other art could.

The 'dynamic' aspect of romanticism, stressed by both the Schlegels, and the idea that art–historical forms arose in succession through the ages in accordance with the onward development of the human spirit, so that Schlegel can even contrast 'modern emotions' with those of the Greeks, were to find important echoes in later writers – notably Hegel and his followers; so, too, was the Schlegelian concept of 'romantic irony', by which the creative artist can demonstrate his independence of and superiority to his own creation by interfering with, or even deliberately destroying the illusion that he has created. Hegel in particular waxed scathing about this aspect of romanticism, devoting a whole section of the Introduction to his *Aesthetics*[1] to it.

1. Music in relation to temporal and eternal life

We have seen that music occupies the dimension of time, one that is universally experienced by the inner consciousness. Time has only one dimension; it is best thought of in terms of a flowing point. Strictly speaking, variety is never experienced at one moment in time; unity must be imposed on it if it is to be experienced in this way. Basically then, music is pure succession, in which variety is experienced successively, rather than simultaneously. As such, it is an image of our restless, mutable, ever-changing life. Yet nothing that is apparently simple in nature is in fact so; all reality is the product of a combination of antinomies. Part of our being derives from the unity that comprises two, three, or a multiplicity of diverse elements. The harmony made up of simultaneously sounding notes that are concordant with each other, and which, though diverse, form a unity, may well, in fact, represent in audible terms the internal structure of life. Thus harmony is the truly mystical element in music, one which does not demand some powerful reaction from progression in time, but which strives for the infinite in the indivisible instant. So we see in fact that the modern development of harmony originated in Christian worship at a time when men had lost that sense of free movement in the phenomenal world, and that energetic rhythm of the ancients, at a time when the psyche was looking inwards in its search for a higher life. The solemn church anthem expresses this striving for spiritual union in the dimension of the suprasensual. Music can express every degree of worldliness, every degree of spirituality, music ranging from the march and the dance to the chorale; the former merely excites coordinated physical movements, the latter inspires an immutable, infinite longing of reverence, altogether throwing off transient, earthly

---

[1] G. W. F. Hegel, *Vorlesungen über die Aesthetik*, ed. Rüdiger Bübner (Stuttgart 1971), pp. 118–25.

passions. In the solemn, steady movement of devotional music there is inherent in every instant a sense of harmony and perfection, a unity of existence which to Christians is an image of heavenly bliss.

2. Romantic and classical art

Countless people, whole nations even, are so subject to the conventions of their upbringing and way of life that they cannot tear themselves free, even when it comes to the appreciation of the fine arts. Nothing appears natural, proper or beautiful to them that is foreign to their own language, their customs or their social relations. Looking at things in this exclusive way, it is doubtless possible, with training, to develop great subtlety of discrimination within tightly prescribed limits. But no true expert can manage without that open-mindedness, without that flexibility that rejects personal prejudice and blind habit, and that enables him to gain insight into the particular qualities of other ages and peoples. Such flexibility helps him to place things in their proper perspective and to recognise and respect everything great and beautiful that seems to ennoble human nature, everything that is hidden beneath the external trappings that people consider so necessary to their existence and that sometimes seems to be so alien to them. . . .

Let us now apply this concept of true critical open-mindedness to the history of poetry and the fine arts. Although there is much that deserves to be known outside this sphere, aesthetic history is normally limited, as is so-called world history, to the consideration of matters that have more or less directly influenced contemporary culture, to the works, that is, of the Greeks and Romans, and to those of such modern peoples as achieved the first and greatest significance in this field.

[p. 163, line 21 to p. 165, line 12 omitted]

Admittedly, human nature is basically simple; but all investigations point to the fact that there is no fundamental power in nature so simple that it may not divide or fragment. The entire interplay of life's dynamic forces depends on harmony and contrast. Why then should this phenomenon not be paralleled in man's entire history. Perhaps this idea might prove to be the real key to the history of ancient and modern poetry and fine art. Those who have adopted it have coined the term romantic to differentiate that unique spirit of modern art from ancient or classical art. The word is certainly not inappropriate: it derives from *romance*, the term applied to the vernaculars that originated from the combination of Latin and Teutonic languages. Similarly, modern culture is a fusion of elements of Nordic tribal society and fragments of classical civilisation in all their disparity. Ancient civilisation, let us not forget, was much more of a piece than ours.

If it could be shown that there is a similar parallel and perhaps even consistent contrast running right through the works of the ancients and the moderns in every field of art known to us, then the above thesis would be highly illuminating. Despite the many penetrating comments and observations that have been made on unrelated aspects of the arts, the task still remains of fully proving this thesis in music and the representative arts as well as in poetry. Certain foreign authors anticipated the work that is being done by German writers. Amongst these, Rousseau drew attention to this contrast in music, demonstrating that ancient music was based on melody and rhythm and modern music on harmony. But he simply dismisses harmony, a course of action with which we totally disagree. Hemsterhuys ingeniously observed of the representative arts that the ancient painter was probably too much of a sculptor, whereas the modern sculptor is too much of a painter. This is precisely the difference, as I shall proceed to demonstrate in more detail, for the spirit of ancient art and poetry is plastic, just as that of the modern arts is picturesque.

I shall try to elucidate this by means of an example from another art – architecture. The Middle Ages saw the development of a universal architectural style, which reached its zenith during the closing years of that era. This style was called the Gothic style, though 'the old German style' would have been more appropriate. The revival of classical antiquity led to the indiscriminate imitation of Greek architecture, all too often regardless of differences in climate, customs, or the function of the buildings. The zealots of this new taste then sweepingly condemned the gothic as tasteless, gloomy and barbaric. The Italians do at any rate have some excuse for this; their heritage of ancient buildings and their climate, which they have in common with that of the Greeks and Romans, ensured an innate preference for ancient architecture. To the Northerner, however, the first powerful impression gained on entering a gothic cathedral is not so easily explained away. He endeavours, rather, to explain and justify these impressions. A moment's thought will convince us that gothic architecture is not only a matter of superlative technical skill, but also of astonishing inventive power. Closer investigation reveals its profound significance, its perfection and its self-consistency, which are the equal of those of the Greek system.

[p. 166, para. 1 to p. 167, para. 2 omitted]

For our purpose, which is to justify our division of art history into two main periods and thus our intention to apply it to the history of drama, it should be enough simply to have established this striking contrast between the ancient or classical and the romantic. But since there are devotees of the ancients who insistently and one-sidedly claim that any departure from their principles is nothing but a passing critical whim, expressed in abstruse language which avoids any valid definition, let me attempt to explain the origin and spirit of *romanticism*, and then you may judge whether the use of the word is justified and whether the concept really means anything.

Greek culture provided a natural training of the utmost perfection. The Greeks were a beautiful and noble race; they were endowed with sensitivity and a spirit of noble calm; they lived in a temperate climate; they led a full, healthy existence and they achieved everything which our limited human nature can achieve, prospering as they did from a rare confluence of favourable circumstances. All their art and poetry expresses an awareness of the harmony of these influences. They invented the poetry of joy.

They deified the powers of nature and earthly life. This worship, which darkened the minds of other peoples with terrifying images, and which hardened their hearts to cruelty, assumed a gentle, noble and dignified form among the Greeks. Superstition, too, which so often enslaves the faculties, seems here to have furthered their freest development. It nurtured the arts that paid it tribute, and idols became ideals.

But however far the Greeks may have developed beauty and even morality, their culture cannot be said to have risen above the level of a refined and ennobled sensuality. Obviously, this is a generalisation; there were exceptional philosophical insights and flashes of poetic inspiration. Man can never wholly ignore the infinite; and chance recollections will always serve to remind him of his lost home. What matters, however, is the main goal towards which he strives.

Religion lies at the root of human existence. If it were possible for man totally to abandon religion, including that innate religion of which he is unaware, everything would become mere surface without any inner substance. When the religious focus of life is disturbed, the whole system of the spiritual and mental faculties must consequently be reordered.

And this is what has actually happened in modern Europe, owing to the spread of Christianity. This religion, as sublime as it is beneficial, has regenerated the decayed and exhausted world of classical antiquity; it has become the guiding principle in the history of modern peoples; even today, when many claim to have outgrown its authority, they find themselves much more under its influence than they think in all things touching human conduct.

Following the advent of Christianity, European post-medieval culture has been mainly dominated by the conquering Germanic race from the North, which brought new vigour to a degenerate people. Life in the rugged North forces man in upon himself; and where the free play and development of the senses are constrained, there is bound to be compensating seriousness of attitude in those of noble character. This explains the warmth with which the ancient Teutonic tribes welcomed Christianity; on no other people did it make so profound and powerful an impact, or become so much a part of the texture of all human emotions.

Chivalry developed from a blend of Christian sentiment and the rough but honest heroism of the northern conquerors. The object of chivalry was to guard the practice of arms by solemn oaths solemnly observed against that crude, base abuse of power into which it is so easy to slip.

[p. 168, para. 5 to 169, para. 2 omitted]

The ancient Greeks held human nature to be self-sufficient; they were unaware of its defects and they aspired to no higher perfection than that which could actually be achieved by the exercise of their own faculties. Superior wisdom teaches us that man, on account of some heinous offence, has forfeited the place for which he was originally destined; and that the whole purpose of his earthly existence is to regain that state which, unaided, he could never achieve. The Greek religion of the senses aimed only at the enjoyment of outward and transitory blessings; and immortality seemed a remote, vague shadow, if it was believed in at all, a faded image of this bright and vivid life. The Christian attitude is diametrically opposed to this. Everything finite and mortal is lost in contemplation of the eternal; life has become shadow and darkness, and the dawn of our real existence lies beyond the grave. Such a religion is bound to awaken the clearest realisation that we seek in vain for happiness here on earth; this is a premonition that slumbers in any sensitive soul: that no external object can ever entirely satisfy the soul, and that every pleasure is but a fleeting illusion. Now suppose the soul, resting as it were beneath the weeping willows of exile, sighs with longing for its distant home, how can the character of its songs be other than prevalently melancholy? The poetry of the ancients was, therefore, the poetry of possession, while ours is the poetry of longing; the former is firmly rooted in its present, while the latter hovers between remembrance and anticipation. This is not to imply that everything is borne away in unrelieved lament and that the prevalent tone is one of endless and unjustified melancholy. Just as the Greeks none the less found austere tragedy acceptable, despite their optimism, so romantic poetry may assume any mood, even the most joyous, yet it will still somehow or other bear traces of its origin. Modern emotions are, on the whole, more introverted, the imagination is more abstract, and ideas are more reflective. In nature, it is true, the boundaries between things are not as sharply defined as they must be if a clear concept of them is to emerge.

The ancient Greeks held as their ideal a perfect concord and balance between the faculties – a natural harmony. Recently, we have again become aware of the inner division that makes such an ideal impossible; modern poetry endeavours, therefore, to reconcile the two worlds, the spiritual and the sensual, between which we find ourselves divided, and to fuse them indissolubly together. Sense impressions are, so to speak, consecrated by their mysterious alliance with the higher feelings; on the other hand, the spirit gives phenomenal shape to its intimations or ineffable visions of eternity through the medium of the senses.

Greek art and poetry originates from an unconscious unity of form and subject; in any modern art that has remained true to its own spirit, a fusion is sought of these two natural opposites. The Greeks solved their problem to perfection; but the moderns can only partially realise their endeavours to reach the eternal; and because they give the appearance of imperfection, their products are in greater danger of being imperfectly appreciated.

Franz Christoph Horn

(b. Brunswick, 30 July 1781; d. Brunswick 5 Oct. 1837)

From: 'Musikalische Fragmente', in the *Allgemeine musikalische Zeitung*, Leipzig, vol. 4, nos. 25, 26; 17 and 24 March 1802, pp. 403–5; 406–9

The 'fragment' or aphorism has a long and distinguished literary history, but it was with the romantic movement that it had its greatest vogue in German letters. The Schlegel brothers and Novalis (1772–1801) in particular used the device to set down scattered *aperçus* on subjects of almost any kind, including of course music. Its advantages are obvious: there is no need to develop a sustained argument; points can be made with irony and concision; the take-it-or-leave-it format gives the writer a chance to seize, hold and then cast aside the reader's attention.

Early in the history of the Leipzig *Allgemeine musikalische Zeitung* (founded in 1798), a series of 'Musikalische Fragmente' were published, whose author was Franz Christoph Horn. Horn, who later became a fairly well-known writer of light novels, and whose reputation was such that Heinrich Heine (1797–1856) felt justified in ridiculing him in chapter 18 of his satirical epic *Atta Troll* (1841), was at the time an undergraduate. He studied law, first at Jena, and then at Brunswick, where he also studied history, aesthetics and philosophy. In 1803 he obtained a post at the Greyfriars Gymnasium in Berlin; and he taught in Bremen from 1805 to 1809. Suspected of harbouring 'dangerous' opinions, he lost his teaching posts and made his living as a tutor and freelance writer, publishing many novels, volumes of poems, essays and literary histories. He died in 1837.

The 'Fragmente' are of particular interest in that they contain the first verifiable mention of romanticism in music, referring to Mozart as a romantic composer and comparing him, as a romantic artist, with Shakespeare.

On musical illustration

There has been much debate as to whether or not music should be *illustrative*. The question is sufficiently answered – and in the negative – by one simple and irrefutable observation: namely that music must be – musical. It must, that is, give form to the highest emotion. Once it strays into the territory of some other art it will be unable to do this. Not only therefore should it avoid the merely illustrative but neither should it engage our reflective powers by being *picturesque*. If it does either it will encroach on the preserves of another art without adopting the specific role that the art fulfils, and it will unavoidably develop a split personality. It will be neither music, nor painting nor plastic art, and it will vacillate insecurely and aimlessly between them. Only poetry can fuse the arts together. In attemp-

271

ting to do so, music will only borrow inessentials from the other arts. The understanding listener will be tossed to and fro from emotion to reflection, and he will only be able to take pleasure in measuring the skill that the composer has mistakenly wasted, and in judging the consistency with which he has pursued his goal.

The case is quite different, though, in respect of one kind of illustrative representation in music – one that is only found in the most perfect work of art. I would call this, invisible illustration, a quality that only belongs to work of sublime genius. Mozart, Cherubini, Cimarosa and one or two others belong to this category. Even to the listener of average imagination, *Don Giovanni* pulses with romantic life; its ever-changing forms shape themselves into bold and significant patterns; they press in on him until dark foreboding eventually becomes reality, and an undefinable, superhuman power engulfs his life in another, full of terror. Who can still be aware of the nothern skies when he experiences Cimarosa's *Secret Marriage*, Paisiello's *Maid of the Mill*, Cherubini's *Les deux journées*, Salieri's *Axur* or Piccini's *Dido*, however dismal and oppressive the weather may be outside? Who is not borne away on soft, southern breezes, as he listens to the first duet in *Axur*, or the delightful trio in the first act of Winter's *Elise*?

[Musical beauty transcends the intellect]

As every art endeavours to express the infinite within the limits of the finite, it is easy to see that a genuine and perfect work of art cannot really be *comprehended* in an intellectual manner. The intellect will find no answers here, for art has a higher task to perform than the mind can demand of it. The man who is wholly intellectual, therefore, will never form a clear idea of beauty; he will still analyse, even when analysis is impossible, art being so to speak the complete and satisfying answer to every question that can possibly be raised. Art is thus beyond the reach even of the most enlightened intellect, the more so the more deeply the intellect strives to analyse. . . . To the limited intellect, art can be nothing more than a facet of a cleverly executed mathematical exercise.

The intellect can at least derive some pleasure from poetry, especially dramatic poetry, and even though such pleasure may be infinitely less rewarding than that which is experienced by the true connoisseur, it will still be sufficiently stimulating to be of some value. The intellect seeks unity in variety: it calculates the merits of the various facets of the work that are assembled so skilfully, and it singles out particular passages which offer it matter for reflection. It may go a step further and find pleasure in the sublime characters that have been so well shaped and so powerfully portrayed . . . in short, the intellect enjoys here an even greater pleasure than it derives from a skilfully-devised *puzzle*.

The intellect contrives to draw a similar pleasure from painting and sculpture, though it inevitably does greater violence to sculpture, which needs to be appreciated in its totality if it is fully to be enjoyed. But how can the intellect possibly derive even the slightest pleasure from music, strive as it may? Genuine music cannot form concepts or express truths, nor can it engage the contemplative faculty. No specific inferences or conclusions can be drawn from musical structures. Music rejects every attempt to subject it to such processes. This may explain the odd ideas that men have about music, men who otherwise judge things profoundly and perceptively. This accounts for the clumsy remark made by one of our most eminent philosophers[1] to the effect that music lacks breeding because it imposes itself on people. Such comment can hardly be serious, for on the contrary music bypasses many people because it is heard from afar, and ignored. Music is ineffable. For that very reason it is not susceptible to pure intellectual perception, nor is it something that can be learned. As soon as it leaves the sphere of the abstract, as soon as it stoops to the servitude of intellectual comprehensibility, it ceases to be music and becomes in effect a parody of itself.

A great deal of our so-called comic music falls into this category for it is not really comic but just vulgarly funny . . . and this is something that music should never be.

---

[1] See p. 223.

Friedrich Wilhelm Josef von Schelling

(b. Leonberg, 27 Jan. 1775; d. Ragaz, 20 Aug. 1854)

From: *Philosophie der Kunst* (Lectures delivered at Jena, 1802–3). Text from *Werke*, ed. Manfred Schröter (Munich 1959), vol. 3 (Ergänzungsband), pp. 142–55

Schelling was the most philosophically-inclined member of the Jena group of romantics and a close friend of the Schlegels. He was admitted at the age of 15 to the Protestant theological faculty of the University of Tübingen, where he met and became friends with Hegel and the poet Hölderlin. A precocious scholar, he had already published a significant philosophical paper (*Ueber die Möglichkeit einer Form der Philosophie überhaupt* (published in part, Landshut 1809; complete text in *Werke*, ed. Manfred Schröter), when he was only nineteen years old. Schelling began as an adherent of Fichte's subjectivist idealism, which explains the universe in terms of the way individual self-consciousness construes it. Schelling soon reacted against Fichte's idea of nature, which the older philosopher construed simply as an instrument for moral action. Schelling interpreted nature as an immediate manifestation of the cosmic spirit – the absolute; and the various manifestations of life within nature were steps in a vast system moving upwards towards the emergence of consciousness and nature's knowledge of herself in and through man.[1]

In 1798, Schelling was appointed to the chair of philosophy at Jena, which became the centre of the first wave of the romantic movement in Germany. In the winter of 1802–3 he devoted a course of lectures to the philosophy of art; and it is this course that forms the basis of this section. In 1803, he married Caroline Schlegel, whose marriage with August Wilhelm Schlegel has been dissolved; and they went to live in Würzburg, where the course was repeated in 1804–5. He continued his work as an academic, but with the rise of Hegelianism, his philosophy never regained the position it had enjoyed in the earliest years of the nineteenth century. Some explanation is needed of the layout and terminology of Schelling's exposition. It is conceived in terms of a series of mathematical axioms, with mathematical terminology and a strange, idiosyncratic use of the preposition *in* followed by an accusative. This usage normally indicates motion towards or into; and it is best rendered in English by a paraphrase such as 'expanding into', though the usage itself derives from mathematics. Hence, when Schelling talks of 'powers', he is using the term in a mathematical sense; and words such as 'unity' and 'dimension' are also to be understood in this way.

Schelling regarded the philosophy of art as the keystone of his whole system of thought.[2] Nature is, as it were, the *un*-conscious poetry of the spirit; the spirit, when

---

[1] For a clear, concise yet detailed exposition of Schelling's philosophy, volume 7 of Frederick Copleston's *History of Philosophy, Part I, Fichte to Hegel* (New York 1965), pp. 120–82 is strongly recommended.

[2] Copleston, *History*, pp. 149 et seq.

working consciously, produces art through the same power that acts unconsciously in producing nature. The satisfaction derived from experiencing a work of art is that art is the supreme objectification of the intelligence to itself. In other words, art conceals – and reveals – the fundamental meaning of the universe. Aesthetic sensitivity thus has a metaphysical significance, not just an emotional or rational one. It is the merging of opposite identities: the conscious and the unconscious; flowing time and static eternity; the phenomenal and the ideal: the objective and the subjective, which gives rise to aesthetic satisfaction.

It would be an overstatement to say that Schelling's ideas on music here quoted actually influenced Schopenhauer. But it is remarkable that Observation 3 of Axiom 83 comes fairly close to Schopenhauer's assertion that in listening to a work of music we are confronted, not with an image of the will that underlies the cosmos, but with the will itself.

Section 77. Music is the art form in which unity of substance purely as such is developed into a power or symbol

[This] follows directly from the two previous axioms. *Rider*: Music may be defined in a number of different ways, but the definition which follows derives from earlier propositions and it leads directly to the following corollaries:

Corollary 1. As an art, music is basically subject to the *first dimension* (it exists in one dimension only).

Corollary 2. The essential form of music is *succession*, for the idea of eternity assumes form as duration by expanding into time, form being regarded as something abstracted from substance. A subject that becomes aware of its own continuity becomes aware of *itself*. Self-awareness can thus be thought of as universal consciousness in the abstract forming itself into a multiple consciousness. This explains the close overall relationship that exists between hearing, music and speech on the one hand and self-awareness on the other. It also suggests how the arithmetical aspect of music can for the moment be explained; its deeper significance will be demonstrated later. Music is substance counting within the soul, though the soul is no longer aware of this subconscious process. (Pythagoras was the earliest person to compare the soul to number.) Thus Leibniz could write 'Musica est raptus numerate se nescientis animae'.

Section 78. Music as form in which unity of substance itself becomes a symbol must necessarily comprehend all other unities

For in art, unity of substance is *assimilated* into itself as a potency simply in order to be *re-established by its own agency* as an *Absolute*. But if this is so, every separate Unity assimilates every other one in its absoluteness; and thus music, etc.

Section 79. Rhythm constitutes the concept of unity expanding into diversity; in other words, unity of substance in music that forms itself into a particular unity

Using the term rhythm only in its most general sense to mean nothing more than a periodic division of something uniform, this proposition may be proved of rhythm by the fact that rhythm introduces an element of variety into that of uniformity. For example, the emotion aroused by a composition as a whole is completely homogeneous and coherent. It may be sad or happy, but by its very nature it is consistently homogeneous, variety and diversity being imparted to it by its rhythmic subdivisions. Rhythm is one of the most wonderful mysteries of art and nature; no concept seems to mankind to have been more directly inspired by nature herself. The ancients consistently ascribed the most intense power to rhythm; and hardly anyone would deny that rhythm is in reality the source of the truly beautiful in music and the dance. But in order to appreciate rhythm as pure rhythm, we must first detach ourselves from anything else in the music that charms and excites us. Notes themselves, for example, also have a meaning: they may express happiness, tenderness, sadness or pain. When considering rhythm, we should remember that its beauty is not material and that it needs none of the purely natural emotional stimuli latent in actual sounds in order to please and charm the receptive soul. To grasp this idea clearly, we may begin by thinking of such rhythmic elements as are in themselves quite neutral: the individual notes of a string, for example, or the beat of a drum. How is it that a sequence of notes or beats becomes significant, exciting and pleasurable?

Pulses or sounds that follow each other without any semblance of a design have no effect on us. In themselves, these sounds are essentially and by nature meaningless; they are not even pleasant. But as soon as they recur at regular intervals and build up into a period, an element of rhythm emerges, albeit in the most rudimentary form, and we are made irresistibly aware of it. Impelled by nature, man thus transforms in rhythm a process which is in itself undifferentiated into one that is varied and diverse. We cannot tolerate uniformity for any length of time in anything that is meaningless – when we count, for instance, we shape the sequence of numbers into periods. Most workers who are engaged on mechanical tasks lighten them in this way; the inner pleasure of subconscious counting causes them to forget the burden of work, detailed actions take on a shape and afford a kind of pleasure which would be impaired if the rhythm were broken.

So far, we have discussed only the most rudimentary type of rhythm, in which the unity is entirely a matter of the simple regularity of the intervals that elapse between successive pulses. An image of this: equal-sized equidistant points. The lowest scale of rhythm.

A higher kind of basic unity in diversity can be achieved when individual sounds or pulses are produced, not with equal force, but according to a specific pattern, alternately strong and weak. With this, *metre* is introduced as a necessary element in rhythm, one which can be observed wherever identical patterns are evident in diversity and variety. It follows that these patterns may be varied in a host of different ways, to give the uniform sequence even greater variety.

Considered in a general sense, then, rhythm is really the conversion of a succession that is in itself meaningless into one that has meaning. Purely as such, a sequence of pulses has a randomness about it. Rhythm constitutes the conversion of what is random in the sequence into what is predictable. The consequence of this is that the whole is no longer subject to time, but has absorbed time *into itself*. Music acquires articulated shape when a series of constituent parts is built up in such a way that several *sounds* together comprise a section, one which is intentionally and regularly differentiated from the others.

Such rhythm, even though it is still of the simple kind, and though it consists merely of a sequence of sounds divided into equally long periods perceptibly differentiated from one another, can none the less be divided into several categories. The rhythm can, for example, be regular or irregular. But several bars can be combined in units, which constitute a higher rhythmic potency: rhythms in combination (in poetry, a distich). Still larger units can be built up from these combinations (in poetry, the strophe) and so on, until the point is eventually reached when the entire order and combination becomes fully apparent to the inner mind. We can learn to discern the complete perfection of rhythm only from the following propositions.

Rider: Rhythm is the musical element in music. For the uniqueness of music arises from the fact that in music, unity forms itself into diversity. Now since according to Proposition 79 rhythm is nothing other than the musical expression of this concept, it must be the music in music. Thus, by reason of the very nature of music, rhythm is the fundamental feature of that art.

Only when we have firmly grasped this fact will we be in a position to differentiate scientifically between ancient and modern music.

Section 80. By reason of its all-embracing nature, rhythm necessarily embodies the second unity: modulation[3] (understood in the broadest sense)

The first part of this proposition goes without saying and it can be understood as having universal application. As far as the second part is concerned, all that is needed is a definition of what modulation is.

The first precondition of rhythm is some kind of unity in diversity. But

---

[3] Schelling clearly does *not* mean modulation in the sense of a change of key: see below p. 278 (eds.)

this diversity does not simply arise from the varied nature of the constituent parts, from their arbitrary or random existence (i.e. their purely temporal existence). The diversity arises from something substantial, essential and qualitative. It arises solely from the musical differentiation between the notes. In this respect, 'modulation' is the art of sustaining the coherent identities of sounds; this is the pre-eminent quality of a musical work, however the work may vary *qualitatively*, just as that same identity is *quantitatively* sustained through rhythm.

I must express myself in this general way because modulation has such different meanings in artistic terminology. My meaning must not be confused with the specifically modern, technical meaning of the term 'modulation'. The technique of determining the course of a composition by leading melody and harmony through several keys to a final return in the tonic is also termed 'modulation'. This is, of course, an exclusively modern device.

It is impossible for me to go into all these technical matters. It would require a theoretical treatise rather than a general exposition. You need note in general that the element we call rhythm is quantitative and the element of modulation is qualitative. Since rhythm is fundamental to music, it must subsume modulation. As an independent parameter, modulation is thus absorbed in rhythm, and music with a harmonic foundation results. The corollary to this statement, *in so far as the second element [modulation] presupposes rhythm*, is that rhythm constitutes the whole of music. This in turn leads us to differentiate between those cases in which the entire musical material is subordinated to the primary element, rhythm, and those in which it is dominated by the secondary element, modulation; for two quite different kinds of music result, each of course valid in its own right.

Section 81. The third element, in which the other two are of equal significance, is melody

As this proposition is really only an explanation; and as there can be no doubt that the combination of rhythm and modulation *is* melody, no proof is necessary. Instead, we shall seek to define these three parameters more clearly by means of various criteria, in order to demonstrate the way in which they relate to each other.

We can therefore state that: rhythm = the first dimension; modulation = the second dimension; melody = the third. Through the first, music achieves reflection and self-awareness; through the second, emotion and judgement; through the third, contemplation and imagination. We may also presume that if the three basic categories of the arts are music, painting and the plastic arts, it is rhythm that makes music musical, modulation that makes it picturesque (which is not to be confused with the *illustrative*, something that only a debased and decadent taste can demand of music, taste of the kind that nowadays enjoys the bleating of sheep in Haydn's *Creation*); and it is melody that gives it shape (*Plastische*).

Section 82. Melody, in which the first of the three unities of music is pre-eminent, is complemented by harmony, in which the second of the three unities is pre-eminent

Harmony is generally recognised to be the complement of melody (even by empirical theorists). Melody is the absolute musical embodiment in time of eternity – in other words, total unity. Similarly, harmony is the musical representation of identity in diversity. Here, the unity is one of contrast: unity, that is, in the ideal sense. A composer is commonly said to know about melody if he can create a monodic line out of rhythm and modulation, and to understand harmony if he can add breadth (extension into the second dimension) to the identity that is combined with rhythm to form diversity – if, in other words, he can combine several parts, each constituting a separate melody, into a euphonious whole. In the first case, we obviously have unity in diversity; in the second, diversity in unity: in the first, succession; in the second, co-existence.

There are cases in which harmony is an element in melody, but only when the latter is subordinated to rhythm (the plastic element). In this present instance, however, I am concerned only with cases in which the harmony is not subordinated to rhythm, in which it is an *entity* in itself, subordinate to the second dimension (melody).

Admittedly, harmony is defined by the theorists in various ways, so that, for example, it may mean the simultaneous combination of sounds in one chord. Here, though, we are considering harmony in its most rudimentary form, as it is manifest, for example, in a single note. For a single note contains various overtones which, however, blend so well that the resultant impression is of one single sound. Applying the principle of diversity in unity to an entire composition, in which the interplay of forces is on a larger scale, we find that harmony clearly involves the combination of different sound-relationships of these forces into a total unity.

This unity in turn requires the integration of all the conceivable constituents of the composition, all the complex developments of sounds into the absolute unity of the whole (the diversity of these complex sounds being perceptible in terms of 'modulation' rather than rhythm). Enough can be inferred from this general concept to state that harmony and rhythm are interrelated, and that melody is, too, since it is in fact integrated rhythm. I would say that harmony stands in the same relationship to rhythm as ideal unity does to phenomenal unity, or as the concept of diversity expanding into unity does to the contrasting one of unity expanding into diversity.

Q.E.D.

Section 83. The forms of music are the forms of eternal things in phenomenal guise

For the phenomenal guise of eternal things is the means through which the infinite takes shape in the finite. But musical form is a process whereby the infinite is embodied in the finite; hence the forms of music are inevitably forms of things in themselves. In other words, they are forms of ideas exclusively under a phenomenal guise.

Since this has now been demonstrated in the general sense, it must also be true of rhythm and harmony, which are the [platonic] forms peculiar to music. In other words, rhythm and harmony can express the forms of eternal things to the extent that those forms are thought of entirely as discrete entities. In this case, rhythm and harmony are forms of phenomenal ideas; they are also forms of the life and being of cosmic bodies in as much as things or ideas assume phenomenal shape in cosmic bodies. Music is accordingly nothing other than the aurally perceived rhythm and harmony of the visible universe itself.

Various observations

1. Philosophy, like art, does not generally deal with tangible phenomena; it deals only with their [platonic] forms or eternal essences. The thing itself, however, is nothing other than some particular mode or form of existence; and through forms, we comprehend (*besitzt*) things. The plastic arts do not, for example, endeavour to rival natural phenomena. Art strives after pure form, the ideal; the material object itself is after all only another aspect of that ideal. If we apply this to the case in point, to music, music brings before us in rhythm and harmony the [platonic] form of the motions of physical bodies; it is, in other words, pure form, liberated from any object or from matter. To this extent, music is the art that is least limited by physical considerations in that it represents *pure* motion as such, abstracted from any object and borne on invisible, almost spiritual wings.

[p. 153, para. 1 to p. 154, para. 1 omitted]

3. Only now can we determine the supreme significance of rhythm, harmony and melody. They are the primal and purest form of motion in the universe; in terms of phenomena, they are ideas in substantive guise. The cosmic bodies are held aloft on the wings of harmony and rhythm; centrifugal and centripetal forces, as they are called, are nothing other than rhythm and harmony respectively. . . .

4. So now it is possible to define music's place in the general system of the arts. The structure of the universe exists independently of other natural potencies; in one sense it represents what is highest and most comprehensive in nature. In it, whatever is confused in its material guise is resolved when it is considered purely rationally; yet from another viewpoint, it is also the highest potency in nature. So also music, which from one point of view is

the most universal of the arts and the one that is closest to being dissolved into speech and reason, is from another point of view only the first potency of the other two.

Cosmic bodies are the primary unities that come from eternal matter; they draw everything into themselves, even though they contract of necessity into more restricted and specific spheres in order to represent in themselves the highest organisations in which the unity of nature achieves perfect self-realisation. In their universal motions, therefore, the cosmic bodies express the type of reason that is inherent in them only as the first potency. So it is that music, which from one point of view is the most recondite of all the arts, expresses only the pure form of these motions, for it apprehends shapes when they are still chaotic and undifferentiated; it is independent of physical phenomena, and it takes on the quality of the absolute only as rhythm, harmony and melody (i.e. as the first potency), even though within its sphere of operation it is the least constricted of all the arts.

(Johann) Karl David (Paul) Reimold

(b. 1757; d. 1834)[1]

From: 'Etwas über den Grundsatz der schönen Künste', in *Apollon* (Penig 1803), vol. 1, No. 7, pp. 17–25

Johann Karl David Paul Reimold was a Minister in the Reformed Church. He wrote hymns and edifying verse, such as *Der Friede, ein Lehrgedicht* in eight cantos, which was published at Heidelberg in 1809; and his *Lyrische Gedichte* came out in two volumes in 1818. He also published theological works, such as *Die angeblichen Apostolischen Liturgien aus historisch-kritischem Gesichtspunkte betrachtet* (Heidelberg 1834).

This interesting attempt to draw parallels between technical devices in the various arts was, of course, nothing new. Reimold's approach, however, is rather different from the conventional one of likening melody to line, harmony to colour and rhythm to design or pattern. It may be compared with Runge's arguments in favour of an art which is 'pure' and 'spiritual'. Note also that, as seems to have been quite a frequent procedure in Germany in the early nineteenth century, the imitation of natural phenomena in musical terms in Haydn's oratorios elicits a certain priggish disapproval!

Four main considerations are of paramount importance in the assessment of beauty. Visually, these are form and colour; and aurally, sound and melodic shape. Although these two senses may differ, they do none the less have this in common: a sensitivity and a responsiveness to phenomena. Since, in fact, they are so inescapably subject to the same laws of beauty, a constant relationship must exist between all kinds of beauty, both visual and aural, for the inner sense responds to both. There are striking and essential parallels between the states of pleasure and displeasure, and the rounded structure of the eye or the coiled shape of the ear. The angular and pointed is less pleasing than the rounded. Angularity seems to be at odds with the structure of the eye, the rounded seems to be more in harmony with it. We do not immediately take in a shape that lacks angular features and in which the parts flow smoothly into one another; the circular movement that the eye must make to encompass the outline of the shape is more naturally suited to its structure than such a movement is to the horizontal or the vertical, or indeed to any combination of *straight lines*. Very prominent features such as protuberances and sharp projections are also to some extent obviously displeasing, for they fundamentally weaken or destroy the

[1] The *Allgemeine Deutsche Biographie* gives 1757–1874, which is unlikely.

impression of unity, a notable fact that will not have escaped the careful observer.

The individual sound that drowns its predecessor is equivalent to the angular and sharp-contoured feature in a visible object. This may occur once or continuously. . . .

It is equally significant that the eye can tolerate only an intensity of light that is compatible with its capacity and sensitivity. Anything that exceeds this intensity is to some extent painful; anything that lacks the requisite intensity affords the eye no pleasure because forms and outlines cannot be distinguished. Even the practised eye, therefore, is unhappy about colours that are strident or excessively bright, or with colours that are matt and dead.

It is precisely here that we can again draw striking parallels with the sense of hearing. Sounds that are too high – piercing sounds – or those that are too deep, correspond to light that is intolerably bright or weak. Colour-music – an invention of little potential – depends on, or at least shows some awareness of, this parallel. A sound that is too high or low for effortless listening is painful; it points us, as it were, either to an unattainable height or to a frightening abyss. People with weak nerves, and consequently a strong susceptibility to sense-impressions, show this most clearly. They often find bass and alto voices painful, whereas they are almost sent to sleep by sounds that lie in the middle register. Sounds that are both deep and indeterminate (sounds that lack brightness) are suggestive for such people of gloom or hostility, fear or terror. Try imagining sounds of higher and higher pitch! There comes a point beyond the normal range of the senses at which the act of imagination becomes pointless, strenuous and painful. Or try imagining a sound that is inconceivably deep; a quite unique sense of discomfort and oppression will be experienced.

Certain types of composition may be compared to the bizarre. By bizarre, I mean anything in which there are such marked and violent colour contrasts that the conflicting hues never blend smoothly with one another according to the principles of compatibility, but are sharply juxtaposed, no attempt being made to harmonise them or to relate them, so that their differences are even more striking than usual. This corresponds in the realm of sound to random groups of notes, as can easily be inferred from the botched and tasteless products of our musical hacks. Lacking the ability to select, or even to join together contrasting ideas by means of unifying transitional passages, they create a patchwork jacket for a musical dandy from totally unrelated scraps: heat and cold, height and depth, joy and sorrow, all are thrown together, provided that the time-signature fits. . . .

From all this it appears *that unambiguous principles exist in the human soul for both the auditory and visual senses*, and for anything that can be construed by the inner sense, however spiritualised such things may be. *The close relationship that exists between the two kinds of beauty can only be explained on these grounds.* Common principles must necessarily underlie the very close parallels and compatibilities that we experience in both fields of sensation with regard to pleasure. But in order to formalise these principles as a basis for the subjective appreciation of beauty and to deduce from them the simplest and most reliable aesthetic laws, we need a terminology that can be applied both to visual and aural kinds of beauty, not a formal systematic terminology, but one illuminating by its very vocabulary the links that bind the heavenly sisters, one that confirms the unshakable family relationship between them. Such a terminology cannot be difficult to work out, bearing in mind that, as has been shown, both senses betray very great *similarities* in their effects, despite the differences that exist between them and between the materials which they employ. It is necessary only to apply certain terms from one field of sensation to the other, as by a happy chance has often been done anyway, to make such terms equally and mutually valid, or choose those that are more suitable and meaningful. The following tabulated summary view will perhaps illuminate my point.

SIGHT		HEARING
The straight line		One single sound persisting at a given intensity
The curved line: (a) circular		The gradual fading away of one sound, which immediately recurs as before
(b) undulating	C O R R E S P O N D S T O	Sounds gently rising and falling in pitch
Smoothness		Sounds united in equal intensity
Protuberant, pointed		Prominent sounds
Corners, angles		Leaping intervals*
Symmetry: (a) overall		Harmony; the overall impression conveyed by a sequence of sounds
(b) of constituent parts looked at in isolation		Particular passages of harmony in a composition considered independently
Colour		Tonality†
Bright colours		High pitch
Dark colours		Low pitch
Bizarre colours		Contrasted passages juxtaposed without transitions
etc.		etc.

* Hence the difficult, leaping, angular flute solo in Haydn's *Seasons*, where the composer has endeavoured to express the jaggedness of lightning.

† *Tonart*. Modern readers may find this a strange parallel. Reimold may, however, mean major or minor tonality (eds.)

I would be the first to admit that not everything in this scheme is quite as it might be. It must inevitably be incomplete, too. Even so, it serves its purpose in pointing the way to a terminology that may be applied equally to all the arts, thus reminding us of their close relationship and furthering the development of aesthetic theory. Once such a terminology has been agreed, it will be easy to define the essentials of beauty by transferring terms from one field to another. Thus, having charted out the main points of beauty, we shall discover its basic principles from these generalisations.

Christian Friedrich Michaelis

(b. Leipzig, 3 Sept. 1770; d. Leipzig, 1 Aug. 1834

From: articles in the Leipzig *Allgemeine musikalische Zeitung* (1806–7), and the *Berlinische musikalische Zeitung* (1805)

Michaelis was one of the first to investigate the application of Kant's aesthetic theories to music. He studied law, philology and philosophy at the University of Leipzig. Among the lectures he attended was Heydenreich's course on aesthetics. Taking his Master's degree in 1790, he then went on to study at Jena in 1792, returning to Leipzig in 1793. After submitting his doctoral thesis in 1794, he began lecturing as a Privatdozent on metaphysics and aesthetics. Never called to the chair on account of his association with the 'atheist' philosopher Fichte, he gradually withdrew from university teaching in favour of private tutoring and freelance journalism. A *philosophe* in the eighteenth-century sense, Michaelis's attempts to reinterpret Kant's ideas as applied to music are of interest; and his activities extended to other fields of music criticism, such as education, ethics, and certain aspects of musical anthropology. He was also interested in the grammar of the German language, painting and drawing and the art of declamation.

His publications, the most important of which in book form was *Ueber den Geist der Tonkunst mit Rücksicht auf Kants Kritik der Urteilskraft* (two parts 1795 and 1800), included translations of Minoja's *Lettere sopra il Canto* (1815), Busby's *General History of Music* (1821) and Burgh's *Anecdotes of Music* (1820); but his clearest and most stimulating comments on Kant's ideas are to be found in his numerous magazine articles, all of which were published after and represent further developments of the *Geist der Tonkunst*.

[The intangibility of music]

Sounds originate in vibrations of the air around us, which are transmitted to our ear. So when we hear sounds, we experience something outside ourselves; it is our outer sense that responds first to music. Now it is true that the sounds are given shape in space, since the air that communicates them is extended in space; but we can no more consider sounds as objects extended in space than we can air as a solid object (we actually infer its existence only from certain physical sensations). We cannot accept sounds as constituents of the physical world interpreted by the sense of sight and of touch. Sounds are to a certain extent un-physical, although they originate from bodies in motion; and just as spiritual things are invisible, so too are sounds. Sounds make a physical impact on our external sense of hearing, but those that we are consciously aware of are rather different from those that merely stimulate the nerves. Such sounds in fact represent a response, the product of mind, imagination and emotion. Hence the ear is only music's external route to our mind; the mere external organ. Musical sounds are in themselves a spiritual phenomenon. Our soul apprehends the sensations we hear and relates them to one another. Since the sounds communicate no tangible or visible material objects, and since they make us conscious of spatial substance other than ourselves (our immediate awareness of music being in no way dependent on extraneous factors) the sounds themselves constitute influences on our personality. Thus music affects our inner sense by means of our external sense, i.e. it affects our imagination and our inner receptivity through our sense of hearing. It enters, so to speak, the spirit and the heart by way of the ear. The external sensations aroused by music are immediately interiorised. We absorb them, shape them into a pattern, and thus they become within us a means of providing the material music uses as a means of artistic communication.[1]

If the intellect is the source of that cognitive clarity which thinks, differentiates between, integrates and coordinates the multiplicity of our sense-impressions, it is natural that an art that does not express itself through words, which makes use of no code of concepts, and which does not appeal directly to the intellect, will lack a certain clarity if one judges it by purely cognitive standards. Music cannot be grasped or understood in this manner in the way that a poem, a speech or a painting can be, the content and meaning of which can be absorbed and understood both in detail and as a whole. But it is precisely on account of this representational vagueness that music more nearly approaches aesthetic ideas the more it distances itself from intellectual concepts. For aesthetic ideas, products of reason and imagination, transcend all the constraints that bind the intellect to the everyday world. Now if music arouses the imagination by its images, which are wordless and merely internally felt and perceived, it simultaneously arouses reason, with which the imagination is closely connected and whose servant imagination is, hinting at or projecting in shadowy outline that very attractive element which is never expressed in full detail and cannot be realised with absolute clarity.[2]

[Musical beauty—form and content]

Music's extension is thus movement in time alone; its essence is origin, growth, change, decline and end. Music can express what is constant only by the repetition of what is similar or identical. But unmodified identical continuation of musical sounds or chords, or the uniform repetition of these will, if unduly extended, prove unbearable. The ear seeks variety and change, whereas the eye is apparently able to lose itself in lasting and rapturous contemplation of the same beautiful column or painting without tiring (*ermüdet*). Thus the maintenance of one fixed unchanging idea, and

[1] *Allgemeine musikalische Zeitung*, vol. 9, no. 43, p. 674.
[2] *Allgemeine musikalische Zeitung*, vol. 9, no. 44, p. 694.

the holding and piling up of dissonances are techniques that are employed in music solely for two purposes: either to express the sublime or to intensify the music's impact and to give it bite (*pikant zu machen*); such procedures always cause a certain degree of unrest or pain, which in turn arouses our vital forces and enhances our joy when the unrest is assuaged. . . . Individual sounds in themselves mean nothing; but certain melodic sequences or complete melodies can symbolise certain moods or modes of feeling. Should then the interest, the charm and the magic of music necessarily originate in what the melodies mean rather than in the manner in which they are shaped? I think it is a matter more of musical form rather than of what the music *expresses*. Whether or not the musician is depicting sadness or joy, our attitude is not conditioned by any sympathetic or other coincidental interest; at least that is not what constitutes *aesthetic* pleasure. But what delights and enchants us is how the composer uses sound to create melody and harmony, thereby evoking a specific reaction: in other words, it is the *form* of the music. Pleasure in music does not necessarily derive from the *significance* of melodies or modulations, which is often indeterminate; we experience such pleasure directly, *before* we have time to reflect on the possible meaning of the music. It seems to me that we do not contemplate the sounds of music in most cases as symbols, but that we derive pleasure directly from the harmonious interplay of the sounds. Melody and harmony do not seem to me to have to be merely symbolic of something else if they are to please; they are in themselves the object of our pleasure, our sense of well being, our admiration. One would have to censure much music that is highly esteemed (e.g. many excellent fugues) if the criterion of judgement were that they should be precisely expressive in one particular way expressed conceptually. What melody and harmony depict or stimulate is an awareness of the beautiful, the sublime, and the noble, which is the product of these two. It is this and this alone that pleases. It does so on its own account, without further significance being implied. In doing this, music may still be *characteristic*: and its power is then that much greater. Music that is of its nature pathetic retains its great value; the truer to life its expression is, the more certain it is to conquer the imagination and the heart. But we should not, I think, require every piece of music to be expressive of moods, emotions or states of mind; for we should have to be shown that the composition in question contained nothing additional that was pleasant, interesting or moving, which I believe not to be the case if its content is purely aesthetic. On the other hand, what *is* essential is that no piece of music should be loosely constructed from sections that effectively cancel each other out and neutralise the overall impression. Everything should possess unity in diversity. If character is definable as a certain satisfying impression left behind by the combination of musical ideas, melodies, chords and modulations – even, indeed, by suitably contrasting effects of light and shade – then every piece of music should in that case possess character. But the music's aesthetic quality, as in everything where beauty captivates us, does not, however, have anything to do with *what* is stated or expressed, but with the order and manner in which ideas are presented. Just as a lover rejoices to hear his beloved speak, bewitched by the sound of her voice and oblivious to what she is saying, so music often enchants us simply by its very existence, by the union of melody and harmony in a manifold interplay of the most intimate kind which reverberates in our innermost being, whatever the content may be.[3]

[The beautiful and the sublime in music]

Music can *either* seek to arouse the feeling of sublimity through an inner structure that is independent of any emotional expression, *or* portray the state of mind aroused by such a feeling. In the first case the music can objectively be called *sublime*, like untamed nature, which arouses sublime emotions; in the second case, the music portrays what is pathetically sublime. The former resembles epic poetry, the latter lyric poetry. In the first case, something analogous to an imitation of the external impact of sublime nature is being aimed at, the idea being to affect us the same way as nature does, to intensify our imagination and to arouse in us ideas of the infinitely great. In the second case, the portrayal is of our own nature, as we are moved, stirred, roused to emotional change and enthusiasm. The composer also expresses sublimity through the use of the marvellous. This is achieved by the use of unconventional, surprising, powerfully startling, or striking harmonic progressions or rhythmic patterns. Supposing, let us say, the established tonality suddenly veers in an unexpected direction, supposing a chord is resolved in a quite unconventional manner, supposing the longed-for calm is delayed by a series of stormy passages, then astonishment and awe result and in this mood the spirit is profoundly moved and sublime ideas are stimulated or sustained.[4]

> The second part of this article is divided off from the first; and the word *sublime* occurs only once. None the less, it is clearly meant as a rider to it, describing as it does, the symphonies of Haydn, Mozart and Beethoven as: 'on an epic scale, with heroic struggles between the themes' and asserting that the contrast throws new light on the material. The conclusion is almost unavoidable that for the reasons already stated, Michaelis regarded these works as examples of the sublime in music.

An essential difference between the beautiful and the sublime is revealed (following Kant's penetrating analysis) in the following: the beautiful relates to *form, outline, limitation*, the easily apprehended *image* of the object in space, or the easily apprehended melody, the gentle harmonic and rhythmic play of emotions in time. Sublimity, on the other hand, must, under certain circumstances, also be considered a constituent of crude unformed, un-

---

[3] *Allgemeine musikalische Zeitung*, vol. 9, no. 43, p. 676.
[4] *Berlinische musikalische Zeitung*, vol. 1, no. 46, p. 180.

shaped objects, and must be based on the idea of infinity or immeasurability. The beautiful depends in this respect on *quality*, the sublime on *quantity*. If the emotions are easily integrated in audible expression and fuse into a whole; if the sounds relate fluently to one another, constituting by their rhythmic symmetry a melody that the imagination can grasp without difficulty, then true *beauty* manifests itself in music. But when the sounds impinge on the ear at great length, or with complete uniformity, or with frequent interruptions, or with shattering intensity, or where the part-writing is very complex, so that the listener's imagination is severely taxed in an effort to grasp the whole, so that it feels in fact as if it is poised over a bottomless chasm, then the sublime manifests itself. The feeling of sublimity in music is aroused when the imagination is elevated to the plane of the limitless, the immeasurable, the unconquerable. This happens when such emotions are aroused as either completely prevent the integration of one's impressions into a coherent whole, or when at any rate they make it very difficult. The objectification, the shaping of a coherent whole, is hampered in music in two principal ways. Firstly, by uniformity so great that it almost excludes variety: by the constant repetition of the same note or chord, for instance; by long, majestic, weighty or solemn notes, and hence by very slow movement; by long pauses holding up the progress of the melodic line, or which impede the shaping of a melody, thus underlining the lack of variety. Secondly, by too much diversity, as when innumerable impressions succeed one another too rapidly and the mind being too abruptly hurled into the thundering torrent of sounds, or when (as in many polyphonic compositions involving many voices) the themes are developed together in so complex a manner that the imagination cannot easily and calmly integrate the diverse ideas into a coherent whole without strain. Thus in music, the sublime can only be that which seems too vast and significant, too strange and wonderful, to be easily assimilated by it. Sublime notes, figuration and harmonies stimulate the imagination, which must exert itself and expand beyond its normal bounds to grasp, integrate and recall them. They offer it, not flowing melodies with gentle cadences, but something that appears intractable to rhythmic laws; they have no immediately pleasant effect on the personality and the imagination, but an almost violent one of frightful and terrifying aspect. To the extent that music can depict greatness exceeding the normal capacity of the imagination, thrilling the listener with horror and rapture, it can express the sublime. But because the sublime does not readily appeal to the mind or to the imagination, but is able to satisfy us only because of its very incompatibility with both and because of its impact on the mind; frivolous, feeble and blinkered temperaments are not responsive to it. It appeals only to men of spirit and sensitivity, men of the noblest intellect.[5]

---

[5] *Berlinische musikalische Zeitung*, vol. 1, no. 46, p. 179.

In the final paragraph of the 'Analytik des Erhabenen', Kant discussed the question of humour in art, allowing it a place among the pleasant arts rather than among the beautiful, and asserting that humour really exists when the practitioner can voluntarily assume the talent 'to assume according to this disposition a particular state of mind in which everything is assessed quite differently from normal (even topsy-turvy) and yet according to certain rational principles' (p. 282).

Michaelis takes this up in an article on 'The Humorous or Comic Element in Musical Composition', dating from August 1807. True, it smacks somewhat of the earnest teutonic professor explaining the point of a string of earnest teutonic jokes, but Michaelis shows that he has grasped at least one vital point obscured from nineteenth-century writers and composers, namely, that there is such a thing as humour in music and that many of the ambiguities and incongruities in the music of, say, Haydn are intentionally humorous.

[Humour in music]

Music is humorous if it displays the composer's wilfulness more than the strict practice of artistic techniques; in such a case, the musical ideas are very odd and unusual and they do not follow on one another as the natural harmonic progressions might seem to imply. Instead, the listener is surprised by quite unexpected turns of phrase, by unexpected transitions, or by wholly new and oddly shaped figures. . . . Established ideas are inverted into new shapes, the notes are syncopated, individual parts are woven into remarkable textures, keys are boldly approached and left, returns to the original key and main theme are equally unexpected and everything concludes in so individual a manner that nothing can be explained in terms of conventional musical techniques, customary musical forms, or natural, regular procedure. The very unexpectedness of it all has precisely the same impact as do the ideas of a comical or humorous narrator who combines the bizarre with a wayward imaginative capacity to give the most familiar things a new look, and who, boldly and openly gives rein to his thoughts without ever offending against good taste.

Humorous music is sometimes comic and naive, sometimes serious and sublime. Deviations from the conventional, wayward combination of the bizarre and the unfamiliar, the inversion of themes, unorthodox openings, transitions, endings, and such like, might at first sight appear clumsy; but because these deviations are still unexpectedly combined with inspired music, because they immediately lose their clumsiness in their proper context, the music assumes a comic quality and it may arouse laughter.

Humorous music is either witty and of a jovial, pleasing character, or else it is on the whole more serious, bearing the traces of a wayward humour in which the impressions conflict strangely with each other and in which the imagination cannot quite enjoy free play. One rarely encounters these categories in their pure form. The term *scherzo* (*scherzando*) is generally used to describe the principal characteristics of the first kind of humour, and *capriccio*, the second. Music that is playfully humorous is designed above all to cheer and entertain us; the composer allows himself a freer rein than he does in the other genre, though he may well make use of ideas that he has himself devised, attractive or amusing themes which he varies and contrasts with other ideas. In a proper scherzo, the structure is more controlled and regular, and the procedure is more obvious, flowing and comprehensible than in a capriccio. For in the latter, the composer seems to be too dependent on his immediate mood and upon ideas that are generated by it to have in mind an audience or to attempt to entertain it and engage its sympathy by means of comprehensible ideas. He seems rather to be impelled by an inner urge to lay bare his immediate soul and to express the strange succession and transformation of emotions and ideas to which he is subject. Whereas the scherzo assumes much of the character of the beautiful, the capriccio tends towards the sublime and easily strays into the pompous or bombastic. .. What I understand in this instance by capriccio our composers often entitle *fantasy* and especially *free fantasy*. In the music of earlier times, humour was extremely rare, since composers preferred to observe strictly regular procedures, and were reluctant to embark on those bold, imaginative essays that transcend the conventional. Handel was perhaps one of the most distinguished composers of genius to introduce into his music an element of the comic now and then. There is, on the other hand, a considerable element of humour in modern music, especially since Joseph Haydn, the greatest master in this genre, set a pattern, particularly in his highly original symphonies and quartets. J. S. Bach frequently wrote in this style, but he confined himself mainly to ingenuities of harmony. C. P. E. Bach, too, often composed in a humorous style; but it was Haydn who first did so at all regularly, thereby influencing a number of composers of the modern era to write in this vein. Mozart's fertile genius, too, was no stranger to humour, but it seemed attuned more to the serious and sublime than to the comic and naive. Skilful though Mozart was at handling musical humour, he rarely exploited the vein at great length, and when he did, he managed to effect a quick smooth transition from the grand and impressive to the intimate and moving. His duos, quartets and quintets for various instrumental ensembles seem especially suited to the humorous style. Not only Haydn, but also Pleyel, Viotti, Rode, Kreutzer, Clementi and Beethoven have drawn upon rich springs of humour to flow in their compositions, a humour that in some has tended more towards roguish wit, whilst in others it has been serious and imaginative.[6]

[6] *Allgemeine musikalische Zeitung*, vol. 10, no. 46, p. 725.

Aubin Louis Millin

(b. Paris, 1759; d. Paris, 14 Aug. 1818)

From: *Dictionnaire des beaux-arts* (Paris 1806)

Millin was destined for the church. Having private means, however, he chose to devote himself to natural history and archaeology, and he probably did more than any of his contemporaries to spread a knowledge of these in France. After a term of imprisonment during the early years of the Revolution he accepted a place on the Bureau du comité d'instruction publique, and he succeeded Barthélemy as conservateur du cabinet des médailles in 1794. He did extensive research on buildings of historical interest in France; his publications include an *Introduction à l'étude des monuments antiques* (1798), the *Discours sur l'origine et les progrès de l'histoire naturelle en France* (1790), and the three-volume *Dictionnaire des beaux-arts*, which draws heavily on the work of Sulzer, and which, in such articles as 'Romanesque', is extraordinarily backward-looking.

The Beautiful (le Beau)

It is easier to sense the beautiful than to define it. Beauty depends on the ensemble and on the arrangement of the constituent parts; it is of interest, not on account of its content or function, but because of its forms. Without a perfect union between the parts and the whole – without this ensemble and structure – there can be nothing in literature or the arts that is wholly beautiful. On the contrary, although the detail may be beautiful, the work as a whole can never merit the description.

Classic (Classique)

A term that is applied to composers who are generally admired and who are regarded as authoritative: Palestrina, Durante, Leo, Piccini, Cimarosa, Handel, Hasse, Gluck, Mozart, Haydn, Méhul, Chérubini, Catel, these are classic composers. The word is used moreover in connection with works that are regarded as masterpieces, or at least as excellent, and which have been adopted as models for teaching purposes. Oratorios by Handel, Jomelli and Haydn, cantatas by Pergolesi, psalms by Marcello, masses by Palestrina, Mozart and Chérubini, Leo's *Miserere*, Pergolesi's *Stabat Mater*, symphonies and quartets by Haydn and Mozart, operas by Sarti, Piccini, Cimarosa, Gluck, Mozart, Méhul and Chérubini are all classics, just as are the fine overtures, duos and choruses that they contain.

293

Romanesque [having a novel-like quality] and romantic (romantique)

These two words are not synonymous. The 'romanesque' is that which belongs to the novel; the 'romantique' is that which is suited to it, or which has the appearance of belonging to it. The subject of a picture could be taken from a novel, and it could consequently be 'romanesque' without being in any way 'romantique'. Things that have something romantic about them might include a certain pleasing extravagance in dress, whimsical ornament, and an ingenious singularity of landscape and scenic layout. As such fantasies belong neither to history nor to daily life, the spectator attributes them to the novel. Many painters, including Rembrandt, Salvator Rosa, and le Feti, have introduced a romantic style into the historical genre. This great error is sometimes excused by the pleasure that such works afford, for we will excuse anything that pleases us. The word 'romantique' comes from the English and German tongues. Several French writers have made use of it, and as there is no direct equivalent in our language its adoption both in literature and painting has much to recommend it.

The Sublime (le Sublime)

Sublime works of taste are generally thought of as those which have in their particular way much greater power and grandeur than one would normally expect and which consequently arouse surprise and excite admiration. Beauty and goodness of themselves please and entertain, both in nature and in art; they create a sweet impression and are enjoyed in tranquillity. The sublime, on the other hand, makes an impact as it were by violent blows. It involves us and it irresistibly grips the soul. The effect is felt, not only at the moment of the initial surprise, but continuously. The more it is subjected to reflection, the deeper is its impact. The relationship between the beautiful and the sublime is parallel to the relationship between a smiling landscape (one that is pleasing to the eye) and a massive group of towering mountains. The sublime is the highest perfection of art and it must be used to excite powerful impressions within the soul: admiration, veneration, violent desire, great courage, and even terror and fear. In a word it is essential whenever intellectual activity is to be stimulated or curbed. The dimension of the sublime can be as effectively expressed by the graphic arts as by eloquence and poetry. There is no aspect of the sublime that Raphael has not touched. The artists of classical antiquity were eminently successful in expressing sublimity of character and feeling, as is evidenced by their writings and by the monuments of art that come down to us. They knew in sublime terms how to portray the divine majesty of Jupiter and the wisdom of Minerva in their sculptures. In only one respect do modern artists seem to lack the power to express the sublime, namely when they strive to express immanent divinity. They have best succeeded when they have not attempted an immediate representation of the grandeur and majesty of God. It is possible to express the sublime, even in architecture. It is easy to imagine a building that could inspire profound impressions of veneration, grandeur and power, and even of violent terror, though architects have rarely succeded in achieving such effects. Music has also its sublime aspects. It has in its power, sublime passion and even sublime tranquillity of spirit. Handel, Graun and Gluck have often achieved sublime heights in their compositions.

An object acquires its sublimity from its inner grandeur, and also possibly from the way in which it is presented. The first could be described as the essential sublime (*sublime essentiel*), the other, the incidental sublime (*sublime accidentel*). One only has to know or to feel certain things, certain ideas, to admire them. Other things may make an extraordinary impression on us at one particular time, although previously we have encountered them more than once, without experiencing any vivid impression.

The sublime artist is not wholly the product of nature; the circumstances in which he finds himself also contribute to the development of his genius. The finest qualities that an artist may have come to nothing when the surroundings are base and ignoble. Simplicity is part of the sublime: simplicity of intention, action and means. Grandeur and energy are most often to be found in the sublime. Unity of intention leads to unity of feeling and action. When a composition is dominated by a single theme to which everything else is demonstrably beholden, there is something sublimely impressive about it. These are the means by which art can strive towards sublimity: economy of object, an uncomplicated arrangement, a single light source, colours lacking studied refinement, a simple, general harmony tending to a unique effect.

Sublime feelings are much more powerful when the artist puts us, so to speak, in the position of looking inwards into the soul, and when he only uses external signs to show us what is going on within. The painter and sculptor who have sufficient genius to reveal the soul within the body can express the most sublime feelings without any violent movement. The artist who sees the body as nothing but inanimate matter, however, is obliged to express the inner workings of the soul by different means. The artist to whose chisel we are indebted for Niobe[1] knew how to express mortal terror on the very countenance of the unfortunate mother. Agisander, Polydorus and Athenodorus[2] had no need to resort to such objective signs as cries and tears in order to express Laocoon's violent anguish. The suffering soul reveals itself in the whole body. The artist can express grief itself, something that poetry denied Virgil, who was forced to make do with the signs of grief.[3]

Concerning the general question of the sublime, Longinus's *Traité du sublime* may first be consulted; there are numerous editions, one of the best

---

[1] A copy, probably Roman, of the original sculpture is in the Uffizi Gallery, Florence (eds.)

[2] The three sculptors who worked upon the Laocoon group (eds.)

[3] Virgil, *Aenid*, ii.

being by Toup (Oxford 1778); Boileau has translated it into French, and there are many other translations in English, German and Italian. There are many critical commentaries on it, too. The following may also be consulted: *A philosophical inquiry into the origin of our ideas of the sublime and the beautyfull*, by Burke (London 1767, 1772 and 1787) [see pp. 69–74]; there is a French translation (Paris 1765); the second chapter of the first part of the *Essay on Taste* (Al. Gerard); the fourth chapter of the *Elements of Criticism*, by Home [see pp. 76–81]; the fourth to sixth chapters of *L'art de sentir et de juger en matière de goût* (p. 112, etc. of the 1788 edition, dealing with the 'sublime').

Concerning the sublime in the arts, and in the arts of design in particular, I would refer to *Essai sur le sublime visible dans les arts du dessin*, by J. P. Melchoir (in German; Mannheim 1781); Richardson, his *Traité de la peinture* (1728, vol I, p. 182); Hagedorn's *Les considérations sur la peinture* (p. 335); and above all Lessing's *Laocoon*, in an excellent translation by M. Vanderbourg (Paris 1802) – I cannot too strongly recommend that artists read and meditate on this work.

Mme de Staël

(b. Paris, 22 April 1766; d. Paris, 14 July 1817)

From: *De l'Allemagne* (the English translation published by John Murray, London 1813), bk 1, ch. 11, pp. 304ff; bk 2, ch. 32, pp. 402ff; bk 3, ch. 6, pp. 71ff

Anne Louise Germaine was the daughter of Jacques Necker, who was from 1767–78 Minister of the Republic of Geneva in Paris and subsequently financial adviser to Louis XVI. Her mother was the centre of a distinguished Salon during this period, her famous 'Fridays' attracting men of the calibre of Marmontel, Grimm (who in 1774 returned from Germany singing the praises of Goethe) and Diderot. From 1786 until her separation in 1800 Anne Louise Germaine was married to the Baron de Staël-Holstein, who was for a time Swedish Ambassador in Paris. Two years after her marriage she published privately her first major work, the *Lettres sur les écrits et le caractère de Jean-Jacques Rousseau*, a tribute to the great *philosophe*; the fifth of the six letters includes an appraisal of Rousseau's writings on music.

She was a woman of great intellect and enthusiasm,[1] and her spirited defence of liberty during the tumultuous years of the Revolution and the Empire did nothing to endear her to any one political cause. She spent much of the time between 1789 and 1814 in voluntary and enforced exile, during which she made contact with many of Europe's leading literary, political and philosophical figures. Through the Hamburg editor Charles Villiers she became acquainted with the work of Kant; she corresponded with Goethe, who translated her *Essai sur les fictions* (1795) and who expressed a high regard for her *L'Influence des passions sur le bonheur des individus et des nations* (1796); in 1803 she visited Weimar and Berlin where she engaged August Wilhelm Schlegel as tutor to her boys. Her *De l'Allemagne* (1810) is one of her most important works: as Goethe observed, 'It was a powerful instrument which made the first breach in the Chinese Wall of old prejudices raised between us and France'.[2] It is a remarkably broad and penetrating study of every aspect of contemporary German culture. It took six years of research and a further two of writing, and when having been approved by the French censor it had been printed and was ready for distribution, all five thousand copies (each of two volumes) were seized by the Minister of Police, and the author exiled. The work was considered to be critical of the French regime and of Napoleon. The first edition to reach the public was in fact the English translation of 1813 which sold out in three days; the text is a good one, and it has been quoted here verbatim.

Mme de Staël returned to Paris in 1814, the year in which the first French edition came out; during the following five years a further four editions were produced. During the brief time that remained she found herself as the focus of a distinguished circle that included Lamartine (an author particularly beloved of Liszt), Sainte-Beuve

---

[1] See p. 513 for her definition of this central concept.

[2] Quoted in Mme la Comtesse de Pange, *Madame de Staël et la découverte de l'Allemagne* (Paris 1929), p. 478.

and Victor Hugo. She was seen by many later commentators as the leader of the early romantic movement in France (see especially 'Concerning the Romantic', in *Le Globe*, and chapter 2 of *L'histoire du romantisme*, F. R. de Toreinx (Paris 1829) (pp. 358 and 406).

For further reading:
A collation of the various editions of the French text is in Mme de Staël, *De l'Allemagne*, ed. La Comtesse Jean de Pange (Paris 1959).
Christopher Herold, *Mistress to an Age* (New York 1958) for a full biography.

Of classic and romantic poetry

The word *romantic* has been lately introduced in Germany to designate that kind of poetry which is derived from the songs of the Troubadours: that which owes its birth to the union of chivalry and Christianity. If we do not admit that the empire of literature has been divided between paganism and Christianity, the north and the south, antiquity and the middle ages, chivalry and the institutions of Greece and Rome, we shall never succeed in forming a philosophical judgement of ancient and of modern taste.

We sometimes consider the word *classic* as synonymous to perfection. I use it at present in a different acceptation, considering classic poetry as that of the ancients, and romantic, or *romanesque* poetry as that which is generally connected with the traditions of chivalry. This division is equally suitable to the two eras of the world: that which preceded, and that which followed the establishment of Christianity.

In various German works, ancient poetry has also been compared to sculpture, and modern to painting; in short, the progress of the human mind has been characterized in every different manner, passing from material religion to those which are spiritual, from nature to the Deity.

The French nation, certainly the most cultivated of all that are derived from Latin origin, inclines towards classic poetry imitated from the Greeks and Romans. The English, the most illustrious of the Germanic nations, is more attached to that which owes its birth to chivalry and romance, and it prides itself on the admirable compositions of this sort which it possesses. I will not in this place examine which of these two kinds of poetry deserves the preference; it is sufficient to show that the diversities of taste on this subject do not merely spring from accidental causes but are derived also from the primitive sources of imagination and thought.

There is a kind of simplicity both in the epic poems and tragedies of the ancients; because at that time men were completely the children of nature, and believed themselves controlled by a fate as absolutely as nature herself is controlled by necessity. Man, reflecting but little, bore the impressions of his soul on his countenance; even conscience was represented by external objects, and the torch of the Furies shook the horrors of remorse over the head of the guilty. In ancient times men attended to events alone, but among the moderns character is of greater importance; and that uneasy reflection, which like the vulture of Prometheus, often internally devours us, would have been folly amidst circumstances and relations so clear and decided, as they existed in the civil and social state of the ancients.

When the art of sculpture began in Greece, single statues alone were formed; groups were composed at a later period. It might be said with equal truth that there were no groups in any art; objects were represented in succession, as in bas-reliefs, without combination, without complication of any kind. Man personified nature; nymphs inhabited the waters, hamadryads the forest: but nature, in turn, possessed herself of man; and it might be said, he resembled the torrent, the thunderbolt, the volcano, so wholly did he act from involuntary impulse, and so insufficent was reflection in any respect to alter the motives or the consequences of his actions. The ancients, if we may be allowed the expression, possessed a corporeal soul, and its emotions were all strong, decided, and consistent: it is not the same with the human heart as it is developed by Christianity; from the repentance it so strongly enjoins, the moderns have derived a constant habit of self-reflection.

But in order to manifest this kind of internal existence, a great variety of outward facts and circumstances must display, under every form, the innumerable shades and gradations of that which is passing in the soul. If in our days the fine arts were confined to the simplicity of the ancients, we should never attain that primitive strength which distinguishes them, and we should lose those intimate and multiplied emotions of which our souls are susceptible. Simplicity in the arts would, among the moderns, easily degenerate into coldness and abstraction, while that of the ancients was full of life and animation. Honour and love, valour and pity were the sentiments which distinguished the Christianity of chivalrous ages; and those dispositions of the soul could only be displayed by dangers, exploits, love, misfortunes, that romantic interest, in short, by which pictures are incessantly varied. The sources from which art derives its effect are then very different in classic poetry and in that of romance; in one it is fate which reigns, in the other it is providence. Fate counts the sentiments of men as nothing; but providence judges of actions according to those sentiments. Poetry must necessarily create a world of a very different nature, when its object is to paint the work of destiny, which is both blind and deaf, maintaining an endless contest with mankind; and when it attempts to describe that intelligent order over which the Supreme Being continually presides; that Being whom our hearts supplicate and who mercifully answers their petitions!

The poetry of the pagan world was necessarily as simple and well defined as the objects of nature, while that of Christianity requires the various colours of the rainbow to preserve it from being lost in the clouds. The poetry of the ancients is more pure as an art; that of the moderns more readily calls forth our tears. But our present object is not so much to decide between classic and romantic poetry properly so called, as between the imitation of the one and the inspiration of the other. The literature of the ancients is, among the moderns, a transplanted literature; that of chivalry and romance is indigenous and flourishes under the influence of our religion and our institutions. Writers who are imitators of the ancients have subjected themselves to the rules of strict taste alone, for not being able to consult either their own nature or their own recollections it is necessary for them to conform to those laws by which the *chefs-d'œuvre* of the ancients may be adapted to our taste, though the circumstances both political and religious which gave birth to those *chefs-d'œuvre* are all entirely changed. But the poetry written in imitation of the ancients, however perfect in its kind, is seldom popular, because in our days it has no connection whatever with our national feelings.

The French, being the most classical of all modern poetry, is of all others least calculated to become familiar among the lower orders of the people. The stanzas of Tasso are sung by the gondoliers of Venice: the Spaniards and Portuguese, of all ranks, know by heart the verses of Calderón and Camoëns. Shakespeare is as much admired by the populace in England as by those of a higher class. The poems of Goëthe and Bürger are set to music, and repeated from the banks of the Rhine to the shores of the Baltic. Our French poets are admired wherever there are cultivated minds, either in our own nation or in the rest of Europe; but they are quite unknown to the common people and even to the class of citizens in our towns, because the arts in France are not, as elsewhere, natives of the very country in which their beauties are displayed.

Some French critics have asserted that German literature is still in its infancy; this opinion is entirely false: men who are best skilled in the knowledge of languages and the works of the ancients, are certainly not ignorant of the defects and advantages attached to the species of literature which they either adopt or reject; but their character, their habits and their modes of reasoning have led them to prefer that which is founded on the recollection of chivalry, on the wonders of the middle ages, to that which has for its basis the mythology of the Greeks. The literature of romance is alone capable of further improvement because, being rooted in our own soil, that alone can continue to grow and acquire fresh life: it expresses our religion; it recalls our history; its origin is ancient, although not of classical antiquity. Classic poetry, before it comes home to us, must pass through our recollections of paganism: that of the Germans is the Christian era of the fine arts; it employs our personal impressions to excite strong and vivid emotions; the genius by which it is inspired addresses itself immediately to our hearts and seems to call forth the spirit of our own lives, of all phantoms at once the most powerful and the most terrible.

Of the fine arts in Germany

The Germans excel in instrumental music; the knowledge it demands, and the patience necessary to execute it well are quite natural to them; some of their composers have also much variety and fruitfulness of imagination; I shall make but one objection to their genius as musicians; they put too much *mind* in their works; they reflect too much on what they are doing. In the fine arts there should be more instinct than thought: the German composers follow too exactly the sense of the words; this, it is true, is a great merit in the opinion of those who love words better than music, and besides, we cannot deny that a disagreement between the sense of the one and the impression of the other would be offensive: but the Italians, who are truly the musicians of nature, make the air and words conform to each other only in a general manner. In ballads and vaudevilles, as there is not much music, the little that there is may be subjected to the words; but in the great effects of melody we should endeavour to reach the soul by an immediate sensation.

Those who are not admirers of painting considered in itself, attach great importance to the subject of a picture; they wish, in contemplating it, to feel the impressions which are produced by dramatic representation: it is the same in music; when its powers are but feebly felt, we expect that it should faithfully conform to every variation of the words; but when the whole soul is affected by it, everything except the music itself, is importunate and distracts the attention: provided there be no contrast between the poetry and the music, we give ourselves up to that art which should always predominate over the others: for the delightful reverie into which it throws us annihilates all thoughts which may be expressed by words; and music awakening in us the sentiment of infinity, everything which tends to particularise the object of melody must necessarily diminish its effect.

Gluck, whom the Germans with reason reckon among their men of genius, has adapted his airs to the words in a wonderful manner, and in several of his operas he has rivalled the poet by the expression of his music. When Alcestis has determined to die for Admetus, and that this sacrifice, secretly offered to the Gods, has restored her husband to life, the contrast of the joyful airs which celebrate the convalescence of the king, and the stifled groans and lamentations of the queen who is condemned to quit him, has a fine tragical effect. Orestes, in the Iphigenia in Tauris, says, 'serenity is restored to my soul', and the air which he sings expresses the sentiment, but its accompaniment is mournful and agitated. The musicians, astonished at this contrast, endeavoured in playing it to soften the accompaniment, when Gluck angrily cried out: 'You must not hearken to Orestes, he tells you he is calm, but he lies.' Poussin, in painting the dance of the shepherdesses, places in the landscape the tomb of a young girl on which is inscribed: 'And I also was an Arcadian'. There is thought in this kind of conception of the arts as well as in the ingenious combination of Gluck; but the arts are superior to thought: their language is colour, forms or sounds. If we could form an imagination of the expressions of which our souls would be susceptible without the knowledge of words, we should have a more just idea of the effect to be produced by painting and music.

Of all musicians, perhaps Mozart has shown most skill in the talent of 'marrying' the music to the words. In his operas, particularly in 'the Banquet of the Statue', he makes us sensible of all the gradations of dramatic representation; the songs are gay and lively, while the strange and loud accompaniment seems to point out the fantastic and gloomy subject of the piece. This ingenious alliance of the musician and poet gives us also a sort of pleasure, but it is a pleasure which springs from reflection, and that does not belong to the wonderful sphere of the arts.

At Vienna, I heard Haydn's *Creation* performed by four hundred musicians; it was an entertainment worthy to be given in honour of the great work which it celebrated; but the skill of Haydn was sometimes even injurious to his talent: with those words of the Bible, 'God said let there be light, and there was light', the accompaniment of the instruments was at first very soft so as scarcely to be heard, then all at once they broke out together with a terrible noise as if to express the sudden burst of light, which occasioned a witty remark 'that at the appearance of light it was necessary to stop one's ears'.

In several other passages of the *Creation*, the same labour of mind may often be censured; the music creeps slowly when the serpents are created; it becomes lively again with the singing of birds, and in the *Seasons*, by Haydn also, these allusions are still more multiplied. Effects thus prepared before-hand are in music what the Italians term *concetti*: without doubt certain combinations of harmony may remind us of the wonders of nature but their analogies have nothing to do with imitation, which is nothing more than a factitious amusement. The real resemblance of the fine arts to each other and also to nature depends on sentiments of the same sort which they excite in our souls by various means. Imitation and expression differ extremely in the fine arts: it is pretty generally agreed I believe, that imitative music should be laid aside; but there are still two different ways of considering that of expression; some wish to discover in it a translation of the words; others, and the Italians are of this number, are contented with a general connection of the situations of the piece with the intention of the airs, and seek the pleasures of the art entirely in the art itself. The music of the Germans is more varied than that of the Italians, and in this respect perhaps is not so good; the mind is condemned to variety, its poverty is perhaps the cause of it; but the arts, like sentiment, have an admirable monotony, that of which one would willingly make an everlasting moment.

Philosophy and morals: Kant

His treatise upon the nature of the human understanding, entitled the *Examination of pure Reason*, appeared near thirty years ago, and this work was for some time unknown; but when at length the treasures of thought which it contains were discovered, it produced such a sensation in Germany, that almost all which has been accomplished since in literature as well as in philosophy, has flowed from the impulse given by this performance.

To this treatise upon the human understanding succeeded the *Examination of Practical Reason*, which related to morals; and the *Examination of Judgment*, which had the nature of the beautiful for its object. The same theory serves for a foundation to these three treatises, which embrace the laws of intellect, the principles of virtue, and the contemplation of the beauties of nature and of the arts.

I shall endeavour to give a sketch of the principal ideas which this doctrine contains; whatever care I may take to explain it clearly, I do not dissemble the necessity there is of incessant attention to comprehend it. A prince who was learning mathematics grew impatient of the labour which that study demanded. 'It is indispensable,' said his instructor 'for your highness to take the pains of studying, in order to learn the science; for there is no royal road in mathematics.' The French public, which has so many reasons to fancy itself a prince, will allow me to suggest that there is no royal road in metaphysics; and that to attain a conception of any theory whatever, we must pass through the intermediate ways which conducted the author himself to the results he exhibits.

The philosophy of materialism gave up the human understanding to the empire of external objects, and morals to personal interest and reduced the beautiful to the agreeable. Kant wished to re-establish primitive truths and spontaneous activity in the soul, conscience in morals, and *the ideal* in the arts. Let us now examine in what manner he has fulfilled these different undertakings.

At the time *The Examination of Pure Reason* made its appearance, there existed only two systems concerning the human understanding among thinking men: the one, that of Locke, attributed all our ideas to our sensations; the other, that of Descartes and Leibniz, endeavoured to demonstrate the spirituality and the activity of the soul: free-will, in short, the whole doctrine of Idealism: but these two philosophers rested their opinions upon proofs purely speculative. I have exposed in the preceding chapter, the inconveniences which result from these efforts of abstraction that arrest, if we may use the expression, the very blood in our veins, until our intellectual faculties alone reign within us. The algebraic method applied to objects that we cannot embrace by mere reasoning, leaves no durable trace in the mind. While we are in the act of perusing these writings upon high philosophical conceptions, we believe that we comprehend them; we think that we believe them, but the arguments which have appeared most convincing very soon escape from the memory.

If man, wearied with these efforts, confines himself to the knowledge which he gains by his senses, all will be melancholy indeed for his soul. Will he have any idea of immortality, when the forerunners of destruction are engraven so deeply on the countenance of mortals and living nature falls incessantly into dust? When all the senses talk of death, what feeble hope can we entertain of a resurrection? If man only consulted his sensations, what idea would he form of the supreme goodness? So many afflictions dispute the mastery over our life; so many hideous objects disfigure nature that the unfortunate created being curses his existence a thousand times before the last convulsion snatches it away. Let man, on the contrary, reject the testimony of his senses, how will he guide himself on the earth? And yet, if he trusts to them alone, what enthusiasm, what morals, what religion will be able to resist the repeated assaults to which pain and pleasure alternately expose him?

Reflection wandered over this vast region of uncertainty, when Kant endeavoured to trace the limits of the two empires, that of the senses and that of the soul; of external and of intellectual nature. The strength of thinking and the wisdom with which he marked these limits were perhaps never exhibited before: he did not lose himself among the new systems concerning the creation of the universe; he recognised the bounds which the eternal mysteries set to the human understanding, and (what will be new perhaps to those who have only heard Kant spoken of) there is no philosopher more adverse, in numerous respects, to metaphysics; he made himself so deeply learned in this science, only to employ against it the means it afforded him to demonstrate its own insufficiency. We might say of him that, like a new Curtius, he threw himself into the gulf of abstraction, in order to fill it up.

Locke had victoriously combated the doctrine of innate ideas in man because he has always represented ideas as making a part of our experimental knowledge. The examination of pure reason, that is to say of the primitive faculties of which the intellect is composed, did not fix his attention. Leibniz, as we have said above, pronounced this sublime axiom: 'There is nothing in the intellect which does not come by the senses, except the intellect itself.' Kant has acknowledged, as well as Locke, that there are no innate ideas; but he has endeavoured to enter into the sense of the above axiom by examining what are the laws and the sentiments which constitute the essence of the human soul independently of all experience. *The Examination of Pure Reason* strives to show in what these laws consist and what are the objects upon which they can be exercised.

Scepticism, to which materialism almost always leads, was carried so far that Hume finished by overturning the foundation of all reasoning in his search after arguments against the axiom, 'that there is no effect without a cause'. And such is the unsteadiness of human nature when we do not place the principle of conviction in the centre of the soul, that incredulity, which begins by attacking the existence of the moral world, at last gets rid of the material world also which it first used as an instrument to destroy the other.

Kant wished to know whether absolute certainty was attainable by the human understanding, and he only found it in our necessary notions – that is to say, in all the laws of our understanding which are of such a nature that we cannot conceive any thing otherwise than as those laws represent it.

In the first class of the imperative forms of our understanding are space and time. Kant demonstrates that all our perceptions are submitted to these two forms; he concludes from hence, that they exist in us and not in objects, and that in this respect it is our understanding which gives laws to external nature, instead of receiving them from it. Geometry, which measures space, and arithmetic, which divides time, are sciences of perfect demonstration because they rest upon the necessary notions of our understanding.

Truths acquired by experience never carry absolute certainty with them: when we say, 'the sun rises every day', 'all men are mortal', etc., the imagination could figure an exception to these truths which experience alone makes us consider indubitable; but imagination herself cannot suppose any thing out of the sphere of space and time; and it is impossible to regard as the result of custom (that is to say, of the constant repetition of the same phenomena) those forms of our thought which we impose upon things: sensations may be doubtful but the prism through which we receive them is immovable.

To this primitive intuition of space and time we must add or rather give, as a foundation, the principles of reasoning, without which we cannot comprehend anything, and which are the laws of our understanding, the connection of causes and effects: unity, plurality, totality, possibility, reality, necessity, etc.[3] Kant considers them all as equally necessary notions, and he only raises to the rank of real sciences such as are immediately founded upon these notions, because it is in them alone that certainty can exist. The forms of reasoning have no result excepting when they are applied to our judgement of external objects, and in this application they are liable to error; but they are not the less necessary in themselves; that is to say, we cannot depart from them in any of our thoughts: it is impossible for us to figure anything out of the sphere of the relations of causes and effects, of possibility, quantity, etc.; and these notions are as inherent in our conception as space and time. We perceive nothing excepting through the medium of the immovable laws of our manner of reasoning; therefore these laws also are placed within ourselves and not without us.

In the German philosophy, those ideas are called *subjective* which grow out of the nature of our understanding and its faculties, and all those ideas *objective* which are excited by sensations. Whatever may be the denomination which we adopt in this respect, it appears to me that the examination of our intellect agrees with the prevailing thought of Kant, namely, the distinction he establishes between the forms of our understanding and the objects which we know according to those forms; and whether he adheres to abstract conceptions or whether he appeals in religion and morals to sentiments which he also considers as independent of experience, nothing is more luminous than the line of demarcation which he traces between what comes to us by sensation and what belongs to the spontaneous action of our souls.

Some expressions in the doctrine of Kant having been ill interpreted, it

---

[3] Kant gives the name of *Category* to the different necessary notions of the understanding, of which he gives a list.

has been pretended that he believed in that doctrine of innate ideas, which describes them as engraved upon the soul before we have discovered them. Other German philosophers more allied to the system of Plato have, in effect, thought that the type of the world was in the human understanding, and that man could not conceive the universe if he had not in himself the innate image of it; but this doctrine is not touched upon by Kant: he reduces the intellectual sciences to three – logic, metaphysics, and mathematics. Logic teaches nothing by itself; but as it rests upon the laws of our understanding, it is incontestable in its principles, abstractedly considered: this science cannot lead to truth, excepting in its application to ideas and things; its principles are innate, its application is experimental. In metaphysics, Kant denies its existence because he pretends that reasoning cannot find a place beyond the sphere of experience. Mathematics alone appear to him to depend immediately upon the notion of space and of time, that is to say, upon the laws of our understanding anterior to experience. He endeavours to prove, that mathematics are not a simple analysis, but a synthetic, positive, creative science, and certain of itself without the necessity of our recurring to experience to be assured of its truth. We may study in the work of Kant the arguments upon which he supports this way of thinking; but at least it is true that there is no man more adverse to what is called the philosophy of the dreamers; and that he must rather have an inclination for a dry and didactic mode of thinking, although the object of his doctrine be to raise the human species from its degradation under the philosophy of materialism.

Far from rejecting experience, Kant considers the business of life as nothing but the action of our innate faculties upon the several sorts of knowledge which come to us from without. He believed that experience would be nothing but a chaos without the laws of the understanding but that the laws of the understanding have no other object than the elements of thought afforded it by experience. It follows that metaphysics themselves can teach us nothing beyond these limits and that it is to sentiment that we ought to attribute the foreknowledge and the conviction of everything that transcends the bounds of the visible world.

When it is attempted to use reasoning alone for the establishment of religious truths, it becomes a most pliable instrument which can equally attack and defend them because we cannot on this occasion find any point of support in experience. Kant places upon two parallel lines the arguments for and against the liberty of man, the immortality of the soul, the temporary or eternal duration of the world; and it is to sentiment that he appeals to weigh down the balance, for the metaphysical proofs appear to him of equal strength on either side.[4] Perhaps he was wrong to push the scepticism of reasoning to such an extent, but it was to annihilate this

---

[4] These opposite arguments on great metaphysical questions are called 'Antinomies' in Kant's writings.

scepticism with more certainty, by keeping certain questions clear from the abstract discussions which gave it birth.

It would be unjust to suspect the sincere piety of Kant, because he has maintained the equality of the reasonings for and against the great questions in the transcendental metaphysics. It appears to me on the contrary that there is candour in this avowal. Such few minds are able to comprehend these reasonings, and those who are able are so disposed to combat each other, that it is rendering a great service to religious faith to banish metaphysics from all questions that relate to the existence of God, to free-will, to the origin of good and evil.

Some respectable persons have said that we ought not to neglect any weapon, and that metaphysical arguments also ought to be employed to persuade those over whom they have power; but these arguments lead to discussion, and discussion to doubt upon every subject.

The best eras for the race of man have ever been those when truths of a certain class were uncontested in writing or discourse. The passions might then seduce into culpable acts but no one called in question the truth of that religion which he disobeyed. Sophisms of every kind, the abuses of a certain philosophy, have destroyed, in different countries and different ages, that noble firmness of belief, which was the source of the devotion of heroes. Then is it not a fine idea, for a philosopher to shut, even to the science which he professes, the door of the sanctuary, and to employ all the power of abstraction to prove, that there are regions from which it ought to be banished?

Despots and fanatics have endeavoured to prevent human reason from examining certain subjects, and reason has ever burst these unjust fetters. But the limits which she imposes on herself, far from enslaving her, give her a new strength – such strength as always results from the authority of laws, which are freely agreed to by those who are subjected to them.

A deaf and dumb person, before he had been under the discipline of the Abbé Sicard, might feel a full conviction of the existence of the Divinity. Many men are as far removed from those who think deeply, as the deaf and dumb are from other men, and still they are not less capable of experiencing (if the expression may be allowed) within themselves primitive truths, because such truths spring from sentiment.[5]

Physicians, in the physical study of man, recognise the principle which animates him, and yet no one knows what life is; and if one set about reasoning, it would be easy to prove to men (as several Greek philosophers have done), that they do not live at all. It is the same with God, with conscience, and with free-will. You must believe, because you feel: all argument will be inferior to this fact.

The labours of anatomy cannot be practised on a living body without

---

[5] In this and the following six paragraphs, de Staël seriously distorts Kant's moral thinking by placing undue emphasis on 'sentiment' (eds.)

destroying it; analysis, when attempted to be applied to indivisible truths, destroys them, because its first efforts are directed against their unity. We must divide our souls in two, in order that one half of us may contemplate the other. In whatever way this division takes place, it deprives our being of that sublime identity, without which we have not sufficient strength to believe that of which consciousness alone offers us assurance.

Let a great number of men be assembled at a theatre or public place, and let some theorem of reasoning, however general, be proposed to them; as many different opinions will immediately be formed as there are individuals assembled. But, if any actions, displaying greatness of soul, are related, or the accents of generosity heard, the general burst will at once proclaim, that you have touched that instinct of the soul which is as lively and as powerful in our beings, as the instinct which preserves our existence.

In referring to sentiment, which does not admit of doubts, as knowledge of transcendent truths, [and] in endeavouring to prove that reasoning avails only when exerted within the sphere of sensations, Kant is very far from considering this faculty of sentiment as an illusion; on the contrary, he assigns to it the first rank in human nature; he makes conscience the innate principle of our moral existence; and the feeling of right and wrong is, according to his ideas, the primitive law of the heart, as space and time are of the understanding.

Has not man been led by reasoning to deny the existence of free-will? and yet he is so convinced of it, that he surprises himself in the act of feeling esteem or dislike even for the animals that surround him; so forcibly does he believe in the spontaneous choice of good and evil in all beings.

The assurance of our freedom is only the feeling we have of it; and on this liberty, as the corner-stone, is raised the doctrine of duty; for if man is free, he ought to create to himself motives powerful enough to combat against the operation of exterior objects, and to set his will free from the narrow trammels of selfishness. Duty is at once the proof and the security of the metaphysical independence of man.

In the following chapters, we shall examine Kant's arguments against morality as founded upon self-interest, and the sublime theory which he substitutes in the place of this hypocritical sophism or perverse doctrine. Different opinions may be entertained as to Kant's first work, *The Examination of Pure Reason*: having himself acknowledged reasoning to be insufficient and contradictory, he ought to have anticipated that it would be made use of against him; but it appears to me impossible not to read with respect his *Examination of Practical Reason*, and the different works that he has written on morality.

Not only are Kant's principles of morality austere and pure, as might be expected from the inflexibility of a philosopher, but he always connects the evidence of the heart with that of the understanding, and is singularly happy in making his abstract theory as to the nature of the understanding, serve as a support to sentiments at once the most simple and the most powerful.

A conscience acquired by sensations may be stifled by them, and the dignity of duty is degraded in being made to depend on exterior objects. Kant, therefore, is incessantly labouring to show that a deep sense of this dignity is the necessary condition of our moral being, the law by which it exists. The empire of sensations, and the bad actions to the commission of which they lead, can no more destroy in us the notion of good or of evil than the idea of space and time can be changed by an erroneous application of it. There is always, in whatever situation we may be placed, a power of reaction against circumstances which springs from the bottom of the soul, and we cannot but feel that neither the laws of the understanding, moral liberty, nor conscience, are the result of experience.

In this treatise on the sublime and beautiful entitled, *The Examination of the Judgment*, Kant applies to the pleasures of the imagination the system from which he has developed such fruitful deductions in the sphere of intelligence and of sentiment; or rather it is the same soul which he examines, and which shows itself in the sciences, in morality and in the fine arts. Kant maintains that there are in poetry and in the arts which are capable, as poetry is, of painting sentiments by images, two kinds of beauty: one which may be referred to time and to this life, the other, to eternity and infinity.

And so impossible is it to say that what is infinite and eternal is intelligible to our minds, that one is often tempted to take even what is finite and transient for a dream; for thought can see no limits to anything, neither can being have a conception of non-existence. We cannot search deeply into the exact sciences themselves without meeting even there with what is infinite and eternal; and those things which are the most completely matters of fact do, under some relations, belong to this infinity and eternity as much as sentiment and imagination.

From this application of the feeling of infinity to the fine arts, arises the system of ideal beauty, that is to say, of beauty considered not as the assemblage and imitation of whatever is most worthy in nature, but as the realization of that image which is constantly present to the soul. Materialists judge of the beautiful according to the agreeable impression which it causes, and therefore place it in the empire of sensations: immaterialists who ascribe everything to reason, see in the beautiful what they call the perfect, and find in it some analogy to the useful and the good which they consider to be the first degrees of perfection. Kant has rejected both these explanations.

Beauty, considered only as an agreeable thing, would be confined to the sphere of sensations and consequently subject to the difference of tastes; it could never claim that universal acknowledgment which is the true character of beauty: beauty, again, considered as perfection, would require a sort of judgement like that on which esteem is founded: the enthusiasm that ought to be inspired by the beautiful belongs neither to sensations nor to judgement: it is an innate disposition, like the feeling of duty, and those ideas which are essential to the understanding; and we discover beauty when we see it because it is the outward image of that ideal beauty, the type of which exists in our mind. Difference of tastes may be applied to what is agreeable, for our sensations are the source of that kind of pleasure, but all men must admire what is beautiful, whether in art or in nature [because they have in their souls sentiments of celestial origin which beauty awakens, and of which it excites the enjoyment.][6]

Kant passes from the theory of the beautiful to that of the sublime, and this second part of his *Examination of the Judgment* is even more remarkable than the first: he makes the sublime, in moral liberty, consist in the struggles of man with his destiny, or with his nature. Unlimited power excites our fear, greatness overwhelms us; yet by the vigour of the will we escape from the sensation of our physical weakness. The power of destiny and the immensity of nature are placed in endless opposition to the miserable dependence of the creature upon earth; but one spark of the sacred fire in our bosoms triumphs over the universe, since with that one spark we are enabled to resist the impressions which all the powers in the world could make upon us.

The first effect of the sublime is to overwhelm a man, and the second to exalt him. When we contemplate a storm curling the billows of the sea and seeming to threaten both earth and heaven, terror at first takes possession of us, although we may be out of the reach of any personal danger; but when the clouds that have gathered, burst over our heads, when all the fury of nature is displayed, man feels an inward energy which frees him from every fear, by his will or by resignation, by the exercise or by the relinquishment of his moral liberty; and this consciousness of what is within him animates and encourages him.

When we hear of a generous action, when we learn that men have borne unheard-of misfortunes to remain faithful to their opinion, even to the smallest swerving, at first the description of the miseries they have suffered confuses our ideas, but by degrees we regain our strength, and the sympathy that we feel excited within ourselves by greatness of soul makes us hope that we ourselves could triumph over the miserable sensations of this life to remain faithful, noble and proud to our latest day.

Besides, no one can define, if I may so say, that which is at the summit of our existence; 'We are too much elevated in respect to ourselves, to comprehend ourselves', says St Augustine. He must be very poor in imagination who should think himself able to exhaust the contemplation even of the simplest flower; how then could we arrive at the knowledge of all that is comprised in the idea of the sublime?

I do not certainly flatter myself that I have been able, in a few pages, to give an account of a system which for twenty years has occupied all thinking

---

[6] The passage in square brackets comes from de Staël and has nothing to do with Kant (eds.)

heads in Germany; but I hope to have said enough to show the general spirit of the philosophy of Kant and to enable me to explain, in the following chapters, the influence which it has had upon literature, science, and morality.

See also Bibliography under: Brion

Victor Cousin

(b. Paris, 28 Nov. 1792; d. Cannes, 2 Jan. 1867)

From: *Cours de philosophie professé à la Faculté des Lettres pendant l'année 1818 sur le fondement des idées absolues du vrai, du beau et du bien* (Paris 1836); tr. as *Lectures on the True, the Beautiful, and the Good*, by O. W. Wight (3rd edn Edinburgh 1854), lecture IX

In 1815 Cousin became an assistant professor at the Sorbonne, where he lectured on the Scottish metaphysicians. In 1817 he visited Germany to become more closely acquainted with the work of Kant, Jacobi, Fichte, Schelling and Hegel. He was dismissed from the Sorbonne in 1821 on account of his liberal views, and in 1824 was arrested in Dresden as a carbonarist (see Mazzini, p. 476). He was reinstated in 1827 and he became an outspoken critic of Charles X's reactionary policies. After the 1830 revolution he was appointed a member of the Comité d'instruction publique, a member of the Académie française, and director of the École normale. In 1840 he became Ministre d'instruction publique and was subsequently a supporter of the 1848 revolution. Thereafter he retired from public life, devoting much of his remaining time to teaching at the Sorbonne. *Du vrai, du beau et du bien* (as the 1852 edition was entitled) originated as a series of lectures, during the years 1817–18; some idea of its influence is indicated by the fact that it had reached its twenty-ninth French edition by 1904, and that it was translated into many other languages during the course of the nineteenth century.

Our true doctrine [Cousin wrote, in his preface to the book], our true flag is spirituality – a philosophy as substantial as it is generous, which began with Socrates and Plato, which the Gospel has spread abroad in the world, which Descartes put under the severe forms of modern genius which in the seventeenth century was one of the glories and strengths of our country, which perished with the national grandeur of the eighteenth century, which at the beginning of the present century M. Royer-Collard re-established in public education, whilst M. de Chateaubriand, Madame de Staël, and M. Quatremère de Quincy transferred it into literature and the arts.[1]

Cousin examines most of the main issues that had been raised during the previous century: the problem of unity in variety (here very much centred on the idea of God as the being in whom there is both absolute unity and infinite variety), the aesthetic principle of disinterestedness, the nature of the beautiful and the sublime, the relationship between goodness and beauty, the qualities of genius and taste, and the purpose of the arts. He is concerned to avoid any confusion between beauty and goodness. He accepted that the artist seeks the ideal forms of beauty (an idea that is central to Batteux's system), the 'imitation' of nature being in effect the 'idealisation' of nature. He agreed, moreover, that 'if the ideal mounts unceasingly towards the infinite, art, which expresses ideal beauty, purifies the soul in elevating it towards the

[1] Author's preface, p. ix.

312

infinite, that is to say, towards God'. He was concerned none the less to emphasise, as Kant had done, that art was in no way the servant of morality, and that the experience of beauty was necessarily a disinterested experience.

In all this Cousin shows himself to be a disciple of Kant. Where he differs is in the specifically Christian interpretation that he gives to the process of idealisation, and in the equivalence that he draws between the 'infinite' (a word much beloved of early-nineteenth-century writers) and 'God', music being the art that awakens, more than any other, 'the sentiment of the infinite'.

The difference here between Kant and Cousin, however, is not one of principle but of emphasis; and if Cousin believed that music's 'proper effects' were 'vagueness', 'obscurity' and even 'infinitude', he did not choose to develop the idea to its logical conclusion, namely that the highest forms of music were purely instrumental. Indeed, the gulf between Cousin and his great contemporary, Schopenhauer (see p. 324) could hardly have been greater. For Cousin placed music not at the head of the fine arts but in a very inferior position – beneath poetry; even beneath painting.

The different arts

Expression is the general law of art. Division of arts. Distinction between liberal arts and trades. Eloquence itself, philosophy, and history do not make a part of the fine arts. That the arts gain nothing by encroaching upon each other, and usurping each other's means and processes. Classification of the arts: its true principle is expression. Comparison of arts with each other. Poetry the first of arts.

A *resumé* of the last lecture would be a definition of art, of its end and law. Art is the free reproduction of the beautiful, not of a single natural beauty but of ideal beauty as the human imagination conceives it by the aid of data which nature furnishes it. The ideal beauty envelops the infinite: the end of art is then to produce works that, like those of nature, or even in a still higher degree, may have the charm of the infinite. But how and by what illusion can we draw the infinite from the finite? This is the difficulty of art, and its glory also. What bears us towards the infinite in natural beauty? The ideal side of this beauty. The ideal is the mysterious ladder that enables the soul to ascend from the finite to the infinite. The artist then must devote himself to the representation of the ideal. Every thing has its ideal. The first care of the artist will be then, whatever he does, to penetrate at first to the concealed ideal of his subject, for his subject has an ideal, in order to render it, in the next place, more or less striking to the senses and the soul, according to the conditions which the very materials that he employs – the stone, the colour, the sound, the language – impose on him.

So, to express the ideal of the infinite in one way or another, is the law of art; and all the arts are such only by their relation to the sentiment of the beautiful and the infinite which they awaken in the soul, by the aid of that high quality of every work of art that is called expression.

Expression is essentially ideal: what expression tries to make felt, is not what the eye can see and the hand touch, evidently it is something invisible and impalpable.

The problem of art is to reach the soul through the body. Art offers to the senses forms, colours, sounds, words, so arranged that they excite in the soul, concealed behind the senses, the inexpressible emotion of beauty.

Expression is addressed to the soul as form is addressed to the senses. Form is the obstacle of expression, and, at the same time, is its imperative, necessary, only means. By working upon form, by bending it to its service by dint of care, patience, and genius, art succeeds in converting an obstacle into a means.

By their object, all arts are equal; all are arts only because they express the invisible. It cannot be too often repeated, that expression is the supreme law of art. The thing to express is always the same, it is the idea, the spirit, the soul, the invisible, the infinite. But, as the question is concerning the expression of this one and the same thing, by addressing ourselves to the senses which are diverse, the difference of the senses divides art into different arts.

We have seen that of the five senses which have been given to man,[2] three – taste, smell, and touch – are incapable of producing in us the sentiment of beauty. Joined to the other two, they may contribute to the understanding of this sentiment; but alone and by themselves they cannot produce it. Taste judges of the agreeable, not of the beautiful. No sense is less allied to the soul and more in the service of the body; it flatters, it serves the grossest of all masters, the stomach. If smell sometimes seems to participate in the sentiment of the beautiful, it is because the odour is exhaled from an object that is already beautiful, that is beautiful for some other reason. Thus the rose is beautiful for its graceful form, for the varied splendour of its colours; its odour is agreeable, it is not beautiful. Finally, it is not touch alone that judges of the regularity of forms, but touch enlightened by sight.

There remain two senses to which all the world concedes the privilege of exciting in us the idea and the sentiment of the beautiful. They seem to be more particularly in the service of the soul. The sensations which they give have something purer, more intellectual. They are less indispensable for the material preservation of the individual. They contribute to the embellishment rather than to the sustaining of life. They procure us pleasures in which our personality seems less interested and more self-forgetful. To these two senses, then, art should be addressed, is addressed in fact, in order to reach the soul. Hence the division of arts into two great classes, arts addressed to hearing, arts addressed to sight; on the one hand, music and poetry; on the other, painting, with engraving, sculpture, architecture, gardening.

[2] Lecture VI.

It will perhaps seem strange that we rank among the arts neither eloquence, nor history, nor philosophy.

The arts are called the fine arts because their sole object is to produce the disinterested emotion of beauty without regard to the utility either of the spectator or the artist. They are also called the liberal arts, because they are the arts of free men and not of slaves which affranchise the soul, charm and ennoble existence; hence the sense and origin of those expressions of antiquity, *artes liberales, artes ingenuæ*. There are arts without nobility, whose end is practical and material utility; they are called trades, such as that of the stove-maker and the mason. True art may be joined to them, may even shine in them, but only in the accessories and the details.

Eloquence, history, philosophy, are certainly high employments of intelligence; they have their dignity, their eminence, which nothing surpasses, but rigorously speaking, they are not arts.

Eloquence does not propose to itself to produce in the soul of the auditors the disinterested sentiment of beauty. It may also produce this effect, but without having sought it. Its direct end, which it can subordinate to no other, is to convince, to persuade. Eloquence has a client which before all it must save or make triumph. It matters little whether this client be a man, a people or an idea. Fortunate is the orator if he elicits the expression: That is beautiful! For it is a noble homage rendered to his talent; unfortunate he is if he does not elicit this, for he has missed his end. The two great types of political and religious eloquence, Demosthenes in antiquity, Bossuet among the moderns, think only of the interest of the cause confided to their genius, the sacred cause of country and that of religion; whilst at bottom Phidias and Raphael work to make beautiful things. Let us hasten to say, what the names of Demosthenes and Bossuet command us to say, that true eloquence, very different from that of rhetoric, disdains certain means of success; it asks no more than to please, but without any sacrifice unworthy of it; every foreign ornament degrades it. Its proper character is simplicity, earnestness – I do not mean affected earnestness, a designed and artful gravity, the worst of all deceptions – I mean true earnestness that springs from sincere and profound conviction. This is what Socrates understood by true eloquence.[3]

As much must be said of history and philosophy. The philosopher speaks and writes. Can he then, like the orator, find accents which make truth enter the soul, colours and forms that make it shine forth evident and manifest to the eyes of intelligence? It would be betraying his cause to neglect the means that can serve it; but the profoundest art is here only a means, the aim of philosophy is elsewhere; whence it follows that philosophy is not an art. Without doubt Plato is a great artist; he is the peer of Sophocles and Phidias

---

[3] See the *Gorgias*, with the *Argument*, vol. III of our translation of Plato. [Plato, *Oeuvres*, tr. V. Cousin, Paris 1822–40) and V. Cousin, *Des Pensées de Pascha* (3rd edn, Paris 1847)].

as Pascal is sometimes the rival of Demosthenes and Bossuet;[4] but both would have blushed if they had discovered at the bottom of their soul another design, another aim than the service of truth and virtue.

History does not relate for the sake of relating; it does not paint for the sake of painting; it relates and paints the past that it may be the living lesson of the future. It proposes to instruct new generations by the experience of those who have gone before them, by exhibiting to them a faithful picture of great and important events, with their causes and their effects, with general designs and particular passions, with the faults, virtues, and crimes that are found mingled together in human things. It teaches the excellence of prudence, courage and great thoughts profoundly meditated, constantly pursued and executed with moderation and force. It shows the vanity of immoderate pretensions, the power of wisdom and virtue, the impotence of folly and crime. Thucydides, Polybius, and Tacitus undertake anything else than procuring new emotions, for an idle curiosity or a worn-out imagination; they doubtless desire to interest and attract, but more to instruct; they are the avowed masters of statesmen and the preceptors of mankind.

The sole object of art is the beautiful. Art abandons itself as soon as it shuns this. It is often constrained to make concessions to circumstances, to external conditions that are imposed upon it; but it must always retain a just liberty. Architecture and the art of gardening are the least free of arts; they are subjected to unavoidable obstacles; it belongs to the genius of the artist to govern these obstacles, and even to draw from them happy effects, as the poet turns the slavery of metre and rhyme into a source of unexpected beauties. Extreme liberty may carry art to a caprice which degrades it, as chains too heavy crush it. It is the death of architecture to subject it to convenience, to *comfort*. Is the architect obliged to subordinate general effect and the proportions of the edifice to such or such a particular end that is prescribed to him? He takes refuge in details, in pediments, in friezes, in all the parts that have not utility for a special object, and in them he becomes a true artist. Sculpture and painting, especially music and poetry, are freer than architecture and the art of gardening. One can also shackle them, but they disengage themselves more easily.

Similar by their common end, all the arts differ by the particular effects which they produce, and by the processes which they employ. They gain nothing by exchanging their means and confounding the limits that separate them. I bow before the authority of antiquity; but perhaps through habit and a remnant of prejudice, I have some difficulty in representing to myself with pleasure statues composed of several metals, especially painted statues.[5] Without pretending that sculpture has not to a certain point its

---

[4] There is a *Provincial* that for vehemence can be compared only to the *Philipics*, and its fragment on the infinite has the grandeur and magnificence of Bossuet. See our work on the *Thoughts of Pascal*, 4th Series, *Literature*, vol. I.

[5] See the *Jupiter Olympien* of M. Quatremère de Quincy.

colour, that of perfectly pure matter, that especially which the hand of time impresses upon it, in spite of all the seductions of a contemporaneous[6] artist of great talent, I have little taste I confess for that artifice that is forced to give to marble the *morbidezza* of painting. Sculpture is an austere muse; it has its graces but they are those of no other art. Flesh-colour must remain a stranger to it: there would nothing more remain to communicate to it but the movement of poetry and the indefiniteness of music! And what will music gain by aiming at the picturesque when its proper domain is the pathetic? Give to the most learned symphonist a storm to render. Nothing is easier to imitate than the whistling of the winds and the noise of thunder. But by what combinations of harmony will he exhibit to the eyes the glare of the lightning rending all of a sudden the veil of the night, and what is most fearful in the tempest, the movement of the waves that now ascend like a mountain, now descend and seem to precipitate themselves into bottomless abysses? If the auditor is not informed of the subject, he will never suspect it, and I defy him to distinguish a tempest from a battle. In spite of science and genius, sounds cannot paint forms. Music, when well guided, will guard itself from contending against the impossible; it will not undertake to express the tumult and strife of the waves and other similar phenomena; it will do more: with sounds it will fill the soul with the sentiments that succeed each other in us during the different scenes of the tempest. Haydn will thus become[7] the rival, even the vanquisher of the painter, because it has been given to music to move and agitate the soul more profoundly than painting.

Since the *Laocoon* of Lessing, it is no longer permitted to repeat, without great reserve, the famous axiom, 'Ut pictura poesis'; or, at least, it is very certain that painting cannot do everything that poetry can do. Everybody admires the picture of Rumour, drawn by Virgil; but let a painter try to realize this symbolic figure; let him represent to us a huge monster with a hundred eyes, a hundred mouths, and a hundred ears, whose feet touch the earth, whose head is lost in the clouds, and such a figure will become very ridiculous.

So the arts have a common end, and entirely different means. Hence the general rules common to all, and particular rules for each. I have neither time nor space to enter into details on this point. I limit myself to repeating that the great law which governs all others is expression. Every work of art that does not express an idea signifies nothing; in addressing itself to such or such a sense, it must penetrate to the mind, to the soul, and bear thither a thought, a sentiment capable of touching or elevating it. From this fundamental rule all the others are derived; for example, that which is continually and justly recommended, composition. To this is particularly

---

[6] Allusion to the *Magdeleine* of Canova, which was then to be seen in the gallery of M. de Sommariva.

[7] See the *Tempest* of Haydn, among the pianoforte works of this master.

applied the precept of unity and variety. But, in saying this, we have said nothing so long as we have not determined the nature of the unity of which we would speak. True unity is unity of expression, and variety is made only to spread over the entire work the idea or the single sentiment that it should express. It is useless to remark that between composition thus defined and what is often called composition, as the symmetry and arrangement of parts according to artificial rules, there is an abyss. True composition is nothing else than the most powerful means of expression.

Expression not only furnishes the general rules of art, it also gives the principle that allows of their classification.

In fact, every classification supposes a principle that serves as a common measure.

Such a principle has been sought in pleasure, and the first of arts has seemed that which gives the most vivid joys. But we have proved that the object of art is not pleasure: the more or less of pleasure that an art procures cannot, then, be the true measure of its value.

This measure is nothing else than expression. Expression being the supreme end, the art that most nearly approaches it is the first of all.

All true arts are expressive, but they are diversly so. Take music; it is without contradiction the most penetrating, the profoundest, the most intimate art. There is physically and morally between a sound and the soul a marvellous relation. It seems as though the soul were an echo in which the sound takes a new power. Extraordinary things are recounted of the ancient music. And it must not be believed that the greatness of effect supposes here very complicated means. No, the less noise music makes, the more it touches. Give some notes to Pergolesi, give him especially some pure and sweet voices, and he returns a celestial charm, bears you away into infinite spaces, plunges you into ineffable reveries. The peculiar power of music is to open to the imagination a limitless career, to lend itself with astonishing facility to all the moods of each one, to arouse or calm with the sounds of the simplest melody, our accustomed sentiments, our favourite affections. In this respect music is an art without a rival: however it is not the first of arts.

Music pays for the immense power that has been given it; it awakens more than any other art the sentiment of the infinite, because it is vague, obscure, indeterminate in its effects. It is just the opposite art to sculpture which bears less towards the infinite because everything in it is fixed with the last degree of precision. Such is the force and at the same time the feebleness of music that it expresses everything and expresses nothing in particular. Sculpture, on the contrary, scarcely gives rise to any reverie for it clearly represents such a thing and not such another. Music does not paint, it touches; it puts in motion imagination, not the imagination that reproduces images, but that which makes the heart beat, for it is absurd to limit imagination to the domain of images.[8] The heart, once touched, moves all

---

[8] See Lecture VI.

the rest of our being; thus music, indirectly and to a certain point, can recall images and ideas; but its direct and natural power is neither on the representative imagination nor intelligence, it is on the heart, and that is an advantage sufficiently beautiful.

The domain of music is sentiment, but even there its power is more profound than extensive, and if it expresses certain sentiments with an incomparable force, it expresses but a very small number of them. By way of association, it can awaken them all, but directly it produces very few of them, and the simplest and the most elementary, too, sadness and joy with their thousand shades. Ask music to express magnanimity, virtuous resolution and other sentiments of this kind, and it will be just as incapable of doing it as of painting a lake or a mountain. It goes about it as it can; it employs the slow, the rapid, the loud, the soft, etc., but imagination has to do the rest, and imagination does only what it pleases. The same measure reminds one of a mountain, another of the ocean; the warrior finds in it heroic inspirations, the recluse religious inspirations. Doubtless, words determine musical expression but the merit then is in the word not in the music; and sometimes the word stamps the music with a precision that destroys it, and deprives it of its proper effects – vagueness, obscurity, monotony – but also fullness and profundity, I was about to say infinitude. I do not in the least admit that famous definition of song: a noted declamation. A simple declamation rightly accented is certainly preferable to stunning accompaniments; but to music must be left its character, and its defects and advantages must not be taken away from it. Especially it must not be turned aside from its object, and there must not be demanded from it what it could not give. It is not made to express complicated and factitious sentiment nor terrestrial and vulgar sentiments. Its peculiar charm is to elevate the soul towards the infinite. It is therefore naturally allied to religion, especially to that religion of the infinite which is at the same time the religion of the heart; it excels in transporting to the feet of eternal mercy the soul trembling on the wings of repentance, hope and love. Happy are those, who at Rome, in the Vatican,[9] during the solemnities of the Catholic

---

[9] I have not myself had the good fortune to hear the religious music of the Vatican. Therefore, I shall let a competent judge, M Quatremère de Quincy, speak, *Considerations morales sur le destination des ouvrages de l'art*, Paris, 1815, p. 98: 'Let one call to mind those chants so simple and so touching, that terminate at Rome the funeral solemnities of those three days which the Church particularly devotes to the expression of its grief, in the last week of Lent. In that nave where the genius of Michelangelo has embraced the duration of ages, from the wonders of creation to the last judgement that must destroy its works, are celebrated, in the presence of the Roman pontiff, those nocturnal ceremonies whose rites, symbols, and plaintive liturgies seem to be so many figures of the mystery of grief to which they are consecrated. The light decreasing by degrees, at the termination of each psalm, you would say that a funereal veil is extended little by little over those religious vaults. Soon the doubtful light of the last lamp allows you to perceive nothing but Christ in the distance, in the midst of clouds, pronouncing his judgments, and some angel executors of his behests. Then, at the bottom of a tribune interdicted to the regard of

worship, have heard the melodies of Leo, Durante and Pergolesi on the old consecrated text! They have entered heaven for a moment, and their souls have been able to ascend thither without distinction of rank, country, even belief, by those invisible and mysterious steps, composed thus to speak of all the simple, natural, universal sentiments that everywhere on earth draw from the bosom of the human creature a sigh towards another world!

Between sculpture and music, those two opposite extremes, is painting, nearly as precise as the one, nearly as touching as the other. Like sculpture, it marks the visible forms of objects, but adds to them life; like music, it expresses the profoundest sentiments of the soul, and expresses them all. Tell me what sentiment does not come within the province of the painter? He has entire nature at his disposal, the physical world, and the moral world, a churchyard, a landscape, a sunset, the ocean, the great scenes of civil and religious life, all the beings of creation, above all, the figure of man, and its expression, that living mirror of what passes in the soul. More pathetic than sculpture, clearer than music, painting is elevated, in my opinion, above both, because it expresses beauty more under all its forms, and the human soul in all the richness and variety of its sentiments.

But the art *par excellence*, that which surpasses all others, because it is incomparably the most expressive, is poetry.

Speech is the instrument of poetry; poetry fashions it to its use and idealizes it in order to make it express ideal beauty. Poetry gives to it the charm and power of measure; it makes of it something intermediary between the ordinary voice and music, something at once material and immaterial, finite, clear and precise, like contours and forms the most definite, living and animated like colour, pathetic and infinite like sound. A word in itself, especially a word chosen and transfigured by poetry, is the most energetic and universal symbol. Armed with this talisman, poetry reflects all the images of the sensible world, like sculpture and painting; it reflects sentiment like painting and music, with all its varieties, which music does not attain, and in their rapid succession that painting cannot follow, as

the profane, is heard the psalm of the penitent king, to which three of the greatest masters of the art have added the modulations of a simple and pathetic chant. No instrument is mingled with those accents. Simple harmonies of voice execute that music; but these voices seem to be those of angels, and their effect penetrates the depths of the soul.'

We have cited this beautiful passage – and we could have cited many others, even superior to it – of a man now forgotten, and almost always misunderstood, but whom posterity will put in his place. Let us indicate, at least, the last pages of the same production, on the necessity of leaving the works of art in the place for which they were made, for example, the portrait of Mlle de Vallière in the *Madeleine aux Carmelites*, instead of transferring it to, and exposing it in the apartments of Versailles, 'the only place in the world,' eloquently says M. Quatremère, 'which never should have seen it'.

precise and immobile as sculpture; and it not only expresses all that, it expresses what is inaccessible to every other art, I mean thought, entirely distinct from the senses and even from sentiment, thought that has no forms, thought that has no colour, that lets no sound escape, that does not manifest itself in any way, thought in its highest flight, in its most refined abstraction.

Think of it. What a world of images, of sentiments, of thoughts at once distinct and confused, are excited within us by this one word, country! And by this other word, brief and immense, God! What is more clear and altogether more profound and vast!

Tell the architect, the sculptor, the painter, even the musician, to call forth also by a single stroke all the powers of nature and the soul! They cannot, and by that they acknowledge the superiority of speech and poetry.

They proclaim it themselves, for they take poetry for their own measure; they esteem their own works, and demand that they should be esteemed in proportion as they approach the poetic ideal. And the human race does as artists do: a beautiful picture, a noble melody, a living and expressive statue, gives rise to the exclamation, How poetical! This is not an arbitrary comparison; it is a natural judgement which makes poetry the type of the perfection of all the arts, the art *par excellence*, which comprises all others to which they aspire, which none can reach.

When the other arts would imitate the works of poetry, they usually err, losing their own genius without robbing poetry of its genius. But poetry constructs according to its own taste palaces and temples, like architecture; it makes them simple or magnificent; all orders, as well as all systems, obey it; the different ages of art are the same to it; it reproduces, if it pleases, the classic or the Gothic, the beautiful or the sublime, the measured or the infinite. Lessing has been able, with the exactest justice, to compare Homer to the most perfect sculptor; with such precision are the forms which that marvellous chisel gives to all beings determined! And what a painter, too, is Homer and, of a different kind, Dante! Music alone has something more penetrating than poetry, but it is vague, limited and fugitive. Besides its clearness, its variety, its durability, poetry has also the most pathetic accents. Call to mind the words that Priam utters at the feet of Achilles while asking him for the dead body of his son, more than one verse of Virgil, entire scenes of the *Cid* and the *Polyeucte*, the prayer of Esther kneeling before the Lord, the choruses of *Esther* and *Athalie*. In the celebrated song of Pergolesi, *Stabat Mater Dolorosa*, we may ask which moves most, the music or the words. The *Dies irœ, Dies illa*, recited only, produces the most terrible effect. In those fearful words, every blow tells, so to speak; each word contains a distinct sentiment, an idea at once profound and determinate. The intellect advances at each step, and the heart rushes on in its turn. Human speech idealized by poetry has the depth and brilliancy of musical notes; it is luminous as well as pathetic; it speaks to the mind as well as to the heart; it is in that inimitable, unique, and embraces all extremes and all contraries in a harmony that redoubles their reciprocal effect, in which, by turns, appear and are developed, all images, all sentiments, all ideas, all the human faculties, all the inmost recesses of the soul, all the forms of things, all real and all intelligible worlds!

Fig. 3. *Liszt am Flügel* (Josef Danhauser, 1805–45). This scene was painted for the Viennese piano-manufacturer Konrad Graf. The enraptured audience includes George Sand, Marie d'Agoult, de Musset, Victor Hugo, the elder Dumas and Paganini. Even Rossini, behind whose head there is a portrait of Byron, seems to be carried away by Liszt's playing, like the others. The portrait of Byron and the prominent bust of Beethoven leave one in no doubt as to the spiritual forebears of this scene of romantic, infinite intensity. (Nationalgalerie, Berlin)

Arthur Schopenhauer

(b. Danzig, 22 Feb. 1788; d. Frankfurt am Main, 21 Sept. 1860)

From: *Die Welt als Wille und Vorstellung*, bk 3 (1819) and 2nd edn (1844), in *Sämtliche Werke*, ed. Paul Deussen (Munich 1911), vol. 1, pp. 301–3; 304; 307–12

Because of his undoubted influence on Richard Wagner, Schopenhauer is probably better known to musicians than most of the other great philosophers active during the period covered by this volume. There can be no doubt that his powerfully argued philosophy and his assessment of the place of music, not only among the arts, but as an element in the cosmos, were bound to arouse a sympathetic reaction among musicians. Yet it will be evident from the preceding extracts that Schopenhauer's aesthetic is an extreme example of certain marked tendencies notable in earlier thinkers, rather than a radical new departure.

Schopenhauer's father was a wealthy banker of intelligence and culture. His mother was a competent writer who lived, after her husband's suicide in 1805, for over twenty years in Weimar, associating with Goethe and his circle. Arthur studied science and philosophy at Göttingen and Berlin, understood English well enough to be able to read *The Times*, and served for a short time in the War of Liberation in 1813. He was a lifelong misanthropist, a man well aware of his exceptional intelligence, and extremely susceptible to music and literature. His interest in the latter subject led him to study the thought of the East, particularly Hindu writings, which certainly influenced his mature philosophy.

Schopenhauer became a Doctor of Philosophy in 1813 and hoped to set up as a university teacher. His first truly original contribution to philosophy came in 1819, with the publication of the first version of *Die Welt als Wille und Vorstellung*. It attracted little attention; and when he moved to Berlin in 1820, hoping to attract a following from the Hegelians there, he failed to make any converts. He then spent ten years in Italy, returning to Germany in 1831, working in Frankfurt as a translator and writer of occasional pieces, mostly on philosophical and ethical issues. *Die Welt als Wille und Vorstellung* was republished in an expanded version in 1844, when it achieved success and a reputation for its author – too late, as he wrily observed, for the success to be of much use to him. He lived on as a crabbed and hypochondriac recluse until 1860.

Schopenhauer regarded himself as the true and worthy successor of Kant. He proposed that the *Ding an sich* which Kant postulated as the ultimate reality, was a universal cosmic Will; and all life – and even inorganic matter – was an individualised manifestation of that Will. The Will proceeded from desire to temporary satisfaction and thence to renewed desire; and the only escape from the vicious circle was a kind of Buddhistic renunciation of desire. One way of seeking temporary relief, however, was in aesthetic contemplation; and as the following excerpts will show, listening to music is not merely the highest form of aesthetic contemplation, but one radically different from all the others.

We have, like all previous translators, had difficulty in choosing a suitable consistent English term for Schopenhauer's *Vorstellung*. It is usually translated as *Idea*; but in his translation (New York 1969), E. F. J. Payne prefers the term *Representation*. *Sich etwas vorstellen* means 'to imagine' in the sense of to project an image in the mind, so we have kept to Payne's term, using the word 'Idea' for Schopenhauer's *Idee*.

Other themes that need some explanation are the *principium individuationis*, or the principle by which the observer can tell of *a* that it is, or is not identical with *b*; and the musical term *Ripienstimmen*, which Schopenhauer uses in the sense of subsidiary harmonic parts of no melodic interest. This, incidentally, is one of the definitions given by Koch (1749–1816) in his *Musikalisches Lexikon* of 1802 (p. 1261).

See also Bibliography under: Copleston, Gardiner, Tengler

[Music – the unique art]

We have now considered all the fine arts in those general terms relevant to our purpose, beginning with architecture, whose aim as such is to crystallise the Will's objectification at the lowest level of its visible aspect. Here it reveals itself as something circumscribed by law, a ponderous striving of inert matter incapable of cognition, yet even at this stage revealing internal conflict and strife, namely between gravity and rigidity. . . . We concluded our exposition with tragedy, which, at the highest level of the Will's objectification, brings that very conflict before our eyes on a fearful scale and with fearful clarity. Yet there is still one fine art that has of necessity been excluded from consideration, since in the systematic exposition of our theory there was no suitable place for it.

This art is music. It stands quite apart from all the others. In it, we do not perceive an imitation or a copy of some idea of the things that exist in the world. Even so, it is such a great and eminently splendid art, it creates such a powerful reaction in man's inmost depths, it is so thoroughly and profoundly understood by him as a uniquely universal language, even exceeding in clarity that of the phenomenal world itself, that we must certainly look for more in it than Leibniz's 'exercitium arithmeticae occultum nescientis se numerari animi', even though Leibniz was quite right, in that he was speaking only of immediate and external significance. However, if music were no more than this, the satisfaction it affords would be akin to that which we experience when we correctly solve a mathematical exercise and it could not be that intimate joy with which we see the innermost depths of our being expressed. Looking at the matter, then, from the point of view of aesthetic effect, we must seek a much deeper and more serious significance, one that relates to the innermost nature of the world and of ourselves, a significance whereby the numerical relationships into which music may be analysed are held to be not what music is but only what it symbolises. We may infer by analogy from the other arts that it must relate to the world in some sense or other as a representation does to what is represented, as a copy does to a model; for all the arts possess this character. Music's effect on us is on the whole similar to theirs, but stronger, more immediate, effective and inevitable. The way in which it relates to the world must also be very profound, infinitely true and really striking, since it is immediately and universally comprehensible; and hence there is a certain infallibility about it in that its form can be reduced to certain definite rules, expressible in numerical terms, from which it may not deviate at all without altogether ceasing to be music. None the less, the point of comparison between music and the world, the relationship in which the one stands to the other as an imitation or copy lies hidden very deep. Music has been performed in all ages without there being any accounting for this relationship. Content with directly responding to it, people renounce abstract understanding of any such direct response.

[How music relates to the Will]

(Platonic) ideas are the adequate objectification of the Will; the object of all the other arts is cognition of these objectifications by means of the representation of individual objects (for that is what works of art themselves always are), and this is possible only when some change takes place in the subject reacting to them. Thus the other arts all objectify the Will only indirectly, i.e. by means of ideas, and as our world is nothing but the appearance of a multiplicity of ideas, through entry into the *principium individuationis* (the form of cognition available to the individual as such), so music, which bypasses ideas, is also totally independent of the phenomenal world; it simply ignores the world, and it could in some sense continue to exist even if the world did not, something that cannot be said of the other arts. Music, in other words, is just as *immediate* an objectification and image of the entire *Will* as the world itself is, as immediate, in fact, as those ideas are which in their multiplicity of appearances constitute the world of individual objects. Music is thus in no sense, like the other arts, the image of ideas, but the image of the *Will itself*, which also takes objective shape in ideas; and for this very reason the effect of music is far more powerful and penetrates far more deeply than that of the other arts; for they communicate only shadows, whereas it communicates the essence. Since, however, the same Will takes objective shape in ideas as in music, only rather differently in each case, there must therefore be, not perhaps an immediate resemblance, but at any rate a parallel, an analogy, between music and ideas, whose appearance in variety and imperfection constitutes the visible world. The demonstration of this analogy will, as an illustration, make it easier to understand this explanation, which the obscurity of the subject has made difficult.

[The analogy between music and the phenomenal world]

I recognise in the deepest notes of harmony, in the fundamental bass, the lowest level of the Will's objectification, inorganic nature, the mass of the planets. All the high notes, light and more rapidly dying away, should clearly be considered as arising out of the secondary vibrations of the deep fundamental, vibrations which simultaneously and gently sound whenever the fundamental does. It is a harmonic law that only those upper notes may coincide with a bass note which really form a consonance with the bass note's upper partials (its *sons harmoniques*). Now this is analogous to the fact that all natural bodies and structures must be regarded as having been developed step by step from the mass of the planet, which both engenders and supports them; and the upper notes stand in the same relationship to the fundamental bass. Depth of pitch has a threshold beyond which no further sound can be heard – this is analogous to the fact that material cannot be perceived unless it has form and quality; in other words, without its being the expression of some power which cannot be more explicitly defined. In this power, however, an idea is expressed. It is also analogous in a more general sense to the fact that no matter can be totally independent of the Will. Hence from sound as such a certain degree of pitch is inseparable just as a certain degree of expression of the Will is from matter. The fundamental bass is thus to us in harmony what inorganic nature is in the world – the crudest mass on which everything is based and from which everything arises and develops. Further, I recognise in the combination of those subsidiary parts (*Ripienstimmen*) generated by the harmonic texture which lie between the bass and the leading melodic part, the entire step-by-step sequence of ideas in which the Will objectifies itself. The parts lying closest to the bass are the lowest of those steps – bodies which are still inorganic, yet well able to express themselves in sound: the higher parts symbolise for me the world of plants and animals. The specific intervals of the scale parallel the specific degrees of objectification of the Will and the separate species in nature. Deviations from arithmetical correctness in intervals occasioned by any kind of tempered scale or chosen tonality are analogous to individual deviations of a type from a species; furthermore, out-of-tune notes that do not correspond to a true interval may be compared to monstrous hybrids of two animal species or of man and animal. But all these bass and subsidiary parts that constitute the harmonic texture lack that coherence in progression that the upper part alone has, moving as it does in rapid and fluent runs and figures, whereas the others move more ponderously and lack any internal coherence. The deep bass moves most ponderously of all and represents mass in its crudest form; it rises and falls only in wide intervals, in thirds, fourths, and fifths, never stepwise, unless it is a transposed bass in double counterpoint. This slow gait is also physically essential; a rapid run or trill low down is inconceivable. The inner parts which move more rapidly, but still without melodic coherence or any sense of progression, parallel the animal world. The incoherent movement and the circumscribed part-writing of all inner parts is analogous to the fact that, in the entire non-rational world, from crystal to perfect animal, no being has a truly coherent sense of self-awareness to shape its life into a significant whole, nor does it experience a succession of spiritual developments. None perfects itself by development of character (*Bildung*); everything remains according to its kind, eternally static and determined by fixed laws. Finally, in melody, in the high, singing, principal part, which dominates the whole and progresses freely in a single, uninterrupted, coherent and meaningful idea from start to finish, a complete entity in itself, I recognise the highest stage of the objectification of the Will, the conscious life and strife of man. Just as he alone, being endowed with reason, is always aware of the past and the future, so that his material existence is complete, coherent, conscious and of infinite potential, so *melody* alone has a significant, purposeful coherence from start to finish. Consequently, it tells the story of the Will as illuminated by self-awareness, the Will which imprints on the phenomenal world its successive actions. But melody expresses still more: it reveals the Will's secret history, portrays its every movement, its every endeavour, everything that reason comprehends under the broad pejorative concept of emotion, being incapable of further abstraction. Thus it has always been claimed that music is the language of emotion and passion, just as words are the language of reason. . . .

Now the essence of man's nature is for his will to desire, be satisfied and desire again, and so on – indeed, his happiness and well-being depend simply on this: every transition from desire to satisfaction is so rapid that failure to be satisfied constitutes suffering, and failure to desire constitutes empty longing, languor or boredom – so, correspondingly, the essence of melody is a continual fluctuation, a thousandfold deviation from the tonic, not only towards the consonant intervals, the third and the fifth, but towards any note, including the dissonant seventh and augmented intervals; but a final return to the tonic always follows. Through these many ways, melody expresses the Will's varying and innumerable desires, but it also invariably expresses satisfaction through eventual resolution onto a consonant interval, and more still onto the tonic. The invention of melody, the revelation in it of all the deepest secrets of human desire and emotion, is the work of genius, whose impact is more immediately apparent here than anywhere else, genius that is so far removed from any reflexion and conscious intention that it could be called inspiration. Such reflexion is barren here, as it is everywhere else in art; the composer reveals the innermost essence of the world and expresses the deepest wisdom in a language that his reason does not understand, as a mesmerised sleepwalker reveals truths of which he has no conception when awake. Thus in a composer, more than in any other artist, the man is separate and different from the artist. The very act of explaining this wonderful art betrays the explanation's inadequacy and limitations: I shall therefore develop our analogy. Now as the transition rapidly takes place from desire to satisfaction and from the latter to new desire, happiness and well-being, so it is that rapidly moving melodies which involve no large-scale digressions are happy; slow ones, founded on painful dissonances which resolve onto the tonic only after several bars, are sad, analogous to delayed, thwarted satisfaction. Delay in the re-excitement of the Will, namely languor, cannot be expressed in any other way than by sustaining the tonic, whose effect would soon become intolerable: highly monotonous, unmemorable melodies come very close to this. Brief, fast, easily intelligible dance movements appear to communicate only commonplace and easily attainable happiness; on the other hand, an *allegro maestoso*, with its large-scale periods, long progressions and wide digressions, symbolizes a loftier, nobler striving after and eventual attainment of some distant goal. An *adagio* conveys the sufferings of a great and noble endeavour which disdains all petty happiness. But how wonderful is the effect of *major* and *minor*! How astonishing that the alteration of a semitone, the substitution of the minor for the major third, should immediately and inevitably arouse in us a mournful, painful sensation from which the major inflection just as immediately releases us! An *adagio* in the minor achieves the expression of the most intense pain, becoming a shattering cry of grief. Dance music in the minor seems to signify the pointlessness of that trivial pleasure that one ought rather to disdain, and appears to convey the attainment of some petty goal amidst toil and vexation. The inexhaustibility in differentiating melodic possibilities corresponds to nature's inexhaustibility in differentiating individuals, physiognomies and careers. The transition from one tonality to another, since it dissolves all connection with what has gone before, resembles death to the extent that it portrays the end of the individual; but the Will manifest in that individual lives on as before, appearing in other individuals whose self-awareness nevertheless has no connection with that of the first.

However, when demonstrating all these analogies, one should never forget that music's relationship to them is not direct, but indirect, as it never expresses the phenomenal appearance, but the inner essence alone, the idea behind the phenomenon, the Will itself. Thus it does not express this or that particular joy, but anxiety, pain, horror, jubilation, happiness, contentment *in themselves*, to a certain extent in the abstract, unaccompanied by any incidentals and thus by any self-interest. And yet we understand them completely in this quintessential form. Thus it is that music so readily stimulates our imagination, which then attempts to give shape to this spiritual world, invisible, directly affecting us, yet so vital, clothing it with flesh and bone and thus embodying it in some analogous concept. This is the origin of the song with words and, ultimately, of opera; for this very reason these should never abandon their subordinate roles and assume the principal one, turning music into a mere vehicle for their expression – a gross blunder and an arrant perversion. For everywhere, music expresses only the quintessence of life and its happenings, not those happenings themselves, the details of which thus do not always affect it. It is, in fact, music's exclusive universality, together with its extreme precision that gives it the status of a panacea for all our suffering. If therefore music allies itself too closely with words and seeks to portray events, it is engaged in speaking a language that is not its own. No one has held more aloof from this error than Rossini; thus his music speaks so purely and clearly its *own* language that it has no need at all of words and it thus creates its own effect even when performed only by instruments.

In view of all this, we can therefore consider the phenomenal world, or nature, and music as two different expressions of the same thing. Thus that thing itself is the sole vehicle for communicating the analogy of either; and cognition of that thing is necessary to any insight into that analogy. Considered as an expression of the world, music is thus a language of the utmost universality, which corresponds even to the universality of concepts in much the same way as concepts relate to individual things. Its universality, however, is in no way the empty universality of abstraction, but is of quite a different kind; and is combined with clear, thorough precision. In this it resembles geometrical figures and numbers, which, applicable *a priori* as universal forms of all possible objects of experience, are still not abstract, but perceptible and thoroughly explicit. All possible efforts, activities and expression of the Will, all those processes that occur within man himself, which reason relegates to the broadly pejorative concept of emotion (*Gefühl*), are expressible through the infinite possibilities of available melodies, but always in the universal guise of form, pure and simple, disassociated from matter, always only as they are in themselves, not as they appear phenomenally, rather as their inmost soul, so to speak, without a body. This most intimate relationship between music and the true essence of all things serves to explain how it is, when appropriate music is provided, that the innermost and secret meaning of the scene, action, process or locality seems to be revealed; the music acting as the clearest and most explicit commentary on it; similarly anyone who fully submits to the impact of a symphony seems, as it were, to be watching all possible events of life and the world flow past him. Yet when he reflects upon it, he cannot indicate any resemblance between the interplay of sounds and the things that have passed through his mind. For music is, as we have said, different in this respect from all the other arts in that it is not an image of phenomena, or, more correctly, of the adequate objectification of the Will, but a direct image of the Will itself. It thus stands in the same relationship to the physical world as the metaphysical, and to everything phenomenal as the Thing-in-Itself. Thus one could equally well call the world an embodiment of music as an embodiment of the Will: hence it is possible to explain why music immediately causes every picture, indeed every scene of real life and of the world, to be invested with intensified significance – in fact, the more analogous its melody is to the given phenomenon, the greater the intensification. This is the basis of our ability to interpret through music a poem as a song, or a visible spectacle as a pantomime, or both as an opera. Such individual images of human life, interpreted in the universal language of music, are never combined with it, nor do they correspond with it through necessity, but they stand to it only in the same relationship as any given example does to a universal concept: in the distinctness of phenomenal reality they represent what music expresses in the universal terms of form alone. For melodies are, to some extent, like universal concepts, an abstraction from phenomenal reality. This reality, the world of individual phenomena, that is to say, presents to us the perceptible, the particular and individual, the single case, be it universality of concept or universality of melody. The two kinds of universality, however, are in a certain sense opposed to one another, concepts being only forms abstracted from cognition and containing, so to speak, the discarded outer husk of things; they are thus quite definitely abstractions. Music, on the other hand, is the kernel that precedes all attempts to shape it; it is, that is to say, the heart of things. This relationship might quite well be expressed in the language of the scholastics by saying that concepts are *universalia post rem*, whereas music is *universalia ante rem* and reality *universalia in re*. The general character of a melody accompanying a poem might equally well fit other instances of whatever *universalia* it expresses; thus the same composition suits several verses, hence *vaudeville*. That any relationship at all, however, is possible between a composition and a phenomenal representation rests, as has been said, on the fact that both are simply very different expressions of the same inner essence of the world. Now such a relationship really is evidenced in a specific case; when, that is, the composer has managed to express in the universal language of music those movements of the Will that constitute the kernel of an event, then the melody of the song or the music of the opera is expressive. Any analogy between the two that the composer discovers must, however, have sprung from his direct awareness, in which reason is not involved, of the essence of the world; an imitation cannot be deliberately and consciously conveyed by concepts, for if it does so, music unsatisfactorily imitates only the appearance of the Will instead of expressing its essence. All really imitative music, e.g. many passages in Haydn's *Seasons* or his *Creation*, where events of the phenomenal world are directly imitated, are like this: the same is true of battle pieces and is to be condemned outright.

The inexpressible inner essence of all music, by virtue of which it flows past us so utterly comprehensible and yet so inexplicable, like a familiar but eternally distant paradise, is rooted in the fact that it reproduces all the movements of our innermost being but quite divorced from phenomenal life and remote from its misery. In the same way, music is essentially serious; the absurd is altogether excluded from its domain. This can be explained by the fact that music's object is not representation, which may involve deception and absurdity, but the direct expression of the Will itself; the Will is necessarily the essence of seriousness, because everything else depends on it. Some indication of the richness of content and fullness of meaning of music's language may be inferred from the very repeat marks and *da capo* signs that are used. In literature these would be intolerable, whereas in music they are both highly practicable and beneficial, for in order to grasp the music fully, it is necessary to listen to it twice.

M

From: 'Upon the philosophy of art', *Quarterly Musical Magazine and Review*, vol. 2 (1820), pp. 148ff

The *Quarterly Musical Magazine and Review* may be regarded as the first serious and extended attempt to establish an English musical periodical. It began, under the editorship of R. M. Bacon, in 1818, and evidently owed a good deal in format, and even in content, to the Leipzig *Allgemeine musikalische Zeitung* which had then been going for some twenty years. 'M', the author of the following communication to the editor was evidently of the opinion that insufficient attention had been paid to the work of English philosophers, *vis-à-vis* music and aesthetics. His appraisal may be usefully read in conjunction with the extracts from the sources he mentions, that are included in the present anthology.

To the editor

SIR,

None of our English writers upon the theory of composition so far as I am acquainted with their works have yet touched upon the philosophy of the art. Shield, Crotch,[1] Kollman, Corfe, King and writers of inferior note have confined themselves to the rules: to the grammar of science if I may so call it. But surely, Sir, this method of proceeding leaves us short of the goal? The art of writing has been illustrated by treatises without end from the days of Aristotle through all the periods of history. Authors out of number have turned their attention to the development of the theory, and have drawn their examples from the works of the poets and philosophers of all times, by which, not only has the structure of our periods been analysed, settled and polished and our numbers refined, but the variety of methods by which the sentiments, emotions and passions of man's nature are best depicted, have been apprehended and distinctly demonstrated. It appears to me, a disquisition of this nature might tend to the advancement of music; I purpose, therefore, to publish through the pages of the *Quarterly Musical Review* the result of such thoughts as I have been able to throw together upon this very interesting branch of scientific pursuit.

I was at first a little surprised at the very few hints upon this matter the earlier writers upon the metaphysics of taste have drawn from music, which led me to presume that they have been for the most part ignorant of or averse to the science. But the principles they examined are, it will be found,

[1] Crotch nevertheless went 'far beyond the rules', in his later *Substance of Several Courses of Lectures on Music* (London 1831) (see pp. 427–42).

very few and simple. I propose in this essay to give a concise review of such opinions put forth by English authors, as may serve to explain those principles which they have considered to be common to music and the sister arts, and from which its influence over the affections is derived, and it will be seen that they are comprehended under not more than three heads. Mr Dugald Stewart says,[2] 'It is obvious that the circumstances which please in the objects of taste are of two kinds: first those which are fitted to please by nature or by associations which all men are led to form by their common condition; and secondly those which please in consequence of associations arising from local, and accidental circumstances. Hence there are two kinds of taste; the one enabling us to judge of those beauties which have their foundation in the human constitution; the other, of such objects as derive their principal recommendation from the influence of fashion.' We find the same opinions previously maintained by Addison, Lord Kames, Burke, Adam Smith, and Beattie, almost in the same words. We may then take them as the foundation laid by the collective judgement of these writers.

I must, however, premise that poetry and painting make their appeal through the medium of senses which all men may be said to possess. That music does not enjoy the same advantage in the same degree is scarcely a matter of doubt. The numbers who are susceptible of the beauties of either of the former arts are far greater than of those who can be said to enjoy the pleasures of music. Hence, we may fairly infer that men are fitted by a peculiar organisation for the gratification the art bestows. When, therefore, I make appeal to the common sense and faculties of men, it must be understood to be with an express limitation to that gifted class,[3] for such I cannot forbear to esteem them who have what is called an ear for music, since we might with as much chance of a right judgement, address ourselves to the blind upon the merits of a painting as to persons not susceptible of the effects of music, upon the truth of the principles I shall endeavour to establish.

The imperfect knowledge of the science and the little sensibility to the pleasures of music which Mr Addison appears to have possessed may probably account for the slight notice he has taken of its objects and its powers in his speculations. His observations are few and scattered. He, however, has remarked, that 'the rising and sinking of the passions, the

---

[2] *Elements of the Philosophy of the Human Mind* (3 vols., London 1792–1827), pt 2, ch. 2, section ii.

[3] Everybody knows that to hear and to have a relish for melody are two different things; and that many persons have the first in perfection who are destitute of the last. The last is indeed, like the first, a gift of nature; and may like other natural gifts languish if neglected, and improve exceedingly if exercised. And though every person who hears might no doubt, by instruction and long experience be made sensible of the musical properties of sound, so far as to be in some measure gratified with good music and disgusted with bad; yet both his pain and his pleasure would be very different in kind and degree from that which is conveyed by a true musical ear. Beattie, *On Poetry and Music*, p. 137 (see pp. 150–6).

casting soft or noble hints into the soul, is the natural privilege of music in general'.[4] The little examination he had bestowed on the subject is further apparent in one of his essays on imagination, wherein he speaks of the imitative powers of music. 'It would be yet more strange', he says, 'to represent visible objects by sounds that have no ideas annexed to them, and to make something like description in music. Yet it is certain there may be confused imperfect notions of this nature raised in the imagination by an artificial combination of notes; and we find that great masters in the art are able sometimes to set their hearers in the heat and hurry of a battle, to overcast their minds with melancholy scenes and apprehension of deaths and funerals, or lull them into pleasing dreams of groves and elysiums.'[5] The gratification thus derived, this philosopher classes with those which he terms *the secondary pleasures of the imagination*, and which arise from comparing the ideas we have received from original objects with those we receive from the sounds, etc., which represent them.

Mr Addison also extracts the basis of recitative from the tones of the voice in speaking, and of course the different expressions of passions in music, as imitative of the tones which passion naturally adopts. Hence he infers that music, in common with the other fine arts, 'is to deduce its laws and rules from the general sense and taste of mankind and not from the principles of those arts themselves or in other words that the taste is not to conform to the art, but the art to the taste'.[6]

I have gone back to the enquiries of the author of *The Spectator*, because, as it seems to me, they exhibit the real foundations upon which succeeding philosophers have erected their more extended speculations, at the same time that they really comprehend the only means by which music produces its effects: firstly, by its aptitude, as Dr Beattie calls it, to move our affections through the sense of hearing; secondly, by employing the fancy in raising, and the mind in comparing images; and thirdly, by association. These are in truth all the original powers and perceptions in regard to music which either the art itself or the mind moved by the art, embrace and entertain. It may yet, however, be useful to observe how philosophers have developed these principles.

Mr Burke,[7] in his *Essay on the Sublime and Beautiful*, part 2, sect. 17, and part 3, sect. 25, has gone no further into the subject than to remark the congruity of our sense of hearing, and of the affections moved by it, with the effect of our other senses. After quoting the well-known passage of Milton, 'And ever against eating cares', he says, 'let us parallel this with the softness, the winding surface, the unbroken continuance, the easy gradation of the

---

[4] *Spectator*, No. 630.
[5] *Spectator*, No. 416.
[6] *Spectator*, No. 90.
[7] It will be highly necessary as we proceed to note the chronological succession of opinions. Addison wrote in 1710; Burke in 1756; Smith in 1759; Lord Kames in 1761; Beattie about 1770; Twinning in 1789; Alison in 1810 [sic].

beautiful in others; and all the diversities of the serveral senses with all their several affections, will rather help to throw light from one another, to finish one clear consistent idea of the whole, than to obscure it by their intricacy and variety'. Thus we arrive at the conclusion, that certain qualities or objects are universally agreeable to the senses.

Dr Adam Smith extends the theories of Addison and Burke, and connects them in some sort with an attempt (an imperfect one it will hereafter be seen) to demonstrate and limit the emotions and passions, which music is calculated to express. The following passage is from his *Theory of Moral Sentiments* [London 1774], vol. 1, part 1, sect. 2.

> When music imitates the modulations of grief or joy, it either actually inspires us with those passions or at least puts us in the mood which disposes us to conceive them. But when it imitates the notes of anger, it inspires us with fear. Joy, grief, love, admiration, devotion, are all of them passions which are naturally musical. Their natural tones are soft, clear and melodious, and they naturally express themselves in periods which are distinguished by regular pauses, and which upon that account are easily adapted to the regular returns of the correspondent airs of a tune. The voice of anger, on the contrary, and of all the passions which are akin to it, is harsh and discordant. Its periods too are all irregular, sometimes very long and sometimes very short, and distinguished by no regular pauses. It is with difficulty, therefore, that music can imitate any of those passions; and the music which does imitate them is not the most agreeable.

Lord Kames carried on Mr Addison's doctrine relative to the melody of speech and the expression of passion. His Lordship maintains there is not only a consent as to the properties of sounds among mankind generally, in regard to the affections they move; there is also a natural expression of those sentiments common to us all in what may be called the language of sound. He says, *Elements of Criticism*, ch. 15,

> Words are obviously voluntary signs, and they are also arbitrary; *excepting a few simple sounds expressive of certain internal emotions, which sounds being the same in all languages, must be the work of nature;* thus the unpremeditated tones of admiration are the same in all men, as also of compassion, resentment and despair. Dramatic writers ought to be well acquainted with this natural language of passion; the chief talent of such a writer is a ready command of the expressions that nature dictates to every person when any vivid emotion struggles for utterance, *and the chief talent of a fine reader is a ready command of tones suited to these expressions.*

Here, then, we have the foundation of the first principles of our associations in the conventional understanding established by nature herself, and we must infer that however remote very many of the modes of musical expression may be from the primitive languages of passion implanted by nature, they have nevertheless their origin in her ordinances. And further, his Lordship, who investigates sentiments and sensations with the express view of deducing from them 'laws and rules for the fine arts', has taken up the same leading opinions as Dr Smith.[8] The emotions raised by music, he terms 'the sympathetic emotion of virtue', thus embracing in a measure the principle of the author of the *Theory of Moral Sentiments*. These he considers among emotions not directed to an object. His Lordship thus carries on the distinction. 'It is beyond the power of music to raise a passion or sentiment but it is in the power of music to raise emotions similar to what are raised by sentiments expressed in words pronounced with propriety and grace, and such music may justly be termed sentimental.' Lord Kames considers the same analogies to hold between music and the passions as Dr Smith and he enumerates them nearly in the same terms[9] I need therefore only refer to the passages in his work [see pp. 76–81].

Dr Beattie, in his *Essays on Poetry and Music*, has enlarged, beyond any of the writers we have yet quoted, upon our subject. The Doctor like them attributes to mechanical effects upon our organization,[10] a considerable portion of the pleasure we enjoy. He however deviates little from Mr Burke's theory of the congruity of our perceptions through the sense of hearing with those of our other senses, though he enlarges considerably upon it.[11]

After Adam Smith and Lord Kames, Beattie held that 'music may both prepare the mind for being affected and determine it to one set of affections rather than to another', and he completely accords with their notions as to

---

[8] *Elements of Criticism*, ch. 1, 2, Part 1.

[9] *Elements of Criticism*, ch. 2, Part 4 (see p. 78).

[10] Nor is it absurd to suppose that the human body may be mechanically affected by them. If in a church one feels the floor and the pew tremble to certain tones of the organ; if one string vibrates of its own accord when another is sounded near it of equal length, tension, and thickness; if a person who sneezes, or speaks loud in the neighbourhood of a harpsichord, often hears the strings of the instrument murmur in the same tone; we need not wonder that some of the finer fibres of the human frame should be put in a tremulous motion, when they happen to be in unison with any notes proceeding from external objects. *Essays*, p. 138.

[11] Nothing is more valued in a musical instrument or performer, than sweetness, fullness, and variety of tone. Sounds are disagreeable which hurt the ear by their shrillness, or which cannot be heard without painful attention on account of their exility. But loud, mellow sounds, like those of thunder, of a storm, and of the full organ, elevate the mind through the ear; even as a vast magnitude yields a pleasurable astonishment when contemplated by the eye. By suggesting the idea of great power, and sometimes of great expansion too, they excite a pleasing admiration, and seem to accord with the lofty genius of that soul whose chief desire is for truth, virtue, and immortality, and the object of whose most delightful meditation is the greatest and best of beings. Sweetness of tone, and beauty of shape and colour, produce a placid acquiescence of mind, accompanied with some degree of joy, which plays in a gentle smile upon the countenance of the hearer and beholder. Equable sounds, like smooth and level surfaces, are in general more pleasing than such as are rough, uneven, or interrupted; yet, as the flowing curve, so essential to elegance of figure, and so conspicuous in the outlines of beautiful animals, is delightful to the eye; so notes gradually swelling and gradually decaying, have an agreeable effect on the ear, and on the mind; the former tending to rouse the faculties, and the latter to compose them; the one promoting gentle exercise, and the other rest. *Essays*, p. 140.

the passions it can and cannot express.[12] He also discusses somewhat more at large the power of association.

Mr Twining, the learned translator of *Aristotle's treatise on poetry*, in his *Dissertation on the word imitation* as applied to music, has introduced similar opinions to those we have cited, with however the addition of some new circumstances. The passages which follow, though they have relation to the same points, are extracted from various parts of the *Dissertation*.

Music can raise ideas *immediately* only by the actual resemblance of its *sounds* and *motions* to the sounds and motions of the thing suggested.

Of all the powers of music, this of raising ideas by direct resemblance is confessed to be the weakest and the least important. It is indeed so far from being essential to the pleasure of the art that unless used with great caution, judgement and delicacy, it will destroy that pleasure by becoming to every competent judge offensive or ridiculous. The highest power of music and that from which it derives its greatest efficacy, is undoubtedly its power of raising emotions.

Between *sounds themselves* and *mental affections* there can be no resemblance; the resemblance can only be a resemblance of effects, the *general emotions, tempers or feelings* produced in us by certain sounds are *like* those that accompany actual grief, joy, anger, etc.

The *expressions* of music considered in itself and *without words*, are within certain limits vague, general and equivocal. What is usually called the power over the *passions* is in fact no more than a power of raising a general *emotion, temper* or *disposition* common to several different though *related* passions, as pity, love, anger, courage, etc. The effect of words is to strengthen the expression of music by confining it, by giving it a precise direction, supplying it with ideas, circumstances and an *object*, and by this means raising it from a calm and *general* disposition or emotion into something approaching at least to the stronger feeling of a particular and determinate *passion*.

I am indeed persuaded that the *analogy* between the melody and rhythm of *music* and the melody and rhythm of *speech* is a principle of greater extent and importance than is commonly imagined. Some writers have extended it so far as to resolve into it the whole power of music over the affections – such appears to have been the idea of Rousseau. He divides all music into *natural* and *imitative*, including under the latter denomination all music that goes beyond the mere pleasure of the sense, and raises any kind or degree of emotion; an effect which

---

[12] Everything in art, nature, or common life, must give delight which communicates delightful passion to the human mind; and because all the passions that music can inspire are of the agreeable kind, it follows, that all pathetic or expressive music must be agreeable. Music may inspire devotion, fortitude, compassion, benevolence, tranquillity; it may infuse a gentle sorrow that softens, without wounding, the heart, or a sublime horror that expands and elevates, while it astonishes the imagination; but music has no expression for impiety, cowardice, cruelty, hatred, or discontent; for every essential rule of the art tends to produce pleasing combinations of sound, and it is difficult to conceive how, from these, any painful or criminal affections should arise. I believe, however, it might be practicable by means of harsh tones, irregular rhythm and continual dissonance, to work the mind into a disagreeable state and to produce horrible thoughts and criminal propensity, as well as painful sensations; but this would not be music, nor can it be for the interest of any society to put such a villainous art in practice. *Essays*, p. 155.

he conceives to be wholly owing to an imitation, more or less perceptible, of the accents and inflexions of the voice in animated or passionate speech. Professor Hutcheson was of the same opinion. In his *Inquiry concerning beauty*, etc., he says 'There is also another charm in music to various persons which is distinct from the harmony and is occasioned by its *raising agreeable passions*. The *human voice* is obviously varied by all the stronger passions; now when our *ear* discerns any *resemblance* between the air of a tune, whether sung or played upon an instrument, either in its *time or modulation* or any other circumstance to the *sound of the human voice in any passion*; we shall be touched by it in a very sensible manner and have *melancholy, joy, gravity, thoughtfulness*, excited in us by a sort of *sympathy or contagion*' [see p. 25].

But the author who has gone the farthest into the development of the means by which music affects us is Mr Alison, in his beautiful *Essays on the nature and principles of taste*, and while he classifies the sentiments to which sounds address themselves, and endeavours to establish some of the principles upon which music, properly so called, addresses itself to the understanding and the heart, he gives much more to the association than any of his predecessors, and thus divides the sounds and the ideas and emotions they excite.

The great divisions of sound are into loud and low, grave and acute, long and short, increasing and diminishing. The two first divisions are expressive in themselves: the two last only in conjunction with others.

1. Loud sound is connected with ideas of power and danger. Many objects in nature which have such qualities are distinguished by such sounds, and this association is further confirmed from the human voice in which all violent and impetuous passions are expressed by loud tones.

2. Low sound has a contrary expression and is connected with ideas of weakness, gentleness and delicacy. This association takes its rise not only from the observation of inanimate nature or of animals, where in a great number of cases such sounds distinguish objects with such qualities, but particularly from the human voice, where all the gentle or delicate or sorrowful affections are expressed by such tones.

3. Grave sound is connected with the ideas of moderation, dignity, solemnity, etc., principally, I believe, from all moderate or restrained or chastened affections being distinguished by such tones in the human voice.

4. Acute sound is expressive of pain or fear or surprise, and generally operates by producing some degree of astonishment. This association, also, seems principally to arise from our experience of such connections in the human voice.

5. Long or lengthened sound seems to me to have no expression in itself but only to signify the continuance of that quality which is signified by other qualities of sound.

6. Short or abrupt sound has a contrary expression, and signifies the cessation of the quality thus expressed.

7. Increasing sound signifies in the same manner the increase of the quality expressed; as

8. Decreasing sound signifies the gradual diminution of such qualities.

I shall leave to the reader to attend to the diversity of expression which arises from the different combinations of these diversities of sound.

The most sublime of these sounds appears to me to be a loud, grave, lengthened and increasing sound.

The least sublime, a low, acute, abrupt or decreasing sound.

The most beautiful, a low, grave and decreasing sound.

Such are the few general principles that, as far as I can judge, take place with regard to the sublimity or beauty of sounds. The innumerable exceptions that there are to every one of these rules affords a sufficient proof of this sublimity or beauty of the sounds themselves. Wherever, however, any new sound occurs, it is I think by its approach to one or other of these classes that we determine its sublimity or beauty.

Mr Alison has also a dissertation upon music or 'sounds united by certain laws'. The whole is extremely elegant and worthy of attention, though too long to quote in this place. It goes to prove what has been laid down by the writers before him, that

Music is productive to us of two distinct and separate pleasures:

1. Of that mechanical pleasure, which by the constitution of our nature accompanies the perception of a regular succession of related sounds.

2. Of that pleasure which such compositions of sound may produce, either by the expression of some pathetic or interesting affection, or by being the sign of some pleasing or valuable quality, either in the composition or the performance.

From hence he deduces 'that it is to this last source the beauty or sublimity of music is to be ascribed, or that it is beautiful or sublime only when it is expressive of some pleasing or interesting quality' [see pp. 209–13].

I have thus, Sir, concentrated much of what has been written with regard to our perceptions of musical sounds by the received authors upon the metaphysics of the fine arts, and here I shall conclude my first letter. In my next, I shall endeavour to furnish a more minute detail and to illustrate the premises I may advance by examples drawn from eminent composers.

I am,

Yours respectfully,

M

Georg Wilhelm Friedrich Hegel

(b. Stuttgart, 27 Aug. 1770; d. Berlin, 14 Nov. 1831).

From: *Aesthetik*, in *Werke* (*Jubiläumsausgabe*), ed. Herman Glockner (Stuttgart 1928, 3rd edn., 1949–59, vol. 14, pp. 135–47, 151–3, 184–90, 208–15)

Hegel's knowledge and experience of music was quite considerable. As a boy he had been uplifted by the sound of trombones solemnly playing from a church tower at a funeral and as a young man had been impressed by Mozart's operas, particularly, or course, *Don Giovanni* and *Die Zauberflöte*. He was certainly a member of a group that met in Jena in the early years of the nineteenth century to listen to song recitals; and when he was professor of philosophy at Heidelberg, he was a member of a musical circle run by the distinguished lawyer, Justus Thibaut, where he heard or even took part in performances of music by Italian composers such as Palestrina, Lotti, Allegri and Durante. The details of Hegel's musical background have been systematically investigated by Alfred Nowak in his *Hegels Musikästhetik* (Regensburg 1971). It is not surprising, then, that music plays a considerable part in his system of aesthetics; and it is even less surprising when it is remembered that his formative years were spent in two centres of the German romantic movement: Jena and Heidelberg.

In 1788 Hegel began theological studies at Tübingen University, where he met and became friends with Schelling and the poet Hölderlin. They studied the works of Rousseau together and like many other young German intellectuals of their day, were excited by the events of the French Revolution.

After a number of years spent as a private tutor, Hegel was called to a university post at Jena in 1801, but after the Battle of Jena he had to resign, and for the following ten years he worked first as a journalist and then as a schoolteacher, becoming headmaster of the Gymnasium at Nuremberg. In 1817 he accepted the chair of philosophy at Heidelberg and the following year at Berlin. He remained at Berlin until his death in 1831 in a cholera epidemic.

Building on the foundations laid by Kant, Fichte and Schelling, Hegel established the final and most complex structure of German idealist philosophy. His aesthetic system is part of his metaphysical system. The Spirit, which objectifies and manifests itself in history, thought and art, has three aspects: subjective, objective and absolute. It is the absolute spirit that operates in the realm of art, religion and thought. In art itself, there are three phases of historical development – the predominantly sensual, the classical and the romantic. Music and painting are the two arts in which the romantic is manifest; and music is the focal point of romantic art (*bildet . . . den Mittel-punkt der romantischen Künste*[1]). It is thus, by the same token, the bridge between the abstract spatial art of painting and the abstract spiritual art of poetry.

Hegel's ideas on music are interesting and were influential. Felix Mendelssohn is

[1] *Aesthetik*, ed. Bübner, Pt 1, p. 148.

known to have attended his lectures on aesthetics in Berlin, for he wrote to his family in a letter dated 24 May 1830 that he had visited Goethe, and had told him about Scotland, Hengstenberg, Spontini and Hegel's *Aesthetik*[2]. The editor of the influential Berlin *Allgemeine musikalische Zeitung*, Adolf Bernhard Marx (1795–1866) was a Hegelian; and in 1842, the *Neue Zeitschrift für Musik*, which had been founded and edited by Robert Schumann some eight years previously, devoted the greater part of ten successive issues (22 July to 23 August, inclusive) to an exhaustive critique of Hegel's ideas on aesthetics in general and on music in particular (see below, pp. 530–8).

Building on the work of the Schlegels, Hegel differentiates between classical and romantic art. Romantic art manifests itself in painting, in music and in poetry rather than in architecture and sculpture; and Hegel goes into considerable detail about music and its nature. In classical art, he claims, external form was the outward expression of the Spirit in terms of beauty, proportion and harmony. Romantic art, however, was the form that corresponded to spiritual subjectivity, the comprehension and expression of its freedom and independence. Such things were infinite and universal and the expression of them in art was of necessity the negation of differentiation: instead of the polytheism of the plastic arts there was now but *one* God, *one* Spirit, *one* absolute self-sufficiency, totally free, totally unified. The true subject of art was the Image (*Erscheinung*) of God; and only in the present romantic era had art attained to the means to express the Absolute in terms of human form and activity.[3]

Hegel is notoriously difficult to translate. His style is complex and often obscure; where we have found obscurity, we have inserted the original text, so that the reader can decide the meaning for himself. We have also wherever possible broken his long incapsulated periods up into shorter, more manageable units. Certain terms need commentary. Hegel distinguished between two kinds of content: *Inhalt* and *Gehalt*. We have reserved the English 'content' for *Inhalt* and translated *Gehalt* according to its context. *Vorstellung*, which is usually translated by *idea*, *representation*, or *mental image*, we have usually translated as *imaginative concept*, reserving *idea* for the Hegelian *Idee*.

[Music and the other arts]

[From αα] The representational arts are concerned with objective plastic beauty. They portray the human being in its universal and idealised form as a unity and avoid specifically individual detail that might otherwise compromise the coherence of the representation. Music must achieve its aim differently. The representational artist needs only to bring to light the idea that is veiled in the material shape, and the form that is already latent in it. Hence, each particular and essential individual feature simply adds more precise interpretative detail to a complete form that is already in the artist's

---

[2] Letter to his family, quoted in *Letters from Italy and Switzerland by Felix Mendelssohn Bartholdy*, translated by Lady Wallace (London 1867), p. 6. Ernst Wilhelm von Hengstenberg (1802–69) was a Lutheran theologian who founded the *Evangelische Kirchenzeitung* in 1827 to strengthen orthodoxy and combat radicalism in the Lutheran church. It is ironic to think, incidentally, that Mendelssohn thought music far more precise in expression than words, though it is perhaps a little unfair to ascribe this belief to his experience of Hegel's lectures.

[3] Hegel, *Aesthetik*, ed. Bübner, pp. 566–73.

mind, because an imprecise notion of the content for which he must find a shape is already latent there. For example, in a work of plastic art a human figure in a given situation will need a body, or hands, or feet or a trunk, or a head with specific expression and in a certain position, together with certain other shapes, and other circumstantial details. Each of these features depends on the others, so that each can combine with the others to produce an overall pattern of which it is an indispensable part. The development of the theme in this case merely involves a more detailed working of the given material. The more detailed the development of the resulting image before us, the more concentrated the unity and the more coherent the precise interrelationship of the parts. If the work is a genuine work of art, the more exact the detail the greater the unity of the whole. Now of course inner organisation and overall coherence are equally essential in music, because each part depends on the existence of the others; but in this case, the material is developed rather differently, and the term 'unity' has a more restricted meaning.

ββ. A musical theme should have a meaning that is complete in itself. If it is now repeated or developed by means of broader contrasts and a wider range of technical procedures, repetitions, key-changes, developments in foreign keys, and so on, these procedures may easily strike us as irrelevant, since they belong more properly to the field of technical musical procedures and to the appreciation of harmonic ingenuity and resourcefulness. Nothing of all this is required nor communicated by the theme itself. In the representational arts, on the other hand, the execution of detail – the whole process, indeed, of going into detail itself – becomes a matter rather of delineating the content more and more precisely and analysing it more searchingly. Yet it cannot really be denied that even in a musical composition some content can be expressed through the more obvious relationships, contrasts, tensions, transitions, complexities and resolutions, that the themes undergo, now being expanded, now added to, now treated in alternation, the one theme now absorbing the other, now hurrying on, now changing, disappearing, reappearing elsewhere, now seemingly overwhelmed, and then triumphantly re-emerging. But even in this case, such development does not achieve any deeper and more concentrated unity, as in sculpture and painting, but a unity that constitutes more of an expansion, a broadening, an extension, a digression and eventual return. The thematic content may well be the unvarying point of departure, but it does not bind the whole together as it can do in the representational arts, especially those aspects of it that confine themselves to the portrayal of the human organism.

γγ. Music, in contrast to the other arts, enjoys enough in the way of inner formal freedom to be able more or less to abandon the content, the material at its disposal. The recall of a theme at will is, as it were, an act of self-realisation on the artist's part, i.e. a discovery of the fact that *he* is the artist, having the power to proceed as his fancy takes him. All the same, improvisation is in this respect manifestly different from a finished piece of music intended as a coherent whole. In improvisation, freedom from restraint is an end in itself; the artist can, amongst other things, demonstrate his freedom to weave well-known melodies and passages into his extempore creation, he can display them in new lights, revealing their detail, he can lead to new ones, and progress even further from his starting point, diversifying his material ever more and more.

On the whole, however, a piece of music may either be developed fairly strictly (it thus in a manner of speaking achieves a unity more akin to that of the plastic arts); it may on the other hand be developed according to the intensity of the artist's feelings, by episodes which depart to a greater or lesser degree from the original, using such means as capricious variations of tempo, by the use of sudden pauses which are then swept aside as the rushing torrent resumes its course. Whilst, then, the painter or sculptor should be recommended to study the forms of nature, the musician has no parallel field of study at his disposal, save for the forms that have already been developed which would have to be adhered to. The limitations and boundaries within which music must operate are largely predetermined by the nature of sound itself; this does not relate as closely to the content of what is being expressed as in the other arts. There is accordingly a great deal of room for freedom in the subjective manipulation of these materials.

This is the main aspect in which music differs from the objectively representative arts.

γ. *Thirdly*, on the other hand, music is most closely related to *poetry*, since both arts affect the senses through the use of the same medium – sound. There are none the less considerable differences between even these two arts, both in the way they make use of sound and in the methods of expression that they adopt. If then a text is a poetic work of art in its own right, music can be expected to add but little to it. The dramatic choruses of the ancients are a case in point, for in these music merely played a subordinate role. But if, on the other hand, music is given greater autonomy, the text must necessarily have slighter poetic value and must deal only with general emotions and broad imaginative concepts. A poetic exposition of profound thoughts will no more make a good text for music than will descriptions of natural physical objects or descriptive poetry in general. The texts of songs, operatic arias, oratorios and such like may well be quite mediocre and of little technical and poetic merit. The poet should be self-effacing if the musician is to be given proper scope for his imagination. In this respect the Italians such as Metastasio have shown great skill. Schiller's poems are, of course, in no way intended to be set to music, and are clearly cumbersome and useless for such a purpose. Wherever music is skilfully developed, little or nothing can be understood of the text anyway, especially the way our German language is pronounced. It is plainly unmusical to focus one's interest on the text. Thus an Italian audience gossips, eats and plays cards and so on during the less important scenes of an opera, but when an important aria or some other important piece of music begins, everyone is all attention. We Germans, on the other hand, concentrate our main attention on what happens to the operatic princes and princesses, and to their servants, squires, confidants and lady's maids, and on what they say. Even now there are probably many people who perhaps regret the flow of the action whenever a tune starts up, and seek relief in chatter. In sacred music, too, the text is usually either a well-known credo or perhaps a compilation of excerpts from the psalms, the words being intended only as an excuse for a musical commentary. The music is thus something to be performed for its own sake; it is not designed to reinforce the impact of the text, but only rather its general substance, much in the way, perhaps, the painting selects its subject matter from biblical history.

Musical interpretation of content

We may ask in what *second* respect music *interprets* (*Auffassungsweise*) things differently from the other arts when it seizes on and expresses a particular content, either as an accompaniment to a text, or independently of it. I have already suggested that of all the arts music has the greatest potential freedom not only from a specific text, but also from specific content. Music therefore achieves satisfactory expression by means of a closed sequence of combinations, variations, contrasts and communication, all of which are part of the musical world of sound. But in such a case the music will be empty and meaningless and unworthy of consideration as art, since it lacks spiritual content and expression, which are essential to art. Music rises to the level of true art only when the sensuous element of sound in its innumerable combinations expresses something that is suitably spiritual. Such content may be more precisely expressed in words, or it may be felt more intuitively(*empfunden*) through the harmonic relationships and melodic animation of the notes themselves.

α. In this respect music's true task is to bring that content to life in the listener's *subjective inner consciousness*, not to present it either as a general and conscious mental *imaginative concept*, or a specific latent physical *shape* – even if such shape were artistically possible. Music has the difficult task of realising in sound this life and movement in which it has its being, or of fusing with the words and imaginative concepts expressed, clothing them in sound in order to throw fresh light on them to stimulate a reaction in us and engage our sympathy.

αα. The inner consciousness itself thus becomes the form in which music contrives to embody its content. It can thus assimilate and clothe in the form of emotion whatever gets through to it. It is for this reason, though, that music must avoid imitating visual objects and must confine itself to making the listener more clearly aware of the workings of his inner self (*die Innerlichkeit dem Innern fassbar zu machen*). It may do this by causing the substantial inner depth of a particular content as such to penetrate the depths of our being. It may, on the other hand, choose to mirror the life and movement of a specific idea (*Gehalt*) in one individual *subjective* inner consciousness, so that this subjective inner consciousness thus becomes its own object.

ββ. The special characteristic relating the abstract inner consciousness most closely to music is *emotion*, the self-extending subjectivity of the ego. Emotion does in fact gravitate towards some content, but it still leaves this content confined within the ego unconnected with anything external and is not thereby formally connected with it. In this way, emotion always remains only the outward covering of the content. It is this field in which music operates.

γγ. From here music extends it range to cover every *specific* emotion of the soul, every degree of happiness, merriment, humour, moodiness, rejoicing and jubilation; similarly such things as the various degrees of anxiety, trouble, sadness, mourning, care, pain, longing, and finally such things as awe, supplication, and love become part of the true sphere of musical expression.

β. The sounds of 'Ahs' and 'Ohs' that function as interjections, cries of pain, sobs and laughter, are the most direct and vital non-artistic expression of the emotions and the states of soul. The soul thereby draws attention to and gives expression to its objective existence in a manner midway between birdsong, in which the bird projects itself in song, without any practical result, and derives pleasure from so doing, and withdrawal to the subconscious and to the world of inner thought itself.

Natural interjections of the kind, though, are not music, for unlike the sounds of speech they are of course not articulate, conscious symbols (*Zeichen*) of imaginative concepts. They thus express no predetermined content under the guise of a universal concept, but they give expression through sound of a mood and emotion which the sound itself directly symbolises. Expressions of the kind afford the heart relief. None the less, such relief is not aesthetic relief. Music, however, by means of specific tonal relationships must express emotions, purging them of intemperance and crudity.

γ. Thus music may well originate in interjections, but only when the interjections are properly shaped does it become music. In this sense music must artistically refine its raw material to a greater degree than painting and poetry do before that material can be used to express some spiritual content. Only later shall we need to look more closely at the manner in which tonal resources are employed; for the moment I shall simply repeat the observation that musical notes in themselves may differ enormously in type and quality, and may divide into or combine in the most varied kinds of compatible, essentially contrasting, related or unrelated patterns. These contrasts and combinations, and the different ways in which they move and change, the way they are presented, progress, and conflict, resolve and dissolve into nothing, reflect to a greater or lesser degree the inner nature both of a particular content and of the emotions that are absorbed (*sich bemächtigen*). Hence tonal relationships of a specific kind are now understood and given shape, expressing a conventionalised code what is latent in the depths of the spirit as specific content.

But the element of sound thus shows itself to be more closely related to the fundamental *inner* nature of a given content than any of the phenomenal material considered so far. This is because sound is not (*befestigen*) associated with spatial patterns nor does it assume material substance in the form of differentiated objects that are extended in space. Sound operates (*anheimfallen*) much more within the ideal dimension of *time*. There is thus no question of any differentiation between simple inner being and the objectively physical. The same is true of the emotional form assumed by any content of the kind music is best suited to express. For in contemplation and mental conception, as the self-conscious processes of thought, a necessary distinction is immediately evident between the contemplating, conceptualising, thinking ego and the contemplated, visualised or thought-of object. In the process of feeling, however, this difference is eliminated, or rather it never arises, the content being inextricably part of the texture of the inner self as such. So whenever music is placed at the service of poetry, and conversely, whenever poetry combines with, clarifies and interprets music, music cannot give objective shape to thoughts and imaginative concepts, nor can it try to project them in the way that they are conceived by the consciousness as concepts and thoughts. Music must either, as we have said, stimulate the emotions to react to tonal relationships, relationships that bear some inner connection with the basic nature of this content, or else it must seek to express more faithfully the emotion itself that the content may arouse. It is by means of notes then that music matches and mirrors the inner nature (*verinnigen*) of poetry as both the author and the listener *experience* it.

The effect of music

Going on from here we can now infer, *thirdly*, the power through which music can affect the very personality (*Gemüt*) itself. The personality neither makes empirical observations nor breaks down impressions into unrelated individualised concepts; it exists rather as a continuum in the unexplored depths and intimacy of the emotions. For it is in just this sphere – in the inner sense, involving self-absorbed contemplation (*das abstrakte Sichselbstvernehmen*) – that music operates (*erfassen*) thus activating the heart and personality, in which all inner changes occur, the one and only, the one concentrated focal point of the whole man.

[p. 148 to p. 150 omitted]

The ego exists in time; and time is the essence (*das Sein*) of the subject itself. Now since time and not space furnishes the essential element in which sound comes into existence as something musically significant, and since the time that is filled by sound is the same time that is inhabited by the subject, sound as such thus permeates the self, absorbs the self's innermost being and activates the ego by its movement in time and its rhythm. Any further emotively expressive patterning of sounds contributes moreover to a more intense self-fulfilment for the subject in that it moves and carries along the self with it, all of which serves to explain why it is that music possesses such elemental power.

β. But more is required for music to make its full impact than merely abstract patterns of sound in time. There is, then, a *second* and essential ingredient, namely a *content*, the soul of which is expressed in sound and which serves to stimulate the personality.

It is not, therefore, necessary to cherish outworn views on the omnipotence of music, views once expressed by ancient theorists, both sacred and secular, in myth and legend.

γ. A final aspect of the subjective effect of sound is the manner is which a work of musical art, in contrast to other works of art, is transmitted to us. Unlike buildings, statues and paintings, sounds do not in themselves possess any permanent objective continuity, but vanish once they have winged past us. A musical work, then, needs constant re-creation in performance on account of its purely ephemeral existence. Even so, the need for such repeated reconstitution has even more profound implications. Music's content is the subjective inner self; there is no suggestion here of creating a physical object existing in its own right. Music's content, then, must directly express a *living subject*, in which the work invests its entire inner being (*Innerlichkeit*).

[p. 154 to p. 183 omitted]

Form, technique and content in music

One and the same melody can be so woven into a contrapuntal texture that a harmonic progression results; totally different melodies can in similar manner be harmonically combined so that the coincidence of individual notes in these melodies results in a harmony as, for instance, often happens in J. S. Bach's compositions. The progress of these melodies takes many and widely different courses, which seem to weave in and out of each other independently, yet which retain an essentially harmonic relationship to one another, one that lends a necessary element of coherence.

Developed thus, then, more serious music should be *required* and not merely *allowed to explore* the boundary that separates consonance from dissonance, even to violate it, before eventually resolving into consonance; it must in fact break up the simple, original consonance into dissonance. For the inevitably deeper and essential harmonic relationships and hidden interconnections are wholly rooted in such contrasts; the profoundly penetrating effects of melodic ebb and flow can thus only be based on such deeper harmonic relationships. A bold musical composition thus abandons purely consonant progressions; it develops contrast, generates very powerful tensions and dissonances; it demonstrates its power by quelling the harmonic conflict and turmoil, secure in the knowledge that it will be able to resolve everything in a final soul-satisfying victory of melodic reconciliation. There is a conflict here between freedom and necessity; a freedom involving the ebb and flow of the imagination and a necessity, imposed by those harmonic relationships which the imagination needs to express itself, and in which its own significance is rooted. But if the main aim is to exploit the resources of harmony or the intense conflict resulting from their exploitation, then the composition easily becomes ponderous and academic, for if freedom of movement does not actually disappear it is at any rate unable wholly to triumph.

Now every melody must above all be singable and self-sufficient whatever the kind of music is. It must not become obscured or lost in ornate expression. There is, in this sense, obviously no limit to the number of notes a melody can have. But the melody must be so developed as to create a total, complete impression in our mind. The whole may well incorporate some variety and development; but it must be fully coherent; it requires a definite beginning and end, so that the middle is only the link between that beginning and that end. Only then, when melody has internal consistency and an internal structure, and when it does not formlessly peter out, only then does it mirror the free subjective self-sufficiency that it aims at expressing. And only then does music become direct expression of the ideal, that sense of liberation which raises the soul onto a higher plane of perception while yet obeying the preordained physical laws of harmony.

The relationship between the musical means of expression and their content

Having discussed music's general characteristics, we then considered the various factors that bear upon the way pitches and note durations are shaped. Now, going on to melody we have now entered the realm of free artistic invention and true musical creation, and are at once faced with the problem of a *content*, which must be artistically expressed in rhythm, harmony and melody. The final aspect of music that we still have to look at is the one of defining the various ways in which music can be expressive. As far as these are concerned the following differences should be underlined: in the first instance, music can, as we have already seen, be an accompaniment. Its spiritual content, that is, can be grasped not only in the abstract and inner sense, not only as subjective emotion, but also as music, the flow of which is influenced by verbal concepts. Music, on the other hand, may break free of any predetermined content; it may assume an independent existence of its own, so that, although it may bear some relationship to some specific concept or other, this is submerged by melody and by the harmonic development of melody; music manages to retain its independence by means of entirely self-sufficient combinations of different sound-qualities (*Klingen und Tönen*) and by means of the harmonic and melodic patterns that are made from them. The difference here is similar to that which we have already noted in the realm of architecture as an independent or as an applied art, though here the dimension is an altogether different one. Even so, accompanying music enjoys a freedom and at the same time a close relationship with its content that are considerably greater than can ever be the case with architecture.

In practical terms this difference means the difference between *vocal* and *instrumental* music. That difference must not be viewed on a purely superficial level as if it were a question of the timbre of the human voice in vocal music in comparison with the more extended range of sounds in instrumental music. What happens is that the voice sings *words*, words which express a particular conceptual content.

Consequently, if the two elements, word and sound, are not meaningless and unrelated, music's sole aim can only be the musical expression of the verbal content as best it can. (This content, *as such*, is predetermined by its imagery and is no longer a matter of indeterminate emotion.) Inasmuch as the content of a pre-existent text has meaning, inasmuch as it can be read, it is something apart from the musical setting and its expression. Any music that is set to a text thus will be accompanimental. In sculpture and painting, of course, the content cannot assume any representational form other than its artistic one. We should, on the other hand, avoid thinking that such *accompaniment* is merely useful, for the very reverse is the case: the text is there to serve the music and it has no higher aim than that of making us more keenly aware of the specific concept (*Gegenstand*) on which the artist has based his work. Music retains this peculiar freedom principally not so much by interpreting the content in the same terms as the text expounds it, but by operating within (*sich bemächtigen*) an element that is not part of contemplation and imagination. In this respect I have already indicated, when considering the general character of music, that music should express our innermost selves. But there are *two sides* to our inner nature; on the one hand, when we comprehend the inner meaning of an object this may imply a comprehension, not of its external phenomenal reality, but its *ideal significance*. On the other hand, it may imply that we experience the content as subjective expression that stimulates *the emotions*. Music is capable of both. I shall attempt to illustrate this in more detail.

In ancient church music – for example, in a *Crucifixus* – the profound concepts inherent in the idea of Christ's Passion as divine suffering, death and burial are realised in several ways; the Passion is experienced not so much as *subjective* feeling, compassion or personal grief at the event that is expressed, but rather as the thing itself, so to speak. Its deepest meaning, in other words, brought out by the harmonies and the melodies that arise from them. It is true that even here emotions are awakened (*für die Empfindung gearbeitet*) in the listener – he is not asked to *contemplate* the pain of the crucifixion or the burial, nor to form a mere general *conception* of it, but rather to experience in his deepest self the deepest meaning of this divine suffering and death; he is required to immerse himself totally in it; it now becomes something that he perceives within himself, something that blots out everything else and takes complete possession of him. In exactly the same way, the composer must have become so intimately involved with it, not merely as a subjective experience, that his work or art acquires the power to induce an impression of such intensity, the intention being to bring the event to life in the inner senses by means of sound, to the exclusion of all else.

Conversely, I can, for example, read a book that tells of some event, expounds a plot, or evokes emotions in words, and be so moved by it, that for instance I might weep copiously. Music is able to arouse in the listener those very *personal* feelings, which may accompany any human activity, feelings that are the expression of an inner life, and that can also be aroused by observing an event and being present at an action. Music can through the impression that it makes, calm, soothe and idealise the feelings that the listener has for the subject. In the case both of music and of literature (*in beiden Fällen*), therefore, the content is addressed to the inner self. The self has a sweeping freedom of thought, imagination, and contemplation; music can control this and also the powers of concentration by focusing the attention on a particular matter, holding the attention, stirring up and nourishing the emotion(s) within that specific field.

It is in this particular sense that the term accompanimental music must be understood. It moulds the first-mentioned [see above, p. 343] aspect of our inner nature according to the content to which our imagination is already preconditioned by the meaning of the text. But as vocal music is particularly suited to fulfilling this function and as, moreover, instruments are combined with voices into the bargain, people generally choose to describe instrumental music of all things as accompanimental. At all events instrumental music is used to accompany the voice, and it is not allowed great prominence or independent expression. In this respect, however, vocal music belongs more specifically to the category of incidental sound; the voice communicates articulated words to the imagination, and the vocal line is only a further gloss (*Modifikation*) on the substance of these words, that is to say it interprets them for the inner emotions. In instrumental music as such, however, such verbal communication is dispensed with and the music must restrict itself to its own methods of purely musical expression.

[p. 191 to p. 207 omitted]

Lyric and dramatic music

Lyric music . . . expresses individual moods of the soul melodically. It must above all maintain its independence of what is merely descriptive and declamatory, although it may also further portray the specific content of a text whether that content is of a religious or any other character. However, dramatic music is much more appropriate to emotions of a tempestuous or unrequited character, to unresolved emotional conflicts or to tensions within us; these are less suited to independent lyric treatment and serve effectively as integral parts of a dramatic design.

There is also *dramatic* music, which can be traced back to ancient tragedy. Music was not the principal element in this, since in works of a truly poetic nature preference must be given to verbal expression and to the poetic development of the imaginative concepts (*Vorstellungen*) and emotions. In ancient times harmonic and melodic techniques had not yet attained the level that was later achieved in the Christian era; music's principal role therefore was simply to enhance the effect of the poetic text by means of rhythms that give life to the words and which thus intensify their immediate physical impact. Dramatic music, in contrast, had an independent role in the field of church music and a large measure of freedom as the lyric component in modern opera, operetta, etc. Operetta is, however, a minor hybrid form of vocal music, in which speech and song, musical and non-musical elements are combined in only a superficial way. It is commonly held that the use of song in drama is completely unnatural, I grant; but this criticism is not a valid one. The criticism can be directed even more against opera, in which every action, emotion, passion and decision is accompanied and expressed in song. Music can in fact be quite justifiably introduced into operetta in those places where the emotions and passions are particularly intense or show themselves amenable to musical expression. The juxtaposition of banal and prosaic dialogue and skilfully composed musical pieces still jars on the audience. Operetta in fact is not a fully-realised art form. In true *opera*, on the other hand, the entire action is developed in music, and we are once and for all translated into a higher aesthetic plane, one that is sustained throughout the work. This plane is sustained as long as the content of the music remains primarily a subjective emotion, the individual and general atmosphere in the various situations, the conflicts and struggles of the passions, provided that the music emphasises all these by expressing their affective emotions in fully developed form. Conversely in a *vaudeville* where well-known, popular melodies are sung to rhymed verse of a unique and striking character, singing takes, as it were, an ironic tilt at itself. The fact that there is any singing at all lends to the piece a quality of light-hearted parody; what matters is that the satirical text should be understood; when the singing stops, we smile at the fact that anything should have been sung at all.

Independent music

We can compare what is melodic, already coherent and complete in itself, to sculpture, the plastic art. Musical declamation on the other hand can be paralleled (*wir wiederkannten*) with painting, which goes more into matters of individual detail. Since, however, a profusion of detail is revealed whenever one attempts more precise characterisation which the human voice cannot comprehensively express, the range of inflections available to it being comparatively simple, instrumental accompaniments are added the more the music extends its range in order to increase its variety and vitality.

Next, apart from setting a melody to a text and apart from expressing what is in the words, there is also the musical process that seeks independence of concepts other than those that can be conveyed by musical sounds. Subjective inner consciousness is the determining principle of music. Now, the innermost quality of the phenomenal self is pure subjectivity. It is not determined by any hard and fast content and therefore not bound to follow any particular course, but is allowed complete freedom in and for itself. If this subjectivity is to achieve full realisation in music, the music must free itself from a specific text and derive its content – the development and manner of its expression, the consistency and development of its structure (*Werk*), the development of its main ideas and any episodic or subsidiary material etc. – purely from its own resources, it must limit itself to purely musical means, since words cannot express the meaning of an entire composition. This applies to what I have already called *self-sufficient* music. Accompanimental music exists to express something outside itself. Its expression relates to something that does not belong to music as such but to an alien art: poetry. Now if music is intended to be purely musical, it must eschew and eradicate this alien element. Only then can it fully liberate itself from the constraints of verbal precision. This point we must now discuss in more detail.

We have already seen the process of liberation at work in the field of accompanimental music. For though it is true that the poetic word has forced music into a subordinate role, music has none the less ignored the *specific* precision of words, and fully freed itself from the expression of precise concepts in order to induce gaiety or grief at will. Now much the same has happened with the listening public, especially in respect of dramatic music. For opera has many ingredients: the locale and the scenery, the dramatic action, incidents, acts, costumes, and so on; there is on the other hand emotion and its expression. In opera, then, the content is twofold – the outer action and the inner emotion. Though the action as such gives coherence to particular elements of the whole, it is worked out for the most part in terms of the plot – and hence in recitative – rather than in specifically musical terms. Now the listener can easily detach himself from the action; he may pay practically no attention to the cut and thrust of speech and simply hold on to what is really musical and melodious. This is particularly the case with the Italians, as I have said before, most of whose latest operas are tailored so that one need not listen to musical small talk or other such trivialities, but one can talk or pass away the time in some such manner, listening with full enjoyment only to the really musical items which may thus be enjoyed purely as music. In this case, the composer and the public have a springboard which can free them from the specific content of words enabling them to develop the music alone as a self-sufficient art.

α. The dimension in which this independence can truly operate is that of *instrumental* music, rather than accompanied vocal music, which is conditioned by a text. For as I have already said, the voice is the very expression in sound of total subjectivity, one that at the same time uses imaginative concepts and words. When the subjective self, suffused with concentrated emotion, seeks to express or to react to the inner world of imagined concepts, it finds its own voice, hence song, the appropriate medium for doing so. The need for an associated text disappears, as far as instruments are concerned, and it is here that music in its narrowest sense may be said to enter into its own domain.

β. Music both for individual instruments and for an entire orchestra, which makes use neither of text nor the human voice nor relates to any clear sequence of imaginative concepts, comprises quartets, quintets, sextets, symphonies. For that very reason it is predisposed towards abstract feelings, such as can be expressed only in general terms. The main thing about it, at any rate, is its purely musical ebb and flow, its harmonic and melodic rise and fall, its progressions, which are now delayed, now complex, now deeply moving, now incisive, now simple, now more fluent. This ebb and flow also comes from the working-out of a melody with all the technical resources of music; the artistic and euphonious combination of instruments in ensemble, the quality of the part-writing, the interplay and interaction of the parts, etc. and so it is in this field that the essential differences become clear between the *amateur* and the *expert*. The layman enjoys above all in music the content, the physical qualities (*das Stoffartige, den Inhalt*), the comprehensible expression of emotions and imaginative concepts; thus he prefers to devote his attention to music as an accompaniment. The expert, on the other hand, loves instrumental music, since he is cognisant of the inner musical relationship of sounds and instruments, in which he appreciates melodious part-writing (*melodische Verschlingungen*), its use of harmony and the interplay of patterns (*wechselnde Formen*). He finds fulfilment entirely in the music itself; his primary interest is to compare what he hears with the rules and laws that he knows, in order thoroughly to judge and enjoy what the composer has achieved, though the artist's inventive genius may offend the judgement even of the expert, whenever he is presented with an unfamiliar progression or transition. The mere amateur rarely experiences such complete fulfilment, and he immediately succumbs to the desire to fill this apparently disembodied sequence of sounds with meaning, to find spiritual points of reference in its progress, indeed to discover more clearly-defined imaginative concepts and a more specific content in anything that strikes a chord in his soul. Music thus becomes to some extent symbolic for him; yet as he attempts to catch its meaning, the problems confronting him whisk past, puzzling, sometimes intractable, and susceptible to the most varied interpretations.

For his part, the *composer* can, of course, invest his work with a specific meaning, with a content of imaginative concepts and emotions as they follow a defined and consistent course. On the other hand, unhampered by such a content, he may concentrate on the purely musical structure of his work and upon the rich spiritual satisfaction of creating such a structure. In this respect, however, musical composition can easily lose intellectual or emotional content, and call for no deep cultural or intellectual awareness. This being so, the gift for composition can be seen to develop quite frequently at a tender age; indeed, throughout their careers, talented composers often remain creatures of little self-awareness and intellectual depth. If the composer is to achieve a greater profundity, he must devote equal attention to both matters: the expression of a content that is admittedly indeterminate, and the musical structure, especially in instrumental music. In this case, the composer is free to give rein now to the melodic and harmonic depth and complexity, now to the descriptive aspect, and to relate these elements to each other.

However, right from the start, we have argued that this stage of unconstrained musical creativity must be based on the general principle of subjectivity. Independence of any predetermined content will have thus to be of such a kind as both to counterbalance to some extent mere capriciousness and to afford it a certain freedom. For even composing in this way must be subject to certain rules and forms that must control mere caprice. Only considerations of a general kind affect these laws, there being an infinite range of detailed matters in which subjectivity may reign unchallenged as long as it remains within the bounds inherent in the very nature of tonal relationships. Indeed, in the exploitation of these relationships, too, subjective caprice (*Willkür*) with its inspirations, whims, interpolations, inspired leg-pulls, deceptive tensions, shock developments, leaps and lightning flashes, amazing and unheard-of effects, is in the last resort the unfettered master over the controlled movement of melodic expression and the textual content of accompanimental music.

See also Bibliography under: Doederlein, Knox

Abraham Rees

(b. 1743; d. 1825)

From: 'Composer of music', *The Cyclopedia* (London 1820), pp. Hhv col. 2–Hhr col. 2

Abraham Rees began his career as a teacher of mathematics and theology. In 1795 he took holy orders. In 1786 Ephraim Chambers's *Cyclopedia* had been reprinted in four volumes, with a supplement by Rees. This 'universal dictionary of the arts and sciences' was the seed for Rees's own work, *The Cyclopedia; or Universal dictionary of the arts, sciences, and literature*, which was published in 1819–20, in thirty-nine volumes, with six supplementary volumes of plates. Many of the musical entries in *The Cyclopedia* were supplied by Charles Burney.

Composer of music, a person who invents a melody and clothes it with harmony, according to the established rules of the art. Under the word *composition* we shall detail the qualities requisite to support this character. Yet these are insufficient to form a complete composer, whose productions will be felt and admired whenever they are heard. All the science possible without the inspirations of genius, is unable to command attention, and interest an audience, at all times, and in all places. They are only gifted men that possess such powers. What is meant here by genius is not a whimsical and capricious imagination that quits a flowery road to ramble in thickets, through briars and brambles; that to render harmony piquant, loads it with discords; and instead of grace and elegance, is labouring to surprise by extraneous modulation, and to divide the whole scale into half notes; true genius is that latent fire which inflames the composer, irresistibly forces him to write, and incessantly supplies him with new melodies, always agreeable, expressive, and natural, accompanied by a harmony, pure, touching and majestic, which embellishes melody without overpowering it. 'This was the guide' says the Citizen of Geneva, 'that led Corelli, Vinci, Perez, Jomelli, and Durante to the sanctuary of harmony; and Leo, Pergolesi, Hasse and Buranello, to that of good taste.' We have to add to these, Handel, whose sublime works were never heard by Rousseau; the elder Stamitz, Piccini, Sacchini, Cimarosa and Paisiello, with Haydn and Mozart who have gone somewhat further in vocal music, and many leagues in instrumental.

[the following three paras. omitted]

Rousseau seems sometimes to regard musicians as mere instruments, incapable of reflection; and that it is the business of philosophers to think for them; so imagine M. Suard, and all speculative musicians; but in the following advice to a composer, Jean Jacques seems to require more meditation and reflexion than the daemon of composition, by which a man of genius is possessed, will allow, who, absorbed in his own ideas, or impelled by the ideas of others, flies to his pen or his instrument, without metaphysical reasoning, or analytical enquiry into the foundation of his art. But Rousseau sums up the article *Composer (Compositeur)*, in his dictionary, with the following instruction, 'In composing, the author has to consider the physical production of sound, and that its sole use is to delight the ear; or if he mounts up to imitative music, he has to move the passions by moral effects. In the first instance, he has to select the most pleasing series of sound and agreeable harmony; but in the second, he ought to consider music with respect to its similarity with the inflexions of the human voice in speech, and the possible conformity between the harmonical combinations of sound and imitable objects.' This is all very fine and profound: but we apprehend that the most happy effusions of genius have been generated without speculative assistance.

François Hénri Joseph Castil-Blaze

(b. Cavaillon, 1 Dec. 1784; d. Paris, 11 Dec. 1857)

From: *Dictionnaire de musique moderne* (Paris 1821); Effect (Effet) [see also Rousseau, 'Natural' and 'Taste', pp. 113–15]

Castil-Blaze went to Paris in 1799 to study law. He had his father's keen interest in music (the family were in touch with leading French composers of the day), and he subsequently became a pupil at the Conservatoire. He played an important role in French musical life, as music critic of the influential and progressive *Journal des Débats* during the 1820s, as the proponent of Mozart's operas (though Berlioz strongly attacked him for daring to tamper with the original scores in his French adaptations), and as the author of several substantial books, notably *De l'opéra en France*, and the *Dictionnaire*, which leant heavily on Rousseau's *Dictionnaire*. In his article on 'Effect', Castil-Blaze first prints Rousseau's, in its entirety, following it with additional comments of his own which show an interesting awareness of certain psychological principles that govern the ways in which we listen to music.

Effect (Effet)

One of the most changeable qualities in music, one that is most threatened by the passage of time is that of 'effect'. Of itself it is nothing; merely an impression that is made on the senses. The force of an impression, therefore, depends upon the fineness of the senses, upon the extent to which they have been educated, and upon the degree to which they have previously been exposed to the emotions. It depends too upon the training (or, if you prefer, the exercise) that the ear has had as to whether the range of its sensations and as it were its needs will have been circumscribed or enlarged.

The first person to create a powerful effect, not only by giving the harmony an unusual and unexpected twist, but by scoring it for full orchestra, doubtless made a great impact. The first person to prolong an expression of terror by the use of low, repeated notes on the strings, doubtless petrified his audience; and if someone had then tried to describe this effect he could justifiably have said that in listening to those terrifying sounds his hair stood on end. If soft, slow and sustained notes followed those violent shocks they would have produced a kind of enchantment. Such alternations of gentleness and strength would give inexperienced and sensitive listeners much satisfaction.

Many such pieces by early masters are still extant, but they do not nowadays have their original effect. The early masters made little use of wind instruments. Many instruments indeed were unknown then; but as

356

they were gradually incorporated into the orchestra, we became acquainted with new effects. Trumpets, trombones, kettledrums and bells (all of which have been much over-used) provide the composer with a superb fund of tragic and brilliant effects.

Every aspect of sound has its related effects. We may thus distinguish effects of intonation, rhythm, intensity, timbre and character, and to these five may be added the effects that spring from harmony, from the union of several sounds. Simple effects stem from a single cause; compound effects from several at once.

In painting the term 'effect' denotes the quality of analogy. In music, effects are equivalent to figures of speech. The same advice concerning the handling of effects, applies to both. The first point is that effects must not be piled one upon another, as they quickly lead to fatigue and distaste. The second is that they must be skilfully used if they are to be effective. Care should be taken that they do not cancel each other or produce violent cacophony. This unfailingly results from the simultaneous use of two effects of the same kind, especially those of rhythm. The wisest counsel that a young composer can be given is this: never use an effect unless you know how to handle it, for the result will be quite otherwise than that which was intended.

Anon

From: *Le Globe*, 24 March 1825, p. 423f

Le Globe, which described itself as a 'Journal philosophique et littéraire', had a short, yet distinguished existence, from September 1824 until 1831. It attempted a most ambitious programme, and it came to be regarded as the mouthpiece of the romantics in their struggle against classicism. It was truly European in outlook, even though naturally enough French affairs were given pride of place. During its first year it covered a remarkable diversity of topics, ranging from Malthus on population theory, the education of the working classes in England, Goethe in old age, Weber's conducting engagement at Covent Garden, a summary of the *Freischütz* plot, a review of the collected works of Descartes, to three lengthy articles covering the Paris Salon of 1824, and in particular, Delacroix's celebrated 'Massacre of Chios', which was exhibited there. Many articles dealt in one way or another with romanticism and classicism, and particularly two entitled 'Du romantique', from which the following paragraphs are taken.

For further reading:
T. R. Davies, *French Romanticism and the Press: The Globe* (Cambridge 1906).
Pierre Trahard, *Le Romantisme défini par le Globe*, *Études romantiques*, no. 3, ed. Henri Girard (Paris 1924).

Concerning the romantic (Du romantique)

Since the time of Schlegel and Mme de Staël this word has been on everyone's lips, although there are probably not two people who interpret it in the same way. To some people the word is synonymous with extravagance; to others it is equivalent to inspiration. In short it is a word, like 'liberal' that has only a relative meaning, an implied sense. Ask a devoted reader of the *Pandore* what he understands by *romantic* and he will reply that it comprises the grammatical inversions of M. d'Arlincourt and the neologisms of MM. Hugo and Devigny. A subscriber to the *Mercure*, of rather more advanced opinions, will readily avow that romanticism is not a question of styles; he would argue that it is a question of the imprecision of ideas, the linking together of the sublime and the burlesque, the neglect of the eternal proportions of the beautiful – as if beauty ever had eternal proportions! Some people hardly bother with such fine distinctions and will quite happily describe everything that appeals to them as 'classic', and everything that they consider to be bad as 'romantic', secure in the belief that they are in the right as opponents of the new school. On the other hand, are the romantics more agreed as to the object of their homage? We doubt it. A whole volume could be compiled from the definitions that they have proposed. Under their banner, as under the crusading banner of our ancestors, march diverse nations, their phalanxes representing opposite extremes; can there be men of more contrasting views than M. de Stendhal, M. Victor Hugo, M. Manzoni and M. Charles Nodier? What have these warriors in common with each other? What is that Jerusalem that they seek to conquer, the enemy that they are so keen to fight? Shall we declare it? In our opinion the enemy is routine, the Jerusalem is liberty; here as everywhere else the old regime struggles against the new, faith against the spirit of enquiry.

How do the men who above all consider themselves to be adherents of the 'classics' go about the task of judging a new work? Do they consult their feelings? Do they ask themselves whether they have been interested and moved, or whether the work in question – lifeless and banal – has painfully dragged itself along the path that has been mapped out by so many others, and to which time has granted the legitimacy of boredom. No. They would consider such matters to be beneath their dignity. No. Peacefully seated at their desks with books dating from the reign of Louis XIV to hand, they may be seen examining the ways in which the new product resembles their favourite works, determining in which category it may be placed, and above all which lines of Boileau they may apply to it. 'Do you hope to do better than Livy or Tacitus?' the Constitutionnel once asked of M. de Barante in connection with the *l'Histoire des ducs de Bourgogne*. This splendid remark would have stunned even Livy and Tacitus since they had been preceded by Herodotus and Xenophon. It can be applied to everything: poetry as well as prose, tragedy as well as history. It seems that every Age has suffered deprivation for the benefit of certain models, and that our classicist critics have been sent to preside over the fulfilment of this terrible decline. They were the ones who criticised *Le Cid*, who insulted Molière and who supported Pradon against Racine. Nowadays they only make use of the illustrious names of Corneille, Molière and Racine to prevent others from doing what these great men did. In short, they are unable to raise themselves above the time-honoured conventions of their countries: were they English they would swear by Shakespeare and Milton; were they Spaniards, by Cervantes and Calderón, but being French they practically regard them as barbarians. If Aeschylus or Aristophanes were now alive they would be labelled as such, for – make no mistake – the esteem that the French profess for the Greeks is merely lip service. They have outlawed M. Soumet for his very classical imitations of Aeschylus and Alfieri whilst they have approved of M. Picard, one of the boldest innovators in the field of French literature. They should stop criticising romanticism for being so ill defined, and above all they should stop taking refuge in the supposed solidarity of their doctrine. Anything that has a resemblance to works that are more than twenty years old is *classical*, as far as they are concerned, and all that departs from that is *romantic*.

Let us compare this arbitrary and narrowminded ethic with that of their adversaries. Seeing how the customs, the ideas and aspirations of each era and each race come alive in literature, even from earliest times, the romantics resolutely refuse to imprison themselves in one fixed system. They believe that it would be the height of absurdity to straitjacket the expressive needs of diverse and changing societies within immutable and constant forms, just as it would be equally absurd to demand the universal observance of one language and one code of behaviour, or to require that modern society should preserve and respect primitive law. Their boldness extends to the point that they believe it is always better to copy nature than to copy copies of nature, to be open to the influences of their own generation than to earlier ones, and to create rather than to copy. In order fully to understand the works of the English and the Germans, as indeed those of the Greeks and the Romans, they seek to understand the civilisations of these diverse peoples, to immerse themselves for a while in their customs and beliefs. In this way hosts of minor imperfections that the classicists so eagerly point out disappear. As far as they are concerned, the age of Louis XIV, brilliant though it was, and a time in which the greatest genius prospered, is none the less as far removed from the spirit of the present age as is that of Pericles and Augustus.

Anton Friedrich Justus Thibaut

(b. Hamelin, 4 January 1774, d. Heidelberg, 28 March 1840)

From: *Über Reinheit der Tonkunst* (Heidelberg 1825); tr. W. H. Gladstone as *Purity in Music* (London 1877), ch. 4, pp. 83ff

It is not only in Germany that significant musicians have sprung from the ranks of those intended originally for the law; but Justus Thibaut was remarkable in that he was a lawyer of international eminence who also considerably influenced at least one composer of international fame. The composer was Robert Schumann, who met Thibaut when studying at Heidelberg in the late 1820s.

Thibaut's father was an officer in the Hanoverian army. The boy read law at Göttingen, Königsberg and Kiel Universities, and by the age of twenty-four had been called to the chair of civil law at Kiel. In 1802, he was appointed Professor at Jena, then a centre of romanticism, and it was at Jena that he completed his chief work, a compendium of pandect law that codified Roman law as it then applied in Germany, relating it to canon law and court practice in a clear and comprehensive system. In 1805, he moved to Heidelberg, where he remained until his death.

Thibaut's great hobby was music, and in particular the study of music of the sixteenth and early-seventeenth centuries. He founded a choral society and sought out compositions for them to perform, eventually amassing a considerable library of valuable music of many kinds. The book from which our quotation is taken is a high-minded justification of the purity of music as an art which may purify and cultivate the mind if it is of the right kind, but may equally corrupt and deprave it if it is not. First published anonymously, *Ueber Reinheit der Tonkunst* was quickly reprinted and remained in demand almost throughout the nineteenth century.

The translation is taken verbatim from Gladstone's 1877 edition.

On the instruction to be derived from good models

Kant says somewhere of mathematics that they are but a poor science because an unfit subject for philosophy. The same might almost be said of music as regards its influence upon education at the present day.

Music, as now practised, abounds in difficulties, but is deficient in zest
Execution and flourish we have everywhere; mountains of amazing difficulty; a plethora of notes in place of completeness and perspicuity; but apart from the satisfaction of vanity or professional whims, little of comfort or pleasure; so that our good maidens, when they get a hearth of their own and can settle down there, gladly throw to the winds all the so-called art they have learnt.

361

A *living principle essential to music, as to other arts*

No art is without a living principle; and this may be eaily found in music by going back to the point where it took its rise and became a want. In other words, music is in its essence nothing but, as it were, the overflowing of emotion – of mental ecstasy – in sound; and whenever a piece of music answers to this description, it will never fail to move and enchant all unprejudiced minds, barring of course that exceptional class that have no sense of tune and to whom music is a sealed book, like a statue to a blind man.

The essence of music is expression of feeling, not conformity to rule

Music requires indeed a code of rules, just as poesy requires a system of versification. But true excellence in a musical work can no more follow from conformity to rule or from artifice than it can in a poem from regularity of versification. A composition that appeals in no way to the heart, or which jars upon the feelings, can never be anything better than a practice-piece, however much in favour it may be with the admirers of bravura. A Dutch preacher succeeded after thirty years' labour in engraving with a pin a whole troop of soldiers upon a small coin; but I imagine that no one would hang up the coin as a worthy companion to a Madonna of Raphael. I freely grant that music may be really embellished by art, just as a fair maiden by dress. But the incidents must not be mistaken for the essence. The divinity of music is only revealed when it transports us into an ideal state of being; and the composer who cannot do this for us is, so far, a mere hewer of wood and drawer of water.

Music pleases according to accidental tastes and habits

If, in judging of musical works, we seek for a common point of comparison in men's sentiments and instincts (such instincts, that is, as are a worthy subject-matter for art, and so may serve in some sort as a standard), we find a hopeless difficulty in attempting to reduce all classes of people to one common measure. For, as to instincts, every one has his own standard, often so interwoven with the whole nature of the individual, that no human power can prevail against it. Take, first, the untamed savage who reproduces in his songs and in his dress his highest idea, brute force; and then go on through innumerable gradations to the languid heroine of romance who recoils from all that is vigorous and pure; where among these is the talent of the musician to find a proper basis for its creations? Take into account, too, the fanciful interpretations and the semi-philosophical, semi-poetical meanings perpetually attributed to plain things in the present day; and that precious indolence which refuses to pursue or acquire anything solid, and so tries to deafen us by rude noise. I know persons who have studied, or pretended to study but twenty or thirty modern pieces, but who imagine that they have thereby rendered themselves such complete masters of musical science that they turn a deaf ear to everything else, loudly talk the silliest nonsense and cannot refrain from a smile of commiseration if any hint is dropped of Lasso, Palestrina, Morales, Lotti and Durante, not to mention Luther's favourite, Senfl whose name, moreover, will not be relished by their dainty palates.[1]

Bad taste must be borne with

Formerly, when I received the first impressions of those great compositions which will ever possess for me a life-long charm, I used to be impatient if others would not understand them and could listen to nothing but the fragments they had in their heads. Now that experience has made me wiser, though I still feel something of the same kind, yet I sit still calmly and civilly and recall to myself the story of a minister of state coming to Frederick the Great and depreciating Homer, Virgil, Plato and such like, while praising to the skies the first catcher of herrings; whereupon the king merely remarked, 'I suppose you are very fond of herrings!'

Music can not make a man; presupposes a healthy nature

In truth, there can hardly be a more erroneous idea than that music can make a man. It can do no more than respond to what good a man may have in him, or else rouse something that lies dormant in him. A cold, vain man of contracted ideas and debased affections will never appreciate a grand piece of music; and if there be added to this a quarrelsome temper or the usual professional conceit, as disagreeable as it is barren, or if – lowest of all conditions – when he attends a concert, his small soul has no room for aught beside the two or three pieces he has at some former time acquired or has heard in his own beloved town, then indeed are all attempts at conversion idle.

Musical taste not to be imparted by lectures

Words and theories can no more enlighten the mind on the subject of music than can abstract principles of painting give a correct eye for colour. Those who talk of musical theorems are much addicted to descriptions, but are not sensible of the small effect produced by them. The human frame admits of description much more easily than an invisible note; and yet no one ever found it on inspection the same as he had imagined from description. But there is one great resource always open to the lover of good music which must always rank as the best means for influencing taste and feeling; and this is the information and improvement derivable from classical models.

Classical authors the great teachers

However much a mistaken culture may warp and narrow most people's minds, it is certain that if the taste is not utterly depraved nor ruined by artificialism, the better element is not wholly quenched but at the worst only

---

[1] The German word 'Senf' being 'mustard' (eds.)

slumbers; and it will be found as a rule that the study of great models leads in the end to a just estimate of their worth.

Personal experience of their influence

I have known passionate admirers of Kotzebue but not one who remained of the same mind after attentively reading Shakespeare; and I used myself, fifteen years ago, to admire musical works, which now with more historical knowledge I scarcely care to look at. And such has been the case with others. It is hardly to be believed how speedily the influence of good examples is felt. I have more than once found one-sided people, who from certain hybrid pieces had conceived a great idea of certain modern composers. These pieces I had sung, having previously selected others by Lasso, Palestrina, Lotti and Sebastian Bach, not exactly of a profound but of pure and dignified character. The question was decided in a moment, and never did a similar experiment fail. What actually occurred, to my great satisfaction, was this: a young man came to me with his head full of wrong ideas, and after listening to a Mass of Lotti's, exclaimed in ecstasy, 'This evening I can bear ill-will to no man.' Effects like this might often be noticed, if people wished for them, and were not content to cling with miserable obstinacy to the approved fashion of the day.

Works of less than the highest order have their legitimate use

Works of mediocrity may have their place, provided only they be healthy and unaffected. Men are not disposed to be reading the Psalms, or Homer, every hour of the day. They crave variety to entertain them and help them to pass the time without mental strain. A large portion of the public have neither taste nor capacity for anything beyond mediocrity. Hence I should not be disposed to criticise several songs now in fashion so severely as some connoisseurs may have done. I merely ask those who can only understand and enjoy indifferent music to abstain from pronouncing upon works of real genius, and not to expect masterpieces like the *Merry Wives of Windsor* and *Don Quixote* from the same pen as *The Provincials* and *The Bard with the Iron Helm*.[2]

Superficial knowledge likely to be misleading

In all this I wish to warn people against a certain prejudice and narrowness which meets one at every turn. For instance, if an amateur has mastered certain pieces and takes due pleasure in them, he is apt for that very reason to think them beautiful, nay more beautiful than all others; and he will very likely take umbrage if it be hinted that there are other more beautiful – far more beautiful – pieces. Such narrowness is mischievous in the highest degree. Music is essentially a matter of taste, but taste is first formed by slow degrees.

[2] By Kotzebue.

Good judgement in music accrues by degrees, and from mature experience

Test it by the analogy of painting and poetry. What pleased the boy fails to satisfy the young man; what transported the young man the grown man often finds empty and defective. By such tests and comparisons we shall at last realise what is truly classical and attain therein a happy repose, because its characteristic is that it can be enjoyed over and over again, and rather gains than loses by repetition. So, if it be that heretofore a person has had but little knowledge, no one can say whither an educated taste may not lead him; and it is therefore mere indolence or want of spirit on the strength of the known, to presume on the unknown and doggedly refuse to go further. There can be wisdom in such conduct only when any one possessed of complete knowledge puts into your hands that which is of the highest and most unquestionable merit, and in this way excludes all that is indifferent and worthless, a most valuable educational help. But in the case of music, it is seldom that such a mentor is at hand, and then many trials must be made before the object is attained. Ambition is not indeed disposed to confess its errors. But what harm can there be in saying, 'What a simpleton I was up to such and such a year!' if you are happily able to add the reflection, 'But how knowing I am now!'

John Feltham Danneley

(b. Wokingham, Berks. 1786; d. 1834?)

From: *An Encyclopaedia or Dictionary of Music* (London 1825)

Danneley established himself as a music teacher in Ipswich in 1812, having mainly been taught by his father who was a lay clerk at St George's Chapel, Windsor. In 1816 he visited Paris to study with Reicha, and while there he met Monsigny and Cherubini. In 1820 he published an *Elementary Principles of Thorough Bass*, and in 1826 a *Musical Grammar*. His *Encyclopaedia*, despite its imposing title, was a lightweight work designed for a popular market. Even so, Danneley evidently considered aesthetics to be important enough to warrant at least a brief, general description.

Aesthetic, a word derived from the Greek, generally denoting an acquaintance with, or power of conveying ideas of the beautiful; or according to Sulzer, that part of the philosophy or theory of the fine arts which is derived immediately from nature and taste. It is likewise used to designate those properties of matter which are adapted to interest the feelings and operate upon taste.

Peter Lichtenthal

(b. Presbourg, 10 May 1780; d. Milan, 18 Aug. 1853)

From: *Dizionario e Bibliografia della Musica* (Milan 1826);
bibliographical articles, vols. 1, 2 and 4

After studying medicine in Italy and Vienna Lichtenthal settled in Milan in 1810, remaining there until his death. Upon the occupation of Lombardy by the Austrians he became 'royal and imperial censor'. Among his extant works are a number of ballet scores for La Scala, and books on various topics: general bass (*Harmonik für Damen*, 1806) music therapy (*Der musikalische Artz*, 1807), composition (*Orpheik*, n.d.), and a translation of Forkel's *Allgemeine Literatur der Musik*. The four-volume *Dizionario* was highly regarded. The first two volumes comprise the dictionary, and the third and fourth, the bibliography: volume 3 covers musical history in a series of chronological chapters, and volume 4, the theory and practice of music. Most of the relevant information on aesthetics and criticism is in the sixth chapter of this volume. Lichtenthal's systematised bibliography is quoted here *in extenso* to illustrate the wide range of sources that were familiar to musical scholars at the beginning of the nineteenth century.

Beauty (Bello)

Most aestheticians define beauty as that quality in which the *form* controls the imagination and the intellect in an easy and regular manner, and which thus becomes a source of stimulating pleasure.

Beauty *pleases*, but so do the pleasant, the useful, the true and the good; the pleasure derived from beauty, however, differs from the pleasure derived from the others.

The *pleasurable* satisfies our inclinations. As a creature with senses, man has a number of instincts and inclinations which may perhaps be reduced to three main ones: namely the instinct of self-preservation, which may be called *egoism*; that of self-propagation, part of which may be called *egoistic* and part of which may be called *sympathetic*; and the social instinct, which is purely *sympathetic*. If these instincts are satisfied, pleasure ensues; if they are thwarted, suffering results. Pleasure that is caused by the pleasurable presupposes desire, otherwise only indifference could ensue.

That which is *useful* may be considered an object of pleasure; it is distinguished by the process of reflexion. Mere instinct (*instinctus brutus*) is limited to the pleasurable, whereas the useful can be recognised only by the intellect, which reflects on causes and effects and on the logical connection between things; for experience teaches us that unpleasant and even harmful things are used, such as medicines, poisons, etc., with a pleasurable end in

367

view. The useful therefore depends on the end for which it is intended. The beautiful may also be pleasant and useful; thus we may experience a kind of sensuous delight in a beautiful picture-frame, whereas a dealer would consider it to be very useful; but all such things are purely incidental to beauty, and the true amateur of beauty, unaffected by desire and cupidity, will only find that they serve to degrade beauty.

Even so the logical and moral pleasures that the true and the useful arouse in us differ from aesthetic pleasure. Thus a fine poem may well conform to the laws of truth and beauty, but submission to these laws is in no way necessary in order to arouse aesthetic pleasure; in fact, such pleasures may occur without them. No one now believes in the existence of the gods of Greek mythology, and no one would approve their worship. None the less sculptures of a Jupiter, an Apollo, a Juno or a Venus give pleasure, just as do the poems that treat of their failures, their passions and their immoralities.

The pleasant and the useful arouse within us a *sensual* interest, the true and the good an *intellectual* interest. Pleasure in the beautiful presupposes neither one nor the other in any absolute sense, but it does engage a very particular interest which may be called *aesthetic*. Sensual and intellectual interest result from the matter, aesthetic interest from the form. All the same, a story may interest us both on account of its content and on account of the beautiful form in which it is clothed; it may give us pleasure, too, on both counts. Another difference between the interest that springs from the matter and that which springs from the form may well be that the one precedes enjoyment, whereas the other follows it. The beautiful, then, interests us because it pleases, whereas the pleasant, the useful, the true and the good please because they interest us.

It follows then that the beautiful is interesting, but that by no means everything interesting is beautiful.

The beautiful may have no practical purpose – a beautiful aria, or a beautiful poem, for instance – or it may have one – a beautiful palace, for instance, or a beautiful piece of furniture.

Among the things that are perceived by the external senses, only those that are seen and heard may be described as beautiful, for the other external senses only derive pleasure from material impressions. Visible and audible things, however, *please solely on account of their form*: those that do not please in this way cannot be objects of aesthetic pleasure.

The things that are perceived by the inner senses are partly external stimuli, and partly emotional reactions to them. It follows from this that if things are to excite aesthetic interest and pleasure, they must be composed or designed in such a way that the form of the design or composition awakens pleasure in the percipient. There are consequently *internal* and *external* kinds of beauty: physical beauty, that is, and intellectual beauty. The latter is the proper basis for the former.

The perception of beauty and the longing for contact with the ideal raises the soul above the finite physical world to the intellectual world which is held by reason to be the infinite totality of all that is, and the point of reference for all its ideas. It follows then that beauty may be defined as something that pleases, because its form presages the infinite within the finite. The beautiful, then, does not offer us the actual contemplation of the infinite, but simply a presentiment of it – a vague idea, that is, of something higher that cannot be described in words.

The rapture that beauty excites in the soul is called *enchantment*, because the beautiful enchants us, detaching us, so to speak, from the world of the senses and bringing us closer to the ideal world. Such enchantment is normally silent, since we cannot express what we are thinking and feeling.

The beautiful, therefore, has something *mysterious* about it, being surrounded, as it were, by a veil which permits us to view the infinite only as an evanescent outline in the dim distance.

Expression (Espressione)

A quality that the musician has, whereby he is enabled to feel keenly and to express forcefully all the ideas that he wishes to portray and all the emotions that he seeks to express. There is expression in composition and expression in performance; together they produce an effect of the greatest power, one that affords superlative pleasure.

Much has been written on this subject but as not everyone is equally sensible to music's charms; some have extended the domain of expression into the infinite; some have relegated it to the ranks of chimera;[1] whilst Rameau, the author of a new system of music and composer of twenty operas, made the astonishing statement that if he were given the *Gazette de Hollande,* he would set it to music. Both extremes are equally far from truth and reason. One would be absurdly partisan either to claim that music could portray minute nuances, the character of which is ill defined, or to carry a love of paradox so far as to deny music any kind of expression, a sophistry that the history of music itself refutes.

Expression in music is at its best only when it is aided by poetry. Music sharpens the darts that the poet aims at our hearts; and the two arts combine to create a divine language. If the composer wishes to achieve such a happy union between words and music, he must read the text with the greatest care and fully enter into the theme of the action. He lives the characters in the poem; he himself is the tyrant, the hero, the lover; he feels the grief, the enchantment of love, the insults, the terror, the pangs of death. He must be outraged or angry; he must hope or, like the character, he will despair; his blood will boil in his veins. In the heat of his enthusiasm he will discover the sounds, the melodies and the harmonies; the poem will spring forth from him expressed in the miraculous language of music.

---

[1] Boyé, *L'Expression musicale mise au rang des chimères* [1779].

Since there are so many subtle gradations of emotion and passion, it is very easy to err in expressing them. The gaiety of a Queen is not the same as that of a peasant woman; the wrath of a hero requires a different expression from that of a simple soldier, etc.

Expression may be inherent either in the vocal line, or in the instrumental part, or in both. Where the emotion is gentle and melting, the vocal line will be pre-eminent; the orchestra will support it, filling out the moments when the actor is silent; in such a case simple harmony and smooth modulations are called for. If the emotions are strong, as are wrath and revenge, the voice alone is insufficient to express them; and the composer will have recourse to the orchestra.

So let the composer, in the spirit of the poem, avoid any discrepancy between the musical expression and the sense of the text, without becoming too misguidedly involved in it. There is no harm in expressing the words *tortuous steps* by a twisting melodic line, but such a line would sound quite ridiculous if the composer used it in connection with the word *slavery* to illustrate the chains fettering the prisoner. Another such composer might turn the 'Agnus Dei' into a pastoral, probably because *agnus* means *lamb*; and lambs need shepherds. In a duet in *La Fausse Magie*, Grétry put a cadence on the word *cadence*, despite the fact that the word referred to the cadence pirouettes of a ballet dancer. As a general rule, subjective expression should not be confused with objective illustration.

Jealous rage, the penitence for a great sin, grief, joy, religious hymns, rustic dances, war-songs, in fact everything with a pronounced character to it, has a convention of expression which the composer ignores at his peril. But things are different with tranquil emotions and sweet passions; joy born of friendship and requited love; the cares and foibles of two lovers; the little perversities that cross our path in life, these are all in half-tones; these may be truthfully but never precisely expressed. It is up to the actor to make the picture convincing by the expression he puts into the vocal line and the way he performs, firmly characterising the melody. In painting, green is always green; red is always red; nothing can change the nature of colour; but it is not so in music and poetry, the phrases of which mean only what one wishes them to mean; the identical *motif* may in turn express ideas that are diametrically opposed. A lover may say to his beloved *Sta sera*; 'This evening': two gluttons, two ruffians, two villains may meet and use the same words. But how many different implications that phrase offers! A lover's assignation, a gambling den, a banquet, a duel, a murder! It is evident that the actor's voice alone can depict the emotion that moves him; the expressive power lies not so much in what is said, but how it is said.

Pitch, tempo, rhythm, key, accompaniment, the choice of voices and instruments, the effect of the harmony, with particular attention to the appropriateness of the mood, all these none the less contribute to the expression of the vocal line. If melodic invention is evidence of the composer's genius, his character, his taste and his skill will soon be revealed in his use of harmony and instrumentation, appropriate to the situation he is dealing with or the emotion he seeks to express. Musical expression is thus the outcome of a combination of vocal line and harmony, and it is the most sublime aspect of the art; the most sublime musical expression results from a combination of melody and harmony, and not even an ensemble in which every instrument is involved could have such a powerful effect. The accompaniment of a religious hymn will differ greatly from a romance, a pastoral or a march. It is self-evident that a lively 3/4 or a 6/8 measure has little dignity and that if either metre is used in a serious context it should not have the character of a dance.

Even though the impact of musical expression derives in the main from combinations of notes, timbre is not unimportant. Being energetic and imposing, the bass voice is more suited to powerful passions and religious arias, but it is too solemn, and, moreover, too rough for the gentler emotions. The tenor voice, on the other hand, is distinguished by sweetness and flexibility; its noble and touching sound gives a most seductive quality to the language of love. The female voice combines power with lightness; it is sensitive and graceful in its middle range, and in its upper registers it has the brightness and vigour that are appropriate to the grand passions.

In conclusion, then, the perfection of a picture depends on three qualities – design, colour and expression – whilst in music the excellence of a composition depends on melody, harmony and expression. Melody is the fruit of invention, the basis and foundation of the other two; it corresponds exactly to design in painting. Harmony gives expression and power to melody, as colour does to design; in both arts, expression results from the combinations of the two other qualities and is nothing but the powerful application of those qualities to a given subject. If the union is skilfully managed the composition will be perfect; but if one of them is overlooked and is faulty, the proportions of the composition will be distorted accordingly.

Imitation (Imitazione)

Cicero said: 'Omnis motus animi suum quendam a natura habet vultum et sonum et gestum.' If all the emotions have their own sounds and if the composer is capable of using the sounds that express them, music, though limited in what it can imitate, is nevertheless an imitative art, since nature provides its models and the means of reproducing them. Aristotle, Rousseau and other writers have accepted this principle.

It is really very remarkable how the imitation in a picture remains cold, whereas that in music straightway warms the soul; and though a painting cannot depict what cannot be seen, the composer can depict what cannot be heard, e.g. nocturnal calm, silence, rest, the horrors of a desert, a cloudless sky, etc.; the picture represents all nature in terms of sound alone, even though the observer is not asleep. The effect of music goes further still, rekindling in our soul the very emotion that the object itself aroused.

Apart from imitation of natural beauty, there is yet another kind, which consists in following the example of other composers, taking them as models. Here it is useful to distinguish between *free* and *slavish* imitation. The slavish imitator may be a man of talent, whereas the free imitator has room to express his own genius.

Romantic (Romantico)[2]

The romantic consists of a combination of the grand, or rather the marvellous, with the gentle and soft. Thus the term is applied to a romantic setting on a summery night, the constituents of which are *imposing*, but which are illuminated by the *gentle* light of the moon. A rugged range of mountains might be sublime on account of its savage and impressive grandeur, but the surroundings must be pleasant if it is to be romantic. Hence the essence of the romantic is the overwhelming enhanced by the pleasant and the attractive.

Sublime (Sublime)

Almost everything that relates to the article on beauty may also be applied to the sublime.

Pleasure in the sublime is distinguished from pleasure in the beautiful, in that whereas the beautiful relates to the *form* of things, that is to say to their *quality*, the sublime is a matter of their *size*, or *quantity* and may be found in objects that are devoid of form, such as enormous masses of rock. Since we tend to recognise the size of an object by comparing it with other objects, it follows that if at the moment of perception a thing seems to be great beyond all comparison, we elevate it quantitatively above anything comparable and give to it the term *sublime*. The division made in the case of the beautiful into *external* and *internal*, or *physical* and *intellectual* is applicable to the sublime as well (as for instance the sound of thunder, the idea of eternity, etc.), which gives a feeling of the infinite within the finite. It is true that the sublime inhibits the imagination and the intellect to start with by its immeasurable size; but it extends and develops the activity of reason, sharpening and developing its vital senses. So the sublime is that which, by its immeasurable grandeur, stimulates the action of reason, increasing its vital senses. Indeed, as Kant and Schiller have said, the sublime comprises the infinite which terrifies the senses and the imagination beyond the powers of comprehension, and it is reason that creates and affirms the sublime.

The *great* is similar to the sublime and is one stage below it; but if it exceeds its limits, and approaches sublimity, it is termed *colossal*. If

---

[2] This article does not appear in the French edition (eds.)

Fig. 4. *The Bard* (John Martin, 1789–1854). The sublime as seen by an artist a mere half-century later than Wright's *Indian Widow*, with its exaggerated contrasts, both in human and landscape terms. The lone Welsh bard defies the advance of Edward I's conquering army from a crag set in an awesome landscape. (Laing Art Gallery, Tyne and Wear County Council Museums)

grandeur relates to the moral, it engenders the *noble*, which to a high degree concerns moral virtues (*che annunzia un grado maggiore di virtu morali*), giving the object a certain *dignity*, inspiring a certain *respect*, whereas the ignoble and the vulgar are scorned.

The *solemn* sets the mind in an analogous mood that is serious or religious, in the way as for instance that sacred music does. The terms *solemn* and *magnificent* are applied to such natural and human things as exhibit *majesty* and are therefore *revered*, or – at a higher level – *worshipped*.

The *pathetic*, properly speaking, arouses the most powerful and noble emotions; in such cases, the sublime and all its associated qualities take on the character of pathos.

The term *moving* is applied, as the word suggests, to anything that causes one to vacillate between pleasure and pain; that is why the sublime is always moving, though not all that is moving is necessarily sublime.

The *sentimental* is a genre of its own, or rather a major subdivision of the moving.

The composer who wishes to express the character of the sublime should create melody that has few ornaments and little embellishment, and that moves in bold progressions with many large leaps; he should adopt a measured tempo and extremely energetic harmonies which he intermixes from time to time with harsh dissonances.

The performance of the sublime requires well-accented and well-sustained notes, a sensitivity to grammatical accent and energetic declamation; the notes should be staccato rather than legato, yet sustained and vigorous.

Unity (Unità)

Unity is the foremost of the two great principles upon which harmony depends, not only in music but in all the arts.

Without unity there is neither sound, concord, cadence, phrase, period nor any kind of music. Given unity and variety, all is well with the arts and with each of their respective parts. The man of genius must constantly keep these two in balance.

The rule that prescribes that there shall be one plot and that interest shall constantly focus upon one object is perfectly applicable to musical compositions. One musical theme can suffice to make an entire symphony. Provided that the modulations are artistically prepared, that felicitous modifications of harmony add variety to melodic restatements, and that the timbres are subtly graded to produce powerful effects, there is no need to fear that thematic repetitions will weary the listener. On the contrary, such repetitions will be experienced with renewed pleasure. Amongst the works of the great masters may be found innumerable pieces that are built upon a single motif. What marvellous unity there is in the structure of these compositions! Everything relates to the subject: nothing extraneous or inappropriate is there. Not a single link could be detached from the chain without destroying the whole. Only the man of genius, only the learned composer can accomplish such a task, one that is as admirable as it is difficult.

The rule that one strives for unity of idea in a composition is not without its exceptions. If for instance an air or a symphony projects a series of varied images, the composer must necessarily have recourse to different melodies if he is to meet the wishes of the poet. Such pieces must however be developed with infinite art if they are not to degenerate awkwardly into a kind of *pot pourri*. Moreover, the composer must often show skill and genius in linking together two or three *motifs*. Broadly speaking a composer who lacks a profound knowledge of the secrets of harmony will never give the perfection and precious unity to his compositions that add so much to their impact and their charm.

Aesthetics (Estetica)

This branch of knowledge was outlined for the first time in the middle of the last century by the German philosopher A.G. Baumgarten, and has since then been recognised by the world of letters as an essential aspect of philosophy. It concerns itself with the beautiful and the sublime, with taste, with judgement of taste, etc.; and thus it is also called the *theory of taste* and the *philosophy of the fine arts*.

Like logic and metaphysics, aesthetics divides into the *pure* and the *applied*. Pure aesthetics deals with aesthetic ideas (*aesthetic ideology*) and with aesthetic judgements (*aesthetic discrimination*); the applied aspect, or *calleo-technical* side, both general and special, deals with the fine arts in general, and also with their individual branches, such as the *arts of sound* (music, poetry and rhetoric), the *plastic arts* (plastic art, architecture, painting, calligraphy, etc.), the *arts of mime* (mime, ballet, gymnastics, etc.) and with the fine arts according to their genres.

Aesthetic theory is further divided into the doctrine of the beautiful (*calleology*), of the sublime (*hyposeology*) and of aesthetic qualities of similar character such as charm, grace, elegance, splendour, the colossal, the majestic, the awe-inspiring, the pathetic, the sentimental and the comic.

Even though history amply demonstrates the existence of the finest works of art before the establishment of the science of aesthetics, never the less aesthetics can be of great value to those creative artists, amateurs and art critics who are endowed with a philosophical turn of mind and who, mistrusting their imperfect and confused feelings and their unclear ideas, seek to prove more deeply the sources of aesthetic power; it follows that it is unnecessary to determine how advantageous this science may be, not only to the composer, but even to the singer.

The literature of musical criticism (Letteratura della Critica Musicale)
On musical aesthetics (Dell' estetica musicale)

The nature and applications of the principles of fine art (Natura, Applicazione e Principi delle Belle Arte)

BATTEUX (Charles), professor of philosophy at Paris: *Les beaux arts reduits à un même principe*, Paris, 1743, 1747, 1755, 8vo.

The author has attempted to apply Aristotle's badly understood principle of the imitation of nature to all the fine arts, expanding his hypotheses further in his *Cours de belles lettres*. Ramler translated this latter work very effectively into German. Of the translations into German of the former work, the following deserve to be mentioned as well as the appended commentaries:

SCHLEGEL (Johann Adolph), consistorial councillor at Hanover: *Batteux Einschränkung der schönen Künste auf einen einzigen Grundsatz; aus dem französischen übersetzt, und mit verschiedenen einzigen eigenen damit verwandten Abhandlungen begleitet*, Leipzig, 1752. *Zweite verbesserte Auflage*, Ibid. 1759. *Dritte Aufl. von neuem verbessert und vermehrt*, Ibid. 1770. Two vols in 8vo. The first volume contains the translation of Batteux and the second, essays by the translator, on: (1) genius in the fine arts; (2) the need to develop taste; (3) the premature cultivation of taste; (4) the origins of the arts, especially the liberal arts; (5) the fine arts listed according to their scope.

RUETZ (Caspar), cantor and director of music at Lübeck: 'Sendschreiben eines Freundes an den andern über einige Ausdrücke des Herrn Batteux von der Musik.' See Marpurg's *Hist. Krit. Beitr.*, 1754, vol I, pp. 273–311.

OVERBECK (—), Rector at Lübeck: 'Antwort auf das Sendschreiben eines Freundes an den andern, über die Ausdrücke des Herrn Batteux von der Musik.' See Ibid., pp. 312–17.

RUETZ (Caspar): 'Beantwortung der vorhergehenden Antwort.' See Ibid., pp. 318–25. Both Ruetz's letters contain well-argued refutations of Batteux's principles by some authors less well-versed in art than he.

[ANON] *The polite arts, or a Dissertation on poetry, painting, music, architecture and eloquence*. London, 1749.

ESTEVE (Pierre), member of the Royal Society of Montpellier: *L'Esprit des beaux arts*. Paris, 1753, 2 vols in 12mo. The second volume contains eleven chapters on the alleged effects of ancient Greek music and a comparison between it and modern music. The author claims that modern harmony is a child of art and melody a child of nature, which contradicts his exposition of the problem. Laborde says that, once the author had read the works of Roussier, he changed his opinion. He is also credited with *Nouveaux Dialogues sur les Arts*, publ. 1775 in 12mo.

CASTEL (Louis Bertrand), learned Jesuit born at Montpellier in 1688: *VIII Lettres d'un Académicien de Bordeaux sur le fond de la Musique,* 1754.

A reply to Rousseau's letter attacking French music, in which the Abbé adds substantially to the ideas developed by Rameau in his works.

[ANON] 'Betrachtungen über die Quellen und die Verbindungen der schönen Künste und Wissenschaften.' *V. Bibl. der sch. Wissensch. und fr. Künste,* 1757, vol. I, Sec. ii, pp. 231–68.

RAMLER (Carl Wilhelm), professor of literature in Berlin: 'Auszug aus der Einleitung in die schönen Wissenschaften, nach dem französischen des Herrn Batteux, mit Zusätzen vermehrt und auf Musik angewendet.' See Marpurg, *Hist. krit. Beitr.,* 1760, vol. v, p. 20–44.

LACOMBE (Jacques), printer from Paris, where he was born in 1724: *Spectacle des beaux Arts, ou considérations touchant leur nature, leurs objets, leurs effets et leurs règles principales.* Paris, 1761, 1765, 2 vols in 12mo.

An extremely superficial work in dialogue form.

MENDELSSOHN (Moses), learned Jew from Berlin, director of a silk factory, b. Dessau, 1729: *Ueber die Hauptgrundsätze der schönen Künste und Wissenschaften.* See Philosophical Works, 1761, vol. ii, pp. 95–152.

By the same author: Letters on the Emotions; a dissertation on the sublime and the simple in the fine arts: which contain much that is relevant to music and its aesthetics.

BUSCHING (Dr Anton Friederich), privy councillor in Berlin: *Geschichte und Grundsätze der schönen Künste und Wissenschaften, im Grundriss.* Berlin, 1772, 8vo.

The observations prefacing the work are completely applicable to music and have been reprinted separately under the title: *Aesthetische Lehrsätze und Regeln.* Hamburg, 1774, 8vo Second ed. Ibid., 1776, 8vo.

SULZER (Joh. Georg): *Die schönen Künste in ihrem Ursprunge, ihrer wahren Natur und besten Anwendung betrachtet.* Leipzig, 1772, 8vo.

ROBERTSON (Thomas), member of the Edinburgh Academy of Sciences: *An Enquiry into the Fine Arts.* London, Cadell, 1785, 4to.

The first two chapters deal with modern and ancient music, the third contains reflections on art, the fourth, fifth and sixth are historical. Music is the main theme of the book. The six chapters are followed by an appendix on music in the South Sea Islands. On p. 428 it is stated that the first true concert was given in England only in 1678 by a certain Britton. See *Journ. Encyclop.,* Dec. 1785, p. 448.

ROSSI (Gian Gherardo): *Memorie delle belle arti.* Rome, 1785, vol. i, p. 91.

CARLETTI (Giuseppe): *Giornale delle belle arti.* Rome, 1785, pp. 405–11.

PREVOST (P.): 'Mémoire sur le principe des beaux arts, et des belles lettres, ou recherches sur la cause du plaisir excité par les beaux arts, et les belles lettres.' See *Mem. de l'Acad de Berlin pour l'an 1786*. Berlin, 1787.

Deals with the relationship between music, poetry, our senses and our mind.

HEYDENREICH (Carl Heinrich), professor of philosophy at Leipzig, d. 1801: *System der Aesthetik. Erster Band*. Leipzig, bei Göschen, 1790, 392 pp. in 8vo.

The author of this extremely valuable work is particularly concerned with the aesthetics of music. Its contents may be found in Forkel's *Allgemeine Literatur der Musik* (Leipzig 1792), p. 453 *et seq*.

[ANON] *Lettere su le belle arti pubblicate nelle nozze Barbarigo-Pisani.* Venice, Carlo Palese's press, 1793, 192 pp. in large 8vo.

Letter XII contains: Sensual Italy. Its sensual music. Considerations on the inconsistency of its music. The Ancient Concert in London. The author also deals later with ancient Greek music.

ROCHLITZ (Friederich): *Blicke in das Gebieth der Künste und der pracktischen Philosophie*. Gotha, bei J. Perthes, 1796.

HEUSINGER (Jh. Heinrich Gottlieb), doctor and Privatdozent in philosophy at Jena: *Handbuch der Aesthetik und Grundsätze zur Bearbeitung und Beurtheilung der Werke einer jeden schönen Kunst, als der Poesie, Mahlerei, Bildhauerkunst, Musik, Mimik, Baukunst, Gartenkunst, etc. für Künstler und Liebhaber, Erster Theil*. Gotha, bei Perthes, 1797, 344 pp. in 8vo.

HERDER (Joh. Gottfried): *Kalligone*, 1800. New edition Karlsruhe 1820 in *Werke: Abtheilung der schönen Litteratur*. Vol. xv, pp. 212–32 deal with music.

EBERHARD (Joh. August), professor of philosophy at Halle, b. Halberstadt, 1738: *Handbuch der Aesthetik für gebildete Leser aus allen Ständen, in Briefen*. Zwei Theile. Halle, bei Hemmerde und Schwetschke, 1803. It is a pity that this excellent work does not go into music more fully.

BOUTERWECK (Fr.): *Aesthetik*. Zwei Theile. Leipzig, bei Martini, 1806. See Leipzig *Allgemeine musikalische Zeitung*, vol. 8, p. 545.

KRUG (Wilhelm Traugott), sometime professor of philosophy at Leipzig, b. Radis, near Wittenberg, 1770. *Aesthetik*, Vienna, bei Franz Härter, 1819, 8vo. Deals with music in particular.

AZAIS (H.): *Cours de Philosophie générale, ou explication simple et graduelle de tous les faits de l' ordre physique, de l'ordre physiologique, de l' ordre intellectuel, moral et politique*. Vols. I–IV, Paris, 1824.

In this work, the author deals with music in relation to its theory and philosophy. One chapter deals with the parallel between music and painting. See *Journal des Débats*, 23 March 1824, 'Chronique musicale'.

Concerning music in particular (Della musica in particolare)
MITZLER (Lorenz), councillor and doctor at Konskin: 'Ungebundene

Uebersetzung von Horazens Dichtkunst durchgehends auf die Musik angewendet.' Can be found in his *Bibliothèque musicale*, 1752, vol. III, pp. 605–33.

ARNAUD (M. L'Abbé): *Lettre sur la musique, a M. le Comte de Caylus, imprimée en 1754.*

This is, as it were, a preface to a musical rhetoric, which in fact never came out. In this letter, the author develops the principles on which such a musical rhetoric should be based. He deals with music as an imitative art, attempting to demonstrate the means it should adopt to imitate. These means he believes are rhythm, melody and harmony. The letter takes up 17 pages in quarto and is printed in 8vo on 36 pages – see *Journ. des Scav.* 1754, p. 175. Stefano Arteaga published it in Italian in vol. III of his *Rivoluzioni del teatro musicale italiano*, and it may be found on pp. 498–532 in Chapter 17 of the German translation of that work.

BLAINVILLE (Charles Henry): *L'Esprit de l'art musical, ou réflexions sur la Musique et ses différentes parties.* Geneva, 1754.

There exists also a Paris edition, 1765, in 8vo and a German translation. See Hiller's *Wöchentliche Nach.*, 1767, pp. 308–73, in eight parts.

HILLER (Joh. Adam), director of music at Leipzig: 'Abhandlung von der Nachahmung der Natur in der Musik.' See Marpurg's *Hist. krit. Beytr.* 1745, vol. I, pp. 515–43.

JUNKER (Carl Ludwig), Pastor at Kirchberg: *Tonkunst*, Berne, 1777, 119 pp. in 8vo.
Betrachtungen über Mahlerey, Ton- und Bild-hauerkunst. Basle, 1778, 190 pp. in 8vo.
Both these short works relate to musical aesthetics.

CHABANON (M. de), member of l'Académie des inscriptions et belles lettres, born in America in 1729, died in Paris in 1792: *Observations sur la musique, et principalement sur la métaphysique de l'art.* Paris, 1779.

Hiller translated this work into German with annotations under the title: *Ueber die Musik und deren Wirkungen*, Leipzig, 1781, 8vo.

A much expanded version of the original was published under the title: *De la musique considérée en elle même et dans ses rapports avec la parole, les langues, la poésie et le théâtre.* Paris, chez Pissot, 1785, 460 pp. in 8vo.

This version differs not only in the order of the chapters and in the addition of new material, but in the addition of a second part. It contains the following:

Part I: Preliminary observations. Chap. 1. Analysis and definition of the art. Chap. 2. Is music basically an imitative art? Is its original aim to imitate? Chap. 3. Continuation of the same essay. Chap. 4. Music pleases independently of any imitation. Chap. 5. How music imitates. Chap. 6. The advantages and disadvantages of imitation and description in music. Chap. 7. Song is not an imitation of spoken language. Chap. 8. Important corollary of the previous chapter. Chap. 9. What song expresses is not an imitation of the inarticulate cries of our passions. Chap. 10. Musical sensations as applied to our various emotions and the natural means of expression proper to music. Chap. 11. Completion of the argument of the preceding chapter. Unity of art resulting from our system. Chap. 12. On dance. Chap. 13. Music considered as a natural language and a universal one at the same time. Chap. 14. What song is for and why nature has endowed us with it. Chap. 15. Under what circumstances is one most naturally disposed to song? Chap. 16. Different types of music, their natural application and their use in imitation. Chap 17. Additional observations on lively, loud and colourful music. Chap. 18. Style in music. Chap. 19. What declamatory imitation adds to musical style. Chap. 20. Reply to various questions about style of execution. Chap. 21. Melody and harmony in combination.

Part II: Chap. 1. The musical qualities of languages. Chap. 2. The musical qualities of prose, of different types of poetry and of differing verse metres. Chap. 3. Sung tragedy; and the relationship of text to music. Chap. 4. Music in relation to its poetic text. Chap. 5. Comedy in music and comic opera. Chap. 6. Oratorio. Chap. 7. To what extent the spirit of philosophy can be applied to the arts and in particular to music. Chap. 8. On the idea that there is much that is arbitrary in music. Chap. 9. To what extent the arts are for the masses and to what extent they can judge them well. Chap. 10. Those arts that please the masses most, and their opinion on them. Chap. 11. On emotional impact in the arts.

Appendix: Observations on the songs of savage races. Thoughts on languages. Chap. 1. On the genius of languages. Chap. 2. On the harmony of languages. Chap. 3. Progress in languages; what decides the concept of what perfection they have attained.

An extensive analysis of this work is to be found in the *Monthly Review or Literary Journal*, Vol. LXXIII, page 490, in which it is praised rather more highly than it merits; admittedly it does not lack good and truthful ideas; all the same the Author's argument in detail is too little based on a profound insight into the art, which is why an expert in philosophy will probably find it superficial.

MARTIGNONI (Don Ignazio), doctor of laws, born June 1757, died 23 March 1814: *Saggio sulla Musica*. See his *Operette varie*. Milan, Giuseppi Galeazzi's press, 1784, pp. 59–92.

Contents: Nature and force of music. Its sway is universal. Its expression is limited to the expression of emotions. Languages become less imitative as they become more abstract and more or less harmonious according to their region or climate. The origin of music. The Greeks transported by it. Examples of musical scales compared with the orders of architecture and their character.

Progress in the art; and why it has the effect it does on us. Appeal to composers to return the art to its original simplicity and naturalness. Analogy between dance and music. How it is a vital language; a universal one. The history of the Greek theatre and the Roman. Details of their aim and their mime. Italian opera. At first spectacular and showy, then gradually returning to truth through Zeno and to perfection with Metastasio. What our recitatives are like and our arias. Discussion whether our music is superior or not to French music. The relative merits of the two languages and the nature of the art.

This essay does not lack good ideas; but on the other hand, the author does not appear to know enough about music, admitting so, in fact in a note on p. 71.

STEINBART (Gotthelf Samuel), consistorial councillor and professor at Frankfurt-an-der-Oder: *Grundbegriffe zur Philosophie über den Geschmack*. First volume. Züllichau, 1785, 17 sheets in 8vo.

Contains general theory on all the arts and in particular on music.

MICHAELIS (Christian Friederich), Privatdozent in philosophy at Leipzig, where he was born in 1770: *Ueber den Geist der Tonkunst mit Rücksicht auf Kants Kritik der ästhetischen Urteilskraft. Ein ästhetischer Versuch*. Leipzig, Schäffer, 1795, 134 pp. in 8vo.

Zweiter Versuch. Ibid., 1800, 160 pp. in 8vo.

In the second part the author deals in particular with music as a fine art, a pleasant art and a useful one and with its relationship with poetry and the plastic arts.

ROTH (Georg Michael): *Ueber die bisherige Unmöglichkeit einer Philosophie des Bildes, der Musik und Sprache*. Göttingen, Dieterich, 1796, 95 pages in 8vo without the preface.

FLEISCHMANN (Friederich), doctor of philosophy, secretary and Kapellmeister to the Duke of Saxe-Meiningen, born 1766, died 1798: 'Wie muss ein Tonstück beschaffen seyn um gut genannt zu werden? Was ist erforderlich zu einem vollkommenen Komponisten?' See Leipzig *Allgemeine musikalische Zeitung*, vol 2., pp. 209–25.

The requisites of a good piece of music are: (1) *Care in invention*: (a) suppleness, well-shaped parts and well-proportioned interrelationships between them; (b) distinctive character; (c) suitable melodies and ornaments. (2) *Regarding counterpoint or harmonic treatment*: (a) grammatical correctness, (b) precision and clarity of modulation, (c) knowledge of the instruments, (d) imaginative use of emotional effect. Hence a well-equipped composer needs: (1) *Inventive genius* and (2) *Knowledge of composition*.

TICK [TIECK] (Ludwig): *Phantasien über die Kunst, für Freunde der Kunst herausgegeben von etc.* Hamburg, Perthes, 1799.

Deals with: (1) the wonders of music, (2) the various kinds of sacred music, (3) the inner essence of music and the psychology of modern instrumental music.

The true author of this little work was Herr Wackenroder, who died in the summer of 1799.

KELLNER (G. Ch.): 'Ideen zu einer neuen Theorie der schönen Künste überhaupt und der Tonkunst ins besondere'. See *Eggers teutsch. Magazin.* Aug. 1800.

MICHAELIS (Christian Friederich), Privatdozent in philosophy at Leipzig: 'Einige Ideen über die ästhetische Natur der Tonkunst und Nachtrag dazu'. See: *Eumonia*, 1801, March and April issues.

'Ueber den Rang der Tonkunst unter den schönen Künsten'. See Leipzig *Allgemeine musikalische Zeitung*, vol. 6. p. 765.

'Ueber die wichtigsten Erfordernisse der Tonkunst als schöne Kunst'. See: *Berlinische musikalische Zeitung*, 1805, nos. 33, 34, 45.

'Vermischte Bemerkungen über Musik,' ibid., nos. 4, 6, 7, 35, 36.

'Versuch das innere Wesen der Tonkunst zu entwickeln'. See Leipzig *Allgemeine musikalische Zeitung*, vol. 8, pp. 673, 791.

SCHREIBER (——): 'Beiträge zur Aesthetik der Tonkunst'. Ibid., p. 337.

GRÉTRY (André Emile), famous operatic composer, born at Liège, 1741, died 1813: *De la vérité, ce que nous fûmes, ce que nous sommes: ce que nous devions être.* Paris, 1803, vol. III in 8vo.

Deals with the emotions and the means of arousing them with regard to musical composition.

SCHUBART (Christian Fried. Daniel), Kapellmeister to the Court of Würtemberg, born at Obersontheim in 1739, died in 1791. *Ideen zu einer Aesthetik der Tonkunst. Herausgegeben von Ludwig Schubart, kön. preuss. Legationsrath.* Vienna, Degen, 1806. 382 pp. in 8vo.

This work, written in 1777, contains the following: Introduction. History of Music. The Hebrews. Greek music. The Romans. The great Italian singers. The German school. Characteristics of famous musical artists. Sweden and Denmark. Russia. Poland. Switzerland. Holland. England. France. The principles of music. Musical instruments. The harpsichord. Use of the hands. Solos. Wind instruments. The voice. Musical style. Musical technical terms. Colour, Genius and musical expression.

MICHAELIS (Christian Friederich): 'Ueber das idealische der Tonkunst.' See Leipzig *Allgemeine musikalische Zeitung*, vol. 10, p. 449.

STEUBER (——) 'Ueber die ästhetische Bildung des komponirenden Tonkünstlers.' Ibid., vol. 12, pp. 321, 793.

BÖKLIN (Franz Fried. von), doctor of philosophy and privy councillor, born at Strasbourg in 1745: *Fragmente zur höhern Musik und für ästhetische Tonliebhaber.* Freiburg and Constance, Herder, 1881. Reviews of this work are not favourable.

BERTON (Henry Montan), opera composer, member of the Académie française: *De la musique mécanique et de la musique philosophique.* Paris, 1812, 24 pp.

MOSEL (J. F. von): *Versuch einer Aesthetik des dramatischen Tonsetzers.*

Vienna, Strauss, 1813, 8vo. *Ueber Kunstdarstellung, besonders in der Musik.* Munich, Lindner, in 8vo.

F.L.B. 'Reflexion über das innere Wesen der Musik.' See Leipzig *Allgemeine musikalische Zeitung,* vol. 17, pp. 761, 777.

WAGNER (J. J.) 'Ideen über Musik.' I. *Vom ästhetischen Charakter der Musik und ihrem Verhältnisse zu den andern Künsten.* Ibid., vol. xxv, p. 197. II. *Was ist Musik?* Ibid., p. 213. III. *Gesang und Instrument.* Ibid. pp. 293, 309. IV. *Die Tonverhältnisse.* Ibid., p. 441. V. *Die Modulation.* Ibid., pp. 697, 713. VI. *Die Composition.* Ibid., vol. xxvi, p. 234. VII. *Die Verwandschaften der Musik.* Ibid. pp. 314, 334, 446, 462, 496.

LAHALLE (P.): *Essai sur la Musique, ses fonctions dans les moeurs, et sa véritable expression.* Paris, Pousselon, 1825, xiv and 96 pp. in 8vo.
The first chapter, entitled: *Prolegomenes,* postulates that music is the most favoured art of this century. Delineating in the second chapter the scope of his work, the author first discusses the music of various peoples and then, in the fifth chapter analyses musical expression, eschewing whatever is extraneous to music so as to define what is peculiar to it (indeterminacy). The eighth chapter contains reflections on national genius; and in Chapter 9, the author sets out the art's limits, asking composers to abandon descriptive music, which is nothing but a villainous embellishment stuck onto the frame of a masterpiece; and finally the author adapts to his own use the value of the idea that music is potentially a universal language. The work concludes with a bibliography (very incomplete and badly arranged). See *Revue musicale,* Aug. 1825, pp. 558–60.

BERTON (Henry Montan): *Épître à un célèbre compositeur françois, précédée de quelques observations sur la musique mécanique et sur la musique philosophique.* Paris, Alexis Eymery, 1826, 48 pp. in 8vo.
The famous composer mentioned in the title is Boieldieu. In his remarks, the author sets out the distinction between our physical and moral capacities. Applying this distinction to music, he notes that the intellectual aspect of this art among the Greeks was considered as an *end* and the physical as a *means.* See ibid., vol. xxix, 1826, p. 894.

Concerning musical genius and talent (Del Genio e Talento musicale)

RAMEAU (Jean Baptiste): *Observations sur notre Instinct pour la Musique et sur son principe, ou les moyens de reconnoitre l'un par l'autre, conduisant à pouvoir se rendre raison avec certitude des différens effets de cet art.* Paris. 1754.
Matheson, in his *Plus ultra,* p. 470, speaks unfavourably of this work.

GERARD (Alexander): Doctor and professor of theology at Aberdeen: *An Essay on Genius,* 8vo.
A German translation under the title: *Versuch über das Genie* was published by Garve of Leipzig in 1776 in 8vo.

DALBERG (Fried. von): *Vom Erkennen und Erfinden*. Frankfurt, Herrmann, 1791, 8vo.

Contains many good ideas both on musical invention and on musical genius.

'Ueber die physiologischen Kennzeichen des musikalischen Talents; nach Herrn Dr Galls Entdeckungen.' See Leipzig *Allgemeine musikalische Zeitung*, vol. 4, p. 65.

MICHAELIS (Christian Friederich), Privatdozent in philosophy at Leipzig, born there in 1770: 'Ueber die Prüfung der musikalischen Fähigkeiten.' See Berlin *Allgemeine musikalische Zeitung*, 1805, nos. 56, 57, 58.

'Ueber die verschiedenen ästhetischen Charakter einiger Komponisten.' See *Der Freymüthige*, Berlin, 1811.

HOHENBAUM (D. C.): 'Von der Verschiedenheit des musikalischen Talents.' See Leipzig *Allgemeine musikalische Zeitung*, vol. 16, pp. 261, 277.

Concerning musical taste (Del Gusto Musicale)

MURATORIUS (Ludov. Ant.): 'Commentatio de recto, de Scientiis et artibus iudicio.' See *Acta Eruditor. Lips.*, Suppl. VII, p. 127.

GRANDVAL (—) French actor: *Essai sur le bon goût en musique*. Paris, 1732, 76 p. in 12mo. A German translation exists also. See Marpurg's *Krit. Mus.*, pp. 109, 117, 125, 133, 165, 183, 191, 199.

CARTAUD DE LA VILATE: *Essai historique et philosophique sur le Goût*. Paris, 1735, 12mo.

The second part contains reflections on music in general, on French and Italian music and on changes in the former in recent years.

GEMINIANI (Francesco), born at Lucca in 1680, lived for a long time in England. *A Treatise on good Taste and Rules for Playing in good Taste*. London, 1739, 1747. Was also translated into French.

MERMET (Bollioud de), secretary of the Académie des sciences at Lyon: *Sur la corruption du goût dans la musique françoise*. Lyon, 1746, 8vo. A German translation was published at Altenburg in 1750 and another in Marpurg's *Crit. Mus.*

GERARD (Alexander), professor of moral philosophy and logic at Aberdeen: *An Essay on Taste. With three dissertations on the same subject. By Mr de Voltaire, Mr D'Alembert, Mr de Montesquieu*, 1756, 8vo.

In the German translation of this fine work, published at Breslau and Leipzig in 1766, the final dissertation by Montesquieu was omitted.

[ANON] *Abhandlung vom musikalischen Geschmacke*. See *Hamburg, Unterhalt.*, vol. I, pp. 41–59, 158–161; vol. II, p. 223.

VOGLER (Ab. Georg Joseph): *Essai de diriger le goût des Amateurs de Musique et de les mettre en état d'analyser, de juger un morceau de Musique*. Paris, Jombert, 1782.

Unpublished work by the Abbé Vogler.

RANGONI (March. Gio. Battista): *Saggio sul gusto della Musica, col*

carratere de' tre celebri suonatori di Violino: Nardini, Lolli e Pugnani.
Livorno, Masi, 1790 (in Italian and French).

ROCHLITZ (Friederich), court councillor of the Duchy of Saxe-Weimar, born at Leipzig in 1770: 'Ueber die Verschiedenheit der Urtheile über die Werke der Tonkunst.' See Leipzig *Allgemeine musikalische Zeitung*, vol. 1, p. 497.
'Ueber den Geschmack an Sebastian Bachs Kompositionen, besonders für Klavier.' Ibid., vol. 5, p. 509.

MICHAELIS (Christian Fried.): 'Ueber musikalischen Geschmack.' See ibid., vol. 9, p. 49.

HEINSE (Wilhelm), court councillor and librarian at Ratisbon, died in 1803 at the age of 54: *Musikalische Dialogen, oder philosophische Unterredungen berühmter Gelehrten, Dichter und Tonkünstler über den Kunstgeschmack in der Musik.* Leipzig, Gräff, 1805.
Posthumous work, written in the author's twenties and not comparable with any of his other works.

SCHAUL (Joh. Baptist), court musician at Würtemberg. *Uber den Geschmack in der Musick.* Karlsruhe, Machlot, 1809.
A work riddled with absurdity.

Concerning beauty in music (Del Bello nella Musica)

MENGOLI (Pietro), doctor of laws, Prior of St Mary Magdalene and professor of mechanical sciences in Bologna, d. 7 June 1686, aged 60. *Discorso accademico recitato nell'Amor tirano, Accademia fatta in casa dell'illustrissimo Sig. Senatore Fantuzzi, composta in musica da Domenico Pellegrini, accad. Filomuso* Bologna 1649 in 4to.
In this essay, Mengoli proves that musical harmony somewhat resembles the harmony of constituent parts that go to make up a beautiful figure.

CROUSAZ (Jean Pierre de), professor of philosophy and mathematics at Lausanne, where he was born in 1663, and where he died in 1748: *Traité du Beau, où l'on montre en quoi consiste ce que l'on nomme ainsi, par des Exemples tirés de la plûpart des Arts et des Sciences.* Amsterdam, 1715 in 8vo.
Chapter 11, in 8 sections, pp. 171–302, deals with beauty in music, derived from physical and mathematical principles.
In the later 1724 edition in two volumes, these sections are missing. In Forkel's *Bibl. crit. music.*, vol. i, pp. 1–52 and pp. 1–125 of vol. ii, there is a German translation.

ANDRÉ (Yves Marie), French Jesuit, professor of mathematics at Caen, where he died aged 89 in 1764: *Essai sur le beau*, Amsterdam, 1760, in 8vo.
Chapter 4, pp. 114–172, deals with musical beauty. The author is in agreement with St Augustine concerning the unity of beauty ('Omnis pulchritudinis forma unitas est'). This work was published in 1741

anonymously. Formey reprinted it with additions in 1759. The other editions (1760 and 1763) were also attributed to Formey and the last-named edition included new material – six new essays. The 1741 edition was translated into German by Ernst Amadeus Baron under the title: *Versuch über das Schöne*, etc., published in Altenburg in 1757, 130 pp. in 8vo.

The four sections deal with: (1) The Beautiful in general and visual beauty in particular; (2) Moral Beauty; (3) Intellectual Beauty; and (4) Musical Beauty. At the end, pp. 131–84 is Gresset's essay on the nobility and function of ancient music, delivered in 1751. 'Betrachtungen über das Erhabene und das Naive in den schönen Wissenschaften.' See *Bibl. der sch. Wissensch. u. fr. Künste*, 1758, vol. II, Sec. ii, p. 229.

CASTILLON (Frederic Adolph Maximilien Gustav de): 'Recherches sur le Beau, et sur son application à la Musique (La Mélodie, l'Harmonie, le Rhythme).' See *Mém. de Berlin*, anno 1804. *Mém. Cl. Philos. spéculat.*, pp. 3–19.

MARTIGNONI (Ignazio), doctor of laws, at Como, b. June 1757, d. 23 March 1814: *Del Bello e Sublime*, Milan, 1810. Second edition, with notes on the author's life and works by Luigi Gatenazzi, Como, 1826, in 12mo.

Chapter IV deals with beauty in music. The author, who shows an evident distaste for harmony in his *Saggio sulla Musica* [see above, p. 380] now says: 'the most outstanding perfection in music is to be found in the miraculous combination of melodic expression enriched by harmonious chords.' This is immediately followed by the assertion that musical beauty, music being an imitative art, consists in the variety and clarity of the expression.

WEILER (– von): 'Ueber den Begriff der Schönheit, als Grundlage einer Aesthetik der Tonkunst.' See Leipzig *Allgemeine musikalische Zeitung*, vol. 13, p. 117.

[ANON] *Saggio sul Bello*, Padua, 1823, pp. 36 in 4to. Sections iv and vi deal with the beauty of sounds and melodrama. See *La Bibliotecca Ital*, vol. II, p. 413.

Concerning expression, character and style in music (Dell'Espressione, Carattere, e Stile nello Musica)

WIDDER (Friederich Adam), D. Litt. and Doctor of Philosophy, Gröningen: *Dissertatio de affectibus ore Musices excitandis, augendis, et moderandis*, Gröningen, 1751. This essay was written as a Doctoral thesis.

AVISON (Charles), English organist at Newcastle, d. 1770: *An Essay on musical Expression*. London, 1751, 1753. Both editions were published by John Brown, who is alleged by some to have been responsible for much of the text. The second edition contains: *A Letter to the*

Author concerning the music of the Ancients, etc. A good German translation of this work was published at Leipzig in 1775; 112 pp. in 8vo.

Remarks on Mr Avison's Essay on musical Expression. London, 1753, in 8vo.

A detailed critique of Avison's original work. Avison published a new edition of his work the same year with a reply to the *Remarks* etc., and with a letter containing various matters relating to music. Gerber, in his *Bibliografisches Lexicon*, attributes the work to one William Hayes. 'De l'expression en musique.' See *Mercure de France*, Nov. 1771, p. 113.

PILEUR D'APLIGNY (M. le): *Traité sur la Musique et sur les moyens d'en perfectionner l'Expression.* Paris, 1779; 174 pp. in 8vo.

Deals with: (1) Music in general. (2) The origins of music. (3) Metric quantity in poetry and music. (4) The nature of ancient music. (5) The melodies of the ancients. (6) The beginnings of modern music. (7) The origins of Vaudeville. (8) Italian arias. (9) Italian recitative. (10) Choruses. (11) Italian opera. (12) Motets. (13) Cantatas. (14) French opera. (15) French recitative. (16) The advantages of French over Italian as a language for music. (17) Accent. (18) Quantity. (19) The advantages possessed by the French language in giving rise to harmony. (20) The opportunities available in French to compose metrical verse. (21) Refutation of objections to metrical verses. (22) The uselessness of rhyme in lyric poetry. (23) The advantages of poetic quantity for expression. (24) On lyric poetry. (25) Observations on the way in which recitative should be noted. (26) Accentuation of ideas. (27) On musical composition. (28) The essential qualities of music. (29) The three aspects of opera. (30) On the overture. (31) On first performances. (32) On the principal character. (33) On expression. (34) On the imitation of nature. (35) Illustrating the passions. (36) The character of people on stage. (37) Situations. (38) Metre. (39) On accompaniments. (40) On musical quantity. (41) The employment of different types of music. (42) Tempo, measure and movement. (43) On speed. (44) On musical periods. (45) Sections of periods. (46) Defects of the Italian aria. (47) On repetitions. (48) On Hyperbation. (49) On transitions. (50) On the study of good models. (51) On imitation. (52) On style. (53) On aspects of style. (54) On taste.

ENGEL (Johann Jacob), professor at Berlin, b. Parchim, Mecklenburg, 1741, d. 1802: *Ueber die musikalische Mahlerei. An den königl. Kappellmeister Herrn Reichardt.* Berlin, 1780, 48 pp. in 8vo.

BOYÉ: *L'expression musicale mise au rang des chimères.* The author prefers dance music to all other kinds on the grounds that it gives general pleasure and arouses gaiety. His work contains: (1) The main aim of music is to provide physical pleasure. (2) There are various kinds of music. (3) Music is analogous to speech but cannot be expressive. (4)

The music that approaches the expressive most closely is the most boring. (5) Music can sometimes be evocative but not truly picturesque. (6) Dance music should take the first place. See *Journ. Encyclop.*, April 1779, pp. 295–307.

MORELET (Abbé): *De l'Expression en Musique.*
A well-written work. The author defines music as 'Succession, ou un ensemble des Sons mesurés dans leur durée; succession dans la Mélodie, ensemble dans l'Harmonie.'

ROBINSON (Pollingrove): *Handel's Ghost. An Ode.* London, 1784, in 4to. Deals with the form of Handel's *Messiah*. The author takes Dryden's *Alexander's Feast* as a model. See *Crit. Review*, 1784, vol. 58, p. 240.

CAMBINI (Giuseppe): 'Differens Solfèges d'une difficulté graduelle, pour l'exercice du Phrase, du Style et de l'expression; avec des remarques nécessaires et une basse chiffrée.' Paris, 1788. See *Journ. Encyclop.* April 1788, p. 329.

WEBER (Friederich August), Doctor of Medicine at Heilbronn, b. there in 1753, d. 1806: 'Von der komischen Schreibart und ihren Grenzen im praktischen Musikwesen.' See *Musikal. Korresp.*, 1792, pp. 363, 369.

[ANON] *Ueber Karakterdarstellung in der Musik.* See *Die Horen*, ed. Schiller, 1795, no. 6, pp. 97–121. The author is [believed to be] Herr Körner of Dresden.

DITTERSDORF (Carl Ditters v.), opera composer, b. Vienna, 1739, d. 1799. 'Ueber die Grenzen des Komischen und Heroischen in der Musik.' See Leipzig *Allgemeine musikalische Zeitung*, vol. 1, pp. 138, 201.

GERBER (Ernst Ludwig): 'Etwas über den sogenannten musikalischen Stil', see ibid., pp. 292, 305.

WEBER (Friederich August): 'Ueber komische Charakteristik und Karikatur im praktischen Musikwesen.' Ibid., vol. 3, pp. 137, 157.

MICHAELIS (Christian Friederich), Privatdozent in philosophy at Leipzig, b. there, 1770: 'Ueber das Humoristische und Launige in der musikalischen Komposition.' Ibid., vol. 9, p. 725.
'Ueber die verschiedenen Gattungen der Musik, ein historisch-ästhetischer Beitrag.' See *Der Freimüthige*, Berlin, 1811.

KANNE (Friederich August), poet and composer for the stage, in Vienna, b. Delitsch, nr Leipzig, c. 1778. 'Ueber musikalische Mahlerei.' See Wiener *Allgemeine musikalische Zeitung*, 1818, pp. 373, 385, 393, 401.

CRELLE (A. L.): *Einiges über musikalischen Ausdruck und Vortrag. Für Fortepianospieler, zum Theil auch für andere ausübende Musiker.* Berlin. See *Handb. der mus. Litt.*, suppl. 7, 1824, p. 85.

The union of music and science (Unione della Musica colle Scienze)
MUNERAT (Jean le), musician of the French Court and theologian at the

Lycée in Paris: *De moderatione et concordia Grammatica et Musica*, Paris, 1490.
Found at the end of the Martyrology of Usuard, a monk at St Germain in Paris, published by Munerat. See *Hist. Littér. de la France, par les rélig. Bénéd.*, vol. v, p. 441.

DOPPERT (Joannes), Rektor at Schneeberg: *Musices cum litteraris copula descripta.* Programme of 1711. See *Godofr. Ludovici Hist. Gymnas. Scholarumque celebr.*, p. 183.

MITZLER (Lorenz), historiographer to the King of Poland, councillor and doctor of medicine at Konskin in that kingdom, born in the Province of Ansbach in 1711; died 1778: *Dissertatio, quod Musica scientia sit et pars eruditionis philosophicae.* Leipzig, 1734, 4to. Second, expanded and amended edition with new preface, Leipzig and Wittemberg, 1736, in 4to.
Untersuchung, ob die Musik ein Theil der Gelehrsamkeit sey? See *Braunschweigische Anzeigen*, 1745, no. 55, p. 898.

WINTER (Johann Christian), cantor and director of music at Hanover, born in 1718: *Dissertatio epistolica de Musices peritia Theologo neque dedecora neque inutili.* Celle, 1749.

ULRICH (Fried. Nicol.), Rektor of Rudolstadt Gymnasium, born at Oberweissenbach in 1712: 'De nexu Theologiae atque artis musicae.' See *Gel. Europa*, vol. xviii, p. 258.

MATTHESON (Johann), councillor in Hamburg, born there in 1681, died in 1764: *De eruditione musica, Schediasma epistolicum. Accedunt eiusdem litterae, ad V. Cl. C. F. L. de codem argumento scriptae.*
Second edition, Hamburg 1752, 30 pp. The third edition dates from 1782.

PETRI (Georg. Godofr.), cantor and director of music at Görlitz, born at Sorau in 1713, died in 1795: *Quod coniunctio studii musici cum reliquis litterarum studiis eruditio non tantum utilis sit, sed et necessaria videatur*, 1765.

ALBERT (Joh. Fried.), Rektor at Nordhausen: *De iucunda artis Musicae coniunctione cum literarum studio.* Nordhausen, 1778. 4to.

MATTEI (Saverio), lawyer, author of a number of writings on music, born in Calabria in 1742, died in 1795: *Se i Maestri di cappella son compresi fra gli artigiani: Probole di Saverio Mattei, in occasione di una tassa di fatiche domandata dal maestro Cordella.* Naples, 1785, 4to.
Cordella taught a deaf person to sing and asked for some reward for doing so. This was refused on the grounds that his action did not merit any remuneration other than that of an artisan. These circumstances inspired Mattei's essay referred to above. It was also quoted in Forkel's *Musical Almanac*, 1789, p. 117.

C. (G. M.): *Sulla questione: Se gli Maestri di Cappella son compresi fra gli artigiani. Anti-Probole.* Naples, Salvatore Palermo, 1785, 43pp. in 8vo.

The author counts Capellmeisters as artisans because they are musical mechanics rather than scholars. Forkel commented: 'But might there not be learned Capellmeisters in Italy? And if one judged them by their knowledge of the pertinent professions, perhaps there are quite a few unskilled doctors and lawyers. Or does the author perhaps purport to believe that all doctors of medicine, theology and law are genuine men of learning?'

DALBERG (Joh. Fried. Hugo Freyherr von): *Blicke eines Tonkünstlers in die Musik der Geister, an Philipp Haake.* Mannheim, 1787, 21 pp. in 12mo.

The idea is not new that the soul and the body react upon one another according to harmonic laws and conditions; but in this short work it is well presented and the style of the whole is elegant.

MONGEZ (M): *Mémoire sur la réunion des littérateurs et des artistes dans l'Institut françois, et sur l'esprit qui doit les animer.* Paris, 1796.

OLIVIER (—), appeal court judge at Nimes: *Troisième étude, ou Dissertation touchant les relations de la musique avec l'universalité des sciences.* 1804, 8vo.

BOISQUET (M. F.): *Essai sur l'art du Comédien chanteur.* 1812, 8vo.

The union and correspondence between music, poetry and language
(Unione e Somiglianza della Musica colla Poesia e la Lingua)

ALDRIGHETTI (Antonio Lodvico), Count and Paduan nobleman, professor of law, born 22 October 1600, died 24 August 1668, wrote among other works, *Raggulaglio di Parnasso tra la musica e la Poesia.* Padua, 1620, 4to. See Mazzuchelli. The author is also sometimes called *Andrighetti.*

OSIO (Teodato), Milanese lawyer: *L'armonia del nudo parlare, overo la Musica ragione della voce continua, nella quale a forza di Aritmetiche di Musiche Speculazioni si pongono alla prova le regole sino al presente stabilite degli osservatori del numero della prosa e del verso.* Milan, 1637.

ENT (Sir George), English doctor of medicine: 'An Essay tending to make a probable conjecture of temper, by the modulations of the Voice in ordinary discourse.' See: *Philos. Transact.* vol. XII, p. 1010.

KÖNIG (Johann Ulrich von), former court councillor at Dresden and well-known German poet, b. Esslingen, 1688, d. 1747: *Von der Vergleichung des Numerus in der Dichtkunst und Musik.* See: *Anhang zu den Besserischen Schriften.*

WINTER (Joannes Christian), cantor and Kapellmeister in Hanover: *De eo quod sibi invicem debent Musica Poetica et Rhetorica artes iuncundissimae. Dissertatio Epistolaris.* Hanover, 1764, 12 pp. in 4to.

CHASTELLUX (le Chevalier de Beauvoir de), member of the Académie des sciences, born in 1734, died in Paris 25 October 1788: *Essai sur l'union de la Musique et de la Poésie.* The Hague and Paris, 1765, 12mo. There is a German translation in the periodical *Hamburg. Unterhaltungen*, vol. VII, p. 525 and a reasoned analysis in another periodical entitled: *Neue Bibl. der sch. Wissenschaften* etc., vol. II, no. 2, pp. 293–316. Two letters relating to this essay, written by the author to Metastasio, can be found in his posthumous works, Florentine edition, vol. II, pp. 46, 61.

The same author also wrote: *Observations sur un Ouvrage intitulé: Traité du Mélo-Drame*, and: *Réponse aux Auteurs du Journal* in the *Calendrier musical universel*, 1788.

WEBB (Daniel), born in the county of Limerick, died 2 August 1798: *Observations on the Correspondence between Poetry and Music*. London, 1769. A German translation by Eschenburg was published at Leipzig in 1771, 169 pp. in 8vo, entitled: *Betrachtungen über die Verwandschaft der Poesie und Musik etc. An Essay upon Harmony of language, intended principally to illustrate that of the English Language*. London, 1774, 8vo. Contains 'Observations on the connexions of Poetry with Music.' See: *Monthly Review*, 1754, vol. 51, p. 304. These works are attributed in Gerber's new Biographical Lexicon to one *John Mitford*.

STEELE (Joshua): *An Essay towards establishing the melody and measure of speech to be expressed and perpetuated by peculiar symbols*. London, 1776.

The author proposes symbols similar to those of music to establish good declamation. See: *Journ. Encyclop.*, June 1776, p. 361.

BEATTIE (Jas), professor of moral philosophy and logic at Aberdeen, born in Kincardineshire in 1735, died in 1803: *Essay on Poetry and Music as they affect the mind*; see his *Essays on the nature and immutability of truth, etc.* London, 1777, 4to, where it is the first essay. A German translation was published in Leipzig in 1779 in 8vo, and a French translation in Paris in 1799, in 8vo, entitled: *Essay sur la Poésie et sur la Musique, considérées dans les affections de l'âme*.

VENINI (Ab. Francesco), member of the I. R. Istituto di scienze, lettere ed arti di Milano, born in Como in 1738, died in 1820: *Dissertazione sui principi dell'armonia musicale e poetica, e della loro applicazione alla teorica e pratica della versificazione italiana*. Paris, 1784. Second edition, ibid. 1798, Molini.

Ch. 1: The principles of musical harmony, and primarily of those resulting from simultaneous or successive shrill and sonorous sounds. Ch. 2: Harmony resulting from the length of notes, or musical rhythm. Ch. 3: The need for and use of harmony, primarily in poetry. Ch. 4: The origin and nature of poetic harmony. Applying this to the versification of the Latin poets, the author demonstrates that harmony in the classics, whether Greek or Latin, consisted in the measure of the tempo. In Ch. 5, he applies the same principles to Italian poetry and shows that this depends on the place of the accents and on the tempo.

The first two chapters, under the title: 'dell'Armonia musicale' can be found in *Opuscoli scelti di Milano*, vol. IX in 4to, pp. 132–59.

WALKER (J.): *The Melodie of speaking delineated etc.* London, Robinson, 1787.

The author's intention is to teach speech-intonation as one does music, adopting signs indicating the inflexions and variations of written and spoken sounds and at the same time setting out rules for intonation and the expression of emotions. See: *Journ. Encyclop.*, July 1787, p. 362.

BAYLY (Anselm), English doctor of laws: *Alliance of Music, Poetry and Oratory*. London, 1789, 319 pp. in 8vo.

According to Forkel, a work of a little value.

ROBBERS (Joan.), organist and campanist of the French church in Rotterdam: *Ueber die Verbindung der Musik mit der Dichtkunst*.

A dissertation which won the Amsterdam Society of Literature's prize in 1790 and which will probably be published.

LANGE (C.), professor of rhetoric at Brunswick: *Attische Unterhaltungen, oder die Vereinigung der Poesie und Tonkunst* (in German and English). See the new Gerber *Biographical Lexicon of Music*.

ROCHLITZ (Friederich): 'Ueber Verbindung der Musik mit der Poesie.' See Leipzig *Allegemeine musikalische Zeitung*, vol. 1, p. 433.

KRUG (Wilhelm Traugott), professor of philosophy at Leipzig: 'Bemerkungen über Sprache und Gesang.' Ibid., vol. 3, p. 57.

APEL (August): 'Ueber Musik und declamation.' Ibid., vol. 4, pp. 129, 145, 161, 177, 193, 209.

'Musik und Poesie.' Ibid., vol. 8, p. 443.

The author considers in this second essay that instrumental music should have such a character as can be rendered in poetry, giving as an example one of Mozart's large-scale symphonies.

FRAMERY (Nicolas Etienne), French man of letters, born at Rouen in 1745, died in 1810: *Discours (qui a remporté le prix) de Musique et de déclamation proposé par la Classe de Littérature et Beaux Arts de l'Institut de France sur cette question: Analyser les rapports qui existent entre la Musique et la Déclamation, déterminer les moyens d'appliquer la déclamation à la Musique sans nuire à la mélodie.* Paris, Pougent, 50 pp. in 8vo.

The same author had previously written: *Avis aux poètes lyriques, ou de la nécessité du rhythme et de la césure dans les Hymnes ou Odes destinés à la musique.* Paris, vol. IV, 8vo.

BURJA (Abel), professor of mathematics at Berlin: 'Mémoire 1 et 2 sur les rapports qu'il y a entre la musique et la déclamation.' See: *Mém. de Berlin*, 1803, 4to. *Mém. mathém.*, pp. 13–49.

The subjects dealt with by the author are: (1) Intonation; (2) Prosody; (3) Stress; (4) Sound Quality and Articulation; (5) Style.

DEPERT (Gabriel): *Du principe de l'Harmonie des langues, de leur influence sur le chant et sur la déclamation. Le 5 Mars, 1806.* See:

Mém. de l'acad. Imp. des sciences, litt. et B. A. de Turin pour les années 1805–6, pp. 241–320.

VILLOTEAU (G. A.), professor of music at Paris, born at Belleme in 1769: *Mémoire sur la possibilité et l'utilité d'une théorie exacte des principes naturels de la musique.* Paris, Renouard, 1807.

These investigations are divided into four parts. The first part deals with the art of music in relation to language and dress. The second part deals with music as an art from the first age of its degeneration since the Greeks to the age of our present knowledge. The third part discusses the state of modern European music and of the measures we can adopt to perfect it. The fourth part examines its origins in detail and its object and scope. Differences between languages manifest themselves only in their articulate features; those features which are inarticulate (in other words tones) are common to every language; whereas the same emotions are active within all men, however diverse their languages. This inarticulate language is that of nature; consequently it is the original language of mankind and the true ideal of music. The true and original scope of this art is the expression of emotion; that of arousing pleasure should be considered as subordinate and the result of the degeneration of the art. The author's main idea is to justify rhetorical music and to show that it is the proper end of music, based on the identical origin of music and language.

RAYMOND (G. Marie), professor of mathematics and physics at Chambery: *Lettre à Mr Villoteau, touchant ses vues sur la possibilité et l'utilité d'une théorie exacte des principes naturels de la Musique.* Paris, 1811, 8vo.

To this letter are appended various essays, two of which have already been alluded to in the section on church music. The third is entitled: *Réfutation d'un Système sur le caractère attribué à chacun des sons de la gamme, et sur les sources de l'expression musicale.*

PANANTI (Dr Filippo), poet from Mugello in Tuscany: 'Saggi teatrali.' See *Giornale italico.* London, 1813. August, p. 408. The first essay is entitled: *Musica e parola*, and deals with the close relationship between words and music.

Comparison between music and painting (Somiglianza e Paragone della Musica colla Pittura)

HARRIS (James), English scholar, born at Salisbury in 1709, died in 1780: *Discourse on Music, Painting and Poetry.* London, 1744, 8vo. Two other London editions, also in 8vo, date from 1755 and 1773. The German translation of the second edition printed at Danzig in 1756 is by Professor Johann Georg Müchler; and that of the third edition, published at Halle in 1780, is by J. C. F. Schulz.

GRÄFENHAHN (Wolfgang Ludwig): 'Rede der Musik von dem Vorzug derselben vor der Mahlerey, Poesie und Schauspielkunst.' See Mitzler's *Mus. Bibl.*, vol. IV, pp. 1–22.

Wettstreit der Mahlerey, Musik, Poesie und Schauspielkunst. Bayreuth, 1746, 8vo.

WILL (Georg Andreas), professor at Altorf: *Der Ton und die Farbe in den Werken des Geschmacks.* Altorf, 1759, 4to.

'Beantwortung der Frage: Was finden sich zwischen der Musik und der Mahlerey für Aehnlichkeiten?' See: Leip., *Wöchentl. Nachr., 1768*, vol. III, p. 89.

[ANON] *Vergelyking tusschen de Musick de Schilderkonst en de Poezy, naan't Fransch.* The Hague, Bouvink, 1778, large 8vo.

HERDER (Johann Gottfried): 'Ob Mahlerey oder Tonkunst eine grössere Wirkung gewähre?' See: *Zerstreute Blätter. Samml. 2, 1786.*

HOFMANN (Johann Leonhard): *Versuch einer Geschichte der mahlerischen Harmonie überhaupt, und der Farbenharmonie insbesondere, mit Erläuterungen aus der Tonkunst und vielen praktischen Anmerkungen.* Halle, Hendel, 1786, 157 pp. in 8vo.

R. S. C.: *Essai sur le perfectionnement des beaux arts par les sciences exactes, ou calculs et hypotèses sur la Poésie, la Peinture et la Musique.* Paris, 1803, 2 vols. in 8vo, with decorations representing the picturesque element in music.

The author of this work is Lt-Col. Jacques Antoine Saint-Cyr Reveroni, born at Lyons of an Italian family. However bold his theories may be, he shows great ingenuity in developing his main idea; and his book contains several excellent analogies between painting and music.

WEBER (Dr Gottfried): *Ueber Tonmalerei.* See: *Caecilia*, vol. III, 1825, pp. 125–72.

The author is of the opinion that musical illustration is suitable only to the genre of comic burlesque; none the less, he admits some slight elements of nobility, pathos and sublimity to it.

Union of music and dance (Unione della Musica colla Danza)

ARBEAU THOINOT di Langres: *Orchesographie*, 1588.

Deals with the history of the dance and music, in the form of dialogues between Arbeau and Capriol.

DUMANOIR (Guillaume): *Le Mariage de la Musique et de la Danse.* Paris, de Luine, 1664, 12mo. See: *Hist. du Théatr. de l'acad. roy. de Mus. en France.*

ANGLEBERMEUS (Pyrrhus): 'De Saltatione et Musica.' See: *Tiraquelli, Comment, de Nobilitat.*, ch. 34, section 26, p. 367.

The author admits that he has made much use of Luciano.

BORIN (–): *La Musique théorique et pratique dans son ordre naturel avec l'art de la Danse*, 1746.

PAULI (Carl), ballet-master at Göttingen: 'Musik und Tanz.' See: *Gothaisch. Magaz.*, 1777, vol. II, no. II.

NOVERRE (Jean George), famous choreographer, Knight of the Order of Christ, born in Paris, died at St Germain in 1810 at the age of 83: *Lettres sur les arts imitateurs.* Paris, 1807, 2 vols. in 8vo.

Hans-Georg Nägeli

(b. Zurich, 16 May 1773; d. Zürich, 26 Dec. 1836)

From: *Vorlesungen über Musik mit Berücksichtigung der Dilettanten* (Stuttgart and Tübingen 1826), pp. 29–34.

Like Sulzer, Hans-Georg Nägeli was a Swiss. The son of a minister of religion, he showed an early talent for music. In 1790, he decided to devote himself to music as a career, so he set up in Zürich as a music teacher, founding a music shop, lending library and publishing firm in 1792. One of the pioneers in the rediscovery of baroque keyboard music including works by Frescobaldi, Handel and J. S. Bach, he then began serial publication of keyboard works, under the title of *Répertoire des clavecinistes* (1803), including modern works by Cramer, Dussek, Steibelt and Beethoven.

Nägeli was also keen on making music available to a much wider public than had previously been dreamed of; and so when the great educational reformer Heinrich Pestalozzi (1746–1827) needed a musician to apply his principles to the musical side of education, Nägeli, together with Michael Traugott Pfeiffer, set about the task. In 1810, he published a series of articles in the *Allgemeine musikalische Zeitung* of which he became editor in 1808. He was also deeply interested in the ethical effects of music; and to this end was active in the foundation and encouragement of male-voice choirs all over Switzerland.

During the 1820s, he made many lecture tours in Germany which attracted much attention, his lectures being published, on Beethoven's recommendation, by Cotta of Stuttgart, in 1826. As a composer, he wrote a considerable number of songs, part-songs and motets, some of which are still popular in his native country.

Nägeli accepted Kant's premises regarding the aims and effects of art and the means whereby these aims were achieved; but he rejected Kant's low rating of music in the aesthetic hierarchy. The quotation given below is taken from the original edition of his *Vorlesungen*, pp. 29–34.

There are ten lectures in all.[1] The first is devoted to an investigation of what a musical amateur is; and it displays at once that Nägeli expected a great deal of his listeners. Lectures 2 and 3 are devoted to the theory of instrumental and vocal music respectively; the fourth deals with the subject of aesthetic procedure. The fifth is on J. S. Bach; the sixth on Emanuel Bach, Haydn and Mozart; the seventh on Beethoven. The eighth provides a sketch history of vocal music; and the two final ones deal with suggestions regarding musical education.

Art manifests itself to man and influences him in the dimension of space through the plastic and pictorial arts; and in the dimension of time through music. Whereas the plastic and pictorial arts generate emotional reactions

---

[1] A very much abridged version of Nägeli's comments on some of the great composers appeared in W. Reich's selection entitled *Von Bach zu Beethoven* (Basel 1946) which has a good introduction.

(*Affekte*), music generates moods (*Stimmungen*). Emotions enslave us; moods, on the other hand, liberate us. Emotions emphasise individual aspects of things; moods, universal ones. Emotional reactions banish moods; moods obliterate emotional reactions.

Our emotional reactions derive from our basic need for love; our moods, from our basic need for pleasure. So the human soul continuously longs both for love and for pleasure. (I need of course hardly observe that in the present context the words 'love' and 'pleasure' are to be understood in the most general philosophical sense.)

Love attracts; pleasure liberates. One of the main tasks of the visual arts is to attract; one of music's main tasks is to liberate. Whenever a visual art attempts to stimulate pleasure, it is infringing the territory of music; whenever music attempts to arouse love or to attract the soul, it forsakes its own territory for that of the visual arts.

It is a well-known fact that the visual arts reached maturity before music did. With the development of instrumental composition, music achieved autonomy, but this happened only with the discovery of harmony, in other words, only a few centuries ago. Before that, music was merely the servant of verse; it was inseparably joined to it and its function was merely to reinforce its impact. Even though the ancients had instrumental music for war and dancing, such music counted for little when it was set against the significance and impact of the visual arts, for it was monophonic (that is to say it was played in unison or in octaves). The visual arts therefore matured earlier and developed their terminology first. Their aims and objectives were transferred to the sphere of music; and thus the functions and dimensions in which both kinds of art operated came to be misconstrued.

Where there is any clear statement of the theory of art, it takes a form similar to that set out below: from this it can be, and indeed often has been, readily concluded that the principles of art theory derive from the study of works of visual art:

'Every work of art must express a specific emotion.'

'Every work of art must possess its own specific character.'

'The more precisely a specific emotion is expressed, the more pregnant and clearly defined its character seems, the more impact it has and the more real it is.'

'Such accuracy of representation (*Bestimmtheit*) is the hallmark of genuine art. Its genuineness is demonstrated by the impression it makes on us and by its lasting effect.'

'The deeper the impression, the more firmly it becomes rooted in us, the more completely art has achieved its objectives.'

'Thus it is possible to evaluate works of art and the effect they have on us in terms of a scale. An individual work of art generates a specific reaction; a more complex work of art, by its very nature, sustains a state of being; the most complex work of all, comprising several states of being, develops a mood or disposition.'

These observations are absolutely true of the visual arts, even if they do not completely cover them. If, however, we apply them to music, they are totally and fundamentally false. Exactly the opposite is true. In any of the senses mentioned above, music has no character. Whenever the word *character* has been used in connection with music (with instrumental music, of course), it has been misused. Whenever mention has been made of the specific character of a musical work, it has always been in such vague terms that no insight could possibly be gained into what was characteristic of it. No one has ever attempted to define the nature of music, either by proposing a theory about it or by studying specific works; other attempts, even those undertaken by men of the greatest genius, have proved equally unfortunate. Quite naturally so. The impossible was being attempted. It is precisely in this respect that the two kinds of art are diametrically opposed. Music sets up movements in us; it does not attract us towards an object. It moves us; it does not generate static moods or states of mind. Its play of movement is inconsistent with anything that might be termed a lasting temperamental disposition. Its essence is play.

The term 'play' has always assumed a role of the greatest significance in the language of art and in the theory behind it; and this could and should have been grasped long ago. As play is music's real essence, it 'plays away' any random elements that move us only momentarily. In doing so, it plays itself into their place. Its essence is play, through and through; nothing else. It has no content of any kind that men have tried to adduce from and give to it. It simply comprises forms, regulated combinations of sounds and sequences of sounds. These varying forms of sound all produce the same effect – one that differs only in magnitude. A prelude or waltz generates a slighter reaction than a sonata or a symphony. A good and effective (i.e. 'play-full') piece of chamber music will generate the same reactions as a concert piece. Nobody has managed to differentiate on formal grounds between the various ways in which music stimulates reactions. It has not been possible, therefore, to assign a specific character to the separate forms – or even to the principal ones. This is surely a tacit acknowledgment that music's play is effective.

We may contrast the free, liberating effect that music has with the fixed, binding reaction exacted by the visual arts. The following observations should fully clarify – perhaps to the point of over-simplification – the conflicting issues:

By its play of forms, music counteracts any tendency of the cognitive faculties to affect our emotions, no matter what reaction may be generated in us, whatever way we may be influenced – by colour, shape or figure. Music endeavours to 'play away' emotion.

The richer a musical work may be in form, the more comprehensive in 'play' a musical work is, the more surely and effectively will it achieve this aim and the more powerful and excellent will it be. It must affect people of the most differing kinds and temperaments. It must dispel all specific moods or combinations of moods. It must, as it were, obliterate any random perception. By doing so, it makes the soul genuinely receptive to the pleasures of its free interplay of forms.

François Joseph Fétis

(b. Mons, 25 March 1784; d. Brussels, 26 March 1871)

From: articles in *Revue musicale*, vol. 2 (1827), pp. 369; 313ff

Fétis became a student at the Paris Conservatoire in 1800, where he studied piano, organ and composition, and where in 1807 he won the second composition prize (later to be called the Prix de Rome). In 1813 he became organist of St Pierre, Douai. On returning to Paris in 1818 he set out to make a career as a composer, and several pieces achieved some success at the Opéra-Comique. The year 1821 marked the beginning of a meteoric academic career which took him in just over ten years from the position of professor of counterpoint and fugue at the Conservatoire, by way of the librarianship of the Conservatoire, to the directorship of the Brussels Conservatoire. During this period he found time to set up France's first long-lived music journal, *La Revue musicale* (1827), and to publish a much praised *Traité du contrepoint et de la fugue* (1824) and a general and very popular introduction to music history, *La Musique mise à la portée de tout le monde* (Paris 1830; many reprints, and translated into English, German, Spanish and Russian).

So numerous were his commitments when he moved to Brussels that it is difficult to believe that he could possibly have found the time to master the enormously wide range of topics that he covered in the *Revue* and in his many other publications. He conducted orchestral concerts in Brussels of the standard Haydn, Mozart, Beethoven repertory; he was in charge of the music of Leopold I's chapel royal; he completed a mammoth *Biographie universelle* (1845) of musicians past and present, which he profitably revised and expanded in 1860; and he continued to compose – including two symphonies, a *Fantaisie symphonique* for organ and orchestra, much piano music, and choral music for the chapel royal.

It is hardly surprising then that Fétis was not always as careful of factual detail as could be wished. Nevertheless, his achievement was quite remarkable and (for all that Berlioz might say) far-seeing: Fétis's reviews of the first Paris performances of Beethoven's late string quartets and of his Ninth Symphony, for example, are sympathetic and penetrating. His breadth of scholarship is best seen in such articles as the survey of musical aesthetics (given in full on pp. 498–512), and in parallel articles on music dictionaries (p. 443) and music journals (given here).

For further reading:
Robert Wangermée, *François Joseph Fétis, musicologue et compositeur* (Brussels 1951).
François Joseph Fétis et la vie musicale de son temps: catalogue of an exhibition held in Brussels (Brussels 1972).

Réponse à une question qui nous à été faite par quelques-uns de nos abonnés

We sometimes make use of a word that is currently adopted in Germany but little known in France; that word is aesthetics. Some of our readers have observed that it would be useful if we defined little-used words which we have occasion to employ from time to time, and they have asked us what the word aesthetics exactly signifies. It is our duty to satisfy them.

In precise terms aesthetics is the philosophy of the arts. This science was sketched out towards the middle of the eighteenth century by the German ideologist, A. G. Baumgarten, and it dealt with the doctrine of the beautiful, the sublime, and of taste and judgement in the arts. It was divided, like logic and metaphysics, into a pure and applied science. Pure aesthetics involves the abstract consideration of concepts of the beautiful, the sublime, and of taste, and so on; it is called *Crimatologie aesthétique*. Applied aesthetics, which is given the name of *Calléothecnie*, embraces the fine arts in general, and their diverse manifestations, which may be subdivided into the tonic arts (music, poetry, and rhetoric), and classic arts (painting, architecture, calligraphy and so on), and the arts of mime (dance, choreography, gymnastics, and so on). The theory of aesthetics further divides into the doctrine of the beautiful (*Calléologie*), of the sublime (*Hypsicologie*), and of aesthetic affinities (*Syngenciologie*), as for example the pleasant, the graceful, the elegant, the magnificent, the colossal, the majestic, the astonishing, the pathetic, the sentimental and so on. (See Lichtenthal's dictionary of music).

Such are the established branches of this science which are to a greater or lesser extent cultivated by German theorists, but little known amongst us.

Revue des journaux de musique publiées dans les divers pays de l'Europe

If all those who practise a science or an art would interest themselves in its progress, its vicissitudes and in the discoveries that are made, periodicals containing historical and critical writings about special matters would secure a rapid and lasting success; but it is not thus. The arts are appreciated for the relaxation that they provide and not as objects for study. Some able people do experience a need for such writings it is true, but they are small in number. The rest are indifferent. Music, for example, is of all the arts the one that is talked of the most and to which men of affairs devote most of their leisure hours. But such people are avid for light articles in the daily journals, commonplace criticisms, couched in conventional phrases that are at least familiar to their ears, even if they do not express ideas of any positive kind; such writings are much to be preferred to the learned discourse of a professor which calls for some effort if it is to be understood. Such are the attitudes of most readers; as long as a man appears to know what he is talking about no one will take the trouble to understand him.

However, from time to time there have been devoted men who, drawn on by a love for music, have sought to challenge public indifference through the medium of periodical journals. Their fruitless efforts, and the number of such publications that have had but the shortest existence, are proof enough that they were mistaken and that they took their own wishes for the needs of society. However, excellent pieces on all subjects are to be found in these journals; the authors then are not to be blamed for the lack of success. It seemed worthwhile, therefore, to summarise these works.

Scheibe was the first to attempt to publish a kind of journal on music; he was Kapellmeister to the King of Denmark. His journal appeared in Hamburg in 1737 under the title of *Critischer Musicus*. It was subsequently reprinted at Leipzig in 1745 in an octavo volume of 1,059 pages. It was rather a succession of scientific dissertations than a true journal. It still merits attention.

Laurence Mizler, who was first a bookseller in Leipzig, then a councillor and doctor at Konskin in Poland, later published a journal entitled *Musikalischer Staarstecher* (musical stargazer); it appeared weekly in Leipzig during 1740. It contains bits of interesting information, but its style is heavy, pedantic, filled with harsh criticism in the manner of Mattheson. It only survived for about a year.

It was followed by an anonymous publication, also weekly, which appeared in Brunswick between 1741 and 1742 and which had as its title *Der muskalische Patriot*. It comprises some good things, but only 30 issues were published.

Marpurg, a remarkable man who set the seal of perfection on everything that he did, displayed his customary perception, erudition and taste in his *Kritischer Musicus an der Spree* (Berlin, 1750, 5 issues in quarto), in his *Historisch-kritischer Beitrag zur Aufnahme der Musik* (Berlin, 1745–60, 30 issues in 5 volumes) and in his *Kritische Briefe über die Tonkunst* (Berlin, 1760–3, 8 issues in quarto forming 1,010 pages). Such writings are perhaps too serious for the general public, but they are invaluable to artists and to anyone who seeks for serious instruction.

During the second half of the century many other music periodicals sprang up in Germany. Among these were the *Wöchentliche Nachrichten und Anmerkungen die Musik betreffend* by Hiller which appeared in Leipzig from 1766 to 1770, the *Betrachtungen der Mannheimer Tonschule* that Abbé Vogler published each month between 1778 and 1781, the *Musikalisches Kunstmagazin* of Reichardt, Berlin, 1782–91, Cramer's *Magasin de musique*, Hamburg, 1783–6, the *Musikalische Bibliothek für Künstler und Liebhaber* by Eschtruth, Marbourg and Giessen, 1784–5, the *Musikalische Realzeitung* published by Bossler between 1788–91, the *Berlinische musikalische Zeitung*, edited by Spazier, which survived only from 9 February 1793 to 4 January 1794, and the *Journal de musique* by Cock, which appeared in 8 issues in 1795.

All these journals were happily replaced by the excellent *Allgemeine musikalische Zeitung* of Leipzig. The journal was started in 1798 and is still in existence, comprising to date 29 volumes in quarto; despite its merits which are indeed considerable, it owes its long existence only to the sacrifices made for it by the house of Breitkopf und Haertel. The first 20 years are the most remarkable; these were edited by Frederic Rochlitz with whom a number of distinguished writers cooperated. An index has been published in two octavo volumes. The periodical contains a mass of interesting and instructive articles on every point of theory, history, and instrumental design; there are excellent analyses of books on music and of compositions of all kinds; there are 165 well-written profiles of the most celebrated musicians and theorists; there is news about music in theatres and concert halls throughout Europe; and finally there are accounts on the state of music in the principal cities throughout the world.

All the journals that have since appeared on this subject are based upon the model of this periodical. Of these the ones that deserve the most attention are (i) the *Berlinische musikalische Zeitung*, which the competent Reichardt wrote for in 1805, and which came to an end in 1806 due to the departure for Russia of Reichardt and the death of Froehlich, its publisher, (ii) the *Allgemeine musikalische Zeitung, mit besonderer Rücksicht auf den Oesterreichischen Kaiserstaat*, edited by the Viennese music-seller Steiner; it is a shame that this enterprise was not more profitable, for the greater part of the articles that were submitted to it by its writers were done with skill and knowledge – it began in 1817 and ended in 1823, the collection forming seven quarto volumes; (iii) the *Berlinische allgemeine musikalische Zeitung*, published by Schlesinger senior, a bookseller and music-seller. This journal appeared for the first time at the beginning of 1824 and it continues successfully. Its principal contributor, M. Marx, is mainly interested in musical aesthetics; he is distinguished as much by the independence of his judgement as by his stylistic talents and the soundness of his observations. M. Marx is a German in every accepted sense of the word and he appears to esteem only German music. His patriotism is to be respected, but I think that he is too severe on our composers and on some of our more celebrated musicians. Mozart and Beethoven are doubtless musical giants; nobody can admire their genius more than I do; but after them Méhul, Boieldieu and Auber deserve honourable mention. Apart from this tendency to run down French and Italian music too much, the writer of the *Berlinische musikalische Zeitung* shows himself to be an informed critic, and he knows how to make his journal very interesting. I should praise him even more warmly if he had not so highly commended me in articles which he has contributed to the *Revue musicale*, for it might seem that I was merely returning his compliments.

There have been and there still are other German periodicals which appear either monthly or at indeterminate intervals. Among these are the *Apollon* that the brothers Werden and W. Schneider have published at Penig in 1803, the *Musikalische Monatschrift* which appeared at Linz in the same year which the Kapellmeister F. X. Gloeggl edited, and the magazine *Caecilia*, an excellent work published by the brothers Schott from Mayence which began in 1824 and is still going, in issues of from sixty to eighty pages. One of the principal contributors to this interesting collection is M. Gottfried Weber, a distinguished theorist and composer, the author of many important works on the art of music.

In 1775 there appeared the first English music journal under the title, *The New Musical and Universal Magazine*: this continued to the summer of 1776 when it ceased to appear for lack of subscribers. This journal comprised articles on many points of theory and history and included vocal compositions. Some of the best contributions to it are by Burney. There then followed an interval of forty-three years after which an enterprise of a similar kind was tried out; this was the *English Musical Gazette* which appeared at the beginning of 1818 but which was so badly edited that it ceased to appear in June of the same year.

From its ruins arose almost immediately a review entitled the *Quarterly Musical Magazine and Review* which, as the title suggests, appeared every three months in issues of about 150 pages. The editor, M. Bacon of Norwich, made of this one of the best periodical publications of the kind. There is little information about music in other countries, but everything that relates to England is dealt with carefully and knowledgeably.

Two other English journals were launched in 1823: one had for its title, *The Monthly Magazine of Music*, but it got no further than the first issue, and certainly deserved no longer existence. The other was entitled the *Journal of Music and the Drama*; it was no better than the preceeding one and lasted no longer.

It is not the same case with *The Harmonicon*, which appears on the first of each month in issues of three or four folios with two folios of music in quarto. It comprises few original articles, almost all being taken from foreign journals, material from the *Revue musicale* now occupying some of its pages; but if it can offer little to knowledgeable musicians it is useful enough for men of affairs. This without doubt is the root of its success and it has already been in existence for five years.

The prospectus of another music journal was issued in London in 1824 under the title of *La Bilancia*, or a journal of theatrical music. This was to appear every Saturday, printed in two columns, one in English the other in Italian, and it was to comprise two volumes per year. I do not know whether this enterprise is still going.

Whatever taste the Italians may have for music, they read very little about it, for all their enjoyment comes from instinct rather than from reasoning. It is thus hardly surprising that they have few musical journals and those that have been attempted have not lasted long. The first of the kind was published by Martorelli, a music-seller in Rome, under the title *Foglio periodico e ragguaglio de spettacoli musicali*. The first issue appeared in 1808 and the last in the month of September 1809. It was a poor work and one which could have been of little use on account of the exaggerated praise that it indiscriminately scattered.

La Polinnia Europea, ossia Biblioteca universale di musica which was subsequently published at Bologna, merited a longer life. It was a good journal, carefully and knowledgeably edited. This year a new enterprise of the same kind has been undertaken, devoted to music drama and the dance, entitled *I Teatri*. The contributors and owners are M. Gaetano Barbieri and Giacinto Battaglia. According to the prospectus the contributors are to include M. Simon Mayr, G. Paccini, All. Rolla, G. Piantanida, P. Bonfichi, Dr Lichtenthal and D. Banderoli; up to this moment, however, these promises have not been fulfilled. One might reproach the editors for supplying no more than superficial articles on musical matters; it is no doubt on this account that those names that we have just mentioned have been slow to contribute articles. All that has yet been published on the theory and history of the art has been taken from some pieces that were published in the *Revue musicale*.

I have already remarked elsewhere that up to now France has lacked a journal of music, although several attempts have been made to establish one. In 1773 a *Journal de musique par une société d'amateurs* was published. One of the principal contributors was Framery; but although this journal was not without interest it found few subscribers and only four numbers were published. An amateur, by the name of M. Cocatrix from La Rochelle, brought out between 1800 and 1804 the *Correspondance des amateurs musiciens*, which primarily contained criticisms of the compositions that were played in concerts. Its aims were too limited to interest either scholars or men of the world; it is surprising then that the *Correspondance* lasted as long as four years.

After an interval of seven years, M. de Garaude, assisted by Cambini and some other artists, sought in 1810 to reawaken the interest of music lovers in musical literature by means of the *Tablette de Polymnie*, a weekly musical journal; but either the time was not ripe, or there were too many articles on concerts and operatic productions of little importance, for this journal attracted an insufficient number of subscribers to cover its expenses, and at the end of 1811 it ceased to appear.

Since this time and up to 1827, a period of sixteen years, no periodical publications appeared in France. In the hopes of being useful I have undertaken the publication of the *Revue musicale*. I hope that I may be allowed to refrain from saying what I think about it; but I may affirm that the encouragement that I have received everywhere from the most enlightened men would suffice to sustain me for a long time to come, apart from the many other reasons that determine me to go on.

F. R. de Toreinx

(fl. Paris 1830); pseudonym for Eugène Ronteix

From: *L'Histoire du romantisme* (Paris 1829), bk I, chs. 1–5, 9

Ronteix was known as the author of a few light pieces for the theatre, and some society gossip on fashions and on the theatrical world in Paris, including a *Manuel du fashionable, ou Guide de l'élégant* (Paris 1829), and a rather more substantial *La Rampe et les coulisses. Esquisses biographiques des directeurs, acteurs et actrices de tous les théâtres* (Paris 1832).[1] His *L'Histoire du romantisme* is obviously aimed, like his other publications at a fashionable and popular market, and it no doubt reflects the kind of conversation that was to be heard in smart society at the time. It should not be despised, for all that. For such an early work it achieves a remarkably modern perspective on many topics. Toreinx argues that in whatever field we look, outworn conventions are being swept away, and new vitality, new realism achieved: in literature, painting, music, historical method (well worth consulting), politics and medicine even. The book divides into two main sections, the first dealing with general concepts, the second with the people who in their various fields were regarded as leaders of the movement, including Mme de Staël, Chateaubriand, Schiller, Goethe, Dumas, Scott, Byron, Lamartine, Hugo, Beethoven, Weber and Rossini. The book reveals, in short, a real awareness of the truly great figures and a disregard for the second rate. Of the earlier French literature on romanticism should be mentioned, *L'Antiromantique* by Saint-Chamans (1816), d'Audin's *Essai sur le romantisme* (1822), and Cyprien Desmarais's *Essai sur les classiques et les romantiques* (1824).

Book I Theories

Chapter 1 Introduction

> There is no salvation other than in romanticism.

My epigraph is neither a joke nor an exaggeration; it is the product of sustained and careful observation. Anyone who has thought at all during the present times will see the truth of it.

Not without difficulty, nor in a day has romanticism reached its present, powerful position. It has fought many battles and confronted many dangers: Multum ille et bello passus (and he went through much in war). Numerous enemies have conspired together against it, right from its infancy (in truth, a somewhat petulant one). Hideous serpents have attempted to suffocate it in its cradle, as they did with Hercules; MM. Dussault,

---

[1] Bibliographical details from *La France littéraire* (Paris 1827–)

Geoffroy, Hoffmann, etc., have greatly persecuted it in its youth. And yet in vain! Despite their combined efforts, despite their outbursts of anger and their shafts of ridicule, and (shall I confess it) despite being outlawed by a power that till then nothing had resisted, it survived, it grew! Now it triumphs; it rules, and who knows whether in the near future it may not take on the role of persecutor?

Nowadays one cannot pass for an intellectual without being a romantic; and who would wish to be thought an idiot?

[p. 3, line 8 to p. 5, end of chapter, omitted]

Chapter 2

> We would still demand novelty, even though nothing new were left in the world!

These lines have always been the motto of the romantics. They were certain then of victory sooner or later. How could fashion not fail to become their accomplice? When has it ever divorced itself from novelty?

It was in 1801 that the child was born in France. Chateaubriand was its father. The five volumes of the *Génie du Christianisme* were the swaddling clothes in which it was wrapped. Since then it has many times changed its dress, but its baby clothes should never be forgotten.

As one now sees it, early romanticism was nothing more than a reaction against the anti-religious spirit that had set the closing years of the eighteenth century in a ferment. Romanticism was no more than the renewed application of Christian ideas to the products of the imagination. These old ideas were reclothed in a style that was occasionally ridiculous but which was more frequently magical, a style in which certain forms were wholly new.

During the twenty years that led up to the Revolution, the French had been bombarded with godless diatribes and academic discussions.

Romanticism appeared. It said to them: 'Sirs, I am going to drive away your boredom, if I can.' The readers, with signs of reawakened interest replied: 'We shall see!', and the attempt succeeded.

But could the academicians, the didactic poets and the materialistic philosophers cede victory to the newcomer? Could they politely take off their hats to it and from that time on wholly give place to it?

This is not how things happen in the republic of letters. Having at first been somewhat stunned by the unexpected blow, they pulled themselves together; they rallied. A bloody war began, and floods of ink began to flow. . . .

There was at the time a lady in Paris[2] whom nature had endowed with all

---

[2] The lady was, of course, Mme de Staël (eds.)

that could be asked of a standard bearer. Having a lively imagination she knew how to give tangible form to ideas of the most abstract kind. She was gifted with a fiery spirit and a cutting sense of irony, and her eloquence was deeply moving, her sheer enthusiasm compensated for any deficiencies that there might be in the argument. She adopted the new-born child and from then on its future was assured.

She saw to begin with that it had to have a name, for a name is a banner. She knew that ordinary folk are swayed by words and never more so than when the words mean nothing to them! She dreamed up a word which – as it had no precise meaning – could be applied to anything.

So it was that the word 'romantic' (*romantique*) came to enrich the French language.

She called her enemies classicists (*classiques*), yet another word that meant nothing in particular.

From then onwards there has been sustained warfare.

The classicists soon saw that they were on the losing side. Time was inevitably against them for they upheld outworn ideas against the new. They sought the support of authority.

It was a straightforward matter: the classicists supported the Master, and the romantics were his enemies. The romantics invoked the name of liberty, as all new factions do at the outset. It was a question of literary freedom, but all freedoms joined hands together.

For Mme de Staël did not limit her interests to the novel or the tragedy. She dared to speak of political institutions and of the inalienable rights that tyranny could never deny mankind! Mme de Staël was exiled. And as she left she was able to say, as Dupont de Nemours had done: 'We have greatly suffered, but the infant is conceived!' (*Nous avons beaucoup souffert, mais l'enfant est fait!*)

Chapter 3

And so it went from strength to strength.

During the last days of the Empire, romanticism was silent, or rather, no one heard it – the noise of cannon was so great! But when all the turmoil had died down it suddenly reappeared. . . . It had grown!

Here was a strange reversal of human affairs! Romanticism had at first declared itself the defender of liberty. Now it was the accomplice of despots. My concern for the truth forces this confession from me, and I blush to make it. For several years romanticism was the servant of a bigoted and servile faction. . . .

There was no question then of theories and general ideas. Save for a small group of enlightened spirits – imperceptible atoms in the midst of revolution – all France was divided into two warring camps that fought each other, not for principles but for personalities. For all that they changed their tune, these romantics did not change their ways.

Incredibly, those who claimed liberty in matters of taste sought servitude in matters of law! . . .

And so the people detested romanticism; and the odes of Victor Hugo were hardly more successful that the speeches of Marchangy, the public prosecutor!

But everything falls into place, given time, and we have seen how the new doctrines gradually spread from the Société des bonnes-lettres at the Sorbonne and laid siege to the portals of the Académie and the vestibule of the Théâtre français.

How did this revolution come about? How was it that public opinion changed so much that the *Joueur* and the *Orpheline moscovite* are now applauded, and *Bélisaire*, *Julien dans les Gaules* and the *Intrigues de cour* are howled down?

It is since the roles have changed that M. Roger and the late M. Auger declared themselves to be classicists, and under the romantic banner appeared this triple devise: 'Liberty in politics, religion and literature!' . . .

Chapter 4   Definition, or what must stand for a definition

Happy is he who can understand the cause of things.

Do you know it? Do I? Has anyone ever known it? Has it ever been defined concisely and exactly?

No! Romanticism is just that which cannot be defined! It is a modification of some kind in the arts of the imagination. It is a new form substituted for ancient ones, too recent to be threadbare and which will become classical (*classique*) like the others as it grows older.

It is the appointed task of genius to create new forms that will rejuvenate literature and win over a section of the public; the critic, who can never foresee the emergence of these forms, will only be able to define them when they have begun to become classics.

And when everything has been determined concerning this, the romantic school will be no more than the one which is disposed to accept ideas that differ from those that are currently in force, whatever the subject in question and whatever the time.

In every century, in every age, then, romanticism must change form, and the romantic works of yesterday are sometimes the classics of tomorrow.

Thus, Pascal was a romantic when he took it upon himself to crack jokes and speak French during the course of a theological discussion. Racine was a romantic when he put Jews on the stage in place of Greeks and Romans.

And do you remember what happened? He was disgraced for his audacity, and in parlour games people were given an act of *Athalie* to read as a forfeit.

The romantics are those who long for something other than what already exists in the arts.

Chapter 5 Drama

> Who will deliver us from the Greeks and Romans?
> That a single deed, accomplished in a single day and in a single place should be able to sustain the drama to the very end!

This was the field of action where fierce battles first raged.

Realism! Interest! How many times were not these words repeated! My ears are still ringing with them!

A scene having been depicted on the stage, the classicists argued, how can the same spot represent a different scene in the same play?

The curtain being raised and the drama begun, the spectator enters the world of the imagination. In his mind's eye he is in Rome, or London, or perhaps Monomotapa. Once there, he sits down, he settles himself.... How can you convince him that within the space of a few seconds you have transported him several degrees along the meridian? How can he feel that he has crossed the Alps or the Atlantic when he has felt neither the movement of a carriage nor the motion of a boat? How can he appreciate that during the interval between the acts his hero has aged by a year?

Is that credible?

And if there is no credibility will not the spectator perceive that none of the objects that you bring before him is real?

And if he no longer believes, how can he be interested?

To this the romantics reply:

Have the Germans and the English totally different minds from us? If they have found pleasure in the representation of the misfortunes of Prince Hamlet and Count Egmont, does this not prove that a drama can be interesting even though its action spans several days and moves to different locations.

This argument alone is irrefutable, for Dr Gall died without having discovered that English or Spanish brains are any different from our own.

You will reproach us for our absurdity in wishing to imitate the Germans, but you – up till now – have you not imitated the Greeks? When it comes to imitation for imitation's sake, is not a new model better than an old one?

God bless us, you have been in the same rut for almost two hundred years; does not such protracted constancy lead to overmuch conformity, and do you not realise what will come of this, one day?

Then, getting to the heart of the matter, as the lawyers say, the *Globe* has examined afresh what 'dramatic truth', 'interest' and 'realism' really are, and it has had some very profound things to say on these matters. I must beware, though, of repeating them for I do not wish to put anyone to sleep.

Even so, I must attempt a short precis, in order to resolve the difficulties as speedily as I can.

When one finds a play interesting, what does this interest stem from? Do we in truth persuade ourselves that the actors who come before us really are the characters whose names they have borrowed? Has Michelot ever passed for the King of Prussia? Has Talma (very correctly clad in a Roman Toga, but speaking French Alexandrines) ever been taken for the first Roman Emperor, pardoning the life of the man who had conspired against him and showering gifts upon him? And what about that other hero next to him bawling out lines that are not remotely natural or correct? In all conscience, can we ever dissociate ourselves from all that? It is exactly when the illusion is most effective that you applaud. Would you do this if for a single moment you were able to forget that you were looking at an actor?

The very basis of your argument is faulty. Not for a single instant is the spectator your dupe. At no time does he find himself, as you maintain, in Rome or Peking; he is quite simply in the pit or the *premier loges* of the rue de Richelieu, whistling you or applauding you in proportion to the pleasure that the performance has given him.

In a similar way we take pleasure in a painting without for a moment forgetting that we are looking at a framed canvas, for we could only otherwise be shocked at the immobility of the figures. In other words, the intellectual pleasure that we derive from a work of imitation depends precisely on the fact that we realise it is an imitation.

[p. 26, para. 1 to p. 27, para. 1, omitted]

With respect to unity of time, your exceptions make no more sense than your rules.

Only one of the two following conclusions is possible: either the dramatic action may last no longer than the time it takes to act, or there is no point in limiting the duration at all.

You have sensed the impossibility of compressing a plot into a two-hour span. You thus allow twenty-four hours, or rather the spectator must understand that there are twenty-four. Would he find greater difficulty in imagining a period of twenty-five hours, or thirty-five, or ninety-nine? Would it be more difficult at the end of an interval to persuade oneself that two days had passed, rather than two hours?

Interest and dramatic illusion have nothing to do with this but rather the fact that the characters are placed in circumstances, the uncertainty of which excites our curiosity, makes us tremble or laugh; interest and dramatic illusion depend, too, on the fact that the characters speak and act as we ourselves would in similar circumstances. Realism springs from truth of feelings, and our interest in a character is proportional to the sympathy that his words and deeds arouse in us.

Notwithstanding these reasons, popular opinion still hesitated. One fact turned up to lend them weight, and it succeeded in tipping the balance.

An attempt had already once been made to acquaint the Parisians with the workings of the English stage, but the time was one of extreme political ferment, and amongst the literary reformers were the declared enemies of liberty who were greatly disliked by the people. *Jacques Bonhomme* turned out to be almost as intractable as *John Bull*; physical force got in the way of purely intellectual discussion. The voice of reason from across the sea was drowned by a clamorous and piercing accompaniment. Disastrous arguments swooped down on their heads, and if we remember correctly, one of these ladies claimed she could spot ineradicable traces of classical energy in Albion.

But all that changed in 1827 when M. Laurent revived the dramatic enterprise. By then the public had become almost well-bred; their minds were calmer and they had learned to reason, listen and understand. *Julien* and *Vingt-cinq ans d'entr'acte* were applauded at the Vaudeville, as were the *Bénéficiare* at the Variétés, and *Trente Ans* or *La vie d'un joueur* at the Porte Saint-Martin; the Comédie Française itself had educated us into following Louis XI from the castle of Plessis-les-Tours to Peronne. Charles Kemble and Miss Smithson continued the great work of reform in *Romeo and Juliet* and *Richard III*, awakening in the French a thousand sensations that they had never known before. They listened; full of surprise and admiration they wept, they trembled; the applause from the Odéon was heard as far away as the Institut. The shock succeeded in toppling classicism from its wormeaten throne, a classicism vainly propped up by the feeble hands of the *Ermite de la Chaussée d'Antin*, and the turncoat author of *Christophe Colomb*. At this point the war was all but over and triumphant romanticism began to lay down its laws.

And so the rule of Boileau is now repealed; we may now extend the time span of a play at will and add to the play a profusion of decorative detail.

But these are not the only matters that the reforms have touched; there are still others that I cannot avoid mentioning to my readers. Classical drama is, rightly speaking, only the allegorical painting of a whim or a mood in a general sense: an abstraction built up from a multiplicity of incidents taken from individual and specific circumstances.

It was thus that Molière depicted the miser (*L'Avare*), the *Misanthrope*, *Le Tartuffe*. Thus Racine revealed to us maternal love in *Andromaque*, ambition in *Athalie*, low ambition in *Mathan*, sweet and tender love in *Bérénice*, love, pride and anger in *Hermione*, in *Roxelane*, and so on.

These are, if I may put it thus, historical paintings; each of their characters – so noble, so exact – is however only a figment of the imagination. Such characters represent humanity as the artist imagines it to be and not as it is in real life.

How, after a century, can this same path be trodden without servilely following what has already been done? How is it possible to avoid endowing the characters with qualities that are already very familiar?

Whilst the human intellect is weak and circumscribed, nature is great and powerful. She creates as many diverse forms as she does individual personalities. Study her works with the greatest attention; note instead of a few general traits the details of each personality. Then your pictures, which up till now have been unfailingly uniform, will become portraits that are as diverse as their models, the resemblance to whom will greatly add to our pleasure.

How may this be done? Descend from those heights where detail is lost to view. Abandon those stilts that you call buskins.[3] Shed that dazzling purple mantle that so fatigues the eyes. Discard the brazen masque with its unchanging features. Show us life as it really is, in all its variety. Show us its people, with all their petty inconsistencies. No longer set before us fine statues, but men of flesh and blood such as we all are. Give us a *Richard III* who is ugly and hunchbacked and not an Apollo-Belvedere, dressed up in leggings and a cardinal's hat.

Let each historical character be true to historical fact. Let him speak, not just as we speak, but as he himself must have spoken. 'Pasque-Dieu', let Louis XI exclaim, and Louis XIV 'jarnicoton', if he must, for realism springs from such individual touches as these.

Another change must come about in tragedy as a direct result of this, namely that the familiar and elevated styles will be mixed together as circumstances dictate.

The art of changing the style of language and speech at will is a difficult one. The example of how to do this comes from abroad, and it has rarely been successful. It has almost always been too poetic or too familiar. I know of but one man who achieved what he set out to do in this genre and he has only once been entirely successful. I refer to Schiller, and to *Guillaume Tell*.

Guillaume Tell has up to now been the major work of romantic tragedy, and it will remain so for a long time. It concerns the noblest and grandest theme that is open to development by poetic genius. It deals not merely with Tell's adventures, but with the liberation of the Swiss nation. The real hero of the work is Switzerland; we are shown all kinds of people from the three cantons in all kinds of situations; they range from Ruodi the fisherman to the venerable Baron Attinghausen whose majestic figure so poetically dominates this vast composition. This noble old man places patriotism before all personal interest and he dies with these prophetic words on his lips that express the whole future of mankind: 'Ah, Our help is no longer needed. I can go down into the tomb without regret. Our time is at an end. A new power will be able to win back the rights and titles of the human race.'

Tell, here, is no fine orator, giving voice to philosophical sentiments at every opportune moment, reciting in measured tones long and impassioned speeches on the virtues of liberty. Tell is a hunter and nothing more. We feel that whatever boldness and poetry are in his speech, they naturally belong

---

[3] Thick-soled boots worn by actors in ancient tragedy to give them added height (eds.)

to his way of life; only when he is on the mountain tops, or when he is there in his imagination is he a poet. He is a courageous peasant, but peace-loving by nature. Only when no other course of action is possible does he resort to arms to defend himself. Listen to him, when Stauffacher is trying to incite him to rebellion:

[Tell]: The serpent only bites when he is tormented. They will ultimately tire if they see we are unmoved.

Stauffacher: We could do so much if we were united.

Tell: When one is alone in the midst of the tempest one can save oneself more easily.

Stauffacher: By being so indifferent, are you not neglecting the common interest?

Tell: One can only depend with certainty on oneself.

Stauffacher: Union gives strength to the weak.

Tell: The strong man is more powerful when he is alone.

Stauffacher: So the country cannot depend on you if, in its despair, it takes to arms?

Tell: (grasping his hand) Tell descends to the bottom of an abyss to rescue a lamb. Would he then desert his friends? Whatever enterprise you have in mind, do not call me to your counsels. I am no good at planning, nor can I remain inactive for any length of time. But if you have need of me for an exploit that you have agreed upon, then call Tell. He will not fail you.

I cannot go into a detailed analysis of Schiller's tragedy, but read it for yourselves.

To recapitulate: there are the following differences between romantic and classical drama:

The one depicts generic, metaphysical beings of a kind that are nowhere to be found in nature; the other depicts people as they were or as they must have been: everyday, ordinary people.

The one puts into every mouth a standardised form of speech, such as has never been used; the other on the contrary seeks to give each person a style that suits his character.

The one restricts dramatic action to a period of twenty-four hours and to one place; the other prolongs it at will, changing the scene as often as the sense demands.

When from this, you recognise the classical style, delay no further! Rise up as one body and set off in hot pursuit!

Chapter 9 About music

The lyre is a blessing of the Gods!

It will readily be seen that this chapter cannot but be an excursion abroad. Up till now the French have been feeble imitators, doing no more than follow in the footsteps of the Italians and the Germans. In this respect we have been classicists, though our models have not.

Of all the imaginative arts, music is certainly the most recent. Since the discovery of harmony and the scale its domain has continually grown. There has been steady progress from perfection to perfection, and who knows where the future may lead?

The public (and I refer here to those few people who shut themselves up in a theatre after having dined well and offer opinions with the greatest aplomb that seem all too often to be utter gibberish), the public, I say, would be not a little astonished if the director of the Bouffes took it into his head to produce Pergolesi's *Serva padrona*, or some other piece by Leo, Durante or Sarti.

These were men of genius, none the less, though they spoke a language that was not yet fully formed. We owe them nothing more than our musical syntax, and yet how many sleepless nights, how much effort, how many groping experiments, how much unfruitful and uncertain labour did not their music cost them!

Sad to say, Gluck was a German, for Gluck greatly enlarged the domain of his art. His most original work was composed in France, and it would indeed be pleasant to think of him as a national figure. But no such self-conceit is permitted us.

Gluck drew from the human voice effects (considered in instrumental terms) that were unknown before. Many of his choruses are of a very high order; he knew how to give meaning to each chord and a sense of shape to progressions of chords.

The energetic expression that he has imparted to his recitatives also gives him another claim to glory. The scene, 'Armide, vous m'allez quitter!' is still and will always be a masterpiece. After Gluck there appeared three men of whom one might say, as is customarily said of Pascal and Boileau, 'They have established the language.' These are Paisiello, Cimarosa and Mozart.

It is not the function of this study, which in other respects has been very impartial, to go into the respective merits of these three great men. As far as we are concerned they are classics, although they were romantics in their day. In one of his letters Gluck speaks of a young madcap who has turned all the rules of music upsidedown, and 'who put into a single duo ideas that were sufficient to make a whole opera'. This young madcap was Mozart.

In those days it was indeed understood that a piece of music should be based on a single idea, a precious principle for those who had little imagination! This was the principle that the connoisseurs described as music's logic, and the pedants as music's science.

What would Gluck have said if he had been able to hear the aria from *The Secret Marriage*, 'Pria che spunti'? A good dressing down to Cimarosa would hardly have sufficed to atone for the violated rules.

Since then, if experience has shown us that though a piece which is constructed out of a single well-managed motif may well give us a high opinion of the composer's competence, one that is built upon several ideas is just as logically satisfactory, provided that the ideas are of such a kind that each seems to prepare for and introduce the other. Such a composition, moreover, has the advantage of variety.

The different types of movement, the way in which the voices are handled, the still more difficult art of accompaniment, the structure of the movements, the art of placing them in a large work with such skill that the spectator listens to the whole without fatigue or boredom, the harmonic progressions, the management of melodic cadences, in a word, everything that comes under the heading of syntax and musical rhetoric, all this has been established by Cimarosa, Paisiello and Mozart.

One or two men have been carried away by excessive zeal, none the less, and have been seen making the attempt to sacrifice themselves on the altar of a new God, when in truth there was no cause for such sacrifice. But they have merely been laughed at, for what can the impudence of the schoolboy do against the glory of the Master?

One has to admit, nevertheless, that much had still to be done by the men of genius who came after. We sense now that our ears have accustomed themselves to new habits. Run through the score of *The Secret Marriage*. Each movement, on its own, will enchant you; indeed, they are all wholly admirable. None others have greater spirit or verve; nowhere else will you find ideas of greater originality, expressed in a more elegant or purer style. But listen to the whole opera, and towards the middle of the first act you will fall into a kind of languor which not even the most striking passage will easily dispel! I must confess that I have often surprised myself by yawning as I exclaim at the end of a movement, 'How fine that was!', even when I felt that the praise had never been more justified!

This even happened to me during a performance of *Le nozze di Figaro*, a work in which genius is certainly not wanting!

We have all experienced the feeling. What is its cause?

There is too great a sameness about the movements. Almost all the pieces of the old school are *andante*, or *adagio* or *largo*. The *allegro* and its derivatives occur but rarely, nor are they as extensively developed. This sameness cannot but produce fatigue, in the long run.

A second cause of boredom is a lack of variety in harmonic procedures. There is a certain timidity about them which in large measure destroys the effect of the modulations and takes the point away from them.

Yet another cause is the weakness of the *forte*; they did not know how to make a loud noise, or perhaps they were afraid to do so. It is clear however that the more the power of an orchestra is increased, the wider becomes the possible dynamic range between *pianissimo* and *fortissimo*.

These are three faults that any artist or well informed amateur cannot help noticing in the ancient school, faults that have been corrected by the modern school.

It is remarkable that in almost every respect romantic criticism has preceded romantic art. In music, however, quite the reverse is true.

The outcry and uproar that first greeted the *Barbier de Seville* will long be remembered! What a concert of bitter and passionate criticism there was in the newspapers, the cafes and salons! The *Barbier* was a ridiculous work which denied one everything that one had a right to expect of a musical work. According to one critic, the composer had the necessary technique and knowledge but no gift for melody. Another said that he had a great deal of imagination and an abundance of melody, but not the slightest idea how to use them, and what, the critic asked, is genius without knowledge?

All were agreed, however, that he was a madman, that he was trying to outdo his masters and that he was not worthy to be compared with them. He had set out to remake Paisiello's *Barbier de Seville*; a single piece of Paisiello's was worth more than all Rossini's compositions, put together.

These remarks were repeated by so many people, so constantly and so loudly, that the director of the Bouffes – a very talented and intelligent man – resolved to put an end to it all, once and for all. He alternated Paisiello's work with that of his young rival.

The Cabaleurs have always suffered from the fact that the public can never be persuaded to go to the theatre with any other object in view than pure amusement.

What was the result of all this then? The goal of the arts simply being pleasure and diversion, the presence or absence of the public will in the last resort decide all those questions on which the critics have fruitlessly expended floods of ink.

This is what happened on that occasion. The theatre, which was consistently full for performances of Rossini's *Barbier* was consistently empty for Paisiello's.

And so the great trial was decided.

Rossini was the man that the state of the art of music and of public taste required. He was the man of his time, as were Voltaire, Mirabeau and Napoleon.

Is there no greater variety, then, than that to be found in the works of this master? Has no one else been able to grip the audience's attention as he has done, and to hold it without a hint of boredom from beginning to end?

How diverse are the movements that he writes; how greatly he has expanded their limits! How broad his *andantes* are, and how lively his *allegros*!

How boldly and felicitously he modulates!

How rich and varied are his accompaniments! How well he subordinates the accompaniment to the vocal line, using it as a support and to give additional emphasis to the voice, without ever a note being wasted!

And then, how vigorous and energetic are his *tuttis*, how rich and varied his instrumentation! How skilled he is in assigning a part of each orchestral instrument, so that each speaks the language that is best suited to it!

Could so vigorous, so brilliant, so unpredictable and so original a talent possibly have escaped such success?

We will have occasion to discuss this great man and his numerous works at greater length in a chapter specially devoted to him. For the moment we will go on to consider some of the other musicians who also have been great and whose innovations have not been less felicitous.

Before Rossini had ever appeared, Beethoven was already a celebrity. Beethoven was one of those phenomena to whom nature declares, as they are brought forth, 'There you are; create!' (*Te voilà, crée!*)

I can say, without contradicting myself in any way, that original genius as he was, Rossini owed much to Beethoven.

And, when we come to think of it, is not the human mind made in such a way that one idea sparks off another, the latest always being dependent on the penultimate one?

Would Beethoven himself have become what he is had he not followed Joseph Haydn and Mozart?

But it is to him alone that we owe those unprepared modulations of the third and minor sixth and the gigantic sounds that accompany them, and which so powerfully grip the listener's imagination.

It is to Beethoven that we must attribute those extremely rapid movements, in which the accompaniment marks out every beat of the measure, while the melody graphically weaves its design overhead.

Yet another man has appeared since Beethoven, one alas who has been very shortlived. He too broke new ground; and who knows where this would have taken him? Like Rossini he had the knowledge to apply to the theatre those immense resources that Beethoven had devoted to instrumental music. Setting out from the same point as his rival he took a different route and he has travelled just as far. Why, though, did he not learn more about the mechanism of the human voice? Weber conceived some astonishing works; he was an admirable symphonist, and indeed his claim to glory would be unimpeachable were he not a permanent nightmare to his singers.

As for us Frenchmen, it is painful to confess that we have lagged very much behind our rivals. Our role up to now has always been to follow in their footsteps. Our composers seem to have taken for their motto: 'Tu longe sequere, et vestigia semper adora'.

One man amongst us, however, is no stranger to this great movement which for the past thirty years has shaken musical Europe. He is Méhul.

Méhul has only dared to go halfway, however, whether out of a sense of modesty, or through lack of powerful inspiration, or whether even through fear of criticism of the kind that often discourages and embitters genius. He is a learned harmonist, but his instrumentation is often weak and dull. His vigorous imagination is at its best in a quartet or a finale, but it allows itself to be imprisoned within the narrow confines of a romance or couplet for two voices (a duo, as it is called). Just imagine a six foot man, enveloped in swaddling clothes, recumbent in a wicker cradle and turning a rattle in his mouth! Méhul is obviously impatient of the yoke of routine, but he dares to do nothing to shake if off. We need a rebellious man such as Rossini, by way of example, who took for his motto: 'Scriro per la canaglia' – 'I write for the rabble', assured in the knowledge that the rabble would soon become the entire public.

For us Frenchmen, then, musical romanticism, can you believe it, is singing in grand opera!

Yes, singing, I repeat. And do you recall the greatest praise that enlightened journalists could pay a new musical work? This music, they said, is declaimed (*déclamé*) to perfection. At that time, indeed, opera was declaimed, whilst on the other hand, tragedy was sung.[4]

It yet remains for all the instruments of the orchestra to be used, not indiscriminately and on every occasion as MM. So and So have done, but freely, without being cramped by the customs that have been followed from time immemorial in our hidebound Académie royale de musique.

It remains also to follow certain rules in the distribution of movements; to avoid beginning an act with a recitative; to avoid following a septet with a concluding solo; to avoid, moreover, placing all the arias at the beginning of a scene and the recitatives at the end.

In tragedy, moreover, we must come down somewhat from the strenuous heights that our predecessors had screwed themselves up to; we must let the august races of Oedipus and Agamemnon rest a little; we must allow our singers to abandon their buskins and mantles, now and again, for modern trousers and shoes, a change that will particularly benefit those who are gifted with fine voices rather than good legs.

As for the opera which is called comic (but which in truth is not always so) reforms are equally necessary, though they will be more difficult to accomplish. No decision has been reached yet as to whether singing is obligatory, and M. and Mesdames So and So will continue to support the opposition for some time to come!

However, the *Dame Blanche* has inflicted a terrible blow on them, from which they will recover with difficulty. *Masaniello* and *Guillaume Tell*, happily rejuvenated by a man of talent, have renewed the demonstration. The fruits of the tree of knowledge have been gathered, and despite MM. Auber, Fétis, Krebuč, etc., etc., the old Adam must sooner or later die!

See also Bibliography under: Keys

---

[4] The author refers here to the singsong style of declamation adopted by the actors, in tragedy (eds.)

Johann Wolfgang von Goethe

(b. Frankfurt-am-Main, 28 Aug. 1749; d. Weimar, 22 Mar. 1832)

From: *Wilhelm Meisters Wanderjahre* (1829) quoted in *Schriften zur Kunst*, ed. Rolf-Dieter Denker (Munich 1962), vol. 2, p. 257

It is perhaps in music that the dignity of art is most eminently apparent, for music has no material element that has to be taken into account. It consists entirely of form and content; and it elevates and ennobles everything that it expresses.

Fétis[1]

From: *La Musique mise à la portée de tout le monde* (Paris 1830);
translated as *Music Explained to the World* (London 1844), pp. 278–9

Suppose that an audience, capable of appreciating music, is assembled at the representation of a new opera; that the name of the composer is unknown; and that the kind of music is new, and of such an originality, that all the musical habits of the audience are disturbed. This, then, I think, would be the proper way to analyse the new composition:

The first effect of a celebrated name is to inspire confidence, and to give us favourable prepossessions; by a contrary effect, we feel a sort of distrust of an unknown name; and the first impulse is to condemn things with which we are not acquainted. We desire novelty, but we must determine what is new. We fear to compromise ourselves; and as, in general, there are fewer good things than bad, we think it safer to condemn, at first, than to approve. There is much security in reputation; it does not require the annunciation of public opinion, and this is already something; then, it is almost certain that beauties as well as defects will be found in the work; and thus we may express opinions which will not compromise us for the future. Such, one cannot doubt, are the causes of the premature opinions which are every day expressed. These things are the results of human nature and society. The first rule to be established before proceeding to an analysis of the sensations which we experience upon hearing a new work, is, therefore, to distrust our prepossessions, and to be satisfied that we rarely escape being deceived by them at first. The difficulty of escaping deception is increased when the style of music is new; for it is very rare that extreme originality does not offend at first. Let one recall the unfavourable judgement which was passed upon the music of the *Barber of Seville* at its first representation, and upon the compositions of Beethoven when they were heard for the first time. These examples ought to serve as lessons. We shall have gained much, when we cease to be precipitate in our opinions; for it costs much less to suspend our judgement than to take back what we have said. How often has it happened to us to persist in manifest errors, only because we have avowed them, and because we are interested in them, by an ill-understood self-love!

There are other reasons which ought to put us on our guard against the tendency to preconceived opinions for or against anything. What music is there, however good, which has not lost its charm in consequence of a bad execution? What insipidity has not fascinated the senses, when interpreted

[1] For a discussion of the author's work see the editorial introduction on p. 400.

by great artists? Music, as it comes from the hand of the composer, is a mere idea: the performance, good or bad, makes something or nothing of it.

It is also a result of human nature to believe that every thing is going on improving in the arts and in literature, as in industry. Hence we think ourselves entitled to call in question ancient reputations, and to pronounce a final opinion upon them. But in these strange decisions, in which we are generally inclined to determine that past generations have done wrong in admiring the productions of their own times, we make no account of the difference of circumstances, of the prevalent forms of fashion, nor of the traditions of execution which are lost. We think ourselves sufficiently informed, after an imperfect hearing, in which we were much more disposed to look for the ridiculous than to listen in a true spirit. How frequent are judgements of this kind!

E. F.

From: *Revue musicale*, vol. 5 (1830), pp. 231–6

This is an unusually explicit statement, inspired no doubt by the 1830 Revolution, of an idea that is to be found more and more frequently during the early years of the nineteenth century, namely that the creative artist is always ahead of his time.[1] France was perhaps a natural breeding ground for such an idea, where opposition to innovation – particularly in the field of opera – was so well organised.[2] The writer none the less shows an awareness of the nature of historical change that is rarely to be found in earlier discussions. As Edouard Fétis (the son of François Joseph Fétis, founder of the *Revue Musicale*) was only eighteen at the time, he is unlikely to have been the 'E. F.' of this article.

Romanticism in music (Le romantisme en musique)

What is this romanticism? And is it necessary? These are questions that for the past fifteen years have been the subject of lively debate. They have resulted in much animosity and are constantly being discussed, but they are, I would suggest, less new than is generally supposed. Romanticism can be identified in every phase of the history of the arts, under different names. It will last as long the arts, and as long as time itself. Have not timid or hidebound men always mistrusted anything that smacked of inventiveness, condemning every infringement of the rules that they have grown to believe are inviolable? They have persuaded themselves that the artists whom they admire are inimitable, and they cannot see that for this very reason these men are not to be imitated. This is so today, and it will be so every time one generation gives place to another. One of our faults is to reject the notion that we can grow old; most men are so in love with the idea of youth that they arrive at an advanced old age with the tastes and opinions of young men, precisely because they lament the times that are gone. They have witnessed the triumphs of works that have brought about revolutions in the arts, and they will not admit that there are other things to be admired. Nor do they remember that they themselves once looked for new delights in new things. What a number of people then inveigh against the bad taste of the times, in which Rossini has replaced Grétry, and Beethoven, Haydn; these are the people who censure Lamartine, Byron and Hugo, because these men

---

[1] An idea that Ernest Newman fascinatingly demolishes in his *A Musical Critic's Holiday* (London 1925).

[2] See for instance William L. Croston's discussion of the claque, in *French Grand Opera: An Art and a Business* (New York 1948; and 1972), p. 41ff.

of genius have broken out of the shackles imposed upon them by a system. The men who reject all idea of creativity do not understand that the idols they worship were never imitative.

Another equally major consideration serves to confirm certain people in the absurd belief that we should not venture outside the all-too-narrow limits dictated by taste and habit. This is the work of the artists themselves. It is natural enough that the men who earn a living from the arts of literature, painting and music show a stubborn opposition to progress since this (if its worth were recognised) would deprive them of part of their livelihood, or oblige them to follow new paths for which most of them are unsuited on grounds of age. These people may be seen defending their art with a pretended disinterest. They have good reason to do so; being forced to continue to work a system that they cannot escape and which is no longer in accordance with the needs of the times, they try to stem the torrent, to seek support from things that they themselves have made threadbare, and they make constant efforts to maintain and preserve the doctrines that they profess.

The many revolutions that have taken place in the arts are a necessary consequence of the movement and progress of the human spirit. Each age has its needs, related to its historical position, its customs and the nature of its society. The music of the most ancient nations was at first confined to a small number of notes. The scales that seem so limited to us were sufficient for their needs because music was then no more than the accessory of poetry. Only long afterwards were other notes added, each innovation in the musical system bringing down accusations of extravagance. At first the new notes seemed superfluous, for men had managed without them before then. If we go through the annals of musical history we shall find that every musical innovation has been the object of violent attack. When the simple melodies of Alessandro Scarlatti were supplanted by the more varied and complicated songs of Leo and Pergolesi, it was said that music was in decline, just as more recently the admirers of Monsigny and Dalyrac have complained that the compositions of these masters have been cast aside. The idols of present taste will likewise be sacrificed, for art cannot go backwards; there may be a moment of pause but when a man of genius comes to the fore, change will again be rapid.

When the first comic opera was mounted, the art of music seemed to have reached its peak. Yet, with each generation, tastes have changed; the arts have been forced to take new directions, and they have obeyed the forces to which they have been subject. Since there have been so many revolutions during the course of musical history how can it ever be imagined that music should restrict its talents, when it ought to seek to multiply them? And why should music alone remain stationary when all the arts, which are modified according to time and place, meet the demands of their day and rule (to put it briefly) over the spirits of those that they are intended to move? When the current musical forms have aged, a new way will open up, an untouched treasure-trove will be offered to those who know how to make use of it. The invention of new instruments and unaccustomed rhythms will give new means for effects that we cannot guess at, but which the future will reveal. A superior being will emerge, having ideas, originality, and faults, one destined by nature to bring about change. He will at first be repulsed, but unjustified opposition will fall away before the profound conviction of an independent genius, and soon the man who was first condemned will be admired. Such is the inevitable chain of events that centuries of experience should have taught us, if only the mind could rid itself of prejudice. But as has already been said, we grow old; in some measure we live on the memories of our youth and we do not notice that minds have undergone fundamental changes.

Are not the arts, moreover, conventional currency, like gold and silver? Do they not, even more than these metals, have a value that derives from the pleasure we take in them? Their whole merit lies in the pleasure that they afford; that is the only balance in which they may be weighed. The people who claim authority to decide on such matters must be out of their minds, people who believe themselves called to judge what we need, who condemn the taste of such and such age, and who praise that of another. Are they so sure of their own judgement? The only difference between one age and another is a difference of feeling. To condemn feeling is a madness; to try to repress it is even greater madness. Indeed, how can an opinion that has been held by a whole nation be ridiculed? How may one set oneself up as a judge of taste and pleasure? There are composers today who seem to lack distinction and yet who have one great merit: that of speaking to their contemporaries in an appropriate language, one that in musical matters meets contemporary needs and knowledge. No one can ask us to account for our tastes. A nation can be instructed in the secrets of music which thereby enhance its musical pleasures; but as to making up a nation's mind for it, can this be ever possible? Feelings of pleasure can never be based upon reason; they are spontaneous; no one can shield himself from them for the very good reason that they are not subject to outside influences.

The natural dispositions of young people must on no account be shackled; this is a truth that few people have understood. Most professors will not bother themselves, for instance, with those of their pupils who refuse to follow blindly the paths that they have mapped out for them. How many young people have raised themselves above the level of mediocrity, curbed as they were in the development of their faculties, but who none the less might have aspired to distinction had they been allowed more freedom! Who could have seen, in view of the scant success that Rossini's operas had when they first appeared, that the same works would echo throughout the whole of France, throughout Europe, and indeed throughout the entire world, and that in the wake of this brilliant genius would follow a host of imitators, gleaning after him in the vast field that he had harvested? Who would have thought that Beethoven, after thirty years of neglect, would succeed at last in overcoming the opposition that had been mounted against him? What can be said of all this? That it was unfair to belittle the works of such composers? No; but that the moment had not yet come for them to be understood; that they were not yet right for the taste of the age. To deny their merits now would be more than unjust, for they have accomplished their work.

Let us allow full and complete liberty then to those who are determined to be independent, and let us place no obstacles in the paths that they have chosen to follow. There is no need to fear that they may obtain undeserved success. The public, which is guided by common-sense instincts well knows what suits it. If it is displeased by the works that are submitted to it, it knows how to do justice by them. Let us wait, though, until it has pronounced judgement before saying that it is seeking such or such thing, or that it rejects others. Complaisant performers, do not publish abroad the judgements of the public before it has itself judged. In music as in literature, let independence of thought be the guiding principle in everything. Free your consciences from every kind of yoke and do not attempt to monopolise the things to which no one has an exclusive right. Liberty! Let that be the sacred word for us all!

William Crotch

(b. Norwich, 5 July 1775; d. Taunton, 29 Dec. 1847)

From: *Substance of Several Courses of Lectures on Music, read in the University of Oxford and in the Metropolis* (London 1831), chs. 1–3

Crotch gave his first organ recitals at the age of three, having taught himself the national anthem (both hands) when only two years and three weeks old. In 1786 he went to Cambridge, studying with the Professor of Music, Dr Randall, and playing the organ at Trinity College, King's College and the university church. By 1789 he had moved to Oxford with a view to studying for the church; for various reasons however the scheme did not materialise, and in 1790 he found himself successor to Thomas Norris as organist of Christ Church. In 1797 he became professor of music at Oxford, and in 1822 first Principal of the newly founded Royal Academy of Music in London. He was an assiduous composer, widely versed in the arts, and like Mendelssohn, a skilled draftsman and painter.

His *Substance of Several Courses* is based upon materials that he prepared for lectures at Oxford and London, 1800–4 and 1820. These reveal considerable breadth of reading, and they include a wealth of practical illustration from all the fine arts that is lacking in most previous discussions of aesthetics.

For further reading:
J. Rennert, *William Crotch, 1775–1874, composer, artist, teacher* (Lavenham 1975).

Ch. 1: Introduction

The good composer must not, therefore, write for the majority of hearers; he must not be discouraged by the inattention or censures of the public. Let him look to Sebastian Bach 'who (says his biographer) never worked for the crowd but always had in his mind an ideal perfection without any view to approbation. He sung only for himself and the Muses.' Were the majority always in the right, why are the Battle of Prague and Pleyel's concertante which they so much admired, now passed into oblivion to make way for similar trash? Were the majority always wrong, we should thus have another rule for determining our own opinions. But they are not to be trusted. And when I attend public concerts and hear, as is too frequently the case, the undeserved applause bestowed on some new trifle, I am tempted to apply to them what Sir Joshua Reynolds says of the public exhibitions of paintings, 'Popularity always accompanies the lower styles of painting. I mention this, because our exhibitions, while they produce such admirable effects by nourishing emulation and calling out genius, have also a mischievous tendency by seducing the painter to an ambition of pleasing the mixed multitude of people who resort to them.' Certainly, however, it is the wish of the composer to please, if possible, all hearers, both the discerning few and the unpretending multitude. He would if he could, acquire both immediate and lasting fame. He would if possible have all men on his side. He therefore argues with them and endeavours to persuade them to adopt his opinions when he cannot agree to theirs. These endeavours are not usually crowned with success. A lasting reputation is seldom acquired quickly. It is by a slower process, by the prevailing commendation of a few real judges, that true worth is finally discovered and rewarded. The opinions of acknowledged critics accumulate in time and are compacted into a mass that irresistibly bears down before it all the opposition of false taste and ignorance. Hence, the artist who lives unnoticed and neglected, often after death acquires immortal fame. Marcello, who was at first too highly extolled and afterwards as much undervalued, has found his true level among the great classical composers. The *Prince of Venosa* was hailed as the brightest of the rising luminaries, then suddenly went down and was no more remembered. 'Giant Handel' was driven by 'the Goddess of Dulness ... to the Hibernian shore,'[1] but is now placed highest in the temple of Fame. The prevalence of true taste would have altered all these cases by immediately determining the merits of the candidate. But it is said that the taste of the critic should even equal that of the composer as in the sister art, 'whatever speculative knowledge is necessary for the artist is equally and indispensably so to the connoisseur.'[2] Taste cannot be too much or too carefully cultivated.

I now have to offer a few hints on the frame of mind which the student should assume if he would derive due benefit from the remaining part of the present work.

He must place little or no reliance, at first, on his own judgement. He must revere the characters of the classical composers of former ages: they have acquired a celebrity which has outlived and triumphed over the false taste of the times in which they flourished. 'He who begins by presuming on his own taste, has ended his studies as soon as he has commenced them.'[3] Neither let him be dazzled with the sudden blaze of newly-kindled reputation. Experienced critics alone are able to distinguish what is good or bad in new productions; and even they do not find the task easy. He will be sure to meet with those who would recommend their own and other modern works in preference to those of the early masters, 'who,' say they, 'however eminent at the time they lived, have been long superseded'. But

> the modern, who recommends himself as a standard, may justly be suspected as ignorant of the true end and unacquainted with the proper objects of the art which he professes. To follow such a guide will not only retard the student but mislead

[1] Alexander Pope, *The Dunciad*, (London 1728–43) Bk. 4, lines 65–70.
[2] Sir Joshua Reynolds. *Discourses on Art*. ed. R. A. Wark (New Haven 1975), seventh discourse, p. 123 (eds.)
[3] Reynolds, *Discourses*, first discourse, p. 17.

him. On whom then shall he rely? Or who shall show him the path that leads to excellence? The answer is obvious. Those great masters who have travelled the same road with success are the most likely to conduct others. The works of those who have stood the test of ages have a claim to that respect and veneration to which no modern can pretend. The duration and stability of their fame is sufficient to evince that it has not been suspended upon the slender thread of fashion and caprice, but bound to the heart by every tie of sympathetic approbation.[4]

Who these great masters were, it may be easy to discover; but the degree of veneration in which they ought to be held, and the comparative excellence of their several productions may not be so obvious to the student. It is probable that, far from being enraptured, he would at first be disappointed and even displeased with their works and tempted to throw them aside as dull, heavy, monotonous, void of feeling, expression and effect. But to experienced judges they constitute what the remains of antiquity are to painters, architects and sculptors. Let him then, 'regard them as perfect and infallible guides; as subjects for his imitation, not his criticism'.[5]

So great indeed ought to be his deference for their superiority that it has been said, 'to feign an approbation of them would be venial, as it would probably terminate in sincerity and true taste'. But as long as sincerity is wanting, a submissive silence is rather recommended.

Ch. 2: On the three styles of music – the sublime, the beautiful, and the ornamental

As there are certain principles common to the fine arts, music may be considered in reference to other arts, with a view of improving the taste, by an analogical application to music of those principles admitted to be true in respect of the other arts. 'To enlarge the boundaries of the art as well as to fix its principles, it is necessary that that art and those principles should be considered in their correspondence with the principles of other arts which, like this, address themselves primarily and principally to the imagination.'[6]

On this plan the founder of the British school of painting whose just sentiments and forcible language I cannot too often quote, raised an academy with which, it is allowed, the similar institutions of other nations will not bear a comparison.

It is by the analogy that one art bears to another that many things are ascertained which either were but faintly seen or perhaps would not have been discovered at all if the inventor had not received the first hints from the practice of a sister art on a similar occasion. The frequent allusions which every man who treats of any art is obliged to make to others in order to illustrate and confirm his principles,

---

[4] Reynolds, *Discourses*, second discourse, p. 28.
[5] Reynolds, *Discourses*, first discourse, p. 17.
[6] Reynolds, *Discourses*, thirteenth discourse, p. 229.

sufficiently show their near connection and inseparable relation. All arts having the same general end which is to please, and addressing themselves to the same faculties through the medium of the senses, it follows that their rules and principles must have as great an affinity as the different materials and the different organs or vehicles by which they pass to the mind, will permit them to retain.[7]

'There is then (says another elegant author[8]), a general harmony and correspondence in all our sensations when they affect us by means of different senses; and these causes (as Mr Burke[9] has admirably explained) can never be so clearly ascertained when we confine our observations to one sense only.' Music is not indeed like painting, an imitative art, but 'applies itself like architecture and poetry, directly to the imagination, without the intervention of any kind of imitation.'[10] 'There are in music as in other arts, certain styles which are more or less valuable in proportion to the mental labour employed in their formation.'[11] Music, like painting, may be divided into three styles, the sublime, the beautiful, and the ornamental. Sir Joshua Reynolds does not avowedly adopt this division. He speaks of the sublime and ornamental only. But that which he calls the sublime evidently includes the beautiful; and that which he calls the ornamental seems analogous to the picturesque. We cannot peruse the celebrated work on the sublime and beautiful, without admitting that the distinction between them is there made manifest.

The sublime and beautiful have been accurately described in an essay, the early splendour of which, not even the full meridian blaze of its illustrious author was able to eclipse. The picturesque has a character no less separate and distinct than either the sublime or the beautiful; nor less independent of the art of painting. The term picturesque (as we may judge from its etymology) is applied only to objects of sight, and indeed in so confined a manner as to be supposed merely to have a reference to the art from which it is named: I am well convinced however, that the name and reference only are limited and uncertain, and that the qualities which make objects picturesque are not only as distinct as those which make them beautiful or sublime but are equally extended to all our sensations by whatever organs they are received; and that music (though it appears like a solecism) may be as truly picturesque according to the general principles of picturesqueness as it may be beautiful or sublime according to those of beauty or sublimity. The English word picturesque naturally draws the mind towards pictures; and from that partial and confined view of the subject, what is in truth only an illustration of picturesqueness, becomes the foundation of it. The words sublime and beautiful have not the same etymological reference to any one visible art, and therefore are applied to objects of the other senses. Sublime, indeed, in the language from which it is taken, means high; and therefore perhaps in strictness, should relate to objects of sight only; yet we no more scruple to call one of Handel's choruses sublime

---

[7] Reynolds, *Discourses*, seventh discourse, p. 133.

[8] Uvedale Price, *An Essay on the Picturesque* (London 1794).

[9] Burke, *A Philosophical Enquiry into the Origin of our Ideas of the Sublime and the Beautiful* (London 1757) [see pp. 69–74].

[10] Harris, *Three Treatises* (London 1744) [see pp. 36–9].

[11] Reynolds, *Discourses*, fourth discourse, p. 57.

than Corelli's pastorale beautiful. But should any person, simply and without qualifying expressions, call a capricious movement of Domenico Scarlatti or Haydn, picturesque, he would with great reason be laughed at; for it is not a term applied to sounds: yet such a movement, from its sudden, unexpected and abrupt transitions, from a certain playful wildness of character and an appearance of irregularity, is no less analogous to similar scenery in nature than the concerto or the chorus, to what is grand or beautiful to the eye.[12]

That this third style may be denominated the ornamental, and that Sir Joshua Reynolds meant no other, I infer from his using the expression, 'the picturesque or ornamental style';[13] and this he opposes to that higher walk of the art which he calls the sublime, and which includes the beautiful. An attempt, therefore, will be made in these lectures to improve the taste of the student by enabling him to appreciate the merits of any composition by considering the comparative value of the style adopted by its author. And if by this mode of considering the subject we find that the art is on the decline, let us not regret that we have discovered Truth, though she may seem to frown on us. Her brightness, which enables us to detect our error, will also help us to recover from it. Let criticism be just, and artists will pay it due respect. Let the higher walks of the art be pointed out, and new productions will soon spring up and adorn them.

Music then, I repeat, like other arts, may be divided into three styles – the sublime, the beautiful and the ornamental – which are sometimes distinct and sometimes combined.

The sublime is founded on principles of vastness and incomprehensibility. The word sublime originally signifies high, lofty, elevated; and this style accordingly never descends to anything small, delicate, light, pretty, playful or comic. The grandest style in music is therefore the sacred style – that of the church and oratorio – for it is least inclined to levity, where levity is properly inadmissible and where the words convey the most awful and striking images. Infinity and what is next to it, immensity, are among the most efficient causes of this quality; and when we hear innumerable voices and instruments sounding the praises of God in solemn and becoming strains, the most sublime image that can fill the mind seldom fails to present itself – that of the heavenly host described in the Holy Scriptures,[14] and thus paraphrased by the poet:

> all
> The multitude of angels, with a shout
> Loud as from numbers without number, sweet
> As from blest voices, uttering joy, heaven rung
> With jubilee, and loud hosannas fill'd
> The heavenly regions.[15]

[12] Price, *Essay*.
[13] I feel much pleasure in finding that Mr Samuel Wesley, in his *Lectures on Music*, has adopted the same division.
[14] Revel. v. 8–14; xiv. 1–3; xv. 2–4; xix. 1–6.
[15] Milton, *Paradise Lost*, bk. 3, lines 344–9.

Uniformity is not only compatible with the sublime but is often the cause of it. That general, equal gloom which is spread over all nature before a storm is, in the highest degree, sublime. A blaze of light unmixed with shade, on the same principle, tends to the same effect; and accordingly, Milton has placed light in its most glorious brightness as an inaccessible barrier round the throne of the Almighty.

Simplicity and its opposite, intricacy, when on a large scale (such an intricacy as from the number of its parts becomes incomprehensible), are sublime. Raphael cartoons are simply sublime; Martin's *Belshazzar's Feast* is a specimen of sublime intricacy. The large portico of the Grecian Parthenon or the long arcade of the Roman aqueduct, illustrate simple grandeur;[16] and the Gothic cathedral is an example of sublimity resulting from a vast assemblage of parts. In music, the great compass of notes employed in a full orchestra conveys an idea of vastness undefined. A uniform succession of major chords, the most agreeable of all sounds, resembles a blaze of light, while the unintelligible combination of extraneous discords conveys a feeling like that caused by darkness. The clearness of harmony in the madrigal of many voices or in the full anthem, and the deep science of the organ fugue produce sublimity from seemingly opposite causes; as also a passage performed by many voices or instruments in unisons or octaves, and one in full and florid counterpoint.

Pathetic expression, which will be treated of more fully hereafter, is not confined to any one of the three styles, but is most analogous to the ornamental. In painting or sculpture, sorrow robs the countenance of dignity and beauty, but is conducive to picturesque effect.

Beauty in all the arts is the result of softness, smoothness, delicacy, smallness, gentle undulations, symmetry and the like. When therefore in music the melody is vocal and flowing, the measure symmetrical, the harmony simple and intelligible, and the style of the whole soft, delicate, and sweet, it may with as much propriety be called beautiful, as a small, perfect, Grecian temple or a landscape of Claude Lorraine.

The ornamental style is the result of roughness, playful intricacy and abrupt variations. In painting, splendid draperies, intricate architecture, gold or silver cups and vases, and all such objects are ornamental – aged heads, old hovels, cottages or mills, ruined temples or castles, rough animals, peasants at a fair, and the like, are picturesque. In music, eccentric and difficult melody, rapid, broken and varied rhythm, wild and unexpected modulation, indicate this third style.

The three styles are seldom found distinct. A mixture of the sublime and

---

[16] Several words are here used, for the sake of variety, to denote the sublime style which are not strictly synonymous. Sublimity, elevation, and loftiness are so; but grandeur and magnificence imply something of splendour and agreeable attraction. The military man well knows the difference between the grandeur of a parade and the sublimity of a battle. The choruses of Haydn, Mozart, and Beethoven are frequently magnificent, but seldom sublime.

beautiful, though at first it might seem incompatible with the opposite nature of their characters, is sometimes found. The wisdom of Minerva's countenance and the majesty of Juno's did not prevent their being candidates for the prize of beauty though it was probably the cause of their losing it. In music, when the melody is simple and slow, the harmony full and plain and the expression chaste and solemn, it will be as difficult to deny the combined existence of the sublime and beautiful as to determine which predominates. Such a combination forms one of the higher walks of our art.

The sublime and ornamental may be combined, as in the landscapes of Rubens and Gaspar. This is closely analogous to the intricate grandeur already described; and it is illustrated in music by those choruses in which the voices are dignified and the accompaniments varied and playful.

Beauty and ornament are still more frequently blended. 'The sublime by its solemnity takes off from the loveliness of beauty.'[17] The ornamental style 'corrects the languor of beauty and the horror of sublimity but renders their impression less forcible. It is the coquetry of nature. It makes beauty more amusing, more varied, more playful but also "Less winning soft, less amiably mild."'

In music, wherever there is flowing and elegant melody with playful and ingenious accompaniment, this union must be apparent; it forms the leading characteristic of modern music.

The three styles may also be found blended, though rarely without a sensible predominance of that in which the composer excels, or that which is the favourite style of the age in which he lives.

Let us next consider the rank and value of these styles as the basis on which all the elements of musical criticism may safely be established.

The rank and value of each style are deduced from a consideration of the mental labour employed in their formation and the mental capacities required for the comprehension and enjoyment of them. From the time of Longinus at least, who wrote on the subject in the early part of the third century, the invention of whatever is sublime has been esteemed the greatest effort of the human mind. This style, which is emphatically denominated the elevated, the lofty style, may well be called the highest walk of any art. But whether we regard this, with Sir Joshua Reynolds, as including the beautiful, or with Uvedale Price, divide the whole into three styles, the lowest and least estimated is the ornamental. The well known rebuke from his master of the young Grecian painter, for having decked his Helen with ornaments, because he had not the skill to make her beautiful, is a striking illustration of the inferiority of this style. Difficult as execution in music or in painting may appear to the ignorant, it is held in comparative contempt by those who seek for the forms or the sounds that can only be produced or enjoyed by the mind. We say then with Sir Joshua Reynolds, that the highest walk of the art is the sublime and the lowest walk of the art is the

---

[17] Price, *Essay*.

ornamental. But if with Burke we separate the sublime and beautiful into two styles, which shall we prefer? Surely the sublime, as requiring most mind in the person gratified and in the author of the gratification. The mental operations required for writing an epic poem, designing a cathedral, painting a storm or composing a full chorus, must be greater and more extraordinary than those which produce a sonnet, a shrine, a miniature or an ariette. Why was the lecturer in a sister art so anxious to impress on his pupils the merits of Michelangelo? Not because he is generally allowed to be the most pleasing of painters, not because he is the last painter or the favourite of the present day, but because he excelled all others in the sublime style – the pure sublime, not including in this case beauty. How many would pass by his productions who would admire and duly appreciate the truth of Wilkie, or the minuteness of Ostade! Many turn from the vast, the incomprehensible, the awful, the terrific, to find a milder gratification from that which soothes and tranquillises the mind. A still greater number seek for amusement and delight from the wit and humour of the lowest style. A multitude may be satisfied with and even prefer, caricatures. A child, a savage, the weakest mind, may be charmed with beauty of any sort in nature or art – distant views, soft scenery, delicate objects, shells, flowers, minerals, insects, elegant buildings, apartments or gardens, while the same mind would perceive nothing but terror in the storm, danger in the precipice, desolation in the ruin, poverty in the hovel, and barrenness in the rocky mountain. Some minds may however feel what is forcibly striking and grand, while the less obtrusive merits of the pure sublime will not appear to them to have any effect. Pope, Scott, and Byron have charms for all readers. Milton is comprehended by few, and that few can remember how long it was before they could perceive his excellence. The mind itself must expand before it can comprehend what is so vast. Admiration, wonder, awe and even terror are produced in the mind by the sublime style; beauty pleases, soothes, and enamours; ornament dazzles, delights, amuses and awakens curiosity. Will it not then be readily granted that the value of any style, singly or predominating if combined, may be ascertained by the nature of its impressions? To be amused and delighted is a meaner enjoyment than that of being soothed and charmed; while both are less noble to the mind than feeling itself elevated and expanded. The humorous incidents of a drama make men laugh; the tender and happy parts excite the smile of approbation: but the tragic scenes petrify them into silent, serious, breathless attention. The superiority of the tragedy over the comedy and of both over the farce, is therefore obvious, though the majority of every audience should deny the statement. Illustrations out of all the arts might easily be multiplied. In Grecian architecture the Doric, Ionic and Corinthian orders are respectively in the sublime, beautiful and ornamental styles. Show them to the world: the bending acanthus, the rich entablature and the light proportions of the Corinthian will be instantly preferred by the majority; the chaste elegance and simplicity of the Ionic will charm others; while the massive strength and bold outline of the Doric will be left to the admiration of the remaining minority. Show them again, the sacred edifices of the twelfth, thirteenth and following centuries in this kingdom. Some would venerate and admire the ponderous strength of the massive columns and impenetrable walls of the Norman fabrics. More, thinking these heavy and barbarous, would prefer the lighter shafts and aspiring arches of the early pointed style; while the many would be dazzled and delighted with the lofty spires and pinnacles and the rich tracery in the roofs and windows of the decorated style; and even more so perhaps, with the superbalance of ornament in the perpendicular style which was the sure indication of the decline of the art.

The student has now obtained a rule for discovering and appreciating the value of any piece of music by observing the effect of its style or of its predominant style on real judges. It is sublime if it inspires veneration, beautiful if it pleases, ornamental if it amuses. Whoever then were the greatest composers of the sublime style, they are to be regarded as treading in the highest walks of the art; those of the beautiful occupy another inferior stage near the summit; but those of the ornamental are far below. When two of these styles are combined, a union of the sublime and beautiful ranks first, one of the sublime and ornamental next, and one of the beautiful and ornamental last; and when all are combined, the predominance of any one over the others must be regarded with a reference to its own peculiar value. Such a combination of the three as preserves their due subordination, not permitting the beautiful to take precedence of the sublime, or the ornamental of either of the others, deserves the highest praise.

When these styles prevailed, and who these composers were, shall be considered hereafter.

Ch. 3: On musical expression

Previous to the application of the foregoing general principles, and the attempt to show when these styles prevailed and who were the greatest masters in each, it will be necessary to detain the student on another subject of considerable importance: that of musical expression.

In extolling the descriptive powers of our art, many writers have exceeded the truth, making it capable of what it really cannot achieve. Composers, encouraged by these praises, have become more daring than their predecessors and have drawn upon themselves the censure not merely of sound musical judges but of others, ignorant of the art and only guided by common sense, 'who, though deaf to the charms of music, are not blind to the absurdity of musicians.'[18] The union of music with poetry (making vocal music) has been one fruitful source of these exaggerations. Praise due to the poetry alone has thus been bestowed on the music. Let the poetry cease altogether, or be in an unknown tongue, and then see whether music can

---

[18] Dr Beattie, *An Essay on Poetry and Music* [see pp. 150–6].

build the walls of a city or civilise a savage race. Music has been called the language of nature; but it is a very imperfect language; it is all adjectives and no substantives. It may represent certain qualites in objects or raise similar affections in the mind to what these objects raise but it cannot delineate the objects themselves. It conveys no imagery and cannot even discriminate very accurately between the affections it does command. It may speak of something serene, joyous, wild, tender, grave, melancholy, troubled, agitated or pathetic; but without poetry lends her aid we remain ignorant of what that thing may be. An argumentative writer tells us that

> the fittest subjects for imitation are all such things as are characterised by motion and sound. Motion may be either slow or swift, even or uneven, broken or continuous; sound may be either soft or loud, acute or grave. Wherever, therefore, any of these species of motion or sound may be found in an eminent degree, there will be room for musical imitation. The glidings, tossings and murmurings of water, the bellowing of a storm and the confusion of a battle are all capable of being in some degree imitated in music.

And again, he says, 'Music is a modification of sound, and rhythm is the time or motion of that sound; musical sounds, therefore, may resemble other sounds, and musical motion other motion.'[19] Let the piece be unaccompanied by words or title, and the gliding, tossing, bellowing and confusion will neither represent water, a storm or a battle. Handel has but one and the same favourite soothing melody to express the murmurings or perhaps the undulations of a flowing stream,[20] the repose of the dead,[21] the beauty of the queen,[22] and the softness of spring.[23] In another place, where waves were to be depicted and the roaring of a giant, but one passage is used.[24] The poet says well of this composer, that 'Jove's own thunders follow Mars's drums.'[25] But the drums are obliged to represent sometimes one and sometimes the other.

The student has learned that awe, complacency, and amusement are severally caused by the sublime, beautiful and ornamental styles.[26] Pain and pleasure are awakened by the use of the minor and major keys, of their appropriate concords and discords, and of the chromatic and diatonic scales. The major key is more agreeable to the ear than the minor, and the diatonic scale and discords than the chromatic. In the diatonic scale there are fewer semitones than in the chromatic, and those further apart. The triads of the major key are the same with the perfect chords formed by any

[19] See Harris, *Three Treatises* [pp. 36–9].

[20] Last song and last chorus in *Acis and Galatea*.

[21] 'I know that my Redeemer liveth.' *The Messiah*.

[22] 'Upon thy right hand did stand the Queen.' *My heart is inditing*. Coronation anthem.

[23] The recitative in *Joshua*, preceding the song, 'Hark! 'tis the linnet.'

[24] 'Wretched Lovers.' *Acis and Galatea*.

[25] Alexander Pope, *Dunciad*, line 68.

[26] See preceding chapter.

note with its five principal harmonics, and are therefore as much a part of nature as light itself, or the colours into which it may be refracted. Again, if two notes of the triad are accurately sounded by two voices or instruments, a third sound belonging to the same triad is formed in the ear by the coincidence of the vibrations. If C and E are produced in the treble clef, the G below is heard; and if E and G, C below. But the minor key consists partly, and sometimes wholly, of minor triads. Now the minor triad is not like the major, a part of nature; nor will two of its sounds generate a third: consequently it is less agreeable than the major; its minor third seems like the string which sounds it to have been relaxed and depressed from the more agreeable and natural major third. While the chromatic scale, abounding in semitones and its discords containing minor and extreme flat and sharp intervals, approaches nearer to the cries and howlings of men or animals in distress, to the whistling of the wind and to other confused and indistinct noises than the diatonic scale. The major key therefore when unencumbered with chromatic passages, is a great source of calm satisfaction to the mind; it causes serenity. By serenity I do not mean indifference but that tranquil pleasure which ever results from the contemplation of the beautiful style. Some pleasure also accompanies the awe and the pain occasioned by the sublime and the pathetic. Much also depends upon the manner of performing any passage. The same notes which, when rendered by a few soft voices, we pronounce beautiful, acquire somewhat of the sublime by increasing the number of the performers, though still very soft; but if loud, the character is totally changed and the beautiful disappears.[27]

Clearness of harmony likewise conduces to serenity; the attention is less fatigued than by what is complicated and unintelligible. Symmetrical rhythm in moderate time also conduces to the same effect. By increasing the velocity, joy and delight are kindled. Long accented notes with short unaccented ones following, convey an idea of firmness and majesty. Very slow notes belong to sublimity, and very rapid ones to ornament. Broken and varied measure is properly used for indecision, as in the song of Jealousy:[28]

> Of different themes the veering son was mix'd,
> And now it courted Love; now, raving, call'd on Hate.

The poignancy of grief in the minor mode is much increased by the agitated rhythm rendering that confused, or mysteriously grand, which in the uniform measure would only have been melancholy.

But if it be demanded whether this is the use always made of the major and minor keys, I am compelled to own that it is not. Many exceptions to the rule may be found in the works of the great masters. Handel has set

[27] In Handel's Hallelujah Chorus, the notes to the words, 'The kingdoms of this world,' when performed soft, are beautiful; but when repeated loud, and with the full band, are sublime.

[28] Collins's *Ode to the Passions*, set to music by Dr [Benjamin] Cooke (1784).

words to the minor key which seemed to require the major.[29] The minor key of itself confers an expression of seriousness and dignity, and is frequently on that account adopted by second-rate composers. But Handel was not of this description. He probably adopted the minor key merely for the sake of contrast to the pieces which preceded and followed. Thus the Italian painter considered '*una nevola che passa*', a sufficient excuse for having thrown a shade over one of his figures that he did not wish to be too prominent.[30] Sometimes, also, he adopted the major key for words of a sorrowful cast. Contrast may account for this also; and, indeed, a succession of pieces in the minor would be yet more fatiguing than in the major key.

The general effect of the oratorio[31] is improved by these contrasts; but had the pieces been composed separately they would probably have been differently treated. Observe in the recitative, 'For behold, darkness shall cover the earth,' and in the air which follows it, how carefully the author has assigned the minor key to the words which speak of darkness, and the major to those of light. The one is set off by the other, like the bright gleam of sunshine in a storm which seems more brilliant than when the whole landscape is illuminated: and this perhaps is the reason why the minor key is preferred by many lovers of music – not because it is more agreeable but that it is a foil to the major key and makes that more attractive.

In some cases, however, sorrow is not meant by the composer where the words may at first seem to require it. In the song, 'He was despised', love to the Saviour, rather than pity for his sufferings, seems intended. And in the movement, 'All we like sheep have gone astray', sorrow for sin was not what the author aimed to excite, but he attempted to depict the thoughtless dispersion and careless wandering of silly sheep, each seeking pleasure its own way. But the practice of disregarding the natural effects produced by the major and minor keys is by no means peculiar to this author. Instances of it are afforded by the greatest masters of the Italian school, both ancient and modern. Sentiments of the most intense pathos are rendered by music, which we should denominate beautiful. Burke remarks that the affection produced by the beautiful approaches nearer to melancholy than to joy, according with our bard,[32] who says, 'I ne'er am merry when I hear sweet music.'

But the Italians are justly accused of having less expression and pathos than the Germans. We may instance a song by the elegant Hasse,[33] 'Pallido

---

[29] 'How beautiful are the feet!'; 'Thou art gone up on high'; 'If God be for us.'

[30] 'Quam multa vident pictores, in umbris, et in eminentia, quæ nos non videmus' (How many things painters see in light and shade that we do not see), Cicero, *Academicae Quaestiones.*

[31] *The Messiah.*

[32] Shakespeare.

[33] Hasse was a German by birth, but is always considered as an Italian composer, as he wrote in the Italian style.

il sole', the words of which describe the sun pale, the sky lowering, troubles threatening and death preparing to strike. Yet the key is major, the time moderate, the melody flowing, the expression soft, the harmony clear, the rhythm uniform and the effect of the whole such as would excite in a hearer unacquainted with its words, nothing short of unmixed delight. 'O quam tristis et afflicta!' in the *Stabat Mater* of Pergolesi, and almost all the opera songs by Sacchini, Sarti, Paisiello, etc. are of this description. This error is not peculiar to our own art. 'Guido,' says Sir Joshua Reynolds, 'from want of choice in adapting his subject to his ideas and powers, or from attempting to preserve beauty where it could not be preserved, has in this respect succeeded very ill. His figures are often engaged in subjects that required great expression; yet his Judith and Holofernes, the daughter of Herodias with John the Baptist's head, the Andromeda, and some even of the mothers of the innocents, have little more expression than his Venus attired by the Graces.' In the above passage the real motive is hinted: it was to preserve beauty. The violent passions of grief and even joy were destructive of beauty; there are therefore but few antique statues which have not tranquil features. And thus the Italian composers, finding themselves unrivalled in the beautiful style, became enamoured of it; and considered it as alone sufficient to constitute perfection. They accordingly threw aside the science which they themselves had invented, abhorring canons, fugues and learned contrivance (on which they bestowed the term 'scelerata'), avoiding all but the simplest discords and even the minor key itself.

Another imperfection in musical expression is its incapability of rendering the negative assertion or the absence of the thing described. In setting the words, 'When thou hadst overcome the sharpness of death', which is the musical composer to lay hold of? He cannot convey an idea of 'overcome'; he therefore adapts the expression 'sharpness of death' to appropriate discords.[34] Great musicians have been censured for this. But would not orators do the same in their way of pronouncing these words? 'Let the shrill trumpet cease' is a sentence which absolutely forbids a trumpet to sound immediately, which would indeed be as ridiculous as to begin with a drum when the poet says, 'Not a drum was heard'; but that the voice in singing these words should use the scale of the trumpet, would only seem to show that the singer was thinking of what was said.[35] In the chorus:

> No more to Ammon's god and king,
> Fierce Moloch, shall our cymbals ring,
> In dismal dance around the furnace blue.[36]

the composer was perfectly right in representing these unhallowed orgies by descriptive music, notwithstanding the two first words of the sentence.

Other imperfections in musical expression require to be noticed. 'To

[34] Handel's *Dettingen Te Deum*, and that for the *Peace of Utrecht*.
[35] Last part of 'O lovely Peace.' *Judas Maccabeus*.
[36] First chorus in *Jephtha*.

express,' says Dr Beattie, 'the local elevation of objects by what we call high notes, and their depression by low or deep notes, has no more propriety than any other pun. We call notes high or low with respect to their situation in the written scale. There would have been no absurdity in expressing the highest notes by characters placed at the bottom of the scale,' or the reverse, 'if custom or accident had so determined. And there is reason to think that something like this actually obtained in the musical scale of the ancients; at least it is probable that the deepest or gravest sound was called summa, and the shrillest or acutest ima, which might be owing to the construction of their instruments.' No person, unacquainted with the fact, could discover that the symphony in Haydn's *Creation*, which precedes the description of the sun-rising, was intended to portray that glorious appearance. The crescendo, indeed, of the loudness aptly represents the gradual increase of light. But the slow progress of the diatonic scale conveys no idea of ascent or imperceptible motion. In censuring Handel's attempt to convey the idea of the sun rising and then standing still at the command of Joshua, Avison[37] has made his ridicule turn upon the composer's endeavouring to make us hear what could only be seen. But that does not seem to be the chief objection, which is rather that the sun is an individual object. Light created suddenly or gradually increasing, though only perceptible by the sight, may be expressed in music[38] or, more correctly, the suddenness or the gradation of some sort of increase, for light cannot be represented, much less the sun.

But when composers (however eminent) endeavour to represent by musical notes frogs hopping, arrows flying, a rainbow, a lamp in a high tower, the depths of the sea, the flight of an eagle, great whales, crawling worms, tigers bounding, the paces of the stag and horse, flakes of snow, forked lightning, a dog running over the fields, the report of the gun[39] and the fall of the wounded bird, we surely must acknowledge that they have exceeded the true limits of musical expression.

Another species of imitation in music remains to be noticed which is occasionally used with great success: the imitation of sounds, whether those which are unmusical – as thunder, cannon, birds, the roar or murmur of waters, the cries of distress or pain, the whistling of the wind; or those which are musical – as the tolling or ringing of bells or of certain instruments which, by their tone and scale and the music peculiar to them, convey the idea of the military, pastoral or sacred styles. Dr Beattie, from whom I have already quoted many excellent sentiments, has the following passage on this subject with which I cannot agree and which I think liable to be made the foundation of erroneous principles:

[37] *On Musical Expression* [see pp. 60–3].

[38] See the opening of Haydn's *Creation*, 'O first created beam' (*Samson*) and the last scene of Weber's *Der Freischutz*.

[39] The report of the gun, as being a sound, is perhaps the least exceptionable of these imitations, but even that is too minute for musical expression.

A flute, a hautboy or a bagpipe is better adapted to the purposes of rural music than a fiddle, an organ or a harpsichord because more portable and less liable to injury from the weather. Thus an organ, on account of its size and loudness, requires to be placed in a church or some large apartment; thus violins and violoncellos, to which any degree of damp may prove hurtful, are naturally adapted to domestic use; while drums, trumpets, fifes and French horns, are better suited to the service of the field. Hence it happens that particular tones and modes of music acquire such a connection with particular places, occasions and sentiments, that by hearing the former we are put in mind of the latter so as to be affected by them more or less according to the circumstances. The sound of an organ, for example, puts us in mind of a church and of the affections suitable to that place; military music, of military ideas; flutes and hautboys, of the thoughts and images of rural life.

Thus there is between these kinds of music and the ideas they excite 'only an accidental connection, formed by custom and founded rather on the nature of the instruments than on that of the music.'

Let us then suppose organs and pianofortes portable: would they suit the purposes of regulating the step and inspiring courage in battle? Let us imagine violins to be so improved as not to be affected by the damp: would the line advance to 'the jocund rebeck's sound'? The trumpet, cymbal and drum are as portable as the flute and bagpipe. Why then do not shepherds amuse their shepherdesses and flocks with these deafening instruments? If an organ were reduced in size and a pianoforte rendered gigantic, might they exchange their situations? It is clear that our author has omitted to make the provision that the instruments should be calculated to excite devotion, pleasure or courage; and also that the music performed on them should always be in the most appropriate style for its purpose. But is our author right in what he has said? Does the sound of the organ always put us in mind of a church? If it did in his lifetime, it too frequently does not so now. It often reminds us of the concert, the drawing-room, the opera and the play-house, even when heard in a church. The remote sounds of the pealing organ are indeed sometimes so blended by echoing along the vaulted roofs of the cathedral and cloister that they produce the most sublime effects, and we might suppose that the style of the music is that which we call sacred; but a nearer approach will often dissolve the charm. We shall find it is the military, or the pastoral, or the pianoforte style, which is used for the voluntary. Again, hear a military band on parade playing the soft adagios of Haydn, Mozart and Beethoven! Though a whole host of armed men surround you, not one military idea is awakened. Hear the same band in the ballroom and here also they produce no military effect. Oboes, flutes and flageolets are not properly military instruments, yet they are added to augment the sound of the band and, by playing the same music, increase its effect. They do not always remind us of pastoral scenes. On the organ, when judiciously played, we may distinguish the church and the oratorio styles. On the pianoforte, though all styles are not equally calculated to suit its peculiar expression, all may be distinctly heard, the sacred, the military, the pastoral, the concert, the opera and its own appropriate style. How then can the style depend upon the instrument alone? The pianoforte does not imitate the tone of the organ, of military or of pastoral instruments. The limited scales of the trumpet and horn indeed are recognised when notes similar to harmonics are used. But the sacred, the military and the pastoral styles are only properly so called when instantly distinguishable from each other if performed on the pianoforte. Whatever is slow and grave may sound well if performed on an organ; but these qualities do not constitute sacred music any more than adagios, pastorales, and dances performed by a military band, however well they may sound, constitute military music. I am fully aware that I am opposed to the majority of English organists and to all foreign musicians in these sentiments. The practice of organists shows that 'the praise and glory of God' is not so much thought of as their own reputation for execution or invention. They perform on the organ during divine service such pieces as are expressly composed for the pianoforte, concert or theatre, or pieces which do not differ from them in style. There is, then, between these kinds of music and the ideas they excite more than 'an accidental connection'; and it depends as much at least on the nature of the music as on that of the instruments. 'If the trumpet give an uncertain sound, who shall prepare himself for the battle?'[40]

Musical expression is then more limited in its powers than is perhaps generally imagined.[41] Music cannot, like painting, seize on a particular action and represent with minuteness, all its parts. Like poetry, her imitation is very inferior to that of painting. Without the aid of music, poetry is necessarily forced to waste many of her richest ideas in attempting to raise the affections, which when united to music she finds raised already. Without the aid of poetry, music can awaken the affections by her magic influence, producing at her will and that instantly, serenity, complacency, pleasure, delight, ecstasy, melancholy, woe, pain, terror and distraction. She can remind us also of the sacred, military and pastoral styles; and when poetry would speak of the thunder-storm, the battle, the howl of pain, the warbling of birds, the roar of the winds or the waves, the breath of the zephyr or the murmuring stream, the solemn curfew or the merry peal of bells, music can by her imitations increase almost infinitely the enjoyment of the description.

[40] 1. Cor. xiv 8.
[41] Harris, *Three Treatises.*

Fétis[1]

From: Articles in *Revue musicale*, vol. 6 (1831), pp. 301ff; 147ff.

Sur les dictionnaires de musique

Part 1

Dictionaries of the arts and sciences have a double role to play: on the one hand they supply ideas to men of the world who have neither the leisure nor the will to acquire them through serious and continued study; on the other hand, these same books have sometimes to facilitate the researches of scholars and artists, guiding them to sources of information that they may draw upon for more extended and specialised study. It is obvious from this that dictionaries of the arts and sciences should be of two kinds: the dictionary that is intended for the ordinary reader must contain definitions that are precise and concise; that which is intended for the scholar and artist can hardly contain too many facts, their arrangement can scarcely be too methodical nor the information on historical, theoretical, critical, and philological sources too extensive. Many lexicographers have tried to reconcile these conflicting interests, and invariably neither condition has been satisfied. A musical dictionary, for instance, cannot at once satisfy the humble amateur and the knowledgeable musician. It is essential that the one which is intended for the former shall be edited in a quite different way to the other. This point has not yet been understood, for although more than twenty dictionaries have come out in various languages, there is not a single one which is wholly satisfactory. The following analysis of the principal dictionaries may serve to demonstrate this.

[p. 301, para. 2 to p. 303, para. 1 omitted]

The work that made the greatest impression when it appeared was Jean Jacques Rousseau's *Dictionnaire de musique* [see pp. 108–17]. Preliminary work for this by the celebrated writer was commissioned for the *Encyclopédie* of Diderot and d'Alembert [see pp. 57–9]. As Rousseau remarked in the preface to his dictionary,

> this enterprise was not mine, it was suggested to me. They told me that the entire manuscript of the *Encylopédie* must be completed before a single line was printed; they only gave me three months to complete my task where three years could hardly have sufficed to read, digest, compare and compile writings that were essential to the subject; but my own enthusiasm and the friendship that I had for

---

[1] For a discussion of the author's work see the editorial introduction on p. 400.

the editors blinded me to the impossibility of the task. Faithful to my word, and at the expense of my reputation, I worked quickly and badly, not being able to do anything well in so little time; at the end of three months the whole manuscript was complete, in fair copy and delivered; I did not revise it after that. If, like the other contributors, I had worked volume by volume, the project would have been better done, and could have been left in an unaltered state. I do not regret having been punctual, but I do regret the temerity of having promised more than I could possibly fulfil.

After these explanations, it would be ungracious to criticise too severely the *Encylopédie* articles that served as a basis for the *Dictionnaire de musique*, for Rousseau was at the time living outside Paris and he lacked the resources of great libraries that are indispensable for work of this kind. Rameau attacked some of the articles in a pamphlet entitled *Erreurs sur la musique dans l'Encyclopédie* (Paris 1755); but his criticisms, spoilt by his pigheadedness, were not directed at the matters that deserved the most censure. Rousseau realised the advantage that the author of the fundamental bass system had given him, and he produced a reply entitled: *Examin de deux principes avancés par M. Rameau dans sa brochure intitulée: Erreurs sur la musique dans l'Encyclopédie*. This little work was not published at the time and has only appeared in the collected writings of the philosopher of Geneva.

Though Rousseau was a man of taste and had a feeling for good music, his knowledge of the theory and practice of music was unfortunately very inadequate. He read music indifferently and his understanding of the art of writing harmony and counterpoint came entirely from books; moreover, the success that Rameau's erroneous theories achieved in France meant that he made use of them in sixteen sections of his dictionary, whilst at the same time neglecting the immense resources that were available in Italian books on accompaniment, harmony and composition, historically treated according to the true principles of the ancient schools. This is why such articles as those on 'accords', 'accompagnement', 'contrepoint', 'fugue' and 'canon' are so imperfect.

Such a defect has prematurely aged a book which has much to recommend it in style and clarity of method. I should add that Rousseau was wrong to attempt acoustics and musical proportions, subjects of which he knew nothing, and which, as he describes them, are almost unintelligible.

In his preface Rousseau shows little regard for Brossard's dictionary. He is all the more to be criticised in this respect, as he has much profited from the work of this learned musician; without it he would have been unable to cover those matters that relate to music of the Middle Ages and the notations of the fifteenth and sixteenth centuries.

One of the most extraordinary facets of Rousseau's dictionary is its total neglect of musical instruments; even the names are lacking. He was not commissioned to cover the subject for the *Encyclopédie*, and when he wished to complete his dictionary he was unable to consult any of the works that would have provided the necessary information, being then exiled in Switzerland; he had no option therefore but to leave this gap in his work.

Despite the faults that I have just mentioned, Rousseau's dictionary has enjoyed a greater popularity than several better works which have been published since then, and in all probability many future works will not enjoy its great popularity. This is due less to the usefulness of the book, than to the justly celebrated name of its author, to the magic of his style and to other circumstances that are well enough known to the world not to need rehearsal here.

Part 2

After the publication of Rousseau's dictionary of music, almost twenty-five years went by during which nothing was written on music in dictionary form. As has already been remarked, the fame of this celebrated writer, his literary disputes, his misfortunes, and above all his *Emile*, his *Lettre à M. de Beaumont*, and his *Contrat social*, all of which appeared at practically the same time, focused attention on the author of the *Dictionnaire de musique*, and in doing so upon that book which was designed to popularise a passionate interest. Rousseau's dictionary was translated into English, but with so many faults that it is almost unreadable. By a remarkable singularity, it was not accorded the honour of translation into German. This is all the more remarkable since Marpurg, a highly gifted writer on music, was misguided enough to adopt after his visit to France Rameau's system of the fundamental bass, and to disseminate it as far as he could amongst his countrymen.

In 1773 a book was published in Germany that made a considerable impression, not only there but in France and England, and which was much improved in subsequent editions. This was Sulzer's dictionary of the fine arts, which goes under the title, *Allgemeine Theorie der schönen Künste* [see pp. 120–39]. There is much about music in it, though there are lacunae; for the first time however important articles were handled in an exemplary manner and developed appropriately. At the end of each article Sulzer appended a list of particularly appropriate books, a very felicitous idea. No other lexicographers have taken such trouble, apart from Millin, whose *Dictionnaire des beaux-arts* (Paris 1806) leans heavily on Sulzer [see pp. 293–6]. After Sulzer died his work was reissued by Blankenburg (4 vols., Leipzig 1786); the same editor produced a much improved version (Leipzig 1792) and to this he added three supplementary volumes sometime later (Leipzig 1796). Everyone who subsequently compiled a dictionary of music would have been well advised to adopt and improve upon Sulzer's plan, but up till now no one has thought of doing this.

While Germany was being enriched by this epoch-making book in the history of the arts, a certain Chevalier de Meude-Monpas – a self-styled pupil of Jean Jacques Rousseau – sought to fill a gap that his master had left and to compile a so-called *Dictionnaire de musique* (Paris 1787) for men of affairs, one that aimed to provide precise definitions without an excess of scientific explanation. His book was very slight, but that was not its worst fault: a dictionary designed for people who know little about music could be a very good one, even though it comprised only a handful of pages; unfortunately, however, Chevalier de Meude-Monpas was very ignorant of music, he was greatly prejudiced in his ideas, and his style was hardly more elevated than were his ideas. His book has justly been ignored.

The *Encyclopédie méthodique*, a vast enterprise, dates from the beginning of the first French revolution (in fact from 1782); it reworked everything that was contained in the first *Encyclopédie*, although the editors aimed to conserve as much as possible from that work [see pp. 110–12]. Ginguené and Framery were entrusted with the articles on music, and they were joined by a certain Abbé Feyton, a systematic dreamer of the same kind as the Abbé Roussier, and just about as ignorant as he was of the principles of the science of music. Ginguené was no great musician, and he had the misfortune to be a member of a coterie and to be predisposed to certain schools of music, a considerable defect in a writer whose task is to discuss the arts in general. He was a musical scholar though and all the articles which he wrote for the work are to be recommended for their factual accuracy. Framery was entrusted with all that related to the technical side of harmony and counterpoint, and he possessed a greater knowledge of the art of composition, backward as this art was in France at the time: the Abbé Feyton was, however, given the task of revising the article on fundamental bass which they obstinately retained. The ideas of this Abbé were certainly not approved by his colleagues; but this disagreement was only one of the causes of that incoherence which characterises the musical contents of the *Encyclopédie;* the very plan of the work was so defective it could only result in a kind of monster, curious to behold, but tragic as far as the progress of music was concerned (in so far, that is, as progress depends on the form of a book!) Further comment is called for.

As I have said, the editors of the *Encyclopédie méthodique* chose to preserve as the basis of their work, articles from the great *Encyclopédie* that had been published earlier by Diderot and d'Alembert. During the intervening twenty-five years, however, great progress had been made, and many of the collaborators in this great enterprise felt the need to escape from the restrictions that this obligation would have imposed on them. Framery and Ginguené alone respected the obligation. They were not long in realising, however, that it spelt death to their work; and so, if you compare the *Dictionnaire de musique* and the *Encyclopédie méthodique* side by side, you will find Rousseau's original article in the *Encyclopédie*, and then another by Framery or Suard criticising Rousseau, and as often as not a third, by Abbé Feyton that quite contradicts the first two. In an attempt moreover to lessen their labours (or from some other reason) the editors have frequently used articles from Sulzer's work, and even articles by the Berlin academician, Castilhon – a prolific but unperceptive writer. All this has the effect of throwing the reader into considerable confusion.

The Revolution interrupted work on the *Encyclopédie méthodique* when only two-thirds of the first volume had been completed. When the editors tried to finish the work, Ginguené and Feyton were dead. The remainder of the musical work was accordingly entrusted to M. de Momigny – author of a treatise on harmony and composition based upon a new system – charging him with the task of coordinating the materials and completing the task. As is generally known M. de Momigny's opinions are very trenchant; he was certainly not the man to reconcile articles by Framery and the Abbé Feyton with those of Jean Jacques Rousseau. He accordingly set to work in all his articles to proclaim that his predecessors did not understand what they were saying, and he devoted the whole of the second volume to his own system. Thus we have the strangest and least useful book, indeed one might say the most harmful book that exists perhaps in the whole of musical literature.

It is appropriate to note here that dictionaries of the arts and sciences should not be repositories of editorial ideas and systems, be these true or false, but they should give information about everything that relates to the history and particularly to the present state of the arts. A dictionary is generally regarded as an authority in which full confidence can be placed; dictionaries are consulted in proportion to the confidence that they inspire. In such a work it is thus an abuse to present personal views as truly scientific and artistic theories. The Italians speak not of an author of a dictionary, but of a compiler; their term is more exact, for the talents of the writer of such a book consist in presenting the assembled facts clearly, in making the nomenclature as complete as is possible, and in ensuring that the proportions of the article are commensurate with the importance of the subject.

There appeared at Weimar in 1786 a small pocket dictionary, the first of its kind, with the title *Musikalisches Handwörterbuch oder kurzgefasste Anleitung, sämtliche in Musikwesen vorkommende, etc*. The definitions that it contains have the merit of clarity and brevity; artists will find it of little use, but its form is convenient for amateurs who are looking in a dictionary for simple ideas. This doubtless explains why the dictionary has gone through so many editions. G. F. Wolf's *Kurzgefasstes musikalisches Lexikon* (Halle 1787), based on a very similar plan, has been no less successful, and it has been published in four editions. However, its nomenclature is very incomplete and many of its definitions lack exactness and precision.

As has been stated, every branch of musical literature flourished in Germany. Many musical dictionaries were published, none of which, however, provided a satisfactory source of information for professional artists on the important aspects of their art. Eventually in 1802 Koch's great *Musikalisches Lexikon* was published, and it is still the best work of its kind.

Although its scholarship is not entirely beyond criticism it is the first dictionary in which artistic and scientific questions are discussed at length in an appropriately technical language. The music examples greatly clarify the argument, and they are generally well written by an able musician who is skilled in the practice of music. Had the dictionary dealt with historical matters in an equally scholarly way, and had a better balance been established between the various articles, it might well have been of use to scholars as well as artists. M. Gottfried Weber, one of the most learned musicians in Germany, was aware of these defects, and he determined to make everything available in dictionary format that had been written; the work was to be as complete as possible. He assembled a vast quantity of material – examples of his work are to be found in the magazine, *Caecilia* – but I understand that this distinguished writer has since abandoned his project for other ideas. Koch has published an abridged version of his great dictionary which has been warmly welcomed by the public. Several editions of this have appeared.

While the Germans were moving towards the production of an ideal dictionary, the work of Grassineau and Rousseau was being disseminated in England by John Hoyle, who in 1790 produced a little octavo volume entitled, *A Complete Dictionary of Music*. This so-called 'complete' diction-ary was little more than an inaccurate assemblage of terms, the choice of which was not readily obvious. Not surprisingly it met with slight success. Ten years later, Dr Busby, the author of two quite different musical grammars, a mediocre history of music based on Hawkins and Burney, and a collection of music anecdotes, produced *A Complete Dictionary of Music* (London 1800). Though not faultless, this better deserved its title, and has been useful to many artists. None the less the want of a substantial dictionary has long been felt in England. The celebrated pianist, Clementi, M. Bacon of Norwich, M. Bishop and other notable scholars and artists together published a very detailed prospectus of a work that was to be called *The Encyclopaedia of Music*.

The dictionary was to comprise two volumes in large quarto. Some expense had been incurred, and the materials were already assembled when M. Clementi decided to leave London for the country. From this moment the association broke up and the projected publication was cancelled. It is sad that the plan of the music encyclopaedia has not been carried through since the prospectus made it clear that its editors well understood the importance of the task which they had undertaken.

Part 3

Amongst those dictionaries of music that have not yet been mentioned, one of the more remarkable is the work of M. Jean Verschuere-Reynvaan, advocate at Flushing published in Dutch, which sadly is incomplete. It was published at Middelbourg in 1789 under the title *Musykaal konst woordenboeck* (*Dictionary of the art of music*). Only the first volume was published, covering A-E; early in 1790 there appeared an advertisement for part two, but the author, who had been keenly aware of the faults of his work, withheld publication. As M. Verschuere-Reynvaan himself declared in the preface, he had based his dictionary on those of Brossard and Jean

Jacques Rousseau; but he had abridged the principal articles of the latter work. His book is not, as one might think, a dictionary of Dutch musical terms but an explanation in Dutch of Greek, Latin and Italian terms that relate to the art. The author intended his work for the use of organists and other professional musicians; but apart from the fact that the nomenclature is incomplete, the definitions are too concise to achieve this aim. M. Verschuere-Reynvaan realised this and started work again on a more extended scheme, the fruits of his labours appearing in Amsterdam in 1796 in a 618 page volume, with many illustrations but only covering the letters A–M. Fate decreed that M. Verschuere-Reynvaan should not see the end of his labours, for the second part has not yet seen the light of day. The title of this first volume is the same as that of the earlier work. As far as it goes this first part may be considered as one of the best dictionaries that has been written. Most of the articles bear witness to solid scholarship, and the definitions are as precise as the genius of the Dutch tongue allows. The polyglot vocabulary that M. Verschuere-Reynvaan uses, is something of a drawback to the readers for whom the work is intended.

M. Charles Envalson, public notary in Stockholm, has followed a similar plan in his Swedish dictionary of music, translating for his compatriots Latin, Italian and French terms; the title of the book is *Svenski musikaliskt Lexicon efter Grekiska, Latinska, Italienska och Franska spraechen* (Stockholm 1802); however, the articles are much less substantial than those by M. Verschuere-Reynvaan.

I have not mentioned a little music word book published at Ulm in 1795 by Justin Henri Knecht (8 folios in octavo) although it has gone through many editions; such works are too incomplete and too concise to be worthy of serious consideration. There is of a similar kind a handbook of music, *Musikalisches Hand-Wörterbuch*, produced in 1830 by M. Gustave Schilling (Stuttgart). In a similar class comes the *Dizionario della Musica sacra e profana* (Venice 1810), by the Abbé Gianelli in three small volumes; it is of little worth. The book, in which are assembled technical definitions and a certain number of biographical notices, is useful neither on historical nor scientific grounds. It has, however, enjoyed some popularity, for a second edition was published in 1820, and a third in 1830, all at Venice.

Amongst the pocket dictionaries must be included the one by M. Danneley, published in London in 1825, and the one by M. Hauser. Despite its ambitious title, *An Encylopaedia or Dictionary of Music*, the first is no more than a collection of very brief definitions, for the use of men of affairs, and contains nothing which is not common knowledge. It does have the merit, however, of including a complete enough nomenclature [see p. 366]. The second, which was published at Meissen in 1828 (two small octavo volumes) under the title of *Musikalisches Lexicon*, comprises more extended discussions of the most important artistic matters; but it is of only narrowly practical use and is of little real value to serious students.

It remains to examine two musical dictionaries that have achieved popular success in France and Italy: namely the one by M. Castil-Blaze, published in 1820 under the title: *Dictionnaire de musique moderne* (two volumes in octavo), and the one by Dr Lichtenthal, published in Milan in 1826: this one, divided into two separate parts, each comprising two volumes, has the title, *Dizionario e Bibliografia della Musica*.

M. Castil-Blaze's chosen title indicates the scope of the book [see pp. 356–7]. It does not cover musical history but is limited to questions that concern the present state of music. The coverage is less extensive therefore than that of most dictionaries, but the work is none the less useful to the amateur. Within these terms of reference, M. Castil-Blaze has certainly done an excellent job. If he is to be criticised, it is not for limiting the work in this way but rather for having written at too great a length for the type of reader he has in mind. For while his dictionary contains nothing that is new to knowledgeable musicians it is too detailed for the amateur. This defect apart (one that only concerns the scope of the book) M. Castil-Blaze is to be praised for the clarity and rightness of his judgements, which are confirmed by most artists. Some German critics have reproached him for his incomplete coverage of musical terminology: had they kept the title of the work in mind, they would not have done so. Some factual errors came to light when the dictionary was first put on sale, notably in the articles dealing with counterpoint and fugue, but errata sheets have been inserted in the later copies, and corrections have been made to the 1825 edition.

M. Mees published a new edition of the dictionary at Brussels in 1828, to which he has added a brief history of music, and biographical notices on some of the more celebrated Belgian musicians.

The first two volumes of Dr Lichtenthal's work comprise a dictionary of technical terms [see pp. 367–75]. Apart from a few slips, that are almost unavoidable in a work of this kind, the dictionary is admirably erudite. It is superior to Koch in its coverage of history, but not its equal in the scientific sections. If the best articles could be selected from these two publications, the minor mistakes being emended, the value of the undertaking would be unquestionable. M. Lichtenthal devotes the third and fourth volumes of the work to musical bibliography; but since this is outside the scope of the present article I shall say nothing further.

Polémique. Du mouvement et de la résistance en musique

As far as politics is concerned the tendency, as I see it, is to pay increasing respect to the absolute and individual rights of nations, and to clarify concepts that up to now have been vaguely formulated, and which have therefore impaired the relationships between governments and peoples, and between the people themselves. There is in short a political movement towards the exercise of reason rather than imagination. As far as the arts are concerned, it would seem that the reverse is true. It is precisely reason that men seek to banish, in order that the imagination shall have total freedom.

In both cases, however, the results are similar, as the changes have done little more than satisfy a few minor whims. Established power clings so tenaciously to its authority that it can paralyse change for a long time, even though in the end the forces of change will triumph. Those who favour change in the arts have been powerless to bring it about, and all that they have been able to do is talk. Yet if they believe that the opposition comes from without, they are mistaken. This particular movement, which goes under the banner of romanticism, mistakenly imagines that it is new, and that the age of innovation dates from now. Every progressive age (and there has always been progress) has been one of reform. Since the eleventh century, when Guido d'Arezzo reformed the musical system, there has hardly been a moment when music has been at a standstill. There is less difference between the symphonies of Beethoven and Haydn or between the operas of Rossini and Cimarosa than there is between the music of Josquin Després and that of Guillaume Dufay, between the purity of the master of the Roman school and the boldness of Monteverdi, or between the *stile osservato* of the late-sixteenth century had the *stile concertato* of the early-seventeenth century. Musical change has continued uninterruptedly for four centuries, that is to say from the time that Binchois, Dufay and Dunstable laid the first foundations of regular harmony. Certainly these venerable artists were audacious romantics; they dared to free themselves from the prejudices of their time and to open themselves to the workings of their inner musical consciousness, and to impressions that were at the same time guided by the light of reason. Although their compositions now seem so heavy, so devoid of taste and feeling, they were then marvels of elegance and audacity. Musical history witnessed a thousand revolutions which were no less striking than the one that is going on before our eyes.

[p. 147 col. 2, para. 1 to end omitted]

Johann Friedrich Herbart

(b. Oldenburg, 4 May 1776; d. Göttingen, 14 Aug. 1841)

From: *Kurze Encyclopädie der Philosophie aus praktischen Gesichtspunkten entworfen* (1831), in *Werke*, ed. G. Hartenstein (Leipzig 1851), vol. 2, pp. 121–5

As a philosopher in the Kantian tradition and as a psychologist, Herbart is in many respects one of the most original thinkers of his age, yet he had virtually no influence on aesthetics. This is all the more strange in that he regarded aesthetics as a branch of psychology, and psychology as a fundamental aspect of education.

After studying under Fichte at Jena in 1794, he worked as a tutor at Interlaken in Switzerland from 1797 till 1800. It was here that he made the acquaintance of J. H. Pestalozzi. Becoming a Privatdozent at Göttingen in 1802, he was appointed professor there in 1805. He went to Königsberg in 1808 to take up the chair once held by Kant, remaining in the post until 1833. He combined his work at the university with the administration of a teacher-training institute. He returned to Göttingen in 1833 and died there in August 1841.

Herbart's philosophical system involves a remarkable attempt to reconcile metaphysics, logic and aesthetics. His striking ideas on psychology, interpreting ideas as *forces*, the conflict between which is latent in the subconscious even when it has apparently been consciously removed, foreshadowed doctrines prominent in twentieth-century psychology. Throughout his investigations, he emphasises the need to prove his points from empirical data, though he is careful to state that what is universal and necessary is not always the same as what is empirically perceived. Herbart believed that formal beauty in music could be established as an empirical fact by careful analysis of the mathematical relationships between notes and note-sequences. Music, he admitted, was capable of arousing powerful emotions; but this was not the basis on which its beauty should be assessed. Associated and not wholly disinterested reactions to a work of art he called 'apperceptions'; and the 'meaning' of a piece of music – the emotions or even the natural phenomena it might be held to portray – was included by him among such apperceptions.

Herbart felt that since harmonic relationships were based on mathematical principles, music's effect on us might be definable in terms of the way those principles operate. He therefore tried at some length in his *Psychologische Betrachtungen über die Lehre des Tons* (1811) and his *Psychologische Untersuchungen* (1839) to investigate what these mathematical relationships were.

The ear, he claimed, has a capacity to distinguish between intervals along a continuum of frequencies. This capacity is based on the mathematical relationship between the frequencies; and it is because of the measurable tension between the two different tendencies inherent in any given relationship of pitches to one another that the ear perceives two forces. One of these forces tends towards unity, the other towards contrast and conflict. This sense is carried over into the ear's capacity to leave successive impressions in the mind that are determined by the vertical (harmonic) and the horizontal (melodic) context of the notes.

452

An incalculable amount must be read into every work of art, without exception; its effect depends much more on the inner reactions of the beholder than on outside stimuli. A learned work of art is a misconception; it might easily presuppose too much and impress rather than please.

The plastic arts have the most immediate, the surest and most universal impact on us, for we are most familiar with the human form and we are all experienced in interpreting expression and gesture. A painting, on the other hand, first demands that we become wholly absorbed in it, in order to generate a sense of optical illusion. The effect of a historical painting depends entirely on the mental effort that the spectator makes to relate the moment represented on the canvas to a continuous stream of action. The more beautiful the landscape, the more the eye draws us into it. An artistic impression is slow to form and time is needed for this to happen. As far as great works of architecture are concerned our reactions are in this respect similar. . . .

Considered as monuments, ancient works of architecture impress us in a way that clearly demonstrates the importance of apperception, apperception being utterly different from simple perception and all the artistic impressions that depend on it. How eagerly does a numismatist inspect an ancient coin! Its value depends on his historical appreciation of it (his apperception of it, that is to say).

But the more incidental apperception is, the more easily it can be dispensed with; and the more important the role of the incidental in the assessment of a work of art, the less will that work be a coherent whole. Not even dynamics are considered in a musical style (such as a fugue); the performer could perfectly well manage without them, as also could his instrument (e.g. the organ). The notes need only be heard (or, indeed, merely read) for them to give pleasure. . . .

It will thus be evident that if the artistic value of a work is to be correctly assessed, the part played by apperception must be discounted in so far as it plays no essential role in perception. In arguing that imitation can in no way be adopted as a principle of aesthetics, we are merely applying this basic premiss to a specific case. It is certainly true that an actor is admired if, as they say, he plays his part naturally; so is a painter who tempts children to grasp fruit he has painted on a canvas. But such artifice does not constitute beauty; and the imitation is at best only as beautiful as its model. One is involuntarily reminded that inner freedom depends on harmony between insight and intention. The realisation of an idea is different from imitation; anyone in whom the dual forces of thought and volition are at work is superior to the mere imitator in proportion to the intensity with which the two combine in him: the imitator always comes second to the one he copies.

No one is likely to accept unreservedly that all incidental, or at any rate inessential apperception shall be discounted in connection with the appreciation of beauty. When he looks at a statue, the beholder will want to know which mythical or historical character it represents. The visitors to an art-gallery will have need of a catalogue; the opera-goer will require a libretto. Otherwise, the complaint will be that the painting or the music is incomprehensible. For much the same reason, many poems are provided with a commentary. Works of art are supposed to mean something, so people busy themselves providing minutely detailed commentaries and interpreting works of art as symbols of this or that in a way that would have been inconceivable to the artist. And worse still, artists do not demur at the advance publication by others of such matters as the texts to their music or the circumstances that gave rise to their poem, or the setting of their picture – in other words the meaning of their work – and from these fantasies they no doubt discover what it was that they were trying to express. What a task of musical expression Haydn took on in *The Creation* and *The Seasons*! Fortunately, his music needs no text; it is mere curiosity that impels us to know what he has just tried to illustrate. His music is simply music, and it needs no meaning to make it beautiful. Other artists are surprised if they are not applauded, knowing perfectly well that their works are highly characteristic of the object that they are portraying and that the flood of emotion that they have tried to express is genuine. How frequently are otherwise competent artists led astray by the premiss that their work must mean something! How many scholars, how many brilliant critics, persist in voicing their own prejudices to the end that their business of exposition and commentary may still prosper! Astrologers and interpreters of dreams have for thousands of years refused to recognise that a person dreams because he sleeps and that the constellations appear now in one position and now in another because they are in motion. So it is that even knowledgeable musicians still argue as though the basis of music were not the universal laws of simple or double counterpoint, but the emotions that music may well arouse, and for the expression of which, should the composer so wish, it may hence be employed. What was it that those artists of ancient time strove to express when they explored the potential of fugue, or, again, those of still remoter times when, by their skill, they created the various architectural orders? They did not wish to express anything at all; their ideas were limited to an investigation of the art itself. But those who rely on interpretations betray their distrust of man's inner nature and a preference for outward appearances.

Fig. 5. *Fonthill from the North-East* (J. M. W. Turner, 1775–1851). The most spectacular English Gothic building of the eighteenth century: originally conceived as an artificial ruin but developed into a vast residence from the centre of which arose an octagon steeple, challenging the spire of Salisbury Cathedral. This was an outstanding instance of the architectural search for the sublime, enhanced here by Turner's romantically conceived view of it from the North-East. (Whitworth Art Gallery, University of Manchester)

Felix Mendelssohn-Bartholdy

(b. Hamburg, 3 Feb. 1809; d. Leipzig, 4 Nov. 1847)

From: *Felix Mendelssohn im Spiegel eigener Aussagen und zeitgenössischer Dokumente*, ed. Willi Reich (Zurich 1970), pp. 203; 238; 331; 358; 417

1. [The importance of imagination]

Now when I thought of a Spontini opera, in which the arts of illusion and imitation are so sedulously practised, I felt that in the end, the performance in Lucerne[1] was nevertheless more natural and created a greater illusion, for all its rough-hewn artificial waves, for it allowed play to the imagination, which was fully engaged, whereas in Spontini the imagination is driven into a corner and its wings are clipped; such things always make me feel like an anxious child.

[Letter to Goethe, 28 August 1831]

2. [Emotion]

I'm hanged if I understand correctly either what your final question means, or what answer I am to give to it. Generalisations and anything touching on aesthetics worry me and leave me bereft of words. I am to tell you how you should react emotionally, am I? You want to distinguish between excess of emotion and true taste; a plant can 'flower to death', you say.

But there is *no* such thing as an excess of emotion; what goes under that term is in fact a lack of it. All the ebb and flow and excitement of emotion that people are so fond of experiencing when listening to music is not an excess. Anyone who reacts emotionally should feel as much as lies in his capacity to do – indeed, more so. If he dies in the attempt, he does not die in sin, for there is nothing more certain than what you feel, or what you believe, or whatever term you care to use for it. Nor can a plant flower itself sick, unless one forces it and forces it and forces it. Such forced flowering is not flowering at all – any more than sentimentality is emotion.

[Letter to Rev. Albert Bauer, 4 March 1833]

3. [The nature of a composer's inspiration]

I can only conceive of music when I can think of a mood that can generate it; I have never in my life been able to abide mere academically correct

[1] Mendelssohn had been to see a somewhat rough and ready local production of Schiller's *Wilhelm Tell* in Lucerne (eds.)

456

sounds which suit the declamation of the words, loud when the words are powerful and soft when they are gentle, sounding pretty and all that sort of thing, but expressing nothing. And yet I can conceive of no other kind of music to this poem than accompanimental, incidental, 'musical' music – music that neither penetrates the nature of things nor is permeated by it, music of a kind that I do not like. In a case like this I am reminded of the fable of the two pots that were going on a journey together, and bumped into one another until one got shattered into pieces because it was made of clay and the other was of iron. Anyway, I find the poem neither cheerful nor sad, neither bold nor cautious, neither emotional nor rational, but positive, practical and much to current taste.

[Letter to Julius Schubring, 27 February 1841]

4. [Music is more precise than words]

People talk so much about music and they say so little. I am absolutely certain that words are not adequate to it, and if ever I found that they were, I should eventually give up composition. People complain that music has so many meanings; they aren't sure what to think when they are listening to it; and yet after all, everyone understands words. I am quite the opposite. I feel not only with whole speeches, but even with individual words, that they have so many meanings, they are so imprecise, so easy to misunderstand in comparison with music, which fills one's soul with a thousand better things than words. A piece of music that I love expresses thoughts to me that are not too *imprecise* to be framed in words, but too *precise*. So I find that attempts to express such thoughts in words may have some point to them, but they are also unsatisfying – that goes for yours, too. But you are not to blame – words are; they just cannot manage any better.

[Letter to Marc André Souchay, 15 October 1842]

5. [Musical progress]

If by chance something happened to bring all creative musical activity to a standstill for a hundred years, while the worlds of politics, religion and philosophy marched on uninterrupted, would the art of music have progressed with the rest of the world in the meantime? Would the works of future masters be a hundred years in advance of those of our time? Not one step! At the very best, they would link up with our best works and continue the sequence unbroken, however far the world might have progressed in other respects. In short, the progress of the art of music has nothing in common with that of science, philosophy, religion or politics; it develops according to the natural laws of artistic progress, the laws of birth, growth and death.

[From a conversation in 1846 with J. C. Lobe]

Fig. 6. *Morning* (Philipp Otto Runge, 1777–1810; see pp. 522–3). A striking example of the more visionary kind of romantic painting. Though the figures are 'realistic', their relationship to the composition is based on a combination of formal and allegorical criteria. (Kunsthalle, Hamburg)

Jean-Paul Richter

(b. Wunsiedel, 21 Mar. 1763; d. Bayreuth, 14 Nov. 1825)

From: *Gazette musicale de Paris*, 11 Jan. 1833

One day the guardian spirit of sensitive men stood before Jupiter and addressed this prayer to him: 'Divine Father, give to your poor human beings a more expressive language, for they have only words to voice the extent of their sufferings, their happiness and their love.' 'Have I not given them tears', Jupiter replied, 'tears of happiness, tears of suffering, and the sweeter tears of love?' The guardian spirit replied: 'O Divine Father, tears alone will not suffice for the overflowing heart. Give to men, I pray thee, a more powerful language in which to express the langorous and passionate desires of the tender soul, the charming memories of childhood, the sweet dreams of youth and the hopes of old age, hopes that are fastened upon another life, as the last rays of the day star sink beneath the oceans. Give them O Father, a new language of the heart!' At this moment the divine harmonies of the celestial spheres heralded the arrival of the muse of song. Jupiter beckoned to her and spoke to her, thus: 'Descend to the world of men and teach them your language.' And so the muse of song came amongst us and taught us her accents, and since then the heart of man has been able to speak.[1]

---

[1] This excerpt, from *Levana* (1807), is also quoted in the Leipzig *Allgemeine musikalische Zeitung* of 3 Jan. 1821 (vol. 23, p. 1) (eds.)

Ludolf Wienbarg

(b. Altona, 25 Dec. 1802; d. Schleswig, 2 Jan. 1872)

From: *Aesthetische Feldzüge* (Hamburg 1834), pp. 213–22

A strong quasi-political reaction against romantic other-worldliness came in literature in the 1830s with the group of writers usually collectively known as Das Junge Deutschland (Young Germany). Significant figures in German culture, Heine and Wagner were for a time associated with the group; and the two writers who set out its aesthetic credo most cogently were Ludolf Wienbarg (1802–72) in his *Aesthetische Feldzüge* and Theodor Mundt (1808–61) in his *Aesthetik*.

Neither Wienbarg nor Mundt was interested in spiritualising the world through art. The true matters for human concern were human life and the human predicament in present, material life. Their political tenets called for a radical reorientation of society; and in 1835, the Federal Diet banned their writings as subversive. It is interesting to compare the fresh, vigorous straightforwardness of Wienbarg's lectures of 1834 (quotations from the original edition, Hamburg 1834) and Mundt's rather more sober, more Hegelian, and more puritanical approach of eleven years later.

Wienbarg went to the Altona Gymnasium and then on to Kiel and Bonn Universities, where he studied philology and philosophy. He was a tutor of Count von Bernstorff's family for two and a half years before continuing his studies at Marburg, where he obtained a Doctorate of Philosophy in 1829. He set up as a Privatdozent at Kiel in 1833 and the *Aesthetische Feldzüge* are taken from his lectures there. He then went to Frankfurt and founded a periodical, the *Deutsche Zeitschrift*, which, together with his other writings, was banned in 1835. After a sojourn in the Rhineland, he returned to Hamburg, where he worked as a literary journalist from 1842 till 1846.

Music – one might think – is the art that is least likely to misconstrue its proper field of operation, but experience continually demonstrates that musicians are always striving to outdo first the painter, and then the poet; in doing so, they lose sight of the true dignity of their art. Ancient Italian music generally created a pattern of notes that conveyed neither emotion nor ideas; it was a pure indulgence in the interplay of sounds, no ideas being involved. By contrast, a characteristic kind of music has now become fashionable; it allegedly consists of purely physical and spiritual allusions; it imitates storms, moonlight kisses, galloping horses – anything that is pictorial or poetic, whatever it may be. The incorporation of all these foreign elements has unnaturally extended music's sphere of operation.

Anyway, gentlemen, one cannot fail to observe the intimate relationship between the arts of music and poetry; when they are combined, as, for example, in opera and song, they excite in us the most wonderful reactions.

[p. 214, line 8 to p. 217, para. 2 omitted]

In his *Kritik der Urteilskraft*, Kant argues that music is the most pleasurable of the arts, but that it is the least edifying because it plays with mere emotions which produce no clearly defined ideas.

The sage of Königsberg did not rate music very highly, therefore, nor did Hegel attach much value to music, because, he claimed, it afforded insufficient scope for *thought*. How differently Luther must have been moved by the magic of music; 'I freely admit,' he declared, 'that after theology, there is no art that can be compared to music.' Luther was a flautist and an even more skilful lutenist, and every evening his home resounded to his light, virile tenor voice. Kant, Hegel and those other philosophers and non-philosophers were prejudiced against music because they lacked poetic sensibility, childlike sensitivity and innate musicality. Music's very material, its very medium, predispose us to value it highly as an art. Music speaks to us through our sense of hearing; its medium – air – is invisible, like the sounds that it conjures up; in its invisibility, it stimulates something invisible in us, something, as it were, from some unknown world; music is not something that is dead, immobile, or at rest, but something that is evanescent, fluid, something that floats over, round and beneath us. Its melodies are to us the images of our spiritual awareness, our silent feelings, our premonitions and hopes; our pains and joys; our hearts are transformed into sound; we feel with redoubled intensity, yet our feelings transcend pain and we enjoy them as sounds that captivate the ear and leave no sting in the heart. Sounds, says Heinse in his musical novel,[1] assault the nerves and the hearing, transforming our inmost feelings beyond anything that we can imagine. Our very emotions are nothing but inner music, a ceaseless rhythm of life's nerves. Music excites them in such a way as to stimulate a unique play, a quite special communication that quite surpasses verbal description. It externalises in the air our inner feelings. 'Hearing', he says in another place, 'is certainly our most important sense and the conviction that this is so springs directly from it.' No painter or draughtsman, however practised he may be, can measure out by eye simple linear arithmetical relationships, such as halves, thirds, fifths and sixths with the hair-splitting accuracy that the musician can achieve by ear. For this reason, deaf mutes are far less fortunate than blind people, because they lack the principal intellectual sense, which guides the other senses towards what is right. Of all the arts, therefore, music is the one that provides the soul with the freshest and clearest enjoyment. It is highly fortunate that the human ear is more discriminating and versatile than that of any animal. Even so, a keen, secure and finely sensitive ear – one, moreover, that is well-trained – is as rare as the loftiest beauty; and this divine faculty can easily be ruined by bad habits.

In fact, just as the body is inferior to the spirit, so it is that every art that is fettered to the visible is inferior to music *in respect of the impact that it has*

[1] *Hildegard von Hohenthal* (Leipzig 1795–6).

on us. For music is spirit, having the same nature as the power that rules us – namely, the soul – activity. Music can convey to man things that he cannot perceive. Everything about it is evanescent, for its significance and its impact depend directly on the relationship between notes that are long and short, loud and soft, high and low. It celebrates its triumphs because its effects come and go, change and vanish. The pictorial arts, in contrast, are constrained to represent specific buildings and objects, and nowadays even local colours, and though all the detail is simultaneously displayed, it can be taken in only gradually.

Music's proper domain is that of the emotions, past and future. It should not *depict* nature, nor represent her *poetically*, as painters, sculptors and poets do; it should purely and simply *excite* us. Music never has a *precise* effect, as a poem does, therefore, but only an indeterminate one. Musical attempts to imitate individual events and phenomena, such as the clatter of a mill, the rattling of wheels, or the grinding of teeth, take on the immediate appearance of some ludicrous and insupportable charade. Music should never descend from its pure ethereal heights to the dull plane of reality. We experience spontaneous emotional reactions to music; we immerse ourselves in its pure, dark, surging tide; we drink in its sounds, we slake our thirst and purify ourselves in the torrent of harmony.

Music may be called the *freest* of the arts because its very immediacy overwhelms the soul and the imagination, filling them with musical forms of beauty. It does so without passing through any intermediate stage involving intellectual concepts, still less, tangible phenomena. In music, the individual communes most readily with the ideal; in the temporal art of music, the eternal achieves its clearest expression.

I do not need to state that sounds derive their irresistible power from the sense of the infinite; sounds, as Jean-Paul says which envelop the heart in the mysterious moonlight shed by ethereal powers, and which so exalt the soul that it listens to itself; sounds that bring forth the sublimest hopes and memories from the depths as if they were whispering to us in their sleep. *Harmony* partially satisfies us on account of its arithmetical relationships, but melody, the vital spirit of music, cannot be explained save in terms of the poetic representation of those cruder sounds that are wrung from us by pain and joy. Music around us begets music within us; and thus all sounds excite us to song.

Gustav Schilling

(b. Schwiegershausen, 3 Nov. 1803; d. Nebraska, USA, Mar. 1881)

From: *Encyclopädie der gesammten musikalischen Wissenschaften, oder Universal Lexikon der Tonkunst* (Stuttgart 1834–8; 2nd edn 1840–2: 7 vols.), vol. 6, pp. 246–50; vol. 1, pp. 522–7; vol. 6, pp. 34–7; vol. 2, pp. 615–17

What Sulzer had set out to do in the 1770s for all the arts, Gustav Schilling attempted for music alone in the 1830s. His *Universal Lexikon* was published between 1834 and 1838; and a second edition came out in 1840–2. Running to seven thick volumes, the *Lexikon* is a mixed bag. Certain of the articles were by Hegelians such as Adolf Bernhard Marx; others by Kantians such as Fink; Schilling himself seems to have been an eclectic.

The son of a protestant preacher, he made his first public appearance as a pianist at the age of 10. He was also, by his own account, a proficient organist, violinist, flautist and cellist. In 1823 he began reading theology at the University of Göttingen, proceeding from there to Halle. Deciding not to take holy orders, he set about earning his living as a teacher. After his marriage in 1830, he went to Stuttgart as director of the Musical Institute founded there by Franz Stoepel that operated on Logier's (1777–1846) system.

Schilling's publications on music were voluminous and varied, but his main claim to fame rests on the *Lexikon*. Between 1839 and 1850 he published no fewer than twenty-one works on music, many of them substantial, and, according to Robert Eitner's article on him in the *Allgemeine Deutsche Nationalbiographie*, many of them plagiarisms. He lived beyond his means, incurring heavy debts, and fled to the United States to escape his creditors in January 1857. He died on his son's farm in the middle west in 1881.

Beauty and the beautiful (Schönheit und Schön)

As we have mentioned in the article on *Art* and elsewhere the aim of the muses is to reveal the highest beauty in a physically perfect shape. Aesthetics thus has no higher object than the investigation of beauty itself. This is particularly true of musical aesthetics, as music ranks second in the hierarchy of the fine arts, being closely related to the muses whose actual name it bears.

Those who have argued that the word *beautiful* (*schön*) is derived from the verb to *shine* (*scheinen*) have much been ridiculed. Yet the verb does mean to be bright or brilliant, and it has been metaphorically transferred from visual phenomena, to which it was originally applied, to anything and everything that shines in the reflected light of something that our inner or outer perception considers to be perfect. As, however, the terms 'beauty' and 'beautiful' have been applied to more and more objects, and as they have thus acquired a broader meaning, it has become more difficult for recent aestheticians to clarify what beauty is, a task which in itself is difficult enough. The Greeks used the word in its original meaning of *shining out*. This is virtually to demand admiration on the part of the beholder. If the beautiful is basically a matter of sheer power, endeavour and excellence there can be no place for slipshod indulgence and pointless decadence. The precision and refinement of the Greek language ensured that the original noble meaning of the word was strictly adhered to, but the idea of decency and honour remained fundamental to it, as was the case with the Latin term *pulchrum* which signified only 'honestum et decorum'. The definitions of these terms only became more involved after Plato had entered into the philosophical investigation of beauty. He recognised that there were different categories of beauty, but he considered them as one. He understood the essence of beauty to be that pleasing harmony, order and balance which is manifest in various ways in the physical and moral world. Beauty, therefore, was to him merely a representation of goodness and truth. Socrates, too, had the same idea in mind when he described beauty as the constant inner form of things, in which justice and goodness are united. Only the Sophists thought to differentiate between these qualities. The Platonists at any rate held on to the original concept, refining it almost out of existence, and it was only after the Greek spirit of learning had been revived, that the idea of beauty was recovered. It was in Italian art in fact, and particularly in the poetry of Dante and Petrarch that the sacred trinity of truth, beauty and goodness first reappeared. This was the foundation upon which the philosophers themselves built. And though the French were to conceive of beauty as merely *pleasurable* (q.v. *angenehm*) commendable studies were made by such men as Rousseau, Diderot and Montesquieu, to name only a few. Although the English may have little practical mastery of the beautiful in the arts, and little taste for it, their philosophers still adhere to Greek ideals, always using the term beautiful with some moral implication. Such men as Lessing, Eschenburg and Garve transplanted the English theories of Addison, Johnson, Hume, and others into German soil. In his *Kritik der Urteilskraft*, Kant subsequently claimed that judgements of taste were an aesthetic matter and that pleasure in the good was nothing to do with beauty; it was only in the object of a disinterested pleasure, he maintained, that beauty could be found. Since then there has been much controversy between aestheticians, which Herder, for instance, carried on in his *Kalligone*. Men have failed, however, to clarify the concept of beauty, ignoring those random and minor meanings that are figuratively employed in connection with the term *beautiful* in everyday life.

As aesthetics is the consideration of the beautiful in art, the term should be examined in the light of its proper and original meaning. The idea of truth is associated with knowledge, the idea of goodness with ethics and conduct; the idea of beauty on the other hand is expressed either completely, or at any rate in large measure, in form, and it awakens a pleasure that is in the highest degree disinterested. As far as aesthetic emotion is concerned, it matters not whether a statue is of bronze or stone, or whether a garden is adorned with idealised fruit trees, firs or pines. Now form is not merely a matter of the shape of a thing, nor can the uninterrupted contemplation of individual words, notes or ideas make them more or less beautiful, or more or less displeasing. Beauty of form really results from the ways in which variety is moulded into a unity according to the rules of taste (see *Art*). Nor does it necessarily follow that beauty is always empirical, simply because it primarily concerns form. It is true that representations of the beautiful in music, painting and poetry, make their initial impact upon the external senses, but there are also spiritually beautiful objects, and if something did not exist inside us to interpret phenomenal stimuli then the term beautiful would be quite meaningless. Colours, sounds and words are symbols by which the inspired artist represents what he feels inside him; by means of these he creates that beauty which in turn affects the observer. The beautiful then mainly plays upon the intellect and the imagination; it affects the intellect by means of regular form and the imagination by means of material representation of something that is spiritually beautiful – the idea of the beautiful *in concreto*. The following definition then would seem to be self-evident: *The beautiful is that which occupies the intellect and the imagination with such uncomplicated and regular form that it much enhances our vitality.*

Some higher spiritual power must at the same time give life to the pleasingly regular form; so it is that morality and truth are not excluded from the creation of true beauty. This obviously is logical enough, for anything that seems to be beautiful must be more or less perfect in form, engaging the faculty of reason, which, as the faculty of the absolute, also strives after the ideal. Untruth and amorality may certainly assume pleasing shapes, but never ones that are truly beautiful. The idea of the beautiful is infinite. Beauty may also be defined as that quality in the form of an object that causes the infinite to be seen or felt in terms of the finite. To summarise then: *The highest beauty is in God; and its brightest image on earth is man*, who not only goes to God but also comes from God and is thus constantly aware through recollection of some previously sacred experience. Man's premonition of and search for ever more perfect beauty is most deeply anchored in this awareness of bliss. If the true nature of beauty is to be more precisely defined, we must now consider the matter from a less abstract viewpoint, one, to use Schelling's expression, that is to be found as the living centre between soul and nature. One of nature's finest and most splendid gifts is the capacity to react to art, which springs from the earth and grows from an inextricably interwoven triple root: form, colour and sound. Art wholly belongs to nature which gives it the rules and patterns for every kind of *beauty*. If we contemplate a work of art with a trained eye, we observe, from what has been said above, that it has certain spiritual and formal qualities, qualities that are not mutually exclusive, but which may none the less be thought of as masculine and feminine and which can be compared with one another in the following way: strength–gentleness; firmness–tenderness; solemnity–innocence; grandeur–simplicity; dignity–grace; nobility–attraction; loftiness–elegance; pathos–ethos; the solemn–the moving; the sublime–the naive. The reason for pairing solemnity and innocence is that they are both inseparable from sheer exuberance. Grandeur and simplicity are juxtaposed simply because one is more or less masculine the other feminine in appeal; they are not mutually exclusive, but they consort well together and in combination they create sublime beauty. The most moving type of masculine beauty is loftiness, whereas elegance has feminine qualities. Pathos and ethos, which the Greeks regarded as contraries, represent virtually the extreme opposites in the sequence of attributes that relate to beauty. But both are essential preconditions of beauty. The passions lend expression and character to art; they are the winds which drive our ships forward on the sea of life, they are the winds by which the poet sails and on which the artist is borne aloft, but the artistic expression of pathos cannot be dissociated from ethos, a disregard for ethos is incompatible with pure and heavenly beauty. By opposing the sublime to the naive, we are arguing that the sublime is merely one category of beauty and not diametrically opposite to it. Aesthetics has long been dominated by the idea of the sublime and the beautiful as opposites, an idea that has destroyed the unity of art. Detailed definitions of *particular* aspects of the beautiful are given under separate headings, each of which will explain how and to what extent these forms of beauty are normally represented in music and to what extent they constitute actual types of forms and representations.

If we glance again at the complete list of types of beauty, the sublime takes the form of a kind of fusion – the sum total of all the masculine qualities of beauty. These all call for a certain clear self-awareness, the antithesis of which leads to the contemplation of feminine or naive beauty. This has its greatest impact when all those qualities that may be regarded as essentially feminine are intimately fused together. In combination with masculine, sublime beauty, they form something that admittedly is very rarely or never encountered in nature but which must none the less be recognised as *artistically beautiful*, something that may well be encountered in art (see *Art*). So it is that the pathos and ethos combine to produce the highest art works; majesty and emotion movingly combine together; solemnity and innocence together form calm beauty; in short the image of lofty beauty may be shaped from almost every conceivable combination of qualities. Qualities that when separately defined had seemed to be opposite, now blend together in pure harmony until finally the eternal source of all creates the highest beauty of the utmost brilliance, one that only may be experienced in art.

Although the images of art attempt to give phenomenal expression to the idea of perfect beauty (an ideal perceived by the soul), they rarely manage to achieve this goal; for man can only reflect nature in his art, and nature herself is never perfect.

When artistic images are created they are merely illuminated by the purest ideal beauty and are but a feeble reflection of it, for God's eternal beauty can, as the ancient Persian poet has so beautifully put it, only be perceived by one eye which thus illuminated becomes sublimely immortal. But even were the ideal none the less an undiluted vision of the Divine, as is perhaps sometimes the case with the inspired artist (see *Inspiration* and *Imagination*) think how much gets lost in the case of the portrait painter, for instance, on the long, laborious journey that leads from the eye of the soul by means of the hand and the tool to the recalcitrant material?

The poet's ideal necessarily becomes obscured in the immense variety of shapes and patterns that succeed each other and through which he must express the images that are within his soul. The lyric poet's brilliant and most intimate vision dissolves even more totally than does that of the epic poet, into disconnected flashes of inspiration, until the *composer's* ideal ultimately illuminates everything like a shaft of light that springs from behind the magic veil to produce an encircling halo of pure enchantment. Indeed, only music manifests, as it were, the principal qualities of beauty in pure physical essence, its substance being the billowing surging waves of air. For all its apparent incoherence it thus brilliantly foreshadows the transcendental, the beauties of which it awakens in our souls by means of notes (See *Music*). Hajji Chalsa, an oriental poet of the eleventh century, said of music in his great and comprehensive work (*Encyclopädie der Morgenländischen Wissenschaft*, p. 308, Leipzig 1804), 'When the soul is charmed by beautiful melodies, it longs to perceive higher beings and spirits, and it yearns for translation to a purer world. Through the medium of music, souls that are darkened by the body's substance are prepared for and made receptive to communication with those superior spirits and beings of light who float in the highest dwelling places round the seat of the Almighty.' The ascription of such magic to sounds, which even here on earth intermittently conjure up heavenly visions, is surely not just a poet's dream of music. Many spiritually receptive people, as the psychologists tell us, are filled with blissful rapture when music unfolds to them in brilliant clarity shapes of marvellous beauty.

Inspiration (Begeisterung)

All inspiration begins with a vivid impression that is created in the soul by some object or other of outstanding aesthetic appeal; but the impression an object makes on a creative artist differs from its impact on the performing artist or on the listener, even if all three ultimately share the same derivation. The *creative musician*, the true tone-poet, experiences this object in much the same way as do all those in whom any kind of divine creative fire is kindled, that of the ideal itself. In his case, this is what he seeks to express in terms of music; the more clearly and brightly this ideal illuminates his inner perception, the more powerful its impact on his sensibility, the more he is inspired by it and the more clearly he will be able to give it shape. At such times, he sees, hears, feels and thinks only of that one thing which must be fashioned, or at any rate of those matters that are closely or tangentially relevant to it. Hence he becomes all soul, all feeling. The notes come to him vividly, with uncommon facility, clarity and immediacy. They become symbols of his own natural language, expressing effectively, spontaneously and in undiluted purity the emotion latent within him. This is the origin of that intensity and expressive power, that urgent, intimate eloquence of tender emotion, that savage turmoil of vehement passion, that rich store of multifarious images, that subtle shading of emotion, that strange, often dreamlike juxtaposition of widely differing things, that note exactly suited to each emotion, and everything else that inspiration brings out in the artist. Perceiving everything with blazing intensity, he seizes his instrument and plays in such a state that sounds pour out from within him in what is called free fantasy. In the moment of inspiration, he snatches his pen and captures for posterity in an act of composition the vision of pristine beauty that his prophetic eye has discerned.

Inspiration gives rise to a different yet not dissimilar phenomenon in the imagination of the performing artist. The performer does not first need to visualise some ideal on which subsequently to base a model; the poetic material has already been provided for him. He does not kindle his own inner fire, for he is not himself a poet, but some work already in being stimulates his imagination. His situation is parallel to that of the composer of vocal music, for whom the poet has provided a pattern in a shape that is already completed. Words, sounds and individual notes in the text may already indeed kindle new and effective ideas (as did perhaps the simple sonorous sound of the word 'Hallelujah' in the sensitive Handel), the more so if he is aware of their higher sense and deeper meaning.

Thus, then, the inspiration of the virtuoso and the vocal composer, in contrast to that of the purely instrumental composer – the real tone-poet – takes the form of an attraction that quickly and powerfully seizes the imagination. It is aroused only by the greatness, the richness of the actual beauty of some pre-existent object. If such an object (the composition to be performed or the poem to be set) is none the less so to affect the spirit that the spirit's powers are properly stimulated, it must be susceptible to clear, precise development, the imagination must discern the variety in it and be genuinely attracted by it. In such a case, the spirit concentrates all its powers, withdraws its attention from all other objects and endeavours only to perceive clearly; and then, just as clearly, to realise what it has perceived.

And this is what all great and genuine artists of our age still do: just observe them sitting or standing, how calm, how divorced from the outside world, as if turned in on themselves, as if they wished to lose themselves in some invisible world, their eye glowing as if illuminated by some intensely brilliant light that was secretly and rapidly passing over their features, as if magic spirits danced around them, or as if they were controlled by some higher power – in this way they create patterns in sound, and after we have listened to these patterns, we are tempted to ask: 'Were you in Heaven, sitting on some Divine throne, when you addressed us in such a language?'

When the ideal rises like the sun on such an illuminated human soul, it is shown to be an intensely brilliant perception of the Divine, of which none the less it is but a feeble reflection. The eternal pristine beauty of God can only, as an ancient Persian bard so beautifully puts it, be comprehended by an eye that is itself inspired to a state of undying bliss. Hence, when some such dedicated being, fired with blissful inspiration, contrives truly and faithfully to reproduce what his inspired vision perceives, moving us to the depths of our souls, we ought all to sink in obeisance. But on the long and arduous journey from the eye of the soul, through the hand and instrument, to the recalcitrant artistic material, far too much of the inner process (*Gang*) is lost; just as the very image perceived by the soul is only a twilit reflection of the highest things, so in turn the artist's most sacred vision will appear to us, even in the most perfect work of art, only as a faint impression. This is so however much the sounds, dissolving like a rainbow behind some magic veil into a pure vision of dazzling radiance and providing a clear premonition of the transcendental, stimulate an awareness in us of those beautiful qualities that their own image reflects and that is clearly recalled by the notes. It is perhaps neither an exaggeration nor an extravagantly poetic attitude to art to suggest that such sonorous magic awakens in our souls even here on earth fleeting visions of heaven. For psychology provides many well-authenticated examples of visionaries before whose spiritual eyes music has miraculously evoked beautiful shapes, brilliant in their clarity, thus filling the beholder with the most blissful rapture.

Romanticism and the romantic (Romantik und Romantisch)

These words must not be confused with, or derived from 'Roman' (novel) or 'romanhaft' (novel-like), though they do have a common origin, namely the *romance languages* [*lit.: language*]. The romance countries of Southern Europe, notably Italy, Spain and France, were the first to explore an intense emotional world that was not as clear or serene as that of ancient Greece nor as inflexible or systematised as that of ancient Rome. The seeds from which that world grew included Christianity, chivalry, the colossal Roman Empire in its final stage of dissolution and the crude but vital spirit of the Middle Ages. It also partly grew from the dynamism of the Saracens' ardent and adventurous outlook, transmitted by the Crusaders as well as left behind by the Saracens themselves when they occupied the near eastern countries. These ideas were identified as romantic. They took firm root and multiplied in every form of art. Hence, on to the stock of oriental romance, rooted in an intense and fervent faith, in honour, love and the idealisation of suffering, was grafted in place of the dark concept of fate a sublime faith in a wise and benevolent Providence. The turning point dates from the time that Christian chivalry, with its ideals of faith, bravery and love, paved the way for a response to a new richness of ideas and for a new way of thought that had previously been inconceivable. The foremost qualities of this romanticism were an innate sensitivity and a belief in the miraculous.

Add to this the bolder speculative idealism in which such pride has recently been taken, and we have the idea of the romantic and of romanticism in its entirety. And if of all the arts music proves to be the one in which romantic ideas are most truly at home, it may well be said that where music is, there, too, is the essence of romanticism. Music is pre-eminently romantic; what other art draws so heavily for its most beautiful and characteristic materials from the profound depths of the emotions? And what other art moulds the material at the same time into a more ideal shape? Musical ideas and musical materials, the very essence of romanticism, are here fused together with the deepest inner feelings and a powerful urge towards an ideal world.

The art of music was beginning to take root at the time that Christinity made its impact upon the spirit of chivalry, at a time when Christian romanticism transmuted earth to heaven wherever Christianity spread. Music was the art which first served the Christian liturgy and through which Christian ideals were most suitably expressed. The religious concepts of classical antiquity were expressed through the medium of the plastic arts, and in them the gods assumed perfection in human form. Christian ideals could be expressed only in an art that aspired to the eternal, the elements of which were evanescent, ethereal and heavenly. It is music that elevates man to the infinite, to God Himself. The visual arts reduce the infinite to the finite. The concept of romanticism is misconstrued if it is explained in any other way. Romantic music is in fact *any perfect* music. The term should not even be applied to a specific genre of music, as the French would have it, of which more later.

Romantic art springs from man's attempt to transcend the sphere of cognition, to experience higher, more spiritual things, and to sense the presence of the ineffable. No aesthetic material is better suited to the expression of the ineffable than is sound, the stuff of music. All music is in its innermost essence romantic. Music on the wings of rhythm can achieve that which no colour, however splendid, no chisel, no word can achieve. The proper realm of true music only begins where speech leaves off. E. T. A. Hoffmann says that instrumental music is the most romantic of all the arts; and he is right. In the realm of vocal music, Mozart accomplished everything that could be accomplished. No other composer has expressed romantic life as fully as he did in *Don Giovanni*; and for this reason, the opera will always remain fresh. Of more recent composers, Maria von Weber and Spohr are particularly attuned to the romantic spirit, Spohr being the more limited and Weber the less disciplined of the two. Of the most recent composers, Mendelssohn, Löwe and Reissiger deserve particular mention. Few others merit comparison with these, for the power to create and imitate freely and unconsciously, inspired by the inner workings of the spirit in an hour of bliss, has become all too rare. Mechanical intellect has usurped the place of inspiration. A feeling for the eternal is steadily diminishing, just as is the pious faith of children, in which religion is rooted.

There is increasing distaste for the romantic and a growing desire for the sensual and the physical. Countless artists are ever ready and willing to satisfy these needs. The outward trappings of romanticism – ghosts and miracles – may have been preserved, but the soul has all but vanished. Meyerbeer described his opera *Robert le Diable* as a romantic opera, but it has everything except the romantic spirit.

Turning away from this somewhat unhappy situation, and briefly recapitulating, profound sensitivity and bold idealism are the principal characteristics of musical romanticism, rather than any quality of materialism. The romanticism that several young French composers are trying to establish at the moment – they even describe themselves as a romantic school – is of a very different kind. In this case, it implies an antagonism to classical procedures and the search for a really novel musical style. Mm de Staël was the first to use the term 'romantic' in order to describe Chateaubriand's pietistic attack upon atheism. Another more general meaning soon became associated with it, one that is certainly better referred to as Neoromanticism. The new French neo-romantic school has as its goal the overthrow of all traditional artistic procedures, arguing that true poetic freedom is to be found in the unfettered imagination, and that any higher standards of taste are subject to the rule of shameless anarchy. The most recent exponents of such ideas include Liszt, Berlioz, Chopin, Auber and Halévy. This school of composers is undeniably responsible for many an aberration, many an adventurous experiment and a good deal of wilful tastelessness. Nevertheless, the school has in many ways helped to liberate French art. The two principles upon which these romantic composers base their work can be identified as easily as can a party flag. These concern the substance and the structure of their music.

The French romantics who, incidentally, already have a following in Germany, are quite unselective in the ideas that they handle: in their music lives the age of égalité, of horror and of bloodshed. Absolutely anything serves them as material; and it is unfailingly treated in the most eccentric manner in order to attract attention. These men merely flirt with truth; they reach out for rain and sunshine, thunder and lightning, slaughter and murder, horror and tumult, because heaven is too remote and because it ignores the sensible world (*Gefühlswelt*). These romantics have discarded as shackles the forms and textures of which the old school was so proud. Their harmonies and melodies are bold, exciting, highly coloured. They assume unprecedented shapes which are quite breathtaking, but they are not infrequently over-ornate and therefore tasteless. That the tasteless may also be epoch-making is neither here nor there. The romantic school is in fact epoch-making, but as far as can be judged, none of its exponents has yet achieved true clarity or balance. It attempts to be descriptive in a variety of ways and it strains after novelty. In the realms of art, at least, aberrations and deviations are no new thing, nor are they any guarantee of artistic originality. These neo-romantics give more thought to the creation of colourful contrast than to basic musical ideas, and yet for all that, beautiful variations of light and shade are quite lacking. This neo-romantic school has sought romanticism above all in the dimensions of the bizarre and grotesque. It has been unaware of the deeper, more inward-looking qualities of romantic music, that spring from the depths of the soul, and which are manifest in Beethoven's instrumental music and in Mozart's vocal music. A piano piece by Chopin gives rise to astonishment: compare it to one by Beethoven. The fact that far fewer people respond to the Beethoven is a reflection of current attitudes, but these provide no standard for the evaluation of the only true and lasting forms of art.

The sublime (Erhaben)

In the literal sense, everything which the observer perceives as incomparably great, and which arouses intense emotions in him, is sublime. There must therefore be something distinguished and commanding about anything that is describable as such. Now sublime grandeur can be either *extensive* or *intensive* and an object may thus be either extensively or intensively sublime. Following Kant, some aestheticians have used the term *mathematical* in place of extensive, and *dynamic* in place of intensive. The trouble is that the alternative terms are quite unacceptable as long as mathematics involves the consideration of intensive size as well. The sublime can be experienced not only in the towering Alps, in the vast oceans, in the pyramids and in the colossus of Rhodes, but also in human nature itself. According to Burke, who was otherwise very sensitive to beauty, the sublime is displayed in titanic acts of human willpower, and in situations of regal splendour. Yet man in his purely natural state is able to create all the effects of the sublime.

The sublime would be better subdivided into the *physical* and the *spiritual* but even this does not exhaust all its aspects, since the spiritually sublime, at any rate, is identical to the intensively sublime. Intensive sublimity too may be found in the physical world; in for example, a volcano, or a storm at sea. Let us therefore stick to our original categories and define the *extensively sublime* as *grandeur extended in space or time*, and the *intensively sublime* as *grandeur of power*. A still more exact understanding of the idea of the sublime (in music as elsewhere) is to be got from an investigation of the theory of the different qualities of sublime grandeur. For something to be sublime it must be on a large scale: large *in itself*, in its power or in its extent or shape. Thus the ideal, the infinite is incontestably of the greatest sublimity; the concept which embraces the eternal, the ineffable, the divine, the supremely transcendental in all its relations with the finite world, dwarfing nature herself. One has only to concentrate intensely on this idea and one becomes aware of the sense of the sublime in its pristine purity, a sense that can moreover be aroused in nature or in art or indeed in the imagination, by anything of any magnitude that is assessed not by mathematical but by aesthetic standards. This implies that the finite spirit is inspired with awe, that it gradually loses itself in a sense of the infinite and assesses things by a standard for which the whole world itself is too puny. The sublime object is usually at the same time both attractive and repellent; it does not arouse an unadulterated feeling of pleasure, but one of pleasure combined with a certain displeasure, a feeling that is none the less intensified by this very mixture. This is the most beautiful and at the same time the most surely and easily recognisable hallmark of the sublime. Here is yet further proof that a higher degree of spiritual training is invariably necessary if the contemplation of the sublime is to afford pleasure. In the *arts* considered in themselves, the sublime is always a special category of the beautiful and a quality of beauty. Taken in its strictest sense, the term beautiful need not normally imply sublimity, nor will the sublime always be beautiful. Even formless, gigantic grandeur is sublime, but it is not beautiful.

As nothing formless is permissible in art, nothing sublime can be created in art without creating beauty at the same time. Something beautiful can certainly exist without sublimity however, for the goal of art is beauty, in whatever form it takes, whether sublime (masculine) or naive (feminine). From this it can be proved irrefutably that the intensive (spiritual or dynamic) sublime is vastly superior to the purely extensive (physical or mathematical) sublime. The power of inner reflection is so vast that it is incompatible with the qualities of grace and naiveté. Beauty in its absolute power flows directly from the depth of self-awareness. It is precisely such reflection that gives rise to a sense of the sublime in art. Man experiences it more from within himself than from without. It is more subjective than objective. It is not the tempestuous sea that is sublime, but the infinite spirit whose physical eye surveys it; the eye in which the world is reflected is more sublime than the world itself. The sublime is here connected to some extent with things that thrill, frighten and horrify, and sublime experience can be sparked off and intensified by what is thrilling. The same also is true in respect of the arts. The sublime always involves an element of the marvellous, and it flows over into the realm of the solemn, the splendid and the noble, where it achieves its finest realisation in union with unalloyed beauty.

This is such an important point that it is necessary to start with an analysis of the sublime both in nature and in art in order to formulate principles that may appropriately be applied to music in particular. This will not take long. In music the extensive and intensive sublime are always found in combination, fused with one another (if that is it is ever possible to speak of external constituents of music). Here as everywhere in the Arts, as in Nature, only grand and large-scale forms produce a sublime impact: this is especially true of music in which the sublime results from rich harmony and strongly emotive rhythms. In order to retain the character of that masculine beauty which alone is sublime, all colourful and pretty embellishment, however graceful and enchanting, must be avoided as being alien to the genre. The sublime is exclusively expressed in beautiful simplicity of layout and execution, and it makes its effect solely by means of its massive power. Thus we find the sublime in many larger-scale sacred works by famous composers, especially in this case because the sublime easily flows over into the solemn and the splendid, as has already been mentioned. The Overture to Handel's *Messiah*, the 'Hallelujah' chorus, the chorus 'Wonderful, Counsellor', the chorus 'God of Israel' from *Samson*, the chorus 'Let my mouth not desecrate his name' from Schneider's *Pharaoh* and many others of similar character are all sublime and hence beautiful. It is the sublime simplicity, the sheer weight of sound that creates the effect in these cases. The first impact is admittedly all but shattering, but the very impact prepares the listener for the sublime emotion that it immediately awakens, and as it unfolds in beauty it increases his pleasure more and more to the point that any attempt at verbal description would be futile.

In all these particular cases the intensively sublime element, the sheer power of the music, predominates; the extensively sublime, in the form of the development of powerful material, takes only a subordinate role. In the act of listening, no one is aware of the musical construction, skilful though this certainly is; only the total effect is felt. In such works as J. S. Bach's eight-part motets and Handel's splendid fugues for instance, things are different. The ear alone cannot absorb in a single act of perception the full power of the harmony and the conjunction of rhythms; it is the marvellous texture and intricate counterpoint that arouse our astonishment rather than the magical intensity and richness of the part-writing. In this case it is extensive sublimity that predominates. It may generally be assumed that in all major contrapuntal works extensive sublimity is the source of our awe, whereas intensive sublimity is its source in all other works that are generally thought of as pure art. In the first case the music principally affects those who are spiritually initiated (those who are educated musicians); in the latter case, on the other hand, music appeals to all sensitive listeners. Even so, the concept of the sublime transcends all physical reality and if religious faith in miracles ultimately stems from the same source as aesthetic feelings for the sublime, then in music too the sublime achieves its most perfect expression and greatest power when it links the finite and phenomenal, so to speak, with the infinite and divine, thereby clothing the sublime with a miraculous radiance. Thus there is still no music of greater sublimity than the passage, 'and there was Light' which follows 'and God said' in Haydn's *Creation*. God's creation of the finest of good things – light on Earth – was a miracle; what a marvellous impression the music makes here too! Haydn, deeply moved by it, once cried out at this point, 'That did not come from me; it came from above!' Some have also called the music to the dungeon scene in Beethoven's *Fidelio* sublime. This can only be intended in the sense that the sublime arouses horror or terror, feelings that are present when we reflect on our insignificance in relation to the grandeur we have felt as sublime. Instead of surging freely and joyfully upwards to the infinite, our imagination becomes more and more self-centred; the infinite of its very nature, however, cannot be expressed in art. Beethoven's music is descriptive, true and beautiful; as such it is deeply moving but it is not sublime, for it strides only in firm, bold steps that are altogether devoid of melodic decoration, often moving by leap and requiring in performance a pithy, very sustained sound, and energetic accentuation.

Giuseppe Mazzini

(b. Genoa, 22 June 1805; d. Pisa, 10 Mar. 1872)

From: *Filosofia della Musica* (1836), in *Scritti Editi ed Inediti* (Imola 1910) vol. 8 *Scritti Letterati*, vol. 2, pp. 121–6

After a brilliant university career Mazzini graduated in law at the University of Genoa in 1826. He speaks in his autobiographical notes of long hours devoted to music, in his youth. The discovery that he was a member of the secret revolutionary organisation, the Carbonari, led to his imprisonment in 1830 and to his exile. It was during his imprisonment that he determined the future mission of his life, the expulsion of foreign powers from Italian soil. Apart from a brief period as a triumvir of the Roman Republic, in the revolutionary year 1848, his hopes remained unfulfilled and he died at Pisa whilst in hiding from the authorities.

The romantic movement was for him a political movement, and he saw music fulfilling a role not dissimilar to that envisaged by the French revolutionary writers, notably Barthélemy (p. 166) and Leclerc (p. 240). Something of the quality of Mazzini's imagination is revealed in the brief autobiographical comment, in which he looks back with a curious pleasure to those early months in prison: 'The cell [he wrote] looked out on the sea, and this was a comfort to me. The Alps only excepting, the sea and the sky are the two sublimest symbols of the infinite. Whenever I went to the little grated window in my cell, there they were before me.'

For further reading:
Edith Hinkley, *Giuseppe Mazzini; the story of a great Italian* (London 1924, repr. New York 1970).

Art is immortal. It is also progressive, for it is the expression in terms of emotion of God's thought as revealed and interpreted in His world. It does not describe a circle, nor does it retrace paths already trod. Instead, it progresses from age to age, continually enlarging its sphere, continually rising to higher ideas as each previous idea has been fully realised, continually renewing itself in the name of each new movement, once the ideas of the previous one have settled into a mere technical routine. This is the law of fate in all matters: one age exhausts its originality and another takes its place. It is for genius to discern and reveal the secrets of the new.

I believe that music has reached such a pass today. The ideas that gave it life have become exhausted; new ideas have not yet been revealed. And until they have been, as long as our young composers persist in reworking the old ones, as long as their inspiration kindles no desire to explore some new heaven, music will be devoid of creative power. School will contest with school without hope of victory; *artists* will wander in confusion among systems and movements, lacking all purpose and hope of progress, for ever copying others and winning no laurels save those reserved for imitators; laurels which, colourful though they are, wither away in a day. We shall have perfect technique and exquisite execution but no creative growth. We shall have diversity of style but no new ideas; flashes of inspiration, but no music; musical enthusiasm, fashion – even feeling – but not faith or belief.

The human intellect is at present poised between two worlds in the gap that separates the past from the future, between an exhausted complex of ideas and a new one yet to be exploited. Every field of human knowledge provides evidence of this truth. Poetry, literature, history and philosophy all express one common factor; they all proclaim to those who have ears to hear: 'We are living in an age of transition, between the last rays of a setting sun and the first feeble glimmer of a rising one.' Modern poetry yearns either for the past or for the future; it is the poetry of *tears* or of *prayer*. Literature either wanders in search of some lost theme or murmurs some hope of some future destiny. History picks an uncertain way between two systems – between the bare and simple chronicling of facts and events and a synthetic interpretation of them. Philosophy is earthbound; either it follows eighteenth-century paths and centres on man as an individual, or it denies reality and the possibility of implementing theory in practice, lost in contemplation of some unattained and perhaps unattainable ideal absolute. Bold attempts are initiated and then abandoned half-finished through discouragement or lack of impetus. Solutions are propounded and then forgotten. There is an air of restlessness. Men sense that they possess powers, yet they do not know how to apply them; they yearn for, yet are troubled by the Unknown, without being spurred on to any positive conquest of it. The intellect thirsts for unity in all things, yet it is either ignorant of, or lacks the courage to follow any path which leads to such unity.

Romanticism, as has been said, though a powerfully destructive agent, could not construct anew. It was essentially a theory of transition, devoid and incapable of any organic conception or idea. Before the human mind could set out on the path of social art, something was necessary to liberate it from the tyrannies of schools and pedants. It is worth stating and re-stating this, because the present dangers facing artistic development do not arise from its enemies, who have been completely vanquished, but from incompetent practitioners, or timid and inexpert innovators, from hotheads who equate current aesthetic anarchy with the height of sublimity, or who worship the Prophet rather than the God. When romanticism hurled the apple of discord among men of letters, it flung it not among Italians, not among nineteenth-century Europeans, but among bastardised Greeks and Romans. The Ancients held despotic sway. Modern elements were suppressed. Christian art, free art, human art, lay stifled beneath the debris of the pagan world. Like the northern invaders during the fall of the Roman Empire, romanticism seized and scattered these dead relics; it revealed *subjectivity* crushed beneath them. And then, whispering a truth that had been forgotten for a good five hundred years, and applying it to art, it rededicated art to freedom with the words 'Forward! The Universe is Yours.' Bid that was all.

Then, however, men of talent could not decide which path to take. They scaled the Heavens and enveloped themselves in clouds of mysticism; they descended into Hell and encountered the unbounded anguish and the satanic sneer that dominate so much French literature; they abased themselves before the relics of the Middle Ages, seeking inspiration in the ruins of cloisters and convents. From all these quests and experiments, by turns tentative, exclusive, even retrogressive, there emerged as a presage of the future one sign of a reborn awareness and power, one idea: the restoration of the human *ego* to its proper place. To those who asked them, 'In whom do you trust?' they were at least able to answer as the barbarians did, 'In ourselves!'

As soon as it became evident, though, that there was still a vast and unbridgeable gap, and that the aspirations of the younger generation could not be satisfied, merely by experiment, men became discouraged and dismayed. They remain so. Science, art, every field of human knowledge lacks a person to reinvigorate it. They need someone to focus their efforts on one goal, to unite them in the brotherhood of a common civilisation. There is no such person now; but he will come. And then the anarchy that presently wearies the mind will be dispelled. The arts will again flourish: each will have its proper place and function, sanctified by the practice of a faith, immortal, revered, each contributing to the other, in harmony and concord. In the meantime it is worth preparing the ground and pointing the path of salvation in every possible way to those who have not lost faith in the arts.

As far as literature is concerned it is not that these and a thousand related matters are unknown, but rather forgotten. Both at home and abroad they have often been expressed and acclaimed, for the powerful Italian intellect recognises truth when it encounters it. Of those however who have discussed or written about music, which of them have ever thought in terms such as these, or even tried to determine the philosophical origins of music's problems? Who has drawn attention to the bonds that link music and its sister arts? Who has even considered that the basic idea of music might be the same as the developing idea of the physical universe itself and that the secret of its development is to be sought in the development of our age as a whole; that the reason behind its present decline is the prevailing materialism, the lack of social belief; and that the path of resurrection can only lie in such belief, in the association of music with the fate of literature and philosophy? Who has even raised his voice, not in protest against incorrigible *academicism*, but in encouragement of the younger generation, wishing to launch out yet not knowing in which direction: 'You are practitioners of a sacred art; and you should be holy too if you wish to be its priests. The art that has been entrusted to your care is closely bound up with the course of civilisation; it can become the air, the soul, the incense of that civilisation; it may become the inspiration of the victory of progressive civilisation, not of arbitrary rules foreign to the laws that determine all things. Music is the harmonious voice of creation, an echo of the unseen world, a note of the divine concord which one day will sound through the entire universe. How then can you capture that note if you do not exalt yourselves to the contemplation of that universe, allying yourselves to things unseen, through faith, embracing all creation, in your studies, your interests and your love? Why be content then to string notes together, at best like minstrels, for the passing hour, when you can dedicate yourselves here on earth to a task that people hold to be the prerogative of God's angels in heaven, alone?'

Alex Br

From: 'Parallelen, Politik und Musik', *Neue Zeitschrift für Musik*, vol. 5, no. 21 (9 Sept. 1836), pp. 84–5

In antiquity, there were world-wide empires; in the Middle Ages, ancient tradition and the Church; in the contemporary world there are dissensions, progress, politics and journalists. Antiquity had its plastic arts, the Middle Ages its painting; and the contemporary world has its music. For whenever there are powerful and forceful political and intellectual influences at work, some kind of compensation for the resultant conflict and tensions must be supplied by the arts to satisfy those human longings that remain unfulfilled. The age provides such a compensation according to its needs. Everything of which the Greeks were aware and everything they fully understood was human; their gods, too, were human in every sense. Nature was their close and intimate friend; nature was a present, a gift whose meaning they easily uncovered in the charming and fantastic imagery of their mythology. There was nothing horrifying to make them frightened, nothing inexplicable to puzzle them. Moreover, they enjoyed political eminence, power, security and triumph. In such a spiritual and political environment, the *plastic arts* were the most appropriate means of expression. They set the material facts clearly before them. Nothing needed to be added, for the spectator beheld the creator's idea in its entirety and immediacy; the meaning was fixed and unshakable.

Such a limited medium could not satisfy Christendom for long, particularly the Christian faith as it had been shaped by the romantic spirit of the Middle Ages. Restless with longing, everything aspired towards *one* point of union; the whole of nature stood in mysterious relationship with the *One*. Every tree, every blossom, every cloud, every wave was a personified object in the mind of the spectator, striving to return to that from which it had been torn. Thus, as a being in the created world, man experienced secret terror. He was aware of his relationship to lifeless matter; everything was sacred and inexplicable. Moreover, he was at once protected and oppressed by the powers of feudalism and religion. Just as the powers of Night vied with each other in the external world, so it was within his perplexed and anxious soul. But this struggle had not yet involved the common man. *Painting* was a more effective medium for the expression of such conditions than the plastic arts. The wonderful paintings of this age and works of medieval architecture bring us close to such feelings even today.

The brighter vision of more enlightened ages has robbed this emotional life of its power. The objective nowadays is pleasurable and easily controlled titillation of the senses. Anything that furthers this objective is welcome; anything that provides a voluptuous thrill is grasped at; and whenever the thrust and unrest of present-day political life leave a residual longing for something different and better, we find it necessary to dissolve that longing in the spirit of art. We have seized hold of *music* – the discontented masses have at last achieved power and influence, which would be desirable and welcome enough if only, motivated by other circumstances, they had different goals.

Our age has reshaped and refashioned music after its needs; it has made it into a courtly and sensuous art, and it has paid a considerable price in the process. The present age is not ungrateful and demands nothing without payment; it asks only subservience and agility and a willingness to please. It has found precisely these things in music – it sees music as a golden egg from which any bird may equally well be hatched: condor, or wren, nightingale or peacock. No art has been so thoroughly permeated by the present as music; no art is more closely attuned to the political climate of the day (or of yesterday) than music is. It is a history of our century written in treble and bass clefs; the Revolutions of 1789 and 1830 may be read in it; the whole history of Robespierre and Charles X, Napoleon and the Archduke of Brunswick, the Württemberg Assembly, Fieschi[1] and the storming of the Catalonian convents. It is at the same time a charter and an oracle; a mirror, an image – in short, the pampered child of the century. And that phrase reveals everything.

---

[1] Giuseppe Marco Fieschi (1790–1836) was a Corsican adventurer who attempted the assassination of King Louis-Philippe of France (1773–1850) on 28 July 1835. Fieschi was guillotined on 19 February 1836 (eds.)

Berlioz

(b. 1803; d. 1869)

From: 'L'Imitation en musique', *Gazette musicale de Paris* (1837)
translated by Jacques Barzun in *The Pleasures of Music* (London 1952),
pp. 211–18

I

Let us begin by discussing *imitation* in music, not in the technical sense
which refers to fugue and the fugal style, but in the sense of producing
certain noises which describe or depict by musical means objects whose
existence we are aware of only through our eyes. This notable element of
art, which not a single great composer of any school has neglected to use,
whether or not his attempts were successful, and which admittedly has
seduced more than one into ridiculous and deplorable errors, has seldom
been treated with any fullness or examined with judgement. I shall therefore
try to throw some light on the darker side of its theory, while seeking the
criterion by which to determine when its application ceases to be art and
falls into absurdity after exhibiting the silly and the grotesque.

M. Guiseppe Carpani, the excellent Italian critic to whom we owe, among
other things, a volume of letters on the life and works of Haydn,[1] will help
us in our search. His views on the matter seem those of a man gifted with
musical good sense and a proper feeling about the true limits of the art of
music. Yet he appears to me not to have sufficiently brought out the main
features of the subject. Hence the present attempt to fill in the gaps left by
his discussion, which I mean to follow step by step.

In one of his letters about the famous oratorio *The Creation*,[2] in which
Haydn makes frequent use of the descriptive style, M. Carpani remarks that
long before Haydn, composers had been making use of the imitative means
open to the musician; of these the critic distinguishes two kinds – the
physical and the emotional. The first he calls direct, the second indirect.

> By direct imitation [says M. Carpani], I mean the imitation of sounds as
> they occur in the throats of animals, or as they are made by the air
> vibrating in different ways around solid bodies. The air soughs through
> foliage, bellows in caverns, murmurs along uneven places, etc., all of which
> it is proper for music to imitate, even though it be not its highest

[1] *Le Haydine* (Milan 1812) by Giuseppe Carpani (1763–1825).
[2] (1798).

prerogative. Such imitations are difficult and deserve credit. It is said that a Greek was once asked to go and hear a man whistle like a nightingale. 'Not I,' replied the Greek, 'I have heard the actual bird.' The reply has been wrongly lauded. 'My dear logician,' I should have said to him, 'it is precisely because the song is not made by a bird that it is worth hearing and admiring. If some one told you to look at a battle painted by Giulio Romano and you replied, "I have seen a real battle," what sense would there be in the rejoinder? It is exactly because you have witnessed real battles that you must find pleasure in seeing art reproduce the likeness with a little coloured earth.'

Here M. Carpani seems to me to go seriously astray by borrowing an argument from a comparison with painting. That art may not indeed have any other object than to reproduce with fidelity, to give a beautiful imitation of Nature; whereas music is in most cases an art *sui generis*. It is sufficient unto itself, and possesses the power to charm without having recourse to any kind of imitation. Painting, moreover, cannot encroach on the domain of music; but music can by its own means act upon the imagination in such a way as to engender sensations analogous to those produced by graphic art. This point, however, belongs to the second part of our subject, that which M. Carpani calls indirect or emotional imitation. As to the first, the direct or physical imitation of the sounds and noises of Nature, here is what I would say about it, and what our author fails to bring out:

If we are to accept imitation among musical devices without detracting from music's independent power of nobleness, the first condition is that imitation shall virtually never be an *end* but only a *means*; that it shall never be considered (except very rarely) the main musical idea, but only the complement of that idea, joined to the main idea in a logical and natural manner.

The second condition to making imitation acceptable is that it shall concern something worthy of holding the listener's attention, and that it shall not (at least in serious works) be used to render sounds, motions, or objects that belong outside the sphere which art cannot desert without self-degradation.

The third condition is that the imitation, without aping reality as by an exact substitution of Nature for art, shall none the less be close enough for the composer's intent to avoid misconception in the minds of an attentive audience.

The fourth and last condition is that this physical imitation shall never occur in the very spot where *emotional* imitation (expressiveness) is called for, and thus encroach with descriptive futilities when the drama is proceeding apace and passion alone deserves a voice.

To illustrate and support the foregoing distinctions, I shall take examples from the great masters of music and poetry (for in this matter music and poetry have a common stake), and I shall begin with Beethoven. It might seem as if the 'Storm' in the Pastoral Symphony were a magnificent exception to our first rule, which allows imitation only as a means and not as an end. For this symphonic movement is wholly given over to the reproduction of the divers noises heard during a violent storm which breaks suddenly over some village festivities. First a few drops of rain, then the rising wind, the thunder grumbling dully in the distance, the birds seeking shelter; finally the approaching gale, the boughs that split, men and animals scattering with cries of dismay, the shattering bolts of lightning, the floodgates of heaven opening, the elements let loose – chaos.

And yet this sublime depiction, which outstrips anything that had ever been attempted in the genre, actually falls within the category of *contrasts* and *dramatic effects*, which are required by the scope of the work. For it is preceded and followed by gentle and smiling scenes to which it acts as a foil. That this is so may be tested by imagining this storm transplanted into another composition in which its presence would not be motivated: it would unquestionably lose a great deal of its effectiveness. Hence this piece of imitation is strictly speaking a means of achieving contrasts, devised and managed with the incalculable power of genius.

In *Fidelio*, on the other hand, a work by the same composer, we find another piece of musical imitation of very different purport from the one just reviewed. It occurs in the famous duet at the grave: the jailer and Fidelio dig the place where Florestan is to be buried. Halfway through their toil the pair unearth a large rock and roll it with difficulty to one side. At this point the double basses of the orchestra play a strange and very brief figure – not to be confused with the ostinato phrase of the basses which runs through the whole piece – by which it is said Beethoven wished to imitate *the dull sound of the rolling stone*.

Now this imitation, being in no way necessary either to the drama or to the effectiveness of the music, is really an end in itself for the composer: he imitates in order to imitate – and at once he falls into error, for there is in such imitation no poetry, no drama, no truth. It is a sad piece of childishness, which one is equally grieved and surprised to have to complain of in a great master. The same could be said of Handel, if it be true – as is commonly said – that in his oratorio *Israel in Egypt* he tried to reproduce the flight of locusts, and this to the point of shaping accordingly the rhythmic figure of the vocal parts. Surely that is a regrettable imitation of a subject even more regrettable – unworthy of music in general and of the noble and elevated style of the oratorio.

Haydn, on the contrary, in his essentially descriptive works *The Creation* and *The Seasons*, does not seem to have lowered his style appreciably when, in order to follow the poem, he applied imitation to such agreeable noises as the warbling of turtledoves – an imitation that is, moreover, quite exact.

This brings us back to Beethoven and the Pastoral. There has been frequent criticism of the song of the three birds toward the end of the 'Scene by the Brook'. As regards the suitability of this imitation, it seems obvious enough. Most of the quiet voices of the waters, earth, and sky naturally find a place here and contribute easily to the serene magnificence of the landscape, but they are not all equally capable of faithful rendering. Beethoven wanted to make the quail, the cuckoo, and the nightingale heard in his orchestra. Now, the first two are unmistakable from the very outset, whereas it is clear that no listener would ever recognize the nightingale in its pretended imitation without being told. The reason is that the fixed sounds of the quail and cuckoo are available in our scale and our instruments, but the voice of the nightingale, sometimes plaintive, sometimes brilliant, and ever irregular, is not imitable. It is odd that this fact of observation has escaped the many composers who have similarly tried and failed to ape the elusive vocalizations of the warbler of dusk.

One may mention other imitations which reason does not exactly reprove but which have been so long in the public domain that they have become vulgar; so that the musician who uses them must show rare tact or strong inspiration to ennoble them or give them the appearance of freshness. In one of the duets of *William Tell*, for example, under Arnold's words 'I seek the field of glory,' there is a prolonged rhythmic pedal point for trumpets. Its effect seems to me commonplace, or at any rate open to criticism of a kind that a man of judgment such as M. Rossini should not make himself liable to. On the other hand, in Gluck's *Armide* the clamour of war with which the composer accompanies Dunois' exclamation 'Our general summons you!' makes the most phlegmatic listener thrill with enthusiasm; it will remain, regardless of the revolutions of taste, as one of the most dazzling strokes of genius.

When, finally, physical imitation is used as a means, there is a pitfall into which some of the greatest poets have fallen, and to which I shall draw the attention of musicians. When Talma, playing Orestes, used to hiss the *s*'s as he exclaimed, 'Pour qui sont ces serpents qui sifflent sur vos têtes?'[3] far from being terrifying he always made me want to laugh. For it seemed to me clear, then as now, that this solicitude of Orestes to imitate the hissing of serpents when his soul is filled with terror, his heart with despair, and his head with ghostly visions, was directly opposed to any idea we may form of what is dramatically natural and likely. Obviously Orestes is not *describing* the Furies; he imagines that he is actually seeing them. He hails them, pleads with them, defies them; and one must be a very docile spectator not to find comic a piece of imitation ascribed to such a sufferer at such a juncture.

As against this, Virgil's many imitative passages strike me as most felicitous, for he has taken care to put them in the narratives made by his characters or in the descriptions for which the poet himself is responsible, e.g. 'Ruit alto a culmine Troia; Nox atra cava circumvolat umbra; Quadrupedante putrem sonitu quatit ungula campum', etc.[4]

---

[3] 'For whom are these snakes that hiss atop your heads?' – from Racine's *Andromaque*, Act IV, scene 5.

[4] From the *Aeneid*.

II

The kind of imitation that M. Carpani calls *emotional* is designed to arouse in us by means of sound the notion of the several passions of the heart, and to awaken solely through the sense of hearing the impressions that human beings experience only through the other senses. Such is the goal of *expression, depiction,* or *musical metaphors.* As regards expressive power, I doubt whether the arts of drawing and even of poetry can equal music. It is only the infatuation of a certain celebrated composer's followers, joined to their total lack of musical feeling and education, that has enabled them to defend their idol on the ground that all musical accents were interchangeable, whence it followed that the composer of *Otello*[5] was not guilty of nonsense or absurdity, since no music could be *true.* He himself refuted them in masterly fashion by his score of *William Tell.*[6] But it would be tedious to dwell on the point.

Musical *depiction*, as I shall show in a moment, is not quite the same thing as a musical *metaphor* and does not seem to me to be nearly so genuine a possibility. The famous naturalist La Cépède,[7] who among his scientific colleagues passed for a very fine composer, says somewhere that 'since music has only sounds at its disposal, it can act only through sound. Hence in order to produce the signs of our perceptions these signs must themselves be sounds.' But how can one express musically things that make no sound whatever, such as the denseness of a forest, the coolness of a meadow, the progress of the moon? La Cépède answers, 'By retracing the feelings these things inspire in us.' And our Italian critic finds this sort of imitation worthy, admirable, enchanting. He deems it the musical sublime. I am far from sharing that opinion, and I incline rather to think him mistaken – deceived, like many other writers, by a play on words or, if you prefer, by the lack of precision noticeable in the terms that define the subject.

Is there, for example, any single, fixed manner in which we are affected by the sight of a forest, a meadow, or the moon in the sky? Assuredly not. The woods whose shade and coolness will draw a reminiscent sigh from the happy lover will make the jealous or jilted man gnash his teeth, and will fill his heart with gall at the thought of his happy rival. Meanwhile the hunter will approach it full of eagerness and expansive joy, whereas the maiden will look upon it with secret fears. Now music will easily express blissful love, jealousy, carefree gaiety, anxious modesty, violent threats, suffering and fear, but whether these feelings have been caused by the sight of a forest or anything else, music is forever incapable of telling us. And the pretension to extend the prerogatives of musical expression beyond these already spacious

---

[5] Rossini (1816).

[6] Rossini (1829).

[7] Count Bernard de La Cépède (1750–1825), known chiefly as a botanist, wrote operas as well as a widely read treatise, *The Poetics of Music* (1785).

limits strikes me as wholly untenable. Hence there are hardly any composers of real merit who have wasted their time in pursuit of such an illusion. Their business was quite other, and their achievement far superior to these so-called imitations. If some few have occasionally given up music in favour of something which, after all, is neither music nor painting – and thus given up substance for shadow – I am inclined to think that art as a whole has not lost much thereby, and that in their case substance and shadow equally lacked merit.

Handel, it is true, tried in one of his works to depict a natural phenomenon which has nothing to do with sound or even with silent rhythm, and which affects no one, I should imagine, in any determinate manner – the phenomenon of falling snow. I find it quite impossible to understand how he hoped to get a grip on such a subject once he had made up his mind to imitate it in music.

I shall be told, perhaps, that there exist admirable examples of musical depiction which must be taken account of, if only as exceptions. But on looking closer it becomes clear that these poetical beauties in no way overstep the vast circle, within which our art is circumscribed by its very nature. For these imitations are not in fact offered us as pictures of objects but only as images or analogues. They help to reawaken comparable sensations by means which music undoubtedly possesses. Yet even so, before the original of these images can be recognized, it is strictly required that the hearer be notified of the composer's intent by some indirect means, and that the point of the comparison be patent. Thus Rossini is thought to have depicted in *William Tell* the movement of men rowing. In point of fact all he has done is to mark in the orchestra a *rinforzando* accented at regular intervals – an *image* of the rhythmic straining of the oarsmen, whose arrival has been announced by the other characters.

Again, Weber is credited with having painted the moonlight in the accompaniment to Agatha's aria in the second act of *Der Freischütz*; this is because the calm, veiled, and melancholy colouring of the harmonies and the chiaroscuro of the instrumental timbre form a faithful metaphor or *image* of the pale light of the moon, and, moreover, admirably express the dreaminess of lovers beneath the moon, whose assistance Agatha just then invokes.

Of certain other compositions one may say that they represent a broad expanse of infinity itself, because the composer has been able to suggest to the ear, through the breadth of his melodies, the grandeur and clarity of the harmony and the majesty of the rhythm – all of these being set off by contrary effects – impressions analogous to those a climber might feel on the summit of a mountain when beholding in space the splendid panorama suddenly unrolled *before his eyes*. And here, too, the truth of the *image* will appear only if the listener has taken the pains to inform himself ahead of time about the subject treated by the musician.

It is evident that the possibility of *arousing emotions by images* that only words sung or spoken can identify, is very far from sustaining the ambitious and vain design of positively denoting by musical means objects that are inaudible or rhythmless.

There is to be sure another kind of *image* that fastens on the words of vocal music, but it succeeds only in shackling expression at large by dwelling on accessory details regardless of meaning. This sort of image is almost invariably childish or petty. How many asininities of this sort could be pointed out in the works of more or less renowned composers! Some cannot come to the word 'Heaven' without leaping to a high note: another would think it a disgrace not to speak of Hell in the lowest vocal register. One makes the dawn rise and another makes the night fall. Nothing is so unbearable as this mania for continually playing on words – a mania which, it must be said, is gradually being cured. For to judge from J.-J. Rousseau's assault upon his contemporaries, it was never more prevalent nor more acute than among the French musicians of the last century.

Robert Alexander Schumann

(b. Zwickau, 8 June 1810; d. 29 July 1856)

From: *Robert Schumann im eigenen Wort*, ed. Willi Reich (Zürich 1967); *Robert Schumann, ein Quellenwerk über sein Leben und Schaffen*, ed. Georg Eismann (Leipzig 1956); *Jugendbriefe*, ed. Clara Schumann (Leipzig 1886)

Eismann, vol. 2, p. 149

1. [The Nature of True Art]
The greatest skill in art is that of spiritualising the material, so that everything material in it is forgotten. But this skill is never the result of contempt for or a cavalier attitude toward the material, for even were such attitudes to be adopted, the material element will still insinuate itself. Skill results from the analysis and re-synthesis of the material.

Reich, p. 119

2. [Music as a Universal Language]
Music speaks the most universal language which arouses the soul in freedom, without specific constraints, yet the soul feels itself at home in it.

Eismann, vol. 2, p. 159

3. [Music with a Programme]
We must confess to a prejudice against this kind of activity, and we share this prejudice perhaps with a hundred academics who usually have, it is true, the strangest ideas on the act of composition, invoking the name of Mozart, who is supposed to have had no thoughts when he wrote his music.

As already stated, however, many people share this prejudice, including those without theoretical knowledge; and if some composer presents us with a programme *before* his music is performed, I tend to say: 'Let me hear it first of all whether it is beautiful and then afterwards maybe your programme will please me too.' There is, after all, a difference between a Goethe writing verse to a given rhyme scheme and some other person doing so.

Hence nobody will dispute the beauties of Spohr's Seventh Symphony – 'Earthly and Heavenly Things in Human Life' – simply because there is a difference between a Louis Spohr setting himself a task to do and some novice.

This matter was already touched upon when Spohr's Fourth Symphony appeared; and the battle has begun to flare up again between the 'One-ought-not-to-think-of-anything-while-composing' party and their opponents. The theorists imagine that things are probably worse than they really are. They are certainly wrong if they believe that a composer works out an idea by sitting down like some parson on a Saturday evening, producing a scheme for his theme under the usual three headings and developing it accordingly.

Yes, they are certainly wrong. Musicians set to work quite differently. And if they have some image in their mind, they will only feel themselves happy in their task if that image comes to them as beautiful melody, borne on those invisible hands like the golden caskets of which Goethe writes somewhere. So keep your prejudices, but at the same time test them; and don't hold the apprentice's clumsy efforts against the master.

Reich, p. 410

4. [Melody]
'Melody' is the amateur's battle-cry; and certainly, there is no music without melody. But let it be properly understood what is meant by the term: for all that they ask for is an easily understood pleasantly rhythmic melody. But there are melodies of a different stamp; and if you open the pages of Bach's, or Mozart's, or Beethoven's works, they will stare you in the face in a thousand shapes and forms. I hope that you will soon tire of the threadbare sameness of the latest Italian opera melodies.

Reich, p. 408

5. [On Being Musical]
What, then, does being musical consist of? You are not so, if you plough laboriously through a piece with your eyes anxiously on the music. You are not so if, when someone turns over two pages instead of one, you get stuck and cannot continue. But you are so if you have some idea of what comes next in a new piece, or if you know by heart what comes next in a piece not new to you; when, in fact, you have the music, not only at your finger-tips, but in your mind and your heart.

(Letter to Clara 13 April 1838)

C. Schumann, pp. 282–3

6. [What my music is about]
I react to everything that happens in the world: politics, literature,

people – whatever it is, I think in my own way about anything that may want to find an escape, an expression in music. This is why so many of my compositions are so difficult to grasp, because they are related to remote interests, interests, incidentally, which are often significant, since anything remarkable in our age seizes hold of me so that I have to give it musical expression. This is why I find so few modern compositions satisfying, quite apart from their technical shortcomings, because they also exist on the lowest plane of musical emotion. Even at their very best they fail to reach the very starting-point of my kind of music. They resemble a flower; my works resemble a much more spiritual poem. They represent a mere natural urge; mine are the product of poetic self-awareness. I am totally unaware of this during the act of composition and I discover it only later – you will certainly know what I mean, as you yourself have climbed so many rungs of this ladder.

See also Bibliography under: Luppmann, Plantinga

Fig. 7. *Strasbourg Minster*. It was a commonplace of romantic criticism to compare the great polyphonic masterpieces of the baroque era with gothic architecture. Becker's essay develops this theme at some length. (Municipal Archives, Strasbourg)

Constantin Julius Becker

(b. Freiberg, 3 Feb. 1811; d. Dresden, 26 Feb. 1859)

From: 'Ideen über Baukunst und Musik', *Neue Zeitschrift für Musik,*
vol. 8, nos. 21–2; 13–16 March, 1838, pp. 81–6

Constantin Julius Becker assisted Schumann with the editorship of the *Neue
Zeitschrift* from 1835 till 1843. In the latter year he left Leipzig to teach singing in
Dresden. He is mainly remembered for his *Männergesangschule* (1845) and he also
wrote a novel *Die Neuromantiker* (1840), translated Berlioz's *Voyage musical* and
composed a symphony and an opera *Die Belagerung von Belgrad* (1848).

Gothic architecture underwent a revival of interest in Germany in the third quarter
of the eighteenth century; and both Herder and Goethe published important essays
on aspects of German Gothic art. Goethe's essay, which appeared in 1772, took as its
subject the cathedral, or rather the minster at Strasbourg, the building which inspired
Becker's two articles in the *Neue Zeitschrift*. Goethe somewhat mistakenly saw the
minster as an essentially German building and his essay is one of the landmarks of
the *Sturm und Drang* period, with its violent sense of the liberating influences of
anti-classical art and its powerful sense of history.

Becker, who was to follow up the articles from which our quotations are taken
with a similar pair of essays on music and painting in 1840, pursues the parallel,
much commoner in the nineteenth century than it is today, between the 'spiritual'
appeal of Gothic architecture and that of the music of Handel and Bach.

Here I sit, in my lonely room, contemplating Strasbourg minster as it towers
into the darkening evening sky, its pinnacles and vaults shrouded in
mystery. The massive edifice resembles some earthly image of the Divine; it
is a magnificent and intricate work of art which seems, as it were, to express
in tangible form the mystery of the Christian church; it is profoundly and
intensely disturbing. Like everything sublime and magnificent, it excites a
turmoil of emotions that threatens to overwhelm clear thought. At a time
like this, no art so closely resembles music as architecture, for it plays, above
all, on our undefined presentiment of some great eternal truth and evokes
through its poetic veil the shimmering image of a transcendental world of
divine clarity. Music can with justice then be described as the art that
symbolises the spiritual idea of truth in the form of beauty. Such truth, on
which the arts are based, necessarily excludes chance and coincidence, be
the work of art simply the idealisation of a model or its complete physical or
moral representation. It follows, then, that what we experience as surprising, or, as we call it, original in music is none the less *necessary*; anything
that is contrived or irrelevant to the idea either makes no impression on us
or causes disquiet.

We encounter this necessary quality of surprise when we look at Strasbourg minster, although we might at first tend to dismiss as purely arbitrary the mass of decorative detail, before we have properly understood it. Further contemplation of the building brought to mind Bach's music; instead of hearing music, I saw it – music, if I may be forgiven the expression, in stone. Indeed, if it were possible to reproduce Bach's music in stone, we should recognise Bach as a contemporary of those venerable masters of medieval architecture. . . .

Italy, once the focus of the organised Christian church, was also the country on which all the arts centred and from which warmth and light were spread abroad. It was there that artists from the Netherlands cultivated music, whilst others – mainly from the East – cultivated architecture. Even if religion was not the mother of music, architecture and painting, she was at least their nurse and governess. A study of the political and religious state of society at the time will serve to underline the undeniable influence that religion then had. At a very early stage, the Christian religion had need of new kinds of temple; later on, as it developed, it required special music. Just, perhaps, as the style of ancient Greek and Roman architecture was alien to the Christian religion, so pre-Christian music was unsuited to the Christian rite. Whereas no pre-Christian music has survived, many works of pagan architecture have not unexpectedly done so. In a short space of time it was inevitable that the architrave, its horizontal lines blocking any aspiration to higher, invisible things, should give way to the upward-thrusting curved arch of the Byzantine style. The basis of this style is essentially the curved arch. Its rounded vault points to and, as it were, symbolises Heaven, and is representative of the Roman Christian Church of its day. The generally smooth and rounded appearance of this style, for all its splendid simplicity and voluptuousness, none the less lacks strength, yet it is highly evocative of the numinous ritual of its age, its religious assemblies and its brilliant festivals. Italian music of a later period took shape in the same climate. It, too, is characterised by rounded forms, and for all its splendour and simplicity, it, too, can be criticised for a lack of drive, resulting from a one-sided emphasis on melody. Even if one absolves the church music of that particular period from the charge, there was none the less a period in which this lack of drive and sensuality tainted it. It was for that very reason, after all, that Pope Marcellus II wished to banish music from the church.

The religious ritual of the South for a long time dominated the North, at the same time infecting its art. After a long-drawn political and moral struggle, however, the North achieved self-sufficiency, not as the South's pampered offspring, but as a free son of the invisible Church. Protestantism, as it may be called, was an innate characteristic of Northern peoples, whereas in the South, it was an acquired one. Small wonder that this protestant spirit slowly but surely developed over a period of several centuries and eventually threw off the foreign yoke as if it were a garment that had become too tight.

It is in the architecture of the Middle Ages that this self-sufficiency is first evident. In Gothic architecture, as it has been called, the pointed arch and the cruciform vault supplanted the rounded arch and the barrel-vault.

The capital and the architrave, with their horizontal lines, and the rounded arch, with its self-contained circular shape, emphasised the finite and the material. The pointed arch achieved something that they had never managed to achieve. It hints at what is revealed rather than what is experienced through the senses and it strives upwards towards the eternal in simple, sublime form. The barrel-vault of the Byzantine style here becomes a bold and upward-thrusting cruciform vault. Instead of columns, there are pillars; their function is not to bear the vault's weight, but to spring from the vault, so to speak, as the blossom does from the seed. In this we observe not only the greatest boldness and power, but also the loftiest grace and charm. . . .

But the masterworks of Gothic architecture not only provide us with intense artistic pleasure, they also lead us to a higher, fuller life, the religious life of the Middle Ages, a life of lofty simplicity, powerful faith and sober, reverent piety, a life that deeply influenced everyday existence and that sought to elevate natural and human affairs to the level of the secret, supernatural and divine.

These works of art do not pretend to embody the transcendental in the material, but to imitate it in the form of beauty, striving to combine reality with perceptive insight.

The impulse that gave birth to Gothic architecture also fathered the music that developed, several centuries later, like a kind of nobler and therefore more slowly ripening fruit, and reached its maturity in Handel and Bach. It is of the same kind, but its form is clearer, for it is created from more spiritual materials and its uplifting effect on the spirit is less restricted. Indeed, rigorous analysis of music and architecture actually yields a comparison between the two. Is not a musical theme exactly like the basic motif that governs the design of a work of architecture? Both create a clear, firm and self-sufficient impression. Such a musical idea is a sort of walled-in emotion, which is focused clearly upon the consciousness, everything alien being excluded. From it, the composer shapes subsidiary themes; these cannot always be related to it note for note, but they are similar in character to it. The architectural development of the sketch is equivalent to the musical development of a theme. The artistic techniques that composers then used are clearly reminiscent of the principles of [Gothic] architecture. Thematic extension, abbreviation, diminution, augmentation, reversal, inversion and the like were artistic techniques. Are not these also to be found in every kind of marvellous, highly characteristic embellishment in a Gothic building?

Here as there, the law of symmetry prevails. However asymmetrical it may seem in itself, every rhythm is very closely and intimately related to the others, and each is necessary, being conditioned, that is to say, by the basic theme. In architecture, this means that any unusual feature of the design can be derived according to geometrical principles from a basic motif. This is the reason why each individual movement of a musical work of that period seems, then, to have been poured out from one source.

[p. 83, col. 2 to p. 84 omitted]

In suggesting that the development is already predetermined to some extent by the theme, I am not saying that the composer has merely to continue the work in a mechanical fashion according to the rules of his craft. The rules that he followed when he began work in no sense restricted his imagination, but his original, unfettered thoughts evolved simultaneously with the form. It is easy to understand why one and the same theme is susceptible to as many developments as the composer can think of. Here, as everywhere, the greatest talent sets the standard. For this reason, no one who lacks inventive talent will ever be able to compose a good fugue, for example, however thoroughly he may have studied counterpoint.

By the way, I should advise you to check my random ideas and develop them yourself by studying some fugue or other (preferably by Handel or Bach). Perhaps you will manage to derive some aesthetic pleasure in a form that is currently so out of favour and misunderstood. Like all older music, it admittedly requires some concentration and a capacity to sustain a single emotion without being feebly diverted into related emotions.

The artist must intensify his emotional concentration to the level that was characteristic of earlier times if he wishes to gain a proper insight into the spirit of the old masters. Laymen can no longer be expected to do this. To launch our apostate age on a crusade on behalf of a confession of artistic faith that no longer holds good would be to mistake the temper of the age. Even though the finest music of the age – that of Bach and Handel – may nowadays be incomprehensible, it still has unique historical greatness, and it will never lose this as long as the Gospel of the Art of Music is preached. To ban it from the Church in favour of modern church music would be a degenerate step to take. This should be avoided, at any rate as long as there is a liturgical need for such music, even if that need currently springs, as does our liturgy as a whole, from pious respect rather than inner compulsion.

I should not care to judge whether Gothic architecture still affects us as it did our ancestors. I should no more deny such an effect than I would deny the effect that the music of Bach and Handel has on our present generation. For whatsoever things are beautiful, whatsoever things are true, whatsoever things are of good report, these will retain their worth to the end of time, even if now and again they may lose some of their effect. Our reactions are certainly so blunted by empty tinkling, elegantly piquant vapidities, loathsome virtuosity and by a craze on the part of some modern composers for originality, that we rise with difficulty to the level of such a classicist as Mozart. The time is none the less coming, let us hope quite soon, when the vain and ephemeral tinsel glitter of such pomp will be forgotten. For the blessed and divine secret of the beautiful will always retain its manifest greatness, a greatness that is revealed to the world by the high priests of art.

Fétis[1]

From: 'L'État actuel de l'esthétique musicale', *Revue et gazette musicale* (1838), pp. 4–7, 44–6, 149–53

That beauty can be the subject of a science is an idea that even now raises an incredulous smile from those superficial people who are only concerned with appearances and for whom the analysis of the faculties of feeling and thinking is quite foreign. For them, beauty is the raw product of an unfettered imagination; it can only be appreciated by a vague and indefinable feeling, one that conforms to no law, other than that of spontaneous pleasure, and one that is the eternal object of uncertainty and mystery.

People who are capable of philosophical thought and serious study, however, find that beauty can not only be the subject of scientific enquiry but it can itself constitute the basis of a science which is as certain as any other can be.

I propose here to examine the present state of this science and to discover what degree of certainty has been reached as far as those matters are concerned that relate to music. For the sake of clarity I must briefly glance at the origin, development and progress of the science.

The very earliest attempt to investigate musical beauty in a scientific manner stemmed from a tradition that is attributed to Pythagoras. According to this philosopher, the basis of the theory of beauty was a numerical one, and it applied to everything in the world. Now numerical relationships are at the root of harmony. These exact relationships result in beauty of proportion and thence in absolute beauty.

Musical proportion, Pythagoras argued, lay in the exactness of the relationships between sounds: the simpler the relationships the more harmonious they are; the more complex, the less pleasing. He proposed that all possible interrelationships are encompassed within the octave and he calculated all the intervals that are contained in it, expressing the relationships numerically in the way that geometricians still do today. The visionary Pythagoras applied these proportions to the universe, and he conceived the idea of a world in which the proportions of all things were identical. He argued that the relationship between the speeds, distances and reciprocal motions of the planets were the same as those of music and that these numerical proportions are to be found in everything known and unknown.

This theory was enthusiastically adopted by a number of Pythagoras's

---

[1] For a discussion of the author's work see the editorial introduction on p. 400.

pupils; it became widely known and it has had a devoted following for some 1,200 years. In modern times it has been given a new lease of life by Kepler, and others. As far as musical beauty is concerned the illustrious Leibniz has summed up the whole of Pythagoras's work in the following proposition: 'Music is a secret calculation that the soul unknowingly makes'; in other words musical judgement is a secret feeling that arises from the congruity and disparity of sounds, one that depends upon the simplicity or complexity of their numerical relationships.

Later on an experiment, or rather several experiments, showed that when a long, thick string was set into vibration in a certain way, a good bell or other weighty and sonorous body gave out not only the fundamental note but several softer notes too which in combination produced a perfect harmony of the major third, the fifth and the octave. Rameau availed himself of this discovery and combined it with Pythagorean proportion to build up a system that was not in a general sense derived from Pythagoras but from musical harmony itself, and which involved all the known chords of the time. He summarised his entire theory in a book entitled, *Observations sur notre instinct pour la musique et sur son principe, où les moyens de connaître l'un par l'autre conduisent à pouvoir se rendre raison avec certitude des différents effets de cet art* (Paris 1754). This was the first time that a French work had attempted to base the rules of musical beauty upon positive principles. In it Rameau established that harmony is the essential foundation of beauty, and that melody and harmony are powerless to create it by themselves. 'A person', Rameau maintained,

> who is engaged in listening to the actual music is never in a sufficiently detached state of mind to be in a position to judge. He may for instance believe that the music's beauty derives from passages that involve a transition from low to high registers, from soft to loud dynamics, from lively to slow speeds, all of which lend variety to the sounds. He will therefore base his judgement on such preconceptions *without reflecting that such things are of only slight importance, that they have little intrinsic merit, and that they have nothing to do with harmony, the sole basis of music and the principle that gives rise to music's greatest effects.* Rameau later goes on to say that passions are stirred up by harmony alone; melody draws its strength from this source alone, from which it emanates. *As for such differences as result from a change of pitch, these modify melody in no more than a superficial way and add almost nothing to it.*

Let us pause for a moment to consider exactly where we have been led, from Pythagoras right through to Rameau, by the doctrine that numerical relationships of sounds are the basis of musical beauty.

At first sight it is not too easy to see how the proportions that merely determine the precision of pitch intervals can produce beauty in music, unless it is by taking care not to shock the ear with discordant notes. On closer examination, however, the conviction grows that this exactness of proportion constitutes a tonal system. Now, since the feeling for a tonal system – for a specific succession of sounds – is one that man spontaneously experiences as he listens to any kind of music, one realises that the proportional system comprising tonality must be the basic principle of musical beauty. It is in this direction that Pythagoras's theory ought scientifically to have been developed. Instead of fulfilling this grand and beautiful design Pythagoras's successors became preoccupied with those mysterious relationships which existed, so they imagined, between musical proportion and the proportions of all other things, both known and unknown, within the universe.

Leibniz took up Pythagoras's system in the general terms that have been outlined above. Though he did not carry all his arguments through to their logical conclusion, there is reason to suppose that he wished his words to be interpreted in the widest possible sense, and that he intended to say this: that music is a secret calculation that the mind unknowingly makes of the relationships of sounds and of their durations, both simultaneous and successive. This proposition cannot be regarded as the exposition of a complete musical aesthetic, but it does suggest the way in which the mind operates when it judges the appropriateness or inappropriateness of successions or aggregations of sounds. Indeed, as artistic beauty necessarily springs from the felicitous relationship of the individual parts, the mind would be unable to judge unless it was continuously involved in the secret calculation of these relationships as it listened to a piece of music.

In Rameau's theories, aesthetic principles take on a more specific and positive form. Intervallic proportion still forms the basis of the system, but it is confined to simultaneously sounding notes. It is this that Rameau proposes as the source of all musical pleasure and even as the necessary basis of melody. Since the theory of beauty is necessarily centred on one specific aspect of the art from which spring all the others, it had to be summed up in a general rule that could both verify the appropriateness of each harmony or aggregation of notes, and the appropriateness of their succession. Rameau presents this rule in a formula that he calls the *fundamental bass* (*basse fondamentale*). As a measure of everything good or bad in music (at least, so Rameau thought), the fundamental bass ought to have been an infallible rule. Alas, it was no such thing, for it led to the approval of things that were not good, and to the condemnation of beauties that were generally approved.

Such, briefly, is the history of the system of proportions which was developed, up to the time of Rameau, by the geometricians, who made it the principle upon which musical beauty was wholly based. As we have seen, the principle is held by its proponents to give rise to two series of identical phenomena: one in the physical world around us; the other within us. In the external world proportion is needed to determine which sounds go together. It is equally indispensable to the mind, if we are to be able to judge the concurrence of sounds.

Another aesthetic principle relating to the appreciation of musical beauty is that which depends on empirical knowledge – the knowledge which we derive from experience. Aristotle is generally considered to be the father of this idea. The principles that this great man expounded in his first book on metaphysics certainly demonstrate that art and logic are of great help to man in his acquisition of a knowledge of beauty. Memory gives him experience; experience gives him art and science. Here, then, experience is established as the basis of feeling and knowledge. But in what ways can experience instruct us as to what is beautiful and what is not? No doubt by simply making us aware that certain things give pleasure, whilst others give pain. Here art is reduced to the level of purely physical pleasure, and there is no question of abstract thought. Such, indeed, is the theory that Aristoxenus taught, one of Aristotle's pupils, in opposition to the theory of proportional relationships propounded by the school of Pythagoras.

One of the consequences of this empirical doctrine – that of experience – is that the knowledge of beauty can only be acquired through the action of natural phenomena on the senses. Art, then, must confine itself to the imitation of that which our senses tell us is beautiful in nature. Thus the aesthetic principle, as far as music is concerned, is the imitation of nature. The chief exponents of the theory in France have been l'abbé Batteux, l'abbé Arnaud, Condillac, de La Cépède, Grétry and Barthez, and in Germany, Hiller, Ramler, Sulzer (though he had reservations), and Herder. These authors believed that beauty in the arts, and particularly in music, is to be defined in the following way: The soul does not have an innate feeling for beauty, but it does have an innate predilection for those things that give rise to the idea of beauty and a feeling for it, things that seem lovely to it.

It is easy to see that musical beauty, when circumscribed in this way, can only manifest itself in propriety of expression, and that its function must be reduced to a faithful portrayal of feelings of love, hate, joy, sadness, grief and anger. This being so, music can only be dramatic, and nothing else. Even when it is purely instrumental it must have a programme, a subject that is present in our minds; our only concern will be to judge the resemblance between the subject and the music. An entire school, both theoretical and practical, was founded upon this premiss, the leaders of which were La Cépède (see his *Poétique de la musique*) and Grétry (see his *Essais*). Several younger artists based themselves upon the work of these two men.

To sum up, the drawbacks arising from the theory of the empirical knowledge of beauty (which necessarily leads to the concept of imitation) are that art is circumscribed, and that the relationship between the soul and art is reduced to a passive one. This principle inevitably denies us the *a priori* creation of beauty. Beauty in instrumental music, then, is necessarily reduced to the imitation of such effects as storms, tempests, rain, wind, the galloping of horses, the noise of war, the sounds of the hunt, and so on; in such a role, music is at its weakest and most limited. This empirical doctrine is most effective in vocal music where the character of the expression produced by the successions of sounds is analogous to that of the words. It is of fundamental importance that the melody shall perfectly imitate the declamation, if this is to be achieved. Gluck, Grétry and their declared admirers gave particular attention to this point.

We now come to the third aesthetic principle, the one which together with the two that have been mentioned above, has divided the world since the age of classical antiquity; it is the principle that Plato has put forward in his philosophical dialogues, and which his followers have developed. According to Plato we have an abstract idea of beauty which relates to the beauty that we experience in things, and which exists independently of the things themselves. This implies, then, that a feeling for beauty is within us before we have any knowledge of external beauty. This theory is the loftiest one and the one that most enlarges the domain of our ideas. According to it beauty can be conceived in a limitless number of ways: beauty is of inexhaustible variety.

Plato's principle had many followers and it was incorporated into a complete philosophical system. It was modified by Hutcheson in his *Inquiry concerning beauty, order, harmony, design* [see pp. 23–7]. In this book the author proposes that we possess an innate sense[1] by means of which we have an *a priori* knowledge of beauty, one that combines with those impressions that it receives from the world around it.

Though Plato's doctrine serves to lend greater authority to judgements that are made of beauty, and of musical beauty in particular, it does raise some very considerable problems. It furnishes no general rule by which absolute beauty can be recognised, and it therefore lacks practical application. Moreover it leaves each of us to the mercy of our own feelings, and it offers no way of reconciling conflicting opinions. In short, it opens the door to the materialistic systems of Gall and Spurzheim and to the theory of nervous stimulation proposed by Broussais and others. These systems explain how it is that certain structures within the brain are better suited than others to comprehend beauty in tonal relationships, and how these organisms must assert themselves over the others in conformity with the law of beauty. In the end though we are left with no rule, other than that of authority, to decide what is beautiful and what is not. Moral despotism of this kind is repugnant to the dignity of man and to the purpose of creation.

Vainly seeking guidance in its search for absolute beauty in the arts (and above all in music, where there are especial difficulties), the world has been divided for many thousands of years between the various doctrines that have been described above. At length, during the second half of the eighteenth century, a new theory sprang up. It was little heeded at first but it has recently attracted widespread attention. You will have guessed that I am referring to the one proposed by Kant. This acknowledges that we acquire

---

[1] Fétis fails here to distinguish between Hutcheson's concept of aesthetic appreciation as an innate sense, and Kant's theory that aesthetic appreciation stems from an *a priori* capacity: see Collingwood, *Principles of Art*, pp. 167–8 (eds.)

knowledge through the action of the external world upon our senses; but it also recognises that the assessment of this acquired knowledge depends on the working of an inner sense. It thus reconciles and brings together the advantages of the empirical and the *a priori* systems.

Once this new approach has been comprehended we can understand the concept of beauty in the external world. Our individuality takes possession of this concept, finding in it a quality to which it can respond. It analyses it, judges it, and draws from within itself more exalted concepts. From this we acquire knowledge and judgement. There is then a rule of beauty; all that we have to do is to apply it.

Difficulties do none the less arise when we come to apply this law to music, ones that were not solved by Kant, for his attempt to determine the law of musical beauty is weak and inconclusive. Herder, his opponent, well understood the advantage that Kant left him in this respect, and he made skilful use of it.

Fichte, Schelling and Hegel greatly advanced the philosophy of beauty, well beyond the point that it had reached when Kant emerged as a powerful reformer. Yet those who have tried to deal with musical aesthetics have found the terrain slippery, and even the most energetic athletes have been hard put to it to remain on their feet. Many specialised and general studies have been published during the past thirty years on the question, and in each one it is evident that once the authors have propounded with greater or lesser force and lucidity their theories of beauty in poetry and the arts of design, they approach the problem of music hesitantly, as if they are walking on live coals.

I now propose, after this unavoidable introduction, to provide an analysis of such books as are unknown, or relatively unknown, in France and in which can be found, if not complete and wholly satisfactory systems, at least some good and fruitful ideas.

The necessary existence of a musical sense that creates and also judges musical beauty is demonstrated by the fact that beauty is created, and by the fact, too, that those of us who are moved by it appreciate it. This musical sense is twofold, comprising *sensibility* (*sensibilité*) and *judgement* (*entendement*), or as Kant proposed, *receptivity* (*réceptivité* and *spontaneity* (*spontanéité*). Kant believed the second of these two qualities to be innate (*a priori*), and he used the distinction as the sole means of reconciling the concept of ideal beauty – one that manifests itself when we imagine beauty in an order of new and hitherto unknown ideas – with the theory of empirical knowledge of musical beauty – the knowledge, that is to say, that we acquire through experience.

In virtue of this theory the philosopher of Königsberg included poetry within the system. Oddly enough, however, he had this to say about music: 'As regards the vital sense of hearing, music greatly stimulates it in countless ways; it even strengthens it. Music is a *regular play of the affections of the soul and it is at the same time a language of pure feeling, having no intellectual content.'* He says very much the same in his *Beobachtungen über das Gefühl des Schönen und Erhabenen* (Riga 1771) and thus falls into the trap of contradicting the very principle on which his system is based. This results from a confusion as to the nature of music, for music is a singular art that in no way deals with the same precisely determined concepts as poetry and painting do, which even in their freest forms are based on subjects that the intellect can readily understand. That an idea should exist, one involving an act of intelligence and a lively if indeterminate sense of pleasure, yet one, being musical, that cannot precisely be defined, is the very thing that most advanced philosophical reformers have hardly begun to comprehend. Thus, every time that they embark upon the subject their intellects begin to falter, and their firmly held principles desert them. As I pointed out in my 'Résumé philosophique de l'histoire de la musique' [*Revue musicale* (1828), p. 385] music is undoubtedly more an art of the emotions than of thought. In this sense I agree with Kant. There can be no doubt, none the less, that if the emotion is profound it does not limit itself to a physical pleasure in sound. We listen to a piece of music. It disturbs us; it transports us and draws from us exclamations of admiration. How beautiful that is, we say: how great, how sublime! In doing so we judge; we express the results of the workings of our reasoning powers. Something then has revealed to us abstract and general ideas of beauty, grandeur and sublimity, formulated by successions and aggregations of sounds. Kant then is mistaken when he reduces the action of music to the level of pure feeling devoid of intellectual content. Thus for the first time, a flaw in his closely reasoned argument has plunged him into a grave and self-contradictory error.

But how is it that ideas of beauty, grandeur and sublimity come to us in the form of configurations in sound? What relationship is there between these patterns of sound and our notions of the beautiful, the great and the sublime, as these terms are most generally and commonly understood? This is precisely the question that critical philosophy has been unable to resolve, because its author has no knowledge of musical feelings, nor has he understood how such concepts may relate to the art of music. It was left to his disciples and successors to apply his principles to musical aesthetics in a fairer and better way, and to get somewhat nearer to a solution of the problem.

Michaelis, a professor of philosophy at Leipzig, was the first to apply Kant's critical philosophy to music. His first essay on the matter was entitled *Ueber den Geist der Tonkunst mit Rücksicht auf Kants Kritik der aesthetischen Urtheilskraft. Ein aesthetischer Versuch.* (Leipzig 1795; *idem, Zweiter Versuch*, 1800). Although Michaelis unfortunately lacked profundity in the scientific presentation of his ideas he at least saw where the philosopher of Königsberg had gone wrong where music was concerned. In the first part of his work he demonstrated that the principles of aesthetic judgement and critical philosophy are as relevant to music as they are to the other arts and that the art of music would, in a sense, be reduced to nothing if it were not susceptible to analysis, and if the mind could not assess the aural sensations. Briefly, he established the fact that there must be a musical sense; without it, indeed, the ear would only perceive a succession of meaningless sounds, When however he gets down to an explanation of the way in which the musical sense arrives at a judgement, he finds himself helpless in the face of the difficulties that have been mentioned above. It was this that doubtless led him in the second half of his book to consider the analogy between music, poetry and the arts of design, although such analogies only apply in a secondary way to music. It is far easier to talk about the way that music paints and expresses certain things, things that are also the domain of poetry and certain other arts, than it is to speak of music's abstract qualities, and Michaelis was much happier when doing so. Limited as he was, he was obviously able to propose no other rule for judging beauty than that of faithfulness to the original, and this is the end result of his theory, no matter how he strives to raise the art of music to the realm of the Ideal.

Amongst those who are greatly attached to Kant's critical philosophy and who devote themselves to a rigorous application of his aesthetic, particularly to music, must be mentioned Heydenreich, Heusinger and C. H. L. Poelitz.

In his *System der Aesthetik* (Leipzig 1790, 4 vols.), Heydenreich devotes much space to the consideration of the beautiful in music. His ideas are close to those of Hutcheson and even to those of Chabanon. In refuting the idea that beauty in music springs from the principle of imitation he establishes, by philosophically transcendent reasoning, that the mind is particularly seized by the idea of beauty when the work of art in question achieves a unity and yet has a variety of means. The mind immediately is cognisant of these qualities when it hears a piece of music, and it rises by its own powers of apprehension to the pure idealism of unity in variety which it conceives as absolute beauty. Although Heydenreich nowhere explains how unity manifests itself in wordless music, there can be no doubt that the principle of unity has long been advanced as the criterion of artistic beauty, and that it may fruitfully be applied to music by virtue of the fact that in the realm of aesthetic judgement, its use has been extended to the area of pure idealism.

J. H. G. Heusinger, a doctor and professor of philosophy at the university of Jena has applied Kant's philosophy to aesthetics in a rather different way to Heydenreich. His *Handbuch der Aesthetik oder Grundsätze zur Bearbeitung der Werke jederschönen Kunst* (Gotha 1797, 2 vols.) deals particularly with music in the first volume (pp. 135, 214). Although, like Heydenreich, he accepted that the feelings produced by music are a subject for aesthetic judgement, he was not wholly convinced that Kant was totally opposed to this approach to the matter. He argued that Kant's ideas on this question are not very deeply thought out, and that the philosopher of Königsberg avoided it because he was not closely acquainted with the art.

Kant believed, moreover, that few musical compositions were of sufficient stature to be worthy of aesthetic judgement, for he argued, most lacked any sense of unity. Take for instance piano sonatas or quartets, he said: the opening allegro expresses joy, the second is of a light and playful nature whilst the third – the finale or presto – is of unbridled exuberance. There is no question here of any connection between them nor of any movement towards a common goal. I must confess that I was somewhat surprised to come across such pitiful reasoning from one of Kant's disciples and from a doctor of philosophy. Can it really be that most musical compositions are powerless to activate the faculty of aesthetic judgement? But anything that you say about music when talking like this is an aesthetic judgement, one that is good or bad, just or unjust, but a judgement none the less, and one that arises solely from the music itself. And then, what analytical method is to be found in the work of a critic who condemns a composition on the sole ground that its several movements have different characters? Obviously this opinion shows that Heusinger understands nothing about wordless music, unless it concerns the imitative expression of a specific thing: music, for instance, such as Beethoven's Pastoral Symphony. Even this work would not have escaped his criticism, for in each movement the composer has expressed a diversity of feelings that we experience at the sight of the countryside, feelings that pass in turn from gentle joy to melancholy, and then to boisterous merriment. Generally speaking, although Heusinger has much to say about music in his *Handbuch* he is much less profound than Heydenreich; he is often manifestly unable to express himself clearly and he is forced to choose almost all his examples from dramatic music. In truth, Heusinger has done nothing to advance the study of musical aesthetics.

The little work by Poelitz entitled *Grundlegung zu einer wissenschaftlichen Aesthetik, oder über das Gemeinsame aller Künste* (Pirna 1800), is more substantial. It comprises a handful of general principles which reveal their author to be a distinguished thinker, possessed of ingenious ideas. Poelitz, who was a professor of history and ethics at Dresden towards the beginning of the nineteenth century, shows in many of his works that he was a student of critical philosophy. The book in question here is characterised by great succinctness of thought and by a dogmatic style that is highly appropriate to the subject. Having concisely outlined the qualities that are fundamentally natural to art and those that are the product of culture, Poelitz sets out the ways in which we arrive at general concepts of art, and a particular knowledge of it; he ends by discussing the metaphysics of ideal sound, and the concepts of subjective and objective beauty. Having established these general principles he goes on to apply them to the different arts, and particularly to music. He argues that when the theme of a piece of music has been heard, the mind uses it as the rule by which it judges; from then on it is satisfied only in so far as the development within the piece is the necessary, or at least the possible consequence of the given opening, there being an identity between the aim of the theme and its development.

Clearly, this is the doctrine of unity in variety; it has already been propounded in earlier books, but it is here formulated in a particularly exact, positive and practical manner. In view of this it is odd that Poelitz's book is one of the least known in the field of aesthetics.

Whilst Kant's philosophical system had many admirers and devotees, it also had many opponents, notably Herder, Jacobi, J. A. Eberhard and Bouterweck; Bouterweck, who began as an enthusiast of Kant's critical philosophy, ended up as one of its most outspoken adversaries.

Herder, who was a man both of learning and of feeling, had a particular admiration for nature. He felt that critical philosophy threatened everything that was beautiful in her. He took up her defence in his *Metakritik zur Kritik der reinen Vernunft* (Leipzig 1799), reinstating experience as an active influence on knowledge, and especially on the knowledge that we acquire of the beautiful. However, preoccupation with critical logic has tended to devalue the fine arts, and it was in his *Kalligone, vom Angenehmen und Schönen* (Leipzig 1800) that he sprang to their defence. The judgement of beauty, grandeur and sublimity, Herder and Jacobi believed, depended above all on the principle of awareness; these two eloquent writers insisted that works of art generate such spontaneous and powerful feelings that it is less a matter of judgement than a surge of true feeling which invades the consciousness.

Bouterweck, a distinguished if uneven thinker, challenged, in his *Aesthetik* (Leipzig 1806), the notion of simple, sense impressions, one that Kant had developed, much to music's disadvantage. Whilst acknowledging that consciousness gives us the certainty of beauty he also believed the process of judgement involving the mind to be absolutely essential. Without it there could be no idea of absolute beauty. This point is indeed of considerable importance, for if a work of art affects different people in different ways, the certainty of beauty vanishes, and beauty no longer exists. Aesthetic judgement alone can give beauty absolute existence. It only remains then to determine the basis upon which judgements can be made.

Having firmly established principles that can lead to a knowledge of beauty, Bouterweck unaccountably went through a period of uncertainty, and only a year later he published a supplement that almost seems to demolish the possibility of a metaphysic of the beautiful.

Of Kant's opponents, Jean-Auguste Eberhard is one who has adopted a properly scholarly approach to music. His *Handbuch der Aesthetik für gebildete Leser aus allen Ständen* (Halle, 2nd edn, 1808–20, 4 vols.) includes in its third volume an extended piece on the theory of beauty in music (pp. 66–123). His fundamental principle is that man has an awareness of the total relationship that exists between music's various elements, and that experience develops a sense of the rightness and wrongness of such relationships. According to him the elements are ordered in this way: first rhythm, then tempo, pitch, melody and harmony.

It is clear from this that Eberhard is more concerned with the way in which music's various elements affect men who have no knowledge of them, than with the discovery of absolute principles within music itself, or with any ideal concept that we may have of its unity. Eberhard recognised, indeed, that those of us who have the least knowledge of music are most powerfully moved by rhythm and metre, then by sonority, and only after that by tune or melody, and harmony. Well founded as these observations are, they cannot, unfortunately, lead to a fundamental understanding of beauty, their only contribution to knowledge being a record of actual experience, notwithstanding the care that the author has taken to relate his observations to those general feelings that we have about beauty.

In a very eloquent passage on p. 77, Eberhard argues for the divine origin of harmony. This will serve as an introduction to the best part of the work which deals with aesthetics and music, and which contains some excellent comments on tonality, intervals and their proportional relationships. These do not depend, however, on any fundamental theory governing this important branch of the art but are merely collections of detailed observations. One of Eberhard's best ideas is that the history of the arts is inseparable from aesthetic theory. In sum, then, although this study contains no transcendental doctrine concerning beauty in music, its author has certainly provided us with an excellent analysis of the moral effects of the separate elements of the art.

Following on from the school of Kant, or rather whilst members of that school were debating the principles of criticism with their adversaries, Fichte came along with his inflexible theories, the origins of which are indeed to be found in the work of his illustrious predecessor, but here developed in the light of the author's rigorous idealism. There is nothing less poetic than Fichte's doctrine, nothing less suited to lead to a knowledge of artistic beauty. At first sight it might seem to be leading to an understanding of how the aesthetic idea is manifested within us, *a priori*, and how it parallels the idea of beauty in the world around us; that would be a great step towards a knowledge of absolute beauty, or rather towards a solution of the whole problem. There exists, Fichte says, in space and time a living force, a free and undefined energy that activates and reactivates. It first takes shape as the 'I'; then in response to this it becomes the 'not I' (*non moi*); perception (*conscience*) lies at the point of equilibrium. The 'I' is what it is because it is. But from whence comes the 'not I' and its action on the 'I'? That, Fichte admits, is something that we shall never know. Sensibility (*sensibilité*) alone tells us that the external world is an active one. We are aware of this but we have no absolute knowledge of it.[2] It follows from this that we can have a feeling for exterior beauty but no knowledge of it. Any theories about it must be purely ideal.

Fichte's stark and rigorous principles provoked a reaction, and the publication of Schelling's philosophy encouraged men once more to develop

---

[2] See Fichte's *Grundlage der gesammten Wissenschaftslehre* (Weimar 1794).

ideas of a more poetic nature and to give freer rein to the imagination. Schelling argued that the 'principle of the absolute' was to be found in everything: in the identity of the subjective and the objective, the I and the not I, the real and the ideal, knowledge and being, unity and plurality, form and matter; it was developed in a scientific manner and it encouraged many distinguished men to explore the new paths that the celebrated author had opened out for them.

Unfortunately, as far as aesthetics are concerned, Schelling only applied his principles to the graphic arts (see his *Philosophische Schriften* (Landshut 1809) in which he discusses the relationship between the graphic arts and nature). Apparently he did not dare tread the slippery slopes of absolute beauty, where the art in question had no model to imitate in the exterior world.

Krug and Krause, the first a declared opponent of Schelling, the second to begin with a pupil and admirer and subsequently an opponent, have each written something on music and aesthetics but neither has advanced this branch of the science. In his general work on aesthetics[3] Krug established that beauty in music may be considered under two general headings. The first is the material one comprising the interrelationship of sounds, their intonation, intensity, timbre, duration, sequence and simultaneous combination. The second involves the intellect and feelings and is a product of form. According to Krug the first kind of beauty is pleasurable for it gratifies the sense of hearing. The second is beauty in itself, aesthetic beauty, absolute beauty. He concludes that most men have a greater awareness of pleasurable or material beauty than of pure aesthetic beauty. For them greatness in music derives from the power of the sound and the impact of the rhythm; that is why, he says, military music has such popular appeal whilst the formal beauty of more serious music goes unrecognised.

Krug's starting point is excellent. He summarises Pythagoras's comments on the relationships of sounds and he recognises the limitations of a natural philosophy of musical beauty and pure aesthetic beauty. He has done nothing, though, to develop these initial ideas, and he has merely drawn attention to the existence of that vexed question, the problem of formal beauty.

Krause was a musician, and he consequently had the advantage of a practical understanding of the art that he set out to consider in philosophical terms. Never the less his comments on musical aesthetics in his *Darstellungen aus der Geschichte der Musik* (Göttingen 1827) are superficial.

The formidable difficulties that surround the question of absolute beauty in music have frightened off the most celebrated minds. Jean-Paul, a writer of audacious originality and one who has many perceptive things to say, has

---

[3] *System der theoretischen Philosophie*, 3rd edn (Königsberg 1825–30, 3 vols.); see vol. 3, p. 331f.

written a large book on aesthetics, but he confines his attention to poetry. Hegel, the latest great philosophical reformer, did not publish the lectures that he gave on this branch of the science. The gap has however been filled by his disciples who have raised in his honour a literary monument in the form of his collected works. In the tenth volume M. Hotho, his pupil, has assembled a voluminous study based on the aesthetic teachings of his master.[4] Poetry, architecture and the other arts are here analysed in detail after certain general principles have been expounded, but not a word is to be found on the subject of music.

Amongst the latest authors who have written on the general theory of beauty in the arts must be mentioned M. Jean-Baptiste Talia, L. Pasquali, C. Seidel, G. A. Bürger, Christian Hermann Weisse and P. Lichtenthal.[5] It may well be that some of these deal with music and that they should be consulted. I have not obtained copies of them as yet, however, and I cannot speak of them therefore at the present time. They will be the subject of a special study that is to complete this series.

While the Germans, the Italians and the English have shown a serious and sustained concern for aesthetics as a part of general philosophy, of no less importance than logic and metaphysics, the French remain indifferent to it and are hardly aware of the possibility of its existence. One book alone, a curious work, attempts to base a theory of musical beauty on the imitation of nature, but in an absolutely novel way. The book is entitled, *Essai sur le perfectionnement des beaux-arts par les sciences exactes, ou calcul et hypothèses sur la poésie, la peinture et la musique* and it is by Reveroni-Saint-Cyr, an officer who died several years ago in a madhouse.

The author starts from the principle that *Music comprises successions of sounds which are designed to be assimilated by the ear, and which depict to the mind images and feelings.* Without further discussion of this definition let us see how it gives rise to Reveroni's system.

Reveroni claims that painting is not alone in being able to create images in the imagination, and that the brain, in which thought originates, is affected by sounds in the same way as it is affected by visual stimuli.

To understand the analogy let us follow the workings of the brain as it receives information from the two senses. What processes does the brain go through in judging the straightness of a line? A visual beam affects the optic nerve of the eye moving parallel to the line in a constant direction. From this the nerve receives an impression that is constant. The brain then takes over and as it senses no deviation it necessarily judges the line to be straight. Now

[4] *G. W. Fr. Hegel's Vorlesungen über die Aesthetik*, ed. D. H. G. Hotho (Berlin 1835–7).

[5] D. Gio. Batt. Talia, *Saggio di Estetica* (Venice 182?); L. Pasquali, *Istituzioni di Estetica* (Padoa 1827); C. Seidel, *Beitrage zur allgemeinen Theorie und Geschichte der schönen Künste* (Magdeburg 1828); G. A. Bürger, *Lehrbuch der Aesthetik*, ed. K. V. Reinhardt (Berlin 1825); Christian Hermann Weisse, *System der Aesthetik als Wissenschaft von der Idee der Schönheit* (Leipzig 1830); P. Lichtenthal, *Estetica ossia dottrina del bello, e delle belle arti* (Milan 1834).

in what way does the brain operate when it perceives a sustained note, or a succession of notes of the same pitch? The tympanum or auricular harp is set into constant vibration by the elasticity of the fluid which has been set in motion by the sound. The brain perceives this one sound alone which it treats abstractly in the same way as the straight line, and indeed the impression that is produced is the same.

[the following two paragraphs are omitted]

He applies his system to some familiar examples and he attempts to show that the gentlest curves are the most graceful and pleasing to the eye. Similarly, he argues, the sequences of sounds that are most closely analogous to a gentle curve are those that seem most beautiful to the mind, whilst successions of angular and disjunct sounds only create an impression of disorder and violence.

[the following two paragraphs are omitted]

I have spent some time on this bizarre system as it is one of the most curious, one of the most original and one of the oddest that I have come across.

I shall take good care to avoid such a system as the one that M. Charles-Ernest de Baer, a distinguished professor at the university of Königsberg, proposes: see his *Vorlesungen über Anthropologie, für die Selbstunterricht* (Königsberg 1824), pp. 288–90. M. de Baer is not only a distinguished scholar but a man of good sense. Nevertheless I cannot accept his system which is based on the idea that feelings derive from the numerical interrelationships of sounds, an idea that was put forward by philosophers of the Pythagorean school, and which depends upon the physiological structure of the ear. While physiologists have gone into great detail about the structure of the ear they have only contributed to an understanding of the mechanism whereby this organ perceives sounds, and they have said nothing about the faculty that the ear has of judging relationships between sounds. Were the ear only a kind of harp, as some would claim, the strings of which vibrated in sympathy with the sounds that struck the tympanum, each sound would surely be an isolated phenomenon; there could be no proof that the organ of hearing is endowed with the faculty of responding to the sounds that it hears. It is the intelligence that seizes upon these relationships and by assembling the sounds together conceptualises the form, thus arriving at the perception and knowledge of aesthetic beauty. Most physiologists tend to attribute to the structure of the ear those operations that are the work of the intelligence, and they even attribute to the physical structure of the brain that power of analysis which can only belong to the ideal 'I'. The distinguished physician, M. Blaud, has not made this mistake: several times in his *Traité élémentaire de Physiologie philosophique* (Paris 1830) he has emphatically denied this materialistic doctrine and he has decisively established that a knowledge of the relationships from which can be deduced the idea of aesthetic beauty results from the most sublime operations of the intelligence.

So far I have analysed the systems and ideas of those authors who have dealt in a general way with aesthetics, and who have considered the arts as a whole. There remain a number of theories dealing specifically with musical aesthetics. After these have been dealt with I shall summarise the few aesthetic certainties that can be gleaned from all that has so far been published, and I shall set out clearly the questions that still remain to be answered if there is to be a future for the science of aesthetics. I shall accordingly attempt a further extended article, very shortly.

Mme de Staël

From: 'On enthusiasm in the arts', *The Musical World*, vol. 4 (1840)

The article is a conflation of material from the last three chapters of *De l'Allemagne* (London 1813) (see p. 297 for further discussion of this work). Although the 1813 translation has evidently been used as the basis for this version, there are significant additions and omissions, chief of which is the deletion of all specific references to Christian beliefs (see footnotes). As the editor of the standard French text has pointed out (de Pange, *Madame de Staël*, v, pp. 187–231) the three chapters on Enthusiasm which end the work seem originally to have formed one; the three primary MSS. show no agreement on the ordering of the material within these chapters. There is nothing to suggest that the editor of the version for *The Musical World* had access to any of the three.

The text printed here is essentially that to be found in the 1813 English translation. Passages enclosed by square brackets however are not to be found in the original English text, whilst passages enclosed in round brackets are editorial corrections of mistranslations.

Many people are prejudiced against enthusiasm, from a misconception of its real nature. It is not an exclusive passion, the object of which is opinion; enthusiasm is connected with the harmony of the universe; it is the love of the beautiful, it is elevation of mind and fervour of soul, a feeling which at once combines grandeur and repose. The sense of this term among the Greeks affords the noblest definition of it; enthusiasm signifies God in us. In fact, when the existence of man becomes expansive, it has something in it divine. Whatever leads us to sacrifice our own comfort, or our own life, is almost always enthusiasm; for the highroad of reason, to the selfish, must be to make themselves the object of all their efforts, and value nothing in the world but health, riches and power. They know nothing of that superfluity of soul which is sweet to consecrate to what is noble and beautiful; they have not that within them which can enable them to taste all the wonders of the heart, and of the thought.[1]

There are also those who play the hypocrite with themselves, almost as much as with others, by continually repressing the generous emotions which struggle to revive in their bosoms, regarding them as so many phantoms of a diseased imagination, which the light of heaven should at once chase away. How impoverished is the existence of those who treat as delusion the source of the most beautiful deeds, and the most noble conceptions! Such men imprison themselves in an obstinate mediocrity, which they might easily

---

[1] Adapted from the 1813 edition, vol. 3, ch. 10, para. 1–2. The remainder of the article is from ch. 12, beginning p. 404 (eds.)

have expanded, to receive the light of knowledge which everywhere surrounds them; they sentence and condemn themselves to that monotony of ideas, to that deadness of feeling which suffers the days of existence to pass, one after the other, without deriving from them any advantage, without making in them any progress, without treasuring up any matter for future recollection.

There are some reasoners, who object that enthusiasm produces a distaste for ordinary life; and that as we cannot always remain in the same frame of mind, it is more for our advantage never to indulge in it; why then, I would ask, have they accepted the gift of life itself, since they well know that it is not to last for ever? Why have they loved – if indeed such men ever have loved – since death may at any moment tear them from the objects of their affection? Can there be any more wretched economy than that of the faculties of the soul? They were given us to be improved and expanded, to be carried as near as possible to perfection, even to be prodigally lavished for a high and noble end.

The more we benumb our feelings, and render ourselves insensible, the nearer (it will be said) we approach to a state of material existence, and the more we diminish the dominion of pain and sorrow over us. This argument consists, in fact, in recommending us to make an attempt to live with as little of life as possible.

[p. 405, last line to p. 406, first seven lines omitted]

But it is very rare that any man can settle peaceably in this confined and desert sphere of being, which leaves him without resource in himself (when) he is abandoned by the prosperity of the world. Man has a consciousness of the beautiful as well as of the virtuous, and in the absence of the former he feels a void, as in a deviation from the latter he finds remorse.

It is a common accusation against enthusiasm, that it is transitory; man would be too much blessed if he could fix and retain emotions so beautiful; but it is for the very reason that they are so easily dissipated and lost, that we should strive and exert ourselves to preserve them. Poetry and the fine arts are the means of calling forth in man this happiness of illustrious origin, which raises the depressed heart; and which, instead of a quiet satiety of life, gives an habitual feeling of the divine harmony in which nature (and) ourselves claim a part. In a word, there is no duty, no pleasure, no sentiment, which does not borrow from enthusiasm I know not what charm, which is still in perfect unison with the simple beauty of truth.

[p. 407, para. 2 to p. 409 para. 1 omitted]

Writers [and composers] who possess not enthusiasm know nothing of the career of literature [and art], except the criticism, the jealousies that attend upon it, and which must necessarily endanger our peace of mind, if we allow ourselves to be entangled amidst the passions of men. Unjust attacks of this nature may, indeed, sometimes do us an injury; but the true, the heartfelt (internal) enjoyment which belongs to talent cannot be affected by them. Long before the public appearance of a work, and before its character is yet decided, how many hours of happiness has it not been worth to him who wrote it from his heart [who poured it forth], as an act and duty of his homage to the beautiful. The creative talent of imagination satisfies, for a time at least, all (our) wishes and desires, it opens to (us) treasures of wealth, it offers to (us) crowns of glory, it raises before (our) eyes the pure and bright image of an ideal world.[2]

How can he who is not endowed with an enthusiastic imagination, flatter himself that he is, in any degree, acquainted with the earth upon which he lives, or that he has travelled through any of its various countries? [Has he in the heart of solitude shed tears of rapture over the wonders of life, love and glory? Has he, in his transports, enjoyed the air of heaven like a bird, the waters like a thirsty hunter, the flowers like a lover who believes he is breathing the sweets that surround his mistress?] Does his heart beat at the echo of the mountains, or has the air of the south lulled his senses in its voluptuous softness? Does he perceive wherein countries differ the one from the other? Does he remark the accent, does he understand the peculiar character of their languages? Does he hear, in the popular song, and recognise in the national dance, the manners and genius of a people? Does one single sensation at once fill his mind with a crowd of recollections?

Is nature to be felt without enthusiasm? Can common men address to her the tale of their mean interests and low desires? What have the sea and the stars to answer to the little vanities with which each individual is content to fill up each day? But if the soul be really moved within us, if it be alive to a sense of the beautiful,[3] of glory, and of love, the clouds of heaven will hold conversation with it, the torrents will listen to its voice, and the breeze which passes through the grove seems to deign to whisper to us something of those we love.

There are some, who although devoid of enthusiasm, still believe that they have a taste and relish for the fine arts; and indeed, they do love the refinement of luxury, and they wish to acquire a knowledge of music, painting and poetry,[4] that they may be able to converse upon them with ease, and with taste, and with even that confidence which becomes a man of the world, when the subject turns upon imagination, or upon nature. But what are these barren pleasures when compared with true enthusiasm? What an emotion thrills the soul when we contemplate, in the Niobe, that settled look of calm and terrible despair, which seems to reproach the Gods with their jealousy of their maternal happiness, what kind of consolation,

---

[2] This sentence is a much shortened version of p. 410 lines 3–25; the editor in the process turned the original plurals – 'our wishes', 'opens to us', etc. – into the singular (eds.)

[3] The 1813 edition reads, 'if, in the universe, it seeks a God, even if it be still sensible to glory and to love' (eds.)

[4] 'poetry' is omitted from the 1813 edition (eds.)

when we turn from this to the beauty and grace of the Apollo Belvedere and the Venus de Medici! In contemplating the St Jerome of Domenichino, we are penetrated with a lofty feeling which tramples under foot all the nothingness of this world.[5] [In listening to the masterpieces of a Handel, a Haydn, a Mozart, how pure, how exalted is the admiration which they inspire!]

Can it be said that there is such an art as that of music for those who cannot feel enthusiasm? Habit may render harmonious sounds as it were a necessary gratification to them, and they enjoy them as they do the flavour of fruits, or the beauty of colours; but has their whole being vibrated and trembled responsively like a lyre, if at any time the midnight silence has been suddenly broken by (singing, or by those) instruments that resemble the human voice? Have they in that moment felt the mystery of their existence, in that softening emotion which reunites our separate natures, and blends in the same enjoyment, the senses of the soul. Have the beatings of the heart followed the cadence of the music? Have they learned, under the influence of those emotions so full of charms, to shed those tears which have nothing of self in them [nothing in them of earth], those tears which do not ask for the compassion of others, but which relieve ourselves from the inquietude that arises from the need of something to admire and love?[6] How great and how sublime is the pleasure that springs from this sweetest and most ethereal of the arts! The interest it excites is freed from all apprehension or remorse; and the sensibility which it calls forth has nothing of that painful harshness from which real passions are never exempt.

[5] This is a much shortened version of p. 412, line 16, to p. 413, line 6; again, specifically Christian comment is toned down: e.g. 'None but the Christian can penetrate the countenance of the virgins of Raphaël and the St Jerome of Domenichino' (eds.)

[6] p. 414, para. 1 omitted: the last two sentences are here adapted from it (eds.)

Hughes Félicité Robert de Lamennais

(b. Saint-Malo, 19 June 1782; d. Paris, 27 Feb. 1854)

From: *Esquisse d'une philosophie* (Paris 1840), Part II, Book 8, ch. 1, ch. 2, and Book 9, ch. 1

Lamennais was one of the most unorthodox and influential members of the French church. He began as an ultramontist, campaigning for the absolute authority of the Pope, and in 1825 he published *De la religion considerée dans ses rapports avec l'ordre politique et social*, in which he saw the church as a major force within the state. From 1830 or so Lamennais came increasingly to believe that the church's future lay in the divorce of church and state; and the publication of his *Paroles d'un croyant* (1833) marks his own separation from the official church. From then on he worked as a catholic in the cause of liberalism and socialism.

Liszt had great respect for Lamennais, to whom he dedicated a march, in celebration of the 1830 revolution (the other dedicatees being Lamartine, Hugo, and Benjamin Constant), a 'De Profundis' for piano and orchestra (1834; unfinished), and the first of the pieces in Book 1 of the *Années de pélerinage* (1840). Something of the relationship between the two can be seen in the extant correspondence.[1] In his *Esquisse* Lamennais sees the arts as the means by which we acquire, through experience of the particular, an intuitive awareness of the infinite, which is God himself. The idea has a Platonic foundation but it is expressed in high-flown, mystical prose that has a strong flavour of Hegelian romanticism about it. Lamennais devotes a substantial section of the work to music, though understandably he is primarily interested in music for the church. Yet, his pictorial description of Beethoven's Sixth Symphony (Part II, Book 9, ch. 1) shows that he was very receptive to great instrumental music, particularly when a direct link could be established with nature.

Book 8, ch. 1

Pure intelligence apprehends truth – the idea as pure essence – independently of the conditions that determine it in an actual being. It comprehends, that is, the world of the ideal in abstraction, one that is quite separate from all the possible manifestations that belong to the world of phenomena. But man develops in such a way that before he can apprehend the pure idea he discovers it in those conditions that pertain to his own created existence, united with phenomena, incarnate in those phenomena, and made manifest in them. Now the idea of truth in the world of phenomena is revealed in finite beauty – that beauty which is the object of

---

[1] See for instance, Franz Liszt's *Briefe*, ed. M. Lipsius (Leipzig 1905), vol. 1, p. 11, 14 Jan. 1835; and vol. 8, p. 40, 18 May 1845.

art. It follows then that a man has a feeling for and a perception of beauty before he comes to know pure truth; thus, in this respect, art precedes knowledge. It will none the less be evident that art involves the intellect since it implies a vision of the idea, and since its progress partly depends on the development of the intellect; the more vivid and clear-cut the intuition of the idea, the finer the intellect. It follows then that no work of art can be created by purely mechanical means: the instrument of art must necessarily be intelligent; anything that is done by machines is a craft.

Since beauty is only in essence a revelation of truth, and since nothing can be brought into existence save in a form that determines and defines the supreme being, beauty must be the expression, within the limitations of form, of that supreme being. It follows then that form is the proper object of art – not merely the necessary, immaterial and eternal form of the pure idea, but form realised under conditions that prevail in the world of phenomena. Art then involves two inseparable elements: the spiritual or ideal element which is necessarily infinite; and the material element, which is finite. The one dissolves itself into that primordial and absolute unity which is its nature; the other reflects those limited, partial and varied aspects which are a consequence of this prime unity. The essential harmony of art lies in the natural relationship that exists between these two elements: unity and variety.

[p. 128, para. 1 to p. 134, line 1 omitted]

No art is self-generating; none is self-sufficient and none exists, so to speak, on its own. Art for art's sake is thus an absurdity. The goal of the arts is the perfection of the individual, to whose progress it bears witness. It is the point at which the physical, intellectual and moral needs of the individual meet, and the arts may indeed be classified according to the relationship that they bear to these diverse needs. Architecture, and its adjuncts, sculpture and painting, arose from the need to create shelter, from the wish to construct increasingly comfortable dwellings and to embellish them, and from the need to have assembly rooms for both civil and religious functions. All these were affected, as they developed, by other needs that are inherent in man's higher nature. Music, the sister of poetry, linked the arts that address themselves directly to the senses, with those that address the mind, all of which have as their common objective the satisfaction of the needs of moral order and the assistance of man, as he strives to achieve his goal. They lift him above earthly things and impart to him a perpetual upward motion. Is it possible to envisage an art that could be good for nothing? An art of building that had no practical use? Or a verbal art that is quite independent of any effect that words may produce? Can we conceive an effect that – for good or ill – is without moral character, either of itself or in the person who sought it out? Not only therefore does art have its roots in man's innate, basic and essential powers, but it is the particular manifestation and exercise of these powers. It is more than this; for by uniting the laws of the body, of the intellect and of love, art directs them to a common goal, namely the perfection of man's noblest qualities. In this wonderful interrelationship we are able to understand by what goes on in us the harmony, the mutual relationships, the factors that are common to every kind of being, the unity of creation, which is the image and reflection of the unity of God himself.

It follows from this that music is in no sense arbitrary nor dependent on the caprice of unregulated thought. Its foundations and laws are eternally fixed, and they cannot be changed without destroying it, for its existence and development, like that of living creatures, is governed by fundamental and essential conditions. These are the product of the union of the laws of physical and intellectual order. Art in this respect corresponds to the faculty that is called the imagination – the power that man has to clothe an idea with a tangible form that has objective existence, and to bring to life in nature eternal forms. Art is to man as is creative power to God.

Book 8, ch. 2

Elusive perfection draws man onwards in her wake, through limitless spaces. And this model, this form that the creative power strives after, what is it, other than the supreme harmony, the speech, the Word or its echo, the sound, the one and infinite voice of God himself? Art is a weak and uncertain echo of that voice. It contains no direct manifestation of that voice. It reveals no pure and clear idea. It imparts no immediate concept or knowledge of that voice to the mind, but through it, man is aware of God, incarnate in his work. It introduces him through the medium of his senses, to the world of the ideal, the direct intuition of which will later enrapture his developing intellect.

Picture yourself at close of day in some vast cathedral. A religious awe seizes you at the sight of the huge nave and the gigantic pillars, the upper reaches of which are lost in the encroaching gloom. Your awe is like that undefined presentiment of the infinite that is inspired by great, natural solitudes. The last sounds die away as day gives way to night. A mysterious silence envelops you. Around you are mute shadows. Inwardly an unknown and invisible power is breathing; it penetrates your being and you are powerless to resist it. It works strangely in you, isolated as you are from those external things that affect the senses. Spirits pass before your inner eye. Your imagination is alive with disembodied phantoms. Time no longer has any measure: it seems to have vanished. Suddenly, far away, a point of light appears; then another; and yet another. You begin to pick out the massive structure of the building: the sharply etched edges, the curving arches, the ribbed vaulting, and the walls, which resemble the flanks of some craggy mountain. The light increases. Harmonious lines unify the mass of the building. You can discern plants, animals and the shapes of myriads of beings springing from the inexhaustibly fertile loins of the edifice. The play of light intermingles and blends, and the shapes take on a thousand dazzling colours. They are as it were a revelation of life to the senses, and their impact is enhanced by the sweet perfume that fills the atmosphere. And when in the midst of this new-born world the organ suddenly springs to life, its harmonies now majestic, now sweet, now austere, when it fills the echoing vaults with its varied and undefinable sounds, is not the instrument the voice of those hosts of beings that have just taken shape before our very eyes? This intangible language however only speaks to the feelings, not to the thoughts. Such is music's nature. It affords us a vision, not so much of the immaterial essence of truth and beauty, as of their inner, physical qualities; in this way it forms a bridge between the arts that directly involve the senses and those that involve the mind. The former struggle towards thought by way of the senses: the latter search for feelings that are in tune with thought. These inverse processes express the twofold movement of creation towards God, and of God towards creation. The first of these – involving an ascent from the world of phenomena to the unchanging idea – spiritualises physical things; the second, in which there is a descent from the idea to the physical world, is the embodiment of truth.

Book 9, ch. 1

Music is necessarily similar to the other arts, being but a fragment of a total art that is essentially one, because art is a manifestation of the divine unity of God and his divine creation. Music's ultimate goal is infinite Beauty. Consequently, it tends to represent the ideal model, the eternal essence of things, rather than things as they are. For as Rousseau has so rightly observed, 'Hors le seul être existant par lui même, il n'y a rien de beau que ce qui n'est pas'. Music does not imitate therefore, it creates. It contributes to the realisation of that incorporeal world in which the spirit (*esprit*) can expand without limit. Through music, man can express his thoughts about God and the universe, thoughts which develop – as he himself does. In expressing, not the idea but the feeling that goes with it, he expresses himself in his relationship to the supreme cause, his fellow beings and nature. In the first place, then, expression springs directly from moral laws, laws of the intellect and love, for the idea is the intellect, and the feeling is love. All song therefore must be expressive. It must speak; it must move the feelings or it is no more than a pointless amalgam of inert sounds, a sort of ethereal corpse that the internal ear instinctively rejects. If it is to be expressive, the sound must have the closest possible relationship with the feelings that it represents and excites – an active yet strictly determined relationship – one that calls for a special power that is latent in sound, a power that springs from rhythm, movement and measure. Now this necessitates the ordering of sounds according to the various kinds of feeling in all their undefinable nuances.

Though in itself a sound may have expressive power, this power has to be applied and set in motion by the artist. The artist then must possess yet another power – that of portraying exactly the feeling that he seeks to communicate. This feeling will then pass from him into his creation, clothed in a form that will be determined by his own particular way of feeling. In expressing the feeling, therefore, he will be expressing himself. He will have impressed his own personality on the general character of his work, and in a curious way he will be reborn in it. And if this is true of the composer – the creator himself – it is equally true of the performer. The singer must discover within himself the feeling that the song expresses. The effectiveness of the representation will depend on the vividness and truthfulness of his inner impressions, and on the subtleties of his own feelings. It is these that comprise what is described as 'accent' both in composition and performance. The accent is the artist's own: it is the echo of his intimate self. United to that power which is inherent in sound, it constitutes artistic expression, expression that comes from two separate and distinct elements.

[p. 312, para. 1 to p. 318, line 8 omitted]

Music has need of ways to express its concepts and give them sensible form. The first of these ways is analogous to the material world, and it comprises instruments (of unlimited number) which represent through their various pitches and timbres the creatures that use their voices in self expression, according to their natures. Man, too, expresses himself through his incomparably more perfect voice. The human voice is music's principal means of expression, and it will never be superseded, even though man is able to reveal something of himself in the instruments that he has made. He animates these with his own life, and thus to some extent he expresses himself through them, just as God manifests himself in the humbler things of creation. There is however an ineradicable difference between the two means of expression – between the two distinct kinds of music, vocal and instrumental. The first kind corresponds to melody, the second to harmony, though these two elements do combine. Instrumental melody originates from and imitates the voice; whilst vocal harmony stems from instrumental chords, which are determined by the fixed laws of sonorous bodies.

The human voice corresponds to all that is most sublime in music, and it is so to speak the tie that binds music to infinite beauty. All the other musical elements must group and order themselves around vocal melody, and in the profoundest sense, accompany it. They provide a harmonious setting for it, in the way that a landscape provides a proper setting for man. And just as there is a place – if a comparatively humble one – for pure landscape painting, so within the art of music there is a place for instrumental music. This is not to suggest, however, that landscape painting and instrumental composition are unconnected with man. Man is at once hidden and present in them: hidden because he is not directly represented, yet present because it is the artist who has expressed and communicated the natural impressions and feelings that nature has awakened in him.

Philipp Otto Runge

(b. Wolgast, 23 July 1777; d. Hamburg, 2 Dec. 1810)

From: *Hinterlassene Schriften*, quoted in *Deutsche Literatur in Entwicklungsreihen, Reihe Romantik*, vol. 12, *Kunstanschauung der Jüngeren Romantik*, ed. Andreas Müller (Leipzig 1934), pp. 20–1

Runge was apprenticed to his brother, the Hamburg merchant Daniel Runge, who financed his studies and edited his writings, publishing them in 1840–1. He studied drawing under Herterich and Hardorff and oil painting under Eckhardt. In 1798 he attended the Copenhagen Academy, continuing his studies at Dresden in 1801. He is the most significant figure in north German romantic painting, and he was particularly interested in the interrelationship between the arts. His painting *The Nightingale's Lesson*, inspired by Klopstock's Ode of the same title, he described in a letter to his brother in August 1802 as resembling a fugue in music.[1]

When he was in Dresden, Runge met Ludwig Tieck, who drew his attention to the seventeenth-century religious mystical writer Jakob Böhme, in whom 'Runge found the original source of his romantic view of life, which identified the universal soul with the individual ego. The cosmic process can be experienced, as the content of individual consciousness and nature is seen as the mirror of the divine.'[2]

On purity in music

Listening recently to a performance of Haydn's *Seasons*, I became quite clearly aware how necessary symbolism is in order to maintain both the purity of nature and that unsullied human nature which both silently understands itself and is at the same time understandable only in terms of itself. This symbolism is true poetry, or the inner music of the three arts, expressed in words, line and colour.

After all, music is always what, in all three of the other arts, we call harmony and repose. Hence, a beautiful literary work is a matter of music in words, just as there must be music in a beautiful painting or building or in any ideas expressed in terms of line. Genuine serene church music expresses only what is pure and permanent in human nature; it leads man back from pain and distraction into the purity of the still calm centre. But simply because it eventually became comprehensible to the common man, or because human powers concentrated on too detailed an expression of human nature, this music – that is to say, large-scale 'narcotic' sacred

---

[1] Ulrich Finke, *German Painting from Romanticism to Expressionism* (London 1974), p. 17.

[2] Finke, *German Painting*. The whole of this section forms a lucid and penetrating introduction to German romantic art and is well worth further study.

music – began to thrill people. What I mean is, this narcotic music demanded more in the way of performing devices, more, that is, of the material and the physical. This manner of expression thrilled people; this led to theatrical music; and similarly, theatrical music led to that of Haydn, in which, as a result, all the physical components – i.e. the treatment of the instruments – are lovingly understood down to the smallest detail, but in which the actual moment of conception, the whole human character in its purity, from which the music developed, is hidden in the obscurity of the background. In this way, good and evil grow up together in confusion.

This is even more the case of German poetry, in so far as I have any knowledge of it. The 'Heldenbuch' and the 'Niebelunglied' are surely the greatest and purest things ever written in which pure music is to be found. The age that created them created the Minnesänger and then the Master-singers, the ancient novels and prose stories, and then modern poetry, which, even at its best, strives more and more to extract material from the physical aspect of the art and transmute it into music, as was the case with Schiller's 'Taucher' for example. The theatre became childish. Eventually Tieck wrote a scene involving stage and auditorium together; the expressive degenerated into mere expressionism. Thus man becomes more and more confused by the physical, consciously thinking thoughts about thoughts.

Painting is in the same state; I need not ennumerate the details.

Ferdnand Adolf Gelbcke

(b. Zerbst, 6 Nov. 1812; d. St Petersburg, 1 June 1892)

From: 'Classisch und Romantisch: Ein Beitrag zur Geschichtsschreibung der Musik unserer Zeit', *Neue Zeitschrift für Musik*, 11 and 14 June 1841, vol. 14, nos. 47 and 48, pp. 187–94

Gelbcke is a fascinating, though somewhat shadowy figure. At the age of 22, he emigrated to Russia, where he spent the rest of his life as a teacher of music, a musical theorist, translator (from 1865 onwards he translated a number of Elizabethan and Jacobean dramas into German), director of the Bjelosselsky Asylum and librettist of a number of works, including an oratorio cantata on the life of Peter the Great (1842). He also wrote a number of dramas, including one on *Albrecht Dürers Tod*. He died in St Petersburg where his son Vassily became an eminent civil servant and lawyer. Gelbcke also published a few *Lieder* (1840) and a number of articles on classical and modern philology, with particular reference to their relevance in the teaching of both classical and modern languages.

It says a great deal for Schumann's broad-minded editorial policy in the *Neue Zeitschrift* that the article below, which defines romanticism in terms quite different from those accepted by Schumann himself, should appear in his journal. The inclusion of Palestrina among the forerunners of romanticism may surprise us today; but Gelbcke's line of argument – that music is at its truest and most romantic when it is directly expressing man's relationship with and reaction to Christianity – is entirely consistent with his action in citing Palestrina as a central figure.

A. (taking a page of the *Musikalische Zeitung* in his hand): Just tell me what in the world these people mean with their romanticism in music. The matter is completely incomprehensible to me; and despite everything that has been said, I am in no position to form any clear picture of it, though others seem to find it so illuminating, particularly in respect of the true nature of the neo-romantic school, as it is called, and the particularly romantic qualities of contemporary music.

B. Many others are equally puzzled; I myself have often wondered how it was that the name came to be applied to a certain style of modern music and to what extent such a name was justified, yet I am no better prepared to answer your question. Even so, I'll answer it as far as I can. To begin with, I must say that in my opinion, modern musical romanticism as it is commonly conceived by critics and public alike is altogether different from the romanticism of the other arts.

A. So you would deny the element of romanticism in modern music?

B. Not at all; any more than I would deny it in music of earlier ages. I cannot accept the use of the term romantic in connection with modern music, for the simple reason that all music is essentially romantic.

A. But could it be that the romantic element plays a more prominent part in modern music than in the music of bygone ages?

B. If that were so, then the term would be applied correctly. But that is simply not the case. As I see it, indeed, the recent tendency has been increasingly to move away from the essential spirit of romanticism, although men would argue that they are still respecting that spirit.

A. I am curious to know how you will justify this assertion, which, after all, goes against everything I have heard.

B. To do that, I must first of all define the spirit of romanticism in classical art. Classical art is object-centred; it is contemplative rather than expressive; and thus it assumes plastic shape. Its quality depends primarily upon the balance between the art which shapes it and the material that is to be shaped.

A. But the perfection that inevitably results from such a balance is not the primary quality of Greek music.

B. I would disagree. Granted that ancient music cannot be compared, as far as we know, with present-day music, it was none the less so shaped and ordered that it completely fulfilled its purpose. In brief, it was nothing more than enhanced declamation and hardly ever was it separated from poetry and the dance. It was in effect recitation, and in this sense, it was excellent music. To judge from the effect that it is known to have produced, it must have been considerably more impressive than anything that has since been achieved of the kind.

A. Just a moment, my friend, you are getting away from the point. First of all, tell me in what respects classic and romantic art differ.

B. The main difference may be attributed without doubt to the tremendous influence that the Christian religion exerted over the free and powerful Western nations that arose after the collapse of the Roman Empire. In these nations, a God was preached and experienced as the source of all love, power and wisdom, a God who could be perceived, though He lacked tangible form and substance, through the imagination and strength that are born of faith. Yet an ideal relationship was never achieved between the artistic materials that were used and the power that shaped them, even in the finest work that was created. Western art, however, was fertilised by faith, hope and love, three ideals that have no part in what we think of as the art of classical antiquity.

A. But what is the relevance of all this to music?

B. I will come to that in due course, old chap. The point must first be made, however, that Christianity was the soil in which this wholly new artistic style, this romantic style, was rooted and it was from this soil that Western music sprang. I do not propose to dwell here upon the way that Western art was influenced by Church and Court and commerce, all of which were products of this initial impetus. The relationship of music to Christianity and to romantic art is paralleled by the direct relationship that was established between the individual and the ineffable, loving and beloved God, about which I have already spoken. Music is the natural medium of communication between the two, and it was from the very beginning a part of Christian worship. Its innermost essence is, like that of faith, hope and love, *emotion*. Its influence operates within the sphere of the mystic and the secret, which cannot be understood in clearly formulated concepts and ideas.

A. And it is still called a language of emotions.

B. Certainly; and that is what indeed it is. Whenever it extends beyond its natural boundaries, it loses its sense of direction and its essential character. But more of this later on. You ask me first to establish that music is a genuinely romantic art. All right; I would argue that the Christian religion has given the individual a higher value and a unique status that spring from his direct relationship with God. If it is true that a particular value is placed upon the individual in romantic art, an art which was the product of Christianity (being subjective in nature just as classical art was objective), then music is a truly romantic art in that it can only be a language of *emotion*, emotion being that which is subjective in the individual. For this reason, music was the latest art to develop. This happened during the Christian era, whilst the other arts – having no such purely spiritual quality – had been through many previous Golden Ages.

A. Excuse me, but does this mean that in your opinion music is only possible in a Christian environment?

B. Certainly its highest calling is to glorify and to serve the Creator. But just as all spheres of human activity, through man's higher destiny, are brought into relationship with God to serve Him, there are no emotions which music cannot express if music is to be considered an independent art. Thus, as society has become increasingly secularised, music has attempted to express all kinds of emotion.

A. Then if I understand you correctly, all music is purely romantic; and when we now speak of classical music, we do not imply an antithesis, but rather excellence and durability of quality. But after all this, what is all this about our new romantic school? You said before that it was forsaking true romanticism. How is this?

B. I have already suggested that music is capable only of revealing feelings and emotions, and it was for this reason that I described it as a romantic art. The more it departs from this proper function, the more it incorporates things that are alien to it, the more it loses of its unique romanticism. This is just what is the matter with most compositions of the so-called neo-romantic school; both the means of expression and the choice of materials are idiosyncratic. The use of atmospheric and descriptive titles, the construction of musical compositions from materials of the most heterogeneous kind in the way that romantic composers do, all this restricts rather than extends the bounds of music, in my opinion. Above all, the tendency to pictorialism is not in any sense a romantic tendency, despite what people say. Does it not betray an inclination towards an objectivity that is otherwise nowhere to be found in romantic art?

A. I quite agree with you, my friend.

B. Moreover, the continual search for subtlety of expression and variety of effect by means that are naturally and simply musical is vitiated by the concern for pictorialism. But are you sure that this interest in visual illustration is peculiar to the romantic school? Are there not illustrative compositions by earlier masters, such as Haydn, for instance?

B. I draw my evidence from the published works of the composers who belong to the romantic school. These betray a particular concern for onomato-musical expression (if I may be excused the term), and they tend, moreover, to use material that belongs more properly to poetry than to music. You mention Haydn in this context. He does write illustrative music, it is true, from time to time; but in his case the illustration is only a small and inessential part of the work, a mere *jeu d'esprit*; and even so, perhaps not always altogether apposite. Most composers of recent times consider illustration to be the true goal of music and its inner essence. Look, for instance, at the music of such composers as Berlioz, Henselt and Liszt.

A. All right. I admit that one of the hallmarks of the romantic school is a penchant for illustration. Other qualities, however, must differentiate romantic music from the music that preceded it. If you cannot identify these, you will hardly be able to answer my question satisfactorily.

B. If we leave the word 'romantic' out of the discussion, the task will be much easier. I have so far suggested that romanticism is the cardinal principle on which music is based. I have tried to show that recent developments deviate from this principle rather than conform to it; and I am now going to argue that the term 'modern' would be preferable to 'neo-romantic'. If Mozart and Haydn were the founders of the previous school of composition (I will confine my remarks to this school in order not to over-complicate the issue) and if Beethoven founded the present school, it can hardly be denied that the artistic principles which Mozart adopted as the basis of his work have been altogether lost. That composure, that peace of mind, that serene and generous approach to life, that balance between ideas and the means of expression which is fundamental to the superb masterpieces of that unique man, these were the most blessed and fruitful characteristics of the age in which Mozart lived, characteristics that we have imperceptibly yet gradually lost, though perhaps through no fault of our own.

A. That may be so; but how do you mean, though, through no fault of our own?

B. For the simple reason that we just could not cut ourselves off from the many non-artistic influences of our times. Now – who creates the spirit of an age? Surely, the man of unquestioned genius who exerts an overpowering influence on his contemporaries. Yet in the first place he is inescapably a child of his time. He can never wholly isolate himself from his surroundings, nor ought he to do so; and he must always work with the materials that he finds around him. The great artist, then, is a product of three separate factors that must happily and successfully be combined with each other: genius, historical context, and the resources that are currently available. Upon these will depend the manner in which genius manifests itself. A brief glance backwards at the history of music in earlier times will provide ample illustration of this point. When the Catholic church stood out against the tide of Reformation under the inspired leadership of a succession of Popes, Palestrina, working within the spirit of his time and his religion, assumed the role of the Reformer of Catholic church music. The artistic medium that had then been most effectively explored was that of vocal music. Thus Palestrina concentrated his attention wholly on that field. When later on an *inspired* form of Protestantism was consolidated in Germany under the protection of the Prussian royal household, which was itself in the ascendant, the contrapuntal style came to full maturity, as did the *Protestant* organ under the imposing leadership of old Sebastian Bach. And later, when the Austrian Empire enjoyed a golden era of security, power, prosperity and peace under the reign of the Emperor Joseph II, was this not the age of Haydn and Mozart? Although the storms were brewing elsewhere, within the Austrian Empire, nothing transpired to disturb the calm. So it was that both great composers were free to develop those qualities that have already been mentioned in connection with Mozart, qualities that they derived above all from the spirit of the age in which they lived. They were, moreover, able to exploit a far wider range of artistic techniques than their predecessors had done, owing to the fact that extensive developments had been and were being made in the construction of musical instruments; this, it should be noted, too, was before the time that the virtuoso had begun to exert such an evil influence on music.

A. As for Beethoven, I still think that this previous age culminates more appropriately in him, since he rose so directly from it; and I cannot understand how it is that you relate him to contemporary developments in music. I prefer to consider that this present age begins with Schubert.

B. No, my dear chap; Beethoven extended musical form and expression far beyond the point that the composers of Mozart's generation had reached, the spirit of his music being altogether different and less balanced. The stormy age of revolution stirred the oceanic depths of Beethoven's imagination, whipping up the most magnificent and restlessly surging breakers. The ceaseless ebb and flow, the constant reshaping of things has since been a characteristic of music; and it is paralleled by the struggle for new political structures, a struggle that is the principal concern of the present age. The artist can easily withdraw from political action and lose himself in mysticism, an extreme form of romanticism (romanticism, I repeat, being the essence of music), even though he may be in painful emotional turmoil. There appears to be such an element of mysticism in Beethoven's last works, which the composer completed after he had withdrawn on account of his deafness from practically all contact with the outside world. Beethoven may thus be regarded as a founder of the modern school (as it is so often called), the music of which exploits the spirit of mysticism to the point at which it has altogether lost clarity, coherence and order. Here again, this development cannot be regarded as one that is properly romantic, but rather as one that in its one-sidedness deviates from the principles of true romanticism. You see, the quest for infinity that is a characteristic of all romantic art can lead to dangerous extremes, in poetry as in music, to a mysticism that is the product of profound contemplative effort, and to pure subjectivity, which results in utter emptiness. These extremes may be traced back on the one hand to Beethoven and on the other to Rossini, and ultimately to Mozart, who is the purest and most eminent of all the romantic composers.

A. Perhaps so, old chap, but I would recommend you to keep such ideas under your hat.

B. Why should I? After all, I am not belittling either composer by saying this. I am merely saying that their music has given rise to two quite different misconceptions. I have not presumed to admonish them for any aberrations they themselves may have committed. As far, at least, as Beethoven is concerned, so much is true and beautiful in his music, so much is admirably conceived and executed, that the element of mysticism is altogether outweighed. Beethoven cannot therefore be held responsible for what has happened since, any more than Goethe and Schiller can be blamed for the fact that countless poets who lacked their inspiration have none the less since made use of their styles.

A. You would therefore conclude that . . .?

B. That modern artists have seized upon the idea of mysticism, which, though deriving from romanticism, was generated by the political and social temper of the times. There has been nobody since Beethoven capable of achieving the necessary aesthetic balance; indeed, I believe that it is quite impossible to do so. If music is to be an adequate and fruitful medium for the composer, the path of mysticism must be forsaken. Heaven grant that this may be so, and that everyone will do his utmost to ensure it.

Eduard Krüger

(b. Lüneburg, 9 Dec. 1807; d. Göttingen, 8 Nov. 1885)

From: 'Hegels Philosophie der Musik,' *Neue Zeitschrift für Musik*, vol. 17, nos. 10–14, 22 July–23 August 1842, pp. 39–40, 48, 51, 53–5, 58–9

Krüger, for some time the standard-bearer of the Hegelians in musical theory, was educated at Berlin and Göttingen. He settled as a schoolteacher in Emden and became director of a teacher-training institute there as well as being active as music critic and conductor. For a short time, he was the editor of the *Neue Hannoverscher Zeitung*. In 1861, he became director of music and professor at Göttingen University.

He was a friend and admirer of Schumann, but having been a regular contributor to the latter's *Neue Zeitschrift für Musik*, became estranged from him after his cool reception of *Das Paradies und die Peri*. Before the break, however, the *Neue Zeitschrift* devoted ten consecutive issues in 1842 to Krüger's detailed and penetrating critique of Hegel's ideas on music, from which the following excerpts have been taken. His *System der Tonkunst* and his *Beiträge für Leben und Wissenschaft der Tonkunst* (1847) may be taken as representing the viewpoint of the Leipzig school of romantic composers, of whom Schumann and Mendelssohn were the most important.

The Relationship between beauty and character

No. 10, pp. 39–40
The difference between character and beauty is most clearly illustrated by means of a few well-known examples. Albrecht Dürer's paintings of saints, like certain paintings of the Dutch school, are typically German in that they concentrate exclusively upon the character of the subject at the expense of beauty. Is it possible to see or feel in these faces of Christ and the Virgin that holy repose, contentment and blessedness which that heavenly apostle of beauty, Raphael, breathed into everything he created? The German paintings are *works* of art that are full of character; to say that they do not measure up to the standard expected of a work of *art* would not be wholly correct, and yet because they are concerned with incidental and external matters, they are far inferior to the works of the best Italian masters. Conversely: beauty may lack character; this is true of the French painter David, who imitates the surface qualities of Raphael. An even more obvious example is provided by Rossini, an artist richly endowed with natural gifts – and by Bellini, his sickly imitator. With these two, feelings of joy,

530

sorrow, love, hatred, turmoil and so on blend into a monotonous and insipid sweetness far removed from any specific or characteristic emotion. The man of informed aesthetic taste finds satisfaction neither in character-less beauty nor in beautiless character, but in a combination of the two: he is, of course, aware of the difference between them, only the greatest artists achieve a balance, and then only in their most perfect works, such as the *St Matthew Passion*, the C minor Symphony and *Don Giovanni*, in which character and beauty are blended in the most profound, most inexplicable manner.

Though we have found that art is fundamentally based on nature, this is no justification of the principle of literal imitation. Hegel defines the limits of imitation in the introduction to his *Aesthetik*, and in the chapter on natural beauty. The aesthetic importance of the principle and the function of such imitation will only later become apparent; there is only space here for a brief discussion. There are aspects of nature and natural properties that are constantly present as a shadowy background; they are the product of no human hand, nor can they be fathomed by human intelligence. They form a barrier between the finite and the infinite that defies speculative analysis, and they should be reinstated in their rightful and recognised place. Just as they constitute the primeval force, whose depth the mind can only sense but never realise, so also are they the last, the final goal, the ultimate boundary of the emotions, of the personality of the artist. To put it more simply: it is the *commensurability*[1] of a work of art. . . . Music indicates more clearly than the visual arts the boundaries of its commensurability. The fact that harmony is based on the simple divisible vibrations of a string is a *natural principle*; the divinely soothing effect of the triad on the human ear has in this respect something *mystical* about it. A good deal has been discovered and deduced about this phenomenon and its effect; however much importance may be attached to the fact that the ear is compatible with this natural principle, there remains that *ineffable* and *eternally feminine* characteristic of music, the legendary rapture that overwhelms the *receptive* listener and draws him into its magic web. This is the beginning and end of all music, the basic law to which all freedom is subject. Indeed, all more advanced harmonic and melodic speculation must be related to this. In his *Musikwissenschaft* Marx[2] will perhaps go further into the question of the *commensurability* and natural law of music than he has done in his *Compositionslehre*. In that work, advanced harmony would eventually dissolve into meaninglessness, if Marx's central principle is taken to its logical conclusion.

In any case, 'sense' protects us from the unthinkable and the monstrous.

[1] *Commensurabilität*. Krüger uses this term to signify the overall limits within which a work of art may operate and still remain recognisably a work of art having a proper effect on the listener or the spectator. These limits can be sensed but never defined and they exist in all the arts according to the canons specific to each of them (eds.)

[2] Adolf Bernhard Marx (1795–1866) (eds.)

Nature, our mystic innate feeling for such things, holds fast within its [proper] boundaries. So, for example, it is certainly possible to add to the interval of a second, a third, a fourth and to these the fifth as well, as J. S. Bach did more than once. On the other hand, it would be unnatural and therefore impossible to add together the intervals of a second, a third, a fourth, a fifth, a sixth and a seventh within the confines of one or more octaves. The limits of comprehensibility are definable, though no proofs can be given as examples of this, unless, that is, speculative philosophy is in a position to determine *why* such a combination is ugly and incomprehensible. No human power can violate nature's boundaries.

Now music's undefinable beauty has to do with the mysterious ebb and flow of the emotions; its content is the ceaseless movement of primeval nature. In this, we are at one with Hegel; but there are gaps in the argument which he builds on this basic premiss. Hegel takes as his starting point the fact that, as it vibrates, the sounding body cancels out its movement by resuming its original shape. In doing so, it obliterates the sense of space. This manner of expression is consistent with the origin of music itself, which comes purely from within and is analogous to the complete withdrawal of the subjective into itself (*Aesthetik*, III, 127–8). Hegel's second point is inadequately formulated: What, he asks, should be the nature of the inner substance if it is to be expressed in an appropriate manner (p. 129)? The ego pure and simple, the inner self *alone*, the self *devoid of further content*, is suited to musical expression: this is the first answer that Hegel gives. Hegel uses the term *content* here far less precisely than he does in the parallel contexts of the other arts. The concept is set out in the first (general) section of the *Aesthetik*, which deals with the definition of the ideal (I. 224). The suggestions in general terms as to what is suitable content for the various arts is to be found in the sub-section on *Activity*, which divides into three main headings: World Condition (Weltzustand), Situation (Situation) and Real Activity (Eigentliche Handlung) (I. 229).

Content in music and the other arts

No. 12, p. 48

Everything in the spatial world is substance for the plastic arts – everything that shines, gleams, and shimmers, everything that has light and colour, these are the things which the artist perceives and to which he responds; it is these that inspire spatial works of art. Similarly, every *movement* in the world, everything that soars, surges, trembles and sounds, everything of this kind is material for the sense of hearing. The artist of musical sensibility responds to them and they are reborn within his soul as a work of musical art. Music most effectively expresses that which is human. It is the human predicament – both as it is seen and heard – that speaks most directly and fully to the heart. The world of nature speaks to man more distantly, more mysteriously, yet in a language that is neither strange nor incomprehensible:

its natural beauties are enjoyed, simply: trees, animals, colourful and attractive scenery, the forest winds, the rippling streams and jubilant birds.

How far such natural phenomena can be transformed into art depends on the extent to which *imitation* is accepted as an artistic principle. To answer this, we must first answer our earlier question: how is the content to be *presented* in music? There is no spiritual value in a mere copy of nature, any more than there is in technical tricks of an artistic kind. Imitation is but *one* aspect of a work of art, and without the element of the ideal, the work lacks content and higher appeal. Modern theories of art agree on this point. If, however, the principle of imitation is regarded as tiresome and awkward, one to be distilled away before the underlying quality of the ideal can be revealed, then the principle has not been exhaustively worked out.

No. 14, pp. 58–9
The content of music, then, is a rich world, a world of the living soul and of the mysterious power of divine natural life. Every art must wholly fulfil its potential if it is to work to the achievement of its goal. Music fulfils its own law when it symbolises the movement of the world in rhythms and harmonies. Symbolism is basic to all art; . . . music is thus symbolic sound, the symbol of animate life in sound; its function is to symbolise life as clearly and as variously as possible. . . .

Irony can be used with care in painting; in music, a more profound humour can be achieved through music's inner movement. Humour in its *fullest* sense cannot manage without words. And yet things that words can only hint at, things that cannot explicitly be expressed because they dissolve into the shadowy world of infinite subjectivity, these can be fully expressed in music; indeed, in a certain sense, only music can express them: such things as waves of subjective emotion, subtle thrills of humour, a lightning glance charged with superabundant energy, laughter in the midst of tears, or joy that overflows in pain. This warm, subjective art is incapable of cold irony; the French and the Italians have attempted irony in their recent operas, and in so doing, they have exceeded music's bounds and introduced ideas that are extraneous to music and which cannot be represented. They have therefore completely failed. More often they have assumed that music should immediately mirror, as a *quid pro quo*, everything that is mentioned in the *text*. On the other hand, the deep, mysterious waves of enigmatic, romantic, cosmic humour can be captured in music's marvellous tone-colours, and reborn in its most characteristic shape. Though Bach's music is far removed in spirit from the pathos of Beethoven's, certain fugues, notably the G sharp minor from Book I of the 48, already have a fleeting quality of magic illumination. Handel, majestic, solemn, regal and festive, had neither the time nor the inclination to be thus sidetracked, yet in 'He trusted in God', from Part II of *Messiah*, one comes across bitter mockery, which lies somewhat between irony and humour. Haydn lives and moves and has his being in a lighter realm of humour. He lacks depth; his elegance and his roguish smile are comparable to Wieland's, though he far transcends Wieland in inner warmth. Mozart's Leporello, his Figaro and his Osmin are humorous characters much more than comic ones. Lastly stands the gigantic son of the Titans. He held aloof from purely *human* song and all but ignored it. Does he not, in the least as in the grandest of his instrumental movements, take hold of us, and almost without respite hurl us into the legendary domain where human joy and suffering have vanished, where jubilation and tears are, as it were, playthings of the gods?

The elements of musical communication

No. 12, p. 51

Music supersedes the plastic arts; in it all spatial dimensions are finally dissolved and transformed into pulsating movement. This at once demonstrates music's *intangibility.* The plastic arts obey specific laws of mass and light, for their static shapes have permanent solidity, a fact that is true even of painting, since its images derive their permanence only from the illusion that they are physically resting on the ground. Music, on the other hand, transcends all such physical limitations, and in doing so, seems to dissolve into the infinite and the intangible. The *definite* element in music is, in fact, that mathematical constraint imposed upon it by the limitations of fine art.

No. 13, p. 52–4

(Music) is characteristically *architectonic.* It must be regular and symmetrical; and thus the familiar image that architecture is frozen music and music fluid structure is wholly apt. A quantitative relationship is implied by this, governing every aspect of music: governing the way in which sounds relate to one another in pitch, rhythm and metre. In order that the subjective consciousness shall not lose its way in fruitless activity, some *point of reference* is needed, to which the *temporal dimension* of continuous and forward movement (a succession of points in time) can be referred. The principle of pulse and metre, in which a constant unit of time is unvaryingly repeated, provides this point of reference. It is here that music's relationship with architecture is most clearly expressed.

In architecture, columns, windows and such like are related to one another at regular intervals. 'Self-awareness discovers itself as a unity in this uniformity, the more so in that unity and uniformity do not spontaneously occur in sounds, but are projected onto the dimension of time by the ego to its own sense of fulfilment. For in the natural order, *unity and uniformity as such* do not exist. Even the heavenly bodies do not maintain a uniform velocity in their movement, but accelerate or slow down.' These words of Hegel's (p. 161) cannot simply be taken as they stand. It is undoubtedly valid to consider the beat as an abstract identity, but living *things* have an extra dimension that cannot be measured in terms of mechanical formulae. The movement of an animal body is subject to mathematical laws, yet never wholly restricted to them. The stars of the heavens do not undeviatingly obey the abstract law of circular motion, since even they wrest concessions from the primal law of gravity, whether they are in conflict, or victorious, or submissive, active or passive. They may thrust outward, or, of their own volition, strive to retract into their own centre of gravity. Similarly, the living ego is not wholly subject to the abstract and primal law of musical metre; the coldest and most inflexible player will demonstrate that even in the strictest tempo, deviations, both lesser and greater, are *unavoidable*. This may be simply proved with the help of a chronometer; not even the strictest time-keeper can maintain an inflexible tempo throughout a 200-bar movement without any deviation whatever from the initial tempo; strict tempo can scarcely be maintained, indeed, in an eight-bar folksong if the rhythm is to have a clear and marked identity.

Musical form

No. 13, pp. 54–5

From this [i.e. rhythmic] regularity are derived a great many artistic principles that can be completely understood only as components of that regularity; they are otherwise lost in uncontrolled subjectivity. *Binary patterns* underlie the simplest period, just as they do the overall pattern of sound in a sonata or symphony. The first inference to be drawn from this is that it is not *subjective* interest that repetition may generate, but the binary principle which is the cause of its regularity. Similarly, a good half of the repetition in fugue stems from the rhythmic element; one can say that fugue as an art form absorbs all lower forms and, as it were, relates the simpler individual elements both to the overall structure and to each other, because it contains the fundamental binary and ternary structure within the theme and its development. It then generates from this source its melodic freedom and its complex textures. Marx's splendid book *Constructions-ordnungen* illustrates the way in which the simple elements of rest and motion are handled even in the most ornate and solid structures, not only in the build-up of rhythm, but also of melody and harmony. Repetition in music has been strongly condemned. Hegel tries to evade the issue by dismissing repetition as a purely *technical* device (pp. 3, 136, 181) irrelevant to the understanding of the content. We are in a position to judge for ourselves, however, the truth of this harsh criticism. It may be true that the simple statement or exposition of the theme contains as it were the quintessence – the *abstract meaning* – of the music, but if this is all that is asked of it, there can be no work of art. What sort of a poem would it be that depended on the mere exposition of a theme? There could be no poem at all, but only a concept, an abstraction, a title, such as, for example: 'Faust seeks the Infinite'; there would be nothing more than a dry abstract *spiritus* instead of a warm and vital account of a man engaged on a divine quest. A beautiful structure depends for its organic and aesthetic vitality upon thematic growth, development and overall shape. Musical variations, incidentally, are similarly to be considered as variations of emotion – i.e. emotion understood in a purely musical sense and according to musical criteria. In other words, the emotion of the music, in so far as the music has an emotional content, is captured anew in ever-changing shapes according to musical principles; every new viewpoint, in profile, *profil perdu*, or full-face, provides a new, precise image of changing inner moods, revealing the content anew in greater depth and concentration.

Franz Liszt

(b. 1811; d. 1886)

From: The Preface to the *Album d'un voyageur, Années de pèlerinage,*
bk. 1 (1842) with lines from *Obermann* by de Sénancour

Liszt prefaced the first book of his *Années de pèlerinage* with a short introduction of
his own, and with a short piece from de Sénancour's *Obermann* that gives
expression to thoughts, similar to his own, on the sublimity of nature and the power
of musical sounds. Etienne Pierre de Sénancour (1770–1846) was influenced both by
Jean Jacques Rousseau and by Chateaubriand. His novel, *Obermann*, first appeared
in 1804, but it only attracted widespread attention in the 1830s. The most
substantial of the eight pieces in the first book of the *Années de pèlerinage* is the
sixth, entitled, 'Vallée d'Obermann'.

Having in recent times visited many new lands, many different places and
many situations consecrated by history and poetry, having felt that these
varied aspects of nature, and the things that take place in nature are not
simply empty images that pass before my eyes but are deep emotions that
move the soul, emotions that link me in an undefinable yet immediate way
to the things that I have seen, having with them an inexplicable yet
unmistakable rapport, I have tried to express in music some of the stronger
emotions that are the fruit of my more vivid experiences.

As instrumental music progresses, develops and frees itself from its first
bonds, it tends more and more to take on an ideal quality of the kind that is
the perfection of the plastic arts; it tends more and more to become not a
simple combination of sounds but a poetic language, more apt than poetry
herself perhaps to express all that transcends within us our customary
horizons, all that escapes analysis, all that relates to the inaccessible depths
of imperishable desires and longings for the infinite.

It is with this conviction that I have undertaken the work that I have
today published, addressing myself rather to the individual than the crowd,
hoping not for success but for the patience of those few who believe that art
has a destiny other than that of whiling away a few empty hours, those who
ask of her something more than the mindless distraction of fleeting
amusement.

[Lines from *Obermann*]

The element of the fantastic appeals to a lively, exuberant imagination, but
only the romantic can satisfy a man of deeper and unaffected sensibility. In

537

primitive countries, nature abounds in romantic effects. In countries that have long been civilised, these effects have been destroyed, particularly on the plains, which are easily conquered by man.

Romantic effects are the accents of a primitive tongue, a tongue that is not universally familiar, and which in a good many countries has become a foreign language. One soon ceases to hear them when one no longer lives with them, and yet this romantic harmony is the only spell that preserves in our hearts the colour of youth and the freshness of life. The man of society no longer is sensible of these effects, for they are too far removed from his style of living. 'What are they to me?', he ends by asking. He is like a man who is worn out by the burning stimulus of a slow and habitual poison. While still outwardly a man he is old in the prime of life, and he has lost all his spring and vitality.

But you, primitive men, who are scattered here and there in this superficial age to preserve the tradition of natural things, you recognise each other and communicate in a language that the crowd can never understand, as the October sun breaks through the mists to the autumnal forests, as the moon sets over a tree-encircled field through which a tiny stream glides and tumbles, as a woman's song rises from the distant walls and roofs of some great city on a cloudless summer afternoon. Because you live simply and because your genius has no intellectual pretensions, or simply because like other people you live, and eat and sleep, the common herd regard you as no different from themselves.

Picture in your mind an expanse of clear pure water, oblong in shape and slightly rounded, stretching away to the south west. It is vast, yet bounded on all sides by majestic oaks and towering peaks. You are sitting on a mountain slope above the northern shore upon which the waves are breaking. Behind you are rocks that rise perpendicularly to the clouds. The bitter polar winds have never breathed upon this happy shore. To your left, a gap in the mountains opens out into a peaceful valley. A rushing torrent pours down from the snowy heights above; and when the morning sun appears between the ice-bound pinnacles that rise above the mists, when voices come down from the mountainside revealing the presence of chalets above the meadows that still lie in the shadows, then the primitive world awakens, a monument to our unknown destiny.

It is the hour of dusk, the hour of repose and sublime melancholy. The misty valley is darkening. Toward the south, the lake is already enshrouded in darkness. The vast encircling crags are set in gloom, whilst above them rises the ice-bound dome, its glaciers seemingly retaining the light of day. The last sunset rays gild the many chestnut trees on the wild mountain slopes; they send long shafts of light between the tall arrow heads of the alpine firs; they tint the mountains brown; they illumine the banks of snow; they burnish the skies. The unruffled water is dazzlingly bright; it merges with the sky and becomes as infinite as the heavens – yet purer, more ethereal, more beautiful. It is of amazing calmness and deceptive transparency; the splendour of the sky, which it reflects, seems to penetrate to its very depths. Thus, seated as you are beneath those mountains that seem to be separated from earth and suspended in mid-air, you may behold at your feet the void of heaven and the expanse of the universe. It is the hour of enchantment and forgetfulness. You no longer know which are mountains and which is sky, nor on what you yourself are resting. There is no longer any horizon or earth; ideas give way to strange emotions; the common world is left behind. And when this valley of waters is deep in shadow, when the eye can no longer perceive objects or measure distances, when the evening breeze stirs the waves, then toward the west only the very end of the lake radiates a pale light; the part that is surrounded by mountains is nothing but a black chasm, and from out of the shadows and the silence may be heard, a thousand feet below, the ceaseless pulse of the waves, washing the shingle of the beach, pouring into the recesses of the rocks, and breaking upon the shore. These romantic sounds seem to unite in a long, echoing murmur from the unseen abyss.

It is in sounds that nature clothes her most intense expressions of the romantic spirit, and it is through the ear that ideas of extraordinary places and things can most readily be conveyed. The sense of smell can stimulate impressions that are immediate and powerful, but which are indeterminate. Visual impressions seem to appeal more to the mind than the heart. You admire what you see, but you feel what you hear. The voice of the beloved is still more beautiful than her features. Sounds that are heard in places of sublime beauty create a deeper and more lasting impression than do appearances. No picture of the Alps can bring the mountains so vividly to mind as can a truly alpine melody.

The 'ranz-des-vaches' does not merely awaken memories: it actually paints a picture. I know that Rousseau denied this, but I believe that he is mistaken. The effect is not imaginary. It so happens that two people who were looking through the engravings in the *Tableau pittoresque de la Suisse* both exclaimed in turn, on looking at the picture of the Grimsel, 'But that is the place to hear the ranz-des-vaches'. If this melody is played in a manner which is not just technically correct, but which is faithful to its spirit, if the player really feels the music, the very first sounds will transport you to those high valleys that lie close to the bare, reddish rocks that lie beneath the cold sky and scorching sun. You are on a pasture-covered ridge. You are deeply conscious of the slowness of things, and of the grandeur of the landscape. You observe the leisurely gait of the cows and the measured swing of their large bells; the clouds almost touch the crest that extends from the granite peaks to the granite of the snowy ravines. The wind breathes through the distant larches, cold and remote. A hidden torrent can be heard at the foot of the precipice that it has hollowed out over the course of the centuries. These solitary sounds in space are followed by the hurried, heavy strains of a Swiss cowherd, as he sings a song, a pastoral expression of pleasure without gaiety, of a joy in the mountains. Presently the song comes to an end; the man has passed beyond earshot, and soon the sound of bells is lost among the larches. Only the impact of loosened rocks may be heard, and the intermittent movement of fallen trees which the torrent carries downwards into the valley. Alpine sounds come and go on the winds, and when there is silence, all seems cold, motionless and dead. This is the domain of the man who knows nothing of hurry. He leaves the shelter of his cottage, which is low and wide and pinned down by heavy stones to ensure security when the storms rage, little heeding whether the sun is burning, the wind is howling or the thunder is rolling beneath his feet. He goes in the direction in which his cows ought to be. They are there. He calls them and they come together. They come to him in turn and he returns laden with the milk that is destined for the lowlands that he will never know. The cows stand and ruminate. Nothing moves. The man has passed out of sight. The air is cold; the wind has died away with the advent of the twilight. Only the ancient snowfields gleam softly. Only the wild sound of the waterfall, rising up from the chasm below, seems to intensify the silent stillness of the lofty summits, the glaciers, and the night.

Soren Aabye Kierkegaard

(b. Copenhagen, 5 May 1813; d. Copenhagen, 11 Nov. 1855)

From: *Enten–Eller* (Copenhagen 1843), translated by David F. and Lilian Marvin Swenson (Princeton 1944), pp. 66–70

Kierkegaard was brought up in a rather gloomy household, cut off from much companionship with other children. He studied aesthetics and philosophy at Copenhagen University, taking a degree in theology. He is nowadays celebrated as the founder of existentialism, which he first developed in his *Enten–Eller*. The main argument of the book is that man goes through three phases of development: aesthetic, ethical and theological – each being on a higher plane than the previous one. *Enten–Eller* investigates aesthetics and ethics, its premiss being that the Hegelian attempt to demonstrate that the world is a rational system is both presumptuous and ridiculous. One of the more important sections of *Enten–Eller* is the so-called, 'Insignificant Introduction', from which the following paragraphs are taken. Much of the Introduction comprises a discussion of *Don Giovanni*. Schopenhauer had claimed that music was a direct portrayal of the Will behind the cosmos. Kierkegaard set out to argue that a particular work of music was one key to the interpretation of human life: *Don Giovanni*. His argument will be set out in the sequel to this volume. For our present purpose it will suffice to outline his general attitude to music and to discover his opinions of its strengths and weaknesses.

Language addresses itself to the ear. No other medium does this. The ear is the most spiritually determined of the senses. That I believe most men will admit. If anyone wishes further information on this point, I refer the reader to the preface of *Karikaturen des Heiligsten* by Steffens. Aside from language, music is the only medium that addresses itself to the ear. Herein is again an analogy and a testimony concerning the sense in which music is a language. There is much in nature which addresses itself to the ear, but that which affects the ear is the purely sensuous, and for that reason nature is dumb; and it is a ridiculous delusion that one hears something because one hears a cow moo or, that which perhaps makes greater pretensions, a nightingale sing; it is a delusion to think that one hears something, a delusion to think that one is worth more than the other, since it is all a case of tweedledum and tweedledee.

Language has time as its element; all other media have space as their element. Music is the only other one that takes place in time. But the fact that it does take place in time is again a negation of the sensuous. What the other arts produce indicates their sensuousness precisely by reason of the fact that it has its continuance in space. Now there is, of course, much in nature that takes place in time. Thus when a brook ripples and continues to

541

ripple, there seems to be in it a qualification of time. However, this is not so, and in so far as one may wish to insist that we have here a qualification of time, one would have to say that time is indeed present, but present as if spatially qualified. Music exists only in the moment of its performance, for if one were ever so skillful in reading notes and had ever so lively an imagination, it cannot be denied that it is only in an unreal sense that music exists when it is read. It really exists only in being performed. This might seem to be an imperfection in this art as compared with the others whose productions remain, because they have their existence in the sensuous. Yet this is not so. It is rather a proof of the fact that music is a higher, a more spiritual art.

Now if I take language for my point of departure, in order by moving through it, as it were, to spy out the land of music, the result appears about as follows. If I assume that prose is the language-form that is farthest removed from music, then I notice even in the oratorical discourse, in the sonorous structure of its periods, a hint of the musical which manifests itself more and more strongly at different levels in the poetic form, in the structure of the verse, in the rhyme, until at last the musical has been developed so strongly that language ceases and everything becomes music. This is a favorite expression which the poets have used to signify that they have, so to speak, renounced the idea, which vanishes from them, and everything ends in music. This might seem to indicate that music is an even more perfect medium than language. However, this is one of those sentimental misunderstandings which originate only in empty heads. That it is a misunderstanding will be shown later; here I desire only to call attention to the remarkable circumstance that, by moving through the language in the opposite direction, I again come up against music, in that I proceed from a prose interpenetrated by the concept, downward until I land in interjections which are again musical, just as the child's first babbling syllables are musical. Here it will hardly be said that music is a more perfect medium than language or that music is a richer medium than language, unless one is willing to assume that saying 'uh' is worth more than a complete thought. But what follows from maintaining that wherever language ceases, I encounter the musical? This is probably the most perfect expression of the idea that music everywhere limits language. From this it is easy to see how the misunderstanding arose that music is a richer medium than language. By saying that when language ceases, music begins, and by saying, as people do, that everything becomes musical, we do not advance but go backwards.

This is the reason why I never had any sympathy – and in this perhaps even the experts will agree with me – with that sublime music which believes it can dispense with words. As a rule it thinks itself higher than words, although it is inferior. Now I might perhaps be confronted with the following objection: 'If it is true that language is a richer medium than music, then it is hard to understand why it should be so hard to give an aesthetic account of the musical; inconceivable that language in this connection should always appear as a poorer medium than music.' This is, however, neither inconceivable nor inexplicable. Music always expresses the immediate in its immediacy; it is for this reason, too, that music shows itself first and last in relation to language, but for this reason, also, it is clear that it is a misunderstanding to say that music is a more perfect medium. Language involves reflection, and cannot, therefore, express the immediate. Reflection destroys the immediate, and hence it is impossible to express the musical in language; but this apparent poverty of language is precisely its wealth. The immediate is really the indeterminate, and therefore language cannot apprehend it; but the fact that it is indeterminate is not its perfection but an imperfection. This is indirectly acknowledged in many ways. Thus, to cite but one example, we say: 'I cannot really explain why I do this or that so and so, I do it by ear.' Here we often use about things which have no relation to music a word derived from music, but we indicate by this the obscure, the unexplained, the immediate.

Now if it is the immediate, qualified spiritually, which receives its precise expression in music, we may again inquire more closely what species of the immediate it is which is essentially the subject of music. The immediate, qualified spiritually, may either be determined so as to fall within the sphere of the spiritual or as falling outside it. When the immediate, spiritually qualified, is determined as falling within the sphere of the spiritual, it may then well find its expression in the musical, but this immediacy cannot be the absolute subject of music, for since it is determined in such a way as to be included under the spiritual, it is thereby indicated that music is in a foreign sphere, it constitutes a prelude which is constantly being annulled. But if the immediate, spiritually qualified, is such that it falls outside the realm of spirit, then music here has its absolute subject. For the first species of the immediate, it is unessential that it be expressed in music, whereas it is essential for it to become spirit and, consequently, to be expressed in language; for the second, on the contrary, it is essential that it be expressed in music, it cannot be expressed otherwise than in music, it cannot be expressed in language, since it is spiritually determined so that it falls outside of the spiritual and, consequently, outside of language. But the immediacy which is thus excluded by the spirit is sensuous immediacy. This belongs to Christianity. In music it has its absolute medium, and from this circumstance it is also possible to explain the fact that music did not really become developed in the ancient world but belongs to the Christian era. Music is, then, the medium for that species of the immediate which, spiritually determined, is determined as lying outside of the spirit. Music can, naturally, express many other things, but this is its absolute subject. It is easy to perceive that music is a more sensuous medium than language, since it stresses the sensuous sound much more strongly than language does.

The genius of sensuousness is hence the absolute subject of music. In its very essence sensuousness is absolutely lyrical, and in music it breaks forth in all its lyrical impatience. It is, namely, spiritually determined, and is, therefore, force, life, movement, constant unrest, perpetual succession; but this unrest, this succession, does not enrich it, it remains always the same, it does not unfold itself, but it storms uninterruptedly forward as if in a single breath. If I desired to characterise this lyrical quality by a single predicate, I should say: it *sounds*; and this brings me back again to sensuous genius as that which in its immediacy manifests itself in music.

See also Bibliography under: Croxall

Theodor Mundt

(b. Potsdam, 19 Sept. 1808, d. Berlin, 30 Nov. 1861).

From: *Aesthetik* (Leipzig 1845), pp. 349–54

Theodor Mundt was more loosely connected with the group, Das Junge Deutschland, than Wienbarg, but the declaration of the Federal Diet condemning the group, issued in December 1835, included him amongst its number. None the less, writings such as his interesting feminist novel *Madonna* (1835), show that he was one of those writers who felt that the *status quo* in the Germany of his day was unsatisfactory and that it was time for a change: 'Men have lain far too long dreaming by rippling streams, listening to the rustling of the leaves. Now they have become restless; they have laid the axe to the tree in leaf, hacking away its decorative foliage; and from its wood they have made themselves a lance and a plough.'[1] With a new desire for a literature of action, he combined an appreciation of the city as a source of life, an attitude that ran quite contrary to the romantics' worship of the country and of nature: 'Amid nature, man is lost among the elements; in the city, he gives himself up to others, finding himself in his neighbour, his neighbour's errors and his neighbour's truth.'[2]

Mundt was the son of a Prussian civil servant. He was educated at the great Joachimsthalsches Gymnasium in Berlin and then at Berlin University, where he read philosophy and philology. He then worked as a literary journalist, editing a Leipzig periodical called *Blätter für literarische Unterhaltung* from 1832. After being condemned by the Federal Diet, he tried unsuccessfully to establish himself as a teacher in Berlin, but his political views rendered him suspect in the eyes of the authorities, and after travelling extensively, he at last became a Privatdozent in Berlin in 1842. In 1848, he was appointed to the chair of literature and history at Breslau, but he returned to Berlin in 1850 to the chair there. He died on 30 November 1861 and is remembered as a writer who was both versatile and volatile. One of the first advocates of a simpler type of literary German, based on the spoken language, Mundt was always at pains to relate the life of the spirit to the world of every day; and he considered any attempt to divide flesh and spirit as an inexpiable suicide of human self-awareness.

In no art, perhaps, are the mighty aspirations and powers of the human spirit revealed with such grandeur as they are in music. A body of works has been created which, in terms of its range and importance, has absolutely no analogy in nature itself. As far as the arts of painting, sculpture and architecture are concerned, nature has herself created significant and analogous works: landscapes in organic living forms, rocks and mountain

---

[1] Quoted by Emil Ermatinger, *Deutsche Dichter, 1700–1900, eine Geistesgeschichte in Lebensbildern* (Frauenfeld 1949), vol. II, p. 409.
[2] ibid.

formations, for instance. Nature's music, however, is rudimentary, and it falls far short of the ideal that has been achieved in art.

We can really speak only of sound in nature. It is the universal expression of the life of the world of natural bodies; and in it there is no spiritual element of measure. The wind rustles in the forest with a confused sound. When it howls through a rocky ravine, it seems to characterise the wilderness of a desolate universe that is powerless to express in sound any awareness of its desolation. Birdsong seems to represent a first step towards the shaping of natural sound, but it has neither the range of the human voice nor any truly musical significance, as its melodies are merely sequences of unmeasured sounds.

The true *sound* of creation is discovered only by man himself, as human nature is nature in human guise. Man thus produces sound which to a certain extent is the sound of nature in an individualised and subjective form. Since the sound is at the same time quantitative and qualitative, it lends meaning to a specific span of time and it assumes dimension in terms of height and depth.

Music creates a remarkable world, and one that is infinite and has no equivalent expression in phenomenal terms, a world that stems entirely from the human spirit and from its insatiable desire for self-expression. The arts represent nothing more than the universal human endeavour to express the totality of life, and they make possible the revelation of its most hidden depths; so it is that this human urge for self-revelation is inherently a part of music. A specific and objective creation is shaped from the inexhaustible potential that lies in the movements and pulsations of our self-awareness, a creation that is inexpressible in words or shapes.

Music is the tonal expression of the deepest things in the human heart. Music represents in tonal terms man's consciousness of everything that lies deep within him and which endlessly longs for an eternal future. It therefore has the power to dissolve the entire human consciousness into the unity of the eternal living idea by incorporating both the past and the future in the immediate present.

In thus entering the eternal life of the idea, music undeniably possesses intellectual significance, even if no logical clarity may be expected of it in the expression of ideas. In this respect, an injustice has often been done to music, especially by philosophers; they have sought to belittle its nature and to define it as a purely arbitrary play of the emotions, in which ideas have no part, since no logical proof was possible of the certainty of music's ideas. Straightway, however, this does violence to the very idea of music. Music can represent just as clearly as any other art those concepts that are its proper concern; it does not have to become the musical equivalent of an exercise in logic.

Some legitimate doubt may none the less exist concerning music's power to express ideas; we may occasionally have just a suspicion that this or that melodic phrase (*Tonreihe*) would equally well express a serious or tragic idea as a serene or jovial one. The tendency for music's expressive potential to become indeterminate and imprecise, however, is not part of the nature of music itself. It always results, in fact, from imprecision or from the defects of a particular musical composition. Ambivalent and imprecise musical expression can perhaps most readily be observed in one particular genre of music, namely in Italian music; this otherwise owes its greatest triumphs to its very volatility and passionate expression and to the supreme artistry of its vocal technique.

Musical sounds have a variety of meanings which the spirit has to resolve into a complete and self-contained composition; this very variety explains why music has widely spread through every aspect of human life, why it has become associated with every national and social event, and why it has played such a profound and intimate role in the spiritual development of mankind. Leibniz has acutely observed, in the sixth volume of his works (p. 306) that the sixteenth-century Reformation was essentially furthered by music, which the reformers esteemed highly and used shrewdly. In Germany and France, the Reformation was largely effected by song, which inspired the people at the most fundamental and intimate level.

Music is involved in many aspects of the life of the people, in *congregational singing*, in *dance* and in the *work-song*. Being associated with such characteristic aspects of life, music – as if of its own accord – strikes its own roots and draws up its own spiritual sustenance; it thus acquires the right to function at every birth or death and at any ceremony on which man celebrates the most beautiful festal occasions.

Harmony represents the most intimate, characteristic and fundamental aspect of modern music. This is essentially something developed by the Christian spirit, something that symbolises the truly Christian life of the spirit, in which creation in all its profusion and variety is united and subsumed in the one fundamental and divine Idea. Harmony in music is, in fact, the simultaneous combination in sound of *different* voices. Such an ideal combination of essentially different elements constitutes an artistic relationship that is both rich and precise; *melody*, on the other hand, is only the rhythmically ordered sequence of sounds of a simple musical idea.

Charles Pierre Baudelaire

(b. Paris, 9 Apr. 1821; d. Paris, 31 Aug. 1867)

From: *Paris Spleen* (tr. Louise Varèse), no. 32;[1] and the *Salon de 1846*, ed. David Kelley (Oxford 1975), pp. 102–3, 108–9

Baudelaire, poet and art critic, is perhaps best known for his one published collection of poems, *Les fleurs du mal* (Paris 1854). He is generally recognised as a founder member of the symbolist movement, and his admirers claim that he has 'revolutionised the manner of thinking, writing and feeling in western Europe'. The *Salon de 1846* contains his most positive statement on romanticism: in his 1859 Salon for example he was much more inclined to recognise its defects: 'le romantisme [he wrote] est une grâce, céleste ou infernale, à qui nous devons des stigmates éternels'.

For further reading:
Joycelynne Loncke, *Baudelaire et la musique* (Paris 1975).

The Thyrsus

To Franz Liszt

What is a thyrsus? In its religious and poetic sense it is the sacerdotal emblem of priests and priestesses when celebrating the deity whose interpreters they are. But physically it is just a stick, a simple stick, a staff to hold up hops, a prop for training vines, straight, hard and dry. Around this stick in capricious convolutions, stems and flowers play and gambol, some sinuous and wayward, others hanging like bells, or like goblets up-side-down. And an amazing resplendence surges from this complexity of lines and of delicate or brilliant colors. Does it not seem as though the curvilinear and the spiral lines were courting the straight line, and were dancing around it in mute admiration? Does it not seem as though all those delicate corollas, all those calyxes, in an explosion of scents and colors, were executing a mysterious fandango around the hieratic rod? But what imprudent mortal would dare to say whether the flowers and the vines have been made for the stick, or whether the stick is not a pretext for displaying the beauty of the vines and the flowers? The thyrsus is an image of your astonishing quality, great and venerated Master, dear Bacchante of mysterious and passionate beauty. Never did a nymph, driven to frenzy by the invincible Bacchus, shake her thyrsus over the heads of her maddened companions with such energy and

---

[1] Published in, Charles Baudelaire, *Paris Spleen* (Peter Owen, London 1951), pp. 72–3.

wantonness as you your genius over the hearts of your brothers. The rod is your will, steady, straight, and firm, and the flowers, the wanderings of your fancy around your will, the feminine element executing its bewitching pirouettes around the male. Straight line and arabesque, intention and expression, inflexibility of the will, sinuosity of the word, unity of the goal, variety of the means, all-powerful and indivisible amalgam of genius, what analyst would have the detestable courage to divide and separate you?

Dear Liszt, through the mists and beyond the rivers, in distant cities where pianos sing your glory, and where printing presses translate your wisdom, wherever you may be, whether surrounded by the splendors of the eternal city, or in the mists of those dreamy countries Gambrinus consoles, improvising songs of joy and of ineffable sorrow, or confiding to paper your abstruse meditations, singer of pleasure and of eternal anguish, philosopher, poet, artist, I salute you in immortality!

Aesthetic curiosities

What is this romanticism?

Few people today are prepared to give a positive and substantial definition to this word. Do they dare to suggest that a whole generation has willingly done battle for several years on behalf of a flag that symbolises nothing? Bearing in mind the recent troubles, it will be seen that if few romantics are now left, the explanation lies in the fact that few of them have found romanticism. Yet all of them have sincerely and devotedly searched for it.

Some have only been bothered about the choice of subject, and have lacked the necessary temperament for the subjects that they have chosen. Others, putting faith in a society founded on catholicism, have sought to reflect that catholicism in their works. For a person to describe himself as a romantic and systematically to explore the past is self-contradictory. Such people have blasphemed the Greeks and Romans in the name of romanticism. Yet, if one is a romantic, one can create Greek and Roman romantics. Many other people have been led astray by realism and local colour. Realism existed long before this great battle took place. Furthermore, to write a tragedy or to paint a picture for M. Raoul Rochette[2] is to expose oneself to contradiction from the first person who comes along, if he happens to be more learned than M. Rochette.

Romanticism is neither a choice of subject, nor exact truth, but a way of feeling.

People have searched for it in external things but it can only be found within.

For me, romanticism is the most recent and up-to-date expression of beauty.

---

[2] A leading archaeologist (1789–1854) of the time (eds.)

There are as many different kinds of beauty as there are traditional ways of seeking happiness.

The philosophy of progress explains this clearly. In the past, people have held as many different ideals as they have had concepts of morals, love, religion and so on. Similarly romanticism is a matter of being in tune with the times and not a matter of impeccable execution.

It is because some men have conceived romanticism as technical perfection that we have had rococo romanticism, which is undoubtedly the least tolerable of all forms of romanticism.

Above all, then, we must familiarise ourselves with those sides of nature and those human situations that artists had previously not known of, or ignored.

Whoever talks of romanticism talks of modern art: of intimacy, that is, spirituality, colour, and a yearning for the infinite, all of which will be expressed in every conceivable way that is within the province of art.

Concerning colour

Harmony is the basis of the theory of colour.

Melody is the unity of colour, or the general colour.

Melody demands a conclusion; it is a whole, in which each particular effect contributes to the total effect.

It is because of this that melody leaves in the mind a profound impression.

Most of our young colourists lack the gift of melody.

The best way to determine whether a picture is melodious or not is to look at it from a distance, neither the subject not the lines being distinguishable. If it is melodious it already has a meaning and it has already taken its place within the repertory of memories.

Style and feeling in colour are a matter of choice, and choice depends upon temperament.

There are shades of colour that are gay and playful, playful and sad, rich and gay, rich and sad, commonplace and original.

Thus, Veronese's colour is calm and gay, Delacroix's is often plaintive, and M. Catlin's, awesome.

For a long time my window looked out to an inn that stood opposite; it was half green and half a crude red which awoke in me an impression of delicious sadness.

I do not know whether someone who has an interest in analogies may have drawn up a reliable scale of colours and feelings, but I recall here a passage from Hoffmann which perfectly expressess what I have in mind, and which will please all those who sincerely love nature:

> It is not only when I dream, or when I lie in that state of disembodied fantasy that heralds sleep, but it is even when I am awake, listening to music, that I find an analogy, an intimate connection between colours, sounds and perfumes. I feel that

everything has been born of the same ray of light and that all must come together again in marvellous concert. The scent of brown and red marigolds has a particularly magical effect on me: it sends me into a profound reverie and I then hear in the distance, as it were, the deep and solemn notes of the oboe.[3]

[3] *Kreisleriana*: from a series of observations entitled, 'Höchst zerstreute Gedanken'.

Theodor(e) Hagen

(b. Hamburg, 15 Apr. 1823; d. New York City, 27 Dec. 1871)

From: *Zivilisation und Musik* (Leipzig 1846), pp. 94–5; 98–9; 102–6; 147–50

Hagen was educated in Hamburg, and, from 1841 till 1842, in Paris. He became a regular contributor to various French and German musical journals, including the *Neue Zeitschrift für Musik*. From 1854 until his death in 1871, he lived in the United States, where he became a well-known and respected figure in New York musical circles, and the founder of a number of musical periodicals.

In addition to his journalistic activities, Hagen wrote a series of novellas on music and a long disquisition on the place of music in society: *Zivilisation und Musik*. This is a work of considerable interest. Hagen's main thesis is that civilisation, by which he means modern urban industrialised society, has ruined mankind and that music of all kinds (except military music, to which Hagen seems to have taken exception) had a great part to play in the regeneration of society. It is clear that his ideas on the corrupting influence of society owe much to Rousseau; his development of them, however, as the following excerpts show, is also influenced by the socialist and anarchist idealists of the first half of the nineteenth century.

Music as a reforming agent in society

[*p. 147–50*]
'Civilisation' is the natural enemy of art, for it undermines spontaneity, the source of all art. 'Civilisation' also undermines the fact that art, by its very nature and quality, contributes to the well-being of mankind. The greater the misery brought about by civilisation, the more necessary is this well-being. Misery is most clearly the lot of the working classes. It is on working people that civilisation weighs down most heavily. If, therefore, we wish to demolish the structure of modern society, we must begin with the part of it that is peopled by the working classes. Modern socialists suggest that this would happen if the living standards of the workers were improved. They would then find the courage and the strength to creep out of their miserable hovels and enjoy the same life as those who work in comfort, they would therefore eat well, drink well and live well. This is certainly an excellent way of reforming things, but only when the workers can play a proper, dignified and serious part in society, only when they can be human beings in the most sacred meaning of the term. This cannot happen, however, for the following reasons:

Once the worker has completed his day's toil, he has nothing left to do but enjoy himself. Our social institutions allow that the worker is capable

552

only of two things: work and enjoyment. Both normally involve no spiritual activity – they are both mechanical. A sudden material improvement would tear the system apart in such a way as to distort the one thing (other than work) that he knew – enjoyment. The reform would merely serve to transform sub-humans into total animals. To prevent this, and at the same time to ensure that the suggested reorganisation of work should bear fruit, only one thing is necessary: the function of enjoyment must be ennobled. And how is this to happen? Through the medium of art, and, of course, through the most comprehensible, accessible and popular of the arts: music. Music strengthens and uplifts; it prepares men for better and higher things. It must therefore prepare the workers for their emancipation. The choral society provides the simplest musical means to this end. So wherever there are workers, whether they be factory hands or country peasants, choral societies must be established. In so doing, a step will have been taken toward the realisation of the splendid ideal that art concerns the well-being of mankind. This would be only a beginning, however, for even if the most significant works of art were easily accessible, they would not be understood by the majority of people. Why? Because they have no popular basis. Art can only contribute to the welfare of mankind if it is popular art. When is it popular? When it reveals nature's message in such a way that both the highest intelligence and the most ingenuous and ignorant minds experience it with equal interest and with equal joy. How is this possible? Most readily by clearing away what has accumulated around nature through corrupt institutions over the centuries, in order that we may again discover our original, true selves. In short, we must abandon the corruption of 'Civilisation'. This, however, can only be achieved in the far distant future; a great deal of time is required to sweep away our current institutions. As I have suggested, music is very well suited to the achievement of this ultimate aim, for, as I see it, music is destined to prepare the way for that great moment when the arts can indeed be regarded as a blessing to all mankind. The development and popularisation of music must therefore lie very close to our hearts. I have attempted to show how this has happened in the fields of dance music, music of the streets, military music, church music and opera. My investigations have clearly shown that there is comparatively little music that is genuinely, universally popular and that it is for the most part poor in quality. So, as I have so often remarked, half of mankind possesses everything and the other half virtually nothing. This cannot surely be the will of the Almighty. For this reason, He will surely be on the side of those who manfully strive to redress the terrifying inequalities in human society. Yes; He is on our side, I am sure. So forward, then, untiringly! We shall achieve our aim!

A revivified church music?

[pp. 94–5]

The Catholic Church is still the foremost example of what a Church should be on this earth: a 'refuge' for rich or poor, young or old, the sick and needy; a little haven of rest enveloped by the rays of the Sun of Divine Grace, which warm every heart that rests there. The Protestant Church can at best mean something to a healthy person, but we are not all healthy. If we were, we should not need the Church. Whether the Catholic 'refuge' might be even better than it is, is another question; for the moment, my task is only to show that it *is* a 'refuge', a fact that will have been felt by anyone who has been inside a Catholic church.

If we ask how the Catholic Church has achieved its hold over men, and how its faith has been able to take such deep root, we find in art a loyal ally and a mighty force which supports the faith. Of all religions, Catholicism has done the most for art. It has built cathedrals that are still a majestic symbol for its committed members; it has inspired paintings; it has created mighty musical compositions that compel us to fold our hands in awestruck devotion, exclaiming, 'how beautiful!'

[pp. 98–9]

If I now consider the Church as a refuge, an asylum, it is self-evident, as I see it, that church *music* must be nothing more or less than one of its adjuncts. The Church exists mainly for the sick; and just as everything in it must aim at reviving and bringing about a state of health, so, too, must music. But music only revives and refreshes (1) if it is inspired; (2) if it is of such a kind that melody is pre-eminent; and (3) if it can be widely understood.

No Church neglects inspiration more than does the Protestant Church, nor therefore does any Church provide less material for art to exploit. The truth of this assertion is based on the realisation that art is contrary to the essential spirit of Protestantism. The reason why Protestantism is not a practical religion is that it misconstrues man's true nature. Relatively few people are satisfied with the Word; the majority require some embodiment of it.

[pp. 102–6]

I have already said that Catholicism has done most for Art. This is as true of church music as it is of the other arts. Admittedly, reservations have frequently been expressed about the value of church music, and they are to some extent justified by the sameness of the material of the Mass, for example. Such reservations vanish, however, if the correct criteria of judgement are applied. These must necessarily be Catholic criteria, the first and primary consideration being that the work of art shall be born of faith and inspiration. The emotions that the work arouses are of prime importance; if these are sincere, deeply felt and true, the influence will genuinely be beneficial. No music, perhaps, arouses so profound and elevating a response as that of the old Italian church composers. Here, the ideas and emotions are so spontaneous and pure that even the most civilised European cannot fail to be moved. Such church music ennobles and purifies the listener; it raises him above the miseries of the society in which he lives, it gives him new strength and confirms his faith; it marks the place where it is performed as altogether holy. Church music of this kind would really seem to be urgently needed. Indeed, the performance of simple melodies by these old masters ought to replace the controversies that rage in the press as to which is the correct faith, and who is the true God. Such music would certainly be of more use than the printed word, which in any case only reflects individual opinion. Church music of this kind uplifts heart and spirit and is the best missionary in the world. If, however, people are ashamed of returning to what is ancient, let them ensure that modern music makes, if not a better or an equivalent impression, then at least a single one and one alone. Even if emotion, faith and inspiration are impossible in the present age, let us at any rate attempt to free ourselves from those rigid conventions that shape and categorise church music, so that something interesting may be permitted to emerge. If the first two preconditions – inspiration and melody – are unattainable, let some effort at any rate be made to realise the third: namely that the music should be widely understood. Religious emotions should be expressed naturally and freely. They should not be deprived of character and sense and imprisoned behind some verbal and musical wall of bombast and sententiousness. If this sententiousness serves only to conceal a poverty of invention, the composer had better give up. Rather no art at all than one into which hypocrisy has insinuated itself. Modern church music seems to have much in common with the Jesuits and Scholastics: lies and deceptions, all to the Glory of God. It might well be a good idea therefore to divest some contemporary church music of the padding with which it is stuffed. Perhaps then the true character of some of our musical pedants would be revealed.

One solution remains that church composers could adopt without loss of integrity; it is one that I have often recommended to them and one which has in fact been used most effectively. It involves setting aside as far as possible everything that civilisation has injected into society – in casting off the skin of civilisation – to seek pleasure and satisfaction from nature alone. This is what Félicien David has done. We are all familiar with the first fruits of his work: in *Le Désert* we find an originality that is – as I have repeatedly said – the essence of all art. This work marks the beginning of a new era, and since above all it has created a highly important new form of church music, a somewhat more detailed account of it may not be out of place here.

Le Désert is particularly interesting, for despite its French origins it is independent of the lyric stage. It is of even greater interest because we encounter at every point in it, depth, originality and truth of expression, and because it expresses in a striking manner, nature herself. It is this above all that marks out the artist. Only when he is able to turn aside from civilisation to reveal nature's secret powers, only then can others feel that wonderful excitement that surges through him as he comes face to face with those powers. In Félicien David's music we feel just this. We can only judge his work properly if we are aware of its origins. Félicien lived in Paris: even he had to drink from civilisation's poisoned goblet. Then, as fate would have it, he came to live among the Arabs. An original personality emerged. Transfigured and purified, David cast himself down before the source of the Godhead and drank deep. And this was the origin of *Le Désert*. David's unconcern for the trivia of daily life, his ability to throw off the lamentably narrow outlook that civilisation forces upon us, his power to absorb the mysterious, natural sounds of the desert and to shape them into an artistic form, these prove that the composer is one of the chosen few. Were the self-styled artists – that multitude of composers and painters – to find themselves alone with God and in that infinite sea of sand which is the desert, they would either be completely overwhelmed by the stupendous impact, or they would people the all-pervading emptiness with the microscopic ideas of their civilised imaginations. A man must be of the very highest artistic calibre to depict the desert as David has done. Consider, for instance, 'La nuit': even Rousseau himself would have been satisfied! Félicien would indeed have been Rousseau's ideal composer: both are in tune with nature's mysteries: both have the feel of her pulse. Both experience the need to cast off the mantle of civilisation, and to express their need in art. Both are to be numbered among the world's great and original minds, and both point the way to better things.

Rodolphe Toepffer

(b. Geneva, 17 Feb. 1799; d. Geneva, 8 June 1846)

From: *Réflexions et menus-propos d'un peintre génevois* (Paris 1848)

Toepffer's father was a minor painter, in the style of Calame. Toepffer spent some time in Paris, from 1819, and in 1833 he became professor of rhetoric in the Académie des belles lettres, at Geneva. He was a prolific author, his writings ranging from novels in the tradition of Rousseau's *Julie* to chatty guides for tourists: his *Voyages en zig-zag*, in which are to be found engravings by himself and Calame, was particularly popular.

Chapter 20: On Haydn

And as for the musician, what does he do, I ask you, in order to imitate? The very first, the essential, the cardinal thing that he does not do is imitate, for as soon as he does so he loses his power. When he imitates he translates. Now in order to move the feelings he must be expressive, and in order to express he must transform. This is his law, even more than the poet's; it is the poet's law, even more than the painter's.

Tell me, what prevents him from imitating cries of grief – its sighs, groans and shrieks? Nothing. And sometimes he does do it. And when he does so your tears dry up. Should the imitation of groaning be prolonged or repeated, then the giggling starts. But if, instead of a straight imitation of the external appearance of things the artist pours out in a language that he has created, the emotions, the griefs and joys, the sublimity which fills his soul – things that are all the more powerful in that they are not clothed in finite form – then at once you understand that this language moves you, transports and captivates you. Its impact will be all the greater in that your soul will not have to reclothe the object of its emotion in finite form.

For this reason, music is pre-eminently powerful amongst the imitative arts. Imitation counts for hardly anything, and expression for almost everything. Sounds are the intermediaries between souls. They are the living and most immediate image of the sweetest and intensest agitation of the human soul; they impart to it joy, ecstasy, ineffable melancholy, tumultuous passion, and the delirium of triumph. While the painter drags himself along on the earth's surface, and while the poet flies astride Pegasus from Pindos to Helicon the musician glides above the earth, above Pindos. He rides above the stormclouds, through infinite space, and his lot is one of unresting motion in the search for expression.

Three men of sublime genius have taken the story of the Creation as their theme: Michaelangelo, Moses and Haydn. Great artist though Michaelangelo was he had to adopt the method of direct imitation, as dictated by the technical procedures of his art. His work is accordingly trivial when set against that of Moses. Working under fewer constraints, Moses expressed in a single tablet (*un seul tableau*) both the hidden thoughts of the Creator, and the magnificence of his creation. The third, being freer still, depicted less but expressed more. At one and the same time he summarises and develops the work of the other two. In his *Creation* is majesty, power, movement and chaos; mountains and plains are for the first time bathed in light; myriads of beings are called forth into their new abode; the coming of man is depicted, and with him, tenderness, passion and poetry! And all these things are willed into existence by Haydn, both simultaneously and successively, things that are more infinite than indeterminate, yet more vital and alive than they are infinite!

Karl August Timotheus Kahlert

(b. Breslau, 5 Mar. 1807; d. Breslau, 29 May 1864)

From: 'Ueber den Begriff der klassischen und romantischen Musik,' in *Allgemeine musikalische Zeitung*, Leipzig, vol. 50, no. 18, 3 May 1848, pp. 289–95

Kahlert showed an early talent for music and literature; and when he was a student in Berlin (1827), he not only took the opportunity to meet many writers and musicians, but attended Hegel's lectures on philosophy. He had intended to become a lawyer, but his health was not strong enough, so he devoted himself exclusively to the study of the fine arts. It was as an historian, however, that he first gained recognition; and in 1840 he was appointed to the chair of history at Breslau. Ill-health compelled him to relinquish the post in 1846, the year in which he published his *System der Aesthetik*, a work much influenced by the ideas of Schelling and Hegel. As well as being a frequent contributor to the *Neue Zeitschrift für Musik* (1834–43) and the *Allgemeine musikalische Zeitung* (1842–50), he was responsible for several volumes of poems and novellas, some of which, such as *Caelestina* (1826), *Donna Elvira* (1829) and *Blätter aus der Brieftasche eines Musikers* (1832) relate to music.

This article is significant in that it is the first one of any importance to define classicism and romanticism in music in terms of the composers and movements which are generally accepted today.

The Year of Revolutions (1848), which saw both the first abortive attempt to establish a pan-German democratic parliamentary government and the fall of Metternich, was watched with varying degrees of interest by musicians. Richard Wagner was driven into exile for his participation in the revolutionary movement in Saxony, for example. The excitement that a new society under a new form of liberal constitutional government might develop certainly invaded the pages of the *Neue Zeitschrift* and the *Allgemeine musikalische Zeitung*; the following excerpts indicate that however other-worldly we may consider them nowadays, the musicians of the period were by no means unaware of the impact that social and political changes may have on art.

However carefully students of aesthetics may have defined the principles of classical and romantic art, difficulties arise when attempts are made to apply these principles to the individual arts and to distinguish works of one kind from another; when, for instance, claims are made that classical works differ from romantic ones. Nowadays, both terms are applied to music whereas previously sculpture had generally been regarded as classical and music as romantic, the one expressing the religious beliefs of the Greeks, the other those of the Christians. There really seems to be little in common between the human form immortalised in stone and the ethereal, evanescent

559

structure of sound; the one served the worship of a God that man conceived in human terms, the other served as the revelation of a spiritual yearning for the infinite. It followed, according to the accepted scheme of things, that no musical composition could be described as 'classical', for music was deemed to be essentially romantic. This is the problem, then, that I shall try to resolve.

If the term 'ancient' is used to characterise Greek art, the word 'classical' can advantageously be reserved for use in another context, namely as an indication of anything that is in its field pre-eminent and exemplary. In every day parlance, indeed, in a non-academic sense, the word has long been used in this way. The use of the word classic in connection with a painting certainly does not call to mind the arts of ancient Greece, any more than it does when applied to the work of some French, English or German author. It is certainly true that philologists are constantly arguing the foundation of our modern culture in its entirety on models provided by the culture of ancient Greece. The argument cannot possibly be applied to those arts that have developed independently of classical models. To avoid any misunderstanding that may arise from the use of the word 'classical', then, we shall make use of the phrases, 'the spirit of antiquity', and 'the spirit of romanticism'.

But how did the antithesis between classical and romantic come about? Through poetry, which for a time imitated that of ancient Greece and then that of the Middle Ages. In every European nation there have been poets who have drawn upon Greek culture and others who have drawn upon their own national traditions. Some thirty years ago there began an out-and-out struggle between the two. A passion for the Middle Ages took the form of a particular interest in the verbal and pictorial expression of Catholicism and the miraculous. The ideals of ancient Greece, on the other hand, continued to appeal more to those who were inclined to Protestantism. It was through the romantics that increasing attention came to be paid to Germany's past history, a history that had been totally ignored in discussions of Greek civilisation, and to this extent the romantics exercised a salutary influence. At the same time clear, rational thought tended to give way to sentimentality, and sober prose to overheated expression. The romantics reached out for the infinite, whereas the classicists sought to establish strictly defined boundaries. The romantics were censured for muddle-headedness, the classicists for triviality. The older generation could not comprehend the new world outlook, and the impetus that it gave to the imagination. Thus the venerable Goethe one-sidedly argued that 'classical means healthy; romantic sick'. Yet he might well have objected that health and sickness were to be found just as much amongst the imitators of the ancients as amongst the romantics, and that he himself had treated the emotions in a very romantic way in *Götz*, *Egmont* and *Faust*. Research into nature's deepest secrets has bred a taste for the miraculous, whereas everything had previously been ordered and explained in abstract, intellectually formulated terms.

If we now turn to consider how music took shape during the early years of the nineteenth century, amidst the turmoil of aesthetic controversy, we shall find that romantic ideas were being pioneered here too. Throughout the eighteenth century a sequence of great masters had ministered in part to German and in part to Italian tastes. The Germans, however, played a decisive role in the history of European music for they achieved such an intimate fusion of Italian and German styles that they were able to create a rapid succession of masterpieces that won universal acclaim. The Germans did much to shape the course of instrumental music, once they had learned to make their music sing in the Italian manner and to implant in their instrumental compositions a melodic quality that was quite new. Instrumental music was emancipated from its purely contrapuntal and ornamental roles; it developed enormous versatility. The composer who most succeeded in this great task was Mozart. He was the most truly classical of all composers; others were classical in only certain specific ways. He was so imaginative, he had such a balanced feeling for musical form, that those who examined his music with a critical eye found it to be as comprehensible as it was inventive. His music possessed lightness and yet the greatest depth and skill. It was universally admired both for its simplicity and for its ineffable profundity. Then along came his great successor, who explored new paths. The romantic movement found expression in music too through Beethoven. He is most intimately involved in the spiritual development of the whole German people. But first we must substantiate the claim that Beethoven is in comparison with Mozart a romantic composer.

From the time of J. S. Bach onwards instrumental music has possessed a greater spiritual potential than vocal music, since vocal music is more subject to natural limitation. To begin with, greater variety of figuration is possible in instrumental music and thus of harmony and texture. Different combinations of instrumental colours, too, can impart remarkable effects even to the simplest intervals and chords. Beethoven mastered these rich resources and exploited them as he strove so astonishingly to break the bonds of the traditional forms that his predecessors had established. What is musical form but the natural body that a piece of music must assume in order to establish itself as a living organism? The laws of nature apply just as much to what is heard as to what is seen.

The creative mind, however, will conquer nature as long as nature's powers are respected. It expands forms; it seems to play with them; but it knows that without them it is nothing, and that if it severs its earthly ties in the process of reaching out for the infinite it will perish. The primeval form that underlies all musical structure was constantly in Beethoven's heaven-storming, Titanic mind. Even when the composer appeared to be acting in an arbitrary manner, he was none the less honouring the eternal law that must be observed if a musical work is to be as comprehensible and enjoyable to others as it is to its creator. None of Beethoven's predecessors had attempted such a daring and hazardous undertaking. They accepted established conventions, he chose freedom. Before Beethoven's day the proportions of a composition were envisaged in terms similar to the proportions of a speech, to its introduction and to its development. Beethoven was however so inventive, so fertile and so original that the proportions of his compositions were obscured, being evident only to the attentive listener. Hand in hand with a concern to break down barriers went a natural mysticism and sense of the mysterious of a kind that hitherto had been quite unknown. Beethoven's music is tense with expectation; so much is pregnant with significance; magnificent themes emerge like beautiful shapes out of the slowly dissolving clouds. The pauses on individual chords, the sheer luxuriance of sound, the very melodic ideas which would have been condemned as boring in a previous age all proved to be just right at that time when people were plumbing the depths of nature's profoundest secrets. Interest in the miraculous supplanted a previous concern to achieve a balance between intellect and emotion. Yet a third romantic element manifested itself in Beethoven's music: humour. This spiritual quality which is so often confused with wit – whimsicality or a sense of fun – is effectively an amalgam of the two mental states of pleasure and pain. It springs from the realisation that nothing in the world, however sublime it may be, is wholly without fault, and that ironically enough, nothing, however terrifying it may be, is free from the temporal limitations of this earthly existence. This Shakespearian characteristic lends Beethoven's music its particular significance. In his symphonies Beethoven frequently plays like a child with the sublimest ideas. Little comic spirits mockingly appear in the midst of the most earth-shattering events. The juxtaposition of sharply contrasting moods most distinguishes Beethoven from his predecessor, the witty and ingenious Haydn.

Beethoven quickly established a tremendous hold over the minds of his contemporaries, and thus music's romanticism made its presence felt. Mozart may by comparison be properly considered as a 'classical' composer, and the model for such later composers as Hummel and Spohr. In less talented hands this classical style degenerated into an easy-going and clever arrangement of regularly constructed but empty forms. In Germany there appeared a flood of squarely constructed musical compositions with threadbare titles, pieces that deserved neither praise nor blame. Men strove to emulate Mozart's simplicity, a simplicity that could not be acquired but which was innate. So it was that interest in the Mozartian school declined in favour of the school of Beethoven. The general public, however, were not satisfied, since they longed only for pretty and voluptuous melodies. Whilst, therefore, a few people enjoyed the romanticism of Beethoven's music, the majority indulged in the undemanding and readily comprehensible melodies of the prolific and artless Rossini. This development did not have an immediate impact, it is true, on instrumental music, in which the Germans took particular pride. The Italians and the French readily left this field to the Germans, and the latter continued to exploit it.

It is noteworthy that the history of romantic poetry somewhat repeated itself in the history of romantic music. Poets quickly shifted their attention from nature-mysticism and the miraculous to ghosts and the fear that they inspire. The devil became fashionable in a variety of guises; Weber gripped the public imagination with his *Freischütz*, much as did Hoffmann with his *Serapionsbrüder*, at about the same time. Quite apart from the fact that *Freischütz* was really the first German national opera, this new genre gave expression to the terrors of the spirit world in instrumental terms: it was Weber who exploited the tremendous power that instruments have to express and illustrate the spoken word. Instrumental music thus lost its imprecise meaning, an imprecision for which it had often been both criticised and praised. Not only did music now express a general mood, but it also clothed and embodied the sense of those specific emotions that were being expressed in words. Every musician is aware of the close parallels that there are between Weber and Beethoven. The difference between the two lies in the fact that what in Beethoven is instinctive, in Weber is calculated. Weber managed to conceal this through his brilliant inventiveness. He had a genuine and beautiful melodic gift which was always at his command. He lacked, however, a simple fluency, because he constantly sought after unusual effects which he had to cobble together. Beethoven, on the other hand, could create structures that were satisfyingly whole and rich. Music now began to stray beyond its former boundaries and to value ingenuity above spontaneity. The introduction of this element of ingenuity, as it has been called, into the art of music resulted in a divorce between the world of phenomenal nature and the use of phenomena to express spiritual concepts that were not purely musical. Intellect and imagination thus diverged. This development had already been foreshadowed in the previous century by a number of Gluck's disciples. Being unaware of Gluck's profound genius, scorning Mozart's simplicity, and altogether lacking any genuine power in invention, they strove for sensational effects. More recently, Vogler made some name for himself on account of his penchant for the bizarre. Even so, many composers were still attracted by the spirit of genuine romanticism. There was, for example, the extraordinarily prolific Franz Schubert, a true descendant of Beethoven, who was taken from the world before he had reached his full maturity.

After Weber, musical romanticism followed two separate paths, the one represented by the music of Mendelssohn, the other by that of Meyerbeer. Though both appeared to owe a good deal to Weber, they otherwise drew from widely differing sources in the formation of their styles. Mendelssohn sought inspiration in Bach and Handel; Meyerbeer turned also to the Italians and to the French. Mendelssohn showed a constant concern for organic construction, for form as it is called in short, and he differed from other of Beethoven's successors in his use of strict contrapuntal techniques based on those of the great composers of the past. Meyerbeer, on the other hand, created a style that was based on elements taken from the three nations, and in doing so he was evidently more interested in the idea of variety than in unity. Though Mendelssohn may have successfully created a genuine unity from the various elements that he took from his predecessors, making each of his works a homogeneous whole, the public was less enamoured of him than of either Weber, who had a prodigious melodic gift, or Meyerbeer. People objected that Meyerbeer's compositions lacked character and that they were best suited for ballet. Mendelssohn and Meyerbeer have at least this in common, that they did not follow the path that had been mapped out by Mozart, although in other respects they differ considerably from each other.

Romanticism found expression in the work of several other talented composers, notably Robert Schumann, Löwe, the Frenchmen Berlioz and David, and in the work of such virtuosi as Liszt, Paganini and Ernst. The gulf separating the two kinds of music has in the meantime widened. On the one hand some composers sink into a dream world, into a silent, inner existence, and they seek to bring hidden treasures to light from the profoundest depths. Their music degenerates into formlessness. Others, who also abandon themselves to the genuinely romantic, mystical impulse, stick small-scale musical ideas together by means of empty phrases. The former kind of composer cannot capture the public attention. The second cannot give effective shape to their ideas because they have no knowledge of how to develop them. In much the same way, a drama or a story cannot be created from a series of anecdotes. In both cases there are substantial musical ideas that simply cannot be given effective form. This formlessness, this striving for a dissolution of the natural boundaries, goes hand in hand with parallel developments in other fields of human endeavour. Everywhere there is a feverish restlessness, as there is in music. Even so, this formlessness promises more for the future than does a sterile adherence to outdated procedures, soulless formality, born of a study, not of the living emotions, but of classical works of art, which had after all originally been inspired by genuine feelings. Musical forms, both strict and free, will continually reshape themselves. Just as the urge to sing gave birth to melody, so it is that melodies will constantly tend to expand, and extend themselves, thus becoming the basis of entire musical compositions. There is a single underlying musical form which is conditioned by the harmonic structure of sound, and this governs the rules of composition. Even so, the potential for the creation of new forms from this basic material is limitless. The contrast between the classical and the romantic will none the less continue, classical composers being more interested in the formal structure of music, romantic composers in free, untrammelled expression. The characteristics of classicism and romanticism may be discerned not only in individuals, but in entire nations, and in specific historical periods too. These will continually recur as they have done from time to time in the past, though in different guises. They assume an infinite variety of forms and are the frequent causes of erroneous judgements. It is precisely those who recognise the constraints of the natural laws of sound who will prevail, the others will lose themselves in chaos or insipid sentimentality as they drift along, entranced by their unfettered imaginations. In this way one acts as a counterbalance to the other.

The political gravity of the present situation has dealt a serious blow to romanticism. The time for dreams is past; such men as Gervinus[1] and Ruge[2] have shown during the course of the past ten years that romanticism has sapped the political strength of the German nation. The need now is to establish the rule of law and order. Anyone who reads a newspaper will know that order without freedom results in despotism and that freedom without order brings anarchy. The arts can degenerate into lifeless routine or into sheer madness. Let us hope that despite the marked polarity between the two musical extremes, new pleasures will be found in living forms rather than in dead procedures or heaped-up effects that only confuse the senses, and that this pleasure will be nourished and intensified by the works that it has conceived. When the life of society as a whole has been galvanised in this way, a healthier mental balance may be expected of the individual, and this will be to the benefit of the arts. Happy are those who experience this pleasure! It will assuage the deepest pain that has been inflicted by the products of many a morbid artistic imagination.

[1] Georg Gottfried Gervinus (1805–1871), German historian and literary scholar, author of a study of Shakespeare, comparing him with Handel (eds.)

[2] Arnold Ruge (1802–1880), German philosopher and political writer, one time co-editor, with Karl Marx, of the *Deutsch-Französische Jahrbücher* (eds.)

Eduard Krüger[1]

From:Beziehungen zwischen Kunst und Politik', in the *Allegemeine musikalische Zeitung*, Leipzig, vol. 50, nos. 25 and 30, 21 June and 26 July 1848, pp. 401–4; 481–4

[No. 25, pp. 401–4]

The age of German freedom has begun in violence, affecting artists, and in some cases driving them into passionately partisan attitudes that have already brought singular results. I say singular, because it is singular to observe how quickly the tides and tempests of the age engulf the stupid, causing them to stand not only themselves but everything else on its head.

'What influence will political freedom have on Music?' people ask. The question indicates that those who ask it understand neither freedom nor art. Political change affects everything; it affects individuals and peoples; it creates and it destroys – these statements may all apply to art as well. From this, the amateur philosopher cheerfully concludes that an obvious interrelationship exists between the two and that it is possible to work out how a political movement may influence the arts. . . .

So what effect will such external events have on the art of music? Is there such a thing as republican or monarchical harmony or melody? Will a republican always play his trombone better in a republic than an aristocrat would? Just remember the outcry a year ago when an organist was appointed to a post somewhere in the capital because he had accepted the religious faith of the royal house. What a fuss there was about it, the result of which was beneficial neither to the post, nor the art – music itself – but only to the King. Neither instruments nor triads, let alone the talents or insights of artists, will be much affected by the Frankfurt Assembly. . . .

But the more thoughtful of our politically-inclined musicians, at any rate, do not construe things quite as crudely as this. After all, they have gratefully accepted freedom of religious belief, so why should they not accept freedom of political beliefs as well? They have, in fact, developed an argument *a posteriori*, which sounds more subtle and persuasive, but is in fact no more watertight than the other and in no way more relevant to art. They claim the following: Of course we will not accept a musical director simply because he wears the red, black and gold colours if he is otherwise useless; on the basis of the principle, however, 'Do good to all men, especially to those that are of the Household of Faith', we would prefer a man who cares

---

[1] For a discussion of the author's work see the editorial introduction on p. 530.

for German liberty if the choice lies between two men of equal talents. As we well know, however, that solves very few problems; and we will happily accept sound aesthetic judgements on Mozart's operas that originate in the land of Czarist tyranny. We will even put up with a Dane writing the best symphonies and be grateful to him for doing so. In fact, these thoughtful Abderites say, it is basically not a matter of any particular views held – and here is the argument *a posteriori* – but a matter of spiritual integrity! An artist must first of all be a good man, secondly a noble one, thirdly one who is politically aware, and fourthly, a man of power, knowing all the significant trends of the time and how to deal with them. Must – must! If only these requirements were automatically self-fulfilling! The artist must be progressive; he must be committed; he must be honest, not tell lies, etc. What, then, is so special about all this? Nothing at all! These are universal moral precepts that everyone should observe; hence nobody does, and everyone ploughs his own furrow as before. But even so, granted that artists might well take this advice to heart, what impertinence to arrogate the finest human virtues to one restricted social order!

The last of these requirements does make some sense; but it is still false and misleading if it is applied solely to artists. The artist must be aware of the trends of his age, and from them he must create beauty. We require of anyone who deserves our confidence such an awareness of the trends of the age; the task of creating beauty from them can be achieved only by a divinely-gifted genius, a task that he performs without even a thought as to how it is done, without so much as a by-your-leave; and he will continue to do so as long as artists exist, till the end of time. Remember, though, that the Deity, not the pedagogue, decides what people must and shall do.

Let us now take one step further into the maze to see if we can get to the heart of the matter. It is often felt that some contemporary phenomenon or something typical of the age should be given artistic shape. This view is often put forward by young intellectuals among artists. It would create, we are told, an absolutely splendid impression, for example, if, instead of eternal sentimental maunderings about love, a heroic patriotic ballad were the centre of interest; instead of languid salon-lions, a Hohenstaufen emperor. That sounds more sensible, if only, as we have said, the artist expresses such things from the heart. Please God some genius even more perceptive than Mozart or Beethoven will be inspired by such themes – for the rest, leave it to the genius in question.

As for embodying the living forces of the age in artistic shape, that is a matter only for those who have honestly dedicated themselves to and experienced the force of the history of art. This is the most difficult problem; and it cannot be solved by the application of logical thought, but only by poetic experience. The interaction of contemporary forces in the world and in life, forces endeavouring to gain acceptance, passionately suffering intense birth-pangs; all these things are ephemeral and hence little to do with art. The poet, like the King, *transcends* party; this deep truth was understood by *Goethe*, but not by *Freiligrath*.[2] It was not during the Reformation, but a hundred years later, that the finest hymns and music were produced by evangelical artists; and Raphael's rapturous angels prove what achievements the Roman church had to its credit and what direction its endeavours were taking long before his divine art had embodied them in permanent form. The poet is not involved in the struggle; but the successfully concluded struggle may be the basis of a poem.

[No. 30, pp. 481–4]

Nobody will deny that there is a relationship between morals, art and the state, just as there is between character, church and religion. This relationship has never been disturbed without damage to all three. Where art is amoral, as it has been for years in Paris, both art and morals collapse – or rather both have been in a state of collapse for some time, amoral art being only a symptom of a previous social decay. Does it follow, then, that every moral action results in beauty? Let us not draw such hasty conclusions. We need to take a look at the history of culture in order to determine what the issue is.

Art has never flourished that lacked a national soil from which to grow and it has certainly never been at its greatest without a climate of social morality. Any evidence that seems to point to the contrary is based on misconceptions that may be refuted by thorough investigation. The same is true of the individual artist. He too cannot reach the peak of artistic achievement without personal and artistic standards of values. . . . A thoroughly corrupt and perverted man will never create the image of incorruptible beauty unless he is inspired from time to time by some memory of a purer state of mind. If he has the power to do this, he is, during those moments of creative activity, not devoid of moral standards. . . .

Applying what has already been said to politics, – for civic life only reflects individual morality on a larger scale – the following conclusion may be drawn. It is out of the question that politics should be directly reflected in the realm of beauty. Conversely, though, the spirit of the age, the moral climate, the political atmosphere, the general mood, must inevitably be reflected in works of art. This is logically, though not morally inevitable. In other words, it is self-evident on psychological grounds and has nothing to do with moral precepts. How wide the gap is between the man of action and the poet can be inferred from the fact that so far in the course of history, no man has ever at the same time been a great king or man of action and an epoch-making artist. There is, however, a close relationship between actions and ideas, morals and love, activity and beauty; and this can be observed from the fact that the hero takes pleasure in the work of the bard; the bard honours the hero; each needs the other and there is a mutual exchange. . . .

[2] German patriotic poet, 1810–76 (eds.)

Having established what action and art have in common and in what ways they differ, we may conclude first of all that political developments in Germany will to begin with have no effect on the fine arts. . . . In purely practical matters, however, it may be that the new political system will influence the world of Art. In this connection, steps could be taken to speed up the practical realisation of new ideas, or at least to set some long overdue reforms in motion. Two points must, however, be borne in mind: firstly, too much should not be expected from new laws and institutions; and then, any gains that are made should be unremittingly exploited, not handed over to the state. Men will err, whatever the political system, just as, conversely, there have been and will be brave, trustworthy people in the worst conditions. Even the best system would not eradicate the greater evils of place-seeking, dissension, poverty, nepotism, wronged innocence, etc., nor would the most influential League of Moral Virtue. We do not need to remind historians of the fact; we merely emphasise it, as we have done recently, to warn the unregenerate. . . .

So: what needs improvement, and how? I hope I shall be permitted to draw parallels with politics, not just because it is such a temptation to do so, but because the parallels are apposite. First of all, more than ever, the maxim holds good – attributed not to a modern liberal but to an ancient king – 'The people are not there for the benefit of officials; officials are there for the benefit of the people.' The same is true of artists. They are there for the benefit of the people, and they must constantly be aware of the fact that they are responsible to the consumer, the people, the world, however highly they themselves are respected. They will testify to this respect most obviously by showing an awareness of the true interests of the people and by striving body and soul to realise them and to let beauty into their lives. 'Salus populi suprema est lex esto': Let the supreme law of art be the creation of beauty for the benefit and joy of the world. Not, then, personality; the ghost of the virtuoso has been laid; living beauty will make its presence felt. Moreover, it is not rank or age that count, but beauty. Let the young artist not be neglected, therefore, because he is young, nor let him be pampered simply because he belongs to some party, or because he treats everyone as his equal, or because he is an intriguer or self-seeker. For that would result in that very nepotism that should be eliminated. The same is true of the dead. It does not matter what he was called, what age he lived in, how famous he was, what movement he belonged to; the only claims an artist may make on posterity are those of truth and beauty. Respect for the public demands of the artist moral integrity, not servile flattery and self-prostitution in search of popular artistic success.

Select Bibliography

This list contains only those sources that are relevant to this volume. Where the title of a work is quoted in full in the main text, only a shortened version of the title is given here. Omissions in such shortened versions are shown in the usual manner.

Primary Sources:

Encyclopaedias and other large reference works:

Allgemeine Encyclopädie der Wissenschaften und Künste, eds. J. S. Ersch and J. G. Gruber (Leipzig 1818–50)

Allgemeine Theorie der schönen Künste, ed. J. G. Sulzer (2nd edn, Leipzig 1792–4)

Biographie universelle, ancienne et moderne, ed. J. F. Michaud (Paris 1843–), 45 vols.

A Complete Dictionary of Music, translated from the French of J.-J. Rousseau, by William Waring (2nd edn, London 1779)

The Cyclopedia, ed. A. Rees (London 1820)

Dictionnaire de musique moderne, ed. F. H. J. Castil-Blaze (Paris 1821)

Dictionnaire des beaux-arts, ed. A. L. Millin (Paris 1806)

Dizionario e bibliografia della musica, ed. P. Lichtenthal (Milan 1826), 4 vols.

Encyclopédie de la musique, eds. A. Lavignac and L. de la Laurencie (Paris 1920–31), 11 vols.

Encyclopädie der gesammten musikalischen Wissenschaften oder Universal Lexikon der Tonkunst, ed. G. Schilling (Stuttgart 1834–8, 2nd edn 1840–2), 7 vols.

Encyclopédie, ou dictionnaire raisonné des sciences, des arts et des métiers, ed. J. le R. d'Alembert and D. Diderot (Paris 1751–72)

Historisches-biographisches Lexicon der Tonkünstler, ed. E. L. Gerber (Leipzig 1790–2), 2 vols.

Journal encyclopédique, ed. P. Rousseau (Liège 1756–93), 304 vols.

Kurzgefasstes Handwörterbuch der Musik, ed. H. C. Koch (Leipzig 1807)

Supplément à l'encyclopédie, ed. J.-B. Robinet (Amsterdam 1776), 5 vols.

Periodicals:

Allgemeine musikalische Zeitung (Leipzig 1798–)

Allgemeine Wiener Musikzeitung (Vienna 1840–8)

Apollon (Penig 1803)

Das Athenäum (Jena 1798–1800)

The Atheneum (London 1828–)

[Berliner] Allgemeine Musikzeitung (Berlin 1824–30)

Berlinische Monatsschrift (Berlin 1785)

Berlinische musikalische Zeitung (Berlin 1805–6)

Caecilia (Mainz 1824–48)

Correspondance des amateurs musiciens (Paris 1802–5)

Correspondance littéraire, philosophique et critique (Paris 1754–1813)

Encyclopédie méthodique, musical eds. N. E. Framery and P. L. Ginguené (Paris 1791–1818)
Gazette musicale de Paris (Paris 1833–5)
Le Globe (Paris 1824–31)
The Harmonicon , ed. W. Ayrton (London 1823–33)
Die Horen, eine Monatsschrift (Stuttgart 1795)
Iris im Gebiet der Tonkunst (Berlin 1830–40)
Journal des Débats (Paris 1814–   )
Journal des Savans (Paris 1665–   )
Magazin der Musik (Hamburg 1783–6)
Le Ménestrel (Paris 1833–   )
Le Mercure de France (Paris 1672–   )
The Musical Magazine (London 1835)
The Musical World (London 1836–91)
Musikalisches Kunstmagazin (Berlin 1782–91)
Neue Zeitschrift für Musik (Leipzig 1834–   )
Quarterly Musical Magazine and Review (London 1818–28)
La Revue musicale (Paris 1827–   )

Books

Alison, A., *Essays on the Nature and Principles of Taste* (Dublin 1790)
André, Y. M., *L'Essai sur le beau* (1741) in *Oeuvres philosophiques du Père André*, ed. V. Cousin (Paris 1843)
Avison, C., *An Essay on Musical Expression* (London 1753)
Ballanche, P. S., *Du sentiment considéré dans ses rapports avec la littérature et les arts* (Lyon 1801)
Barthélemy, J. J., *Entretiens sur l'état de la musique grecque au quatrième siècle* (Paris 1777)
    Voyages du jeune Anacharsis en Grèce (Paris 1788)
Batteux, C., *Les beaux-arts réduits à un même principe* (Paris 1746)
Baudelaire, C., *Paris Spleen*, tr. L. Varèse (London 1951)
    Salon de 1846, ed. D. Kelley (Oxford 1975)
Baumgarten, A. G., *Aesthetica* (Frankfurt-an-der-Oder 1752–8), 2 vols.
Beattie, J., *An Essay on Poetry and Music as they affect the Mind* (Edinburgh 1776)
Berlioz, H., *Oeuvres littéraires*, eds. R. Dumesnil, H. Barraud, J. Chailley etc. (Paris 1968–   )
    The Memoirs, tr. D. Cairns (London 1969)
Blainville, C. H., *Histoire générale critique et philologique de la musique* (Paris 1767)
Blair, H., *Lectures on Rhetoric and Belles Lettres*, ed. T. Dale (London 1845)
Boileau, see Longinus
Brown, J., *A Dissertation on the Rise, Union and Power. . .of Poetry and Music* (Dublin 1763)
Burke, E., *A Philosophical Enquiry into the Origin of our Ideas of the Sublime and the Beautiful* (London 1757)
Burney, C., *A General History of Music*, vol. 3 (London 1789)
Busby, T., *A Grammar of Music* (2nd edn, London 1826)
Castil-Blaze, F. H. J. (see *Encyclopaedias*)
Chabanon, M. P. G de, *Observations sur la musique* (Paris 1779)
Chateaubriand, F. R., Vicomte de, *Le Génie du christianisme* (7th edn, Paris 1823)

Chênedollé, C. J. L. de, 'A l'aube du romantisme', in *Oeuvres complètes* (L'Académie française, Paris 1864)

Chorley, H. F., *Modern German Music* (London 1854)

Choron, A., *Principes de composition* (Paris 1808), 3 vols.

Coleridge, S. T., 'On Taste', *The Collected Works of Samuel Taylor Coleridge*, ed. K. Coburn (London 1969–)

Condillac, E. B. de, *Traité des sensations* (London 1754), 2 vols.

Cousin, V., *Du vrai, du beau et du bien*, tr. O. W. Wight as *Lectures on the True, the Beautiful and the Good* (3rd edn, Edinburgh 1854)

Crotch, W., *Substance of Several Courses of Lectures on Music* (London 1831)

Dahlberg, F. H. von, *Die Aeolsharfe, ein allegorischer Traum* (Erfurt 1801)

d'Alembert, J. le R., *Élémens de musique théorique et pratique, suivant les principes de M. Rameau* (Paris 1752), 4 vols.

Mélanges de littérature (Amsterdam 1767–73)

(see also *Encyclopaedias*)

Delacroix, E., *The Journal of Eugène Delacroix*, tr. W. Pach (London 1938)

Deschamps, E., *Un manifeste du romantisme: la préface des Études françaises et étrangères*, ed. H. Girard (Paris 1923)

Desmarais, C., *Essai sur les classiques et les romantiques* (Paris 1824)

Diderot, D., *Oeuvres complètes* (Paris 1875–9)

(see also *Encyclopaedias*)

Du Bos, J. B., *Réflexions critiques sur la poësie et sur la peinture* (Paris 1719)

Critical Reflections on Poetry, Painting and Music, tr. T. Nugent (London 1746, enlarged edition 1748)

Eckermann, J. P., *Gespräche mit Goethe in den letzten Jahren seines Lebens*, ed. E. Merian-Genast (Basel 1945), 2 vols.

Engel, J. J., *Ueber die musikalische Malerei* (Berlin 1780)

Fétis, F. J., *La Musique mise à la portée de tout le monde* (Paris 1830), tr. as *Music Explained to the World* (London 1844)

Fichte, J. G., *Werke*, eds. R. Lauth and H. Jacob (Berlin 1965–)

Forkel, J. N., *Allgemeine Geschichte der Musik* (Leipzig 1788–), 2 vols.

Ueber der Theorie der Musik (Göttingen 1777)

Framery, N. E., *Avis aux poëtes lyriques de la nécessité du rhythme et de la césure dans les hymnes ou odes destinés à la musique* (Paris 1796)

Discours qui a remporté le prix de musique et déclamation (Paris 1802)

(see also *Periodicals*)

Gerstenberg, H. W. von, *Vermischte Schriften* (Leipzig 1815–16), 3 vols.

Goethe, J. W. von, *Werke*, ed. E. Trunz (Hamburg 1948–60), 14 vols.

Schriften zur Kunst, ed. Rolf-Dieter Denker (Munich 1962)

Grétry, A. E. M., *Mémoires ou essais sur la musique* (Paris 1789)

De la verité (Paris 1801)

Hagen, T., *Zivilisation und Musik* (Leipzig 1846)

Hamann, J. G., *Sämtliche Werke*, ed. J. Nadler (Vienna 1949–57), 6 vols.

Harris, J., *Three Treatises. The First Concerning Art, the Second Concerning Music, Painting and Poetry, the Third Concerning Happiness* (London 1744)

Hastings, T., *Dissertation on Musical Taste* (Albany 1822)

Hawkins, Sir J., *A General History of the Science and Practice of Music* (London 1776), 5 vols.

Hegel, G. W. F., *Werke*, ed. Herman Glockner (Stuttgart 1928), 18 vols.

Vorlesungen über die Aesthetik, ed. Rüdiger Bübner (Stuttgart 1971)

Heine, H., *Sämtliche Werke*, ed. G. Karpeles (Leipzig n.d.), 12 vols.

Heinse, J. J. W., *Werke*, ed. K. Schuddekopf (Leipzig 1906–25), 10 vols.

Hemsterhuis, F., *Oeuvres philosophiques* (Paris 1809), 2 vols.

Herbart, J. F., *Werke*, ed. G. Hartenstein (Leipzig 1851), 8 vols.

Herder, J. G., *Sämtliche Werke*, ed. B. Suphan (Berlin 1877–99), 33 vols.
    Kalligone, ed. H. Begenau (Weimar 1955)

Heydenreich, K. H., *System der Aesthetik* (Leipzig 1790)

Home, H., *Elements of Criticism* (Edinburgh 1761)

Hume, D., *An Enquiry Concerning Human Understanding*, ed. A. Selby-Bigge (Oxford 1894)

Hutcheson, F., *An Inquiry into the Original of our Ideas of Beauty and Virtue* (London 1725), ed. with an introduction by P. Kivy (The Hague, 1973)

Jones, Sir W., *Poems . . . with two Essays on the Poetry of the Eastern Nations and on the Arts called Imitative* (Oxford 1772)

Kant, I., *Gesammelte Schriften* (Berlin 1900–55), 23 vols.
    Kritik der Urteilskraft, ed. G. Lehmann (Stuttgart 1966)

Kierkegaard, S. A., *Enten–Eller*, tr. as *Either/Or*, David F. Swenson and Lilian M. Swenson (Princeton 1944)

La Cépède, B. G. D. de, *La poétique de la musique* (Paris 1785), 2 vols.

Lamartine, A. de, *Oeuvres* (Paris 1849–   ), 14 vols.

Lamennais, F., *De la religion considerée dans ses rapports avec l'ordre politique et social* (Paris 1825)
    Paroles d'un croyant (Paris 1833)
    Esquisse d'une philosophie (Paris 1840)

Leclerc, J. B., *Essai sur la propagation de la musique en France* (Paris 1796)

Leibniz, G., *The Monadology and Other Writings*, tr. R. Latta (London 1898, 7th reprint 1971)

Le Sueur, J. F., *Exposé d'une musique une, imitative et particulière à chaque solemnité* (Paris 1787)

Lichtenthal, P. (see *Encyclopaedias*)

Liszt, F., *Briefe*, ed. M. Lipsius (Leipzig 1905)

Longinus, *On the Sublime*, ed. and tr. W. R. Roberts (2nd edn, Cambridge 1907)
    Longinus on the Sublime: the Peri Houpsous in Translations by Nicholas Boileau Déspreaux (1674) and William Smith (1739) (Scholars, Facsimiles and Reprints, New York 1975)

Mazzini, G., *Scritti Editi ed Inediti* (Imola 1910–   )

Mendelssohn, Moses, *Werke* (Stuttgart 1971), 6 vols.

Mendelssohn-Bartholdy, F., *Letters*, ed. Gisela Selden-Goth (New York 1945)

Merle, Jean T., *De L'Opéra* (Paris 1827)

Michaelis, C. F., *Ueber den Geist der Tonkunst* (Leipzig 1795 and 1800), 2 vols.

Millin, A. L., (see *Encyclopaedias*)

de Momigny, J. J., *Cours complet d'harmonie et de composition* (Paris 1806), 3 vols.

Moritz, K. P., *Ueber die bildende Nachahmung des Schönen* (Brunswick 1788)

Mundt, T., *Aesthetik* (Leipzig 1845)

Nägeli, H.-G., *Vorlesungen über Musik* (Stuttgart and Tübingen 1826)

Novalis (Friedrich von Hardenberg), *Briefe und Werke*, ed. E. Wasmuth (Munich 1943)

Price, Uvedale, *An Essay on the Picturesque* (London 1794)

Rameau, J.-P., *Complete Theoretical Writings*, ed. Erwin R. Jacobi (American Institute of Musicology, Rome 1967–72), vol 6.

Rees, A. (see *Encyclopaedias*)

Reynolds, Sir J., *Discourses on Art*, ed. R. A. Wark (New Haven 1975)

Richter, Jean-Paul., *Sämtliche Werke*, ed. E. Berend (Weimar 1922–)
Rousseau, J.-J., *Oeuvres complètes*, ed. P. R. Auguis (Paris 1825)
  (see also *Encyclopaedias*)
Runge, P. O., *Hinterlassene Schriften*, ed. D. Runge (Hamburg 1840–1), 2 vols.
  Kunstanschauung der Jüngeren Romantik, ed. A. Müller (Leipzig 1934)
Sand, George., *Oeuvres de George Sand* (Paris 1896)
Schelling, F. W. J. von, *Werke*, ed. Manfred Schröter, (Munich 1958–60), 12 vols.
Schiller, J. C. F. von, *Sämtliche Werke* (Leipzig n.d.), 12 vols.
Schilling, G. (see *Encyclopaedias*)
Schlegel, A. W. von, *Sämtliche Werke*, ed. E. Böcking (Leipzig 1848–   ), 12 vols.
  Die Kunstlehre, ed. Edgar Lohner (Stuttgart 1963)
  Schriften, ed. Walther Flemmer (Munich, n.d.)
Schlegel, (K. W.) F. von, *Kritische Schriften*, ed. W. Rasch (Munich 1956)
Schopenhauer, A., *Sämtliche Werke*, ed. P. Deussen (Munich 1911), 6 vols.
Schubart, C. F. D., *Ideen zu einer Aesthetik der Tonkunst* (Vienna 1806)
Schumann, R. A., *Gesammelte Schriften* (Leipzig 1854)
  Jugendbriefe, ed. Clara Schumann (4th revised edn, Leipzig 1910)
  Robert Schumann, ein Quellenwerk über sein Leben und Schaffen, ed. G.
    Eismann (Leipzig 1956)
  Robert Schumann im eigenen Wort, ed. W. Reich (Zurich 1967)
de Sénancour, E.-P., *Obermann* (1804), tr. J. A. Barnes (New York 1910)
de Staël, Mme A. L. G., *Lettres sur les ouvrages et le caractère de J.-J. Rousseau*
    (Paris 1788)
  De L'Allemagne (Paris 1814)
  Germany (London 1813), 3 vols.
Sulzer, J. G. (see *Encyclopaedias*)
Thibaut, A. F. J., *Über Reinheit der Tonkunst* (Heidelberg 1825)
  Purity in Music, tr. W. H. Gladstone (London 1877)
Tieck, L., *Sämtliche Schriften* (Berlin 1828–54), 28 vols.
Topffer (sic), R., *Réflexions et menus-propos d'un peintre génevois* (Paris 1848)
Toreinx, F. R. de, *L'Histoire du romantisme* (Paris 1829, Slatkine repr. Geneva
    1973)
Twining, T., *Aristotle's Treatise on Poetry Translated* (London 1789)
Villoteau, G. A., *Recherches sur l'analogie de la musique avec les arts qui ont pour
    objet l'imitation du langage* (Paris 1807), 2 vols.
Wackenroder, W. H., *Werke und Briefe*, ed. L. Schneider (Heidelberg 1967)
  Sämtliche Schriften, eds. C. Grützmacher and S. Claus (Munich 1968)
  Mit der ganzen Ungeduld des Herzens, Briefe deutscher Klassiker, ed. Kurt
    Fassmann (Munich 1969)
Webb, D., *Observations on the Correspondence between Poetry and Music* (London
    1769)
Weber, C. M. von, *Sämtliche Schriften*, ed. G. Kaiser (Berlin 1908)
Wieland, M., *Werke*, Historisch-kritische Ausgabe (Berlin 1909–   ), 50 vols.
    projected
Wienbarg, L., *Aesthetische Feldzüge* (Hamburg 1834)
Winckelmann, J. J., *Ausgewählte Schriften und Briefe*, ed. Walther Rehm (Wies-
    baden 1948)

Secondary sources

Allen, Warren D., *Philosophies of Music History* (New York 1962)

Babbitt, I., *Rousseau and Romanticism* (Boston 1919)

Baldensperger, F., *Sensibilité musicale et romantisme* (Paris 1925)

Bardez, J.-M., *Diderot et la musique* (Paris 1975)

Barry, K. M., *The Image of Music in Early 18th Century English Poetry*, (M.A. degree thesis, Univ. College, Dublin, Sept. 1973)

Barzun, J., *The Pleasures of Music* (London 1952)
  Classic, Romantic and Modern (Chicago 1975)

Begenau, H., *Grundzüge der Aesthetik Herders* (Weimar 1956)

Bellague, C., 'Balzac et la musique' in *Revue des deux mondes* (Oct. 1, 1924)

Boulton, J. T., *Edmund Burke: A Philosophical Enquiry* (London 1958)

Bowra, M., *The Romantic Imagination* (London 1956)

Bray, R., *Chronologie du Romantisme, 1804–1830* (Paris 1963)

Brenet, M., *Les Concerts en France sous l'ancien régime* (Da Capo Press; reprint of Paris, 1900 edn, New York 1970)

Breuillac, M., *Hoffmann en France* in Revue d'histoire littéraire de la France, vols. 13 (1906) and 14 (1907)

Brion, M., *L'Allemagne romantique* (Paris 1963)

Bronson, B. H., 'When was neoclassicism?', *Studies in Criticism and Aesthetics (1660–1800)*, eds. Howard Anderson and John S. Shea (Minneapolis 1967)

Bruford, W. H., *Culture and Society in Classical Weimar, 1775–1806* (Cambridge 1962)
  Germany in the Eighteenth Century (Cambridge 1935)

Bukofzer, Max, *Die musikalische Gemütsbewegung* (Leipzig 1935)

Cannon, B. C., *Johann Mattheson, Spectator in Music*, Yale Studies in the History of Music I (New Haven 1947)

Cardinal, R., *German Romantics in Context* (London 1975)

Carritt, E. F., *The Theory of Beauty* (London 1914, University paperback edition 1962)

Chantavoine, J., *Le Romantisme dans la musique européene* (Paris 1955)

Charlton, W., *Aesthetics, an Introduction* (London 1970)

Chastel, A., 'Etude sur la vie musicale à Paris à travers la presse pendant le règne de Louis XVI' in *Recherches sur la musique française*, vols. 16–17 (1976–7), pp. 37–70, 118–48

Clark, R. T., *Herder's Life and Work* (Berkeley & Los Angeles 1955)

Collingwood, R. G., *The Principles of Art* (London 1937)
  The Idea of Nature (Oxford paperbacks 1965)

Copleston, F., *Arthur Schopenhauer, Philosopher of Pessimism* (London 1947)
  A History of Philosophy, vol. 7 (New York 1965)

Crosten, W. L., *French Grand Opera; An Art and a Business* (New York 1948)

Croxall, T. H., 'Kierkegaard on music', *Proceedings of the Royal Musical Association*, vol. 73 (1946–7), pp. 1–11

Dahlhaus, C., 'Zu Kants Musikästhetik' in *Archiv für Musikwissenschaft*, vol. 10 (1953), pp. 338–47

Davies, T. R., *French Romanticism and the Press: The Globe* (Cambridge 1906)

Dean, W., 'Opera under the French Revolution', *Proceedings of the Royal Musical Association*, vol. 94 (1967–8), pp. 77–96

Doederlein, J. L., 'Hegel und die Aufgabe der Musikphilosophie', *Hegel-Jahrbuch* (1965), pp. 65–9

Dowd, D. L., *Pageant Master of the Republic: Jacques Louis David* (Lincoln 1948)

Draper, J. W., *Eighteenth-Century English Aesthetics: A Bibliography* (Heidelberg 1931)

'Poetry and music in eighteenth-century English aesthetics' in *Englische Studien*, vol. 67 (1932–3), pp. 70–85

Eggebrecht, H. H., 'Das Ausdrucksprinzip im musikalischen Sturm und Drang', *Deutsche Vierteljahrschrift für Literaturwissenschaft und Geistesgeschichte*, vol. 29 (1955), pp. 323–49

Eichner, H., 'Friedrich Schlegel's theory of romantic poetry', *Proceedings of the Modern Language Association*, vol. 71 (1956), pp. 1018–41

Elwart, A. A. E., *Histoire de la société des concerts du Conservatoire impériale de musique* (Paris 1864)

Ermatinger, E., *Deutsche Dichter, 1700–1900, eine Geistesgeschichte in Lebensbildern* (Frauenfeld 1949)

Fellinger, I., *Verzeichnis der Musikzeitschriften des 19. Jahrhunderts* (Regensburg 1968)

(Fétis, F. J.) *François Joseph Fétis et la vie musicale de son temps* (catalogue of an exhibition held in Brussels in 1972)

Finke, U., *German Painting from Romanticism to Expressionism* (London 1974)

Fricke, G., *Wackenroders Religion der Kunst* (Frankfurt 1956)

Funder, A., *Die Aesthetik des F. Hemsterhuis und ihre historischen Beziehungen* (Bonn 1913)

Furst, L. R., *Romanticism in Perspective* (London 1969)
  Counterparts: the Dynamics of Franco-German Literary Relationships (London 1974)

Gardiner, P. L., *Schopenhauer* (Harmondsworth 1963)

Gilbert, K. E. and Kuhn, H., *A History of Aesthetics* (New York 1972)

Girdlestone, C., *Jean Philippe Rameau. His Life and Work* (London 1957)

Gossman, L., 'Time and history in Rousseau', *Studies on Voltaire and the Eighteenth Century*, vol. 30 (1964)

Hagan, D., *French Musical Criticism Between the Revolutions* (Ph.D. dissertation in Musicology; Univ. of Illinois 1965)

Hampson, N., *The Enlightenment* (Pelican History of European Thought, vol. 4, Harmondsworth 1968)

Hilbert, J. A., *Die Musikästhetik der Frühromantik* (Remscheid 1911)

Hiller, J. A., 'Abhandlung von der Nachahmung der Natur in der Musik' in F. W. Marpurg, *Historisch-kritische Beiträge zur Aufnahme der Musik* (Berlin 1754), vol. 1, pp. 515–43

Hinkley, E., *Giuseppe Mazzini; the story of a great Italian* (London 1924, reprinted New York 1970)

Hobsbawm, E. J., *The Age of Revolution* (London 1962)

Honour, H., *Neo-classicism* (London 1969)
  Romanticism (London 1979)

Huch, R., *Die Blütezeit der Romantik* (Leipzig 1901)

International Index of Periodical Literature. See *Current Musicology* Vol. 1 (1965), p. 121, for a list of musical articles in the above

International Review of the Aesthetics and Sociology of Music (Zagreb 1970–)

Isherwood, R. M., *The Third War of the Musical Enlightenment* in Studies in Eighteenth Century Culture, vol. 4 (Cleveland 1975), pp. 223–45

Jacob, M., *Die Musikanschauung im dichterischen Weltbild der Romantik* (Freiburg 1949)

Jacobs, R. L., 'Beethoven and Kant', *Music and Letters*, vol. 42 (1961), pp. 242–51

Jones, H. Mumford, *Revolution and Romanticism* (London 1974)

Kassler, J. C., *The Science of Music in Britain, 1714–1830: a catalogue of writings, lectures and inventions* (New York 1977)

Keys, A. C., 'Schiller and Italian opera', *Music and Letters*, vol. 41 (1960), pp. 223–37

de Keyser, E., *The Romantic West* (Geneva 1965)

Killy, W. (ed.)., *Deutsches Lesebuch, vol 2: Klassik und Romantik* (Frankfurt-am-Main & Hamburg 1960, 4th edn, 1970)

King, A. Hyatt, 'Mountains, music and musicians', *Musical Quarterly*, vol. 31 (1945), pp. 395–419

Klingender, F. D., (ed. and revised by Arthur Elton) *Art and the Industrial Revolution* (London 1968)

Kluckhohn, P., *Das Ideengut der deutschen Romantik* (Tübingen 1966)

Knight, Frida, *Beethoven and the Age of Revolution* (London 1973)

Knox, I., *The Aesthetic Theories of Kant, Hegel and Schopenhauer* (London 1958)

Koerner, S., *Kant* (London 1955)

Kohn, H., *The Mind of Germany* (London 1961)

Kristeller, P. O., 'The modern system of the arts', *Journal of the History of Ideas*, vol. 13 (1952) pp. 17–46

Lang, P. H., *The Creative World of Beethoven* (New York 1971)

Lessem, Alan P., ' "Imitation' and 'Expression": opposing French and British views on music in the Eighteenth Century', *Journal of the American Musicological Society*, vol. 27:2, pp. 325–30.

Lipking, L., *The Ordering of the Arts in Eighteenth Century England* (New Jersey 1970)

Locke, A. W., *Music and the Romantic Movement in France* (London 1920)

Lombard, A., *L'Abbé Du Bos: un initiateur de la pensée moderne* (Paris 1913)

Loncke, Joycelynne, *Baudelaire et la musique* (Paris 1975)

Lough, J., *Essays on the Encyclopédie* (London 1968)
The Encyclopédie in Eighteenth-Century England (London 1970)
The Contributors to the Encyclopédie (London 1973)

Luppmann, E. A., 'Theory and practice of Schumann's aesthetics', in *Journal of the American Musicological Society*, vol. 17 (1964), pp. 310–45.

Maniates, M. R., 'Sonate, que me veux-tu? The enigma of french musical aesthetics in the eighteenth century', *Current Musicology*, 1969, pp. 117–40.

Marks, P. F., 'Aesthetics of music in the philosophy of Sturm und Drang: Gerstenberg, Hamann and Herder', *Music Review*, vol. 35 (1974), pp. 247–59

Menhennet, A., *Order and Freedom; Literature and Society in Germany from 1720 to 1805* (London 1973)

Moenkemeyer, H., *François Hemsterhuis* (Boston, Mass 1975)

Monk, S. H., *The Sublime: A Study of Critical Theories in Eighteenth-Century England* (New York 1935, repr. Ann Arbor paperbacks, Michigan 1960)

Mornet, D., *Le Sentiment de la nature en France de J.-J. Rousseau à Bernardin de Saint-Pierre* (Paris 1907)
Le romantisme en France au XVIIIe siècle (Paris 1912)

Nisbet, R., *The Social Philosophers* (London 1974)

Novotny, F., *Painting and Sculpture in Europe, 1780–1880* (London 1960)

Nowak, A., *Hegels Musikästhetik* (Regensburg 1971)

O'Connor, D. J., *John Locke* (Harmondsworth 1952)

Oliver, A. R., *The Encyclopèdistes as Critics of Music* (New York 1947)

Osborne, J., *Romantik* (*Handbuch der deutschen Literaturgeschichte, Abteilung Bibliographien*, vol. 8, Berne & Munich 1971)

de Pange, J, *Madame de Staël et la découverte de l'Allemagne* (Paris 1929)

Pascal, R., *The German Sturm und Drang* (Manchester 1953)

Pfrogner, H., *Musik: Geschichte ihrere Deutung* (Freiburg 1954)

Pierre, C., *Sarrette et les origines du Conservatoire* (Paris 1895)

    Musique des fêtes et cérémonies de la révolution française (Paris 1899)

    Les Hymnes et chansons de la révolution française (Paris 1904)

Piert, B., *Friedrich Schlegels ästhetische Anschauungen* (Berlin 1910)

Plantinga, L. B., 'Schumann's view of "Romantic" ', *Musical Quarterly*, vol. 52 (1966), pp. 221–32

    Schumann as Critic (Yale Studies in the History of Music, 4, New Haven and London 1967)

Prang, H., *Die Romantische Ironie* (Darmstadt 1972)

Prawer, S. (ed.), *The Romantic Period in Germany* (London 1970)

Quatremère de Quincy, *Essai sur la nature, le but et les moyens de l'imitation dans les beaux-arts* (1823), tr. J. C. Kent (London 1837)

Raynor, H., *A Social History of Music* (New York 1972)

Refardt, E., *Verzeichnis der Aufsätze zur Musik in den nichtmusikalischen Zeit-schriften der Universitätsbibliothek Basel* (Leipzig 1925)

Reich, W. (ed.), *Felix Mendelssohn im Spiegel eigener Aussagen und zeitgenössischer Dokumente* (Zurich 1970)

    Von Bach zu Beethoven (Basel 1946)

Reiff, P., *Die Aesthetik der deutschen Frühromantik* (Urbana, Univ. of Illinois Press 1946)

Rennert, J., *William Crotch, 1775–1847, composer, artist, teacher,* (Lavenham 1975)

Ringer, A. L., 'J. J. Barthélemy and musical utopia in revolutionary France', *Journal of the History of Ideas*, vol. 22 (1961), pp. 355–68

Roche, K. F., *Rousseau, Stoic and Romantic* (London 1974)

Rosen, C., *The Classical Style* (London 1971)

Russell, B., *History of Western Philosophy* (London 1946)

Salomon, O. F., 'La Cépède's la poétique de la musique and le Sueur', *Acta Musicologica*, vol. 47 (1975), pp. 144–54.

Saw, R. Lydia, *Leibniz* (Harmondsworth 1954)

Schaefke, R., *Geschichte der Musikästhetik in Umrissen* (Berlin 1934)

Schafer, R. Murray, *E. T. A. Hoffman and Music* (Toronto 1975)

Schenk, H. G., *The Mind of the European Romantics* (London 1966)

Schulz, G., *Novalis* (Hamburg 1969)

Scruton, R., 'Absolute Music', *The New Grove Dictionary of Music and Musicians*, VI (London 1980)

    'Programme Music', *The New Grove Dictionary of Music and Musicians*, VI (London 1980)

Seifert, W., *Christian Gottfried Körner ein Musikästhetiker der deutschen Klassik* (Regensburg 1960)

Sengle, F., *Wieland* (Stuttgart 1949)

Serauky, W., *Die musikalische Nachahmungsästhetik im Zeitraum von 1700 bis 1850* (Münster 1929)

Sesonske, A. (ed.), *What is Art? Aesthetic Theory from Plato to Tolstoy* (London 1965)

Snyders, G., *Le goût musical en France au XVIIe et XVIIIe siècles* (Paris 1968)

Stolnitz, J., ' "Beauty": some stages in the history of an idea', *Journal of the History of Ideas*, vol. 22 (1961), pp. 185–202

    'On the origins of "aesthetic disinterestedness" ', *Journal of Aesthetics*, vol. 20

(1961), pp. 131–143

Strich, F., *Deutsche Klassik und Romantik* (Munich 1924)

Strunk, O., *Source Readings in the History of Music* (New York 1950)

Taylor, R., *The Romantic Tradition in Germany* (London 1970)

Temperley, N., 'Beethoven in London Concert Life, 1800–1850', *Music Review*, vol. 21 (1960), pp. 213–14

Tengler, R., *Schopenhauer und die Romantik* (Berlin 1923)

Thorlby, A. K., *The Romantic Movement* (London 1966)

Trahard, P., *Le Romantisme défini par le Globe*, *Études romantiques*, no. 3, ed. Henri Girard (Paris 1924)

Tymms, R., *German Romantic Literature* (London 1955)

Vischer, H., *Aesthetik, oder Wissenschaft des Schönen* (Leipzig 1846–57), 6 vols.

Wangermée, R., *François Joseph Fétis, musicologue et compositeur* (Brussels 1951)

Weber, M., *Music and the Middle Class. The social structure of concert life in London, Paris and Vienna 1830–1848* (London 1975)

Weber, W., 'A propos of the figure of music in the frontispiece of the Encyclopédie: theories of musical imitation in d'Alembert, Rousseau and Diderot', *Proceedings of the twelfth Congress of the International Musicological Society* (Berkeley 1977)

Williams, M. (ed.), *Revolutions, 1775–1830* (London 1971)

Williams, R., *Keywords: a Vocabulary of Culture and Society* (London 1976)

Willoughby, L. A., *The Romantic Movement in Germany* (London 1930)

Wiora, W., 'Herders und Heinses Beitrag zum Thema "Was ist Musik?" ' in *Die Musikforschung*, vol. 13 (1960), pp. 385–95

Die Musik im Weltbild der Deutschen Romantik (Regensburg 1965)

Wynn Reeves, J., *Body and Mind in Western Thought* (Harmondsworth 1958)

Zoltai, D., *Ethos und Affekt, Geschichte der philosophischen Musikästhetik von den Anfängen bis zu Hegel* (Berlin 1970)

Index of names, titles and places

General Index